# OXFORD IB DIPLOMA PROGRAMME

## 2013 EDITION

# THEORY OF KNOWLEDGE

## COURSE COMPANION

Eileen Dombrowski
Lena Rotenberg
Mimi Bick

**OXFORD**
UNIVERSITY PRESS

OXFORD
UNIVERSITY PRESS

Great Clarendon Street, Oxford OX2 6DP

Oxford University Press is a department of the University of Oxford. It furthers the University's objective of excellence in research, scholarship, and education by publishing worldwide in

Oxford New York

Auckland Cape Town Dar es Salaam Hong Kong Karachi Kuala Lumpur Madrid Melbourne Mexico City Nairobi New Delhi Shanghai Taipei Toronto

With offices in

Argentina Austria Brazil Chile Czech Republic France Greece Guatemala Hungary Italy Japan Poland Portugal Singapore South Korea Switzerland Thailand Turkey Ukraine Vietnam

Oxford is a registered trade mark of Oxford University Press in the UK and in certain other countries



First published 2013



British Library Cataloguing in Publication Data

Data available

ISBN: 978-0-19-912973-7

10 9 8

MIX
Paper from responsible sources
FSC www.fsc.org FSC® C007785

Printed and bound in Great Britain by Bell and Bain Ltd, Glasgow.

**ACKNOWLEDGEMENTS**

The author and publisher are grateful for permission to reprint extracts from the following copyright material:

Lilian Na'ia Alessa: 'What is Truth?' *The Alaska Native Reader: History, Culture, Politics*, ed. Maria Sháa Tláa Williams, Duke University Press, 2009, reproduced by permission of the author.

Richard Axel: 'Scents and Sensibility: A Molecular Logic of Olfactory Perception', Nobel Lecture in Physiology or Medicine 2004, copyright © The Nobel Foundation (2004), http://nobelprize.org, reprinted by permission.

Roger Barnhardt and Oscar Kawagley: *Anthropology & Education Quarterly*, Volume 36, Issue 1, pp8-23, March 2005, reprinted by permission of the American Anthropological Association, not for sale or further reproduction.

Duncan Bell: *Memory, Trauma and World Politics*, published in 2006 by Palgrave Macmillan, reprinted by permission.

Carol Black: *Occupy Your Brain*, from http://schoolingtheworld.org/blog/, reprinted by permission.

John Brockman: *The Third Culture*, copyright © 1995 by John Brockman, reprinted by permission of Scribner, a Division of Simon & Schuster, Inc., all rights reserved.

Ernst Cassirer: *An Essay on Man*, published by Yale University Press, 1952, copyright © 1944 by Yale University Press, copyright renewed, 1972, by Henry Cassirer and Anne Applebaum, reprinted by permission.

Tobias Dantzig: *Number: The Language of Science, Fourth Edition*, copyright © 1930, 1933, 1939, 1954 by Mac Publishing Company copyright renewed 1958, 1961, 1967, 1980 by Anna G. Dantzig, 1982 Mildred B. Dantzig, reprinted with the permission of Scribner, a Division of Simon & Schuster, Inc., all rights reserved.

'Declaration Toward a Global Ethic', copyright 1993, Council for the Parliament of the World's Religions, 4 September 1993, reproduced by permission.

Keith Devlin: *The Math Gene: How Mathematical Thinking Evolved and How Numbers Are Like Gossip*, copyright © 2000 K. Devlin, reprinted by permission of Basic Books, a member of the Perseus Books Group.

Kieran Egan: *The Educated Mind: How Cognitive Tools Shape Our Understanding*, published by The University of Chicago Press © 1997 by The University of Chicago, reprinted by permission, all rights reserved.

T. S. Eliot: 'Burnt Norton' from *Four Quartets*, copyright 1936 by Houghton Mifflin Harcourt Publishing Company, copyright © renewed 1964 by T. S. Eliot, reprinted by permission of Houghton Mifflin Harcourt Publishing Company and Faber & Faber Ltd.

Thomas Hylland Eriksen: *Small Places, Large Issues*, published by Pluto Books 1995, www.plutobooks.com, reprinted by permission.

Milton M. R. Freeman: 'The Nature and Utility of Traditional Ecological Knowledge' from *Northern Perspectives*, Vol. 20, no. 1, summer 1992, published by the Canadian Arctic Resources Committee, www.carc.org, reprinted by permission.

Chief Dan George & Helmut Hirnschall: *The Best of Chief Dan George*, published by hancockhouse.com, reprinted by permission of Hancock House Publishers.

John L. Graham and N. Mark Lam: 'The Chinese Negotiation', Harvard Business Review, October, 2003, copyright © 2003 by Harvard Business Publishing, reprinted by permission of Harvard Business Review, all rights reserved.

A. C. Grayling: *The Meaning of Things*, The Orion Publishing Group, London, copyright © 2001 A. C. Grayling, reprinted by permission.

Gert Jan Hofstede, Paul B. Pedersen and Geert Hofstede: *Exploring Culture: Exercises, Stories, and Synthetic Cultures*, Intercultural Press, Inc./Nicholas Brealey, reprinted by permission.

'How to Talk to Real People', reprinted by permission of Dr Patricia Marstellar, Emory University.

Samuel P. Huntington: 'The Clash of Civilizations', reprinted by permission of Foreign Affairs, Summer 1993, copyright 1993 by the Council on Foreign Relations, Inc., www.ForeignAffairs.com.

George Lakoff: *Women, Fire and Dangerous Things*, published by The University of Chicago Press © 1987 by The University of Chicago, reprinted by permission, all rights reserved.

Dalai Lama and Alexander Norman: 'No Magic, No Mystery' from *Ethics for the New Millennium*, copyright © 1999 by His Holiness The Dalai Lama (Tenzin Gyatso, the Fourteenth Dalai Lama of Tibet, used by permission of Riverhead Books, an imprint of Penguin Group (USA) Inc. and Aitken Alexander Associates.

Frances Moore Lappé, Joseph Collins and Peter Rosset with Luis Esparza: *World Hunger: Twelve Myths*, copyright © 1998 by The Institute for Food and Development Policy, used by permission of Grove/Atlantic, Inc., and Food First, any third party use of this material, outside of this publication, is prohibited.

John Lennon: 'Imagine', © 1971 John Lennon, reprinted by permission, all rights reserved.

Mario Vargas Llosa: 'Elogio de la lectura y la ficción' (In Praise of Reading and Fiction), Nobel Lecture in Literature 2010, copyright © The Nobel Foundation (2010), http://nobelprize.org, reproduced by permission.

Louis MacNeice: 'Sunlight on the Garden' from *Collected Poems*, published by Faber & Faber, reprinted by kind permission of David Higham Associates Ltd.

Michael Marker: 'Teaching History from an Indigenous Perspective: Four Winding Paths up the Mountain' in Penney Clark: *New Possibilities for the Past*, reprinted with permission of the publisher © University of British Columbia Press 2011, all rights reserved by the publisher.

Donella Meadows: from *Thinking in Systems*, copyright 2008 by Donella Meadows, reprinted by permission of Chelsea Green Publishing (www.chelseagreen.com).

David G. Meyers: 'The Powers and Perils of Intuition', November/December 2002, *Psychology Today* © Copyright 2002, www.psychologytoday.com, reprinted by permission.

'Mission and Strategy' from http://www.ibo.org/mission/, © International Baccalaureate Organization 2013, reprinted by permission.

Devorah Romanek: 'Cross-cultural map for a changing world', reprinted by permission of Devorah Romanek, former Curator for the British Museum.

Oliver Sacks: *Musicophilia: Tales of Music and the Brain*, copyright © 2007, 2008 by Oliver Sacks, used by permission of Alfred A. Knopf, a division of Random House, Inc., any third party use of this material, outside of this publication, is prohibited, interested parties must apply directly to Random House, Inc. for permission.

Oliver Sacks: Seeing Voices, copyright © 1989, 1990 by Oliver Sacks, used by permission of The Wylie Agency LLC and Vintage Books, a division of Random House, Inc., any third party use of this material, outside of this publication, is prohibited, interested parties must apply directly to Random House, Inc. for permission

Arielle Saiber and Henry S. Turner: 'Mathematics and the Imagination: A Brief Introduction' Configurations 17:1-2 (2009), p.18, © 2010 by The Johns Hopkins University Press and the Society for Literature and Science, reprinted with permission of The Johns Hopkins University Press.

Ella Shohat and Robert Stam: *Unthinking Eurocentrism: Multiculturalism and the Media*, page 2 of 'Introduction', published by Routledge 1994, reprinted by permission.

'Statement of Apology' – to former students of Indian Residential Schools, http://www.aadnc-aandc.gc.ca/eng/1100100015644/1100100015649,

Aboriginal Affairs and Northern Development Canada, 2008,

reprinted with the permission of the Minister of Public Works and Government Services Canada, 2013.

Xwelixweltel (Hon. Steven Point): from the essay "Getting Back our Dignity" found in the book *A Sto:lō-Coast Salish Historical Atlas*, published in 2001 by Douglas & McIntyre and Stó:lō Heritage Trust, reprinted by permission of the publisher.

Any third party use of this material, outside of this publication, is prohibited. Interested parties should apply to the copyright holders indicated in each case.

Although we have made every effort to trace and contact all copyright holders before publication this has not been possible in all cases. If notified, the publisher will rectify any errors or omissions at the earliest opportunity.

The publisher and authors would like to thank the following for their kind permission to reproduce photographs and copyright material:

**P5:** Courtesy Of U.S. Geological Survey; **P6:** Tom Van Sant, Geosphere Project/Planetary Visions/Science Photo Library; **P7tl:** Strebe; **P7tr:** Map Resources; **P7m:** NASA; **P7b:** Fao, Ifad And Wfp. 2012. The State Of Food Insecurity In The World 2012 **P9:** © The Trustees Of The British Museum; **P10:** Pierleb; **P30bl:** Sergio Carena/© UNESCO; **P30br:** Eman Mohammed/© UNESCO; **P33:** Gabrieldome/Istock; **P34:** OUP; **P35:** OUP; **P41tl:** Jim Mckinley/Getty Images; **P41bl:** Linda Shen/© UNESCO; **P41br:** Ministerio De Educación/© UNESCO; **P44:** © Ian Nellist/Alamy; **P52:** Wiley Miller/The Washington Post Writers' Group/Universal Press Syndicate; **P53:** Bartosz Hadyniak; **P59:** Christie's Images/Bridgeman Art; **P60:** Theo Dombrowski; **P61:** OUP; **P73tl:** OUP; **P73tr:** OUP; **P74tl:** © Marka/Alamy; **P74tr:** © Dunca Daniel Mihai/Alamy; **P75:** © Tetra Images/Alamy; **P80:** John William Waterhouse/Getty Images; **P82:** Ivan Kuzmin/Shutterstock; **P83:** OUP; **P84:** Thomas Pullicino/Istock; **P89:** Kaj R. Svensson/Science Photo Library; **P91:** NASA.; **P92tl:** OUP; **P92mr:** NASA, ESA, And The Hubble Heritage Team (Stsci/Aura); **P98:** © Urban Zone/Alamy; **P99:** OUP; **P105:** OUP; **P106:** © Theo Schneider/Demotix/Demotix/Corbis; **P114:** © Ocean/Corbis; **P115:** © Matthew Doggett/Alamy; **P118:** Shutterstock/Sandra Caldwell; **P130t:** © Richard Laschon/Alamy; **P130b:** © Richard Laschon/Alamy; **P133t:** © Patrick Guenette/Alamy; **P133b:** OUP; **P134l:** Department For Transport (Crown Copyright); **P134r:** Tonn/Shutterstock; **P136:** © Imagezoo/Alamy; **P138:** © Brian Mitchell/Corbis; **P139:** © The Trustees Of The British Museum **P140tl:** OUP; **P140tr:** OUP; **P143tl:** OUP; **P143bl:** OUP; **P143r:** OUP; **P150:** OUP; **P155:** OUP; **P155:** OUP; **P155:** OUP; **P155:** OUP; **P155:** OUP; **P155:** OUP; **P155:** OUP; **P155:** OUP; **P155:** OUP; **P155:** OUP; **P157:** Giraudon/Bridgeman; **P163:** Photo Credit **P168:** © David Bleeker Photography/Alamy; **P174l:** © Dvarg/Alamy; **P174r:** OUP; **P175l:** © Af Archive/Alamy; **P175r:** OUP; **P176:** © Henn Photography/Cultura/Corbis; **P177:** © Yadid Levy/Alamy; **P178:** OUP; **P190:** © Interfoto/Alamy; **P194:** OUP; **P202:** © Fleyeing | Dreamstime.Com; **P221:** © Rtimages/Alamy; **P227:** OUP; **P227:** OUP; **P227:** OUP; **P227:** OUP; **P227:** OUP; **P227:** OUP; **P234:** Image Courtesy Of The Materials Research Society (Www.Mrs.Org) Science-As-Art Competition And Dong Chan Kim, Sungkyunkwan University.; **P235:** OUP; **P235:** OUP; **P235:** OUP; **P236tl:** © The Trustees Of The British Museum; **P236r:** © The Trustees Of The British Museum; **P236ml:** Guernica, 1937 (Oil On Canvas), Picasso, Pablo (1881-1973)/Museo Nacional Centro De Arte Reina Sofia, Madrid, Spain/The Bridgeman Art Library; **P236bl:** © The Art Archive/Alamy; **P236tr:** OUP; **P236:** © David Wei/Alamy; **P238:** OUP; **P247:** OUP; **P249:** OUP; **P254b:** Calvin And Hobbes ©1988 Watterson. Dist by Universal Uclick. Reprinted With Permission. All Rights Reserved.; **P254t:** OUP; **P257:** OUP; **P257:** OUP; **P257:** OUP; **P258:** © Imagezoo/Alamy; **P269:** OUP; **P269:** OUP; **P273:** Hubble Heritage Team, ESA, NASA; **P274:** © The Trustees Of The British Museum; **P284:** Shanghai Renmin Meishu Chubanshe/Landsberger Collection; **P288:** © Akg-Images/Alamy; **P289:** OUP; **P289:** OUP; **P289:** OUP; **P289:** OUP; **P289:** OUP; **P290:** © Pictorial Press Ltd/Alamy; **P294:** © The Trustees Of The British Museum **P298:** Cteconsulting/Istock; **P299:** © Imagezoo/Alamy; **P303:** © Jim Zuckerman/Alamy; **P304:** © Photoalto/Alamy; **P306:** OUP; **P306:** OUP; **P306:** OUP; **P306:** OUP; **P306:** OUP; **P306:** OUP; **P306:** OUP; **P308:** © Neil Leslie/Alamy; **P313:** Calvin And Hobbes ©1988 Watterson. Dist by Universal Uclick. Reprinted With Permission. All Rights Reserved; **P318tl:** © The Trustees Of The British Museum **P318b:** Paweł Zdziarski; **P321:** OUP; **P323:** NASA And ESA; **P325tl:** Peter Halasz; **P325tr:** Hubble/NASA; **P325b:** Fotolia; **P328bl:** NASA, 2009; **P328br:** © Images & Stories/Alamy; **P329:** © Blend Images/Alamy; **P333:** Scott Bauer/Us Department Of Agriculture/Science Photo Library; **P337:** © Rubberball/Alamy; **P339l:** Robbie Shone/Science Photo Library; **P339r:** Philippe Psaila/Science Photo Library; **P342:** CERN; **P344:** British Antarctic Survey/Science Photo Library; **P346:** Monty Rakusen/Science Photo Library; **P348:** OUP; **P348:** Dr Seth Shostak/Science Photo Library; **P348:** OUP; **P349:** OUP; **P350:** OUP; **P354l:** © Archive Images/Alamy; **P354r:** Science Photo Library; **P356:** OUP; **P356:** OUP; **P356:** OUP; **P356:** OUP; **P356:** OUP; **P356:** OUP; P**359:** OUP; **P359:** OUP; **P359:** OUP; **P362:** © Ken Welsh/Alamy; **P364:** © Bob Thaves/Dist. By NEA, Inc; **P372:** Tokyo Fuji Art Museum, Tokyo, Japan; **P374:** OUP; **P374l:** © View Stock/Alamy; **P374r:** © The Art Archive/Alamy; **P380:** Tim Clayton/Corbis; **P382:** Marilyn Angel Wynn/Getty Images; **P383:** Ray Barnhardt/University Of Alaska Fairbanks; **P387:** Ben Knight/Schoolingtheworld.Org; **P394tl:** © Hollis Photography.Com/Alamy; **P394tr:** © Bill Bachman/Alamy; **P396:** Courtesy of The Office Of The Lieutenant-Governor; **P402t:** OUP; **P402lt:** OUP; **P402tb:** © Asp Religion/Alamy; **P402b:** © Dinodia Photos/Alamy; **P403t:** © Andrew Mcconnell/Alamy; **P403m:** OUP; **P403b:** Stewart Smith Photography/Shutterstock; **P410:** © The Trustees of The British Museum **P414:** OUP; **P427:** OUP; **P431:** OUP.

**Cover photo:** Surelocke/Shutterstock

All other photos courtesy of Eileen Dombrowski. Illustrations completed by Q2A Media.

# Course Companion definition

The IB Diploma Programme Course Companions are resource materials designed to support students throughout their two-year Diploma Programme course of study in a particular subject. They will help students gain an understanding of what is expected from the study of an IB Diploma Programme subject while presenting content in a way that illustrates the purpose and aims of the IB. They reflect the philosophy and approach of the IB and encourage a deep understanding of each subject by making connections to wider issues and providing opportunities for critical thinking.

The books mirror the IB philosophy of viewing the curriculum in terms of a whole-course approach; the use of a wide range of resources, international mindedness, the IB learner profile and the IB Diploma Programme core requirements, theory of knowledge, the extended essay, and creativity, action, service (CAS).

Each book can be used in conjunction with other materials and indeed, students of the IB are required and encouraged to draw conclusions from a variety of resources. Suggestions for additional and further reading are given in each book and suggestions for how to extend research are provided.

In addition, the Course Companions provide advice and guidance on the specific course assessment requirements and on academic honesty protocol. They are distinctive and authoritative without being prescriptive.

# IB mission statement

The International Baccalaureate aims to develop inquiring, knowledgable and caring young people who help to create a better and more peaceful world through intercultural understanding and respect.

To this end the IB works with schools, governments and international organizations to develop challenging programmes of international education and rigorous assessment.

These programmes encourage students across the world to become active, compassionate, and lifelong learners who understand that other people, with their differences, can also be right.

# The IB learner profile

The aim of all IB programmes is to develop internationally minded people who, recognizing their common humanity and shared guardianship of the planet, help to create a better and more peaceful world. As IB learners we strive to be:

**Inquirers**   We nurture our curiosity, developing skills for inquiry and research. We know how to learn independently and with others. We learn with enthusiasm and sustain our love of learning throughout life.

**Knowledgeable**   We develop and use conceptual understanding, exploring knowledge across a range of disciplines. We engage with issues and ideas that have local and global significance.

**Thinkers**   We use critical and creative thinking skills to analyse and take responsible action on complex problems. We exercise initiative in making reasoned, ethical decisions.

**Communicators**   We express ourselves confidently and creatively in more than one language and in many ways. We collaborate effectively, listening carefully to the perspectives of other individuals and groups.

**Principled**   We act with integrity and honesty, with a strong sense of fairness and justice, and with respect for the dignity and rights of people everywhere. We take responsibility for our actions and their consequences.

**Open-minded**   We critically appreciate our own cultures and personal histories, as well as the values and traditions of others. We seek and evaluate a range of points of view, and we are willing to grow from the experience.

**Caring**   We show empathy, compassion and respect. We have a commitment to service, and we act to make a positive difference in the lives of others and in the world around us.

**Risk-takers**   We approach uncertainty with forethought and determination; we work independently and cooperatively to explore new ideas and innovative strategies. We are resourceful and resilient in the face of challenges and change.

**Balanced**   We understand the importance of balancing different aspects of our lives—intellectual, physical, and emotional—to achieve well-being for ourselves and others. We recognize our interdependence with other people and with the world in which we live.

**Reflective**   We thoughtfully consider the world and our own ideas and experience. We work to understand our strengths and weaknesses in order to support our learning and personal development.

The IB learner profile represents 10 attributes valued by IB World Schools. We believe these attributes, and others like them, can help individuals and groups become responsible members of local, national and global communities.

# A note on academic honesty

It is of vital importance to acknowledge and appropriately credit the owners of information when that information is used in your work. After all, owners of ideas (intellectual property) have property rights. To have an authentic piece of work, it must be based on your individual and original ideas with the work of others fully acknowledged. Therefore, all assignments, written or oral, completed for assessment must use your own language and expression. Where sources are used or referred to, whether in the form of direct quotation or paraphrase, such sources must be appropriately acknowledged.

## How do I acknowledge the work of others?

The way that you acknowledge that you have used the ideas of other people is through the use of footnotes and bibliographies.

**Footnotes**   (placed at the bottom of a page) or endnotes (placed at the end of a document) are to be provided when you quote or paraphrase from another document, or closely summarize the information provided in another document. You do not need to provide a footnote for information that is part of a 'body of knowledge'. That is, definitions do not need to be footnoted as they are part of the assumed knowledge.

**Bibliographies**   should include a formal list of the resources that you used in your work. 'Formal' means that you should use one of the several accepted forms of presentation. This usually involves separating the resources that you use into different categories (e.g. books, magazines, newspaper articles, Internet-based resources, CDs and works of art) and providing full information as to how a reader or viewer of your work can find the same information. A bibliography is compulsory in the extended essay.

## What constitutes malpractice?

**Malpractice** is behaviour that results in, or may result in, you or any student gaining an unfair advantage in one or more assessment component. Malpractice includes plagiarism and collusion.

**Plagiarism** is defined as the representation of the ideas or work of another person as your own. The following are some of the ways to avoid plagiarism:

- Words and ideas of another person used to support one's arguments must be acknowledged.
- Passages that are quoted verbatim must be enclosed within quotation marks and acknowledged.
- CD-ROMs, email messages, web sites on the Internet, and any other electronic media must be treated in the same way as books and journals.
- The sources of all photographs, maps, illustrations, computer programs, data, graphs, audio-visual, and similar material must be acknowledged if they are not your own work.
- Works of art, whether music, film, dance, theatre arts, or visual arts, and where the creative use of a part of a work takes place, must be acknowledged.

**Collusion** is defined as supporting malpractice by another student. This includes:

- allowing your work to be copied or submitted for assessment by another student
- duplicating work for different assessment components and/or diploma requirements.

**Other forms of malpractice** include any action that gives you an unfair advantage or affects the results of another student. Examples include, taking unauthorized material into an examination room, misconduct during an examination, and falsifying a CAS record.

# About the authors

## Eileen Dombrowski

Eileen Dombrowski has most recently been mentoring online for Theory of Knowledge (Triple A Learning), instructing online for Global Citizenship (University of British Columbia), and blogging on both topics. She taught English A and TOK for over 20 years for the United World Colleges, mainly Lester B Pearson College in western Canada. During that time, she was extensively involved in international residential student life and in CAS activities.

She has led numerous TOK workshops, face-to-face and online. Her home is on the Canadian west coast.

## Lena Rotenberg

Lena Rotenberg is an educational consultant whose business card states "Director of Impossible Projects." Formally trained in Physics, Brazilian Law and Instructional Technology, she is currently engaged primarily in environmental education, community-building, and dental office management.

She started teaching TOK at Escola Graduada de São Paulo in 1985, and has led numerous TOK workshops. Lena's home is in Keedysville, Maryland, a small town in the eastern United States.

## Mimi Bick

Mimi Bick is currently Academic Director at Craighouse School, a full continuum IB institution in Santiago, Chile, where she continues to teach TOK. Mimi previously worked with the Chilean Ministry of Education's Curriculum and Assessment Unit to improve the state educational system. More recently she has worked as consultant on national projects in Ecuador and Peru, the aims of which are also to raise standards of education.

She has been a member of two TOK curriculum review teams, and has led numerous workshops. A Canadian from Montreal, she makes her home in Santiago.

# Acknowledgements

Above all, I wish to thank Lena Rotenberg and Mimi Bick, who have given me tremendous support throughout the writing of this book. They have brainstormed with me, advised me, and acted as critical readers. They have also, as dearly valued friends, given support and encouragement when my energies flagged.

With all my heart, I also thank my husband Theo Dombrowski, who has read critically every word of the text, with the astute "red pen" so fabled among generations of his English A students. He has also been my resident illustrator on request.

Very special thanks go to all of the topic experts who contributed "voices", interviews, or activities to this book: Carlos Anciano Granadillo, Réal Carrière, Jim Cavers, Manini Chatterjee, Jane Clarke, Sylla Cousineau, Miles Davenport, Patrick Decowski, Anne Enright, Charles Freeman, Maarten Jongsma, Shahla Kanji, Julian Kitching, Heidi Li, Susan McDade, Fearghus O'Conchuir, David Pinel, Oded Rose, Manjula Solomon, Richard Underhill, Todd Waite, Michael Watson. Many of these contributors are also IB Diploma graduates.

Thanks, too, to the contributors preserved here perpetually as TOK students: Mona Aditya, Giorgina Alfonso Rodriguez, Chen Arad, Nathan Bowman, Phiriyaphong Chaengchenwet, Christy Drever, Ruakiri Fairhill, Nakhshab Farhikhtah, Naja Hendriksen, Priyanka Karuvelil, Shobha Lalwani, Tanaka Lesedi Mhambi, Yeshey Lhaden, Lindsay Lloyd, Janeen Madan, Kohei Noda, Isaac Sadaquah, Mohamed Shakir, Adam Spooner, Kati Temonen, Toi Yam Karyn Wong. I greatly appreciate, as well, my many other former students who posed for my camera.

Huge appreciation also goes others who helped in time of need with specific subject matter: Conrad Dombrowski, Jedrzej Zieleniak, Laura Fulton, Leah Macfadyen, Megan Dombrowski, and Michael Watson.

Last, I want to give an affectionate thank you to all the students who shared with me their lives and perspectives on the world over my years of international teaching. They have all contributed, in their ways, to this book: they gave me the great pleasure of being their teacher and learning along with them.

*Eileen Dombrowski*

# Contents

# Introduction

## Foreword to students

Have you ever wondered, "Why don't they ever agree?" or "Do they really know?" Have you ever thought, "I'm not sure what to believe" or "Aha! This is the answer!"? It's likely that you have, and that your own thinking has prepared you for the theory of knowledge course. It's an unusual course for most educational systems, in that it is about everything you and others have ever learned or will learn in the future: it's about knowledge itself. In this course, you'll be taking a giant step back from the knowledge you've gained personally through your family, community, or school to see it all more broadly – to gain the Big Picture of how knowledge is shared, and how it all fits together. You'll take part in the process of asking and trying to answer questions that seem simple only on the surface – questions that emerge from the mother of them all, "How do we know?" You'll heighten your awareness of some big ideas, your capacity to understand different perspectives, and your ability to evaluate knowledge critically and appreciatively. In all probability, you'll really enjoy the discussions and reflection of the course and find they reinforce the habits of mind encouraged throughout the IB Diploma, toward a better future. Welcome to TOK!

## Foreword to teachers:

### How to use this book to support inquiry teaching

Using a course book has the potential to undermine the spirit of inquiry that we try to foster in theory of knowledge. As teachers, we want to awaken students more fully to the *questions* that give knowledge its impetus, its different directions, its methods of investigation, and its humanity. We do not want to hand them distilled answers that preempt their own thought.

Why, then, do we offer this course book to support "inquiry teaching"? Simply because, if its different features are used as intended, it does not bypass thinking but stimulate it! Using this book well has the potential to encourage exploration of ideas, build student capacities for open mindedness and analytical evaluation, give broad support to the topics of the TOK course including the final assessment, and encourage students to take TOK awareness and critical thinking into their lives as global citizens.

## 1. Aims of this book

We have embraced the following major aims in writing this book, attempting to combine idealism and practicality:

- **To place TOK firmly in context of IB educational goals.**
  Taking on ideals of the learner profile, we encourage inquiry and reflection, emphasize the interdependence between being open minded and thinking critically, and contribute, we hope, to students becoming more effective thinkers and communicators. Throughout the book, we stress the need to respect and appreciate cultural, political, religious, theoretical, and other perspectives, but at the same time to evaluate their conclusions for the nature and quality of their justifications. We aim to develop international-mindedness and apply TOK thinking to issues of significance in the world, to build the understanding important for action.

- **To work within a pedagogy of exploration and discussion.**
  We have set up this course book to trigger student inquiry and discussion on central knowledge questions of each topic being examined. Through discussion prompted by activities, students investigate ideas to articulate and stretch their current understanding. Then they place their own inquiry within the broader realm of shared knowledge. The interchapters add to students' own growing awareness: the Overview pages provide diagrams building concepts cumulatively, and the Thinking Critically pages prepare analytical skills for application to the world.

- **To give support to teachers and students for the whole of the current course, including assessment.**
  We have provided discussion activities, reflective questions, and topic background for all the central concepts and skills of the course. The final chapter gives students guidance toward successfully planning and fulfilling the assessment tasks of the presentation and the essay.

Our goal throughout has been to provide a rich resource for students and teachers, one that supports different paths through the ideas of the theory of knowledge course.

## 2. Using different parts of the course book

We have designed this book for ease of access to its different features and levels of navigation. The ongoing chapter text deals with the course ideas, but it is accompanied by complementary ways of developing them. These are formatted and colour-coded to be recognized at a glance.

### Using discussion activities

Roughly a hundred discussion activities, presented in salmon-coloured boxes, offer a great variety of ideas for guided discussion. From them, select the ones that you find most interesting and relevant to your way of doing TOK – and lay aside the others with a practical awareness of the ticking clock.

Some of these are short, intended just to open or punctuate a class, while others set up a sequence of discussions that may structure more than one lesson. They include a considerable variety of focusing activities and, in every case, lead to discussion that furthers the ideas of the chapter and the course. Some of them also set up approaches to analysis that feed into the critical scaffolding of the course.

We recommend entering new topics through discussion, so that students connect with the ideas from their own backgrounds and have a chance to think about them. Only after they have taken the ideas as far as they can themselves do we suggest that teachers pull them along further with reading (such as the chapter text) or any of the other ways we teachers customarily use (e.g. speakers, films, articles).

### Using reflections

Numerous blue boxes entitled "For reflection" offer questions for further thought. Usually they invite students to connect knowledge questions or shared knowledge with their own personal experiences. You may want to leave the reflections to students, to read and think about; students are likely to find that some of them provoke their own quiet thought. However, the questions for reflection can also be used toward student TOK journals or TOK blogs if you ask your students to write in such a way. Many of them also invite class conversational response, perhaps in a looser, more anecdotal way than the guided discussion activities.

### Using the voices, interviews, and quotations

In this book, we include the voices of many people from around the world contributing to a discussion of knowledge. Some are scholars quoted for their insights. Some, though, are past TOK students whose comments are likely to stir current students to respond. Significantly, too, many of the personal "voices" and interviews feature IB Diploma graduates who are now professionals and experts in their fields. Their individual photos and personal commentary support one of the central contentions of the book: that knowledge is humanly constructed, from different perspectives, in different contexts, using different methods, toward different aims.

### Using Thinking Critically interchapters

The interchapters on Thinking Critically are formatted to stand out from the chapters and are identified in the Table of Contents as separate from the main chapters. They compress into quick guides many skills that are associated with the topics of the chapters, and sometimes also offer activities to apply those thinking skills. We encourage teachers to use these interchapters as guides to analysis, and to have their students apply them to current issues in the world.

These interchapters are developed most substantially through the section on ways of knowing in order to help students engage critically with the everyday world – using those ways of knowing with care! Recognizing of the importance of critical thinking is likely to give them a fuller appreciation of the role of methodology in areas of knowledge.

### Using the ongoing chapter text and overview interchapters

In each chapter, we provide background on central TOK ideas. The chapter text flows coherently around the inset activities, reflections, interviews, voices, quotations, photographs, and graphics. Addressed to students, it provides reading that extends the reach of class discussion and enables students to integrate their own exchange of ideas into major ideas of TOK. This is the "textbook" aspect of our course book.

The ongoing text provides background knowledge on topics, analysis, examples, and stories. With a light style, it makes the more abstract course ideas accessible to students. Or so we hope!

- Part 1 establishes key concepts, core vocabulary, and basic analytical approaches.
- Part 2 presents the eight ways of knowing of the TOK course; disentangling them to consider their characteristic features, but also treating their dynamic interconnections.
- Part 3 deals with the eight areas of knowledge of the TOK course. It uses the TOK knowledge framework to structure exploration and comparison.
- Part 4 guides students to preparing good presentations and essays for assessment.

The "overview" pages give a graphic form to ideas presented in the text.

## 3. Planning your route

We have designed this book to support different routes through the TOK course. For one thing, we treat all the ways of knowing and areas of knowledge, though the course does not require that they all be considered in class. (The subject guide suggests that it would be appropriate to study in depth four of the eight ways of knowing and six of the eight areas of knowledge.) For another thing, we use considerable cross-reference to help students build on their previous ideas – and to fill in ideas missed in taking shortcuts through chapters.

It is extremely useful, however, no matter what route you take, to get a sense of the territory through which you will be moving. You'll gain a quick impression by doing the following:

- read the Table of Contents
- have a look at the interchapters, from first to last
- check out the main chapters of transition: chapter 4 introduces ways of knowing, chapter 13 bridges from ways of knowing to areas of knowledge, and chapter 14 introduces areas of knowledge and the knowledge framework
- glance at the refreshment to core concepts that opens Part 4 on assessment.

If you are familiar with the general direction of the book and where it pauses for summary and transition, you'll find it easier to ignore some of the trails, but still gain from the cumulative exploration of ideas.

That cumulative exploration is what the TOK course is all about. Knowledge is complex – multifaceted and interconnected. For the purposes of discussion, we disentangle to the extent we can the components of knowledge for reflection and examination, using the model of eight WOK and eight AOK. But these are never to be treated as though they exist in isolation from each other: the relationships of concepts, the connections between parts of the model, and the broad comparisons we draw across all knowledge are truly the essence of theory of knowledge.

You will find that we treat ways of knowing as interactive. You will also find that within areas of knowledge we refer back extensively to ways of knowing for the creation, communication, and evaluation of knowledge, including justifications of knowledge claims. Throughout, we keep in play central ideas from the beginning of the book – primarily that we construct our knowledge humanly, from different perspectives, and that for exchange of knowledge in any context we benefit from the interdependent combination of thinking critically and keeping an open mind.

Connecting the concepts of the course and the parts of the TOK model is essential to developing a sense of the holistic nature of knowledge. Indeed, the most recent curriculum review group has recommended teaching ways of knowing almost entirely within areas of knowledge in order to ensure that such interconnection is achieved.

## 4. Bon voyage!

We end with our very best wishes to you as you pick up our book to consider its role in your own teaching. Education is one undertaking that is never finished, that is always to be tackled afresh with each year's group of students. It is oriented toward the future and, in TOK, toward inspiring goals. When we take our students along the road toward achieving them, we contribute something worthwhile to the world.

*Eileen Dombrowski*

## 1. Recognizing Perspectives

### Opening activity

Please don't read the box below yet! First, make sure you have a sheet of blank paper and a pen or dark pencil. Write your name and nationality clearly at the top of the paper. When you are ready (or, if you're in class, when *everyone* is ready) read and follow the instructions. May your journey begin!

### Get ready to draw

You have seven minutes in which to draw, as accurately and completely as you can, a map of the world. Don't waste time telling yourself that you can't. Just do your best and discover what you carry (or don't carry) in your mind as your picture of the world. You will not be marked on the accuracy of the results. When you have finished, be prepared to show the results to others in your class.

### Introduction

➔ "How, old one, may I find the Flame? Long have I heard it fabled, but never have my eyes beheld it."

➔ "Young one, the adventure is yours to seek. The journey brings untold riches to one who is true to the spirit of the quest."

➔ "I have heard of dangers on the way, of false paths and sinking swamps. How may I journey safely?"

➔ "Take from me these three magic weapons. Don this golden helmet, the helmet of vision; seek always for the truth. Fasten over your young shoulders this gossamer cape, the cape of compassion; care always for others. And take from my hands this silver sword and shield; the shield will protect you from hostile barbs and the blade will cut through forests that would lose you in their tangles."

➔ "But how shall I find the way?"

➔ "That, my young Quester, you must find for yourself."

And so, in the pattern of many a narrative, starts the journey. A young quester, who is armed with symbolic powers passed on from a figure who is old and wise, searches for Truth or Love or Fortune. He must overcome foes and surmount barriers to be fully tested and victorious. There is something fundamental about seeking and questioning, something archetypal about answering riddles, something deeply appealing about uncovering mysteries.

In our own lives, we often find some personal resonance with such patterns of the quest and the journey: the path ahead of us is not always clear; the way seems tangled, but alluring in its adventure. But alas, in the narratives of our own lives, no Wise One comes along to hand us ready-made golden helmets from some handy helmet supply in the cupboard.

In order to find out what's true, we have to do the work ourselves – devoid of helmets of vision and swords that slice through tangles of confusion. But what is the *goal*? Without an all-purpose mythic Flame burning away on some mountaintop to be sought as our heroic Task, we have to figure out ourselves what goal we're trying to reach.

If you're going our way, would you like to join us? We are about to go exploring. Our own goal is fairly clear: we want to understand why people believe so many different things all around the world, and why people do not agree on everything, even in our own societies. We hope to figure out what it means to "know" something, since ice skaters, scientists, and sculptors *all* seem to "know", but in very different ways. We will ask the question "What, then, counts as 'knowledge'?" We also want to gain some skills, so that we can join the social and academic discussions around us and be able to make a valuable contribution. These are our goals.

We think the journey will be quite an adventure. There will be no magic forests or dragons to slay, but if you can do without them, we can offer some tangled thinking to cut through along the way. We can also show you some ancient questions that, when you touch them, will instantly spring to life. Best of all, we can give you some craft sessions where you take the basic raw materials of your own thinking and shape them, with growing skill, into your own helmet of vision or cape of compassion.

But be warned that the path to our goal will not be wide and straight. If you choose to join us, you'll find it keeps looping back to the same central question of "How do we know?", moving in on it from different angles and adding shades of meaning to it with each pass. However, you'll find that we also move forward, carrying with us, as we go, the question of "How do we know?", along with plenty of others that go with it. They're light to carry. When you leave us, you'll be taking them with you in your own way.

What we can promise you, if you're hesitating, is that we will not let you get lost. You will have to make the journey yourself, but we'll be there to guide. We'll give you the tools you need: not exactly a silver sword, but at least a map of the territory, and a ready supply of relevant concepts and vocabulary. You'll also have some good companions along the way. Others are joining us in the journey, so we can expect some good discussions around the campfires.

We're off. Are you coming? If so, you have to undertake your first task. If you haven't done the opening activity of this chapter yet, go back and do it before you continue. It will take you seven minutes. And then you'll be ready to join your fellow travellers.

## Our map

If you want to glance ahead to the territory we will cover in this book, first go back. Flip to the table of contents. There you will find two simultaneous sequences. If you trace the main chapter headings, you will find the topic outline for the theory of knowledge course. If you then trace the sequence of features that follow many of the chapters, emerging from their contents, you will find that

they give a skeleton for the cumulative thinking skills you will acquire during the course.

As for the values that guide us – you'll find those distilled in the IB learner profile. We hope that its overriding aim will find support in the book ahead:

> The aim of all IB programmes is to develop internationally minded people who, recognizing their common humanity and shared guardianship of the planet, help to create a better and more peaceful world.

Of all the qualities identified in the learner profile, we hope above all to foster the precious balance between being open-minded and thinking critically. The two are tightly interconnected, and together provide us with enough motivation to write all the words that fill this book and to guide our journey into knowledge.

And the method? Inquiry! Join us.

## Your own map of the world

Look at your own map that you drew as the opening activity of this chapter and place it with the drawings done by your classmates. If they are quite similar to each other, can you suggest reasons why? If they are quite different from each other, why might this be the case?

- What part of the world is in the centre of your map?
- What parts of the world have you drawn in greatest detail? What parts of the world have you drawn in little detail or even left out?

### Discussion Activity

#### Match the maps

The hand-drawn maps on the next page were sketched by students from

- Japan
- Greenland
- Italy
- Costa Rica
- Canada.

Can you match each map with the student that is most likely to have drawn it?

What clues are provided by what's in the centre and what is drawn in greatest detail? Did you notice first the relative accuracy of the drawing of your own part of the world?

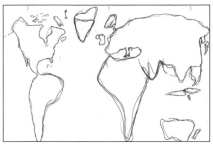

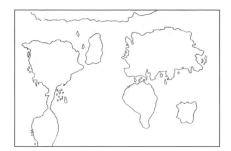

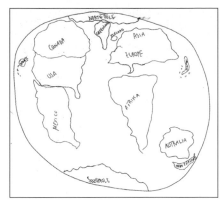

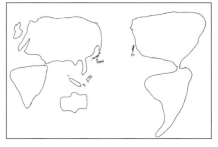

As you matched each map to the nationality of the student who drew it, from the list given, how did you know?

## Voices

### Some student voices

What's in the middle when west and east are just relative directions on a spinning globe?

Toi Yam Karyn Wong, China: In Chinese the name for China is "Middle Kingdom". Historically we thought of ourselves in the centre of the world. We didn't actually need anyone else. You can see the idea of "middle" in the first character of the name.

中 国

Does north have to be at the top? What is "up" on a globe in space?

Ruakiri Fairhill, New Zealand: Our Maori map (on the next page) always puts the south at the top because the map is actually a picture of the creation of the islands of New Zealand.

The name of the south island, Te waka-a-Maui, means "Maui's canoe" and the name of the north island, Te ika-a-Maui, means "Maui's fish". In the story, Maui, our god ancestor, had travelled from faraway islands with his four brothers. His canoe hit a rock (Rakiura, Stewart Island) and got stuck. It never moved again and became the south island. There the brothers decided to go fishing, sensing that there was something big under the sea. Maui hooked a giant fish and dragged it to the surface. His brothers jumped on it and killed it with their oars. It turned to stone and became the north island. You can see the fish in the shape of the island. It's a stingray. The map has to put the fish's mouth at the top because that's how Maui pulled it out of the water.

Besides, the head has to be at the top because it's the most significant part of the body – it's the first part the Sun sees, it's the first part that you see when someone appears over a hill, and it's the part that holds all knowledge. Our picture of the islands as the canoe and the fish is part of our everyday speech in Maori. I live on the north island, and my region is referred to as "the fish's stomach". If I go to the south island, I'd say, "I'm going up to the canoe". And we refer to Wellington as "the fish's mouth".

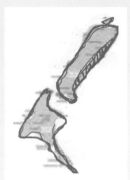

### How many continents are there?

Adam Spooner, England: There are seven continents — Antarctica, North America, South America, Europe, Asia, Africa, and Australasia (or Oceania). This is what I learned in school and all continent maps colour these seven differently.

The division of North and South America is just common sense. They have completely different histories as they were colonized differently. The Panama Canal divides them, though it does leave Central America in a rather grey zone.

Europe and Asia are different continents, divided along the Ural Mountains and the Black and Bosphorus Seas. I learned that Istanbul (or Constantinople) was seen historically as the gateway to Asia and the last step of what was known. This vision was tied to the idea of the Roman Empire as the civilized world.

I can see now the inconsistencies in division of continents, in that some have a geographical justification and some have a political or historical justification.

### How many continents are there?

Giorgina Alfonso Rodriguez, Uruguay: North America, Central America, and South America – they are all one continent. They are naturally joined together. The Panama Canal was man-made.

If it's more than one, it has to be three if you are dividing geographically, to recognize Central America. How can some Europeans say that it's two continents and call Europe, which is joined to Asia, a continent?

I think that when some people divide America, they are thinking about culture and not the land at all. When they talk about North America, they're really talking only about Canada and the United States.

### What determines where borders are drawn?

Priyanka Karuvelil, Canada: I lived in India until I was 15. When I came to Canada, I realized that the map I had of India wasn't accurate by international standards. We don't really have half of Kashmir. Still, it was difficult at first to overcome my views. I have felt very patriotic and proud that India would not compromise its ideals.

Janeen Madan, Pakistan: It's like my history books. What I studied in India was not what was studied in Pakistan. Gandhi is glorified in India and called "father of the nation", and so is Mohammed Ali Jinnah in Pakistan. But each country minimizes the historical role of the other's leader, or treats him disparagingly. Watching news and popular media, you don't see an alternate view and you believe what you see.

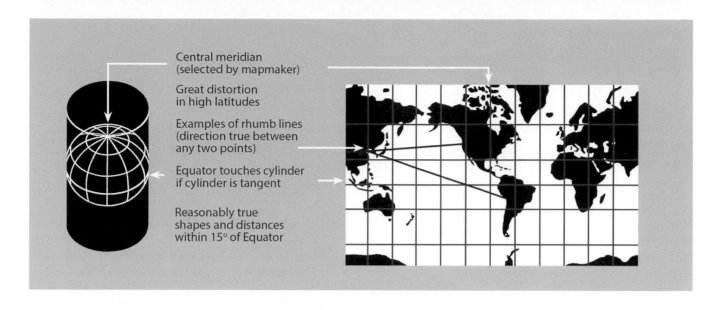

Central meridian (selected by mapmaker)

Great distortion in high latitudes

Examples of rhumb lines (direction true between any two points)

Equator touches cylinder if cylinder is tangent

Reasonably true shapes and distances within 15° of Equator

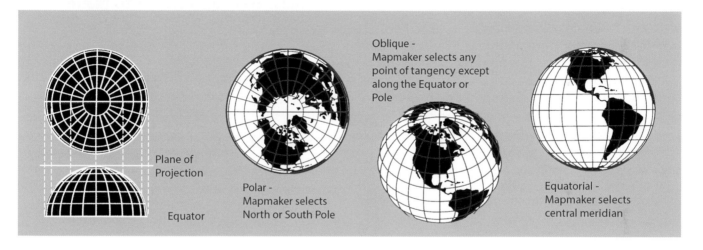

Plane of Projection

Equator

Polar - Mapmaker selects North or South Pole

Oblique - Mapmaker selects any point of tangency except along the Equator or Pole

Equatorial - Mapmaker selects central meridian

## The maps of cartographers

It is understandable that student maps sketched from memory will vary. However, shouldn't the maps made by professional cartographers give a correct version of the world?

There's a problem. It is impossible to make an entirely accurate representation of the world. Shrinking the whole world even to a three-dimensional globe means that so much is left out and so much is made tiny at such a large scale. Any map of the world represents the ground at a very, very high level of overall generalization.

It is also impossible to show a sphere on a flat surface without warping and distorting it. Imagine peeling an orange or other round fruit. The peel removed simply does not lie flat. Facing this problem, cartographers are compelled to make choices of what

to preserve as most accurate and what to allow as distortion. They use different projections to peel the earth in different ways, with each way stretching and warping the "peel" differently. Conical, cylindrical, and single-centred projections all provide different approaches and all have different merits.

Maps are made, in general, for a practical purpose. They are used to show relative position of one country to another, to navigate, to trace geographical features such as fault lines, or to represent a connection between the physical world and other information (such as population growth, spread of HIV/AIDS, incidence of hunger, distribution of the world's languages or religions, and so forth). For example, the Mercator map, devised originally by Mercator in Germany in 1569, was devised as a mariner's map, useful for nautical purposes because it gave constant courses

## Discussion Activity

### What is the "right" view of the world?

Of the world maps pictured in this activity, which is most familiar to you? Does the familiar one seem "right"? Do any of the maps seem "wrong"?

### What is selected to be shown by each map?

- Do the maps represent the physical geography of the world, human political divisions, or other information connected with territory?
- Does each map have an identifiable purpose?

### What is emphasized in each case?

- What is in the centre or both in the centre and at the top?
- Does the map give as much attention to the water as it does to the land?
- Is the equator central in the vertical plane?
- What is distorted, and how, by the particular projection chosen?
- Does the particular distortion give greater importance to any particular part of the world, or any idea about the world?
- Is colour or naming used in an attention–grabbing manner?
- If we see Earth from space, where do we freeze the frame on the rotating planet? Is the cloud cover given or removed?

### Which map orientations reflect the natural world and which ones are invented for human purposes?

- How do we determine north, south, and the equator on a planet spinning in space?
- Does north have to be "up" on a map?
- How do we determine east and west when all points are relatively east of something and west of something else?
- Historically, what determined where the prime meridian of longitude was placed?
- Do lines of latitude and longitude "really" exist?
- What political and economic ideas come with "north" and "south", "east" and "west"?
- What determines where we draw the lines which separate countries?

The maps selected here represent only a few of the many, many possibilities of representation. Can you find other representations that introduce further ideas into your discussion?

We can now view world maps on the Internet and zoom in to study places of our choice. What effect does this have on the pictures of the world we carry in our minds?

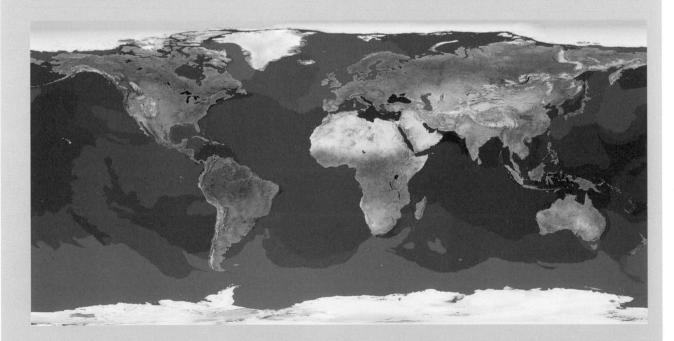

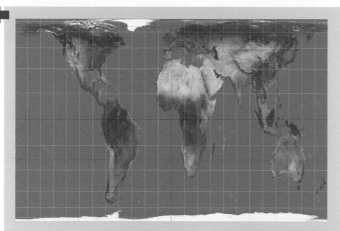

*Fighting Hunger Worldwide*

The cost of hunger to developing nations is an estimated US$450 billion per year.

It takes only 25 US cents for WFP to give a hungry schoolchild a cup of food with all the nutrition needed for the day.

The number of undernourished people worldwide is just under 1 billion – equivalent to the population of North America and Europe combined.

# Hunger Map 2011

WFP
**World Food Programme**
wfp.org

| Category | 1 | 2 | 3 | 4 | 5 | Incomplete data |
|---|---|---|---|---|---|---|
| Undernourished | <5% | 5–9% | 10–19% | 20–34% | ≥35% | |
| Description | Extremely low | Very low | Moderately low | Moderately high | Very high | |

## Adventuring off the map

Wandering around Colorado with Duncan for two weeks [in 1972] seemed almost as good as running away. I'd shown my father, on a topographical map, more or less where we meant to go, but all I really knew was the spot where we planned to get off the train. There were no cell phones or G.P.S. devices or Park Service Web sites in those days, and we hadn't read a guidebook about the region, and there was no one to check in with before we set out. Today, on Google Earth, I can zoom down on jade-colored mountain lakes that must be ones we camped beside, but at the time I felt almost as though we'd crossed into another dimension, that we had become invisible to the rest of the universe as soon as the train was out of sight. The world seemed much bigger then than it does now." David Owen[1]

of navigation as straight lines. The distortion of the size and shape of continents, especially as the scale increases from the equator to the poles, was a by-product of a map that served its own purposes very well.

Used as a representation of the world outside the context of navigation, however, the Mercator map is striking for its distortion of size and shapes: South America is actually almost double the size of Europe, but Europe appears larger; India is roughly three times the size of Scandinavia, but Scandinavia appears larger; the southern hemisphere is squashed into one third of the map's surface, while the northern hemisphere takes up two thirds. It is a view of the world with Europe top, centre, and enlarged, so it is visually dominant.

Historically, the Mercator map became an icon of Eurocentric thinking because of the way in which it was adopted by colonial powers and spread by them to their colonies. So familiar did the map become that most Europeans throughout the era of major colonialism would have been unaware of the extent of the distortion or the way that it reinforced their own perspective on the world. As they introduced the map into the educational systems of their colonies, they passed on their own vision of the world.

## Maps and views of the world

"Oops, I forgot that bit that sticks down in the Far East!" remarked a student from Europe (from which the East is Far) as she examined the map she had just drawn. As we dredge up from memory our pictures of the world and attempt to draw them, we are obviously doing so as individuals with differing past attention to geography, differing memories, and differing drawing skills. As well as being individuals, we are also members of our own social groups in our own home spot on the planet. The students who call the Far East "home" are not likely to forget, accidentally, the Southeast Asian peninsula – though they might not remember all the bumps of Europe. Our pictures of the world, and our knowledge of the world, are learned within our own contexts and our own cultural worldviews.

Our maps, often beautiful and enticing, are images not just of our planet but of the *way that we think about our planet*. As we flatten planet Earth for viewing, we choose a particular projection (with its influence on shape and size), up/down orientation, and centring. We overlay the image with conceptual schemes that cannot be seen in nature: the grid lines, borders, colours, and names. These precious images, which pack so much knowledge onto a small surface, are a product of our history, our technological skill, and our politics. It is strange to think that, aside from recent astronauts, no one throughout history has ever seen the Earth from far above with our own eyes. It may seem stranger still that the astronauts could *not* see what is so often most important to us about the surface of our planet – the invisible *ideas* that we tie to it. We link the Earth with ideas of time (zones), economics (developed/developing world), and culture (for example, the west/the east). We link ourselves to it with ideas of belonging to certain places and not to others. And, sometimes with grim consequences, we link it with ownership through our placement of borders and selection of names.

"Owning" land, after all, is a cultural concept, an *idea* of a relationship between human beings and their natural environment. At the time of European conquests in the nineteenth century, many indigenous peoples made no distinction between themselves and the land that they lived

---

[1] Owen, D. 19 March 2012. "Scars, A Life in Injuries". *The New Yorker.* P 44.

on. They did not think of the grazing lands or hunting grounds that sustained them as "property". Moreover, even indigenous groups who considered the rightful use of a particular territory to be theirs rather than a neighbouring tribe's had no systems of proving entitlement that could convince invaders of their ownership of the land. Any arguments they might employ, such as customary uses of the territory, stories connecting the people to the land, and sacred geography, did not "translate" into systems recognized by their conquerors. In any case, why would invaders *want* to consider alternative cultural means of laying claim to land that they were intent on taking over themselves?

One major cultural system of claiming "ownership" of land, in this example as in others, has been the map. As an idea-tool, maps have long been used for controlling empires: map knowledge was once the knowledge of rulers. Maps are at the heart of many of the fiercest conflicts around the world because maps represent not only *what we see* in terms of territory, but also *what we believe* about that territory. With a map, the nineteenth century European colonial powers carved up their territorial possessions from a distance, imposing borders and ownership that created a reality with vast consequences for those that lived there. With a map, technologically advanced nations have dropped bombs on targets without ever having seen the faces of the people killed by the blast, as was the case with the so-called "smart bombs" of the Iraq war.

Yet a map is an idea-tool that, in itself, is neutral. Although it can be used for conquest, it can also be used for representing, guiding, or contextualizing knowledge of many kinds. Maps give a means of connecting ideas with geographical regions, including ideas concerning distribution of physical resources, interaction through trade or other forms of exchange (such as the spread of the International Baccalaureate worldwide), or relative current conditions (such as hunger or literacy). It would be more difficult to pursue ideas in many areas of knowledge without maps.

## The concept of "perspectives"

Is it wrong to place ourselves in the centre of our own maps of the world? Surely not. Often we learn by moving outward from our own centres of self, family and society as we learn more about the world. Imaginatively entering a different vision of the world that is "off centre" or "upside down" according to our own conventions and beliefs can bring an exciting new revelation about how we think of ourselves, compared to how others view us.

"I never knew Africa was so big," commented an African student from a former European colony, realizing for the first time that the map on his classroom wall at home had exaggerated the size of Europe. "Maybe I'm not from 'down under' after all!" declared an Australian student enjoying the upside-down map of the world.

## Native American buckskin map

This map from the 1770s was probably made by the Piankashaw people on tanned deer hide. From the combination of native markings and English words on it, it appears to have been used within a land transaction. The curator of the British Museum notes:

While the European handwritten words, as well as perhaps the use of commercial inks, indicate the participation of Europeans in making this map, the conventions are Native American. The lines and symbols on the map are drawn in a symbolic and cosmological manner, as opposed to topographically. The Wabash River, drawn down the middle of the hide, is not rendered literally, but rather follows the spine of the deer, mapped out following the life force of the animal as an indication that this river would have been the life force of the people who drew this map.[2]

↑ Native American buckskin map

2   Devorah Romanek, curator, British Museum. "North American buckskin map". http://www.bbc.co.uk/ahistoryoftheworld/objects/-UqCYd_4Rfy85epzSvpaQA.

"I didn't know that India's map of Kashmir wasn't everyone's," acknowledged a student from India, painfully recognizing at least the existence of alternative political claims. Each of these students had achieved a realization of differing ways of presenting the mapped world and the ideas those representations carried with them.

Does recognition that maps can be drawn within different systems of representation and from different points of view mean that all maps are equally right? Yes, if all we ask of a map is that it would represent someone's worldview or be useful for a practical purpose we have chosen. If these are the criteria for an accurate map, then we need only ask for that map to *be coherent* with one particular way of thinking. However, as soon as we expect the map's picture of the world to *correspond* to how the world really is, we will have to recognize that some images are better than others – better, as a picture of the world outside our minds. If a version leaves out (or invents) an entire continent, it is faulty. If a version changes sizes or shapes of land masses in a way inconsistent with its projection, it is faulty. If a version imposes borders that are not accepted by the world community, it may be harder to declare it faulty by reference to geographical data but we still have political criteria for doing so. Our picture of the world needs to be checked against the world itself. Later in this course, we will be further exploring both *coherence with our thinking* and *correspondence with external reality* as major checks for the truth of statements we make about ourselves and the world.

And so, here is one of the major challenges for all of us, human beings building our understanding of ourselves and our world. Can we simultaneously appreciate the variability of perspectives, and at the same time insist on some standard of accurate representation with which to evaluate them all? How do we deal with perspectives that flatly contradict each other in their assertions and interpretations, such as conflicting accounts of historical events, conflicting theories in the sciences, or arguments in ethics? How do we deal with worldviews that clash? Are we compelled to accept *one* or the *other*, or is there a way of finding common ground that includes plural possibilities? In attempting to understand, evaluate, reject, or reconcile multiple views, we are taking on possibly the most interesting and significant challenge of living in an international and intercultural world. We are aiming to combine two major goals: *being open to alternative perspectives* and *being able to assess them critically.*

## The role of perspectives in knowledge

Let's now try to get to grips, a bit more firmly, with this important concept of *perspectives*. When we talk about "perspectives" on knowledge or within knowledge, we are speaking *metaphorically*: we're using a common physical experience of seeing an object from different sides to illustrate a conceptual experience of seeing the same question from different sides. We may use expressions such as, "From where I stand, it looks like …". We may talk about personal, cultural, or theoretical "points of view", "different angles" on a topic, and "different sides" to the same story. We may speak of "converging" and "diverging" points of view. The term "perspectives", which can be illustrated graphically in the visual arts, has become a pervasive metaphor for the recognition that the

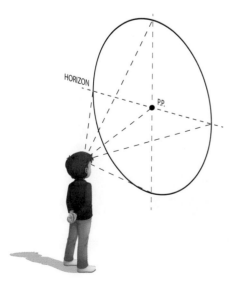
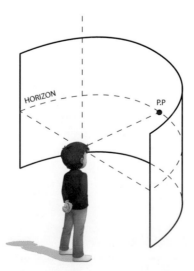
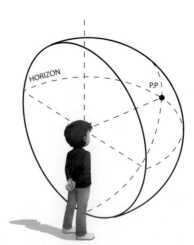

> It is my hypothesis that the fundamental source of conflict in this new world [of the future] will not be primarily ideological or primarily economic. The great divisions among humankind and the dominating source of conflict will be cultural. Nation states will remain the most powerful actors in world affairs, but the principal conflicts of global politics will occur between nations and groups of different civilizations. The clash of civilizations will dominate global politics. The fault lines between civilizations will be the battle lines of the future.[3]
>
> *Samuel Huntington*

same object or the same idea can be "viewed" or *thought of* differently. It is easy to *see* that a perspective drawing anchors the vision in one moment of time from one point in space – and that other versions are possible.

Up to this point, we have been using world maps to take the idea of perspectives a little further than a simple drawing from different angles. Maps, like perspective drawings, demonstrate to us, graphically, that what we observe changes with our chosen vantage point. They also show us the inevitable simplification of the world in our useful representations of it, illustrate the influence of our histories and worldviews on what we consider to be "natural" or "normal", and demonstrate the difficulty of separating what we observe in the world *perceptually* from what we think in our minds *conceptually*.

Nevertheless, both drawings and world maps prove to be limited in the extent to which they can act as effective metaphorical equivalents for perspectives within knowledge. Perspectives in knowledge cannot be pointed to physically; they are intangible, and they shift and change as people do. They are immensely complex, and they exert huge influence on how we gain knowledge, what we consider it to be, and how we might evaluate it. They hold together whole bodies of beliefs.

Differing perspectives within knowledge can apply to fairly superficial matters of interpretation or opinion that have little importance in our lives. However, they apply more significantly to large conceptual frameworks that give us our ways of integrating and making sense of what we know. In this regard, we may speak of cultural perspectives, political perspectives, or religious perspectives, for example. These are generally learned from an early age within the family, school, or community. We may speak, too, of perspectives within areas of knowledge, which are provided by overarching academic explanations such as theories within the sciences or interpretations within history. Similarly, we may speak of perspectives on society involving concepts of gender, race, or class. We can see these perspectives informally within the community and media, or more formally within social research and analysis. Perspectives draw together assumptions and values, bodies of beliefs, knowledge held in common, and shared practices of validation.

People's differing perspectives, tied closely with what they *already* know or *already* believe, affect the further knowledge they seek, understand, and accept. Often, too, people group together with others who share their perspectives and thereby reinforce their own prior beliefs and limit their exposure to alternative views. Indeed, it is possible for groups of people to live almost as if in bubbles isolated from each other, even if they live next door. This can happen to such an extent that, when they speak about their world, they do not appear even to be living in the same one!

## Cultural perspectives

### What is "culture"?

To understand how knowledge is constructed, it is important not to ignore its deeply influential human context. People build their knowledge from birth surrounded by many shaping forces from their families and communities, which are broadly clustered within the general term "culture".

Every reader of this book is likely to have an idea of what "culture" means. The trouble is that we might not all know the same thing. The word is ambiguous; it shifts meaning with context and is difficult to define. It applies to the intellectual and artistic products of a society, for one thing, so "culture" might make many of us think first of attending symphony concerts or reading great

---

[3]  Huntington, SP. Summer 2003. "The Clash of Civilizations". *Foreign Affairs.*
    http://www.foreignaffairs.com/articles/48950/samuel-p-huntington/the-clash-of-civilizations

literature; people who do so are sometimes spoken of as "cultured". It also applies, though, to a much wider range of characteristic features that we can observe: the food, the way of dressing, the way men and women interact, the wedding rituals, and the characteristic dances or games, for instance. In one definition supplied by the American Anthropological Association, the circle is drawn even wider to encompass "the learned patterns of behaviour (i.e. traditions and customs) characteristic of a society".[4]

Here, we want to go wider still with the concept of culture. In order to consider perspectives on the world, we are talking of culture as an entire worldview, involving the underlying assumptions and beliefs that are invisible to the eye. Anthropologist Clifford Geertz gives a definition that digs deep into how people think and feel: "Culture is the fabric of meaning in terms of which human beings interpret their experience and guide their action." He considers it the "framework of beliefs, expressive symbols, and values in terms of which individuals define their world".[5]

This is a definition we can adopt. However, you will immediately recognize that we have accepted with it a lot of complexity – features that are immaterial and elude direct observation, and ideas that are difficult to pin down.

The complexities grow when we try to identify the features shared by a particular cultural group. Group identities are not composed of a neatly definitive list of component elements on which all anthropologists or sociologists will agree. Nor are they homogeneous: there can be considerable diversity within a group, to the extent that we can speak of many cultures within a larger society. Nor are cultures static, frozen forever and immune to change! And certainly we cannot expect that any one individual thinks just like others of the group to which he belongs. It is likely, in any case, that any one person belongs to several different groups and so will share in a whole host of different worldviews.

Indeed, if we recognize all of these difficulties in just finding the group characteristics that we are talking about as culture, we have to acknowledge that we can generalize only in the broadest of terms.

Yet, despite its elusiveness, the concept of culture is hotly contested for many of the real-life implications that come with it:

- Do we accept *at all* that cultural identity exists in a meaningful way and that it is to be respected and preserved (if it's not too late)?
- Do we accept the culture as worth preserving, though, only if its values accord with a standard external to the group (such as human rights)?
- Do groups affirm the concept of culture to reinforce ideas of ethnicity and nationalism, possibly with dangerous consequences to those who do not belong to the group?
- Do groups deny the existence of cultural identity in order to remove barriers and forcibly assimilate peoples as they also absorb their geographical resources?
- What does "multiculturalism" mean in societies of the world characterized by diversity?

If we want to understand how groups of people interact with each other in the world, we clearly have to try to get to grips with "culture" – not just to comprehend how the word is defined, but to understand how it is used in argument.

So, yes, the concept is complex and the word "culture" is ambiguous when it is not given precise definitions in specific contexts. Let us be aware of this complexity. But let us not be deterred from using the word.

## For Reflection

As you think about the way language is used around you, are you aware of words or expressions that seem to take on different meanings for different people, or seem to be used in arguments in different ways? Thinking about what words mean involves far more than consulting an alphabetical list in a dictionary (as we'll consider further in chapter 8 on language as a way of knowing).

---

4   American Anthropological Association. http://www.aaanet.org/committees/commissions/aec/resources.htm
5   Geertz, C. 1973. *The Interpretation of Cultures*. New York. Basic Books. P 145

## Culture and knowledge

The relationship between culture and knowledge is an intimate one, since culture affects what we consider to be important knowledge. In this course, we want to understand the influence culture has on how we use our ways of knowing – our observations, language, reasoning, emotions, memories, intuitions, imaginations, and faith. We want to understand the impact of different cultural views in our areas of knowledge. How do we start to gain this knowledge?

Do you recognize any of these voices? In this book, from our perspective, we are presenting cultural perspectives as inherently interesting and valuable to explore, regardless of whether we find them inspiring or disturbing. This, too, is an assumption and set of values to notice in reading. What are your own thoughts on this issue?

**For Reflection**

Here, we make a distinction between shared knowledge gained from sources such as books and teachers, and personal knowledge gained from your own experience. In your own life, which kind of knowledge have you gained more extensively about cultural characteristics of different groups? Do the two forms of knowledge stay separate in your mind?

If we treat culture as "the fabric of meaning in terms of which human beings interpret their experience and guide their action" as Geertz does, it is so much part of our thinking that we notice it no more than the air we breathe. We take in our cultural "fabric of meaning" as we grow up within a community, learning our languages and appropriate behaviour, absorbing the assumptions and values of our group. People who are familiar only with one way of doing things are likely to consider it *the* way. They are not likely to even consider that there are other possibilities.

It is often through encountering differences that we discover how we think and what we believe ourselves and come to see the social context within which knowledge, both our own and others', is constructed. That encounter can take the form of gaining greater *shared knowledge*, public knowledge that others have previously gained and communicated. Through reading news, watching documentaries, or studying academic subjects which deal with human beings and society, for example, we have the chance to consider more consciously the diversity of ways of thinking – and the effect of that diversity on the exchange of knowledge in our academic disciplines, our workplaces, and our world.

The arts may have a particular role here, since enjoying music or dance from different cultures, or reading literature in translation, can give us a small window into other ways of experiencing and viewing the world. Losing a sense of "strangeness" of unfamiliar customs helps to create a more receptive attitude towards the people who practise them.

The encounter with cultural characteristics which are foreign to us can also come through personal experience. Through travel, we can extend our awareness of how differently things can be

## American and Chinese perspectives

### "The View from Both Sides"

It is tricky to make generalizations about specific cultures without stumbling. Broad generalizations about groups can too easily feed into stereotypes, oversimplified pictures that distort reality and blind people to the variations within culture that actually exist. Yet without recognition of broad cultural characteristics, it is difficult to be sensitive to differences and prepared to modify one's own style of communication. It is also difficult to interpret the behaviour one encounters. Well founded generalizations on culture can be immensely informative, keeping in mind the possibility that they might not apply in all cases.

One beneficial strategy towards better understanding of cultural generalizations is to consider the context within which they are offered, and the perspective from which they are given. Here, the comparison of American and Chinese views is from the perspective of experts on business negotiation, writing an article to the *Harvard Business Review*. This was aimed towards an American audience and was written to help them understand how they appear to the Chinese. John Graham and Mark Lam, the authors, are speaking specifically about the cultural context of making business deals.

Their goal in writing is to give the practical benefit they announce early in their article:

> The challenge of mutual understanding is great; American and Chinese approaches often appear incompatible. All too often, Americans see Chinese negotiators as inefficient, indirect, and even dishonest, while the Chinese see American negotiators as aggressive, impersonal, and excitable. Such differences have deep cultural origins. Yet those who know how to navigate these differences can develop thriving, mutually profitable, and satisfying business relationships.[6]

In the table that Graham and Lam provide, only a couple of terms are likely to need explanation. Chief among them is the opposition between

American negotiators seeking "the truth" and Chinese negotiators seeking "the way". The article is comparing American emphasis on factual information with Chinese emphasis on finding the harmony between forces, the "Middle Way" associated with taoism.

# The View from Both Sides

## American Chinese

### Their basic cultural values and ways of thinking

| American | Chinese |
| --- | --- |
| individualist | collectivist |
| egalitarian | hierarchical |
| information oriented | relationship oriented |
| reductionist | holistic |
| sequential | circular |
| seeks the truth | seeks the way |
| the argument culture | the haggling culture |

### How they approach the negotiation process
#### nontask sounding

| American | Chinese |
| --- | --- |
| quick meetings | long courting process |
| informal | formal |
| make cold calls | draw on intermediaries |

#### information exchange

| American | Chinese |
| --- | --- |
| full authority | limited authority |
| direct | indirect |
| proposals first | explanations first |

#### means of persuasion

| American | Chinese |
| --- | --- |
| aggressive | questioning |
| impatient | enduring |

#### terms of agreement

| American | Chinese |
| --- | --- |
| forging a "good deal" | forging a long-term relationship |

---

6  Graham, J.L. and Lam, N.M. 1 October 2003. "The Chinese Negotiation". *Harvard Business Review*. P 2.

IB Diploma Programme students: Fostering international-mindedness

Every IB Diploma Programme student brings his or her own perspective on the world to enrich our TOK class discussions. We all benefit from the exchange as we consider multiple views and traditions, and their roles in constructing knowledge. However, it is not necessary that your TOK class have a variety of cultures within it to achieve the international-mindedness that the IB encourages. Being open to other perspectives and able to approach differences with interest and inquiry will take you far towards this ideal, even if you and your classmates never set foot outside your own home region.

photos by Eileen Dombrowski

done – though many of us will find abundant diversity in our own home communities. Through knowing individuals from other backgrounds in a multicultural setting, we can blend both knowing people (our classmates, our co-workers, our friends) with knowing, through them, some aspects of their worldviews that grow out of their cultures. When we stumble on moments of difference, we might, if we are alert, be able to talk about them and learn more.

Personal experience of complete immersion in an unfamiliar culture, though, can often be extremely challenging. Many people experiencing what has become known as "culture shock" report similar experiences – confusion over what is happening

around them as they do not understand unfamiliar social cues and conduct. They often also report exhaustion and deep loneliness.

A major cure for culture shock is increased *knowledge*, a growing familiarity with how to interpret words and gestures, and a greater understanding of how to fit in personally with the new codes of behaviour and meaning.

Living well with people involves *cultural learning*. For those who are open-minded and emotionally receptive, recognition of alternative possibilities can be transformative: it can open up some of the richness of diversity in the world that we share with others. It can also lead to greater appreciation of the huge range of human thought and expression.

This kind of knowledge can have important implications, too, if we extrapolate to a world scale. The UNESCO Universal Declaration on Cultural Diversity[7] connects a genuinely open and respectful attitude towards differing cultural perspectives with a worldwide reduction in conflict: "respect for the diversity of cultures, tolerance, dialogue and cooperation, in a climate of mutual trust and understanding [is] among the best guarantees of international peace and security". It affirms cultural diversity to be "the common heritage of mankind" and proclaims its value, stating, "As a source of exchange, innovation and creativity, cultural diversity is as necessary for humankind as biodiversity is for nature".

## Recognizing cultural perspectives

Clearly, the knowledge gained through encounter with diversity goes further than simple recognition that different worldviews exist. Greater understanding also affects *how we think*. If we can enter into alternative views to "stand in someone else's shoes" or "look through their eyes" we can begin to understand *how perspective works*. With awareness and attention, we begin to notice the assumptions, beliefs, and values that come with different perspectives. We notice, too, the ways in which perspectives affect the terms in which different groups talk about issues, the kind of language they use, and the facts that they select as important. We also start to recognize the differing procedures and processes that groups use to validate and communicate their ideas.

As we learn increasingly to recognize these features of perspectives, we begin to listen more actively and possibly form better questions for further inquiry. In this way, we can understand better the impact on the knowledge we possess

of the different perspectives that can be taken on it – cultural, political, or historical perspectives, for instance, or perspectives from within different areas of knowledge.

It could be argued that this capacity for shifting perspectives also has some significant implications: it can improve relationships, reduce frictions at work or in the community, generate new ideas for problem-solving of all kinds, and help us understand the ways of thinking that, for better or for worse, drive the world. Understanding the range of cultural patterns can also give us ideas on how to deal with problems within our own cultures.

## Cultural characteristics: the observable surface

Few of us will ever take culture as our formal lifetime study. Yet an awareness of some of the broad differences between cultures can help us recognize why cultural communities sometimes see issues differently and can increase our alertness to gaps in communication.

The small differences we can easily see often seize our full attention. Students entering an international school or staying with a host family when travelling, for instance, may meet a range of differences in behaviour. If they come from backgrounds where introduction or greeting involves standing at a distance or shaking hands, for example, they may feel quite shocked if someone from a different background steps close and kisses them on both cheeks. If they come from backgrounds where it is appropriate to refuse food at first when it is offered and wait until it is offered again, they may be quite dismayed (and hungry) to be taken immediately at their word. These

### Discussion Activity

#### What we don't know can hurt us: recognizing invisible assumptions of culture

**Case 1** A German IB student and an Argentinian IB student are sharing a room in residence at an international school. Both make a real effort to get to know each other at first, but for some reason things go wrong.

*Argentinian*: I've really tried to get to know her, but she's very cold. She hardly even greets me. I've tried to include her in conversations with my friends, but they don't feel very welcome in our room either. When it comes to the 10:30pm privacy time, she tells them to leave even if we're in the middle of a conversation. I think she

➡

---

[7] http://www2.ohchr.org/english/law/diversity.htm

cares more about rules and schedules than about relationships with people.

*German*: I want to share a room, but she wants it all. She's noisy and intrusive. I don't like her kissing me on the cheek but not really caring about my feelings or respecting my space. She has her friends in the room all the time and they talk and play their music loudly. Even when it comes to 10:30pm, when we're supposed to have privacy in our room, I have to speak to her friends before they'll leave. She doesn't even care about the code everyone's agreed to.

What cultural behaviour does each of these students notice in the other? Try to identify the assumptions that each makes, including the values according to which each judges the other. Are they genuinely *getting to know each other?*

*You might find it useful to consider some of the following concepts, which are aspects of culture: sense of time, sense of space, sense of fairness and justice, sense of individual or group identity. You might also consider greeting patterns and relative explicitness of communication.*

**Case 2** An American student and a Japanese student are going together on a school trip by bus. The American student values open honesty, expects frankness in communication and disagrees with others comfortably in public. The Japanese student values harmony, expects understanding of indirect suggestion and would not expose someone else publicly as making a questionable statement. Can you imagine their discussion over whether the bus window should be open or closed? The American student wants it open while the Japanese student wants it closed. Will it end up open or closed? Will both students *know why?*

**Case 3** Representatives of a Canadian mining company and a Chinese mining company meet to consider doing business with each other. Each does a presentation involving a talk and a slide show. On the surface, everything seems to go well. However, the contact between the companies falters and dies. What has gone wrong in the exchange of knowledge across cultures?

The Canadian presentation is led by one of the Canadian company's up-and-coming young executives, who has brought the company fresh ideas, including this outreach to China. He speaks dynamically about the company's future, with lively gestures and amusing anecdotes, and accompanies his talk with a slide show. It shows photographs of active mining sites, maps of their locations, and numerous informative graphs and tables on products and profits based on the Annual General Report of the previous year. The Chinese audience is very complimentary, telling the Canadians that they appreciated the fine presentation.

The Chinese presentation is led by one of the Chinese company's senior figures within middle management. He speaks formally of the company's past and accompanies his talk with a slide show. It shows first a photograph of the company's Chief Executive Officer, followed by a brief biography of the education and professional history of the CEO. It then lists all the other companies with which their own has done business over the previous decade, with numerous pictures of the CEO shaking hands with other CEOs. Several members of the Canadian delegation look puzzled, furrowing their eyebrows. One person asks whether they could be given the business information for the previous year, acting a little annoyed at the apparent evasion of real facts.

*You might find it useful to consider some of the following concepts, which are aspects of culture: hierarchy of age and position, sense of time, value given to relationships and insider/outsider distinctions (guanxi), value given to information and disclosure, directness or indirectness of communication.*

**PS** The window in #2. It'll be open, as you probably concluded. If the American student found out somehow that his Japanese classmate was distressed, his response could be total surprise: "Then why didn't he *just tell me*? Why didn't he speak up? I wouldn't have minded!" If the Japanese student were told of this reaction, he might think, "Do I have to be rude in order for him to notice what I was *really* saying? Is he so insensitive to people?"

differences in codes, even though they may cause disturbance, are quite superficial differences of customs regarding a sense of social space or a way of offering hospitality.

Some larger differences between cultures are also external differences. We might see others doing roughly the same things we do, but differently. We can readily observe the variations in what languages people speak, how they dress, how they worship, and what and how they eat. Also visible might be the ways in which men and women interact, the ways that older people are treated, and the degree to which members of the group mix with others beyond it. However, these external and observable features of culture are not the whole of culture, but merely its surface.

## Cultural characteristics: worldviews

Sometimes, external cultural differences provide windows into deeper cultural differences which lie below the surface. For an understanding beyond our own experiences and the limited stories we have heard, we must turn to the shared public knowledge given us through research and publication within fields such as anthropology and sociology (we will be considering human sciences as an area of knowledge later in the course). Through awareness of broad patterns identified by cultural theorists, we can grow more alert to assumptions and values that affect different features of our knowledge. We might also understand better the gaps that open up in communicating with others from different backgrounds.

## Three theoretical approaches to cultural differences

One of the major theories starts with a view of cultures as dealing with a limited number of

### For Reflection

Consider the culture or cultures to which you belong. What do you think its values are for each of Kluckhohn and Stodtbeck's five questions? How do you know?

universal human problems. Their central cultural values, then, are grounded in the solutions that they have preferred. In their **Values Orientation Theory,** Florence Kluckhohn and Fred Strodtbeck in 1961 picked out five problems that they argued are centrally important to all societies. How do cultures differ, they asked, in the answers they give to these questions?

- On what aspect of time should we primarily focus – past, present or future?
- What is the relationship between humanity and its natural environment – mastery, submission or harmony?
- How should individuals relate with others – in a hierarchy (which they called "Lineal"), as equals ("Collateral"), or according to their individual merit?
- What is the prime motivation for behaviour – to express one's self ("Being"), to grow ("Being-in-becoming"), or to achieve?
- What is fundamental human nature – good, bad ("Evil") or a mixture?[8]

Kluckhohn and Strodtbeck then undertook the challenging task of putting their questions in forms that made sense in the real-life context of the people they interviewed, and managed to develop value profiles for five different cultural groups. Their theory, which has sparked considerable further research since then, has been used to help communication across cultures and to examine changes in cultures over time.

A second major theorist, Geert Hofstede, took a different approach. From questionnaires administered to employees of an international company, living and working in their own countries, he determined four clusters of values that he called **"dimensions of culture"**. The framework that he developed in 1980[9] used a continuum between extremes to identify the values of any one culture relative to others.

- *Power distance:* the degree of inequality expected and accepted within a society.
- *Individualism/collectivism:* the spectrum between people being seen primarily as individuals who look after only themselves and immediate family and people being seen primarily as groups who look after their members and expect loyalty in return.

8  Hills, M. D. (2002). Kluckhohn and Strodtbeck's Values Orientation Theory. Online Readings in Psychology and Culture, Unit 4. Retrieved from http://scholarworks.gvsu.edu/orpc/vol4/iss4/3

9  Hofstede, G. 1980. *Culture's Consequences: International Differences in Work-related Values*. Beverley Hills, CA. Sage Publications.

- *Masculinity/femininity:* the spectrum between values associated with masculinity (being tough, assertive, and concerned with material success, achievement, and heroism) and values associated with femininity (being modest, cooperative, concerned with quality of life, and caring about the weak).
- *Uncertainty avoidance:* the degree to which uncertain or ambiguous situations are avoided or seen as threatening, ranging from weak uncertainty avoidance (e.g. accepting unfamiliar situations, allowing protest) to strong uncertainty avoidance (e.g. creating rules, repressing protest).

Based on ongoing research, Hofstede added a fifth dimension in 1991, and in 2010 a sixth.[10]

- *Long-term orientation:* the degree to which societies are guided by traditions and a sense of time horizon that encourages thriftiness and perseverance; short-term orientation is also associated with establishing absolute Truth, and long-term orientations with seeing truth as depending on context.
- *Indulgence vs restraint:* the spectrum between allowing gratification of human drives to enjoy life and, at the other extreme, regulating or suppressing them.

Hofstede's model of cultural values has been developed and applied within organizational cultures such as those within companies but also broadly identifies the ways in which societies differ. If we want to understand the perspectives of people who differ from ourselves, his six clusters of values are extremely useful.

A third major pair of theorists, Fons Trompenaars and Charles Hampton-Turner, built on Hofstede's work and examined the ways in which culture affects business and management. In 1997, they identified seven dimensions of culture.

- *Universal/plural:* Is greater importance given to rules that apply universally or to more particular relationships and circumstances that require special consideration?
- *Individualist/communitarian:* Is greater importance accorded to the individual or the collective group?
- *Specific/diffuse:* Is greater attention given to the parts or the whole?
- *Neutral/affective:* Are feelings concealed in a neutral demeanour or expressed in an affective one?

- *Achieved status/ascribed status:* Is status gained by achievements or accorded by other features such as birth, age, position, and connections?
- *Inner directed/outer directed:* Do people control the environment or do they adapt themselves to it?
- *Sequential time/synchronic time:* Is greatest importance given to the past, present, or future? Do people treat time as sequential, doing one thing at a time and planning towards the future, or as synchronic, doing several things at once and considering all of past, present, and future?[11]

All of these theories have their limitations – a study based on employees of a large international corporation may not be entirely representative of the population at large, for instance – but all of them provide us with insight into the assumptions and values of different cultural groups. The *theoretical perspectives* give us tools for recognizing *cultural perspectives*.

As we said earlier, few of us will ever take culture as our formal lifetime study. However, all of us can benefit from a serious attempt to recognize different perspectives on what we know and the reasons that people hold their differing views. We learn more by keeping our minds open to the differences we encounter and finding ways of combining curiosity and sensitivity as we inquire further into the differences.

## Political perspectives

The ideas and values within political discussion did not begin in the modern era. Concepts of the worth of individuals and groups within a society, ideas on who should rule a society and how, and

### For Reflection

Have you had experiences yourself of awkward communication or misunderstanding that might be explained by differences in cultural perspectives?

To what extent would you agree with the following assertion?
"As knowledge flows between us, it runs in channels dug deep by our ancestors."

---

[10] http://geert-hofstede.com/national-culture.html

[11] http://www.provenmodels.com/580/seven-dimensions-of-culture/charles-hampden-turner—fons-trompenaars/

## Political perspectives in liberal democracies

### Reading this comparison

Political perspectives in a liberal democracy compete within the framework of a constitution, free and fair elections, and peaceful transfer of power. The differing perspectives share a common belief in the rule of law and the need for social organization. They diverge, however, in their understanding of how society *does* function and how it *should* function. These political views are generally understood in terms of a spectrum of ideas and values, from left wing to right wing.

The views "left" and "right" can be combined differently: an individual may lean to the right economically but not socially, or an individual leaning towards the left may be concerned with economic issues but give little attention within his priorities to racism or women's issues. Moreover, the whole political leaning of a society can shift left or right at a particular historical moment, or shift on specific issues (e.g. women and the vote, initially an issue supported by the left).

Although what we give here is simplified, it provides an example of how "perspectives" are not just random opinions, but bodies of beliefs with their assumptions and values, which influence how we see the world.

### Left

Of greatest importance is collective well-being; all members of a society should share fairly in the common wealth created by its social division of labour for the benefit of the society.

The extent to which individuals can shape their lives is affected by initial positions of wealth, privilege, and power (gender, race, class, possession of citizenship etc). Through social programmes to reduce exclusion and alienation and provide basic education and health care, a just society provides opportunities for all.

In addition to internal infrastructure and national defence, government should take a social role for collective well-being. Government should administer programmes of social inclusion and mitigate inequalities as a matter of social efficiency and fairness.

Government should, in certain ways, regulate business to ensure that workers receive a fair wage and safe working conditions, and to minimize environmental harm even when doing so compromises short-term profits.

Government should control public services and certain natural monopolies and resources according to the principles of social need and non-market criteria.

Taxation should be progressive, taking a larger share from those who have accumulated more of the social wealth.

Social control of private life should be kept to a minimum. Traditional values of the nuclear family and those of the society should accommodate, with a degree of flexibility, alternative models of marriage and family structure. Sexuality, gender roles, and childbearing are private matters; legislation should protect rights.

Considered to be in systemic opposition to ideal government: the wealthy who benefit unfairly from the work of others through unequal distribution of economic and political power, corporations which pursue profits above all.

Considered to be allies (if not all in the same way or at the same time): environmental groups, labour unions, poverty activists, feminist movements, multicultural and First Nations groups, non-governmental organizations committed to such issues as liberal human rights, peace and/or social development.

Saying frequently quoted: The rich get richer and the poor get poorer.

## Right

Of greatest importance is freedom of the individual; the common good should be achieved through maximizing the opportunities for individuals to benefit from their chosen pursuits.

Individuals make choices freely and deserve their successes and failures. Those who take initiative and risk are entitled to their success and justly rewarded. Those who do not create opportunities for themselves are responsible for their own limited standard of living. Society as a whole has little responsibility to help them.

Beyond basic internal infrastructure, national defense and security, government has little role. Government should not take on large social programmes. Individuals can give to social charities as a matter of personal choice.

Government should not interfere with the free market. It should not impose undue environmental regulation in order not to impede economic efficiency and growth within the capitalist system.

Resources and public services should, for the most part, be owned and managed by private business according to principles of competition and profit maximization.

Taxation should be kept to a minimum and should not penalize those who have been more financially successful.

Social control of private life is necessary to uphold traditional values of the nuclear family and those of the society. Those who do not follow traditional values and models of relationships are under some circumstances considered immoral. Legislation should protect the ideal model of family life.

Considered to be in systemic opposition to ideal government: "free riders" who benefit unfairly from the work of others through welfare systems, individuals and unions that impede production by protest rather than adapting to the economic climate.

Considered to be allies (if not in the same way or at the same time): large businesses and corporations, the financial sector, some international economic institutions, non-governmental organizations such as church groups and those committed to family values and/or entrepreneurship.

Metaphors frequently used: A rising tide lifts all boats. Wealth trickles down.

## Political perspectives and knowledge

Seeking knowledge with awareness of political perspectives demands conscious engagement. For the general public following the news within the social reality of any liberal democracy, there are some basic challenges:

- the need to follow news and views critically with awareness of media leanings and the importance of alternative sources of information,
- the need to be informed as well as possible as voters on issues which are often complex and hotly contested,
- the need to recognize the competing nature of political views such that many individuals and organizations give warped interpretations of opponents, their facts, and their views in order to look better themselves.

Understanding is challenging, yes – but also fascinating. It could also be argued (as we do) that seeking such understanding is significant to our own responsibilities as citizens within our societies.

visions of the relationship of one society to another are all ideas that have a long history. We call them "political", distinguishing them from cultural perspectives primarily for their specific focus on the impact of authority and power on a society.

Some political perspectives are closely allied with different kinds of government. Arguments in favour of different ways of organizing a society start with different **assumptions** and **values**.

Can you suggest some of the likely differences in the assumptions and values of those in favour of these government types?

- Monarchy (or chiefdom or emirate), where someone rules because of his or her social position at birth. This may be established or reinforced by religious beliefs.
- Theocracy, where an elite rules because of their greater knowledge of religion and thereby the will of God for society.
- Democracy, where those people who have the vote rule themselves through their elected representatives.

What assumptions in each case are made about human equality? What assumptions are made about who knows best how to govern a society? What are the likely sources of the values to guide the society?

In practice, countries often have combinations of different types of government, and have within them various perspectives on the ideal relationship between the people and the state. These are often supported or challenged by force. After all, concepts of social relationships do not emerge from a vacuum but a context that involves the distribution of wealth, privilege, and power.

Other sets of political perspectives arise over the degree to which the rulers of the society – in whatever form – should have control over the people and the undertakings of the society. In liberal democracies, the rule of law, the system of government, and methods of transfer of power are established in the constitution. However, within this context many issues remain a matter of hot debate. The relative importance of national security and civil liberties is a prime example of this: should the government ever be entitled to suspend laws that guarantee citizens their privacy or civil liberties (for instance, for suspects of terrorism)? This contemporary example provides an illustration of the more general question in democracies: how should the power

of government be exercised or limited? Over what aspects of life are governments granted control, and by what means should it be enacted?

In more authoritarian societies, public debate on such topics among citizens is limited or non-existent, as a government can exercise power over individual citizens following its own judgment. Disagreements between the government and the citizens involve not discussion but conflict. This political issue of exercise of power has considerable impact on the way that knowledge flows within a society.

## Political control of knowledge

One such impact is on the kind and degree of control that a government possesses over the flow of knowledge. In an authoritarian state, the government may own the media or be able to censor the press or shut it down. It may control, or attempt to control, citizen access to the Internet or other forms of electronic communication such as social media. It may also exercise control over what can be said, with punishment for statements considered to be against the religion or against the state. Within such a context, the state can restrict access to knowledge and provide information very much from its own perspective. We leave it to you to provide your own examples of censorship and propaganda, as anyone following current events or studying history should be able to do.

It is fair to say, though, that even states that would not recognize a description of themselves as "authoritarian" do have restrictions on what kind of statements can be made, what information or images can be circulated, or what knowledge can be explored. Hate literature and pornography, however defined, are frequently subject to restrictions, but also information whose circulation is argued to be against the national interest. The central questions to be asked about such restrictions, perhaps, are: for whose good is the restriction in place? Who decides, according to what criteria, what information is against the national interest? And what precedent does a restriction set? Despite some such restrictions, often controversial, a government in a liberal democracy does not usually exercise direct control of knowledge.

However, political and economic interests can scarcely be separated in this case. A strong influence on news and public discussion is exercised primarily by corporations who own the media and can affect what is presented and how.

## Discussion Activity

### From which perspective?

A newspaper reports on a demonstration in the city, a march through the streets protesting the government's lack of action on poverty and homelessness. The news report is placed on the fifth page and features a photograph of someone, apparently a protestor, breaking a window. The article quotes a shop owner calling the protestors "hooligans" and voicing anger over the downtown "chaos" and lack of respect for property. *Is this news coverage given from a left-wing or a right-wing perspective?*

An Internet site features extensive coverage of a demonstration in the city. It includes an article outlining issues of poverty and homelessness and the actions the government should take instead of its "immoral inaction". It includes photographs and video clips of protestors peacefully chanting and carrying large banners. A feature photo shows three policemen in riot gear crowding demonstrators in what seems a threatening manner, and two policemen roughly throwing a protestor to the ground. *Is this news coverage given from a left-wing or a right-wing perspective?*

An opinion columnist is pointing out the impact of climate change on the Arctic ice cap and the impact of rising sea levels on low-lying island states. She voices the view that all countries must not only sign international agreements to reduce environmentally harmful carbon emissions, but they must also actually follow through on their promises by imposing limits on polluting industries. *Although concern over climate change may come from either the left- or the right-wing, what perspective is dominant in this columnist's identification of cause and solution? What questions or disagreements might come from the other wing?*

An opinion columnist is referring to a new trade arrangement between her country and another one, whereby businesses in her country are now able to open factories for production in the other. She comments that the goods produced will give a competitive edge to the business investing in the factory abroad, meanwhile creating new jobs within the producing country. She voices the view that globalization through international business and trade will bring advantages to all. *Although interest in creation of jobs may come from either the left- or the right-wing, what perspective is dominant in this columnist's view on globalized business? What questions or disagreements might come from the other wing?*

The business interests that advertise in the media similarly have an influence: if they do not accept what is being said they can threaten to withdraw their advertising and the funding it provides.

This economic control of much media is a significant political issue in a democracy because public response to political candidates, government decisions, citizen protest, and major issues of public debate depends largely on the nature of the coverage they are given in the press. Yet a democracy depends on citizens making well informed choices by considering a full range of information and views. Knowledge is crucial! As part of their role in a democratic state, consequently, citizens might develop their skills of consuming media critically and finding alternative views.

## Political perspectives and public discussion

Anyone developing skills of critical literacy in a liberal democracy actively seeks out a range of media sources, with local possibilities extended by the Internet. The reward is a fuller understanding of social issues, as different sources often pick out different kinds of events or issues for detailed coverage. They also often identify problems in unlike terms, drawing different connections of cause and effect, and therefore favour unlike solutions. Understanding that perspectives shape the news in this way is significant because the views that become publicly accepted have implications for the actions of governments within their own countries and the world.

For consideration of how perspectives work, look now at the table "Political perspectives in liberal democracies" in this chapter. It illustrates political perspectives from what are known as the left and the right. Although this simplified summary does not necessarily equate to political parties in any one democracy, it does identify broad political leanings. It provides an illustration of the way political perspectives, like cultural ones, come with differing assumptions, basic concepts, and values. With the table and your own background knowledge as a

23

guide, can you hazard a likely answer to the questions in the discussion activity "From which perspective"?

In none of the examples in this discussion activity are we suggesting that anyone is deliberately distorting information – that's quite a separate topic. We aren't suggesting that journalists do not often strive for accurate and balanced coverage, nor that columnists do not often comment insightfully on events and issues. Yet the world is full of differing ideas and views, and the complex human experience that is reported to us in the media *cannot* be rendered in a single neutral way. Moreover, the variability of editorial opinions and policies characteristic of different sources is not in itself a fault, since the story of who-does-what-in-the-world has to be a *selection* from possibilities far too numerous to cover. The story must also contain, to some extent, an *interpretation* that makes the information relevant, comprehensible, and meaningful to readers or viewers. What we *are* suggesting is that information has to be understood, always, by taking that process of selection and interpretation into account, particularly as it can consistently reflect a particular perspective.

## Politics and you

Before we leave political perspectives, though, we really must correct one impression we might have created – that politics is only about government. It is not. Politics is not just men in suits, and occasionally women in suits, emerging from grand chambers in cities to make media announcements at microphones. Politics, rather, is engagement in communities and countries to try to help them run in the way that fits what you believe is right. Volunteering to help out in a project for the betterment of the community is politics at the ground level, helping to build supportive social connections and healthy goals. The community within which you contribute your energies could be defined in numerous ways – by village boundaries, religious or cultural affiliations, sports associations, youth organizations, or the like. Taking a stand against bullying or racist slurs, or reducing waste of energy or water are also political actions in the broad sense. They emerge out of what we have been considering here – the *perspectives* we hold about how our society should function, and the *implications* that follow from them.

To illustrate the way in which different views are grounded in dominant concepts and values, we have used the difference between the political left

and the political right. Yet it has been said that the biggest political difference of all in a democracy is not between left and right but between those who are passive and those who are engaged – engaged in informing themselves, thinking, and taking action.

After all, who is "the society" if not you, your family, your friends, and your immediate communities, multiplied over and over again? If you care about issues that directly affect you – for example, whether you are entitled to schooling, under what circumstances you can be asked for identification or arrested, whether you must do compulsory military service, whether you have civil rights of appeal to the law if someone assaults you or steals your property – if you care about any of these, you are not "apolitical". People who say "I'm not interested in politics" have simply not yet made the connection between what happens in the society around them and the decisions that shaped it to be that way.

## Perspectives within knowledge

Perspectives within knowledge? The heading we've given above is, actually, a little misleading. We have no intention of trying to tackle in the first chapter much of what belongs to the rest of this book. Here, we will give only a quick preview so that you will see how the topic of perspectives of this chapter links with what we will be considering ahead.

### Ways of knowing

Later in this course, we will look more closely at how perspectives affect our different *ways of knowing*. For example, dealing with sense perception, we will raise questions about how what we think affects what we see and notice. Dealing with language, we will raise questions about the way that naming and describing, within different languages or different theoretical contexts, affect how we are likely to understand and respond. When we treat memory, we will consider the impact of our developing perspectives on our stories of the past. Perspectives affect how we use all of our ways of knowing, and recognizing perspectives in all cases is important to understanding how knowledge is created.

### Areas of knowledge

When later in the course we look closely at areas of knowledge, we will find ourselves surveying the territory from different vantage places, at different levels of generality and abstraction. At each level, perspectives are involved in considering the knowledge questions that arise.

## 1. Perspectives *on* knowledge

*What perspectives can be taken on how knowledge is constructed? How do different areas of knowledge take differing approaches to knowing?*

At the highest level of general overview, different perspectives exist about *how knowledge itself is constructed*. What is knowledge and how do we gain it? Different areas of knowledge provide their own responses appropriate to their subject matter and methods. What are their similarities? What are their differences? What is gained by comparison?

## 2. Perspectives *within* areas of knowledge

*How do conceptual frameworks or theories provide perspectives within particular areas?*

At a lower level of generalization, different perspectives exist *within* areas of knowledge, interacting in ways characteristic of the discipline. In the natural sciences, for instance, theoretical perspectives (theories) provide shared ways of understanding the natural phenomena that they study. As better evidence and fresh reasoning push the discipline along, the perspectives on natural phenomena change with them.

In history, perspectives operate rather differently: explanations in history often co-exist without one disproving another because they trace different causal connections through human experience in the past; they illuminate it in different ways. (You have just been reading different theoretical frameworks of cultural values. They approach the topic in different ways but do not conflict.) Some interpretations, though, are rejected. What, then, makes one perspective accepted over another, in the sciences and in history, or in other areas of knowledge?

## 3. Perspectives *from* areas of knowledge on global issues

*How can different areas or their sub-disciplines provide valuable perspectives on issues in the world?*

At a lower level yet of generalization, different areas of knowledge provide their perspectives on very specific issues in the world. Take the global issue of poverty, for example. How could we even *begin* to understand poverty without turning to the human sciences (for instance, psychology, anthropology, economics, and political science) for analysis and explanation of the way people think and act? But how could we fully understand the causes of poverty without also appealing to history for an account of the effect of the past on the present? For further understanding of causes, we need to turn to the natural sciences to grasp such factors as geographical distribution of natural resources or the biological effects of deprivation on the human body. For deeper understanding of the human experience of poverty, thereafter, we would gain immensely from the communicative power of the arts. For a holistic understanding of poverty, or any other issue of global concern, we need the subject content that all the different areas provide – the explanations, the research and conclusions, the information and the insights.

Theory of knowledge does not get right into the subject content of different disciplines (other than as demonstration of how knowledge works). What it contributes to an understanding of a global issue such as poverty is an overview – awareness of what knowledge questions are urgent to ask, where to turn for different kinds of answers, and how to think critically about these responses. TOK might ask, for instance: What makes the particular issue important to consider, and at this particular time? Do different perspectives on this topic complement each other or conflict? How do we evaluate most effectively any competing claims and arguments? What are the implications of the conclusions we reach? Does knowing about this issue bring any responsibility to act?

If we want to understand any complex issues in the world, we need both the particular knowledge on the ground provided by specific areas of knowledge and the holistic overview developed in TOK. That holistic, questioning overview depends to a large extent on being able to stand outside different perspectives, with an open and critical mind, to understand how they affect what we know. Those different perspectives are crucially important; they are intertwined with the whole way we construct our knowledge.

## Your own personal perspective

Your personal perspective on the world is somewhat shaped by all the influences upon you as you have grown and gained knowledge. Yet, as you begin taking an active role in shaping your own knowledge, you also begin to develop your own personal perspective on the world – a way of looking at things that is distinctly your own. This personal perspective, which will develop and change with your increasing knowledge throughout your life, is your own blend of influences and experiences, combined with all of your reflections upon them.

Take a few minutes now to write quietly, trying to pick out from your own background some major features that seem to you to affect what you know, how you know it, and what your attitude is towards knowledge. The following questions are likely to prompt some ideas, but do not be confined by them if you recognize other major influences on your own formation.

## Your personal profile: a snapshot of this moment

1   How old are you? How might your age affect both what you know and your attitude towards gaining knowledge?

2   What is your mother tongue? What other languages do you speak? How might your particular language(s) affect your knowledge?

3   What sex are you? Does your gender role affect how you see the world? Does it influence your expectations of what knowledge you should gain in your education?

4   Did you grow up in an urban area or a rural one? How might living in a city or living in the countryside affect what and how you know?

5   Have you always had enough to eat, felt safe and been able to get an education? How do you think that having these needs met – or not – affects your present knowledge?

6   How would you describe your spiritual worldview? How might following a religion, or not doing so, affect your knowledge?

7   In this chapter we have treated some broad features of culture identified by theorists. Are any of them useful to you in picking out cultural influences upon how you see the world yourself? Do you identify yourself with a particular culture?

8   Are there any particular fields of knowledge at this point that appeal to you strongly? Does your interest affect your current knowledge and your knowledge goals for the future?

## Personal and cultural perspectives

The students pictured in this chapter wearing their national costumes all posed for these photographs, enjoying the chance to show and share something of their heritage. All of them, at one time or another during their IB studies, expressed the view that their cultures and languages were important to them and influenced how they saw the world. All of them, too, learned a lot during their IB years about treating their own cultural perspectives both as views to be cherished for their contribution to intercultural dialogue, and also as views to be widened in order to understand issues more broadly, by taking into account the perspectives of others.

## Becoming "internationally minded"

Awareness of yourself and the influences on you comes with recognition that others have developed differently from you. They may not know much about your way of looking at the world, and you may not know much about theirs. Finding out, learning about each other, is truly one of the most fascinating possibilities offered by an international education. The world is wonderfully diverse and the knowledge you gain about it is alive with different perspectives.

The International Baccalaureate encourages this learning in your courses and the outlook on the world that goes with them. If, like many of us, you rarely leave your home community, that does not prevent you from becoming "internationally minded" by recognizing your own place in the world in the context of others. Without ever leaving home, you can learn to see your own perspective in the context of other possibilities within a large and varied world. By being open to diversity of points of view, locally and globally, you enrich your own understanding and your own capacity to contribute positively to the way you gain and share knowledge.

# Exploring differing perspectives

The aim of all IB programmes is to develop internationally minded people who, recognizing their common humanity and shared guardianship of the planet, help to create a better and more peaceful world. As IB learners we strive to be:

**Open-minded:** We critically appreciate our own cultures and personal histories, as well as the values and traditions of others. We seek and evaluate a range of points of view, and we are willing to grow from the experience.

**Thinkers:** We use critical and creative thinking skills to analyse and take responsible action on complex problems. We exercise initiative in making reasoned, ethical decisions.

**Communicators:** We express ourselves confidently and creatively in more than one language and in many ways. We collaborate effectively, listening carefully to the perspectives of other individuals and groups.

From the IB learner profile

As we seek knowledge with awareness of differing perspectives, we are likely to find that the question *"How do we know?"* becomes "How do *I (or we) know* in comparison with how *other people* know?" With contemporary information flow and contact between peoples, we often have the opportunity – or can seek it out – of encountering diversity. Awareness of differences then puts our own capacities to the test. If another perspective involves concepts or frameworks of thinking that are very unfamiliar to us, or if it contradicts our own beliefs, it is important not to have the reflex to turn away, but instead to try *sincerely* to understand.

1. **Listen open-mindedly.** Listen to others who hold views unlike your own with a desire to learn, not blocked by eagerness to find fault and refute.

2. **Inquire.** Unfamiliar perspectives are not always easy to understand at first, especially if they are very different from your own. If you are puzzled, activate your curiosity and (with sensitivity and tact) try to learn more.

3. **Try to see from the other point of view.** Empathy and imagination help in entering into a different worldview. The challenge is to grasp the perspective not as described by an outsider but as held by an insider.

People are more likely to follow the steps above in a context of safety and goodwill. At the same time, it is the development of the attitude behind these steps that can help to create that context.

## How do we explore perspectives?

Different perspectives can open up alternative ways of seeing, introduce fresh ideas for solving problems, prompt a search for new knowledge, and give much broader understanding. Coming to understand the broader perspectives that affect communities and the world, moreover, can lead us to greater understanding of the urgent issues of our times.

With a goal of understanding, then, we need to complement an open-minded attitude with skills of critical thinking. Looking more analytically at differing perspectives involves informing ourselves more fully and examining different stands for their major components.

1.  Do the most apparent differences seem to be embedded in larger worldviews with differing **assumptions** – implicit beliefs about the human relationship with the natural world, for instance, or about whether the community or the individual is of central concern? Are the groups aware of each other's assumptions, or even apparently conscious of their own? Do their assumptions influence the language in which they express their ideas?

2.  Do they differ in the **values** that guide what they consider to be most important or most moral? Do groups differ in their goals for living, learning or acting? Do they differ in their views on how the world and people *should be*?

3.  Do the groups holding unlike perspectives differ in the **set of facts** they consider relevant or essential? Do their values seem to affect their *selection* of facts and their *emphasis* on particular ones – such as facts about contemporary or historical events, information about the beliefs and practices of other groups, or research findings in science or medicine? Do they *know* the same things about how the world and people *are*?

4.  Do they differ in their **processes for validation** of claims and views – their practices for communication or procedures for settling differences? Do they use different forms of justification to support their conclusions, with different views on what a good reason is for believing something? Are they familiar with each other's processes or methods?

5.  Do the **implications** of what they believe take them in different directions for making decisions and acting? Once they have accepted a certain perspective, what follows from it that they will also believe? To what extent are the implications for personal behaviour or social action a factor in persuading them to accept the perspective to begin with?

"Other people, with their differences," says the IB mission statement, "can also be right." No thoughtful evaluation of perspectives is possible without this recognition and without a sincere first step: an open-minded attempt to become more knowledgeable about how people construct their perspectives and what the perspectives mean to them.

In its conciseness, the mission statement does not go further to add that other people, with their differences, can be wrong – and so can we. It is the role of a course in critical thinking to take the further steps to give scrutiny to the distinctions between right and wrong, true and false, inclusive and exclusive perspectives, and the ways in which these categories become more nuanced on closer examination. It is the role of theory of knowledge in the IB to consider closely how perspectives interplay in the creation of knowledge and what forms of evaluation are appropriate to apply to them in various contexts.

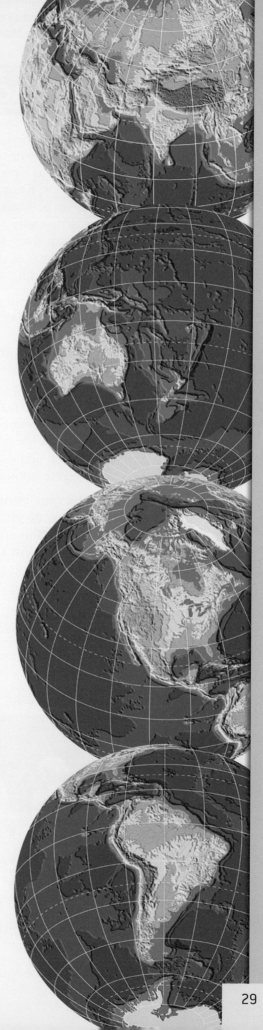

# 2. Gaining Knowledge

There is no such thing as "knowledge" lying around in the world waiting for us to notice it, pick it up, classify it by colour, or to weigh it, measure it, and cut it neatly into slices. Knowledge is not a concrete substance but an abstract concept that we construct ourselves, personally and socially, throughout the whole of our lives. It takes the shape that we give it in all parts of the world, across all memory. Think about it for a moment!

- Imagine yourself to be a warrior riding with Genghis Khan across central Asia in the thirteenth century.
- Imagine yourself to be a contemporary coffee farmer on the slopes of the Andes in Colombia.
- Imagine yourself to be a Christian monk or nun of the ninth century in western Europe.
- Imagine yourself to be an Ethiopian runner in training for competition at the next Olympics.
- Imagine yourself to be an acclaimed musician in northern India playing traditional rāgas.

What might you consider important to know in each of these contexts? How do you think you would gain the knowledge? How much would you be taught by others, and how? And how much would you add of your own?

The vast range of knowledge gained across centuries around the world is staggering, with much of it specific to the context in which it was gained. To a large extent it is the characteristics of that context that shape what knowledge the people need who live there. And it is the social context that influences, then, what is considered important for the next generation to learn.

## Education and knowledge

What should that next generation learn? How should the society direct the thoughts and talents of its children and young adults? An educational system, a method of passing on knowledge in a conscious and planned way, always has goals.

Should the education aim to give children a broad sense of their history, cultural traditions, and place in the world? Or should it aim to teach practical skills relevant to the historical moment in the society, perhaps technological facility and marketing? What balance should be given to valuing tradition and valuing innovation, as the school reflects its surrounding society? What kind of people do different school systems want to develop?

## Your IB studies

One of the contributors to your current knowledge is, of course, the International Baccalaureate Organization. As an educational organization with consciously developed goals, it articulates them clearly and publicly. No system of education is

### Walking to school: same world, different worlds

Kyoto, Japan

Jabalia, Gaza

## Discussion Activity

### Education in social context

- To what extent is education in your own part of the world available to all children, as their right? To what age? Is the kind of education or its quality affected by a child's gender, class, or family's economic position? What social factors seem to you to affect education in your society?
- "In addition to their academic goals, national school systems aim to cultivate civic responsibility and pride in heritage." Do you agree with this statement? In what ways might a school encourage its students to take pride in their country or become good citizens of their communities? What is the ideal of the "good citizen" that is fostered in your own school system, and how?
- How would you distinguish between education and indoctrination? Are you aware of any particular examples in history or in the world today of education being strongly influenced by propaganda?

neutral, since all are embedded in a perspective on what is good for students, good for the society, or good for the world. The IB is remarkable, though, in the extent to which it has declared its goals consciously and worked to develop a curriculum to fulfill them:

> The International Baccalaureate Organization aims to develop inquiring, knowledgeable, and caring young people who help to create a better and more peaceful world through intercultural understanding and respect.
>
> To this end the organization works with schools, governments, and international organizations to develop challenging programmes of international education and rigorous assessment.
>
> These programmes encourage students across the world to become active, compassionate, and lifelong learners who understand that other people, with their differences, can also be right.[1]

This articulation of goals is complemented by the IB learner profile, a copy of which is included in the first pages of this book. It opens with a declaration of the guiding values and goals of the programme, as it introduces the characteristics the IB aims to develop in you.

> The aim of all IB programmes is to develop internationally minded people who, recognizing their common humanity and shared guardianship of the planet, help to create a better and more peaceful world.

What fundamental values can you pick out of the mission statement and IB learner profile? Are there recognizable ethical principles? It should be clear that these statements of values are embedded in a perspective on what an ideal education should be. The benefit sought is not only for students but also, through you, for the communities and the world of which you are a part.

In theory of knowledge, we want you to be aware of what you are learning, including the framing values around knowledge you are gaining. We hope that you share the IB goals and even feel inspired by them. We hope too that you will be an active participant, reflective and critical, in your own growing knowledge.

## What knowledge are you gaining?

But what is this knowledge that you are gaining through your IB Diploma Programme studies?

It would seem that those things we call "knowledge" do not come all in the same size, colour, and flavour, metaphorically speaking. The word "know" sometimes seems extremely elastic. It stretches to cover kinds of learning that, on reflection, do not seem to have a great deal in common.

We ask you to plunge in now. We ask you to give full attention to an activity that, on the surface, is merely an exercise in sorting – blue goes with blue, orange with orange, and so forth. However, if you look closely, you are likely to find that categorizing is not quite so easy, and maybe that

---

[1] "Mission and Strategy" International Baccalaureate Organization, http://www.ibo.org/mission/, accessed 27 May 2012.

## Discussion Activity

### Twenty statements: how many kinds of knowledge?

Below are twenty statements. All of them are about knowing. Can you group them, finding features in common that allow them to be sorted into kinds of knowledge that they represent? On looking at them closely, you may discover more than one system of classification that works to cluster similar statements.

To communicate how you have grouped them, use whatever means works best for you – a diagram, a table, a colour code, or another way of your own. You may want to use 20 squares of paper with the statement numbers on them to shuffle into appropriate piles. Be prepared to communicate your system of classification to your classmates.

1  I know my closest friends.

2  I know how to solve problems between my friends.

3  I know that Brazil's economy is stronger than Argentina's.

4  I know that God created the world.

5  I know my home city of Buenos Aires really well.

6  I know that my girlfriend Maria is very, very beautiful.

7  I know how to play football, or soccer as some call it.

8  I know how to solve problems at my level in mathematics.

9  I know this feeling I get when I see Maria, as if the whole world is suddenly coming awake.

10  I know that Argentina was discovered by a Spanish explorer in the early sixteenth century.

11  I know that Spain won the FIFA World Cup in 2010.

12  I know that I cannot fully explain my love of playing football.

13  I know that a right triangle has a 90° angle.

14  I know that atoms have protons and electrons.

15  I know that tomorrow morning the sun will rise.

16  I know that I'm going to die someday.

17  I know that if I tease my sister her cheeks will turn red.

18  I know that empanadas are delicious.

19  I know that I am wearing a blue shirt and holding a cup of hot coffee.

20  I know when to stop arguing about something.

If you are comparing classification schemes in class, you may discover that classmates have come up with ideas that did not even cross your mind. What criteria did others use for grouping statements? In what ways are their systems similar to yours, or different?

What other languages are spoken within your class group? Do any of these languages use the word "know" in a way that would affect the classification you have done here?

the difficulties are what make it interesting. The activity is "Twenty statements: how many kinds of knowledge?" Please do it before moving on in this chapter.

## Categorizing knowledge

Dealing with abstract ideas certainly hands us a challenge. If we do not name our concepts, we cannot speak about them to each other. We even struggle to think about them clearly in our own minds. But when we *do* sort our thoughts and categorize our concepts in language, what extensive communication we open with each other!

We hope that sorting twenty knowledge statements has not paralysed your mind entirely, and that you were able to think and talk with others about your own thoughts. Doing so has a very practical purpose in laying the groundwork for a lot of good future discussions.

Dealing with those same statements, we are going to offer you categories that we use ourselves, categories that we have found extremely useful.

The first distinction we draw is between personal knowledge and shared knowledge. The second is between different kinds of knowledge. If you and your classmates had other ways of grouping the statement, please do keep a note of them. They will almost certainly prove relevant later on.

## First distinction: personal knowledge, shared knowledge

This is our first distinction – between personal knowledge and shared knowledge. All of the twenty statements are personal knowledge because they start "I know…". We can conclude, at least, that they are personal knowledge for the first person speaker, the "I". Unless you love playing football and eating empanadas, and come from Buenos Aires, you will have to use a bit of imagination to be able to put yourself in his place.

Some part of his personal knowledge will always remain only his own, unshared: "I know that I can never fully explain," our footballer says of his own love of playing his sport. His own experience, personally lived, cannot be completely communicated. We might also recognize (or think we recognize) the feeling he gets on seeing his girlfriend: "I know this feeling I get when I see Maria, as if the whole world is suddenly coming awake." Although we can recognize something common to the human experience and so call it "being in love", we canot feel the emotion as he feels it himself.

On the other side of the same coin, even our personal experiences are, to an extent, shared. Although our Argentinian possesses personal knowledge of his friends (Maria, Jorge, Adriana, Carlos, Ignatio) and

*"I know that empanadas are delicious." How did you categorize this knowledge claim yourself? Is being delicious a fact? How would you put this statement to the test?*

his home city (Buenos Aires), most of us also know our friends and home region. And all of us, when not in denial (or members of a strange cult), might also share the recognition of mortality: "I know that some day I will die." This shared component makes it possible for us to use language meaningfully to communicate with each other and to build our knowledge together of the human experience.

Some of the personal knowledge possessed by our empanada-eating Argentinian, moreover, is more particular knowledge that is shared with plenty of other people. Whose knowledge is it? In the case of empanadas, the knowledge is culturally shared; it extends across South America to include a huge number of families within cultural communities knowing how "delicious" are the empanadas made in their own special way. But the secret is out! This particular form of cultural knowledge has spread around the world to make its welcome entrance into many a community's meals. Could this be intercultural sharing at its finest?

Some of the other personal knowledge in the twenty statements actually *depends* on being shared. It is possible to imagine just one mother making a particular recipe and one son devouring it, but not just one person playing a team sport. Knowing how to play football depends on agreed rules, teams, and socially organized competitive games. Our Argentinian friend has his knowledge of the ball and the field, yes, but this knowledge is also shared with a considerable proportion of the world's population. Whose knowledge is it? Think for a moment about all of those football players and their fans, of all those people who are involved worldwide in organizing local matches or the World Cup. Imagine them to be a "community" – a community of people sharing a particular kind of knowledge.

Some of our Argentinian friend's other knowledge is probably spread even more widely, if you take into account generations in the past: "I know that a right triangle has a 90° angle" or "I know how to solve problems at my level in mathematics." Who has shared this knowledge? What is the nature of the large and loose "community" that holds this particular kind of knowledge? For almost all of us, we possess conventionalized mathematical knowledge only because it has been taught to us within our educational systems. But the community of knowledge we thereby enter goes back thousands of years.

Some knowledge, though, is not taught to us in this way and never reaches us in any other way, either. Millions of people might share it, but we are not in that number. Considering the vast extent of the world's knowledge, we have to accept that we will encounter only a small part of it in all our lives. Most of it lies beyond any possibility that we will ever incorporate it into our personal knowledge and be able to say, "I know....".

## The personal meets the shared: the zone of exchange

To think of personal knowledge and shared knowledge as two isolated categories would be to ignore the vitality and creativity that is generated as they meet.

It is *exchange* between the shared and the personal that stimulates questioning and exploration, debate and testing, and active acceptance or rejection. As others give us their knowledge, we do not, if we are active thinkers, simply accept it and passively join those who share it already. We want to understand why this knowledge has persuaded so many other people and why it would be reasonable to accept it ourselves.

Here, in the contact zone between shared knowledge and personal knowledge, we think and question. Why should we believe what others tell us? How do we know it is true? Is there another way of thinking about what we are taught? We wonder and ask questions, consider answers, examine different perspectives, and investigate further. Our own conclusions may end up being the same as those taught to us by parents, community leaders, or textbooks, but in engaging our own minds, we have made the conclusions our own.

But we might not accept the conclusions. Here in the exchange zone, new possibilities are being created. Fresh minds encounter the knowledge shared by different knowledge communities: cultural communities, faith communities, professional communities, recreational communities, generational communities (teenagers, seniors), communities of scientists or historians.

Fresh minds, with their personal ways of thinking, question and engage, and sometimes change forever the knowledge that they were given. Robert Boyle establishing a relationship between the pressure and the volume of a gas, James Joyce adventuring with language, mythology, and popular culture in writing the novel *Ulysses*, or Steve Jobs pushing the limits of computer technology, all drew on shared knowledge in their fields. However, they not only added to it but changed and revitalized it with their contributions. This dynamic interaction between shared and personal knowledge pushes the development of any field.

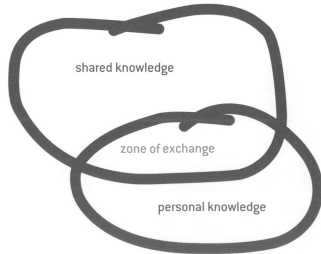

shared knowledge

zone of exchange

personal knowledge

Of all the possible classifications and schematizations of those twenty statements, though, why have we chosen this one between personal knowledge and shared knowledge to offer you? Because…it's useful. This distinction helps to focus on the creative process in all areas of knowledge. It also allows us to talk more easily about the ways in which we know, and the methods we use in order to construct our areas of knowledge. Finally, it provides a good way of reflecting on your own personal process of knowing as you recognize IB goals, set your own, and build your own understanding during your education.

## Second distinction: three kinds of knowledge

Our second classification of those twenty statements takes a different approach, so push the distinction between personal knowledge and shared knowledge to the back of your mind for the moment. In this second classification, we have divided those statements into three kinds: experiential knowledge (hiking the mountain path), skills (knowing how to use a map and compass), and knowledge claims (knowing that the lines on the map represent contours of the landscape or that the marked trail leads to the summit). They are deeply interconnected and interdependent, but have features of their own that are worth considering. Indeed, it would be difficult to talk about educational goals or critical thinking without this distinction.

## 1. Experiential knowledge: experience + reflection

Experiential knowledge depends on living in the world, having sensations and emotions, learning language and thinking (we will consider soon the "ways of knowing", as we call them in TOK). It also involves our capacity to draw from past experiences to shape how we live new experiences. Experiential knowledge, as we are treating it here, has two components that we will try to disentangle: the component of direct experience and the component of reflection.

The component of direct experience includes our own encounters with the natural world, with people, and with all the artifacts and social systems around us that people have made. It is our raw and immediate contact with the things that happen in our lives. It requires our active involvement in doing: other people's descriptions, no matter how good they are, are not the same as actually singing, hiking, working as part of a team, grieving over loss, taking care of children, organizing an event, or feeling love for another person. Being *told about* something does give us knowledge, but *living it ourselves* gives us a different kind of knowledge.

In fact, direct experience itself is often equated with knowledge – a direct personal familiarity. This is individual and personal – it is the most basic form of personal knowledge. Others can share this experience with you by being there with you, but no one else lives it exactly as you do;

your own immediate experience is unique. This lived contact with the world lies behind many of the twenty statements that we have been sorting into categories – the direct experiences of falling in love, watching the sun rise, or eating those delicious empanadas. It comes before them and provides the raw material for being able to say, "I know that empanadas are delicious."

In this way, personal experience interacts with the other two categories of knowledge that we are considering here. Personal experience helps to develop skill (*knowing how* to do something): experience is crucial if you are to learn how to grow crops and run a farm, how to play the drums, how to work well with other people, or how to be effective professionally. Personal experience also provides understanding that you might formulate into language at some point to make knowledge claims (*knowing that* something is so): you might, for example, tell someone else that maintaining soil fertility requires crop rotation, from the knowledge that you have gained first-hand.

Personal experience especially contributes to your growing personal knowledge if accompanied by reflection. Noticing what you are experiencing and turning it over in your mind adds to the benefit you gain. Reflection involves not simply having

### How shall I talk of the sea to the frog?

How shall I talk of the sea to the frog

If it has never left its pond?

How shall I talk of the frost to the bird of the Summerland

If it has never left the land of its birth?

How shall I talk of life with the sage

If he is a prisoner of his doctrine?

*Chuang Tze (Zhuangzi) 3rd century BC*

*What is Chuang Tze suggesting about knowledge and experience?*

experiences, but asking yourself what they mean to you and what you can learn from them. It involves being sufficiently aware that you are not simply receiving impressions, but instead guiding your own interpretations and responses.

With reflection, even experiences that were themselves distressing or hurtful can enrich your growing knowledge of yourself, your own capacities, and the world around you. "Why didn't

### Voices

### Personal knowledge

Naja describes fruitlessly trying to convey to others, across a huge gap in experience, her own direct personal knowledge. Between the two years of her IB Diploma Programme, she did a year of volunteer work in an orphanage school in Uganda.

*Naja Hendriksen, Greenland*

The children were really interested in where I came from, but how could I tell them about my country without mentioning snow? I have so much experience of snow and so many words for it in my language, since it is so much part of daily life for the Inuit. But how could I explain snow when they have no experience of it at all? It's on the top of distant mountains in Uganda, but the children had never seen it.

I could have taken them to a local shop where there was a freezer and shown them the ice and frost, but that still wouldn't have given them the experience of snow. I tried to explain in English. Later, a little girl in the class looked up at a cloud and called to me, 'Look, Madam. Snow!'

## Voices

### Respecting knowledge

Respect for knowledge is a Buddhist principle, and in Bhutan we are deeply affected by Buddhism in all we do. In Dzongka, our language, one form of "knowledge" is gained through schooling. Education is valued. Just as an example, I would never knowingly step on or step over a book, because it holds learning.

*Yeshey Lhaden, Bhutan*

The other form of "knowledge" is gained through experience. The older person has seen more of life and has more wisdom. Most highly respected is the wisdom gained by lamas. Some lamas go on solitary retreats for as long as three years, talking with no one and not washing or cutting their hair. They come back wearing just old rags and are detached from the superficial world. They gain control of emotions, thoughts, and actions so they can advise us on how we can live a virtuous life. They are on the pathway to enlightenment.

I act more quickly?" you might ask yourself. "Why didn't I see that emergency coming?" Or else, "I was upset to watch her treat him with so little respect. Should I have spoken up? What would be the best way of handling the situation?" As you think back over an event, you prepare yourself to act more effectively another time.

Our own experience provides us with the raw material, and then our own reflections on it shape it in our own way. Not only do no two people have the same experience in exactly the same way, but different people certainly appear to have different responses to experiences they have lived. (Did you hear the joke about the optimist and the pessimist?)

Yet does reflection always *follow* the experience? As we encounter more and more situations in our lives, the new experience may change the earlier reflection, and that reflection in turn affects the next experience. Experience and reflection seem less and less to resemble a chronological sequence as we add layers upon layers to our lives, extending experiences, forgetting experiences, and renewing or changing our reflections and memories.

As we process our experience, perhaps silently talking with ourselves or mulling over the meaning of something we have just noticed, we may then use it to form our statements of

"I know…", the personal knowledge of our previous classification. Personal knowledge, put into words, loses something of the actual experience itself. Nevertheless, awareness of the personal experience and some sense of its meaning allow us to articulate what we have concluded, as in statements from our batch of twenty: "I know that if I tease my sister her cheeks will turn red." Or, with personal experience of loss extended by shared knowledge and realizations of its implications, we might acknowledge, "I know that I'm going to die someday." And yet, despite our loss, "tomorrow the sun will rise" and our life carries on.

## Critical reflection

Some people seem *not* to learn from past experience, and make the same mistakes over and over again in their lives. "That experience was wasted on her," observers say. "She's learned nothing." Although there may be an abundance of other explanations for lack of learning, there is one sadly simple one: maybe she was not paying attention at the time and was not reflective then or afterwards. What a loss!

When we deliberately take on experiences in order to learn from them, the quality of the knowledge gained is much improved by reflection on how we planned, took part, and learned. The experience itself will pass, but the thoughts remain, and

## Discussion Activity

### Experiential knowledge: experience + reflection

Gather your own ideas in response to the questions below, and prepare to share your thoughts with others in your class.

1.  In what areas of your life do you think that most of your knowledge is experiential knowledge? To what extent is experiential knowledge part of your learning in school?

2.  Do people always learn from their experiences? If not, why not?

3.  If you are looking for someone to talk to about a problem you are having, do you take into account whether someone has "been there" and might know what you are talking about? Can you find an example? Do you think experience tends to give greater understanding and empathy, and perhaps relevant expertise and authority? Does it ever seem instead to *block* understanding?

4.  Is your own personal experience, even if it is unique to you, gained entirely as an individual? As you have grown up, has it been guided or mentored by family or others in your community? Has your own experience been lived at least in part through taking into account the perspectives of others?

5.  Do you ever go looking for kinds of experience, with an idea in advance about what they are likely to give you (e.g. service projects, travel, leadership roles)? Do you place yourself in situations where you have to find out what strengths you have inside?

6.  Why do job applications ask for past job experience?

ideally strengthen for the future the habit of reflection.

Reflection also needs to be consciously critical of the conclusions we reach, since our own experience can be very powerful in persuading us wrongly. One or two encounters with frustrating situations or people, for example, can make us jump to conclusions or make unfounded generalizations: "It's always like that. Let me tell you what happened to me." A single accidental correlation, experienced ourselves, may block us from questioning our causal conclusion: "Well, all I know is that as soon as I started wearing that bracelet, my symptoms just disappeared."

Soon in this TOK course we will be thinking about our ways of knowing and how to use them critically. Things are not always as they appear to be and our own perspectives influence our interpretations. Still, watching out for errors in thinking can improve tremendously the quality of our reflections on our experiences.

### Experience and reflection in the IB

In all of your IB courses, you are learning through experience to some extent. Even those courses that are most academic and text-based have personal experience in the process of gaining knowledge and applying it in different forms in different subjects.

It is in the core of the IB Diploma Programme, though, that you will find the strongest element of experiential learning: in creativity, action, service (CAS). The CAS programme requires you to take on experiences of quality for your own growth, and to reflect on them thoughtfully.

In the core of the IB Diploma Programme, along with CAS, you also find theory of knowledge. This course will help you develop your skills of critical reflection on CAS and on all the other experiences of knowing you will encounter in your life.

## 2. Knowing how: skills of thinking and acting

This category of knowledge (knowing how to do something) interconnects with the other two. To a large extent, it is *experience* that helps us learn a skill, to the point that truly possessing a skill could be argued to require experience. It could readily be argued, too, that the development of a skill is a subcategory of "experience and reflection". Here, we are suggesting that it overlaps but adds

## Discussion Activity

### In what ways does the IB encourage experiential learning?

Gather your own ideas in response to the questions below, and prepare to share your thoughts with others in your class.

1. Think of each of your IB courses in turn and identify the experiential component. Do you find yourself, through experience, becoming more familiar with methods of inquiry and more confident using concepts and skills? Can you give examples?

2. Think about your own experiences in CAS and try to pick out just one incident or moment of realization that you could describe to your class as significant in your own learning. As you and your classmates describe these moments, do you find any common features emerging?

3. According to the IB learner profile, learners are risk-takers: "They approach unfamiliar situations and uncertainty with courage and forethought, and have the independence of spirit to explore new roles, ideas and strategies." Can you see places in your own CAS programme where you have tried something new that extended your capacities in any way? Can you describe it?

4. Experiential learning, reflected upon and articulated, yields personal knowledge. Has the experiential knowledge that you have gained also been shared knowledge? Has any experience of collaboration or teamwork, or of working under guidance, made you feel as though you were learning not only as an individual but, in a connected way, as part of a group? Can you give an example?

characteristics of its own. Remember that what we are doing here is not insisting that our three-part categorization is the only way of classifying the ideas. Instead, we're offering a useful way to think about different features of knowledge.

It could be argued, too, that knowing how to do something, such as how to make empanadas, is equivalent to having the *information* you need to do each part step by step: "I know that first I go online to find a recipe. I know that next I get out a large bowl from the cupboard. I know that next I measure the flour into the bowl. I know that…". Empanada makers of the world and recipe websites of the Internet, thank you for this shared knowledge!

However, have you ever tried to assemble furniture from a box following step-by-step instructions, or to learn a computer skill from a manual or a training video? "Yes, I know how to do it. It tells me how right here." But do you *really* know how? If you can recall any moment of struggling to figure out what instructions mean, you will probably acknowledge that having a set of steps in the process for reference is not the same thing at all as actually being able to do it. Indeed, some of us (personal confession here!) can end up having the results – the assembled bunk bed or wheelbarrow, or the video edited in a movie

programme – without actually…quite…knowing how to do the same thing another time. It's not until you reach the point of putting aside the instructions and being able to apply what you've learned that you can say (with triumph or with gentle modesty), "I know how." You have a skill. You can apply it and demonstrate it.

When it comes to making empanadas, though, the demonstration might be intensely controversial. "Yes, maybe you've learned how to make empanadas. But you don't know how to make them the delicious way my mum does!" Is it ever possible to pass such a test? "Knowing how" is almost always on some kind of scale of expertise and often evaluated by criteria that include an element of subjective impressions – and sometimes downright bias (don't compete with anyone's mother!). In major world competitions of skills, such as in playing the piano or doing gymnastics, the judges are experts and have criteria to guide them, but there can still be disagreement between members of a judging panel. Nevertheless, none of them at that level would dispute that the contestants *know how*. This kind of knowledge is often called "procedural knowledge" and stored, as we will consider later, in your "procedural memory".

## Discussion Activity

### Knowing how: suggested class activity

*To students*: Identify one thing that you know how to do that can be demonstrated in under two minutes and could possibly be taught in not much more (taught at least to a recognizable level). The skills should be something easy and enjoyable to bring into class: juggling, playing a simple melody on a recorder, singing a short song in another language, a dance step, a shortcut in a mathematical problem, a handy method of organizing time, a trick of manipulating photographs on a laptop computer, whistling, a card trick, a way of putting on a cultural garment, a culturally appropriate way of giving greetings or conducting a ceremony that is unfamiliar to most in the class, and so on. (It's possible that two or three students might want to work together to demonstrate some kinds of skills.) When you have thought of something that you could demonstrate and teach, write down your proposal and hand it in to your teacher.

*To the teacher*: Take in the proposals in advance of the class in which you will do the activity. With your awareness of how much class time is available, select three or four of the proposals to be put into action and give the students advance warning to prepare to demonstrate and teach the skills. Depending on the nature of the skill, it could be taught either to one or two other individuals in front of the class or to the entire class. Ideally, your selection will showcase skills of quite different sorts.

On the day you have scheduled this, arrange the classroom for the demonstrations – and enjoy the results. When the students have finished and been applauded, it is time to move into discussion provoked by the skills demonstrated. You will probably want to run through the other proposals as well so that all of the possible skills can come into the discussion.

> Is knowing how to do something essentially different from knowing information?

> How are skills learned? To what extent does the learning depend on the kind of skill? What different ways of teaching and learning can you identify for the skills demonstrated in your class?

To what extent is the skill the thing that can be demonstrated? To what extent is it also the understanding on the part of the person possessing the skill? In knowing how to do something, is there often an experiential understanding, or an attitude, or an emotional component involved?

Can you state precisely in language what your skill is? Is it "to run fast", "play hard", or "make an excellent cup of tea"? Or is there a dimension of the skill that is difficult to put into language?

Of the skills demonstrated in class and the others proposed, what ones seem to fit into a larger body of knowledge? Do they contribute to areas of knowledge or social skills, or skills for public competition?

What skills are you learning in your IB subjects? In what ways do you have to demonstrate them to get credit for your courses? In what ways do you expect to apply them in the future after your IB studies?

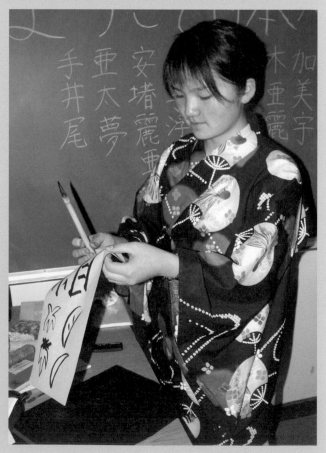

**Transferable skills**

"If I know how to make empanadas, surely I know how to make pancakes or breads." "If I know how to make many different dishes, surely I know how to cook."

What kind of skill is implied by these confident declarations? What examples of transferable skills can you find in your different courses and CAS, such as doing research, keeping careful records, and drawing graphs?

At this point, does this category of skills-based knowledge seem to you to include a rag-tag assortment of skills? In our twenty statements, there are three that are phrased as personal "how-to" knowledge, yet they represent entirely different kinds of skills. Each skill here would be learned, experienced, demonstrated, and evaluated in quite different ways:

> I know how to solve problems between my friends.

> I know how to play football, or soccer as some call it.

> I know how to solve problems at my level in mathematics.

Our range of possible skills is so great that we are likely to put the above statements in completely different categories of abilities.

Psychologist Howard Gardner has gone so far as to theorize that human beings actually have "multiple intelligences". In 1983 he proposed seven distinct kinds of intelligence and has since then accepted an eighth and considered two more. Although his theory has been criticized on several grounds, the categories that he developed were a serious attempt to come to grips with the many different forms of human ability:

1. linguistic intelligence (language)

2. logical/mathematical intelligence

3. musical/rhythmic intelligence

4. bodily/kinesthetic intelligence

5. spatial intelligence

6. intrapersonal intelligence (understanding oneself)

## Learning how

What skills are involved in what the girls are demonstrating here? To what extent does almost all learning in school involve background social skills and facility with language? These skills have been associated with forms of intelligence.

Sana'a, Yemen

Florida (Valle), Colombia

7. interpersonal intelligence (understanding others)

8. naturalistic intelligence (relating to nature, classifying natural forms).

You might want to read further on these forms of intelligence. You could look at the additional intelligences Gardner has considered in subsequent decades, and critical reactions to the distinctions he drew. Some theorists contend that these multiple intelligences cannot be established or refuted by evidence, so are not to be accepted as scientific. Some insist that all intelligences are aspects of a single integrated intelligence. While psychologists research and debate, many educationalists have accepted the concept of multiple intelligences as usefully directing attention to differences in the ways that students learn. Here, we accept these eight intelligences as a non-rigorous identification of human abilities, in all of which it is possible for individuals to be highly skilled.

Although for some skills we need only observation and practice, for many others we benefit from deliberate teaching. We take music lessons to learn how to play an instrument, or follow the advice of a coach to learn how to play a sport more effectively. To develop skills of thinking critically, we also gain from deliberate attention to goals and practice in achieving them.

In this book, you will be given abundant opportunity to develop your thinking skills, particularly as listed in the box "How to think critically: some TOK skills". If you develop these skills successfully, you will be making them part of your own personal knowledge. You will also be able to see more clearly how the shared knowledge of different disciplines is constructed.

In the end, though, all thinking skills are useless unless they are applied. You have to think critically *about something*. And this brings us to our third and last kind of knowledge, the knowledge claim.

## 3. Knowing that...: knowledge claims

In this last kind of knowledge, we are concerned with statements we have accepted. Knowledge claims are what we know – or, rather, what we say we know.

What we say we know includes assertions of many different kinds. Much of it is information or factual report: you know that you are reading this book, that theory of knowledge is a subject in the International Baccalaureate Diploma Programme, that the word "football" indicates different sports in the United States and England, that water boils at 100° centigrade at sea level, that the Statue of Liberty in New York City was a gift from France, that the pyramids of the ancient pharaohs are in Egypt, that taxonomy is the classification of living things, that molten rock flows out of volcanoes. For many questions on examination papers, you are expected to be able to state what you know and will be graded on whether you are factually accurate.

Much of what we say we know extends beyond factual information into our statements of values and other declarations of beliefs. You might say that sunsets are beautiful, that winning the Nobel Prize is admirable, that deliberately hurting other people is deplorable: all these statements are statements of values. You might also say that you know that there is (or is not) a Supreme Being, that after death we go (or do not go) to an afterlife, or that there is (or is not) a purpose for life: all of these statements are statements of metaphysical beliefs.

Certainly, we will never say anything at all about a lot of things we know. Much of what you know you will never put into words, even though you could. For one thing, it may be too personal to share. Even living in an era of electronic social media with the split-second impulse to tell all, most of us retain a sense of what is personal and private, and we prefer to keep some knowledge to ourselves.

Moreover, you may not want to say that you know something simply because it is trivial and irrelevant to any concerns or questions you might have. It is entirely possible, for example, that you know very well that the window is open or that the table in the corner is dusty, but these bits of knowledge are not likely to loom large in your mind. If you did choose to communicate this knowledge to others, they would probably not consider you to be a fascinating conversationalist.

However, when you do choose to put into words what you know, you are taking that giant step into the third kind of knowledge we treat here: the knowledge claim. You are asserting that you know something: "I know that Spain won the FIFA World Cup in 2010." "I know that God has created the world." Rarely are you likely to express the "I know that" part. However, it is implicit, it is

## How to think critically: some TOK skills

We hope you will learn better how to:

- recognize different perspectives and analyse them, first to understand them, and then to evaluate their claims to knowledge. This skill gives a better understanding of debates in academic and public spheres and prepares you to deal with conflicting ideas.
- classify and compare concepts: to draw distinctions and see ideas in relationship. This skill illuminates how categories and terminology affect academic discussion or social and political debate.
- identify common errors of thinking, so that you can avoid making them yourself and prevent being misled by poor arguments. This skill is immediately applicable to everyday life. It also highlights why different areas of knowledge take care to develop their methodologies.
- distinguish between different types of knowledge claims in the world around you and generate good knowledge questions. These skills are basic to any critical inquiry.

- evaluate different sources of information for their perspectives, credibility, and contribution to knowledge and understanding. This skill is important for doing research, reading media, or accepting advice in any area of life.
- make broad connections between ways of knowing, areas of knowledge, and knowledge as a whole. This skill is an unusual one for a course to teach, since most courses specialize. Whatever you choose to do in your studies and your life, you benefit from a more holistic overview.

All of the thinking skills listed above are applicable to academic disciplines and almost all parts of life. They work together for one final, much broader application, which is how to:

- apply critical thinking to situations or events in the world to understand them better and see where you can make a positive contribution.

understood to be there even if it is not spelled out when you make an assertion.

Of the twenty statements that we shuffled into groups earlier, many of them are in this category. They have in common the essential features of a knowledge claim:

1. First, the knowledge claim is expressed in language. Gestures, photographs, music – all of these communicate between people. However, with language (or mathematical statements) we move our ideas into a more public zone to share them with other people in words, terms with definitions. We are entering the zone of exchange between personal and shared knowledge.

2. Second, the knowledge claim above regarding Spain's victory at the World Cup is phrased as a statement, It is not a question: it's not "Who won the World Cup in 2010?" It is not an exclamation: it's not "What a triumph for Spain in the 2010 World Cup!" It is an assertion: "(I know that) Spain won the World Cup in 2010."

3. Third, the knowledge claim is presented as being true, even if it is highly questionable or turns out to be false. "South Africa won the 2010 World Cup", though false, is still a knowledge claim.

4. Fourth, knowledge claims are not solely information or factual statements. They include any assertions that are being presented as true, including opinions and beliefs of all kinds. If someone or some group is saying that they know, then they are making a knowledge claim.

A glance at the knowledge claims that figure among our original twenty statements, though, certainly raises a lot more questions. They do indeed have these features in common, but you might be more struck by their differences.

## Kinds of knowledge claims

How, then, are we going to group the knowledge claims made by each of these twenty statements? We want to recognize differences that actually matter in knowledge and that take us somewhere

## Discussion Activity

### "Knowledge claims"

The term "knowledge claim" is not a familiar expression to many people. A "claim" sounds in many contexts like an official procedure, such as when someone submits a claim to be reimbursed from a budget for an expense. It might even sound legal, such as when people face claims against them in court or when different groups are laying claim to a piece of land. In a TOK context, we use the expression when someone is laying claim to knowing. That is, whenever we say we know something, or make assertions that something is true, then we are making "knowledge claims".

Knowledge claims put what we know into the zone of exchange between people and groups. Because ideas are stated in language, they can be examined and discussed, questioned, evaluated, refuted, or published and passed on. Knowledge claims enable us to learn from each other and build our shared knowledge.

### Activity

Look closely at the photograph taken in Venice, Italy during Carnival, when people in costume parade in the streets. Simply prepare five statements about what you see in the photo. You can describe what you see, interpret any of the behaviour you see pictured, give your own opinions, or provide background explanation if you can. If you are looking at the photo with classmates, tell them what you think and listen to what they think.

Bravo! You have just made and exchanged knowledge claims!

Note that photographs, whatever they show, are not themselves knowledge claims; knowledge claims are what you put into words as what you *say* you know.

in our future thought. Below are the categories we created ourselves, but others are surely possible.

**Statements of personal observation** are assertions of what we know through our senses – what we see and hear, for instance. Observational statements can be checked. You can look again to see the colour of your shirt or ask someone else to confirm. "Yes, it's blue!" "It's a fact."

> *I know that* I am wearing a blue shirt and holding a cup of hot coffee.

As we will discuss later, saying, "It's a fact!" or "It's true!" may be a bit more complicated than it first appears.

> *I know that* empanadas are delicious.
>
> *I know that* my girlfriend Maria is very, very beautiful.

To say that something is delicious or someone is beautiful is a **statement of values, or a value judgment**. Whether something is virtuous or evil, important or trivial, hot or cold, interesting or boring is a matter of the values of the onlooker(s). The scale is qualitative and subjective. "It's hot today" is a value judgment; someone in the Caribbean is likely to have a different "scale" for what is hot from someone in Iceland. Even if hundreds of people agree that it is a hot day, it is still a value judgment. Value judgments are opinions that cannot be proved true or false, even though in many cases we can put forward persuasive reasons for agreeing or disagreeing.

Some value judgments can move from opinion to fact if the scale of judgment changes to one that is quantifiable and objective. "The temperature is 42 degrees Celsius (106.6 degrees Fahrenheit)": this is a statement of observation of the reading on the thermometer, using an established scale of measurement.

These next three statements are also **statements of observation,** but not the personal observation of the speaker. They are shared knowledge based on observations made by others – many others – and then on the records they made and passed on. They are statements of fact, though the three statements have different sorts of facts.

> *I know that* atoms have protons and electrons.
>
> *I know that* Spain won the FIFA World Cup in 2010.
>
> *I know that* Argentina was discovered by a Spanish explorer in the early sixteenth century.

These next three statements are *based* on statements of observation. They are not themselves observations, but take general patterns established through observation and reasoning and extrapolate from them. The first two are **predictions**: they apply observations of the past to the future, in expectation that regular patterns observed over time will continue.

> *I know that* tomorrow morning the sun will rise.
>
> *I know that* I'm going to die someday.
>
> *I know that* if I tease my sister her cheeks will turn red.

The third is a general **hypothetical statement**: it is based on past observation and places two actions in a causal relationship. If one happens then so does the other. Do you think that this particular "if/then" relationship is likely to stay constant over time? Will the Argentinian lad be able to get away with pestering his sister forever? What will it take to prove this statement false?

An assertion of spiritual belief is a **metaphysical statement** – a statement about the nature of reality beyond the material world, such as claims about the nature of time, the soul, or God. These claims differ from observational claims in that they cannot be tested with sense perception and

> *I know that* God created the world.

## Discussion Activity

### Playing with knowledge claims

#### 1 Claims and categories

Cut a piece of paper into six pieces. On each one write one knowledge claim, without identifying its category. Make sure you have at least three categories covered, with duplications permitted. The categories are: statement of observation, value judgment, prediction, hypothetical statement, metaphysical statement, and definition.

Then work in pairs within a group of four. Pairing up with a classmate, exchange papers. Identify the category of your partner's claims while he or she does the same to yours. Check the results with your partner. If you do not agree, wait until the other pair has finished and submit your disagreement to them for further judgment.

Be warned that we often phrase our knowledge claims as a blend of these categories and that words can often be understood in different ways, so that some disagreement is to be expected. The conclusion you reach is less important than identifying the reasons for categorizing as you do, and the difficulties in doing so.

#### 2 Cards and categories

Divide your class into groups of three to five people, each with a pack of cards. In your group, place the cards face down and take turns pulling out a card. If you pull a spade, you must give a definition, if a club an observational claim, if a heart a value judgment, and if a diamond a metaphysical claim. If others think that you have given a claim that is not an example of the category pulled, they must help you to reformulate it until it is. Do two quick rounds.

---

demonstrated to others. We cannot do the God lab: we cannot use litmus paper or a chemical reaction to demonstrate the existence and characteristics of a Supreme Being. We cannot weigh the soul or calculate the trajectory of reincarnation. The very absurdity of the idea underlines the nature of these claims: they are "meta" – meaning "beyond" – the physical.

This statement about a right triangle is a **definition**, which places ideas in relationship with each other using language. The 90° angle is the characteristic that makes the triangle a right triangle. It is not a statement of observation – even though every right triangle you observe will have a 90° angle. But then, how could it possibly not have one? If it didn't, it wouldn't be a right triangle.

> *I know that a right triangle has a 90° angle.*

Clearly, what we know is expressed in a huge variety of knowledge statements from all of our areas of knowledge and all other areas of our lives.

The public nature of a claim allows it to be questioned, tested, supported, refuted, or reformulated. It allows it to be published and archived, and used by others in their own work. Individual claims feed into whole bodies of interconnected claims, and enable us to develop together our shared knowledge.

## Knowledge questions

Inquiry is the very life of knowledge. Without our curiosity and questioning, our wondering and dreaming, we would have little knowledge at all. Without creatively imagining other ways of expressing, doing and making things which question what we already have, how could we generate our works of art, attempt to run our societies better, improve our methods of investigation, or invent technology? Without trying to figure things out – examining them and testing our ideas in pursuit of truth – we would not have the understanding of the world that we possess or the methodologies for learning more.

In aiming that its students be inquirers, the IB is wishing them a fine life, with active minds and the pleasures of chasing interesting ideas: "They develop their natural curiosity. They acquire the skills necessary to conduct inquiry and research and show independence in learning. They actively enjoy learning and this love of learning will be sustained throughout their lives." What a life-enriching wish for your future!

When we direct our spirit of inquiry towards the very idea of what we know, we end up asking the most fundamentally structural questions of all: *knowledge questions*. These are questions about knowledge itself and the methods by which we create it. In TOK, we ask questions centrally about "ways of knowing" and the methods by which they yield personal and shared knowledge.

These questions do not come with answers already implied. Instead, they are *open*. They invite different ways of exploring the ideas they raise and different lines of investigation and argument in posing possible answers. They do not come with their answers implied, but open up varying perspectives.

Knowledge questions are *general*. They are broad questions that can apply to many particular examples of knowledge. They deal with concepts, methods, or applications, for example. Their degree of broad generality can vary, with the overall question "How do I know?" taking on more focused forms as it is applied to knowledge of different kinds.

For the degree of generality of knowledge questions, it might be helpful to think of shifting slowly from the wide angle lens of a camera to the zoom lens, from general overview of knowledge to close-up detail. It might also be helpful to think in terms of circling out of the sky down to the earth, moving from vast overview towards more specific examination of particular knowledge. We will demonstrate with the example of moving in on knowledge in the human science of anthropology, from broad knowledge questions to narrower ones.

## Knowledge questions, broad to narrow

*Overview Circling 1.* How do I know? This hugely general knowledge question floats above all of the other questions we apply in TOK at much lower levels of generality and abstraction.

*Circling 2.* Still in overview, the high-in-the-sky questioning starts to circle closer to earth as we apply it to areas of knowledge. Although still broad, the questions become narrower in their focus. They deal with the scope and application of the particular area of knowledge, perhaps, or its methodology. Typical questions at this level might include: What do we seek to know in the sciences? How do we gain the knowledge? How do we test it? Why do we accept or reject scientific knowledge claims? What do we mean by "uncertainty" in science? Are there ways of investigating that, ethically, we should not use?

In TOK, we use a "knowledge framework" to identify both our overview questions that apply to *all* areas of knowledge and the somewhat zoomed-closer questions that apply to *particular* areas of knowledge.

*Circling 3.* These questions, although high in the sky, begin to loop closer to earth with application to particular areas, where the differences emerge as well as the similarities. For example, we might ask: How do we know in the human sciences as compared with the natural sciences? How does the methodology change as the subject matter changes – as we investigate human beings rather than the natural world?

*Circling 4.* Then, spiraling earthward and moving closer to the details of knowledge, we can ask close-up questions of more particular disciplines within the human sciences, such as: How do we know in anthropology as compared with economics? How does the specific subject matter affect the methods of investigation that are possible or appropriate?

*Circling 5.* Looping lower, moving earthward, we can ask increasingly detailed questions about more particular theories and methods of investigation of anthropology: what characterizes the method of participant observation? What are its goals and advantages in gaining knowledge? What difficulties must be overcome?

A dizzying trip from general overview to particular subject! We have circled over knowledge as a whole, moved in on the sciences, then in on the human sciences, then in on anthropology, and then in on its internal methods of gaining knowledge.

*Circling 6. Stop.* When we come almost to earth with the method of participant observation, we are into the subject matter of anthropology. Here we stop. Here we turn over the questioning to the anthropologists. They ask questions with considerable overlap with TOK – overlapping at least from the point where their own field started to come into view in our spiraling descent. However, as they build and examine knowledge in their own area they give attention not only to the characteristics of anthropology as knowledge, but also to the actual knowledge *content* – the specific knowledge claims of the field and the specific research that supports them. Meanwhile, we in TOK leave the further up-close exploration in their capable hands! The knowledge content of any one subject remains relevant for TOK primarily for providing illustration and examples of how the whole process of knowing works.

## Knowledge questions, narrow to broad

To get used to circling widely in the sky with TOK, you might want to start close to the ground instead and move upward, moving from particular examples to more general questions. To do so, you can take any knowledge claim that catches your curiosity and start thinking about all the different features of its knowledge. As examples here, we'll take three of our familiar twenty statements.

*CLOSE-UP QUESTIONS: What evidence or other justification (reasons for belief) is available for the date of discovery? How do we know this discovery even happened?*

> I know that Argentina was discovered by a Spanish explorer in the early sixteenth century.

*BROADER QUESTIONS: From whose perspective was Argentina "discovered"? Was anyone already there who might have a different perspective?*

*BROADEST QUESTIONS: How do perspectives influence interpretations in history? What is the nature of evidence in history? How do we know what happened in the past?*

Further knowledge questions arise when we start to look at the *assumptions* behind the claim. First, we see assumptions embedded in the perspective that Argentina was "discovered", as if no one had known before that it was there. Second, we can recognize the perspective of the speaker as he looks back into the past. In naming the discovered land "Argentina", he is thinking in terms of a country that only later came into being.

It is possible to trace further *assumptions* behind the wording: the way we measure time in centuries, for instance, involves a way of numbering that is assumed to be known in the knowledge claim; the way we name countries "Spain" or "Argentina" is also assumed. In some contexts, our naming and numbering systems would be relevant to examine, so it is a matter of judgment to select what questions are worth asking at a given time.

it would be hard to understand its full *meaning* without an idea of the implications for that history.

*CLOSE-UP QUESTIONS: What justifications (reasons for belief) can be put forward for knowledge of an invisible supernatural being? Is this knowledge claim personal knowledge or shared knowledge?*

**I know that God created the world.**

*BROADER QUESTIONS: What justifications can be given for metaphysical knowledge claims? Can such knowledge claims be tested? What is the role of definition in examining knowledge claims? What is faith, and what is its role in the acceptance or rejection of knowledge claims?*

*BROADEST QUESTION: What is the difference between knowledge and belief?*

As in the previous example from history, this one can hardly be grasped without raising further questions about the *assumptions* that lie behind it and the *implications* that follow from accepting it. In many parts of our lives, our individual knowledge claims are set within bodies of interconnected knowledge claims that collectively reinforce each other in our minds.

The most obvious *assumption* in this particular case is the existence of God, as it is a prior condition for His creating the world. The *implications* in this particular example are extensive, as they form the basis for an entire religious worldview.

*CLOSE-UP QUESTION: If the sun always rose in the past, can we be sure that it will rise in the future?*

**I know that tomorrow morning the sun will rise.**

*BROADER QUESTIONS: How much observational evidence do we need to consider a generalization to be well founded? Is it possible for a generalization to be so well*

Further knowledge questions arise with the *implications* of this particular knowledge claim. The implications of a knowledge claim are what follows from accepting it. If we accept a certain claim, what else do we open the door to accepting? Claiming a date of discovery, for instance, is one way of establishing ownership of land (and, in research, of ideas). In the case of this particular knowledge claim, its role in possessing and colonizing the New World is immensely significant. Although it is possible to understand all the *words* in this knowledge claim with no familiarity whatsoever with the history of South America, *justified that there is no longer any doubt? If a general pattern has been firmly established in the past, can we predict the future with certainty?*

The major *assumption* that lies behind this knowledge claim is perhaps less obvious to us than in the previous two examples simply because it is so broadly shared. We observe numerous regular patterns in the world, and incorporate them into our understanding of how the world around us works. We have good reason to expect that they will continue, because we have so much evidence that they have existed for so long. However, in projecting into the future we are still making an assumption – that these patterns will not change.

The *implications* of accepting this knowledge claim are numerous as we look to the future. We plan our lives in expectation that tomorrow will come, and that the laws of nature will not change overnight. We apply for courses and jobs, plan weddings, and note appointments in our calendars. We make decisions about present choices in the light of our expectations of the future. We certainly hope that the sun will rise tomorrow!

## But how do we know if the knowledge claims are true?

How do we know if a claim is true? This knowledge question is daunting and intriguing in the complexities it opens up. The twenty knowledge claims that we have played with in this chapter are very direct and simple. Yet even such simple statements take us into knowledge in such different forms that the question "Is it true?" can take us down a number of paths. They can be tricky underfoot at points, but have been signposted by others who have already ventured this way. They offer, at points, some big smiles and excellent views! Take a break, and then join us for the next chapter!

### Discussion Activity

#### Do it yourself! What knowledge questions will you ask?

What knowledge questions will you ask about each of the knowledge claims below? What broader knowledge questions will you ask about them? Remember that the broadest high-in-the-sky question of all is "How do I know?" but that you don't have to fly quite that high!

Not all knowledge questions are equally relevant to all examples, so discard ones that do not lead you into an inquiry on the nature of knowledge. You might consider asking about any of the following: how we interpret the language to determine what is meant by the knowledge claim, how the knowledge is gained, what justifications can be offered in support, whether it is viewed differently from different perspectives, how it is either confirmed or rejected, whether it seems to be set within a particular perspective, and whether it is recognizably a kind of knowledge that comes with characteristic questions.

Can you identify any assumptions that lie behind the knowledge claim? Can you identify any implications that come with accepting it?

The knowledge claims we give you here are familiar to you from your twenty statements. However, you and your classmates might prefer to substitute different ones that you take from the day's media or your course textbooks.

I know that Brazil's economy is stronger than Argentina's.

I know that atoms have protons and electrons.

"How do we know?"

# Kinds of knowledge

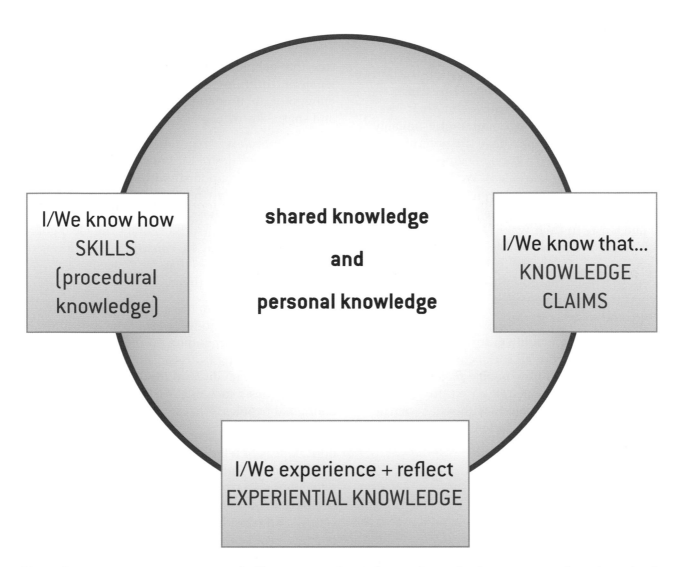

Naming our concepts and diagramming them in relation to each other help us draw distinctions useful in thinking and talking about knowledge. In reality, however, the three kinds of knowledge represented around the perimeter are interacting constantly, as are our shared knowledge and personal knowledge overall.

# 3. Seeking Truth

Ideas, it is often said, drive the world. The huge abstractions of nationalism, wealth, or justice, for instance, can inspire human progress or provoke destruction. They must be handled with care.

One of the most powerful of all these abstractions is the concept of truth, and it assuredly carries this danger. When people believe that their own perspective is uniquely right and unquestionably superior to all others, they have the potential to treat the welfare of other human beings as less important than their own ideas. We have witnessed in the world's history the harshness of dogma and the viciousness of ideological certitude – and the lives laid waste in their wake. *Possessing The Truth*, in this sense of narrow-minded, exclusionary, and passionate conviction, is the dark side of the concept of truth. It stands at the far pole from the concepts that we value within this course: *telling the truth* and *seeking the truth*.

*Telling the truth*, we would venture to say, is a guiding ideal in almost all social contexts – even if that ethical ideal of how people *should* act is not always fulfilled in how people *do* act. In the ideal, our words correspond exactly with what we truly believe to be so; we do not deceive. In the ideal,

we can trust each other fully as we enter into agreements of all kinds: working together and doing business, marrying and developing families, and collectively building societies. It is certainly true that people do not consistently live up to ideals of truthfulness but enough people do so enough of the time to facilitate social interaction and shared knowledge.

*Seeking the truth* is a major drive in our lives and certainly in our desire for knowledge. At a basic level, we need to understand how the world works to be able to survive in it – and that need is as present today as it has ever been. As we build our areas of knowledge, truth becomes the ideal goal to which we aspire as we construct descriptions of the world and societies that are as accurate as we can manage to make them.

Seeking the truth also has a scope that takes us beyond knowledge in its sense of the disciplines we study in the IB. Depending on the cultural context, that goal of finding truth can involve prayer, study of sacred texts, meditation towards enlightenment, or vision quests such as those of North American aboriginal peoples.

Although we will encourage inquiry later on into ethical ideas of telling the truth and metaphysical concepts of seeking the truth, in this chapter we will choose a narrower path. We will be dealing primarily with knowledge in terms of knowledge claims, and considering ways in which we might begin to evaluate them. Are they true? Are they false? Or are the binary categories of true and false too limited for effective evaluation?

## Foolish gullibility or knee-jerk rejection

Seeking the truth – even in the restricted sense of judging knowledge claims to be true or false, or their interpretations to be accurate – is part of our everyday reality. We want to find out what happened when a child is crying; we want to know the real reason someone we depended on just gave us a flimsy excuse; we want to understand why we lost a job; we want to know whether we can believe information given us by our car mechanic, doctor, employer, financial advisor, elected representatives, or media. We want to know why a local lake has become so polluted that it no longer

THE OPENING AND CLOSING CEREMONY OF THE ANNUAL DOGMA DAY PARADE

has fish; why a peaceful protest march has become violent; whether a new medical procedure can, in fact, treat multiple sclerosis. We want to pin down what is true, sometimes within circumstances where the investigation might be difficult. At the same time, we need to be able to accept what we're told to the extent that we are not paralysed in a state of constant doubt and questioning.

Trying to think critically in a constructive way depends, first, on recognizing when it would be

**"Seeking the truth"**

"Seeking the truth" takes on different meanings in different contexts. In this chapter we are treating it as critical evaluation of knowledge claims, using reasoning and language as primary means. In other contexts, it suggests looking for understanding of the meaning of life, possibly by silencing reasoning and language, and using other ways of knowing. Whether the truth lies within the human mind or in a transcendent state beyond the human is then a matter of the cultural and religious perspective. Images of journeys and mountaintops are often associated with spiritual concepts of seeking the truth.

valuable to question. If we are too gullible – that is, if we accept too readily without asking questions and checking – we can easily be manipulated into buying what we do not need, taking remedies that are not good for us, or voting or campaigning against the benefit of our society. "Wanna buy this bracelet? Wanna buy this ideology? It'll cure all your ills." We could end up feeling duped and foolish, or damaging ourselves and others.

Thinking critically equally depends on avoiding the opposite extreme – being so ready to reject what we are told that we become scornful and impervious to good reasons. Blanket distrust is not a thoughtful stand: knowing that the media present information from different perspectives does not mean that it is reasonable to reject news reports as "all lies"; knowing that an issue is disputed by people with different perspectives does not mean that all of them are wrong or that it is reasonable to turn away with a disengaged shrug. "Who knows? You can't believe what you hear."

Thinking critically means raising good questions and looking for good answers. It is not a posture of accepting all with unthinking gullibility or denying all with unthinking rejection or cynicism. Nor is it a dismissal of all inquiry, declaring that all opinions are equally false or true, adopting a posture of feigned open-mindedness in order to avoid thought.

In order even to be ready to think critically, we may have to deal in part with our own temperaments – too trusting or too rejecting – and our own mental laziness. Then, in order to ask good questions but not drown in them, we might want to cultivate our capacity for *constructive doubt*: recognition of when critical questions are valuable to ask.

## The constructive doubt response

But what triggers your doubt? The first step in thinking critically is being aware that there is something not to be taken simply at face value, not to be accepted exactly as presented. However, if you do *not* thereafter give some serious attention to what makes you doubt, you are not likely to get very far as a critical thinker. Recognizing and refining your doubt becomes a major means of sorting out the false from the true.

Test your own response now by reading the article on the next page. If you doubt, why? What reasons can you give? Ideally, you will exchange ideas with others in your class.

# Daily World News

MARCH 15, 2011

# VOODOO DOC DANCES UP A STORM

by Ken U Bleevit, correspondent

The amazing Medicine Man Doc Juru conjures up hurricanes with his dance spins in the jungle!

BRAZIL. Doc Juru may be the greatest wonder of the world. The Amazonian medicine man appears to possess the power to change the weather patterns of the planet.

"It's easy," says the Doc through an interpreter. "I dance hard and fast, I make it rain. I spin, I make a hurricane."

Scientists are baffled by the powers of this quick stepping witch doctor of the Pira tribe, deep in the Brazilian jungle. They have been closely observing his dances ever since 2004 when the tribe was first discovered by adventurous anthropologists.

"I wouldn't have believed it," declares Dr. Hans Wolfgang of the Climate Change Commission. "But our data show consistent correlation between the steps of his dances and the weather across the world. I was a skeptic but now I feel I have to accept that there's something here that we just don't understand with our current science."

Doc Juru, the medicine man of his tribe, is held with great respect by all the Pira. He is a descendent of an ancient line of weather makers who have preserved the jungle's climate for longer than anyone can remember.

"We have to keep his location confidential," says Dr. Wolfgang. "Can you imagine how many groups would like to get their hands on this guy and his powers? He's worth billions."

Doc Juru himself is untroubled by all the attention. He is far too busy dancing daily, resisting outside influences such as jive, hip hop, and ballet. He is also very happy with the gifts he has been given by his paleface visitors, especially the latest model digital music device and the unlimited supply of dancing shoes with arch support.

## Billionaire Sunbather Bursts into Flames

COTE D'AZUR, FRANCE.

THE SPONTANEOUS combustion of oil tycoon Harold Hammer has French police shaking their heads. "There is no evidence of foul play," insists the Chief of Police. "One minute he was soaking up the sun and the next minute he was a ball of fire."

Eyewitnesses to the bizarre barbeque are still in shock. Pierre Blanc, ice cream vendor, saw the human bonfire. He wonders still whether eating an ice cream might have cooled the oily oil magnate enough to save his life. "I will have to live always with asking myself if I could have prevented this catastrophe. But these fat billionaires, they soak up so much. Maybe this was divine justice."

## Discussion Activity

### Do you believe it?

We are presented with many knowledge claims – in class, in the media, in shops, at work, in all the institutions and social circles of our lives. They are part of our conversations and part of the news and gossip of the background of our lives. They thread their way through the information and views we exchange in our work and our family lives. But do you believe them all? What means do you use, often quickly and with little attention, to filter out what's false?

### Voodoo Doc Dances Up a Storm

Please read the article opposite on the Voodoo Doc and give attention to your *reasons* for accepting or rejecting the information it presents. The questions below are useful in focusing your thoughts and class discussion on specific features of the text.

1   Look at the overall visual presentation of the article. Even before you read the words, are there features that would make you inclined either to accept or doubt the information? What background knowledge of the media are you drawing on for this evaluation?

2   When you read the article is there anything about the way it is written that might make you inclined to accept or reject it?

3   "Do you believe it?" the heading above asks you. But what is the "it"? Identify at least roughly the knowledge claims made in turn by Doc Juru, Dr Wolfgang, correspondent Ken U Bleevit, and, it seems, the *Daily World News*.

4   Do you consider those making the knowledge claims to be reliable sources? Why or why not? How can you check their reliability?

5   Are you able to check the information given in this article? Why or why not?

6   What stereotypes of indigenous people do you recognize in this article? Is Dr Wolfgang also a stereotype? Are there any others?

7   The article on Doc Juru is placed next to another about an unfortunate bonfire. Does association with this second story affect your evaluation of the first?

8   What reactions do you find in yourself? Are you inclined to dismiss the article with impatience or irritation? To laugh? To be offended? To look for the possible bits of truth in the article? Do you think that your own prior beliefs about science, magic, and the unexplained, or about human groups, their cultural practices, and their interactions affect how you respond?

### Does it matter if you believe it?

In the case of this particular article, does it make any difference whether you believe the knowledge claims or not? Could believing them affect your thinking or your actions?

### Reflection

Now leave the Voodoo Doc behind. Take your pen, paper, and about 20 quiet minutes to think and write more generally in response to these questions:

*Does it matter if what we believe is true? Is there any harm in believing knowledge claims that are false? Give reasons for your response.*

It's likely that you were inclined to dismiss this article before you even read it, or by the time you had finished reading the first sentence. Although we do want to stay open-minded and not discard what we are told simply on reflex, an inclination to doubt the Voodoo Doc article is an indication of a healthy "doubt response".

Developing this response depends on your pausing to ask questions relevant to the credibility of any report. What questions did you come up with in your consideration of the Voodoo Doc article?

- Did you consider the *reliability of the source* of the article – author Ken U Bleevit and the newspaper the *Daily World News*?
- Did you pick out particular knowledge claims and ask about *supporting evidence*? Did you point to knowledge claims and ask if they even *made sense* in the world as you know it?

**Voices**

### Does it matter if what we believe is true?

### Some student voices

Not always, because...

- When it comes to some claims, I don't really care if they are true. It doesn't make much difference to me whether my friend's uncle drives a truck.

- Some claims can't be proven anyhow, and I prefer to believe. Believing in God gives my life meaning so I'd rather believe even if I'm wrong.

Generally yes, because...

- I just prefer truth. I don't want to mess up my mind with lies. I want to feel truthful inside.

- I think I'll make better choices based on truth. I want to take medicine that will actually cure me and apply to universities that are likely to accept me.

- I think that the way people treat me would be better if they didn't accept stereotypes. It's really insulting sometimes. And I wouldn't like to treat other people ignorantly, either.

- I want to pass my IB exams, so I hope the examiners have the same version of things that I do!

- It's kind of pointless to be studying stuff that's false. How can that be knowledge?

---

- Did you look at the article as a whole and at features of the way it was written?
- Did you reflect on your own inclination to accept or reject articles making claims about powers that appear to be supernatural?

If you raised these questions, or some form of them, then you have already moved from simply rejecting a report to thinking about *why* you reject it. The questions above, easily generated in response to an article that is fairly silly, can apply seriously to any article in any publication.

However, in trying to identify knowledge claims in the article, did you find that more was implied and left unsaid than actually given in the form of knowledge claims? Much is conveyed, after all, not by what is stated directly but how it is suggested by narration and use of language. Attitudes are more difficult to pin down for examination than the outright statements of knowledge claims.

Is there any harm, though, in reading silly stories without an active "doubt response"? After all, we seek out fiction without concern and we often relish absurdity, and neither fiction nor comedy damages us! One major problem in reading without active doubt is that if we confuse condescending or inaccurate stories about people from other cultures (funny faraway folk) with reliable information, we erode our critical responses to stereotypes and distortions. Repeated often enough, they stop seeming so obviously absurd.

**knowledge claim**

doubt response

questions

accept

accept    not sure    **reject**

## Working backwards: rejecting what's false

Does this seem backwards to you – to seek what's true by rejecting what's false? Certainly the approach of discarding misinformation and errors does not guarantee that the rest is error-free. Yet this backwards approach does at least help to maintain those critical screens, the ones we place around our minds to control, to the extent that we can, the quality of what we allow in.

As we will consider later in the course, this backwards approach is the one taken in reaching conclusions in major areas of knowledge. When a new hypothesis is proposed in the natural sciences, for instance, it must undergo testing. If it is found to be wrong, it is discarded or revised for further testing. Only conclusions that have withstood considerable testing are accepted as true within science. Even then they are considered only *provisionally true*, that is, accepted for now but open to being overturned at some later date if further testing and evidence disqualifies them. Science works by "falsifying" hypotheses – testing them to discover what is false – not strictly by proving them true.

## Working forwards: accepting what's true

Our goal in gaining knowledge is to seek what is true. Instead of working backwards to reject what's false, can we work forward to establish what's true?

If this process were easy, if we could all readily agree on what is true and how we reach it, then the world would be witness to far less disagreement. However, we do have some ways to approach the concept of truth, and we have some very useful critical questions that come out of them. It would not be at all surprising if your own approach to the Voodoo Doc article already raised the central ideas of major theories of truth.

As you give your attention to the three major "checks for truth" below, think about the useful ideas they provide but also about their limitations.

| Albanian | Dhivehi | Greenlandic |

## Three "truth checks"

The three truth checks below deal with different concepts of truth – what it is and how it is established. The concepts of truth they give us are not the only ones; philosophical exploration of the nature of truth has generated numerous ideas and subtleties of thought. Here, though, we have selected these three as central ones and simplified them enough to make them useful for this level of critical thinking. All three give us ways of thinking about truth, and all three prompt questions that send us to the next stage of critical evaluation.

| Maltese | Shona | Arabic |

## 1 Coherence check for truth

**(Question: Is this knowledge claim consistent with what I already know? How to answer it: Think. Use your ability to reason. In research, see if the documents and data are free from contradiction.)**

If on reading the Voodoo Doc article you said, "That's ridiculous. No man can control the weather," then you were using *coherence* as a check for truth. Your response to doubt and to question was triggered because the claims that the story presented or implied were not consistent with what you know already.

The coherence concept of truth demands that all the knowledge claims held to be true should not conflict or contradict. It is when a new knowledge claim does *not* fit – when it is *not* compatible with what we already believe – that this check for truth becomes most conscious and active. "That's odd! It doesn't seem right to me." Where does the error lie? Is it in the knowledge claim that we have just encountered – or is there error within the body of beliefs we

## Discussion Activity

### Three truths and a lie

First, write four knowledge claims about yourself. They can be of any kind, but should be quite varied. But here is the trick: three of your claims must be true and one of your claims must be false. Yes, you are being asked to lie.

### Some examples

I am 130 cm tall, I never drink tea, I have two brothers, I am in pain right now, I have a good sense of humour, I won a dance competition when I was 12 years old, I have been twice to New Zealand, I had an argument with my friend yesterday, I want to be an engineer, I believe that poverty is the most important issue facing the world today.

### The interrogation

Divide yourselves now into groups of three or four.

It's time for the interrogation. Can your classmates, by clever questioning, discover which of your claims is the lie? Can you, by your own clever questioning, discover the lies that your classmates have given you? (Note: "clever questioning" does not include directly asking, "Is your third claim true?")

Each person in your group, in turn, is in the "hot seat" answering the interview questions. Someone else in the group is appointed to watch the time. The interviewers have no more than 6 minutes maximum to ask their questions of each person and give their guesses on which statement is the lie.

### The reflection

Now return to the full group. The big overarching question you must face together is the central one of the theory of knowledge course: *How do we know?*

The following questions are more specific and applied:

- What kinds of knowledge claims were the easiest to test with your questioning? Why? What statements were difficult? Were any of them impossible?
- What questioning strategies seemed to work best? Did they differ with different kinds of claims?
- What did you consider "evidence" for a truth, or a lie? What kinds of reasons seemed to be most convincing to you, and why?
- Did your relationship with the person in the "hot seat" affect your questioning or your conclusions? Did what you already knew about the person help you decide whether knowledge claims were plausible?
- In judging the truth of the claims, did you use only language, or did you find other clues in body language or tone?
- Is it acceptable for the person in the "hot seat" to answer the interview questions with lies? If anyone did lie, how did you figure out that he was not honestly answering the interview questions?

Through the interrogation and reflection, you will notice numerous features of how we investigate and how we interpret the information we gain.

>
>
> The scientist seeks system, simplicity, scope; and when satisfied on these scores he tailors truth to fit. He as much decrees as discovers the laws he set forth, as much designs as discerns the patterns he delineates.[1]
>
> *Nelson Goodman*

already hold? A check for coherence does not look at statements one at a time, but instead looks at whole bodies of statements for whether they fit together in a rationally consistent way.

We use this check often, when a report of any kind raises doubts in our minds. When we hear a report about the way someone we know has acted, or

---

[1] Goodman, N. 1985. *Ways of Worldmaking*. Indianapolis. Hackett. P 18.

### The Butterfly Dream

"Once Zhuangzi dreamt he was a butterfly, a butterfly flitting and fluttering around, happy with himself and doing as he pleased. He didn't know he was Zhuangzi. Suddenly he woke up and there he was, solid and unmistakable Zhuangzi. But he didn't know if he was Zhuangzi who had dreamt he was a butterfly, or a butterfly dreaming he was Zhuangzi."[2]

*Zhuangzi (Chuang-Tzu, 369–298 BCE)*

The Butterfly Dream is a well known piece of writing, largely because of all the questions that it stirs up. However, "Is Zhuangzi *really* a butterfly?" is not likely to be chief among them. The inquiry is less literal and more reflective. What is he suggesting about sense perception, experience, and our sense of self? Is he suggesting anything about shifting perspectives, preconceptions, and relative truth? Is he hinting at awakening to a realization of uncertainty? To what extent does the effect of the story depend on the choice of a butterfly and not some other animal?

Poetic writing does not generally gain its impact through making knowledge claims that can be checked for truth. Often it suggests rather than states and evokes rather than describes. Often it appeals to our experience and imagination rather than our articulated and tested knowledge and leaves us with reflections rather than formulated fact.

As we give our attention to knowledge claims and ways of checking them for truth, we might pause to remember that not all of our knowledge takes the form of claims, and that even many of our knowledge claims cannot be checked effectively using these concepts of truth.

---

[2] Watson, B (translator). 1968. *The Complete Works of Chuang Tzu*. New York. Columbia University Press. P 49.

## Discussion Activity

## A coherent worldview

The coherence check for truth involves accepting or rejecting a knowledge claim depending on whether it fits harmoniously within the entire body of beliefs. In areas of knowledge contradiction alerts us to errors, though these may lie not in the new knowledge claim but in what we have already accepted.

To understand more fully how coherence works, have a look at this graphic representation of the worldview of the European medieval period; it is easier to see the assumptions of a worldview we do not accept than to see our own.

The concepts of order and hierarchy penetrate all areas of life. God's Great Chain of Being accounts for everything created in a grand hierarchy, descending from the throne of God to angels, through man, to animals, plants, and minerals. Every living being and all inanimate objects have a rank in the continuous chain. All categories within the chain also correspond to each other, so that referring to a lion (the top animal) can be understood as referring to the king (the top human being). All elements in the chain aspire upward towards God.

The cosmos is divinely ordered. The planets (including the sun) move in circles around the earth; the circle was the perfect eternal form, with no beginning and no end. The nine orbits are cared for by nine ranked orders of angels ($9 = 3 \times 3$, with 3 being the holy number of the trinity).

The closest orbit is the moon's, and it marks the boundary between the eternal cosmos above and the perishable realm below. Beneath the moon, substances are not eternal but decay because

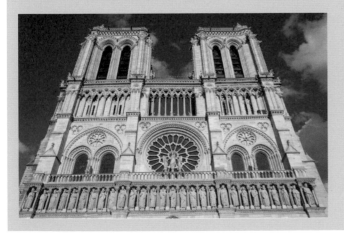

the four elements (earth, air, fire, water) are not in perfect balance. The elements correspond in human beings to the four humours, the components of personality. ($3 \times 4 = 12$, the number of the apostles. $3 + 4 = 7$, the number of virtues or deadly sins.)

The "microcosm" of man possesses a hierarchy (reason at the top tugging upward towards God, and appetites tugging downward towards the beasts), just as does the family and the society.

The tidiness of the worldview as it comes down to us can in part be explained by the fact that it was monks doing much of the recording, but this account of the worldview does appear consistently within religious text and literature of the time.

## Discussion

Now, knowing what you do from this quick picture, can you predict some of the ideas that would be accepted or rejected as coherent with the beliefs of the time? Try to trace some of the implications of the worldview.

- What would be the attitude towards social mobility? How readily would people be able to change their class or station in life?
- What would be the attitude towards rebellion against the social order?
- What would be the interpretation of physical illness, and mental illness?
- Would the people be inclined to give greater admiration to reason or to emotion?
- Can you guess what their attitude would be towards numbers and geometrical shapes, and to reasoned, ordered mathematics and numerology?
- The planets in the picture move in perfect circles to celestial "music of the spheres". What ideas do you expect would be encompassed in a concept of "harmony"?
- Which is more likely to be their method of gaining knowledge: observation of the world or philosophical reflection on how it must be?
- Seeing the progressive divisions and subdivisions of the view of order, what structural characteristics would you expect in medieval painting, cathedral architecture, and stained glass windows?

about an action taken by our government, or about a development in science, we ask, "Is this claim plausible?" "Is it consistent with what I know?" "Does this make sense to me?" In our personal knowledge, we seem to be capable of believing contradictions when we really do not want to face uncomfortably conflicting beliefs ("He loves me, he loves me not.") or when we have given a topic little reflection. However, we are pushed to notice our contradictions when our knowledge is shared. Indeed, the methodologies of areas of shared knowledge are designed to a large extent to notice and scrutinize contradictions.

But think about it!

- What are some problems that you can immediately identify with using a body of beliefs that you already hold to judge the truth of a new knowledge claim?
- Is it possible for two people checking for truth by coherence to reach different conclusions?

### Limitations of coherence as a check

To use this check for truth effectively, we must strive to be open-minded and acknowledge that we could be wrong in the beliefs we have previously held. Otherwise, as we check the truth of a new knowledge claim by its compatibility with what we believe already, we may end up discarding any challenges to our ideas and simply reinforcing our prior beliefs.

In the quotation from Nelson Goodman given earlier he goes so far as to claim that scientists fall into just such a weakness, that they impose a version of reality by tidying the world into their systemized theories. In giving this picture of scientists at work, Goodman may be doing what he accuses scientists of doing, since he tidies his own description of scientists to ignore corrective methods that are part of the public nature of science, and he excludes any possibility of a cross-check from a different concept of truth that he does not accept himself. However, he does bring attention to the human tendency to notice and accept primarily what confirms the ideas we have already. This inclination is known as "confirmation bias".

In considering limitations of the coherence check, we have to question the degree to which we accept truth being subjective and relative, of being

no more than a matter of perspective, reinforced through *confirmation bias* of all kinds.

In drawing on our own concepts and beliefs, the coherence check for truth leads us not outward to the world but deeper into our own minds. If what matters is *only* internal consistency, any worldview of any group has an equal claim to truth, as long as their beliefs form a coherent whole. Medieval beliefs about medical cures, according to this concept of truth, were as true as are current scientific ones, given that they were internally consistent within the worldview of the time; there can be no external measure of progress. This view of truth is known as "relativism".

Relativists would not place their views under the heading of "limitations" as we do here. On the other hand, they cannot argue very convincingly for others to take their particular perspective on truth very seriously, since by their own measure it would be only one view among others, with no special status as true.

### The coherence check and critical thinking

Do the limitations of the coherence concept of truth destroy its usefulness as a check on the credibility of knowledge claims? No, not at all. When a statement contradicts the beliefs we hold already, we are alerted to doubt and ask questions. The difference between the check used sloppily and the check used well lies in two of your IB educational goals: being open-minded and thinking critically.

---

### Overcoming confirmation bias: a tip

Although the coherence check is important for evaluating rational consistency and finding contradictions, it can backfire in our less-than-rational minds! We tend (sadly) to notice and accept only whatever agrees with what we think already – not even noticing contrary evidence. To develop your own open mind, why not look for evidence *against* your current views? Consider knowledge claims and arguments counter to your own – even if you do not, after thought, accept them.

Yiec — Dinka
Añete — Gurani
Liciniso — Siswati

## 2 Correspondence check for truth

**(Question: Does the knowledge claim correspond to how things actually are in the world? How to answer it: Observe. Find evidence.)**

> If it disagrees with experiment it is wrong. In that simple statement is the key to science. It does not make any difference how beautiful your guess is. It does not make any difference how smart you are, who made the guess, or what his name is – if it disagrees with experiment it is wrong. That's all there is to it.[3]
>
> *Richard Feynman*

If on reading the Voodoo Doc article you said, "Why should I believe this? There's no evidence given and no way of checking the facts," then you were using the correspondence concept of truth, which takes us outside our minds and into the external world. This check for truth demands that the knowledge claim match or "correspond to" what really happens in the world.

You cannot apply this check by simply thinking, as you do with the coherence check. You go and look for yourself, or check what observations others have reported within the pool of shared knowledge. For instance, the statement "Canberra is the capital of Australia" is true if and only if Canberra, when you have checked appropriate sources, turns out actually to be the capital of Australia. This concept of truth is so widely accepted that it may appear to be obvious and unproblematic.

Think about this test, too.

- What problems can you identify in establishing truth on the basis of sufficient evidence?
- Is it possible for two people using the correspondence test to reach different conclusions?

### Limitations of correspondence as a check

One limitation of this check – or at least the *scope* of this check – is the fact that not all knowledge claims can be checked by correspondence, since not all are observational claims. (Remember the distinctions we made at the end of the last chapter between kinds of knowledge claims?) It is easy enough to check to see whether someone is wearing a blue shirt and holding a cup of coffee: you look and see. Similarly, for observational statements that are part of the shared knowledge of science, you can check research reports and scientific articles. As long as knowledge claims are based on observation and evidence, then correspondence works well.

Metaphysical statements cannot be checked in this way, though. You cannot look and see God or Allah, or an afterlife in heaven; the very nature of metaphysical knowledge claims is that they are beyond ("meta") the physical, and not material. Value judgments cannot be checked in this way either. Certainly, we can look and see a beautiful girl, but whether or not the girl is beautiful is still a judgment that cannot be established by evidence (even though in some cases we might all agree).

Finally, the reliability of the correspondence check for truth depends on the quantity and quality of the observations, and the way they have been used as evidence in an overall argument.

### The correspondence check and critical thinking

But do these limitations of the correspondence concept of truth undermine it as a check on the truth of knowledge claims? No. As long as we expect

---

3   Richard Feynman. 1964. From Lecture 7, "Seeking New Laws", delivered at Cornell University, as part of the Messenger Lectures: The Character of Physical Law. *http://www.cosmolearning.com/video-lectures/the-relation-of-mathematics-physics-16-9945/ minute 17:20.*

to use it only on observational statements and on knowledge claims based on evidence, it is effective. See the quotation from Feynman!

What this check does bring to the surface is numerous underlying critical questions regarding the quantity and quality of evidence, and the nature of generalizations based on observation.

The need to be responsive to changing evidence, and to evaluate constantly the correspondence between the knowledge claim and the world itself is ultimately not a limitation of this check. Instead, it could be seen as its critical strength. It allows a grounding for knowledge claims, but an open mind towards change.

Basque          Dutch          Hausa

## 3 Pragmatic check for truth

**(Question: Does it work? How to answer it: Test for practical consequences.)**

If on reading the Voodoo Doc article you said, "This knowledge claim is about weather control by some man in a jungle – there's no point to giving further attention to this article" and turned your mind away, then you were using a pragmatic concept of truth. You evaluated the knowledge claim for whether it provided any concepts that could be put into practice in any useful way, and rejected it.

Evaluating what is *true* by trying to establish what is *useful* is not, for most people, the most evident approach to seeking truth. Yet it underlies much

> Ideas … become true just in so far as they help us to get into satisfactory relations with other parts of our experience.[4]
>
> *William James*

of our knowledge: pragmatism allows us to accept assumptions and function effectively in the world. For example, we may not be able to *prove* that the world exists, or that we exist, to someone who is determined to doubt, but we do not (usually) live our lives wondering if we are real. The world and other people may be real or not; we may be real or may be figments in someone's dream. But what is the point of empty inquiry, a pragmatist asks, if we can't tell the difference anyhow in practical terms? Looking at the practical consequences of belief, pragmatists give credence to many of our basic assumptions, accepting them as "givens" so that we can grasp the world and build knowledge.

When we do not understand fully the factors involved in a complex situation, the practical consequences as we try out our theories or models may be our best approach to the truth. We look for a medical treatment that helps patients, or an approach to management that yields a more harmonious and efficient workplace. Technology puts ideas to the test pragmatically: the airplane does fly, the computer development does increase speed and capacity. The practical results of a theoretical concept may give us reason to trust it.

Think about this truth test, too.

- What problems can you see with a society accepting what works for it, and calling it truth?
- Is it possible for two people using the pragmatic test to reach different conclusions?

**Limitations of pragmatism as a check**

One of the limitations of pragmatism is less its own flaw than a quirk of human psychology. When people find a way that works – an agricultural method, a system of medicine, an approach to raising children, a first aid technique, a way of running a business – then they often close out the possibility that another way might work *better*. "The old ways are perfectly good! Why do we have to be bothered with all these new notions?"

As soon as we use pragmatism as a test for truth, moreover, we have to ask, "What do you mean

Tâpwê          Katotohanan          सच्चाई          Ukweli          ความจริง

Cree          Filipino          Hindi          Swahili          Thai

---

4   James, W. 1975. *Pragmatism: A New Name for some Old Ways of Thinking*, Cambridge MA. Harvard University Press. P 34.

ISTINA   Totuus   igazság   Sanning

Croatian      Finnish      Hungarian      Norwegian (Nynorsk)      Urdu

by usefulness?" The concept of what "works" or "has practical benefit" is not clear or consistent within the pragmatic tradition. For William James, it seemed that a knowledge claim "worked" if the consequences were beneficial for the believer. If believing in the teachings of a religion benefited the believer, for instance, then the teachings were true, pragmatically. On this basis, if anything that gives us benefit can be declared to be "true", then we can readily claim almost anything we want – that we are owed a greater share of communal wealth, or that our own group is superior to our neighbours, or that disputed territory belongs to us. The racial segregation of apartheid in South Africa certainly worked – for some. Applied subjectively, this check for truth can reinforce self-interest and fragment society into factions with equal claims to truth.

### The pragmatic check and critical thinking

Do the limitations of the pragmatic check make it useless? No. Applied to the physical world, a pragmatic concept of truth may give us confirmation – sometimes our only initial confirmation – that we are at least researching in

the right direction. We do not fully understand the complex world we investigate, but sometimes we find methods or solutions that really do seem to work and provide grounded and meaningful ways of understanding.

But *why* do they work? The pragmatic concept of truth deals not with the explanations but only with the consequences. However, if a knowledge claim is true pragmatically, then we are stimulated to ask further critical questions to find the further answers we seek, using the other two checks for truth where relevant.

## The three "truth checks" and critical thinking

   PRAVDA   真实

Mongolian      Slovak      Chinese simplified

These three truth checks, in summary, do not establish whether a knowledge claim is true or false. What they do is provide different concepts of truth,

## Knowledge questions, high-in-sky level:
### What is truth? How do we know if a knowledge claim is true?

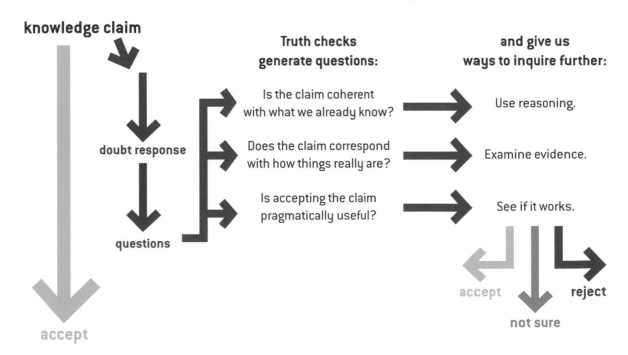

Sandhed — Danish
Vérité — French
Kebenaran — Indonesian
truth — English
Sự thật — Vietnamese

different ways of thinking of *what truth is*. Each of the three concepts then sends us down a particular path with the critical questions that they generate.

The three "truth checks" are synonymous with the term "truth tests" used in other contexts. "Tests", however, sound much too decisive regarding the possibilities for passing and failing. As we suggested earlier, it is possible for knowledge claims to *fail* decisively – to be rejected as false. It is not quite so easy to *pass* decisively. If we want to establish knowledge claims as true, we have to go further, to follow where the questions lead. Moreover, we may also have to content ourselves with imperfect answers.

DINA KEI NA DODONU. — Fijian
נכון — Hebrew
सत्य — Nepali

## Believing and truth

We may have to accept, in short, that knowledge is imperfect. Accepting the truth of a knowledge claim depends, in the end, on human judgment. To be able to discuss such judgment, we should first look more closely at the connection between concepts of *belief* and *truth*, and what we mean when we speak of being *certain*.

Belief and truth have an intimate sort of relationship. If you think a knowledge claim is true, then you believe it. If you believe it, then you think it is true. You would not say to anyone, "I believe it but I think it is false". The expression "it's true *for me*" means that you believe it, nothing more.

However, the two concepts in this relationship – belief and truth – apply to quite different things. Belief is psychological, and applies to acceptance by the mind. Truth, in contrast, applies to the knowledge claims themselves.

### 1. Degree of belief

First, you might want to consider the broad range of degree of belief. To say that you *believe* a knowledge claim can sound terribly solemn. Earnest declarations carry connotations of religious credos or national oaths. You probably believe, for instance, that Canberra is the capital of Australia, but you are hardly likely to proclaim this belief in the resonant tones of deep emotional conviction. (Try it: "I *believe* that Canberra…") Some of the things we believe do not make a big difference in our lives, but some of them significantly shape our perspectives on our lives in the world. However, they all get swept up in the verb category "believe". You may want to find some nuanced synonyms!

If you do believe a knowledge claim, then it is no longer a statement that someone else is giving you and which you are considering. It becomes part of *your own* interconnected beliefs, and part of *your* personal knowledge. You may have reason at some point to pass this belief on – and then it's *you* who is making a knowledge claim, saying "(I know that) Canberra is the capital of Australia". If people hearing you respond with doubt…well, then they can use the truth checks, go off and look for evidence (the Internet is so handy!) and decide for themselves.

> " The expression "it's true *for me*" means that you believe it, nothing more. "

casual acceptance — certainty

belief scale of psychological acceptance:
certainty – or complete conviction – is an extreme on this scale

## 2.   Degree of probability of truth

After our consideration of the checks for truth in this chapter, one major point should be very clear: that they do not function to establish that knowledge claims are true, but instead to point the way towards more detailed critical inquiry in their three different ways. If we accept the limitations of our truth checks, we have to modify the clear and tidy categories of "false" and "true" to accept a more finely calibrated scale: the claim may be held with a *degree of probability* of its truth.

The fact that truth checks do not readily stamp "true" on knowledge claims certainly does not mean, though, that nothing is really true! It would be foolish to expect tidy tests as we attempt to deal with ideas of the greatest abstraction and complexity. Moreover, it is one of the paradoxes of the search for truth that many of the beliefs that matter most to us – our values and our religious beliefs, probably most significantly – are least able to be evaluated according to the methods of these truth checks, which lend themselves best to matters of fact in the physical world. It is the more detailed inquiry that the truth checks prompt – inquiry into different ways of knowing and justification – that enables us to deal appropriately with the full range of our knowledge claims. We will get there next chapter!

Is this conclusion acceptable – that we need to assess the truth of observational statements about the physical world as degrees of probability? Whether it is acceptable depends to some extent on personal temperament. For some people, it appears to be extremely important personally to have no doubt whatsoever and to be totally sure, to the point that they may draw little distinction between whether that certainty is based on psychological commitment or degree of proof. For other people, living with likelihood rather than certainty appears to be entirely comfortable.

### Uncertainty and public debate

For anyone wanting to believe what is true – perhaps all of us – ours is a fascinating time in which to live for some of the major debates around us focus on our actions as human beings on this planet. For instance, a major topic for contemporary society is climate change, and the debates are, to some large extent, about concepts of truth.

> Do we accept that all perspectives, if they are internally coherent, are equally right about what is happening to the natural world? Do international scientific organizations provide just one perspective among others in public debate on scientific conclusions, not to be taken more seriously than any others?

> If we use internal consistency as our check for truth, to what does it apply: the rational consistency of the data or the agreement of all the people interpreting it? If the former, who is most reliable as an interpreter of the consistency of the data? If the latter, where should the agreement be reached – among climate scientists or among members of the public and interest groups?

> If we use, as our check for truth, not internal consistency but correspondence of knowledge claims to reality, then what evidence is available, gained how, and interpreted most accurately by whom? What do scientists mean when they say of scientific conclusions, "We cannot be certain"?

The search for truth is not just an academic, philosophical issue, interesting though that might be in itself. What we consider truth to be, how we search for it, and what sources we consider to be reliable as our informative guides have major implications for the decisions we make about how we live as individuals, as societies and countries, and as a world.

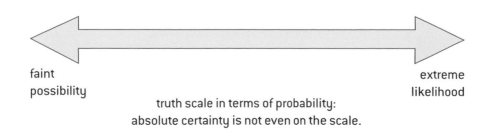

faint possibility ← → extreme likelihood

truth scale in terms of probability:
absolute certainty is not even on the scale.

# Inquiry: asking questions about knowledge

## Experiential knowledge

Is knowledge that I/we gain through experience different from what we gain by being told?

## Knowledge claims

How do I/we know if a knowledge claim is true?

## Skills of critical thinking

How do I/we inquire effectively to create and evaluate knowledge?

### What checks can I/we do for truth?

If a body of claims is consistent, with no contradiction, is it true?

If a claim corresponds to the world, as far as we can tell from checking evidence, is it true?

If a claim works in practical terms, is it true?

## Applied questions:

What justifications support these particular knowledge claims? Who is making these claims? From what perspective?

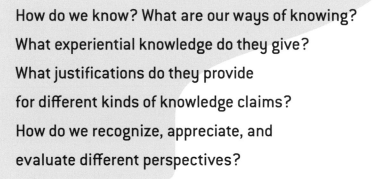

How do we know? What are our ways of knowing?

What experiential knowledge do they give?

What justifications do they provide

for different kinds of knowledge claims?

How do we recognize, appreciate, and

evaluate different perspectives?

How is knowledge constructed?

How is knowledge evaluated?

What skills of critical thinking

can be applied to the world?

## 4.  Exchanging Knowledge

Gaining knowledge, exchanging knowledge, and evaluating its truth: these active pursuits connect us with the people around us. In sharing news and gossip, we come together in communities held together by a flow of knowledge.

> "Did you hear about that young couple down the street? Did you know that...?"

> "Really? I can't believe that of him!"

> "Well, her father saw him on Friday..."

> "Yeah. But you know what her father's like! I wouldn't trust a word he says!"

> "Maybe not. But the other day, when I was passing their door, I could see..."

We talk together about other people, the health and happiness of friends and family, our problems and solutions, social events, current political events, and holidays. We share information, exchange perspectives, and construct around ourselves a web of human connections – our communities with their shared interests and concerns.

In this era of electronic communication, the metaphor of a "global village" is often used for the ways in which we are connected beyond our places on the planet to a degree unprecedented in past generations. We exchange knowledge, swiftly, with people we will never meet. We send and receive instant messages, check the Internet quickly for information, catch a moment on video and pass it in a flash to everyone on a mailing list. In these ways and more, we join networks of communication that link us across a city or across the planet on the marvelously named World Wide Web. Questioning, researching, and writing, we add to the constant hum of exchange in our academic and professional communities as knowledge flows in and out of a shared pool.

These exchanges that connect us raise numerous knowledge questions about the information and views that flow back and forth. In this chapter, we will look more closely at this flow of knowledge. We will be considering the ways in which we gain our knowledge, and the ways in which we justify our knowledge claims as we pass them on.

Be warned! This is a crossroads chapter – a chapter where we are concerned above all with checking the map to see where we have been and to see where we are going. This is a chapter of summary and transition, anchored in this central idea: that we as human beings create our knowledge, and that we keep it constantly alive in exchange.

## Our growing map of knowledge

Where have we been so far in this book in our exploration of knowledge questions and ideas?

Let's look back. First, look once again at the pages that have followed the chapters so far, especially the one at the end of chapter 3. Can you see, in this diagram, the path we have followed in the knowledge questions we have already posed?

Next, take an overview based on lists rather than pictures. Flip back to the table of contents of this book. Can you see that the opening chapters give you concepts and vocabulary for the whole rest of the book and course: *perspectives*, *knowledge*, and *truth*? In this chapter, we will be adding two more key concepts: *ways of knowing* and *justifying*.

Finally, think in terms of knowledge questions and the inquiry that propels this book.

**Discussion Activity**

**Quick drawing activity 1: knowledge exchange**

**1. Your own knowledge exchange**

Within a single day of your life, both inside and outside school, what would a picture of your own flow of knowledge look like? Try using arrows in and arrows out, moving along the timeline of your day, to do a quick sketch. Include:

- the messages you exchange with others
- the information and views you are told or taught
- knowledge claims that blare themselves at you from posters or media
- the gossip and subtle messages passed within groups of friends

- your own contributions, light or serious, to the knowledge exchange.

Compare your results with the sketches done by your classmates. What similarities do you find? In what ways are they different, and why? What kinds of knowledge are exchanged?

**2. Global knowledge exchange**

Within a single day of the life of the world, what would such a picture look like? Take just five minutes more to diagram global exchange of knowledge, using whatever schematizing system makes sense to you, and again compare with classmates. What approaches have different people taken to representing such an elaborate flow of knowledge? What similarities do you find, and what major differences?

## Some major knowledge questions so far

- How do the different perspectives people hold affect the knowledge they gain? What are the role of assumptions and values in knowledge? How can we recognize and analyse different perspectives? (Chapter 1)
- In what ways does education, the conscious passing on of knowledge, reflect social needs and values? (Chapter 2)
- What is the difference between knowledge we gain through experience and knowledge we gain through being told? Can we identify different kinds of knowledge? (Chapter 2)
- In what ways does our personal knowledge interact with shared knowledge? (Chapter 2)
- How does understanding terminology such as "knowledge questions" and "knowledge claims" help in communicating and sharing ideas? (Chapter 2)
- What kinds of answers can we give to the question "What is truth?" To what extent do we have to evaluate the following in the search for truth: rational consistency, evidence, and practical implications of belief? (Chapter 3)
- Can we ever be "certain" in the knowledge we gain? (Chapter 3)

## Some major knowledge questions ahead

In Part 2 of this book, we'll be moving deeper into the construction of knowledge. We'll have a look at how we build it, and how we can build better when we use our tools with care. The central knowledge questions ahead are, as always, ones that circle high above knowledge, looking down upon its general features. In the chapters ahead, we hope you'll enjoy the view of the territory below.

- What ways do we have of knowing?
- How do they give us knowledge, by themselves and in interaction with each other?
- How do we use them with care, keeping an open mind and thinking critically, in order to gain the most reliable knowledge possible?

## What are our ways of knowing?

The IB theory of knowledge course offers eight "ways of knowing" – ways that people have claimed lead them to knowledge. The eight ways of knowing are as follows: sense perception, reason, language, emotion, intuition, faith, memory, and imagination.

You do not have to accept this list of eight as fact, or the only possibility. It is given to you for exploration, reflection, and evaluation. We can certainly promise you that these eight will raise significant and intriguing knowledge questions. All of the eight are equally important in the discussions and investigation of knowledge ahead. How we regard them and use them shapes what we consider knowledge to be, and how we gain, communicate, and evaluate it.

The names of the eight ways of knowing are fairly self-explanatory upon first glance. Although we will encounter ambiguities as we deal with each one, for now probably only three of them require some clarification.

By *"reason"* we mean rationality: the capacity of the mind to be logical and figure things out.

Often in this book we use "reasoning" as well as a synonym, to stress the active nature of the thinking process. We do *not* mean "giving reasons". For providing good reasons for believing a knowledge claim, we use the word "justifying".

The second way of knowing that requires clarification is *"sense perception"*. We are not using "perception" in its loose conversational sense, "His perception was that the meeting was totally pointless." We are using it instead for our contact with the world through our senses – our seeing, hearing, tasting, and so forth. This way of knowing deals with observation and interpretation.

A third way of knowing that needs some explanation is *"faith"*. We will not be restricting this word to its religious context but treating it more generally, considering different definitions.

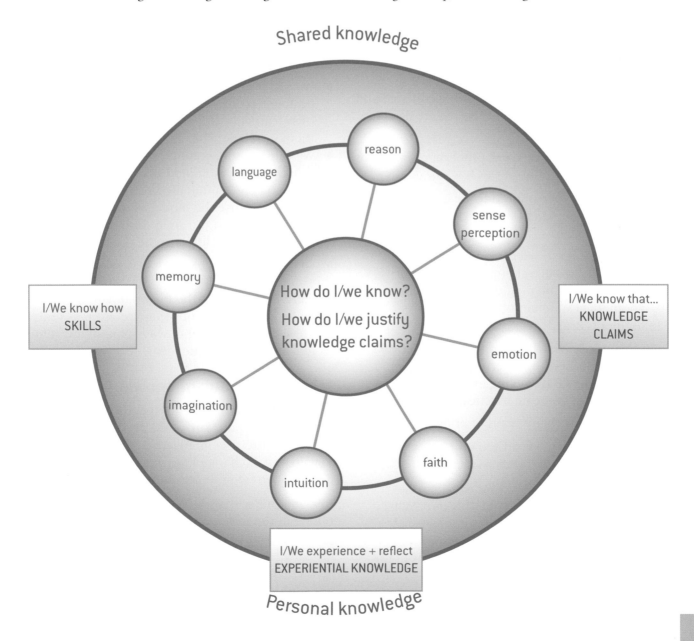

### Quick drawing activity 2: ways of knowing

In our diagram, we are representing the eight ways of knowing suggested by the theory of knowledge subject guide as though they are all alike: we have given them the same shape and the same amount of space, and have spread them equidistantly around a circle with crossroads.

Would you picture them differently in shape, size, or relationship? Would you even use a diagram, or would you paint or draw them otherwise to demonstrate how you think about them and their relationship to one another?

1. Please pick up your pencil once again and take ten minutes to do your own sketch of the relationship of these ways of knowing to each other before we open discussion on any of them. You are free to draw them in any way that you think captures their relationship. Compare drawings with classmates to exchange different ways of thinking about ways of knowing and their relationship.

2. Save your drawing in order to return to it after we have explored the ideas of the upcoming chapters to see if at that point you would represent them differently.

## Diagrams, models, lists: relationship of ideas

This schema of eight ways of knowing is not, of course, a representation of something concrete and material in the world. Remember, we are dealing here with *concepts*.

Have you noticed all the conceptual representations we have given you so far in this book?

1. In chapter 2, we explored three kinds of knowledge: experiential knowledge, skills, and knowledge claims.

2. Also in chapter 2, we considered different kinds of knowledge claims: statements of observation, value judgments, predictions, hypothetical statements, metaphysical statements and definitions. How many is that?

3. In chapter 3, we looked at three truth checks: coherence (checking internal consistency), correspondence (checking evidence), and pragmatism (checking practical implications).

4. And now how many ways of knowing? Eight?

Are you beginning to wonder if you can solve the mysteries of knowledge with a calculator?

This is a good spot to pause and consider the role of a conceptual picture like this one. What it does *not* do is represent something material in the world, or even a conceptualization of knowledge recognized beyond the bounds of the TOK course. What the schema of eight ways *does*

do is provide us with a working model of ideas in relationship, so that we can aim more effectively for certain goals:

- we can disentangle interconnected concepts to be able to consider each in greater depth for its own features – but at the same time see all of them in relationship with each other

- we can communicate more clearly with each other in discussion of knowledge by using a common conceptual picture and vocabulary

- and we can use the model as a whole to develop and test our own thinking as we use it, and possibly modify it in the process.

Models in all areas of knowledge, whether they aim to place concepts in relationship or to represent things in the material world, are simplified representations that are *useful* as tools for thought. Our wheel of ways of knowing allows us to clarify and critique ideas.

## Interactive ways of knowing

Our ways of knowing work together, giving us information on our surroundings and a grasp of how to interpret it. Together, they enable us to gain and exchange knowledge, and to make decisions on what to accept and how to act.

Imagine this scenario. You and five friends are hiking in the mountains, on an expedition led by an adult from your community. The afternoon is growing late, but a couple of hours of tramping still remain before you expect to pitch your tents for the night. Your leader, though, gathers you together as the trail comes up into an open meadow. "We're going to want to stop very soon and get camp set up. There's a storm coming."

You're disappointed. The weather looks fine to you. You protest, "But how do you know?"

"I can just feel it," he explains. "I know these mountains. Call it *intuition*. I'll explain more later."

He knows *intuitively?* You don't understand, but accept his judgment all the same. You have *faith* in this leader – he has led student groups for many years and everyone you know trusts him completely.

"Should we camp by the stream?" asks one of your friends. He's hiked this route before, and through *memory* can propose a site that your group hasn't reached yet. "We'd have water and a fairly flat tent site."

Your leader nods approval and the group sets out across the flank of the mountain, above the tree line. As you stride along, pack on your back, you see dark clouds gathering ominously overhead and feel the wind rising: your *sense perception* is giving you new information. You recall past storms through *memory* and you *reason* that your general past experience applies to the particular darkening sky above. You have come to the same conclusion your leader had reached more quickly: a storm is coming. You *imagine* pitching your tent in a downpour. Obviously you are not the only one. Your group has quickened its pace.

You reach the stream. Should you camp close to the stream or far from it? Should you camp up on that raised bluff nearby, or by the grove of trees? How do you know? Your leader is asking your group to look closely at the terrain and figure it out.

From the distance, over the valley below, comes a low rumble of thunder. You count seconds. Ten seconds – and a flash of lightning!

"We don't want to be up there on that bluff," declares one of your friends, nervously. "Lightning strikes the highest point."

"I don't think we want to be close to the water," says another. "Doesn't water conduct electricity?"

"The trees in that grove are quite old," says another. "They don't seem to have been hit by lightning themselves, so maybe we're safe near them."

**How do they know?**

What combination of ways of knowing does the girl use as she learns to play the flute?

What combination of kinds of knowledge is she developing – experience, skills, knowledge claims?

To what extent would you say that she is gaining personal knowledge, and to what extent shared knowledge?

When musicians play in groups, do they use further ways of knowing, or perhaps a different combination of ways, from learning and playing on their own?

A gust of wind hits you, and you add, "Maybe we'd be better on the far side of the trees, out of the prevailing wind." Like your friends, you are combining *memory* of knowledge gained in the past, *reason* to apply it to the present case – and the unacknowledged *emotion* of fear that is heightening your attention. Someone is starting to make nervous jokes about being flash-fried. You know how your friend feels, through your own *emotional* and *imaginative* empathy, but decide *rationally* not to contribute to the dark humour.

Another rumble. Eight seconds – and then the flash. The storm is coming upon you fast. With your leader's encouragement, you all scramble to the spot in the shelter of the grove, quickly set up your tents, and tie up sheltering tarpaulins between nearby trees. Your hands move swiftly to peg down the corners of the tent and its protective fly sheet – and your ways of knowing whir together! *Memory* – you know how, and you know why, from the past! *Sense perception* – you can see and feel the nylon loops and the plastic pegs under your quick fingers. *Reason* – you have figured out that anchoring the tent might be important tonight, and that its door should face away from the wind. *Imagination* – you can picture to yourself the consequences of not pegging down the tent, and despite your haste you laugh at the absurd scenario of sailing away in a tent-balloon.

**How do they know?**

In these photos, one of the women is a Muslim in a mosque in Iran and the other is a Christian in a church in Europe. Do you think they are both using the same ways of knowing?

Is prayer a means towards personal knowledge, shared knowledge, neither, or both?

*Language* – you can hear your leader calling instructions about putting on rain jackets, getting your sleeping gear into your tent, and moving your packs under the tarpaulins.

Rumble. Flash. And the rain hits. A downpour soaks the hillside, the grove, and your small camp in the mountains. But your group stays dry, settling to cook your meal under a sturdy tarp.

Later, at home, you will tell your family of your adventure in a storm, with lightning flashing all around and your camp set up -- just in the nick of time. "But how did you know that the storm was going to hit?" your younger sister will ask. "How did you know what to do?" And you will answer confidently, "Oh, we had plenty of ways of knowing."

## Communicating and ways of knowing

It is not only when we are *gaining* our knowledge that we use combinations of the eight different ways of knowing. It is also when we are *sharing* it with others and building our knowledge communally. A different combination of ways might dominate when we try to pass on what we have learned.

How do we reach out to other people to contribute to a pool of common knowledge? If you do not

clearly recall the distinction we made back in chapter 2 between personal knowledge and shared knowledge, look closely once again at the interconnecting circles in the diagram (page 34). As we offer our knowledge to others, we are entering that dynamic zone of exchange.

When we try to pass on our *experiential knowledge*, we might falter immediately. How can we ever convey to someone else exactly the experiences we have had ourselves, with all the associations of memory and emotion that they carry for us? Yet in the process of reflecting on what the experience was, what it meant to us, and what we learned from it, we have already distilled something that has greater potential to be expressed. Moreover, we are not helpless to communicate, as long as we accept a degree of ambiguity.

In trying to convey to others what we have experienced ourselves, we use our ways of knowing to create the channels between us. We can describe (through *language*), and use facial expressions and gestures (through *sense perception*). We can also show the results of our experiences. The results do not communicate the process, but suggest something of it to anyone who already shares a common pool of knowledge: we can offer a tour of the garden we have grown, introduce others to the healthy children we have helped to raise, or point out the display that

**How do they know?**

In this photo, two scientists are doing research in a laboratory.

What ways of knowing do they use to gain their knowledge? What ways of knowing – or what combinations of ways of knowing – do they use to justify their conclusions?

What are the relative roles of experiential knowledge, skills of investigation, and knowledge claims?

To what extent do you consider the natural sciences to be personal knowledge and to what extent shared knowledge?

## For Reflection

### Ways of knowing in your personal knowledge

Consider now how these ways of knowing might operate as you try to gain some everyday knowledge of your own.

- Suppose that you want to know more about your family history. How will you do so? What ways of knowing will you use?
- Suppose that you want to learn how to enhance digital images on a computer and use them creatively. What ways of knowing will you use?

As you follow the IB Diploma Programme subjects and the core, you are drawing on numerous ways of knowing.

- Do you use a different combination of ways of knowing in your science course from the ways that you use in your literature course?
- Do you use a different blend for the activities you do within creativity, action, service (CAS)?

we have assembled for a science project, and they will largely understand. We may also find in the arts some medium – music, visual arts, film, creative writing, for instance – to convey more of our experience than we can put into words, using *emotional and imaginative appeals* combined with the *senses*.

In trying to communicate experience, we depend to a large extent on the similarity between ourselves and our audience. We expect that other people can, to an extent, fill in the gaps – not only because they might have had similar experiences

but also because they are using the same *ways of knowing* that we used to gain the experiential knowledge. Using *reasoning* as a way of knowing, they might think by analogy and then draw inferences. Using *emotion* and *imagination*, they might feel empathy and sense what it would be like to be in another's place. Using *language*, they pick up both what we say explicitly, and what we leave implied "between the lines". Our common ways of knowing enable us to connect with others, even at the very limits of what can be expressed, as long as we accept that what we experience, what we convey, and what they understand are not precisely the same thing.

Similarly, when we pass on *skills* – knowledge of how to do something – we use our ways of knowing to create the channels for communication. We can demonstrate how to play scales on a piano, how to do the swimming stroke known as the crawl, how to set up equipment in a science lab, or how, in that lab, to use aluminum and lye to produce hydrogen. We can make our demonstrations serious or funny, using *emotion* to make the demonstration more memorable or to connect better with the

## Discussion Activity

### Ten knowledge claims

### Do you believe them? Why or why not?

Probably the most beneficial way of managing the following activity is in small groups, so that each individual has a chance to give a gut reaction to each of the questions first, fairly quickly, and then to discuss the situation with the others. The ten knowledge claims in this activity are simple. However, for each of the situations, there are many ideas that might come up.

### Ten situations: how do you react?

1   Your friend has just told you that a vending machine for soft drinks has been installed today in your school. Do you believe her? Why or why not? Do you ask her questions in order to evaluate her claim?

2   Your friend has just told you that the math test was extremely difficult. Do you believe her? Why or why not? What exactly do you believe? Are you more inclined to ask her questions than you were in situation 1? Why or why not?

3   Your friend has just told you that she really regretted not having studied harder for the math test and that she feels sure she will fail. Do you believe her? Why or why not? What exactly do you believe? Does knowing your friend affect your conclusion?

4   Your friend, a student in mathematics standard level, has just told you that the probability of tossing a coin 10 times and getting heads every time is less than 1 in 1000. However, if the result of the first 9 tosses is heads every time, the probability of heads on the 10th toss is still 1 in 2. Do you believe her? Why or why not?

5   Your friend, obviously very upset, has just told you that 15 little green men have landed in a flying saucer in front of the main school building. Do you believe him? Why or why not? Would you be more inclined to ask your friend questions than you were in situation 1? (Would you be inclined to take any other actions?)

6   Your chemistry teacher has just told you that one mole of any substance contains $6.02 \times 10^{23}$ molecules. Do you believe him? Why or why not?

7   Your biology teacher has just told you that biology is the most fascinating subject in the world. Do you believe her? Why or why not?

8   Your parents have always told you that it was important to report your classmates if they cheated on exams. Do you believe them? Why or why not?

9   You read in the local newspaper that a politician running for re-election to the district's school board has announced that the past four years have been the best in the school's history. Do you believe the candidate's declaration? Why or why not? Are there questions you would like to have answered before deciding?

10   Your grandfather has told you that there is a God in Heaven who loves you. Do you believe him? Why or why not? (Note that in this question you are not being asked to comment on anyone else's belief, but solely to reflect on what your justifications might be for accepting or rejecting the claim yourself.)

When you have discussed all the situations above, think back over your conversation to consider more generally the following questions.

- Did you find yourself using the truth checks of chapter 3 in some form? Do you react "That's not possible – according to what I know already" or "Where's the evidence?"
- What justifications – supporting reasons – came up in your discussion for believing or not believing each of these knowledge claims? How would you complete the following sentence: "I would believe (or not believe, or partly believe) this knowledge claim because…"
- Do the knowledge claims offered in the situations here fit at least roughly into different categories, as treated at the end of chapter 2? Do you find it useful to distinguish between: definitions, observational statements, value judgments, metaphysical statements, and predictions?
- Knowledge claims do not exist on their own. Somebody makes them. Did you find yourself affected in your own reactions by who made each of these claims?

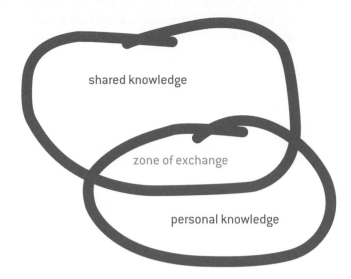

shared knowledge

zone of exchange

personal knowledge

audience. For all skills, we can also use *language*, explaining and giving instructions. Onlookers use their own ways of knowing to take in and interpret the communication: they can hear and see a demonstration using their *sense perception*, they can respond to the *emotional* overtones, and understand the *language*.

When we pass on our *knowledge claims*, our methods of communication narrow. Knowledge claims are always statements in *language*. Yet is language the only way we use as we pass on the assertions that we accept? Depending on the context, we can phrase our knowledge claims with appeals to other ways of knowing such as *reason, emotion, memory, or imagination.* We can accompany the knowledge claims with images that appeal to the senses or emotions, or with graphs and formulae that appeal to reason, all of which extend the understanding we communicate. Language, very often, is used in conjunction with other ways of knowing to enforce the legitimacy of the knowedge claim we're making. Ultimately, the acceptance of a knowledge claim might depend on one of the concepts of *faith* – that is, placing trust in the source of the knowledge.

## Justifying: supporting knowledge claims

As we exchange knowledge in the flow of communication between us, however, we do not simply pour it back and forth through wide-open channels. Our communication of knowledge involves far more control than this metaphor suggests. Indeed, we take care to shape the channel – to deflect some of what would flow through it and to screen the rest. And so do other people. We all construct our screens.

To consider what is worth accepting from all of our knowledge exchanges, we have already considered in chapter 3 the role of the constructive doubt response ("That doesn't seem right to me!") and checking for truth. And now those truth checks send us onward to consider what counts as a good reason to accept a knowledge claim, drawing on our ways of knowing. When we give our reasons for believing a knowledge claim, we are giving our *justifications.* To "justify" is to provide good reasons in support of a knowledge claim or an argument.

In a thoughtful knowledge exchange, we expect other people to *justify* what they are telling us and they expect us to *justify* what we are telling them. We do not demand rudely, "Give me one good reason or I won't believe you!" However, the questions that we pose and answer, and the explanations that we exchange regarding our ideas, often do include our background thinking. As we exchange knowledge claims in a thoughtful and critical manner, we exchange right along with them accounts of the ways of knowing that took us to them, and the justifications that convinced us to accept particular conclusions. Knowledge, as we construct it and exchange it, constantly involves assertion, inquiry and response.

The need to make a decision most particularly activates this process of evaluating and justifying. If you face a decision over whether to undergo major surgery, for example, you want to know what your doctor thinks and why, and what other sources of information you can consult to help you evaluate the risks. If you are choosing which university to attend, you want to investigate its location, facilities, size, policies, and many other features before you feel you have sufficient supporting information for a good decision. This process of checking and evaluating before reaching a conclusion is an important part of your everyday critical thinking.

The interaction between your personal knowledge and shared knowledge provides an impetus for you to sharpen your thinking in this way. When you step into the public zone of exchange, you cannot mumble and evade, but have to be ready to articulate your reasons for accepting or rejecting a particular knowledge claim or argument. Although this push to formulate your arguments clearly and provide justification can be a little intimidating at times, it is immensely beneficial for developing your critical and communicative skills. In many

Why do you accept and learn the information given you in your IB courses (assuming that you do)?

Why do your teachers accept the knowledge offered by their fields? What justifications convince them? Do they tell you in class about the different perspectives and debates that arise within their fields?

Are the justifications given by teachers and textbooks the same in all of your subjects? Do the "good reasons" for accepting particular knowledge claims, interpretations, theories, or techniques vary depending on the subject matter and methods of the particular subject?

In the essays you write for your different subjects, are you asked to provide justification for what you say? Are you asked to support your arguments or give reasons for the conclusions you reach?

ways, the assessment requirements for the International Baccalaureate Diploma Programme are training for being able to take part more effectively in the knowledge exchanges of your life. When the TOK essay and presentation expect you to make convincing arguments, evaluating and supporting them, these tasks are pushing you to apply and develop your thinking skills.

Conversely, you might well ask, before you bring knowledge shared by others into your own personal knowledge, "Why would I accept these knowledge claims and the perspectives they carry? What justifications are offered in support, and which are most convincing? How can I test or verify these claims?" Your role as a student is one in which you are encouraged to think in terms of ideas, arguments and justifications.

## Justifying knowledge claims: combining ways of knowing

A knowledge claim may certainly be justified on the basis of a single way of knowing: you might support a knowledge claim in mathematics solely on the basis of *reason*, or support a knowledge claim about the past solely on the basis of *memory*. Yet the justifications that we give for believing knowledge

claims, or for accepting arguments based on a body of knowledge claims, very commonly do not align themselves with a single way of knowing, but instead draw on several at once.

What ways of knowing does "scientific evidence" use, for example? Certainly not one single way! Sense perception is involved, obviously, in scientific observation, but surely reasoning is equally involved in setting up the testing and drawing conclusions. What about language? Yes, language is essential in an area of knowledge in which findings have to be published. The one word "evidence" as a justification combines at least three ways of knowing.

In fact, many of the justifications we commonly offer for knowledge claims combine elements of several ways of knowing at once. Have a look now at the discussion activity "What ways of knowing are involved in the justifications offered by these speakers?" You will see some common justifications that people have been known to offer in support of their knowledge claims. In each case, what ways of knowing are somehow involved in that justification? Is all justification equally convincing?

## A loop in the journey: ways of knowing

As we opened this book, we invited you on a journey into knowledge that would move forward across the terrain, but would also loop back again and again to some of the same knowledge questions, approaching them from different angles and adding layers of ideas with each pass. Prepare yourself now for a large loop outward, visiting each of the eight ways of knowing in turn.

You will return, in effect, to exactly this spot on the map. You will bring with you, though, increased awareness of our diverse ways of gaining knowledge and of the human factors involved in the knowledge exchange. You will return, as your focus, to how ways of knowing interact to create areas of knowledge, which we will treat in Part 3 of this book.

Interestingly, the more closely we look at the methods by which we construct our knowledge, the more crucial turn out to be three of the qualities of the IB educational profile: an open mind, critical thinking, and effective communication.

Enjoy your loop through the eight ways of knowing.

## Discussion Activity

### What ways of knowing are involved in the justifications offered by these speakers?

"I saw it with my own eyes."

"Results of a recent government survey say…"

"Hidden cameras at the scene of the crime show a man of exactly his stature."

"The novelist says this of her own work: 'I intended to…'"

"Experts in the field have reached consensus that…"

"I have a gut feeling that…"

"I read it in a scientific journal…"

"I read it in a fashion magazine…"

"My dad says so."

"Scientific evidence indicates that…"

"I remember that he was carrying it in his hand…"

"The Qur'an says…"

"For generations people have done it this way…"

"It will help the economy grow, so it must be…"

"It makes sense."

"I really want to do it, so it has to be OK."

"The Bible says…"

"Statistical analysis of trends indicates…"

"Interviews conducted with the recipients indicate…"

"I worked it out mathematically."

"Excavation has uncovered artifacts that reveal…"

"I knew it was going to happen because I dreamt about it."

"It's always worked in the past, so…"

"After repeated observation, the group has concluded…"

"An oil spill has never happened before, so it can't…"

"It was very sad, very moving, so I feel I must…"

"The President, responding to reporters, declared that…"

"According to this morning's weather prediction, it will…"

Diagram — "Ways of knowing" at centre, surrounded by: reason, sense perception, emotion, faith, intuition, imagination, memory, language.

# 5. Sense Perception as a Way of Knowing

Sense perception is the source of much of the pleasure in our lives: we savour a good meal, listen to favourite music, touch the people we love, and with pleasure lift our eyes to green leaves and white clouds drifting in a blue sky. It can also, alas, be the source of much pain. Sense perception, moreover, provokes many of our most intriguing questions of what we know and how we know it.

Even though we have more understanding of our senses now than at any time in the past, human sense perception continues to be something of an enigma. How is it that as humans we convert physical stimuli into meaningful objects and events? You hear not just noise, but the song you danced to the night you first fell in love. You see not just light, colour, and shade, but your father who is waving to you as you step onto the station platform.

The world is not always as we sense it – we do not know how it "really is". As we learn more about our own brains and more about the world, we gain further understanding that tells us, in some ways, how little we still know. Indeed, some philosophers have argued that we cannot know that the world even exists outside ourselves at all, as all we know is our sense impressions of it, and not the world itself.

At the same time, though, perhaps nothing seems more obviously real than what we can sense.

*John William Waterhouse*, The Shrine

### The nose and the brain

In his speech upon winning the Nobel Prize, Richard Axel gives the research question that guided his work: "Put simply, how does the brain know what the nose is smelling?" He and Linda Buck jointly won the Nobel Prize in Physiology or Medicine in 2004 for their addition to knowledge on the sense of smell. Axel elaborates on his interest in investigating the sense of smell.

Why would a molecular neuroscientist interested in perception choose to focus on the elusive sense of smell? In humans, smell is often viewed as an aesthetic sense, as a sense capable of eliciting enduring thoughts and memories. Smell however is the primal sense. It is the sense that affords most organisms the ability to detect food, predators, and mates. Smell is the central sensory modality by which most organisms communicate with their environment. Second, humans are capable of recognizing hundreds of thousands of different odours. For molecular neuroscientists studying the brain, the mechanism by which an organism can interact with the vast universe of molecular structures defined as odours provides a fascinating problem in molecular recognition and perceptual discrimination. Finally, the problem of perception necessarily involves an understanding of how sensory input is ultimately translated into meaningful neural output: thoughts and behaviour.[1]

1   Richard Axel. 8 December 2004. "Scents and Sensibility: A Molecular Logic of Olfactory Perception", Nobel Lecture, Pp 235–6 http://www.nobelprize.org/nobel_prizes/medicine/laureates/2004/axel-lecture.pdf.

We are not inclined to doubt the existence of what we hear, see and feel, touch, and taste. It seems *obviously there*, exactly as it appears. Our senses provide the very basis of our knowledge of the world: they give us a way of knowing that contributes significantly to experiential knowledge and provide observational knowledge claims. Can the very basis of so much of our knowledge be doubted?

In this chapter we invite you to explore this intriguing way of knowing. What is sense perception? What are its characteristics in connecting us with the world? What are its limitations, and how can we attempt to overcome them?

## Characteristics of our senses

In the most general of definitions, sense perception is the physical response of our senses to stimuli. First, sense receptors in different parts of our bodies, our fingertips or our eyes for instance, are stimulated by sensory information. That information then travels as electrical impulses to the brain, which interprets sensations such as sound, taste, temperature, pressure, smell, or sight. Finally, the brain either ignores the sensations or recognizes them and their meanings based on networks of past association and expectation. The process is experienced as instantaneous. It *seems* to us, as we recognize a tree or a chair, that it is *simply there* – as if we are passively recording what surrounds us, with no active engagement of our senses.

This process integrates the sensory stimulation into our understanding so swiftly that we often use the word "perception" to describe our *interpretation* of what our senses tell us, rather than what our senses are actually *perceiving*. "Perception" is sometimes even used as synonymous with "opinion". It is difficult to separate completely the sensations that we receive physically through our senses from the interpretations that we build upon them but, in seeking truth, we are challenged to do so.

How do we *know* through sense perception? To what extent can we distinguish between what we gain through our senses and how we interpret it? We will start here by focusing our attention on four characteristics of sense perception: it is human, variable, selective, and interpretive.

## 1. Our senses: human

By definition, every sentient creature has receptors that capture a certain kind and range of stimuli from the external environment. Other animals have senses we do not share. For example, bats and dolphins use sonar for navigation. And homing pigeons and sockeye salmon have deposits of magnetite in their bodies that enable them to detect the Earth's magnetic field to find their way through sky and ocean. Even the senses that we do share with other animals we possess to different degrees: we don't smell as keenly as wolves or see as well as eagles.

What we have learned about other animals tells us a great deal about our own human capacities and their limitations. We are sensing in a human way, and building our knowledge from a limited range of all the sensory abilities of all the species on this planet.

To place our human sense perception within the context of a range of other sense perception abilities, try the activities and reading here, entitled "Our human senses". The questions raised within them will encourage you to find out more, and to use another way of knowing – your imagination. What is the world that an animal inhabits when its senses give it fundamentally different information from what our senses give us? What are we missing?

Supposing our sight was poor and our sense of smell was extremely sensitive, would we:

- greet each other differently?
- organize the directional signposting in our cities differently?
- have different rituals within our wedding ceremonies?

Supposing we had chemoreceptors (taste receptors) on our palms and fingertips.

- How would our knowledge be affected?
- Would we have different metaphors in our poetry or different research methods in the natural sciences?

Are the basic assumptions that we make about the world the product of a particular set of senses?

**What do they have that we don't?**

Echolocating bats can navigate swiftly in total darkness, using sense perception in a strikingly different way from human beings. They emit sounds that bounce off objects around them and return to give them a soundscape of their environment. Human beings do not echolocate naturally, but have developed the technology of sonar.

---

## Discussion Activity

### Our human senses

With your class, do some research and use your imagination to explore beyond our human range.

Find out, alone or in a small group, as much as you can about animal senses unlike our own. Here are some suggestions:

  **i.** the lateral line system of fish for sensing pressure

  **ii.** echolocation and barometric sensitivity of bats

  **iii.** use of the tongue by snakes for smell and taste, and their sensitivity to vibration

  **iv.** electrosensing of sharks

  **v.** chemoreceptors on the entire bodies of earthworms

  **vi.** compound eyes of insects.

Drawing on the information you found out about other species, choose any one and be prepared to enter imaginatively into the sensory world it inhabits. Without revealing your choice to others in your group, take 15 to 20 minutes to write a description of your classroom as if you are this animal. (Imagine that your classroom is underwater if necessary!) When finished, volunteer to read your description if you feel comfortable doing so. Others will try to guess what animal you have chosen. While someone else is reading a description, take note of the number of times the description involves each of the senses.

Speculations like these are called "counter-factual": they imagine possibilities that are simply not the case. Some people, as a result, treat them as pointless. Other people, though, fly away with the question "What if…?" to imagine alternatives, and thereby often understand better *what is true*, by reflection on *what is not true*. We understand much better that the world is not exactly as we sense it when we have entertained other possibilities, through research for the facts, and through imagination for the fictions. Those of you who read science fiction or fantasy may have discovered that imaginative exploration of worlds with "counter-factual" sense perceptions have illuminated your awareness of the assumptions about the world that you make based on your own set of senses (Perhaps you would enjoy reading the H.G. Wells story "The Country of the Blind".)

## 2. Our senses: variable

As a species, we share our human sense perception as one of our primary ways of knowing. The knowledge we build using our senses starts with the nature of our human bodies – our sensory receptors, nervous systems, and brain. However, we don't all sense the world in exactly the same way!

From person to person, our senses are variable in their range and acuity. Through comparison with others, we recognize that some people can see or hear what most of us miss, or others miss what most of us see or hear. Very quickly we – as individuals and as groups – develop an idea of what is "normal". This term denotes simply the most common usage of the senses, as far as we can tell.

Is our own personal experience of sense perception, though, the same as the norm?

### Flush, The Spaniel

*by Virginia Woolf*

*Observe the descriptions of smells and textures in this extract from Virginia Woolf's Flush: A Biography (1933).[2] Often described as a biography of the poet, Elizabeth Barrett Browning, from the point of view of her dog, some may think it is in fact the biography of the spaniel himself.*

…it was in the world of smell that Flush mostly lived. Love was chiefly smell; form and colour were smell; music and architecture, law, politics and science were smell. To him religion itself was smell… Flush wandered off into the streets of Florence to enjoy the rapture of smell. He threaded his path through main streets and back streets, through squares and alleys, by smell. He nosed his way from smell to smell; the rough, the smooth, the dark, the golden. He went in and out, up and down, where they beat brass, where they bake bread, where the women sit combing their hair, where the birdcages are piled high on the causeway, where the wine spills itself in dark red stains on the pavement, where leather smells and harness and garlic, where cloth is beaten, where vine leaves tremble, where men sit and drink and spit and dice – he ran in and out, always with his nose to the ground, drinking in the essence; or with his nose in the air vibrating with the aroma. He slept in this hot patch of sun – how sun made the stone reek! He sought that tunnel of shade – how acid shade made the stone smell! He devoured whole bunches of ripe grapes largely because of their purple smell; he chewed and spat out whatever tough relic of goat or macaroni the Italian housewife had thrown from the balcony – goat and macaroni were raucous smells, crimson smells. He followed the swooning sweetness of incense into the violet intricacies of dark cathedrals; and, sniffing, tried to lap the gold on the window-stained tomb. Nor was his sense of touch much less acute. He knew Florence in its marmoreal smoothness and in its gritty and cobbled roughness. Hoary folds of drapery, smooth fingers and feet of stone received the lick of his tongue, the quiver of his shivering snout. Upon the infinitely sensitive pads of his feet he took the clear stamp of proud Latin inscriptions. In short, he knew Florence as no human being has ever known it; as Ruskin never knew it or George Eliot either. He knew it as only the dumb know. Not a single one of his myriad sensations ever submitted itself to the deformity of words.

[2] Woolf, V. 1961. *Flush: A Biography*. New York and California. Harvest Books, Harcourt Inc. Pp. 130–2.

Does the world you live in "look like" the world in which your classmate lives? Our personal knowledge, especially our personal experiential knowledge, could vary considerably from other people's without our even knowing.

If you and your classmate are both able to use language to refer to colours, smells, and sounds around you, for instance, can you be sure that the shared use of words does not conceal a difference in your experience of the sensation to what they refer?

Our informally pooled personal impressions suggest our variability. Scientific investigation of the senses then gives us a more reliable form of shared knowledge about them. With simple vision and hearing tests, medical professionals can check us from childhood to find out if our sense perceptions fall within the normal range of the surveyed population. For some people who are "abnormal" an illustrious career might beckon them: they could become perfume-blenders, tea-tasters, or musicians. For others, the abnormality is considered a deficiency and the solution is medical and social: we wear glasses or hearing aids to help us to live effectively within a society geared towards the norm. The sheer number of people wearing glasses – or avoiding doing so through contact lenses or laser surgery – does suggest that departure from "normal" is … well, quite normal.

Many individuals who do not have the usual range of the senses may compensate for weak access to the world through one sense by developing the strength of their other senses. The story of Cristina Frias (see "How did she know?") is striking in the degree to which she compensated for her lack of sight by developing her other senses and her attention to them. She did this to the point that she gained information from her environment that sighted people around her missed entirely.

Understandably, many communities insist that it is much more accurate to replace the term "disabled" with "differently abled", and the term is increasingly in common usage.

Variability exists not only, though, in the degree to which we possess the standard senses. Some people seem to have an extra sense: they have a neurological condition called synesthesia, an intriguing crossover of the senses in which the stimulation of a cognitive pathway for one sense can involuntarily stimulate another. In effect, some synesthetes can "smell" colours and "feel" tastes. Some associate colour with letters, seeing A as red, for instance, or S as yellow. The condition, not yet well understood, is interesting for what it indicates of unusual human abilities, including differences that can go unnoticed because they do not interfere with managing everyday life. They can remain within personal knowledge, never fully shared.

But how much of the variability of our senses is biological, and how much of it is cultural? As we talk about correcting vision towards a norm, for instance, or acknowledging and developing senses,

## Discussion Activity

### Sense perception and naming

With your class, do some research and use your imagination to explore beyond our human range.

1. How do you know that what you call "red" is the same sensation as what your classmate calls "red"?

2. How can you tell if your ability to perceive is in the "normal" range? How is that norm defined?

3. Can you see the central number in the circle? People with a common form of colour blindness cannot. If you are one such person, perhaps you would like to describe to your class what you see when you look, for example, at traffic lights or an apple tree?

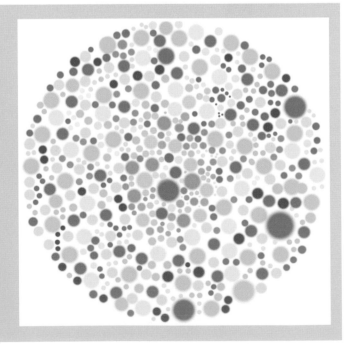

are we not talking about cultural modification of our biological heritage? Do we develop and use our senses as biological creatures (nature), or cultural ones (nurture)?

Interestingly, anthropological literature tells us that there can be a very strong cultural influence on which senses are given emphasis, both within societies studied and within the methods of researchers. You may want to turn ahead to chapter 13 to read an anthropologist's summary of what is known so far.

Social and cultural attitudes toward variations in senses also, unfortunately, sometimes limit understanding. Such has been the heartbreaking story of deaf people in many parts of the world. Not able to hear, and therefore not able to learn spoken language and interact with others, they were treated in Europe before the eighteenth century as imbeciles – as people without functioning minds.[3] With the development of sign language and schooling (in France in the mid-eighteenth century, in the US in the early nineteenth) deaf people were at last able to "speak", overcome profound isolation, gain education, and demonstrate that they were fully capable of thinking and exchanging ideas. It was only hearing that they lacked!

The Congress on Education of the Deaf in Milan in September 1880, however, plunged deaf people back into relative isolation and limited education. This infamous conference banned sign language and substituted oralism, a system of education to teach deaf children, with difficulty, to articulate sound. The goal was to overcome their difference and integrate them into the mainstream.

It was not until a century later that researchers came to grips with the devastating impact of these decisions. Oralism did not fill the gap in the sense perception of the deaf, but instead almost completely denied them another way of knowing: sign language. Since the 1980s, the importance of sign language has been increasingly acknowledged and deaf people using it have been able to connect with others, to gain an education and exchange knowledge. But the struggle to be able to exercise their rights and take a full place in society is not over.

Of particular interest to us, as we consider sense perception as a way of knowing, is what many

**How did she know?**

Cristina Frías worked as counsellor in a school in Santiago, Chile, attended by about 1800 students. Generations of alumni remember her well. She had a beautiful Labrador guide dog – clearly the only canine on the school premises. Rain or shine, Cristina walked to and from school to her house in the neighbourhood. But first and foremost Cristina is renowned to generations of teachers and students because, despite being blind since childhood, she had an uncanny ability to identify individual people. She would cheerfully call out, "Good morning, so-and-so!" even if one tried to pass unnoticed. When asked how she accomplished what seemed to many others to be quite a feat, she said she recognized individuals by how they walked up stairs and down corridors, by their unique odours and by the ways they knocked (or didn't!) on her office door when it was shut.

people in the deaf community are now saying, through sign. They reject the "pathological model" or "medical model" of deafness that treats it as a medical condition, a defect that can and must be fixed.[4]

---

3   Sacks, O. 1990 *Seeing Voices*. New York. Picador.

4   SignMedia. 4 April 2012. "Perspectives on Deaf People", http://www.signmedia.com/info/adc.htm

Instead of the outsider view, they put forward an insider view, a "cultural model", that treats deaf people as possessing a language and culture – and a form of knowledge – of their own. Some Deaf people embracing this model have no desire to hear, and even reject medical intervention as cultural violation. They have adopted the capital D on Deaf for those who have been born without hearing and have made the Deaf cultural community their own, with pride in their achievements. These two perspectives on being deaf – the medical and the cultural – clearly come with contrasting assumptions and values regarding lack of hearing. Accepting one or the other has implications for your own attitudes and potentially how you interact with people who, to a significant degree, cannot hear.[5]

We might also reflect, as we leave this topic, on the difficulties and dangers of "knowing" what is best for other people, and the challenge of keeping our observational knowledge claims separate from our value judgments.

## 3. Our senses: actively selective

Clearly, we do not catch all the sense information about the world that other species do, and we do not all gain the same information even within our human range of senses. Even so, a vast amount of stimulation still reaches us from our own internal states and the world around us. Do we take it in as fully as our senses permit?

You can probably hear a "no" coming, and anticipate the characteristic of the senses that we turn to next: they are *selective* in what they catch out of all the possibilities around us. Far too much is going on around us, and we cannot handle it all. Unconsciously, we ignore many stimuli.

In order to bring to life for yourself some of the further knowledge questions that attend sense perception, we recommend that you try, as a class, the "Activities in observation" on the next page. They do not take long, and they are fun to do.

It should be clear, from doing these activities, that many factors influence what we perceive and remember: out of all possible sense observations that we might make, we catch only a few, and out of all that we might remember, we recall even fewer. Perception is an actively selective process.

Yet the extent to which we can *simply not notice* what is clearly there can be astonishing. In a well known psychology experiment,[6] participants were asked to watch a video of six people, three in black shirts and three in white shirts, and to count the number of passes with a basketball made by the people in white shirts to each other. While the participants watch and silently count, someone in a gorilla suit walks slowly through the middle of the group of people passing balls, pauses to thump his chest, and then exits. People watching the video *did* count the number of times the ball changed hands. But half of them *did not* see the gorilla. A gorilla! And they did not notice!

Christopher Chabris and Daniel Simons have their experiment available online, so you can try it yourself – though you now know what to expect. Their various experiments on the limits of what we notice when we are paying attention to something else have shed light on a feature of the brain they called a "cognitive bias", an innate tendency to handle sense perception in a swift and impressionistic way. They call this particular cognitive bias "inattentional blindness".

### For Reflection

To feel the extent of what we screen out of our attention, take just four or five minutes to pay attention to what you are gaining at the moment through your senses. Close your eyes and listen carefully to all the sounds around you for one full minute. Which sounds had you not been aware of, prior to this exercise?

Do the same by focusing your attention for one minute respectively on:

**a)** the smells around you,

**b)** the feelings your body is experiencing such as the pressure of your hands holding this book, and

**c)** the images in your environment.

Which ones had you not been paying attention to before? Would you say your knowledge of your surroundings has changed in the past five minutes?

5   Ladd, P. 2003. *Understanding deaf culture: in search of deafhood.* Multilingual Matters Ltd. Cleveland, Buffalo, Toronto, Sydney.

6   "The Gorilla Experiment", http://www.theinvisiblegorilla.com/gorilla_experiment.html. A variation on this experiment is called "The Monkey Business Illusion," currently available online: http://illusioncontest.neuralcorrelate.com/2010/the-monkey-business-illusion

Simons comments on a further realization as a result of his work with Chabris and colleagues: that most people *are totally sure* that they would not miss unusual things. "Ninety percent of people say they'd notice. Regardless of how you ask that question, you get high confidence. That's the intuition that's interesting, and that's the one that's dangerous."

"If we were completely aware of these limits on attention, we wouldn't do things like talking on cell phones while driving. We would know that it would make us just that much less likely to notice something. But we don't have that insight into our own awareness. It's only in that rare case where you actually have an accident that you become aware that you've missed something."

He refers in particular to car drivers failing to see motorcycles, even when they seemed to themselves to be paying attention. "The reality is that the driver probably never saw them, because the motorcycle is unexpected. When you're looking for cars, motorcycles are rare; they're not what you're looking for, even when they're distinctive."[7]

There are serious implications to recognizing inattentional blindness and the fact that we tend to be so very convinced by our own first-hand

## Discussion Activity

### Sense perception and observation

### Activity 1: seeing and recording

Choose, in advance, someone to prepare an object for observation. It could be an object with considerable detail found anywhere in the school or at home, or it could be an object made by the appointed person. All members of the group should sit in a circle, eyes closed, while the person places the object in the centre. When told to do so, you should open your eyes, observe the object, and then make a record of your perceptions on a sheet of paper either in words or in drawing. When everyone is finished writing or drawing, place your papers around the object in the centre so that all of you can see all the different records. Consider together the following questions:

- In what ways do your different records of perception vary, and why? Pin down as many factors as you can that might have influenced your record.
- Is it possible to *separate* sense perception entirely from interpretation in the records that you have made? Does it matter to do so?
- What are the recording methods used by different students? Is any method particularly effective, in the judgment of your group?
- If all the different records by all members of your group are combined, do you then have a better record of the object? Why or why not? If all are combined, is the record complete?

### Activity 2: sense perception and memory

Choose together something within your school that all students in the class could have had access to within the past day or two, even if they did not give it close attention. Choose something with abundant sensory detail that could have been observed – but might not have been. It could be, for example, a school noticeboard or web page that regularly updates notices, or a school play, or visiting speaker.

Impose a time limit of roughly five minutes, in which everyone is to write down, as swiftly as possible, as many observations as you can remember. For instance, can you list and describe all the notices on the board? Can you recall what the visiting speaker was wearing, the quality of her voice, and her gestures and props? Then consider together the following questions:

- Compare your lists and descriptions. What influenced the things each of you noticed and remembered? Compile a list of factors.
- Even allowing for personal variability, are some observations simply wrong? How do you know?
- If your versions are combined, do you have a good record? Explain why, or why not.

### Follow-up summary

In both activities, you are asked to identify fully the factors that you think influence what you noticed and recalled in the activities above. Having done so, you may want to compare your list with the brief one placed at the end of this chapter.

---

[7] Dave Munger, 22 April 2012. "Why Invisible Gorillas Matter", Seed Magazine, http://seedmagazine.com/content/article/why_invisible_gorillas_matter/

observations. It is often said that "seeing is believing". However, even when their senses are functioning perfectly well, and even when they have the strongest of intentions to tell the truth, observers vary considerably in their accounts of events.

Indeed, all may tell the truth, and still not give the same account because of all the factors that influenced what they selected, consciously or unconsciously, and then what they remembered. The status of eyewitness testimony as evidence in court cases is under serious review in the United States, with the state of New Jersey leading the way in ordering a review of its reliability. The review committee has concluded that memory is highly susceptible to error, and recommending changes in procedures for witness identification of suspects.[8]

It is strange that there still persists in the general public a common and erroneous idea that our senses simply record the world.

## 4. Our senses: interpretive

Here is where the fun really starts – with the interpretive nature of our sense perception. Even when we are not consciously aware of interpreting our sense information, our brains are actively engaged in doing so. If you did the activities on observation, you probably already commented on interpretation as you identified factors that affected what you noticed.

But this characteristic of our sense perception – the way the brain interprets the sensory information – is particularly intriguing. Even in the act of recognition our brains are interpreting what our senses recognize.

The process of recognition is so basic and so instantaneous that we do not call out the steps as the electric impulses hurtle to our brains. If we were to do so, it would go something like this: Here it comes! A sensation! It's a sensation of light and colour – that is, electromagnetic energy with a wavelength of between 400 nanometres and 700 nanometres shining on an object – and it's stimulating the retinas of my eyes. What is the object? I recognize it! It's my black cat! But – wait! – here comes a new sensation! The olfactory

receptor neurons in my nose are stimulated by … by a combination of molecules … it's an odour! Yes, I recognize it and attribute meaning, plenty of meaning. Freshly baked chocolate cake!

What we experience is never as conscious as a play-by-play narration. It seems that we look – and simply see the cat. Simply? Are the characteristics of colour and smell really in the cat and the cake, or are they in our brains? It seems to us, as we see the black cat or smell the sweet cake, that the blackness and sweetness are in the cat and the cake rather than in their effect upon us. Yet our conscious experiences of cats and cakes are the product of the electrical and chemical organization of our brains. "Our conscious world," declares one biopsychologist, "is a grand illusion!"[9]

It seems, too, that cats and cakes do not grab our attention as compellingly as do certain other objects in our environment. One of these is faces. We see them everywhere – in rocks and clouds, in the texture of walls and curtains, in the configuration of screws and buttons in our technological devices. Can you see the face in the rocks in the photograph opposite? This tendency of our brains to find significant patterns in random sensory information is known as *pareidolia*, and faces – significant in so many aspects of our lives – take a prime place.

Look now at the drawing we offer here and first ask yourself the question "What do I see?" Once you have answered, ask yourself what is "really there" in the image.

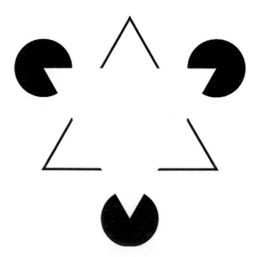

8  http://caselaw.findlaw.com/nj-supreme-court/1578475.html?utm_source=feedburner&utm_medium=feed&utm_campaign=Feed%3A+FindLawNJSu p+(FindLaw+Case+Law+Updates+-+NJ+Supreme+Court

9  Johnston, V.S. 1999. *Why We Feel: The Science of Human Emotions*. Reading, MA, USA. Perseus Books. P 13.

Now, read the text below. Can you read it? Is it English?

> I cdnoult blveiee taht I cluod aulaclty uesdnatnrd waht I was rdanieg. The phaonmneal pweor of the hmuan mnid! Aoccdrnig to a rscheearch at Cmabrigde Uinervitisy, it deosn't mttaer in waht oredr the ltteers in a wrod are, the olny iprmoatnt tihng is taht the frist and lsat ltteer be in the rghit pclae. The rset can be a taotl mses and you can sitll raed it wouthit a porbelm. Tihs is bcuseae the huamn mnid deos not raed ervey lteter by istlef, but the wrod as a wlohe. Amzanig huh? Yaeh and I awlyas thought slpeling was ipmorantt.

The text can be understood by English speakers because repeated encounters with the correctly spelled words generated neural networks in our brains. Stimuli are not being processed by the brain as if it were a blank slate. Rather, the resulting sensations are being integrated, compared, and contrasted with everything you have perceived before. This kind of seemingly simple and involuntary filling in of missing information to form a recognizable pattern or interpretation was what generated the lines and figures in the examples above.

According to the Gestalt theory of psychology, we tend to perceive objects visually as meaningful patterns or groups, rather than as collections of separate parts. When you look at a friend, you recognize her face immediately without being aware of all its separate components. In the Kanizsa triangle illusion above, we "read" the white triangle from empty space and the black outlined triangle by completing the lines in our minds. In this way, we tend to simplify visual information, grouping it in patterns that are easier to process. This process works quite well for us, except that what we notice is sometimes not actually there.

Mirages and optical illusions, too, bring to our attention how quickly and unconsciously we interpret, and how easily our senses can be fooled. If you are interested in exploring optical illusions, many are available in books or on websites, and are circulated so widely that their original source becomes lost. Their popularity, like the popularity of magic shows, suggests that we often enjoy being tricked when we have consented to be so. In this case, we let go of our hold on knowledge with – of course – the knowledge that we have the power to get it back.

Indeed, we *expect* perception to provide quick recognition and to fill the gaps. As your father passes quickly in the distance, you recognize him with very little sensory information: you have noted instantly his characteristic way of walking, caught a quick flash of a familiar coat, or heard his laugh. As your friend calls you on a telephone with a poor connection, you can usually still understand (up to a point) what she is saying, despite words being cut out by static or seconds of silence.

The fact that our brains interpret new stimuli based on past experiences is critical to our being able to use perception as a way of knowing. If we perceived every new sensation as a unique experience, without any associations from the past, we would not be able to apply any of our past learning. We are not neutral observers of the world. We are interpretive observers of the world.

# Overcoming limitations of sense perception

Our senses, as we have seen, do not give us complete and neutral information. This is not a new thought, and neither is the common reaction to it: that our sense perception is inherently limited.

But is it? Factually, our capacity for sense perception is what it is. It is we who create the *idea of limitation*, based on wanting it to be something else, or something more. It is when we compare ourselves with other animals that we acknowledge that we have senses of lesser acuity, that we are missing out on information from the world. Recognizing that our sense impressions are selective and interpretive leads us into wanting to understand how and why, and to wondering how we might gain fuller, more accurate information.

It is our *other ways of knowing*, too, that contribute to the judgment that our senses are limited: our *emotional reaction* to recognizing that we are missing out; our *rational conclusions* about how our sense perception works; our *imaginative response* to wonder if we could overcome our limitations in this way, or that. Altogether, the conclusion that our sense perception is limited – compared with an ideal we have generated – strongly provokes us to want to know more.

Long before our modern investigation of the brain, philosophers and scientists have tackled the limitations of sense perception. Among the many attempts to understand ourselves and overcome barriers to greater knowledge, we will pick out two here for further discussion. First, we will touch the surface of a huge topic of knowledge: our development of technology. Then we will open up a few avenues into thinking critically.

## 1. Extending sense perception with technology

What do you think of first when asked, "How does technology affect our sense perception?" You might think of glasses and hearing aids that adjust the use of our senses. You might think also about progress in science through telescopes, microscopes, and all of the investigative tools that allow us to see far out into space and deep into cells and atoms, or the devices such as sonar that enable us to use sound in ways we do not naturally as a species.

You might also think of the revolution in communication technology that has connected us with the sights and sounds the world over. Indeed, psychologists, cognitive scientists, and educators are posing very interesting questions on the extent to which the use of computers and social media are influencing the very processes our brains use to handle information and gain knowledge.

The development of technology, it is fair to say, has extended our observational knowledge spectacularly. From our own homes in industrialized regions of the world, we can observe nature as no past generations have seen it: a webcam on a computer lets us hear great blue herons land in their nest and watch them lay their eggs,[10] or a film on a television or computer screen can take us deep into the ocean to see strange creatures[11] or high into the sky to witness birds in migration.

With technology, we can also extend our senses to aspects of our universe that no one has seen until recently. We can study subatomic particles such as quarks and neutrinos; or explore galaxies whose images meet our eyes light years after the light has left them; and even dark matter not directly accessible to our senses at all. Observation becomes *indirect* as we gain our "picture" of the world from data on a computer. What we *see and hear*, the starting place for observation, has been developed and overlaid by what *we know* – as has ever been the case with our maps of the world.

Despite its immense power to extend our observations, our technology has potential, paradoxically, also to block them. We can be "blinded" to the real world around us as we are absorbed in technological representations of it. The story is told of the woman in Paris who, intent on her handheld device combining web access, telephone, and a global positioning system, could not gain satisfactory information on her own location. Where, she asked a passerby, would she find the Arc de Triomphe? The passerby gently encouraged her to turn around and raise her eyes. The giant monument, centred dramatically in a huge traffic circle, was just up the street.

---

[10] The Cornell Lab of Ornithology, http://watch.birds.cornell.edu/nestcams/home/index
[11] BBC Earth, http://bbcearth.com/

## For Reflection

In your everyday life, do you yourself use technology to improve how you see, hear, or use your other senses?

If you use a telescope to see farther, you are still gaining observational knowledge through sense perception. But does the observation using technology somehow seem *different* to you from what you gain with your naked eye? If the telescope is one that is out in space and connected with a computer, is your observation still based on sense perception?

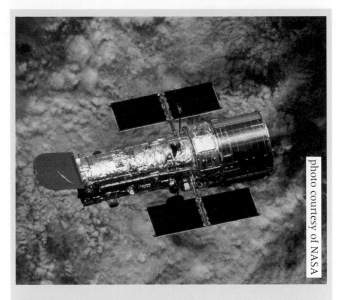

photo courtesy of NASA

**The Hubble Space Telescope**

When Galileo trained his telescope on the sky in 1610, he could not have foreseen the development of the telescope in the centuries that followed. The Hubble Space Telescope, named after astronomer Edwin Hubble, was placed in space in 1990 to give an unobstructed view of the universe. It has photographed planets and galaxies, sending back "sights" that have propelled scientific knowledge of the universe and, in image galleries, given glimpses of its beauty.[12]

Technology, indeed, may be responsible for much of the sensory overload that our brains shut out protectively. Bombarded by flashing images, rumbling traffic, and pounding digital music, urban dwellers unconsciously screen out a high proportion of their sense perceptions.

With so much sensory information available to us technologically, we face not only sensory overload but also information overload. At times, we also face dilemmas in dealing with the knowledge that we gain. At the touch of a button, we can see protestors in faraway cities being shot down in the streets by the military, long queues of hungry people waiting for rations in refugee camps, and the parched wastelands of drought. Sense perception as a way of knowing, extended by technology, gives us contact with a complex and often troubling world. How do we deal with this knowledge? What responsibilities does it bring? We will leave you, for the moment, with these knowledge questions.

## 2. Thinking critically

Technological developments for extended observation, however, do not overcome our other limitations, such as limitations in our own processing and understanding of what our sense perceptions tell us. To overcome the limitations of our own minds, we have to seek a different cure. We have to increase our awareness of our own foibles and try to think critically in order to be on guard against them. Better knowledge of how our senses work can lead to knowledge of how to use them better, and in turn gain better knowledge.

### a. Pay attention

Aware that our senses do not simply suck in the world and store it up for us, we can try to use them attentively. We can train ourselves, to some extent, to be more observant and more curious about what goes on around us. A good exercise for developing an observant eye is one that art students often use – sketching *exactly* what they see. They are training their powers of observation at the same time as their drawing skills. Admittedly, such an activity may not be transformative, but it can help to develop tendencies to observe better. Trying to listen more closely in classes, to notice the herbs and spices in a meal, or to register the responses of people in a group around you: simple "tuning in" of this sort can help to develop habits of attention.

Consciously paying attention, though, still does not make us reliable eyewitnesses, considering all of the difficulties we have raised regarding seeing and attention. Perhaps the most important step we can

---

[12] http://hubblesite.org/gallery/

## Seeing the stars

Over many centuries, the sight of the starry sky has inspired myths and stories, systems of navigation, concepts of time measurement, beliefs about our destinies, and creative works of art. With industrialization and urbanization, though, our experiential knowledge of the natural world is now profoundly different from that of our ancestors. In 1800 3 per cent of the world's population lived in cities. In 1900 it was 14 per cent, by 1950 it had grown to 30 per cent, and in 2008 it had reached 50 per cent.[13] With smog, high buildings, and electric lights affecting visibility, half the people in the world see the stars far less than our ancestors did – and than rural people still do.

At the same time as much of the world's population has lost personal observational experience of nature, we have gained greater shared observational knowledge with technological extension of our vision. We now have amazing access to observations of the universe. Have you ever browsed through photo galleries on the web of images captured by the Hubble telescope? The image below is of a group of interacting spiral galaxies called Arp 273. The photographic image is not one that people have seen with their naked eyes. It is a composite of data from Hubble's Wide Field Camera, using different filters that allow a broad range of wavelengths. The data is constructed into an image that inspires both science and poetic imagery: NASA calls this image a "rose made of galaxies" and presented it in April 2011 as a celebration of the 21st anniversary of the deployment of the Hubble Space Telescope.[14]

take to use sense perception as a way of knowing is to recognize its fallibility and regard conclusions based on it as not completely reliable. When our conclusions matter, our sense perceptions need to be doubted and checked.

### b. Suspend expectations

To observe more fully and accurately, we can attempt to suspend our expectations – to see what is there and not what we expect to see. In trying to do so, we are struggling against our own tendencies, tendencies that generally serve us very well. After all, intuitions of what is likely to be there, or what might happen a moment from now – these can guide us safely past areas of danger and can give us fast reactions in case of emergency. Our intuitions, moreover, are often very well grounded in experience. Yet, if we hope to observe accurately what meets our senses, we need to be conscious of the blocking influence of expectations.

Some striking stories are told of the way expectations interfere with observations. A group of medical students, in one account, was learning to detect telltale signs of heart problems. The instructor told them to listen closely to the opening and

---

[13]  Population Reference Bureau, http://www.prb.org/Educators/TeachersGuides/HumanPopulation/Urbanization.aspx.

[14]  NASA, http://www.nasa.gov/multimedia/imagegallery/image_feature_2134.html.

closing sounds of a patient's heart valve, and issued them all with stethoscopes. All of the students pressed their stethoscopes to the patient's chest, listened hard, and reported that they had heard the characteristic sound. Had they heard it? Their instructor silently opened one of the stethoscopes and revealed what was inside: cotton wool. None of their instruments was functional. The students could not possibly have heard anything at all.

The lesson was not on the heart but on observing accurately, and *not* imagining they could hear what they expected to hear. It was also on not being influenced by what they thought the rest of the group heard and the instructor expected them to report. This story may ring true to any student doing a lab who is helped considerably by knowing in advance what the results are supposed to be. It may also sound familiar to anyone who knows the story "The Emperor's New Clothes".

A similar account is given of the explorer Columbus, setting out from Spain in 1492, and expecting to encounter the humanoid monsters who were believed to live beyond the limits of the known world. The Native Americans he actually met clearly did not fit his expectations, so he gave their appearance considerable attention in his records. Yet he persisted in his inquiries about humanoid monsters, and he recorded reports that seemed to fit: descriptions of human beings with tails, for example. "The tales to which Columbus paid attention, and the manner in which he interpreted them, undoubtedly reflected both his expectations and his hopes. The poor communication between Columbus and the Indians … gave him considerable leeway in imposing his own meanings on the Indians' stories."[15] In listening for stories of monsters and even seeking them out, Columbus was not particularly foolish. He was merely responding with the beliefs of his culture and historical time.

This tendency to perceive what we expect to perceive is known as *confirmation bias*. It works in two reciprocal ways: we notice what supports our expectations, and we do not notice what counters them. This latter form is particularly dangerous in matters of prejudice – about "aggressive immigrants", about "overemotional women" and so on. In everyday life, people can be influenced by their own prejudices such racism,

sexism, homophobia, and classism. In research, too, confirmation bias exerts its influence: even when scientists are trying to keep open minds and observe neutrally, they can be influenced to see what the current theory leads them to expect.

If you think back to the coherence check for truth in chapter 3, you will recognize that confirmation bias can undermine the effectiveness of this check. We evaluate the plausibility of a knowledge claim by whether it makes sense in terms of the rest of the claims we have accepted. But what if we are inclined to reinforce our own beliefs by noticing mainly what we already expect?

### c. Disentangle observation from interpretation

Where suspending expectations can be extremely difficult, disentangling observations from interpretation is even more so. Our senses, as we have said, are interpretive: we sense and interpret in a flash. Being able to do so makes us good observers – up to a point. Along with that quick understanding , however, comes the potential for abundant misinterpretation.

Picture this scene: three businessmen are deep in discussion of a deal as they walk purposefully by; a shifty-looking man loiters by the shop door; an angry couple stops by the corner in noisy conflict; a wealthy woman tugs along her tiny dog on a long leash.

But how do we know that the three men are businessmen, and what in their manner of walking is "purposeful"? What makes us think that the man by the shop door is "shifty-looking"? Is he really "loitering" or simply standing there? Do we know that the man and woman on the corner are a couple, or that their noisy words are "angry"? Can we really know that the woman is wealthy or that the dog is even her own?

To help develop a critical sense of your own interpretations, practise making distinctions between observations (what meets our senses), inferences (what we think the observations imply), and value judgments (how we evaluate subjectively).

> *Observation:* A man and woman on a street corner are speaking to each other at a louder volume than you think is usual in this place.

---

15  Cohen, B. December 1992. *"What Columbus 'Saw' in 1492"*. Scientific American, P 56.

They are waving their hands and have a lot of passing facial expressions.

*Inference:* They are angry with each other. They are a couple having an argument.

*Value judgment:* They are making a spectacle of themselves fighting in a public street. They should have such disagreements in private.

Making these distinctions helps to expose the buried interpretations. Is it possible that the observer is British or Asian, with customarily restrained voice and gestures, and that the man and woman are Spanish or Italian, with customarily more expressive voice and gestures? They might not be fighting at all. Does the value judgment placed on their behaviour then change?

Next, try an activity to break through some of the barriers of value judgments you have already constructed. Can you identify a kind of music, for instance, that you are convinced that you do not like, but which you have rarely heard – perhaps opera, jazz, or traditional folk music from another part of the world? Why not talk with someone who really likes a form that you have rejected, and get some guidance on listening in a more receptive way? Learning more about music or any other product of creativity and culture can help you overcome the common reflex to judge and possibly reject *before* you listen and learn. Indeed, the most useful counter to fusing observation and value judgments together in a way that blocks knowledge is – somewhat paradoxically – greater knowledge.

The knowledge that guides interpretation is often gained, cross culturally, through an initial phase of complete confusion! Anyone who has travelled very much will have stories of struggles to interpret correctly. We will conclude these comments with the small story of Mrs. Ngo and the flight of stairs:

> Mrs. Ngo, a woman from Cameroon, was studying at a Dutch university. A professor whom she was having an interview with showed her out of his office at the end of the interview. As she was heading toward the long way out of the building, he pointed out to her a staircase that provided a shortcut. "Oh," she exclaimed, "I thought that stairway was for staff only." This greatly amazed the Dutch professor, because stairways for staff only do not exist at Dutch universities, so he asked her

what had made her think that the stairway was limited to staff use only. She replied that she had seen a staff member use it.[16]

Clearly, Mrs. Ngo was paying attention to how people acted around her, trying to make sure that she behaved correctly herself in the new context. Her interpretations were based on cultural assumptions. Do you recall the broad cultural characteristics we presented in chapter 1, with Hofstede's identification of "power distance", the degree of inequality and hierarchy expected and accepted within a society? Think in terms of power distance and identity (individualist or collectivist):

> Mrs. Ngo comes from a collectivist country where rights and privileges vary by group, whereas the teacher comes from an individualist culture where everybody is supposed to have the same rights. Also, Mrs. Ngo comes from a culture of large power distance, and the university lies in a country of small power distance: the Netherlands. This combination of circumstances made her expect that she would have to use another staircase than the one reserved for people of higher status [the university staff].

Mrs. Ngo makes a single observation of a member of the university teaching staff using the staircase, and infers quickly that it would be inappropriate for her to use it herself. (It is easy to imagine a reverse situation, in which someone from the Netherlands innocently causes offence by seeing people taking stairs but not "seeing" the hierarchy as he takes the wrong ones himself.)

### d. Check your own observations

A final way in which we can attempt to apply critical thinking to our sense perceptions is to check what we thought we saw or heard or otherwise sensed already. Doing so involves all the other ways we've already considered: paying attention, trying to suspend expectations, and disentangling observations from inferences and value judgments. After all, once we have observed and reached conclusions, it is hard to check what we sensed earlier without our previous interpretations getting in the way. Our eyes can be wide open, but our minds can be closed.

If we can manage this openness, then repeated observation gives us a much better basis for any

---

[16] Hofstede, Pedersen, and Hofstede. 2002. *Exploring Culture: Exercises, Stories, and Synthetic Cultures*. Intercultural Press Nicholas Brealey Publishing Inc., Boston, and London. P 69.

## Voices

### Cows: seeing and interpreting

"As a Hindu, I've grown up seeing the cow as a mother. A cow gives us milk to nourish the population, and holds an honoured place in society. You would never do anything to hurt a cow any more than you would hurt your mother. If you see a cow roaming the streets alone, you wouldn't honk your horn or overtake it but drive behind it and be respectful. I wouldn't eat beef or any other meat either. I'm completely vegetarian."

*Shobha Lalwani, Barbados*

"When I see a cow, I see meat first thing but I also immediately recognize several breeds. Some people think that Angus

*Christy Drever, Alberta, Canada*

meat is the best, but others prefer Charolais. I would never become vegetarian because that would be a slap in the face of my family. Cows are our staple food and our income, but to me they also mean home and a whole lifestyle. We have about 1000 cows of several breeds, and for me the cattle drives and calving are just part of normal life. It's amazing that people don't know how to chase cows. I thought it was a natural thing."

"In traditional Shona culture, cows were often a measure of wealth. It was common for cows to be used as payment of the bride price. Cows were sometimes dedicated to

*Tanaka Lesedi Mhambi, Zimbabwe*

ancestors, in which case they would not be killed. Cows are used for their milk and meat, and oxen are usually used to draw carts or plough the fields."

conclusions we might reach. Our experiences with people, organizations, or processes of communication, extended over months and years, can provide sense perceptions that justify our generalizations about them, possibly our inferences and value judgments, and perhaps even our predictions of how they are likely to act in the future. There are good reasons for employers wanting to hire or consult people with experience, who have built an understanding through involvement and observation over time.

In areas of knowledge that depend on observation, such as the human sciences and the natural sciences, repeated observation is a requirement for credibility. Researchers working in a laboratory

run experiments again to reduce or remove errors, and researchers in the field seek out similar events or behaviour, often over time, as further opportunities to gather information.

This recognition of the many possibilities for error in our sense perceptions and interpretations of them is a major reason for the development of methodology in the sciences. It is not just one scientist who repeats an experiment and reasons towards conclusions based on it. It is a whole community of scientists, peers who undertake to check observations and correct errors. Personal knowledge, contributed to a group, gains reliability from the methodology of shared knowledge.

## Sense perception and observation: follow-up summary

You might want to compare the factors you and your classmates identified as affecting perception with the following list.

- Characteristics of the object or incident under observation: size, colour, shape, loudness, composition, distance away, familiarity or unusualness, simplicity or complexity, number of sense-stimuli it provides.
- Characteristics of the observing conditions or context: angle of observation, closeness of observation, frequency of observation, length of time the object or incident can be seen, heard, smelled, tasted, touched, quality of light, amount of background noise or other distractions, emotional intensity of reactions of others drawing attention to or shying away from the object or incident, comments and interpretations of others at the time.
- Characteristics of the observer: normality of the person's senses at the time, person's emotions, degree of interest in what is being observed, degree of background knowledge that affects capacity to discriminate details, personal biases, verbal skills to articulate observations, length of time after event for memory decay, personal prejudices that might be relevant, and (confirmation bias once again!) the observer's expectations.

## Sense perception: a TOK way of knowing

Much of the splendid achievement of our knowledge starts with sniffing odours in the air, hearing the sounds around us, and feeling sensation in our fingertips. Human, variable, and actively interpretive, our senses are basic to our knowledge of the world.

When we look more closely later on at different areas of knowledge, we will recognize that they deal with many of the topics of sense perception and critical thinking that we have raised here already. All of them, in characteristic ways, draw on sense perception as a way of knowing. Scientists working in teams to observe the galaxy, musicians playing together in symphony orchestras, archeologists exposing the remains of great civilizations of the past – all of them combine sense perception with other ways of knowing to give us their forms of personal and shared knowledge. What we catch with our senses, how we extend them with technology, and what we may miss altogether – these influence the shape of our shared knowledge just as they influence our own observation, from urban centre or rural pasturelands, of the starry sky. When next you look up to the constellations of the night sky, think about all the people around the world who, like you, are gazing upward. You are not all seeing the same thing.

# 6. Memory as a Way of Knowing

**Opening activity**

Read the following list of words out loud *once* and try to remember as many as you can. Then, without looking, write down as many as you can remember. *After* you have done so, look for the comment at the end of this chapter.

door, glass, pane, shade, ledge, sill, house, open, curtain, frame, view, breeze, sash, screen, shutter[1]

> " "Memory . . . is *knowledge from the past*. It is not necessarily *knowledge about the past*."[2]
>
> *Avishar Margalit*
> "

## Does memory work like a video camera?

Read the following five statements. True or false? What do you think?

1. Amnesia makes one unable to remember one's identity.

2. Unexpected objects generally grab attention.

3. Memory can be enhanced through hypnosis.

4. A confident eyewitness should be sufficient to convict a defendant on criminal charges.

5. Memory works like a video camera.

In a large survey conducted in the United States in 2009, the majority of respondents agreed with three of these statements:

- 83 per cent of respondents thought that amnesia makes one unable to remember one's identity
- 78 per cent thought that unexpected objects generally grab attention
- 55 per cent thought that memory can be enhanced through hypnosis.

Although fewer agreed with statement #4, the number was significant for its social implications:

- 37 per cent of respondents thought that the testimony in court of a confident eyewitness should be sufficient to convict a defendant on criminal charges.

Significant for an assessment of the reliability of memory altogether was that:

- 48 per cent thought that memory is permanent
- 63 per cent thought that memory works like a video camera.

However, experts working in memory research reject *every single one of these common beliefs*. All five statements are false. It would seem that, at least in these regards, a common understanding of memory differs from what psychologists have discovered.[3]

## How do we know through memory?

Through our memories, we carry with us the knowledge we are gaining – our skills, our past experiences, and the shared knowledge we have developed informally and formally through our lives. Through our memories, we grow our personal sense of identity and our sense of our place within the shared knowledge and shared life of our communities. Whether our memories of our lives are distressing or happy, we often feel them to be deeply significant to how we understand the world. But how reliable is memory as a way of knowing?

Even to ask this knowledge question can be disturbing. How could we doubt our own pasts? Memory intertwines with our sense of our own personal identities to the point that denial of the accuracy of our memories can feel like an assault. Little feels as convincing as a vivid memory: "I was there. I saw it. I felt it. I remember." What we remember, moreover, affects who we consider

[1] McRaney, D. 2011. *You Are Not So Smart*. New York. Gotham Books. P 176.

[2] *Avishar Margalit, The Ethics of* Memory (Harvard University Press, 2003), page 14

[3] Simons, D.J. and Chabris, C.F. 2011. What People Believe about How Memory Works: A Representative Survey of the U.S. Population. PLoS ONE 6(8): e22757. doi:10.1371/journal.pone.0022757 http://www.plosone.org/article/info:doi%2F10.1371%2Fjournal.pone.0022757 accessed 21 May 2012.

## For Reflection

What is your earliest memory? Are you aware of parts of your own life that, for the moment at least, have escaped your memory?

Do you personally keep photographs, written messages, or personal objects from the past? If so, why does it matter to preserve memories? Do you choose to preserve bad memories and good ones equally?

Do you think your memories of the past influence your interpretations of the present and your choices for the future? If so, in what ways? What, besides the memories themselves, would be lost – to you and to others – if all of your knowledge of your past were erased?

ourselves to be in the present and what decisions and actions we might take. Yet surely almost all of us also acknowledge that we cannot remember very clearly what happened in an event even last week, and treasure photographs and keepsakes to preserve moments as they blur into the past.

What, then, do we need to understand about memory as a way of knowing? An accurate appraisal of memory leads to our being able to judge how best to *use it* and how to *evaluate it* as a justification for the knowledge claims. In the chapter ahead, we will touch on remembering and forgetting, the intersection of memory and other ways of knowing, and the role of memory in personal and shared construction of our sense of the past. Memory certainly does not work like a video camera, but how does it work?

It seems that not all memories are treated in our brains in the same way. Psychologists tell us that the distinction we treated in chapter 2 between types of knowledge – between skills and knowledge claims – is borne out in the different ways they are retained. Our knowledge of skills –
our ability to ride a bicycle or play a guitar, for example – is stored and processed in our brains as *procedural memory* – encoded information that we do not consciously recall. Even after years of not having ridden a bicycle, we can still get on one and off we go, riding it so "automatically" that it is intuitive. (We will return to intuition in a later chapter.) Facts and events in the past are processed

differently from skills. We retrieve facts about family or information we have learned in school, or recall events from the past, in the form of *declarative memory*, with subgroups semantic memory (memory based on information) and episodic memory (based on experiences in time and place). As we make knowledge claims, we have reason particularly to question the dependability of our declarative memory as a justification for belief.

## Eyewitness testimony: memory on trial

"I was there. I saw it." The testimony of eyewitnesses has a ring of truth about it, especially when the witnesses themselves are convinced. Eyewitness reports have long been considered to provide convincing evidence for reaching conclusions in everyday conversations, media reports, social research, and courts of law. Yet scientific study of memory has prompted some critical questions about how much we can trust such reports, especially when the implications are serious.

So concerned was the Supreme Court of the American state of New Jersey that they ordered a special inquiry into the reliability of eyewitness identification of suspects. The legal system was putting memory itself on trial with the knowledge question: How reliable is eyewitness testimony?

Investigators set out to examine the current findings on memory by the human sciences,

**'Eyewitness testimony: memory on trial'**
Witnesses in some courts of law swear to "tell the truth, the whole truth, and nothing but the truth". What features of eyewitness memory might make it difficult for even the most honest of witnesses to tell the truth of what really happened?

particularly consulting psychologists. They also looked closely at their own procedures, with full access to all of their past records, in order to consider both factors within the legal system and particular characteristics of witnesses as they identified suspects. The unanimous Supreme Court ruling in August 2011 (State v. Henderson) was conclusive: memory is not a reliable record of the past – it doe *not* work like video tapes of events stored in a vault. As the ruling put it, "Memory is a constructive, dynamic, and selective process".

The document, moreover, gave extensive summaries of susceptibility to error, based on actual court records from the past. The conclusion cited memory expert Elizabeth Loftus, and three stages of memory: the *acquisition* of the memory in the past, the *retention* of the memory between its acquisition and recall, and its *retrieval* in testimony. In his summary, the judge declared:

> . . . At each of those stages, the information ultimately offered as "memory" can be distorted, contaminated and even falsely imagined. The witness does not perceive all that a videotape would disclose, but rather "get[s] the gist of things" and constructs a "memory" on "bits of information and what seems plausible." The witness does not encode all the information that a videotape does; memory rapidly and continuously decays; retained memory can

be unknowingly contaminated by post-event information; [and] the witness's retrieval of stored "memory" can be impaired and distorted by a variety of factors, including suggestive interviewing and identification procedures conducted by law enforcement personnel.[4]

The factors that the investigation identified as influencing testimony are likely to bear a strong resemblance to those you picked out yourself if you did the activities in "Sense perception and observation" in the last chapter (page 87). You might want to look back to the follow-up summary at the chapter's end.

The investigation also included factors regarding the *methods* of eyewitness identification of suspects from a line-up: witnesses were asked to pick out from several people the one person they had seen commit a crime. Problems included: the nature of the instructions given to witnesses, the amount of time between observation and identification of the suspect, the construction of the suspect line-up, and the administration of the identification so that the administrator also has no information. (The latter is called a double-blind system.) As we will consider more fully when we treat areas of knowledge, the *methodology* of study is immensely important for eliminating possible sources of error. Significantly, the New Jersey Supreme Court ordered major changes in the state's eyewitness identification system.

## Memory and intuition: some common biases

Even if we experience memory decay over time, can't we at least depend on our everyday memories and the things that just "pop to mind" as we remember them? Our quick, intuitive access to events of the past gives the recall a sense of immediacy, of reliability. And yet, here again, it seems that we have to be aware that we are filtering our memories as we look back.

In one common error, we tidy up the past to create the narrative that leads to the present as we know it. This *hindsight* bias is sometimes called the *I-knew-it-all-along fallacy*. We might find out that a man we know has been regularly cheating his customers, and "realize" that we had been suspicious of his actions all along. We might learn that a bridge

4   http://caselaw.findlaw.com/nj-supreme-court/1578475.html?utm_source=feedburner&utm_medium=feed&utm_campaign=Feed%3A+FindLawNJSup+(FindLaw+Case+Law+Updates+-+NJ+Supreme+Court.

## Voices

*Jane Clarke, IB graduate 1979*

Jane Clarke is a poet and management consultant with a background in psychoanalytic psychotherapy. www.janeclarkepoetry.ie

### Memory in Psychotherapy and Poetry

*What matters in life is not what happens to you but what you remember and how you remember it.*
*Gabriel Garcia Marquez*

As a psychotherapist I learned the power of memory in shaping our story of ourselves and our sense of identity. I learned that memory is both tenacious and fragile, that it is formed and reformed in the recalling. I saw how our emotional experience, assumptions, expectations and associations influence our memory of an event. I experienced the mystery of how we protect ourselves from some memories and yet burden ourselves with others. At first I found it disconcerting to realise that various members of a family could each remember the same event differently. I had to let go of the notion of objective truth in relation to memory. I came to see that what matters for the individual is finding the truth of their memories and exploring how that memory has shaped how they experience themselves as adults. What is interesting is why we remember particular

moments when so many moments of our lives are lost to us, and how we relate to what we remember.

This understanding of memory as mutable and individual is liberating for me as a poet. My memories are my own to explore, to learn from, to play with and shape. The process of retrieving bits and pieces of memory and giving them form is an endless source of creativity. Through my writing I have come to question where memory ends and imagination begins. Perhaps they work side by side making stories. They seem to be mutually dependent as I have found that the more I recall of my own life story the more I can imagine the stories of others and the more I use my imagination, the more I seem to remember. Often one memory releases another. Sometimes it's like as if, out of the blue, a new memory comes knocking on the door of consciousness wanting to be heard, to be seen and to given expression.

The process of working with memory, which began for me in my own psychotherapy, led me to poetry. When I began to write poetry in my early forties I was surprised that so much of my writing brought me back to the farm in the west of Ireland where I had grown up. As a psychotherapist I was ever conscious of the influence of our earliest relationships on our development but through writing I discovered that it was the old house and farmyard, the fields and hedges, ditches, rivers and turloughs of county Roscommon that shaped my imaginative landscape.

Working with memory is the bread and butter of both psychotherapy and poetry. Sometimes when I have written a poem around a memory it is as if I have given that memory a home. It is a joy to me when readers resonate with the memory and can read themselves into the poem. Writing a poem can be a way of making meaning of a memory, of coming to understand a memory for the first time or of putting a more bearable distance between myself and a painful memory.

I see memory as the springboard but the poem is the dive. While a poem is often sparked by memory, it must be free to go beyond memory to wherever the poem needs to go. This is where memory, imagination and craft meet. When I read aloud my poem "Honey", people often ask me, "Did that really happen?" I have vivid memories of the dog and of that morning in the farmyard but, knowing that memory has a life of its own, all I can truly answer is, "That is how I remember it."

## Honey

Away, away, he shouts, sending her up the hill,
through furze and bracken, to gather scattered sheep.
Listening for his whistle to bear left or right,
she snakes towards them, belly to the ground.

They raise their heads, sniff, ears pricked,
then flock together and run for the gate.
She comes back panting, stands at his side,
eyes bright, tongue lolling out.

She had the herding instinct from birth;
when she was just a pup he'd find her

in the haggard rounding up the hens.
*You'll make a right cod of her*, he gives out,

when we dress her up like our teacher
in our mother's headscarf and glasses.
We sit her at the kitchen table,
offer her a cup of tea and a scone.

A Sunday close to lambing, three men in the yard,
one with a rifle under his arm. *Your dog and Dunne's
wreaked havoc last night, thirty ewes dead or dying,
mangled in barbed wire, lamb beds hanging out.*

From an upstairs window we watch him
walk to the shed. He drags her by the scruff,
leaves her at their feet. He says nothing
when he comes in, says little for weeks.

## Jane Clarke

*haggard: a part of the farmyard where hay is kept
a cod: a fool or a good for nothing
he gives out: he scolds*

has collapsed in a nearby town, and "recall" that we've noticed it swaying; in fact, the accident was inevitable, wasn't it? We can even blame authorities for not having taken the preventative actions that were obviously necessary – but only "obviously" as we look back. ("The authorities must have known!" And thus is born many a conspiracy theory.) You'll recall *confirmation bias* from the last chapter – a tendency to notice what we expect to notice. *Hindsight bias* is a similar cognitive bias, but looking back in memory.

In a related bias, *consistency bias*, we interpret our own past in a way that is consistent with how we are now. We edit out of our memories actions that we would presently condemn as foolish or hurtful, for example, or interpret past actions in ways that lead to the qualities that we approve of in our present selves.

We tend to retrieve our memories, too, in a very anecdotal way. As intuition interacts with memory, we are prone to the *availability heuristic:* we assess how *likely* it is for something to happen based on how *easily* examples can be retrieved from memory. The memories instantly available seem more important, more representative, more

likely to happen – for instance, airplanes crashing, terrorists attacking, people winning the lottery. But what determines the memories that are *available* for our intuition to grab? Probably recent personal experience or the extent of coverage of events in the media! With the quick judgments of intuition, we are very bad at using memory to calculate probability.

## The role of forgetting

Memory decay, distorted memory, hindsight bias, consistency bias, the availability heuristic – what a lot of problems beset the reliability of our memories! Take heart! The same memory decay that contributes to making us unreliable eyewitnesses in a court case also appears to contribute to our being able to manage our lives.

Memory expert Elizabeth Loftus explains, "We seem to have been purposely constructed with a mechanism for erasing the tape of our memory, or at least bending the memory tape, so that we can live and function without being haunted by the past. Accurate memory, in some instances, would simply get in the way."[5]

Forgetting can also help us to recover from distressing past events, neuroscientists report. Much of our forgetting can be willful, as if we are weeding out memories we do not want. Apparently the "neural circuit underlying this skill [is] analogous to the one that inhibits impulsive actions".[6] At least in this regard, the conclusions of cognitive scientists do not counter commonly held beliefs about memory: common advice for dealing with romantic heartbreak is to try to get over it and move on! (How many sad songs are about forgetting?)

Even when the past events are not distressing, though, forgetting seems to have a positive role. It enables us to leave behind clutter and trivia to retain memories that seem more important. As science writer Ingrid Wickelgren comments, "The act of forgetting crafts and hones data in the brain as if carving a statue from a block of marble. It enables us to make sense of the world by clearing a path to the thoughts that are truly valuable."[7]

The story of Solomon Shereshevsky is a wrenching example not of the *failure to remember* but the *failure to forget*. He could remember every word of a speech he had heard only once, and could quickly memorize even poems in foreign languages and complicated mathematical formulae. However, he could not sift through all the irrelevant details in his memory to pick out characteristics of whole events. Feeling that his mind was full of chaos, he even wrote down what he wanted to forget and burned the paper as an attempt to rid himself of these unwanted memories.

## The suggestibility of memory

Perhaps more troubling for reliance on memory is not just that it is susceptible to error and forgetting, but that it can be entirely created by suggestion. Have you ever been convinced that you remember something from your early life, only to realize that you probably constructed the memory based on a photograph you had seen or stories told within your family? Have you ever wondered whether

a memory could have been a dream, or even something from a film or book?

As part of her research into the reliability of memory, psychologist Elizabeth Loftus investigated the ways in which memories could be modified by techniques of suggestion. She was examining an issue with serious and immediate implications, because of the numerous memories of childhood abuse reported during the 1990s. Much psychological research of the time claimed that victims had repressed their traumatic memories for years and were recovering them in the present as they were encouraged to do so. As they "recovered" their memories, they accused people, often family members, of having sexually abused them in their childhoods and thereby having caused symptoms from which they presently suffered. The memories, if true, testified to past damage, and, if false, unduly created present damage, ruining reputations and splitting families.

In her research on "recovered memory", however, Loftus discovered how easily memories can be created. It was entirely possible that the abuse had never taken place, but that patients were instead responding to suggestions from their therapists – therapists who were unaware of the extent to which they were influencing or planting the memories themselves. Although debate continues to surround what is known as "recovered memory" or "false memory syndrome", in 1998 a working group of the Royal College of Psychiatrists reported, in summary, that "no evidence exists for the repression and recovery of verified, severely traumatic events, and their role in symptom formation has yet to be proved."[8] More overtly condemning of arguments for emotionally-induced amnesia is Berkeley psychologist John Kihlstrom: "Laboratory analogs of traumatic amnesia are models in search of a phenomenon; theories of traumatic amnesia are explanations in search of facts."[9]

---

[5]  Elizabeth Loftus, cited in William Saleton, "The Memory Doctor". 4 June 2010. Slate. http://www.slate.com/articles/health_and_science/the_memory_doctor/2010/06/the_memory_doctor.html accessed 11 June 2010.

[6]  Wickelgren, I. January/February 2010. "Trying to Forget". *Scientific American Mind.* Pp 33–8. http://www.delanceyplace.com 1/11/12, accessed 14 January 2012.

[7]  Wickelgren, I. January/February 2012. "Trying to Forget," *Scientific American Mind.* Pp 33–8. http://www.delanceyplace.com 1/11/12, accessed 14 January 2012.

[8]  Brandon S, Boakes J, Glaser D & Green R (1998). "Recovered memories of childhood sexual abuse: implications for clinical practice". *British Journal of Psychiatry* **172**: 296–307.

[9]  John F. Kihlstrom, "Trauma and Memory Revisited", paper presented at the 6th Tsukuba International Conference on Memory: Memory and Emotion. March 15, 2005 http://socrates.berkeley.edu/~kihlstrm/Tsukuba05.htm

More broadly applicable to memory as a whole was what came out of Elizabeth Loftus' research: that memory is much more susceptible to suggestion and modification than had previously been realized. Her work also raised numerous issues of ethical concern for the ways that knowledge of techniques of memory modification could or should be used.

Loftus posed questions for an entire society to answer: "When we have mastered the false memory recipes, we will need to worry about who controls them. What brakes should be imposed on police, lawyers, advertisers? More than ever, we'll need to constantly keep in mind that memory, like liberty, is a fragile thing."[10]

## Memory, sense perception, and emotion: trauma

What do we edit out of our memories in a normal process of forgetting? Are emotional events more likely to be remembered, and more accurately?

Partial answers emerge from recent research. For instance, a collaborative group of memory researchers have tracked the memories of Americans of the terrorist attacks of September 11, 2001 that have become known as "9/11".[11] They were investigating "flashbulb memories" – memories that seem incandescently lit by their emotional impact at the time. They surveyed 3,000 American within days of the event, then at intervals thereafter. After one year, participants were roughly 60 per cent right about the details as they remembered them and after three years roughly 50 per cent right. Yet the decay of memory did not affect the vividness of their recall or their faith in the accuracy of their memories.[12]

As the research continues, though, it appears that direct experience and emotion affect the accuracy of memory: "the closer we are physically and mentally to the event, the more we get it right,

and the more we can recount every sight, sound and smell we experienced."[13]

In other contexts, it seems clear that the emotional impact of direct experience can affect not only the content of memory but also the way memory processes the past. A medical researcher working with child soldiers traumatized by violence explains that there is a difference between emotional memories and memories of learned knowledge: "It is entirely possible for facts to vanish completely from the memory, whereas in extreme cases emotional recollections remain stored for a whole lifetime. Active intervention is necessary to reduce the priority level of negative memories."[14]

Dr Schauer-Kaiser, international director of Vivo, an organization of health professionals that works with rehabilitating child soldiers, comments on their nightmares, flashbacks, depression, debilitating attempts to keep bad memories at bay, and high suicide rates. The past will not stay in the past: its effects live on in the present, through emotionally traumatic memory. Some children have lost any trust in the world and any sense of self-esteem. Others have learned to enjoy cruelty and killing. Their negative emotional memories will not fade away on their own, but have to be replaced, actively and clinically, by positive ones.

The implications not just for individuals but for their societies and the world are significant. Duncan Bell of Cambridge University, professor of international relations and political thought, draws strong connections between personal histories and the developing history of nations:

> The connections between memory, trauma and identity have been drawn in various and often-conflicting ways. It is a fairly common assumption, however, that certain harrowing events, including genocide, war, terrorism, civil and ethnic strife and radical regime transitions, generate serious and often catastrophic

[10] Elizabeth Loftus quoted in William Saleton, "The Memory Doctor", 4 June 2010. Slate. http://www.slate.com/articles/health_and_science/the_memory_doctor/2010/06/the_memory_doctor.html accessed 11 June 2010.

[11] "9/11 National Memory Survey on the Terrorist Attacks", http://911memory.nyu.edu/

[12] Hamzelou, J. 7 September 2011. "Manhattan memory project: How 9/11 changed our brains", *New Scientist*. http://www.newscientist.com/article/dn20873-manhattan-memory-project-how-911-changed-our-brains.html, accessed 24 May 2012.

[13] Murray Law, B. September 2011. "Seared in our memories", American Psychological Association. Vol 42, number 8. P 60. http://www.apa.org/monitor/2011/09/memories.aspx accessed 24 May 2012.

[14] Peter Popham, "Helping killers choose life", The Independent, 27 December 2012 http://www.independent.co.uk/voices/comment/helping-killers-choose-life-8431686.html

challenges to communal self-understandings, and that the "memory" of such "traumas" plays a significant and sometimes elemental role in shaping subsequent political perceptions, affiliations and action.[15]

## Personal testimony and the shared record

When memory is fallible, and when facts fade more quickly than the emotional impact of trauma, how much trust can we place in the eyewitness testimony of child soldiers, refugees, survivors of attempted genocide, or the many other victims of violence who tell their stories? How we answer this question has serious implications for contemporary tribunals, the shifting political landscape, and the record we distill into one of our major areas of knowledge – history.

What evidence, then, contradicts or fortifies the individual recall? For some memories, perhaps no further evidence is possible – either because the event in the past "recovered" in memory may never have happened, or because other participants or witnesses are silent or dead. Yet for large social catastrophes, there often is a landslide of evidence – hundreds and thousands of voices corroborating the general story with their accounts contributing to a written archive, physical evidence of destroyed villages or cities, remains of concentration camps or torture chambers, and in recent times the technological recordings of photographs, films, audio records. We also have the documents and images of organized attempts to give medical aid and emergency shelter, and the evidence of people mobilized to help. We may be uncertain about the factual recall of a single testimony, but doubt declines with mounting and converging evidence. Although people hearing each other's stories may be influenced in their own, such that stories begin to resemble each other and become more fixed in the telling, on a large scale it does become possible to recount what happened to a whole group.

The collective story of a social upheaval is probably more factually reliable, with accumulation of evidence, than one individual's story. Moreover, as people pool their experiences, remembered from different vantage points and perspectives, we gain a more extensive communal record.

" . . . one might almost say: no memory, no identity; no identity, no nation . . . . Collective memories . . . are active components in the creation and reproduction of nations."[16]

*Anthony Smith*

Yet surely our knowledge still gains in communication of knowledge from individual voices, speaking of their own personal experiences. Can we truly understand unless our imaginations, and often our emotional responses, are engaged? The personal memory may contain factual flaws, but it may, at the same time, give us greater understanding of what the experience has meant to the people who lived it.

## Collective memory and history

The collective memory, passed on through language, influences a sense of a collective identity. But who will determine the boundaries of the "society" and tell our collective story? What are the dominant voices that tell us *who we were*, and the implications for *who we are* – and will dissenting voices be heard? For what purposes *in the present* will our collective memory of the past be used?

When interpretations of today are shaped by cultural and political perspectives, we can expect the stories of yesterday to be similarly shaped; the creation of a sense of group identity with a collective story is a social and political issue, with competing narratives. But whoa! We will return to history as an area of knowledge later in this book.

## Shared memory and knowledge

The area of knowledge of history, however, is not the only one that depends on memory, with all of its supporting artifacts and language. It could be argued, indeed, that every area of knowledge is largely knowledge of the past – knowledge accumulated and passed down over millennia. In treating areas of knowledge later in this book, we will be considering the different ways in which each of them builds on knowledge created in the past. In its development, too, each one has its own history.

---

[15] Duncan Bell, "Introduction" *Memory, Trauma and World Politics*, Palgrave Macmillan, 2006. page 5

[16] Anthony Smith, "Memory and Modernity: reflections on Ernest Gellner's theory of nationalism", The Ernest Gellner Memorial Lecture. European Institute, London School of Economics and Political Science. http://gellnerpage.tripod.com/SmithLec.html. accessed January 28, 2013.

## Discussion Activity

### Memory and trauma: child soldiers

"Suddenly all the death I had seen since the day I was touched by war began flashing in my head. Every time I stopped shooting to change magazines and saw my two lifeless friends, I angrily pointed my gun into the swamp and killed more people.... My childhood had gone by without my knowing, and it seemed as if my heart had frozen."[17]

*Ishmael Beah, former child soldier,*
*Sierra Leone, taken as a soldier at the age of 12*

"What has humanity created?" demands Romeo Dallaire. "What have we permitted to be created?" As a general and a peacekeeper, he has witnessed children used as a weapon of choice. They are easy to catch, light to carry, and easy to manipulate through drugs and indoctrination once they have been ripped from their families. "Man has created the ultimate cheap, expendable, yet sophisticated weapon, at the expense of humanity's own future: its children."[18]

### Information questions for background

- What is the definition of a "child soldier"? Why is child participation in conflict a particular concern?

- Find out about international conventions against child soldiers, numbers involved, and organizations that work to protect children from military recruitment.

### Knowledge questions to apply to this topic

- concepts and language: Who and what determines what "childhood" is, and when it ends? Who and what determines what a "soldier" is? In what ways is it important to clarify concepts and define terms in exchange of knowledge?
- memory as a way of knowing: To what extent is "memory" the *content* of what we recall, and to what extent the *process* of recollection? In what ways is either affected by emotion?
- memory, emotion, faith/trust, and sense perception: In what ways do these ways of knowing interact? How is their interaction affected in the case of child soldiers?
- memory, language, and truth: What are the problems of reliability associated with eyewitness accounts? Is a child soldier necessarily remembering events as they really happened? What factors can make the memories doubtful? On the other hand, what factors can make personal testimony particularly convincing and valuable as evidence?
- history: To what extent could history be called "the collective memory of the past"? How is the present – and possibly the future – affected by how we understand the past?
- ethics: Is it wrong for children to be recruited into armed conflict? If so, why?
- ethics: Does awareness of a problem bring any responsibility to correct it? Why or why not? Whose responsibility is the problem of children traumatized by violence?
- CAS (Creativity Action Service): TOK explores knowledge questions, including those of ethical responsibility. For practical action, however, it passes the questions to another part of the IB Diploma programme, CAS. What can be done toward solving the problem of child soldiers – or, more broadly, toward creating a better and more peaceful world?

---

[17] Ishmael Beah, "The Making, and Unmaking, of a Child Soldier". New York Times. January 14, 2007. http://www.nytimes.com/2007/01/14/magazine/14soldier.t.html?pagewanted=all&_r=0
[18] Romeo Dallaire, They Fight Like Soldiers, They Die Like Children: The Global Quest to Eradicate Child Soldiers. Random House, Canada. 2010. pages 4, 3

## Discussion Activity

### Shared Remembrance

In this photograph from a ceremony in October 2011 in Berlin, Germany, participants place white roses on the railway tracks in memory of the first deportation 70 years earlier of members of the Jewish community to their deaths in concentration camps. In many parts of the world, rituals of remembrance are part of regular public ceremony, and monuments of commemoration are part of the public space.

- What monuments or ceremonies of remembrance exist in your own society? What do they commemorate? Do they mark sad and happy memories equally? Are there any major differences of perspectives on what, exactly, they mean?
- Do ceremonies of remembrance preserve the personal knowledge of the participants, or the shared knowledge of the society? Is there such a thing as "collective memory" and, if so, what is it?
- Are remembrances of the past relevant only to our understanding of the past? In what ways are commemorations relevant to the present, or even to the future?
- In what ways might knowledge of history be important to decision-making of the present?

"Memory is the highest, and perhaps the most meaningful tribute one can pay to the victims of genocide. Those who commit genocide do not only intend to kill, but to erase their victims from the collective memory of the world."[19]

*Richard Sezibera*
*former Ambassador of Rwanda*

Oral history is particularly dependent on the combination of memory and language, and on the unbroken connection between generations as the stories that carry knowledge are told again and again. "My people's memory reaches into the beginning of all things," declared Chief Dan George of the indigenous Coast Salish nation, commenting on traditional stories that reached back to human creation. "If the legends fall silent, who will teach children of our ways?" A chief and a poet, he reflected late in the 20th century on the importance of transferring knowledge from an oral tradition to a written one, to preserve the memory of his people:

We have suffered much,
now we stand to lose all
unless we preserve whatever is left
from the days of our ancestors.
To do this, the spoken word is not enough. . . .
Therefore we must write about our ways,
our beliefs, our customs, our morals,
how we look at things and why,
how we lived, and how we live now.
. . . . To those who believe in the power
of the written word these books
will proclaim our cultural worth.
It has been done so for other races
and their teachings.[20]

---

[19] Richard Sezibera, cited in Robert Krell, "My Journey as a Child Holocaust Survivor", adapted from his keynote address at the United Nations International Day of Commemoration in memory of the victims of the Holocaust, 27 January 2012. http://www.un.org/en/holocaustremembrance/docs/paper18.shtml

[20] Chief Dan George. My Heart Soars. Saanichton, British Columbia: Hancock House Publishers, 1979. http://www.umilta.net/chief.html

We will return in chapter 8 to the role of language as a way of knowing, both oral and written, and to the preservation and sharing of memory through the written archive.

## Memory: a TOK way of knowing

Memory, clearly, does not operate on its own as a way of knowing. It interacts with sense perception and emotion, intuition and language – not just in the *content* of memories retained of the past but also in the *process* as we recall the past, reshape it, or forget it. As the New Jersey judge summed it up, "Memory is a constructive, dynamic, and selective process."

As we build and question our knowledge, we certainly do want to be aware that memory is not totally reliable, and want to know what further questions to ask, or fallibilities to take into account, before reaching conclusions with memory as the justification. At the same time, though, we do not want to be so doubtful that we fail to appreciate the fine role of memory in our lives.

Fragile and malleable though it may be, memory nevertheless allows us to build our knowledge as we learn from past experience, storing our skills in our procedural memory and our experiences and information in our declarative memory. Memory allows us to create our identities, understand increasingly our place with other people in a society, and gain a sense of continuity in our lives. Assuredly, memory is not perfect. But can't we still manage with imperfection, recognizing it as such and simply doing our best to overcome its limitations?

In situations where the truth of the past does have significant implications, we really must confront the fallibility of memory and seek corroboration before accepting knowledge claims. The truth matters, for instance, in trials and tribunals, in records that affect the decisions of the present, and in explanations that influence our understanding of how we came to stand where we are. In such cases, we aim for *objectivity:* we try to confirm memories with other memories (coherence check) and seek out any other forms of evidence that would corroborate or revise our versions of the past (correspondence check).

In many situations, though, we can probably function cheerfully with a blurry sense of the past. We are often content with our own *subjectivity:* we care about what the memories mean to us, and how they function in the stories we tell ourselves of our lives. Does it really matter what song was, *in fact*, playing on that special evening long ago, the one with the full moon – or whether the moon was, *in fact*, full? For much of our lives, we might accept our personally edited fuzziness of memory and realize that, when our memories conflict with someone else's, we could both be wrong. We might recognize the deficiencies of our memories and, instead of despairing over imperfections, take appropriate action: keep the keepsakes and take the photographs, and enjoy them. *And* – write our upcoming appointments into the calendar, so that we don't forget.

### For Reflection

How can memories of the past be checked for accuracy?

What are the dangers to knowledge of over-emphasizing the reliability of memory?

What are the dangers to knowledge of over-emphasizing the unreliability of memory?

### Activity on words from the beginning of the chapter:

Most people taking this test will include "window" in the list of words they recall, even though it is not one of them. Can you suggest why? Could such collective agreement on a false detail of memory ever have disastrous consequences?

# Subjectivity and objectivity

We use our words as tools for exploring thought. The terms "subjectivity" and "objectivity" are often used in discussions of knowledge. What do they mean? How are they used?

## Ways of knowing

Place TOK's eight ways of knowing on a spectrum from those which seem overall to be most subjective to those which seem overall to be most objective. Then think about how these ways interact with each other in practice. Does the spectrum become more complex and questionable?

### Objectivity

One concept we create, subjectively, is the ideal of OBJECTIVITY. Using reason, we aspire to overcome the diversity of subjective interpretations of reality to achieve logical and factual knowledge that can be universally accepted as true.

### Subjectivity

Subjectivity involves our human diversity in interpretation of reality — our individuality, cultural variability, and many differences of perspectives. Our emotions, imaginations, and worldviews give us an array of experiences and understandings of our lives and our world.

### Areas of knowledge

Even before discussing TOK's areas of knowledge in class, place them roughly on a spectrum from those which seem overall most to employ subjectivity and those which seem overall most to employ objectivity. Then think about how subjective and objective qualities interact within each area of knowledge, in creating knowledge and justifying knowledge claims. Does the spectrum become more complex? After discussing areas of knowledge in class, return to your initial impressions to consider them further.

# 7. Reason as a Way of Knowing

> "
>
> The conflicts which attract most attention in the news tend either to be political and military in nature, or they involve the struggle between people and the natural environment when, in floods, drought and plague, it turns hostile. But behind these, and detached from them because it is a struggle whose proportions are those of history itself, is another struggle, a profound and consequential one because it shapes long-term human destinies. This is the struggle of ideas, expressing itself in terms of ideologies, politics, and the conceptual frameworks which determine beliefs and moralities. Our understanding of the human situation, and the choices we make in managing the unruly and difficult complexities of social existence, are founded on ideas – usually, ideas systematised into theories. Ultimately it is ideas that drive people to peace or war, which shape the systems under which they live, and which determine how the world's scarce resources are shared among them. Ideas matter; and so therefore does the question of *reason*, by which ideas live or die.[1]
>
> *A.C. Grayling*
>
> "

In the quotation above, philosopher A.C. Grayling, sweeps across history to emphasize "the struggle of ideas" that lies behind the conflicts of the world. He touches on "conceptual frameworks"– perspectives that are often systemized – and suggests that they drive the struggle. His vision is a powerful and persuasive one. But it comes to an astonishing conclusion: that it is *reason* that controls "which ideas live or die".

Is it truly *reason* that governs what ideas we accept or reject?

We would question whether reason does, in fact, take this role: we doubt that people worldwide are primarily rational in accepting ideas. We also doubt that *reason* is enough in itself to deal with the conflicting perspectives of our world: *emotions* must be involved at the very least to shift from antagonism to good will, and *imagination* to see that another worldview is possible.

In the essay from which the quotation above was taken, Grayling calls "anti-rationalist"[2] those who oppose the idea that reason is the best guide to knowledge. At the risk of being considered anti-rationalist, we protest that reason cannot be fully separated from our other ways of knowing, and that by itself it cannot resolve any of the problems of the world. We are compelled to agree, however, that reason has a powerful role in gaining knowledge and that reason "rightly used, can settle disputes and guide us to truth".

In the chapter ahead we will tackle reason as a way of knowing. We will leave, for the moment, its role of guiding "long-term human destinies" to treat it less ambitiously in terms of our everyday experience and areas of knowledge.

## Reasoning

Reason, as a way of knowing, is our capacity to think beyond our immediate experiences. We use reasoning to build our knowledge and to evaluate it – every person does so in every place in the world, as part of everyday life. Reasoning comes to us so naturally that we rarely pay close attention to the capabilities it offers us.

Indeed, we employ our rational capacities throughout our lives to understanding of all sorts. Children as well as scientists – though with different degrees of rigour – question, put forth hypotheses and test them, seek evidence, analyse the results, and reach conclusions. We select, compile, include, exclude, compare, contrast, count, estimate, and calculate. We build from generalizations about falling rocks to laws of physics about gravity, or from generalizations on buying potatoes in the neighbourhood store to economic correlations between supply and demand. We recognize alternatives and make decisions. We set goals, and then control our actions in order to see them through. We organize, research, plan, and predict. We solve problems on many scales, from figuring out how to tie a shoelace to how to build an International Space Station. Our own reasoning grows within the context and perspectives of our societies: the

---

1   Grayling, A.C. 2002. *"Reason", The Meaning of Things: Applying Philosophy to Life.* Phoenix, P 153.
2   Grayling, P 155.

basic assumptions that feed into our reasoning process are often cultural ones; the linguistic terms in which we think are those of our own language; and the categories into which we place people and features of our world are, at least initially, those to which we have been exposed. Our capacity for reason is born in us, but both *how we think* and *what we think* are influenced by our place in the world.

Significantly, we can use reason to recognize the biases of our own experiences: we can use reason to *think about our thinking*. As a result, we can be critical of our shortcomings and construct methodologies that help us to check ourselves: using reason, we can learn to reason better.

We can also, in our research, investigate in various ways the very *process* of how we think, through running experiments on human behaviour, and more recently through taking images of our brains in action. Cognitive science – an area of psychology devoted to learning how the brain works, and how we know – is the product of reasoning. It uses evidence gathered through technology to make generalizations about our brain patterns. Sophisticated thinking, right? And what does this science tell us as it holds up the mirror to our reasoning?

It tells us that we are not very rational creatures!

## We're not so rational…

It's quite a delicious irony that the rational conclusions of research should reveal how extensively we use our brains to avoid thinking much. Cognitive scientists now tell us that a lot of our errors in thinking and resistance to changing our minds are built right into how our brains work.

According to cognitive scientist Daniel Kahneman, we have already reached conclusions before we are aware that we are even thinking.

> "
> …that pretty marvellous machinery we have in our heads…generates a lot of our behaviour, a lot of it without our being aware of what is happening and without our having the sense that we are doing it.[3]
>
> *Daniel Kahneman*
> "

## Intuitive system 1 and rational system 2

To explain the results of his research, conducted through psychological experiments and fMRI scanning of the brain, Kahneman refers to our swift, unconscious thinking as System 1 (intuition), and our slower, conscious thinking as System 2 (reason). He calls the distinction a "psycho-drama between two fictitious characters" that makes it easier for people to think about the brain.

"System 1," he says, "is a storyteller. It generates interpretations – fairly complete interpretations – which if possible include a cause… So you have a reaction that interprets the past, interprets the present, and prepares for the future, all of this happening within a fraction of a second and without your *intending* to do anything. This is what associative memory does – this is what System 1 does – so it provides a coherent interpretation and prepares a potential response to events."

System 2 then draws on the quick version of reality to think consciously, arrive at beliefs, and make choices. This is the thinking of which we are aware. It is more deliberate and analytical, and when it takes charge it can override our quick System 1 thinking and adjust our thoughts and actions. However, it is lazy. It is inclined simply to endorse the automatic, swift, unconscious conclusions of System 1 rather than to make the effort of directed thinking to scrutinize whether or not they are logical and accurate.

System 1 has its strengths and weaknesses. To our benefit, it does manage many actions that are so familiar as to seem automatic, such as driving or responding to social niceties, and it takes shortcuts in thinking that can lead to conclusions that are roughly right. In emergencies, when we need to react quickly, it is especially important – though not, of course, always reliable.

However, the shortcuts or rule-of-thumb thinking (sometimes called "heuristics") that bypass a rationally thought-out process can lead straight to error; it is characteristic of shortcuts that they take us by a faster route, but eliminate the information of the longer way.

The "cognitive biases" act in this way to cut out background clutter not seemingly important to

---

3  Daniel Kahneman, 30 March 2012. "The Machinery of the Mind", audio podcast Big Ideas, http://itunes.apple.com/ca/podcast/daniel-kahneman-on-machinery/id129166905?i=112461861.

the task, for example, in the *inattentional blindness* (invisible gorilla!) that we considered in chapter 5. They also reinforce the beliefs that we already hold, with resistance to contradictions and questioning. If you think back to our *coherence check for truth* (chapter 3), you will instantly see that *confirmation bias*, also considered in chapter 5, undermines the effectiveness of the truth check: we tend to notice *only* what confirms our beliefs, and simplify the world. Cognitive biases, in short, do speed up pattern recognition and interpretive associations, but at the cost of complexity and often accuracy.

We associate System 1 and System 2 in this book with two different TOK ways of knowing. System 1 is intuition, swift processing by the brain before we are even conscious of thinking. System 2 is reason, conscious and deliberate. It is slower but more accurate. Human beings, it seems, do not reach conclusions primarily through rational and analytical thinking. To activate our System 2 thinking – to use our reason – we might have to outsmart our own brains.

## Overcoming our limitations

Our splendid human capacity for reason, then, seems to involve playing mind games with ourselves simply to overcome our tendencies to resist thinking rigorously. Critical thinking, as a result, becomes considerably more entertaining. If we are to steer a clear path through the knowledge claims around us and try to build our own knowledge as well as we can, we need to take into account our quirky minds, our societies (with all of our interacting cultures and politics), and all our ways of knowing. Far from being a process of cold computation, critical thinking becomes an adventure in the strategies and missteps of human thinking.

How will we begin the adventure? First, lay aside any lingering notions of human beings being fundamentally rational, and accept the way we are. As we observed regarding sense perception, we ourselves invent the idea of "limitations" because we want our senses – and our brains – to be something *other* than, or *better* than, what they are inclined to be. But if we do want to think more clearly, it seems best to start with some self-knowledge of fundamental characteristics as a species!

Then, we might use our reasoning *(Go, System 2, go!)* to figure out how we might do our best to reason well. With the biases of our brains in mind, we are going to make some suggestions, to which you are free to add your own:

- Make the effort to think purposefully and carefully, to check your own conclusions. And learn about the reasoning process to be able to apply it better.
- Learn more. Wouldn't it help your swift thinking, beyond the reach of your awareness, if it had good material accessible to grab?
- Recognize that we are *all* inclined to be biased and to resist changing our minds in face of contrary interpretations – and try to be patient with other people in exchanges.
- Enlarge your awareness of different perspectives and increase the flexibility of your thinking so that new ideas are less likely to trigger stress and rejection.
- In study and research, pay attention to methodology developed to overcome sloppy tendencies. In shared knowledge, we gain a collective strength through weeding out individual errors.

Do you want to add any further advice? Enough for now?

Our limitations are really nothing new, even if we understand better now how some of them are built right into the workings of our brains. Although there have been periods in the history of thought when we conceived of human beings as being more rational than we do now, we have long recognized

### Culture and cognitive style

Based on the evidence available, it is clear that styles of thinking vary from culture to culture, sometimes dramatically. The abstract, analytical, pragmatic approach of Americans is very different from the European style emphasizing theory and organic concepts. And as a group, the Western styles vary substantially from the relational style of the Japanese and the Chinese who are more likely to think by means of analogy, metaphor, and simile.[4]

*Edward Stewart and Milton Bennett*

---

4   Stewart, E.C. and Bennett, M.J. 1991. *American Cultural Patterns: A Cross-Cultural Perspective.* Intercultural Press, Boston. P 44.

> When there are rational grounds for an opinion, people are content to set them forth and wait for them to operate. In such cases, people do not hold their opinions with passion; they hold them calmly, and set forth their reasons quietly. The opinions that are held with passion are always those for which no good ground exists; indeed the passion is the measure of the holder's lack of rational conviction.[5]
>
> *Bertrand Russell*

## Reason and passion

British philosopher Bertrand Russell (1872–1970) asserts above that possessing rational justification for an opinion is *always* associated with behaving in a certain way. Do you agree? Is this just the cultural preference of a philosophical British male? In what contexts do you expect to encounter this manner of calm exchange of rationally justified opinions? Is a calm manner of expression and "rational grounds for an opinion" characteristic of the public discussions of your country?

## Rationalism and empiricism: perspectives on ways of knowing

Sense perception and reason work in such interconnected and complementary ways that you might not expect to find philosophers arguing in support of one or the other. Yet many philosophers have taken opposite sides in an historic debate within western thought: rationalists emphasize that reason is the source of knowledge, and empiricists emphasize that sense experience is the source of knowledge. The justifications that they offer for their opposing views take the form of thought and argument, with debate pushing them to find the flaws in each other's points of view and refine their own thinking. This philosophical approach to inquiry is unlike the research methods of cognitive psychology, even though both fields offer their ideas on *how we know*.

that clear reasoning is an achievement. And, in spite of all our tendencies to be biased and irrational, we have still managed to overcome our limitations to construct some pretty amazing knowledge.

## Kinds of reasoning

As we deal with reason as a way of knowing we are not leaving sense perception entirely behind, because it is largely to our sense perceptions of the world that our reasoning is applied. In *inductive reasoning*, we make many particular observations of the world, and then generalize from them to broad statements on their common characteristics. In *deductive reasoning*, we take broad statements as our starting point, and apply them to particular cases that we can observe or to other generalizations that we have accepted. Language as a way of knowing also accompanies reasoning, facilitating its process and communication.

If this process and relationship appear unfamiliar to you, let us tell you a very short story about a small child meeting the world.

## Woofs, wags, and ways of knowing

If you have contact with very small children, the following scene might seem familiar to you. A toddler sees a large brown animal. As he looks at it, Mummy says, "Doggie". The toddler then sees another large brown animal, and Mummy says, "Doggie" – and maybe they both "woof" together. The next time the toddler sees a large brown animal he says, "Doggie". If he has recognized common features and used the right general category, Mummy confirms happily, "Yes! Doggie." If he has categorized incorrectly, Mummy corrects, "No, *cow*." The child continues to learn "doggie-woof" and "cow-moo" by using reason – or the faster cognition of intuition – to recognize categories and generalize his sense perceptions. He also uses other ways of knowing. He draws on the symbolic capacity of language to name categories,

---

5   Russell, B. 1941. *Let the People think*. London. William Clowes. P 2.

applying the classifications given by his "mother tongue". He associates the category with emotions (fear of doggies, or delight).

But notice that, within the blend of ways of knowing, the child has reasoned both inductively and deductively. He has experienced particular doggies and moved towards the general category of doggies. All those animals with four legs, a wagging tail, and a woof are doggies. Here, he has reached an inductive conclusion (a generalization) and stored it in memory.

Moreover, that generalization can now be applied deductively to the next doggie he sees: "Look, mummy. Doggie." And mummy may help him refine his category: "No, darling. Cow."

Reasoning of this sort involves a continual interplay between the particular example and the general concept, though it is so much part of pattern recognition that it becomes intuitive rather than conscious. As the child encounters more particular experiences – dogs that do not bark or do not have tails, dogs as large as wolfhounds and as small as chihuahuas – he modifies his understanding of the general features of the category and makes new generalizations, inductively, about subcategories. He thus has a better general understanding to apply next time to a new particular experience, deductively.

Cognitive scientists tell us that such thinking – handled for familiar recognition in the intuitive mode of System 1 of the "psycho-drama" – is innate to human beings, and developed right from infancy. They also tell us that from an early age this child not only learns to recognize things and name them, but also grasps *causality*. He learns quickly, after few particular experiences, that if he presses a button the television comes on, if he pulls the cat's tail it will hiss and run away, and if he dances the child in the mirror will dance too. He can apply this memory of correlations deductively to a new experience, make a prediction as to the outcome, and test the prediction: "If I drop this, it will fall." This child also quickly grasps correlations between dropping things and responses in people around him. If he can gain the reaction he wants, he will continue to pitch his toys overboard and expect them to be handed back. (Who, we wonder, is training whom?) As we head into treatment of the reasoning process, we are not dealing

with anything unfamiliar to you. You have long known the basics of inductive reasoning, deductive reasoning, correlations, causal inferences, hypotheses, and testing.

## Inductive reasoning

At this point, we turn to more deliberate and conscious reasoning, first to consider the way we move from many particular examples to construct our broad generalizations. Inductive reasoning provides a justification for general statements of observation in many areas of human endeavour. For example, in marketing, business administration, farming, government, education, and telecommunications we gather and analyse data about a large number of particular objects, people, kinds of behaviour, places, or events over time. We then use this information we've gathered about particular instances to identify general patterns.

Inductive reasoning is also basic to our broad understanding in the natural and human sciences as we test our hypotheses through repeated observations, either in the field or in the laboratory. We aim to provide a solid base of evidence to justify our general conclusions regarding categories, relationships, correlations, and causes. We want our generalizations to be *true,* using the correspondence check for truth (chapter 3). How general, though, can these conclusions be, and how reliably true?

The major limitations of inductive reasoning concern this relationship between the particular examples observed and the breadth of the general statement: *How many particulars does it take to make a good generalization?* Or, phrased differently: *How much observation is enough to justify an inductive conclusion? When can we say, "This is true" or, more strongly, "This is certain"?*

## "All" and "none" generalizations

The most wide-reaching of all our generalizations are universal statements that apply to every single member of a population observed: "All members are this way, or have these characteristics, or behave in this way, or cause this outcome." Sometimes universal generalizations are also expressed in sentences that start with the word "no" or "none", such as "no dogs are five-legged", or "none of the dogs is five-legged". (Can you

## Discussion Activity

### General observations: all those fish

### Activity instructions

1 Write two "all" statements (called "universal positive generalizations") about what you observe in the photo here of tropical fish.

2 Write two "no" or "none" statements ("universal negative generalizations") about what you observe.

3 Write two "some" statements, noting that any number between "none" and "all" is "some".

4 Imagine yourself to be a biologist investigating tropical fish in the southern Pacific Ocean off French Polynesia where this photo was taken. Write three rough research questions for what you would investigate to know more about the fish.

### Questions for discussion

1 Of the first three sets of statements – all, none, or some – did you find some easier to write? If so, why?

2 Which of the three sets of those statements, if true, would be most informative, helping you prepare for your next marine observation? Why?

3 Compare your most informative biological research questions with those proposed by classmates. Are they mainly questions about none, some, or all of the fish? Did you find yourself dividing the fish into sub-populations in order to ask questions about *all* or *some* of the fish?

4 Did any of your research questions ask about the *attitudes* of the fish? If not, why not? If this school of fish were a school of human students of your own age, in what ways would your questions would be affected? How do you think your methods of investigation would be changed? Can you offer any tentative generalizations about the differences between the investigations of the natural and human sciences?

5 Did you or any of your classmates attribute to that fish in the foreground any kind of thought or attitude? Tempting, right? If you do not know the verb "anthropomorphize", look it up. What does this tendency tell us about ourselves and knowledge?

convert these two sentences into a sentence starting with "all"?)

Brace yourself. Here comes the example used in logic textbooks with such relentlessness that you cannot escape the tradition. It is your turn to think about observing white swans! The example given by philosopher of science Karl Popper is such a classic that not being familiar with it would exclude you from multitudes of cultural references – within certain knowledge communities, at least.

*I saw a swan and it was white*
*I saw a second swan and it was white*
*I saw a third swan and it was white*
*…*
*I saw an 'Nth' swan and it was white*
*All swans are white*
(A general statement is the conclusion.)

How many cases of white swans do you think you should observe before concluding that all swans are white and putting the generalization forward as a true statement? How many instances of

**The black swan**

"All swans are white." How many black swans does it take to refute this generalization? "Most swans are white." How many observations does it take to refute that generalization? How many to justify it?

Philosopher Karl Popper used the example of the single black swan to illustrate what he called "the problem of induction", the fact that a universal generalization ("all") can be falsified – that is, proved false – by just one single counter-example. The example of the black swan has lodged itself firmly in discussions of scientific reasoning.

## Universal generalizations: precious, fragile statements

Sentences starting with "all", "no" and "none" are thus fragile statements, and should be used carefully. And watch out. The "all" does not need to be explicitly stated. In fact, we usually do *not* state it, even if we talk in general terms. If someone says, "Teenagers are comfortable with electronic gadgets," this general statement refers to *all* teenagers in the world. Women talking about how men behave, and men about how women think, might remind themselves of the shaky nature of universal generalizations!

The words "always", "never", "everyone", "no one", "everywhere", and "nowhere" are used similarly; they also describe every single instance. What would you have to say to contradict the following statements? Take a moment to go through them.

1. You never talk to me.
2. You can find this kind of laptop everywhere.
3. Nobody cares about famine in Sudan.
4. Demonstrations always end in violence.
5. I have nothing to wear.

You might have given the following correct contradictions, speaking very particularly: "I talked to you *on Wednesday*," "I can't find this kind of laptop *in my village*," "*Your mom* cares about famine in Sudan," "*Saturday's demonstration* did not end in violence," or "You have *that beautiful green shirt*."

You could also have contradicted particular statements using "some": "*Sometimes* I talk to you," "There are *some* villages in my country where I can't find this kind of laptop," "*Some* organizations have sent aid to Sudan," "*Some* demonstrations remain peaceful to the end," and "You have *some* things to wear in that full closet of yours," and in all cases you would have refuted the universal generalizations.

Clearly, universal generalizations are vulnerable to being overturned, given that it is possible that sometime, somewhere, we might find counter-evidence – that is, we might find observations that contradict the generalization. No matter how many particular instances we can offer – no matter how extensive the research and data – by its very nature inductive reasoning cannot give certainty. Universal inductive conclusions ("all", "none")

sunrise do we need to see to believe that it occurs every morning, and that we can trust the sun to rise tomorrow? When we repeatedly observe instances of a particular phenomenon, it might not seem too rationally risky to cross the line and draw a conclusion. But it is.

Alas, there is no magical number that can tell us when we have enough evidence to conclude that a universal inductive generalization of this kind is true beyond doubt. Imagine taking a voyage around the globe to observe swans. After tens of thousands of instances of white swans in Africa, Asia and North America you arrive in the UK, take a walk in a central London park. And there on the river, right before your now-expert eyes, is one (just one!) black swan. One false instance is enough to topple the general conclusion you had painstakingly reached through observing many thousands of white swans.

Just one? Well, if you make a generalization that is so inclusive that it applies to every single member of the population, then that is seriously all it takes, logically. You can now say "almost all" – or, if you continue to spot black swans in that park, you might reduce the breadth of your generalization to encompass only "most".

can never be proved true (except in the case of a closed and defined population: "all students in this class"). They can only be not-proved-false-(yet).

## Uncertainty and science

A misunderstanding of this demand of inductive reasoning lies behind the occasional dismissal of well founded scientific conclusions in the media:

*"We can't be certain," prominent scientist says.*

Of course we can't be certain – not if the possibility always exists of new and better evidence leading to revision of current conclusions! With awareness of logical demands, scientists usually speak not of the "certainty" but of the "likelihood" or "probability" of their conclusions. Evaluating the degree of justification for their conclusions, they often present findings with ratings for their probability of being right – for instance, "90 per cent sure". Yet even if research findings are overwhelmingly in favour of a conclusion, scientists will usually say, "We can't be certain", or "We can't be 100 per cent certain, even though the evidence is strong". As a result, scientists with overwhelming evidence can sound much less convincing to the public than confident charlatans with none.

Acknowledging the impossibility of 100 per cent certainty, we still carry on effectively in our areas of knowledge, in many of them using generalizations backed by repeated observation of phenomena: objects falling to the ground with an acceleration of 9.8 m/s², mitosis of cells demonstrating specific phases of cell division occurring in a specific order, and chemical reactions consuming the same proportions of each compound each time. When a generalization has been consistently confirmed, we do put aside our doubt and treat it as true.

## Trends and tendencies

The natural and human sciences look for universally applicable patterns and relationships ("all", "always") and prize universal laws of science. Yet, depending on the phenomena under observation, they often make the much rougher generalizations of how natural phenomena or human beings act *most* of the time. In the human sciences particularly, variability is expected to prevent universal generalizations. For instance, in economics the "law of large numbers" is often invoked – the idea that if you have a large group

of people, you can broadly observe characteristic behaviour and generalize with a considerable degree of justification, but that the generalizations you make will not apply to everyone. The conclusions are expressed not as "all" statements but as statements of "many" or "most", to the level of trends and tendencies.

The knowledge questions, however, remain the same as those we gave earlier: *How many particulars does it take to make a good generalization?* Or, phrased differently: *How much observation is enough to justify an inductive conclusion?* The method for dealing with these questions becomes somewhat less exacting when we are looking for trends and tendencies rather than absolutes, since we are under no threat that a single black swan – or any single counter-example – will refute our generalizations. If we generalize that *most* swans are white, evidence that *some* swans are black does not act as refutation. Both can be true.

However, to make well justified generalizations on trends and tendencies, we still face the need to employ good research techniques, following the established methodologies of the field in which we are working. In the surveys of the human sciences, for instance, researchers have to ask themselves critical questions such as the following:

- What does the survey attempt to measure, and in what quantifiable terms?
- How is the group of individuals to be studied defined?
- How will the sample be taken? Will it be a random sample?
- How large should the sample be?
- How accurately, in sum, will the survey represent the whole population?

## Statistics

When we talk of trends or likelihoods and want to be informative, it is plainly insufficient to speak of "some people" or "many people". We want to know much more precisely the *degree* and *likelihood*. Statistics tells us exactly that and uses numbers to represent the intervals between "none" and "all".

Statisticians make statements about an entire population using data based on a sample. They seldom have access to an entire population, and have built methods of representing the whole by a part as they run opinion polls, administer questionnaires, or analyse population data of

## Voices

*Chen Arad*

What do the numbers mean?

Nizkor, Nizkor et achinu veachyotenu…[6]

Almost since I can remember myself, I can remember these few words, words that originate in a religious Jewish prayer, read every year in "Yom HaShoa", the Israeli Remembrance Day for the Holocaust. Every year, all over Israel, infants, youth, adults and elders all mention the murder of six million Jews in the Holocaust. Six million victims; this inconceivable number is emphasized time and again, specifically during this day, but all year long as well when talking about the subject, everywhere, by dedicated educators, by loving parents, by publicist media and by charismatic politicians. The consequence of this, which can be debated, is that when asked about the subject, any child will easily utter the number. Even if this will be followed by true sadness and a shed tear, a question must be asked: if this child, even if genuinely and truly sad, can really grasp the pain, sorrow, tragedy and remorse that this calamity, represented by a number, holds in it? Does his sadness truly come from a realization that six million living, unique stories with unique motives, needs and loves were systematically brought to death? To what extent are we all (experienced and educated as we may be) small children when we refer to such a complex, intriguing, yet deeply disturbing point in human history with a number?

all kinds. On such a basis, they can express generalizations numerically to transform "plenty of people" to "67 per cent of people" – and tell us, much more accurately, what we want to know.

Indeed, statistics are pervasive in our knowledge of the world. Each of the quantitative measures of "some" listed below comes with a story behind it (which is far more complex than the swan counter's notes, with entries such as "Monday: 21 white swans. Tuesday: 15 white swans…").

- "14% of the population of the developing world lived below $1 a day in 2008 – 801 million people. This is down from 31% in 1990 and 42% in 1981." World Bank[7]
- "World Internet Usage, December 31, 2011: penetration by % of population: Africa 13.5%, Asia 26.2%, Europe 61.3%, Middle East 35.6%, North America 78.6%, Latin America/Caribbean 39.5%, Oceania/Australia 67.5%." Internet World Stats[8]
- "More than one-third of U.S. adults (35.7%) are obese. Approximately 17% (or 12.5 million) of children and adolescents aged 2–19 years are obese." Centers for Disease Control and Prevention[9]
- "France derives over 75% of its electricity from nuclear energy." World Nuclear Association, February 2012[10]
- "Since the beginning of the epidemic, more than 60 million people have been infected with the HIV virus and approximately 30 million people have died of AIDS." World Health Organisation[11]

---

[6] The Hebrew word "Nizkor" (נִזְכּוֹר) means "we will remember".

[7] http://siteresources.worldbank.org/INTPOVCALNET/Resources/Global_Poverty_Update_2012_02-29-12.pdf accessed 21 April 2012.

[8] http://www.internetworldstats.com/stats.htm accessed 21 April 2012.

[9] http://www.cdc.gov/obesity/data/trends.html accessed 21 April 2012.

[10] http://www.world-nuclear.org/info/inf40.html accessed 21 April 2012.

[11] http://www.who.int/gho/hiv/en/index.html accessed 21 April 2012.

Statistics need to be treated critically for how they are derived, expressed, and used. Like language, they are susceptible to bias and manipulation – as we will consider later. Nevertheless, thinking critically involves recognizing strengths as well as being on guard against weaknesses. As we draw inductive generalizations, we can appreciate the valuable role of statistical representation to convey the degree of evidence in the spectrum from "none" to "some" to "all".

## Deductive reasoning

In reasoning deductively, we do not observe as we do in inductive reasoning. We take generalizations we already accept and apply them to particular instances or cases, or to further generalizations, in order to bring our understanding to bear in new situations. The fact that we can do so, and that every new experience is not a unique one encountered with no prior understanding, is basic to building our knowledge. Despite the familiarity

### Discussion Activity

### The IB genie deduction puzzle

In legends spread through IB Lands
We find the story told
Of a genie in a magic lamp
Who turns all marks to gold.

The seven friends had heard the tale
And wished that it were true.
"Just find the IB Knowledge Lamp!
Success will come to you."

"It can't be true, inductively,"
Sad Sally softly wailed,
"I've tested all the lamps in town
And all of them have failed."

"It takes just one," Christina cried,
"To overturn your doubt.
Extend the search beyond the town!
Find the genie! Let him out!"

The seven friends searched everywhere
Till each felt quite a fool.
Abandoning the quest, they met
In the library at school.

And there between the lofty shelves,
The seven puzzled sadly,

"But could there be another way
To knowledge we want badly?"

Then eerily behind the books
Suffused a golden glow,
And from it came the husky growl,
"What do you want to know?"

"I give you wishes for a week –
I'll grant you one each day.
So take your turns and wish before
I vanish far away!"

The seven friends by accident
Had found what they did seek.
So there amidst the books at school
They planned their magic week.

The first to wish chose *"eloquence"*
Upon a Sunday noon
"Let others understand my thoughts!
Oh, grant this language boon!"

On Wednesday eve another friend
Chose *"rationality"*.
"I want to understand the math
That often puzzles me."

"It's talents of the heart that count,"
Another day cried Lee.
"True understanding that I seek
Consists of *empathy*."

After Lee had made her wish,
The next turn went to Paul,
"*Athletic prowess*, give me please –
Hot shots in basketball."

"I want to *sing amazingly*,"
Said Saturday's friend, doing trills.
Another day Maimouna begged,
"Please give me *essay skills*."

On Friday in the setting sun
A friend (not Sally) said,
"I'd like to *understand myself* –
These thoughts inside my head!"

Chiara one day took a turn
And later also Tim
It wasn't Tim who wished to sing
Or know himself within.

The seven friends were jubilant
And eager now to learn,
With knowledge skills thus granted them
As each had had a turn.

And off they went to practice scales
Or basketball or math –
Or introspection, kindness, or
Whatever was the path.

The genie snug behind the books
Dimmed down the lamplight's glow
And, smiling to himself, intoned,
"What do you want to know?"

*by Eileen Dombrowski*

## Instructions

"The IB genie" is a deduction puzzle. First try to solve it, and then consider, preferably as a class group, the questions on the kind of reasoning you used to reach the answers. (You can find the solution at the end of the chapter.)

Your task is to determine: which friend wished on which day, and for what? Use a table in three columns: days of the week in order, friend's names, and their wishes.

- Hint: Which day, according to you, is the first of the week? Unless you make the cultural assumption that Sunday comes first, you will not be able to do the puzzle. (Being aware that what you are assuming has an important role in reasoning.)
- Pay attention to your process, in order to answer the following questions:
  a) As you were solving the puzzle, how did you know if you made a mistake?
  b) How did you know that you solved the puzzle successfully?

## Follow-up questions

1 What is the name given to the approach of testing many lamps and reaching a general conclusion about them? (Hint: the name you want is included in the poem.)

2 When you solved the puzzle, you knew things you did not know before. How did you achieve that new knowledge? How did the approach differ from the one in question 1?

3 Why do you think stories that deal with magic, which defies rationality, are so popular?

4 If your own school library had an IB genie, what form of knowledge would you wish for and why?

---

of this thinking process, though, we pause to notice its features. Awareness will help to prevent errors in thinking and will illuminate ways in which much of our knowledge is constructed.

First, note that the new *knowledge* you gain through deductive reasoning is *not* new information or data. You are using ideas and information you already possess – but by combining them in the process of reasoning you are drawing conclusions that you did not realize before. If you have not yet done the "IB genie deduction puzzle", we suggest that you do it now. You already have all the information that you need to solve it but it is not until you have used your own mind to think it through that you can find the answers. At the end you have added

no information from outside the bounds of the puzzle, but you *know more* – through the process of reasoning.

## Inference and implication

The process of reasoning that you have used to solve the "IB genie deduction puzzle" is *logical inference:* by thinking about the logical relationships between concepts and information already in your possession, you have drawn conclusions that tell you more. In everyday conversation, we use the word "inference" in a similar way, to suggest that someone has read between the lines or "inferred" an idea that was not stated.

## Implication and inference

*Husband:* We'll have to be out the door in about ten minutes. The performance starts at 8:00pm.

*Wife:* OK. You're right. I'll just send this message and shut down the computer. It'll take me only a minute to change my clothes.

The communication in this ordinary domestic exchange works "between the lines". The husband makes *explicit* comments about time, but *implies* (or leaves *implicit*) what he really means – that he sees his wife absorbed at the computer and not ready to go to the performance, and is concerned that they will be late.

The wife *infers* his unstated message from what he *implied*. She agrees not just with the information about the time but with the implicit suggestion, agreeing, "OK. You're right". She recognizes the *implication* that they will be late if she doesn't get moving, and counters it with reassurance. The implication is what *follows from* his statements – what the statements are pointing towards logically – which, in this case, is that his wife needs to get ready quickly.

Vocabulary: imply, implicit, implication, infer, inference, implicit vs explicit, follow from.

In deductive logic, the process of inference is laid out clearly so that the buried reasoning comes to the surface to be examined. It is laid out in an argument.

## Argument

In reasoning, an argument is a sequence of ideas put forward, involving rational connections between the different ideas, and a conclusion drawn from those ideas. In deductive arguments specifically, an initial statement is accepted and then applied to a secondary situation to reach a conclusion that tells us more.

So many problems in thinking can arise when we try to extend beyond our generalizations (which could be faulty themselves) to new situations! So many difficulties stand in the way of our trying to identify the big ideas that lie behind our thinking and so many more in our ways of combining ideas!

In order to make sure that we do not simply bypass major ideas that contribute to an argument, and that we do not fall into error when combining them logically, logicians have developed the form of the syllogism, a tool for analysing the step-by-step process of reasoning that makes both the *content* and the *process* absolutely explicit. Although you are unlikely to take to using syllogisms

yourself, it is immensely helpful just to see how they work. They help to blow the dust off the reasoning process for one way of checking what lies beneath.

The reasoning is laid out in a particular *form* – hence its name "formal logic". The syllogistic form makes the steps in reasoning easy to see and follow. The concepts or information that we already possess are identified in the form of "premises", with the first premise being a universal general statement and the second premise being either another general statement or a particular statement to which the first is applied. These universals can be negatives ("no") or positives ("all"). Then from them a conclusion is drawn.

1. Premise 1 (major premise) – The necessary "all" or "no" statement.

2. Premise 2 (minor premise) – A related "all", "no", or "some" statement.

3. Conclusion.

The form also makes errors easy to spot. If the reasoning has been done correctly, the syllogism is called "valid". If it has not been done correctly, it is "invalid". All syllogisms that follow the form of the first example below are valid. All syllogisms that follow the form of the second example are invalid.

| Premise 1 | All students at Top Bridge School are taking International Baccalaureate courses. |
|-----------|-----------------------------------------------------------------------------------|
| Premise 2 | Patrick is a student at Top Bridge School. |
| Conclusion | Patrick is taking International Baccalaureate courses.<br>VALID |

| Premise 1 | All students at Top Bridge School are taking International Baccalaureate courses. |
|-----------|-----------------------------------------------------------------------------------|
| Premise 2 | Patrick is taking International Baccalaureate courses. |
| Conclusion | Patrick must be a student at Top Bridge School.<br>INVALID |

In the first example, it is easy to see that the reasoning is correct, or *valid:* the conclusion "follows from" the premises, inescapably. In the second example, it is easy to see that the reasoning is incorrect, or *invalid:* Patrick takes IB courses, but could do so at some other IB school.

Deductive reasoning is not, however, confined to examples such as courses and schools where the connections are familiar and obvious. Imagine for a moment that you are taking part in a tribunal on war crimes, and are examining documentation for the involvement of Blackhawk mercenary soldiers in the atrocities. You have to reach conclusions based on shreds of evidence – a photograph here, an eyewitness identification there, a record of a telephone call, a memo – and reason your way through the connections. A particular soldier, Braggman, seems to provide the link to mercenary involvement. You examine a photograph and start to apply your general knowledge to this particular case:

— *All the soldiers wearing Blackhawk uniforms are mercenary soldiers.*

— *Braggman is wearing a Blackhawk uniform.*

— *Braggman is a mercenary soldier.*

From numerous sources you have further information on Braggman.

— *All the soldiers in the tank that plowed into a house and killed eleven sleeping occupants including five children are open to charges of war crimes.*

— *Braggman was one of the soldiers in that tank.*

— *Braggman is open to charges of war crimes.*

You can bring those two conclusions together to contradict denials that mercenary soldiers were involved or should be charged: you know that at least one mercenary soldier (Braggman) was involved in the incident with the tank.

It is important to recognize that *when the premises are true and the reasoning is valid, then the conclusion is also true.* What a powerful tool deductive reasoning can be – to be able to take true statements and from them create more!

We bring in this last example to demonstrate two main points: that this kind of reasoning does have application to the world, and that when details are involved the statements can become difficult to manipulate quickly as you reason. (We did not phrase the premises formally because the expression would be altogether *too* clumsy.)

To clarify the reasoning process, we often substitute letters for entire terms in syllogisms – removing language to deal with the pattern of thinking in more abstract terms. Rather than details of uniforms and mercenaries, try this:

All A are B.
C is A.
Therefore C is B.

Much easier! Are you experiencing a moment of appreciation for the clarity and compactness of mathematical symbols in a field that requires extensive reasoning?

We will not go further into formal logic here. It is too time-consuming in proportion to the benefit it gives in this course to learn to do all the steps well enough for formal logic to be a very handy tool for analysis. You would have to be able to transform ordinary language into the correct form of statements for syllogisms and then to recognize and name the different syllogistic patterns. What matters here is that you understand the following:

- the term "logical inference" as the deductive process of drawing further information out of information already possessed

- the term "argument" as used in logical context
- the role of the premises as foundational to an argument
- the difference between "truth" and "validity".

As you give attention yourself to constructing arguments and planning presentations or essays, write this sentence large and tape it above your desk:

> A sound argument has true premises and valid reasoning.

Given their importance, we will now give a little more attention to premises and the distinction between validity and truth.

## Premises

In a deductive argument we start with generalizations that we have already made, ready to apply them to new cases. But where do we get those sweeping generalizations that act as the premises?

As we have just seen, some of them come from *observations* (through sense perception) and then *inductive reasoning*. When the inductive generalizations are true, what useful premises they make! As we apply scientific laws deductively, we achieve knowledge of *any* gas anywhere (Boyle's law) or *any* electric current anywhere (Ohm's law) or *any* masses gravitationally attracted anywhere (Newton's law of universal gravitation). Even our more tentative generalizations of tendencies (such as consumer trends) give us likelihoods or probabilities.

Often, too, the premises come as *assumptions* – beliefs that are part of our cultural worldviews: these beliefs are so woven in with our sense of how things are that we may not even recognize them, any more than we notice the air that we breathe. They may be sound generalizations based on generations of experience and wisdom, but they may also be laced with superstition, prejudice, and quirky thought. Unless we have reason to call them to attention and examine them, we simply use them to interpret the world – for good or for ill.

The generalizations that act as our premises may also come from *any other area* of our beliefs, such as our personal experiences, values, or spiritual beliefs. Any of the following, for example, can become a premise for an argument:

> "People are basically honest."
> "People can't be trusted."
> "There will always be poor people."

"Environmental problems are too complex to be tackled."
"A democratic vote always leads to the best decision."
"Cultural practices are always to be respected."
"Parents know what is best for their children."

Regardless of whether you agree with general statements such as these ones, you will probably recognize that many people do. When they are the starting point for building an argument, it is important to call them to attention.

We can construct a logical argument perfectly well, though, with premises that are open to dispute. Remember that we are looking only at the form of the reasoning and its logical sequence, not the truth of the conclusions. The following compressed arguments are all valid: that is, once you accept the premises, you have to accept the conclusions. They follow…logically.

- (All) IB Diploma Programme candidates are students of TOK. She is an IB Diploma Programme candidate. Therefore she is a student of TOK.
- (All) IB Diploma Programme candidates are purple with pink spots. He is an IB Diploma Programme candidate. Therefore he is purple with pink spots.
- Old people need to use canes to walk. He is an old person, so he needs a cane to walk.
- _____s are greedy, calculating, untrustworthy people. She is a _____ and therefore she is greedy, calculating, and untrustworthy.
- People who do X are sinners who will go to hell. He is a person who does X. Therefore he is a sinner who will go to hell.
- People who do Y are valuable leaders of society. I do Y, and so I am a valuable leader of society.

It is entirely possible, though, that you may not accept the premises! The arguments are valid, but the content may be false.

## Validity and truth

Clearly, the validity of the reasoning is not the same thing as the truth of the premises.

*Questions of validity apply to the argument*, to the process of logic, quite independent of what the premises say. The premises could be total nonsense, but still be manipulated logically in exactly the same way. (All fleebles are geep. Tubby is a fleeble. Therefore Tubby is geep.) If the logic follows the correct steps, the reasoning is valid.

*Questions of truth apply to the statements themselves*, the premises of the argument. Are all IB Diploma Programme candidates students of TOK? Are all IB Diploma Programme candidates purple with pink spots? Are the premises true?

If either of the premises in a syllogism is false, the conclusion will be false (unless you make another mistake that happens to cancel out the first one). If our arguments are based on faulty premises, we will not reach true conclusions.

If we combine validity and truth, we have a very powerful step toward greater knowledge. If the premises are true and the reasoning is valid, then the conclusion is true. This recognition is a very powerful one as we build further knowledge on what we have already, working from true statements to create more – using logical inference to recognize what we did not already know.

## Causal inference

Inference is a powerful move in reasoning: filling in the connections between pieces of information we already have, taking statements we already believe and from them pulling out more. Some forms of inference, though, demand examination for all the errors that can creep in between the lines. Among them is reasoning about causes.

We do not see cause. We infer it. What we see is the dirt, the seeds, the sprouting, the rain, the sun, and the blossoms opening on the bush. It is our minds that connect these observations to understand the connection between that hard little brown seed and the large green bush, fragrant with purple lilac. Then, with that understanding, we look for causes when the leaves of the beloved bush start to turn yellow and curl. Is the bush getting enough sun, or too much sun, not enough water, not enough calcium in the acidic soil, or possibly a disease? Figuring out causes is a process of reasoning familiar to everyone.

We will wait until we treat areas of knowledge to deal more fully with different concepts of cause and different methods of trying to draw causal connections. At the end of this chapter in "Fallacies of argument" we will touch on a couple of the most common errors of thinking when we try to infer cause. Since inferring possible causes

can often lead to forming a hypothesis, it is first important to consider hypothetical reasoning.

## Hypothetico-deductive reasoning

The picture of reasoning we have given you so far in this chapter has sketched in first our shortcuts and biases and then our interconnected inductive and deductive thinking. The picture is not yet sufficient, however, because we have not yet considered problem-solving and testing, developed into the hypothetico-deductive method. Here, we think more dynamically and imaginatively than we have acknowledged so far.

When attempting to solve problems, we often have to consider a range of possible solutions. We consider various possibilities and then try them out. We discard each in turn if it does not work. You may have faced the most infuriating problem of all: a computer problem. What could be worse? You call a friend (the same friend everyone calls when facing computer problems!). His questions follow a familiar pattern: "Have you tried this?" "Have you tried that?" (Yes, of course you did!) "Now go into the Preferences menu, and let's try something else." Aha! He finds that changing a setting seems for several steps as though it will be the solution. Yes, it looks as if he's figured it out! But finally that leads

> "
>
> The hypothetico-deductive system seems to me to give a reasonably lifelike picture of scientific enquiry, considered as a form of human behaviour. It makes science very human in its successes as well as in its failures....The scientific method is a potentiation of common sense, exercised with a specially firm determination not to persist in error if any exertion of hand or mind can deliver us from it. Like other exploratory processes, it can be resolved into a dialogue between fact and fancy, the actual and the possible; between what could be true and what is in fact the case. The purpose of scientific enquiry is not to compile an inventory of factual information....We should think of it rather as a logically articulated structure of justifiable beliefs about nature. It begins as a story about a Possible World – a story which we invent and criticise and modify as we go along, so that it ends by being, as nearly as we can make it, a story about real life.[12]
>
> *Peter Medawar*
>
> "

---

[12] Medawar, P. 1969. "Induction and Intuition in Scientific Thought". London. Routledge. P59

to a dead end, too. He then does what you *could* have done yourself without phoning him: he checks the web for a forum discussion on the problem, taking advantage of widely shared knowledge to find out whether others have faced and overcome the same problem. He finally concludes that multiple factors converged to create it. He corrects one, then two, then three – and reaches a solution. (Problem-solvers are the heroes of our lives!)

This process of conjecture, testing, and elimination becomes much more complex when applied to the interconnected variables that science studies when trying to identify broad general patterns and causal connections. The search for a cure for cancer, for instance, is immensely complicated, and the more so because environmental factors and human behaviour add variables to the already complex biological ones. In choosing paths through a labyrinth of variables, researchers have to take the routes that seem most promising.

In active research, then, scientists do not investigate and reason entirely inductively, amassing huge mountains of data before tentatively drawing conclusions. Instead, they interpret much more actively, and conjecture far ahead of the information they possess already. Purposeful research does not depend exclusively on reason as a way of knowing, or even reason combined with sense perception. It demands other ways of knowing as well: possibly *intuition* as the way of knowing that catches the first emergence of pattern and *imagination* as the way of knowing that fuels speculation on what *might be*.

Enter the *hypothesis*, an informed conjecture. Amid all possible explanations of a phenomenon, what seems to be the most likely? Could it be true? With their time and funding limited, scientists do not chase every possible idea, but direct their inquiry towards the most promising explanation. If this idea is right, what predictions can it provide? How can they test them to see whether they correspond with reality?

And test them they must, as is the basic expectation of science. If a hypothesis is wrong, researchers discard it. Even when an enticing hypothesis turns out to be false, though, the process of testing it may have uncovered further possibilities. Moreover, false hypotheses possibly point the way towards another directed investigation. Even the deadest of dead ends has a role in inquiry.

Science in the process of discovery is clearly considerably more dynamic and speculative than science in the process of justification and publication, when it goes public. Most of us, interested wholly in the results, miss out on the backstory.

## Thinking creatively

The thinking that generates the fresh hypotheses is not itself a process of logic. Logical reasoning takes us down paths that are familiar and often quite prescribed as we gather evidence and use logical inference. To generate new explanations that interpret data in an insightful way we need to draw on other ways of knowing – possibly *intuition* for seeing in a flash a new possible pattern or possibly *imagination* for rearranging familiar reality to conjecture, invent, and envision beyond the confines of the known. Where does it come from, that creative impulse that takes us into new knowledge in every area?

Creativity has so far never been satisfactorily explained. We admire the gifted individuals who create the arts, solve long-standing problems in mathematics in entirely new ways, or come up with fresh ideas in science. They contribute their personal insights to our shared knowledge, and we all benefit. But we cannot – at least so far – explain how they do it.

Even the problem-solving of everyday life often demands that we think in new ways. Although introspection does not tell us reliably how our minds are working, do you have any sense of how you are using creative thinking as you solve the following puzzles? (You'll find answers at the end of the chapter.)

1.  A man is found dead hanging from a rope around his neck in the centre of a room with no furniture. A small puddle is on the floor below him. He had no apparent way of hanging himself but the police declared it a suicide. Explain.

2.  A woman had two sons who were born on the same hour of the same day of the same year. But they were not twins. How could this be so?

3.  There are six eggs in a basket. Six people each take one egg. How can it be that one egg is left in the basket?

4.  A father and his daughter are in a car crash. The father is killed. The daughter is rushed by ambulance to the hospital for emergency surgery. But the surgeon on call insists that another doctor be summoned. "I can't operate on this patient. She's my own daughter." Who is the surgeon?

## Argument in thinking and writing

In previous pages, we have used the word "argument" and put it in terms of rational connection of ideas. This is certainly not our everyday use of the word! An "argument", in everyday usage, can be tempestuous: it is a conflict in language, often involving rising tempers. In social situations, people who dislike friction often avoid others who are "argumentative" and in homes with fighting children, parents can be heard to bark, "That's enough! I'm sick of these arguments! You two break it up!"

An argument in thinking and writing is simply not the same thing. Yes, ideas often oppose each other as if in a debate, but there's not a yell to be heard anywhere. In this context, far from being an angry outburst, an "argument" is a clear and orderly progression of ideas from the opening, which usually takes a stand on a topic, to the conclusion, which draws together the case that has been made. (Yelling is often easier!)

Arguments of this kind can be mellow or fierce, but they are governed by the demand to reason. Speakers and writers have to think. They use inductive reasoning and deductive reasoning; they use hypothetical thinking and a host of other ways of connecting ideas. They have to consider what they want to say, what *ideas* they want to put forward, and then choose a sequence that connects them and offers them one at a time, coherently, with justifications given. Or – at least – this is an ideal.

Yes, this is an ideal – one fostered within academic contexts and many traditions of thought. It has often been put forward, too, as important in the public debate of a democracy. Yet the arguments we hear around us are not always very well reasoned or coherent, and not always easy to follow. Human beings, after all, do not always think clearly and do seem, in some contexts, inclined to drop the reasoning and yell.

This situation hands us a challenge if we want to understand the different points of view expressed around us and the different arguments people offer in support of their perspectives. We have to make the effort ourselves to sort out what is being said on a huge range of important social topics around us: interpretations of events, explanations of trends, recommendations on the best way to do things and the best decisions to make. If we do want to understand the arguments that shape our societies and our lives within them, we have to be ready to be patient, to sift through confused thought and expression, and, we would suggest, to make sure we treat people respectfully even when we find their ideas unconvincing.

## Reason: a TOK way of knowing

"Ultimately it is ideas that drive people to peace or war, which shape the systems under which they live, and which determine how the world's scarce resources are shared among them."

In this quotation from A.C. Grayling with which we opened this chapter, he argues that it is reason that determines if ideas live or die. While we do not agree with his description of how human beings really do shape their ideas, we share his wish that reason actually *would* be used more fully as a way of knowing because of its immense potential to help us think clearly and reach understanding. Reason enables us to think coherently and build knowledge in our everyday lives. It can also illuminate the nature of different perspectives: it helps us to analyse them, recognize their assumptions, follow sequences of thinking, and finally assess different views and different angles on topics for what they contribute to our own understanding. Reason gives us the capacity to create and investigate knowledge, evaluate evidence, and reach sound conclusions. Reason helps us to think about how we think – in order that we might learn to think better.

### Solutions

#### Solutions to the IB genie puzzle, pages 116 and 117.

| | | |
|---|---|---|
| Sunday | Chiara | eloquence |
| Monday | Lee | empathy |
| Tuesday | Paul | athletic prowess |
| Wednesday | Tim | rationality |
| Thursday | Maimouna | essay skills |
| Friday | Christina | understanding self |
| Saturday | Sally | singing amazingly |

#### Solutions to lateral thinking puzzles, page 122.

1. He was standing on a block of ice.

2. She had triplets.

3. The last person took the basket along with the egg.

4. Her mother.

# Fallacies of argument 1: Errors in the reasoning process

Fallacies are common errors in the reasoning process. We urge you to learn to recognize them. Don't be persuaded to accept poorly reasoned arguments – and do try not to make muddled arguments yourself!

## 1. Jumping to conclusions

How much evidence is sufficient for a reliable conclusion?

### a. Argument from ignorance.

This first fallacy in reasoning is quite astonishing. Why would anyone believe a claim on the basis of *no evidence at all?* Yet chilling examples have been part of the pageant of history: claims have been believed and acted upon because there was apparently no evidence to the contrary. Accused of being witches, many women during the Inquisition in Europe were drowned or burnt at the stake, because they could *not* prove they were *not* witches. But how could they possibly do so?

It is absurd to claim that whatever has not been proved false must be true, or what has not been proved true must be false. If space aliens have *not* been proved *not* to visit the earth, does it follow that they must have done so? If weapons of mass destruction were *not* proved *not* to exist in Iraq in 2003, did it follow that they must have been there, just well concealed? If God is *not* proved *not* to exist, does it follow that He does – or if He is *not* proved to exist, does it follow that He does *not*?

The fallacy becomes an argumentative tactic also when evidence is simply denied. Cigarette manufacturers in the 1950s argued that smoking was not harmful, in that no one had actually proved that it was. The disturbing feature of this particular example is the extent to which some cigarette companies had suppressed the evidence for damage to health, until they could do so no longer.

### b. Hasty generalization.

The hasty generalization is a conclusion reached on the basis of insufficient evidence. Quick to infer patterns from scant data, people can jump to conclusions after only one or two examples – conclusions about the likelihood of a particular person showing up drunk at a party, the competence of a new employee, or the relative honesty of an entire ethnic group. Unfortunately for the truth, and sometimes for relationships, people often cling to their initial judgment.

As a device for persuasion, the hasty generalization is fueled by striking stories of particular experiences. One or two atrocity stories may encourage negative beliefs about entire groups of people. One or two miracle stories may sell a health product or a religious cult. By the power of narrative, what is called "anecdotal evidence" may persuade people to believe more effectively than many a carefully administered general survey with all its extensive evidence.

## 2. Misinterpreting the grey scale

As we look for pattern in evidence, we may also be inclined to over-emphasize certain positions on the spectrum of interpretation. The metaphor of a grey scale between opposing interpretations helps to illustrate three main fallacies of thinking.

### a. Truth can be only black or only white.

**Black-and-white thinking or oversimplification** presents opposing views as the only possible alternatives. The range of possible views between the extremes is not recognized, and no mention is made of alternatives outside that particular scale: "You are either with us or against us." Yet if groups are opposed to a particular conclusion, does it necessarily follow that they are in support of the opposite? Is a reluctance to join in a particular measure that is claimed to be against terrorism an indication that you support terrorism?

Polarized thinking is often coupled persuasively with an appeal to belonging. If those supporting a speaker's stand are called "true patriots" then what are the others? In propaganda, black–and–white thinking is often used to present *our* heroes and *their* villains.

### b. Truth disappears into infinite gradations of grey.

**The argument of the beard** denies such extremes, obscuring real differences between opposing positions by considering only shades of grey. How many hairs make a beard? Not three? Not four? Not seventy? By insisting that there is no point at which one hair tips the balance, this argument denies the very real difference between a shaven face and one with a shaggy beard.

Thinking in small increments in this way can be surprisingly seductive. It is the procrastinator's plague: "I'm so late with handing in this essay, what harm can one more day do?" But it is the dieter's delight: "Just one chocolate won't make any difference." It is far too easy to blur the difference between a job done and a job not done, or a full box of chocolates (or a full bank account) and (oops!) an empty one.

Turned to persuasion, this fallacy can be used to sell cars or vacation packages, for instance, as the purchaser is encouraged to add just one more little feature (not expensive) and then another (not expensive) and then another.... It can also be used as a defence against charges of wrongdoing, from lying to committing war crimes, for surely, on a sliding scale of grey, perpetrators' offences are seldom worse than those of others they could point to!

### c. Truth is in the middle, at mid-point grey.

**Truth is in the middle** appeals, unfortunately, to people who make a sincere attempt to be balanced in their judgments. While compromise may be admirable in situations where opposing positions are based on opposing desires or interests, compromise is not a sound way of judging between factually opposing knowledge claims.

Between the claims that $5 \times 7 = 35$ and $5 \times 7 = 41$, would it make sense to conclude that the correct answer is the mid-point of 38? Does it make sense to call a woman "a little bit pregnant" or the targets of a bomb "a little bit dead"? Sometimes the truth really does lie at one end of the spectrum, with the position depending on evidence.

This tendency of fair-minded people to look at both sides, but assume uncritically that both are *equally* right, is exploited in gossip and mud-slinging campaigns. Between the accusations and the denial, will listeners compromise halfway? If so, even if the person accused is innocent of any wrongdoing, some of the mud clings – and the damage is done.

In scientific matters that should be decided on the basis of evidence interpreted by experts, this same tactic is used. Even though climate scientists have long confirmed the reality of climate change, the creation of the illusion of debate keeps alive a public sense that "truth is in the middle". The false controversy has been fueled in large part by industries whose interests are furthered by public doubt and by some media whose sales benefit from the simulation of debate, regardless of its merits.

## 3. Problematic premises

### a. Missing premises.

The premises of an argument determine all the logical conclusions that follow thereafter. In much exchange of ideas, though, the initial premises are not stated but assumed. A key skill of critical thinking, as a result, is spotting unstated assumptions. This involves listening or reading carefully, inferring what people think from what they actually said and the language in which they put it. Resolving conflicts – for example over information, relationships, values, or procedures – may depend in large part on uncovering the differing assumptions that furnish premises for opposing perspectives.

### b. False or dubious premises.

The dubious premise – possibly true, possibly false, and certainly contestable – plays an important role in argument. If someone claims firmly that immigrants are a drain on the economy, for example, then it is only a short step in argument from that premise to a conclusion that the country should accept no more foreigners. Evaluating the argument depends in large measure on examining the truth of the premises.

### c. Implied premises.

The implied premise is also sometimes used to influence attitudes or conclusions. "Have you stopped cheating in IB exams? Give me a direct answer – yes or no!" Try it. No matter which answer you give, you confirm the buried premise that you have cheated in IB exams in the past. This device plants suggestions about a person or a situation that are difficult to dispute without drawing greater attention to the implied situation in the past. Gossip thrives in this way on innuendo and hints of unrevealed scandal: "Are things better now between her and her husband?" (Were they ever bad?) Similar are the implied charges of many a political exchange: "Can we trust this government to improve its record on handling of land issues?" (Was its record ever bad?)

## 4. Flawed cause

Two common errors draw a faulty causal connection between variables.

### a. Post hoc.

This fallacy confuses a sequence of events in time with a causal connection. It is usually known by its Latin name of *post hoc ergo propter hoc*, meaning "after this, therefore because of this", and is shortened (affectionately) to *post hoc*.

This faulty connection of variables is the basis of many superstitions. A person walks under a ladder and then later has an experience that he interprets as bad luck. So what does he do? He blames walking under the ladder for the bad luck. He does not reflect

that he also ate breakfast, opened his mail, and talked to his friends, and considers none of them to be the possible cause. *Post hoc* in political argument is frequently used to apportion praise or blame – to blame the crisis in the economy on a prior decision by an opposing political party, or to take credit for the crisis not being worse because of a prior decision of your own. It can be used as veiled accusation, such as to point out that a suspicious fire that burned down the community centre happened just after refugees were housed in the neighbourhood.

### b. Confusion between correlation and cause.

There may be good reason to hypothesize and test for a causal connection if two variables seem to be related. But the existence of correlation is not enough to establish cause. Recent research emphasizes the nearly overwhelming intensity of this inbuilt tendency of the human mind to see causal connections – even where none actually exists.

The world around us abounds with situations in the process of change, sometimes rising or falling with positive or negative correlation. If the unemployment rate rises by 3 per cent – and so do divorce rates, frequency of natural catastrophes, number of new infections from HIV/AIDS, numbers of deaths due to cancer, and sales of chocolate – then does it follow that the rise in unemployment rates (or chocolate sales) caused all the others? When variables are complex and interrelated, as they are, for instance, in biological systems (for medicine) or society (for social policy), a direct causal connection is not easy to draw.

A recent medical example is provided by hormone replacement therapy (HRT) taken by women to relieve some symptoms of menopause. Those taking it not only gained symptomatic relief but also showed reduced incidence of coronary heart disease. For many years doctors recommended it to patients to protect them from heart disease. Further trials, however, indicated that it actually seemed to *increase* the risks of heart disease. Re-examination of the data led to the conclusion in 2004 that the women taking HRT in earlier epidemiological studies were from higher socio-economic groups, with better diet and exercise activity which contributed to their heart health. It was their socio-economic position that had enabled them *both* to have ready access to HRT *and* to have lower risk of coronary heart disease: the two correlated variables had a common cause which was not apparent at first.[12]

---

[12] Lawlor, A.D., Davey Smith, G. and Ebrahim, S. 2004. "The hormone replacement-coronary heart disease conundrum: is this the death of observational epidemiology?" *International Journal of Epidemiology*. Vol 33, issue 3. Pp–464-7. http://ije.oxfordjournals.org/content/33/3/464.full. accessed 29 May 2012.

> I used to think that when two events were obviously sequential, the first really did cause the second.

> I'm taking TOK this year and I have realized my error!

> That course obviously caused you to think more clearly!

> Did it? I'm not sure...

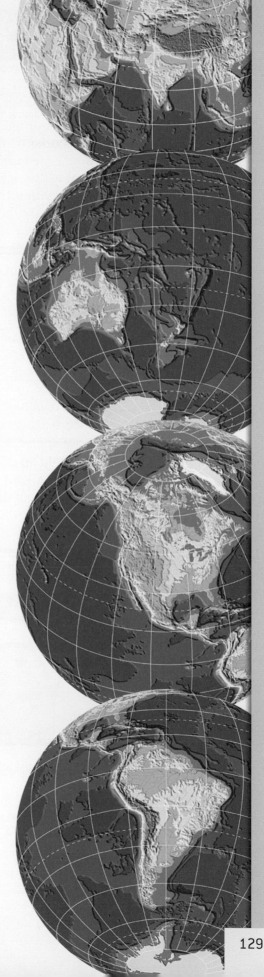

## 5. Straw man

In TOK we consider knowledge claims. We also consider counterclaims – in other words, what can be said *against* those claims, such as evidence that might raise questions or doubt. In making arguments, we take into account *counterarguments*, alternative or opposing interpretations from different perspectives. Our goal is to be open-minded in our evaluation and genuinely look for the best evidence and interpretation before favouring one view over another.

As you tune in your ear to counterclaims in public debate, we urge you not to pick up the intellectually dishonest tactic of the straw man. It takes the goal solely of persuading listeners and introduces counterclaims only to set them up as targets to be shot down. It willfully distorts an opponent's position in order to make it an easy target.

The speaker generates the fake counterclaim – the false representation of what could be said to oppose the speaker's view – in several common ways:

- by inventing a contrary position that no one is actually on the record as holding, in order to establish his or her own stand as more energetic: "There are those who say that we are being too idealistic, that we should attempt less. But I say that we must aim high and follow our vision."
- by utterly misrepresenting opposition views so that they are easily refuted or mocked
- by quoting real words out of context and reinterpreting them to remove nuances or even to make them mean something different
- by finding an unimportant error, exaggerating it, and characterizing it as typical
- by finding a silly proponent for the view and acting as if this airhead's manner and expression typifies the opposing group
- by making up things that the opposition might have said…even though they didn't.

In handling counterclaims in discussion or in essays yourself, play fair. TOK exploration requires an attempt to understand other perspectives and engage honestly with what people have really said.

# 8. Language as a Way of Knowing

## For Reflection

Think of a single day in your life. How, during it, do you use language? Do you use it to gain or give knowledge in the form of information? Probably. But what else? What are the first words you utter as you wake up in the morning? Are they carefully formulated knowledge statements?

Seriously, do this. Think of all the different roles that language plays in your life during a typical day. Language is something we live with so constantly that we hardly notice it most of the time.

In this chapter, we will be considering language as a way of knowing – what we do with all those words – and how much of it is constructing knowledge. We will return to the roles of language at the end, expecting that, by then, you will appreciate language all the more.

## Language: human capacity

No matter where we go in the world, people possess the amazing ability to make noises to each other with their mouths and convey this thing we call meaning. In many places, they also make marks on paper or other surfaces and expect others to be able to understand meaning from the marks. This capacity for language is a human characteristic, with children everywhere learning the language passed on to them by their own speech community, joining in mouth noise (or the movements of sign language) and in most places learning marks on paper – and thus communicating. Language is so much part of our lives that its power can escape us: we may give no thought to how language serves to give us knowledge and affects our understanding of the world and ourselves. By the time you've considered the ideas we raise in this chapter, may this not be said of you!

## How do we learn language?

Language is part of our human heritage, passed from parents to children and developed to take its particular form within the speech communities

> " When we study human language, we are approaching  what some might call the 'human essence,' the distinctive qualities of mind that are, so far as we know, unique to man and that are inseparable from any critical phase of human existence, personal or social.[1]
>
> *Noam Chomsky*
> "

## For Reflection

What would you say, right from the outset, is the role of language in knowing? How does it influence what we know and how we know it?

---

1   Chomsky, N. 1972. *Language and Mind.* Harcourt, Brace, Jovanovich. P 100.

where we live. A child growing up in Beijing will probably speak Mandarin Chinese; a child growing up in Washington will probably speak English; a child growing up in Jordan will most likely speak Arabic. If those children were traded around at birth, they would grow up speaking whatever language they heard around them. Whatever differences there might be among the languages of the world, every child at birth has the capacity to learn any particular language. How is it that we all learn language in this way, or at all?

Different possible views have been given in the twentieth century, notably the contrasting theories of B.F. Skinner and Noam Chomsky, both of whom contributed to our shared knowledge of how we learn language.

B.F. Skinner's view of language emerged from the theories of behaviourist psychology dominant in the 1950s, of which he was a leading figure. Skinner's ideas, summarized in his 1957 book *Verbal Behavior*, he assumed no innate capacity and focused on the impact of experience on learning. He approached language through the general principles of stimulus, response, and reinforcement. Treating language as a form of behaviour, he gave attention to imitation, practice, and correction.

Noam Chomsky, developing his ideas through the 1950s and publishing *Language and Mind* in 1972, rejected the behaviourist theory of Skinner entirely as an explanation of language learning. He argued that the capacity for learning language is innate in human beings – already present from birth as a feature of the human brain. Children do not learn solely by imitating, but absorb the grammatical patterns they hear around them and very quickly learn to generate language constructions they have never heard. For instance, they will put the present tense "I go" into the past "I goed" (logically enough!) or make the word "foot" into an invented plural "foots". Immersed in language all around them, children do not have to be formally taught and corrected, because they will learn in any case – and learn far more than they have been taught. Chomsky's views explain far more than behaviourist views about language acquisition, and accord far better with what we now know about innate capacities and the human brain.

## Is language exclusive to the human species?

When we treated sense perception in an earlier chapter, we compared the senses characteristic of human beings to those of animals in order to recognize the distinctive features of our capacities. We do the same with language. To what extent is the human species distinct in having language?

Certainly, animals communicate with each other, often extensively. We have only to think of the danger signs of different species, or the elaborate mating rituals, to recognize that individual members can exchange messages effectively with each other. Animal communication often involves chemical messages, released as pheromones that relay information and provoke particular behaviour: rabbits release a pheromone that stimulates their young to nurse, for instance, and dogs mark their territory with their urine. Sometimes the content of messages that animals communicate can be extremely detailed, such as the information that a forager bee can communicate to others from the hive. Its dance

## Discussion Activity

### Exchange and debate in shared knowledge

We did not tell you the story of Skinner and Chomsky only because these particular people are important to your understanding of language. We give it to you also as an example of the creation of shared knowledge. With your class, consider the following questions:

1 What are the implications – the logical and practical consequences – of accepting Skinner's behaviourist theory or Chomsky's cognitive theory as true? If you were designing a programme to teach a foreign language, how would the theory affect what and how you taught? Which theory would lead to each of the following: drills to repeat words and structures, practice in reproducing responses to particular situations, immersion in conversation and films with unfamiliar vocabulary and expressions?

2 Can you picture Skinner and Chomsky energetically involved in that zone of exchange between their personal work and shared knowledge? They were extremely

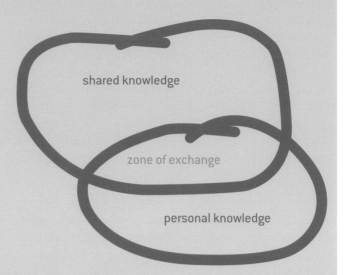

active within it: researching, lecturing, and publishing. They argued with each other, affirming or revising traditions of thought, and discussed ideas intensely with other psychologists, linguists, and cognitive scientists. Can you find other examples of this kind of exchange and debate within your IB subjects? Language makes it possible.

conveys the distance and direction to a food source, and also its quality.[2]

Animal communication is not, however, of the same kind as human language. For the most part, it remains instinctive and limited. Although animals can swiftly signal "danger", they do not move from the instinctive behaviour of the moment to abstract conversations about danger. Beavers do not slap their tales on the water to discuss the concept of danger; birds don't make raucous calls to propose new strategies of avoiding risk. Bees don't move beyond the information dance innate to their species to improvise new dance routines or chat about gathering food. Animal communication, instinctive and fixed, is grounded in the biological characteristics of the species.

And so, we believe, is human communication: we are biologically different from other animals in our capacity for abstract, symbolic language. As soon as we make this statement, though, we hope that you will immediately recognize the precarious

nature of "all" statements and recall that such huge generalizations can be overturned by even a little evidence to the contrary. Continuing research on chimpanzees, for instance, and some whales, indicates that human beings are not alone in the capacity to use symbols in communication at least to an extent. There remains much that we do not yet know.

*Most* animals, then – if not all – communicate in a way that is essentially different from human language, not just in the degree of communication but (with exceptions under study) in the kind of communication. As a species, human beings use *symbolic* communication.

## Language: symbolic system

How exactly language creates meaning has so far eluded full understanding, though different theories have suggested different ways: through the way our symbols create the stimulus and response of language behaviour, through the way they refer to things and ideas, or through the way

2 Animal Communication. http://sitemaker.umich.edu/ling111ec/home, accessed 4 May 2012.

## Discussion Activity

### Signs and symbols

Consider these symbols associated with different religions or worldviews. How many of them are familiar to you? Are any of them significant to you in the context of your own community? Could anyone outside your community, looking up the meaning of the symbol or being told it, understand it as you do? If not, why not?

### Flags

What does a flag symbolize? If, as we have said, the relationship between the flag and what it refers to is a matter of convention (which could easily have been otherwise) why does it matter to people what colour and design are on the chunk of cloth that they flap from the top of a pole? Why does waving a flag – or burning it – reflect and generate passion? Are you aware of laws in your own or other countries that restrict how you may treat the flag? Try to explore, honestly, your own cloud of thoughts and emotions that surface when you see your own flag:

**a.** in a ceremony

**b.** in a casual setting

**c.** when you are in another country.

If you do find that your emotions are stirred, how did that piece of cloth come to have that effect on you?

they stir associations of ideas.[3] Central to meaning, though, is symbolism – the use of one thing (an object, an image, a sound, a word, for example) to stand for something else, with a connection between them that we create ourselves according to our own conventions.

We pause here to clarify some possible confusion over the meanings of words – an appropriate move considering which way of knowing we are considering! In linguistic theories and literary criticism, the terms "sign", "signal", and "symbol" are used with somewhat different meanings and intent. Here, we are *not* talking of connections that can be observed in nature, such as smoke being a sign of fire. We are talking only about the conventional connections we create ourselves and calling them all symbolic.

Symbolism exists on spectrums of kind and complexity. Does the thing we use as a symbol clearly represent one idea, or does it gather more ideas for us as we use it? Does it exist on its own, like a road sign, or does it exist, like a word, as part of a system that is itself symbolic? As we treat language, we are dealing with human creativity in constructing meaning, and with ambiguity that annoys some people intensely and delights others.

Language, our primary form of symbolic communication, is complemented by mathematics, music, painting, sculpture, photography, film, maps and scientific models, all with their own

---

3   Alston, W.P. 1964. *"Theories of Meaning," Philosophy of Language.* Englewood Cliffs, NJ, USA. Prentice-Hall Inc.

forms of communication. Through all of these symbolic representations, we create and exchange meaning. Indeed, our symbolic representations are our major means of creating the knowledge that we share.

To understand better what distinguishes language from our other use of symbols, let us consider the difference between signs that we post and sentences that we speak and write.

## Signs: simple symbols

Signs convey a direct and fixed connection, a one-to-one representation that we have invented and learned. The precision and limitation of the representation are what make the sign useful to us in communication. In fact, at moments it seems to us pretty self-evident what a sign is indicating. For instance, isn't it obvious what the road sign represents when it pictures falling rock?

Consider, however, all we have had to learn to be able to "read" that sign. First, we need the concept of traffic and triangular warning signs – warning not about immediate danger here and now (such as would provoke the bird to call or the beaver to slap the water with its tail) but *possible* danger of a particular kind somewhere along the road ahead. Then, we need to be able to decipher what the black on white is representing: the round blobs are rocks in the process of falling down a slope, pictured statically mid fall. Altogether, reading the sign involves considerable familiarity with conventions of representation. We do not actually have to decipher its meaning, however. We just learn it.

Similarly, is the image for the toilet door not self-evident for its meaning? Considerable conscious attention has gone into trying to make it so. Like the sign for falling rock, this one is aimed to compress a good deal of information into a few shapes that will ideally create no confusion.

Yet, again, how much learning goes into recognizing the signs and acting appropriately? We have to recognize the design as representing a man or a woman, first of all, even though men in some places wear robes and women wear trousers. We have to be familiar with the social convention of separating men and women in public toilets, and recognize what the design then represents when attached to a door. We can then respond with the appropriate behaviour. On the other hand, we may not have gone through any reasoning process at all: we simply recognize a convention and its associated meaning.

Simple though their one-to-one representation may appear to be, our signs demand that we use our human capacity for symbolic communication: we have to be able to abstract our indicators from the world around us (the image of the rocks or the people), use them representationally (that is, to stand for something else), grasp conventionalized meaning (that is, that we make up and assign), and recognize the implications for our own learned behaviour.

## Words: complex symbols

When the sign is not pictorial the connection becomes even more obviously a learned one. When we look to our languages, we are moving into a much more complex use of symbolism than the one-to-one fixed equivalence of signs.

Take, for example, the way we abstract entirely from the physical world received through our sense perceptions as we use our words. The traffic warning sign was already a removal from the physical world as it used blobs of black paint to represent rocks falling down a slope. But the removal becomes much greater when we use not black paint that at least *looks like* a rock (more or less) but instead a word whose connection with our sense perception is arbitrary: "rock" or "pierre" or "piedra" or "sten" or "bato" or "carraig" or "iezis" – depending on the language. The sound we use could be anything. If we called that experience of sense perception a "gooble" or a "fingfang" we would still communicate just as well as long as everyone in our speech community had learned the same convention.

This capacity to move into symbolism, using our sounds meaningfully, opens to us as human beings vast possibilities for thinking and communicating: we can think and talk in abstractions removed from our immediate sense experiences. We can speak not just of what is here before us but of what has been, will be, might be, or could be only in the imagination. We are able to connect our own lives with the lives of others in our language community, giving words to categories of experiences that we seem to share and allowing us to exchange meaning socially. Words group the sensations that we associate in the neural networks of our sense

> Words, words, words. They're all we have to go on.[4]
>
> *Tom Stoppard*

> Words strain,
> Crack and sometimes break, under the burden,
> Under the tension, slip, slide, perish,
> Decay with imprecision, will not stay in place,
> Will not stay still.[5]
>
> *T. S. Eliot*

perception, or possibly give us a grouping that influences our perception of them. This capacity for symbolism to group and classify our experiences, with its impact on thought and culture, profoundly affects what and how we know.

## Words and grammar: the symbolic system

Focusing on the words within language can give us a ready grasp of symbolism, with its abstraction from the world of sense perception and its learned, conventionalized references.

---

### Discussion Activity

#### Ambiguities and overtones of meaning

Try these three quick activities:

1 Choose a simple word of your own and play with it as we do with "rock" in the section "Words and grammar", to get the feel of how meaning can shift. If you don't know what word to choose, try one of these: time, dog, part, down.

2 Have volunteers from your class attempt to stage a short dialogue, using only a single word such as "yes" or "no" or "tomorrow" or "difficult". See if you can create a meaningful exchange between people solely by shifting your intonation, for example, to question, to argue, to imply.

3 Designate one person to choose a word for some familiar object or animal, preferably one with which most people in the group are likely to have had experience. The rest of the class should prepare to hear the word – and then, as the designated person utters the word, catch what rises instantly in your mind. Now, find out what associations came first to others by going from person to person in your class. Does the word stir the same associations for all of you? Are these associations part of the meaning of the word?

---

4   Tom Stoppard, Guildenstern speaking in *Rosencrantz and Guildenstern Are Dead.*
5   T.S. Eliot, "Burnt Norton", from *Four Quartets.*

a drink with ice cubes is also "on the rocks") and a dilemma with equally difficult alternatives is described as "being between a rock and a hard place". Rocking as an action can take part in further common metaphors: "He doesn't want to rock the boat" implies that he prefers the status quo to continue.

The meaning conveyed by a word can also be shifted by its position in speech – whether it is emphasized or merely background, or whether it is given emotional colouring in the tone of voice. "He really rocks!" can be enthusiastic or heavily sarcastic and "rock solid" can be made into a question implying grave doubt simply by a lift of the voice. When used in poetry or song, a word gathers further layers of meaning: the Christian hymn "Rock of Ages" and the lullaby "Rock-a-bye-baby" surround the word "rock" with all the associations of the contexts. Even though the word "rock" is far from being a complex word, it is quite clearly different from the painted black blob for a rock on the warning sign for falling rock. It is a symbol that takes its meaning from its use within the operating system we call grammar.

## Sign language and the Deaf

The resourcefulness of human beings in use of symbolic communication is well demonstrated in the sign language of the Deaf, who communicate in a fully symbolic system with a grammar created by movement in space. Far from being a mere collection of gestures, Sign is a fully symbolic language. People who can hear often find it difficult to conceive of such a thing, so different is it from our own way of speaking. Oliver Sacks, researching his book *Seeing Voices*, describes his reaction to visiting Gallaudet College in the 1980s:

> I had never before seen an entire community of the deaf, nor had I quite realized (even though I knew this theoretically) that Sign might indeed be a complete language – a language equally suitable for making love or speeches, for flirtation or mathematics. I had to see philosophy and chemistry classes in Sign; I had to see the absolutely silent mathematics department at work; to see deaf bards, Sign poetry, on the campus, and the range and depth of the Gallaudet theater; I had to see

Yet those words are not isolated. They gain their force in relationship to one another as we manipulate them within the operating rules of our language. We do not possess just independent word-symbols; the entire system with all its underlying connections is symbolic and gives us vast possibilities for meaningful combinations.

The word "rock", for instance, can be shifted into combinations with other words to take on different meanings and different functions: it can refer to a single stone ("a rock"), or refer to a material of which cliffs or buildings are made ("of rock"); it can become an action, to "rock" a cradle or "rock" from side to side and be shifted into all the verb tenses of the language; it can be used as the name for a kind of music in "rock and roll" and from there give rise to slang expressions of approval: "That really rocks!" We can invoke its qualities by describing reliable choices as "rock solid" and then bestow those associations by giving a name to a baby – though "Peter", which means rock, is more common in English than "Rock"! Conversely, rocks can be combined with metaphors of sailing to suggest threat, such that a relationship that is heading for a breakup is "on the rocks" (though

## Discussion Activity

### Grammar: the operating system of language

It is possible that you have become aware of grammar only when your errors in language have been corrected, or when you study another language. In language classes, you encounter an analysis of patterns that native speakers have absorbed ever since they were babies. To notice the way that language is rule-bound, and then to appreciate the generative and creative flexibility of those rules, try the following two activities.

### Activity 1: shuffled sentences

Work with one other person. If in class, divide up into pairs. Take a sheet of paper and write on it a single sentence of roughly 10 words, spacing the words far apart. Then cut it apart with scissors so that each word is by itself. Shuffle the words into a random order, and let your partner try to make your nonsense order into a meaningful sentence. He is free to make a new sentence rather than duplicating yours.

Sample sentences:

- The horse in the stable quickly ate its crunchy oats.

- The paramedics carefully carried the wounded patient into the hospital.

Did you find it easy to put isolated words into an order that made sense? Why? Did you find more than one way to combine words for meaning?

### Activity 2: description

Now try in your group an exercise in placing ideas in relationship to each other. Look at the cartoon, and write one single sentence that puts into words what is illustrated visually in the two frames. Please *do not read the follow-up instructions* until you have written your sentence.

Only AFTER you have written your sentence should you read the follow-up questions.

### After you have written your sentence on the cartoon...

Read the following questions and keep them in mind as each of your classmates in turn reads out his or her sentence.

### What kinds of connections are being made?

- Is the emphasis on sequence ("and"), on consequence ("because", "causes"), on time relationship ("after", "before"), or on another form of relationship of ideas?
- Listen for what is placed in the main clause of the sentence, and what is placed in a subordinate position. Ideas in the main clause are in a position of greater emphasis.

It is likely that, even given the same pictures of a simple sequence, no two people wrote exactly the same sentence. Although the grammar of the language does dictate that only certain word orders are possible, it also allows much flexibility. We may possibly generate utterances that no previous speaker of the language has ever used.

### What kinds of interpretations?

But let us not, while concentrating on language, forget entirely about sense perception as providing the information about which we were writing. Consider the following questions.

- Did you or any of your classmates mention a ball? Can you see a ball?
- Did any of you say that the man had been hit? Does the cartoon show him being hit?
- Did any of you mention the emotional state of the girl or the man, or their intentions? How do you know what they are?

In putting what you saw in the cartoon into a sentence, did you include things that you did not see at all, but inferred by making connections between the frames? If so, you have just given yourself a good example of seeing interpretively.

- In this book, the cartoon is framed with text in English. If the same cartoon were framed with Hebrew or Arabic text, read from right to left, how might you interpret it?

the wonderful social scene in the student bar, with hands flying in all directions as a hundred separate conversations proceeded – I had to see all this for myself before I could be moved from my previous "medicalization" of deafness.[6]

As a result of their decision at the Milan Conference of 1880 to ban sign language and impose oral education, educators deprived deaf people of language almost entirely for most of a century in Europe and North America. This

**Sign language**
Two deaf schoolgirls sign to each other in their classroom.

decision stands as an example of the implications of believing a particular set of knowledge claims when in a position of decision-making power: those educators, not themselves deaf, believed that it was best for the deaf to be forced to integrate into the mainstream of people communicating through sound. The consequences of their decision, and the failure to impose a follow-up evaluation in case they were wrong, were devastating for the deaf. Not only did they lose effective education, but they also lost the language that connected them with other people.

## Language in writing

Written language is so much part of our contemporary experience of language, and so fundamental to how we learn and exchange ideas, that it is difficult to imagine our lives without it. Even though oral traditions of passing down knowledge included a wealth of information and understanding, writing opened up new possibilities that have transformed our knowledge.

Anthropologists have suggested that the development of the technology of writing has influenced even the way we think. For example,

---

6  Sacks, O. 1990. *Seeing Voices.* New York. Picador, P 129.

**Early writing tablet, from roughly 3000 BC**

This clay tablet, 5,000 years old, is written in "cuneiform", the oldest known writing in the world. It comes from ancient Mesopotamia, in the region of modern-day Iraq. And what does it record, in its non-alphabet language that derives from pictographs? All the earliest tablets were administrative records, with the earliest of all being a record of workers' daily rations of beer.[8]

Jack Goody has argued that writing has implications for both thought and social organization: writing turns words into things as it detaches them from the passing context and moment; it allows us to store and examine accumulated knowledge; it facilitates political administration of large numbers of people. As anthropologists point out, though, societies cannot be neatly divided into literate and non-literate, and it is important to be tentative in generalizations about people and cultures.[7]

Certainly, we cannot dispute that writing has changed knowledge. Whether we use writing to communicate information and ideas in social contexts or in our areas of knowledge, the possibility of exchanging knowledge beyond face-to-face contact, and also archiving for access beyond the moment, has shaped the way we construct knowledge.

## Shades of meaning

If you have tried the activities given here in "Ambiguities and overtones", you are likely to be appreciating afresh just how much is going on *around* our words as we use them to communicate. As poet T.S. Eliot says, "Words... slip, slide, perish, Decay with imprecision, will not stay in place, Will not stay still." Surely, our words have made it possible for us to construct our knowledge. But what meanings do they attempt to fix in place, and what meanings are they given by the millions of others who might read and interpret them? Our languages are, beyond doubt, an amazing way of knowing in enabling us to share knowledge. But how do we manage such sharing with words that "decay with imprecision"?

We do make various attempts to pin down and hold in place the core meanings of our words, prime among them being the move we take to define our terms. If we want to make sure that we are all talking about the same thing when we exchange ideas, we check our basic understanding. Many a discussion has reached a frustrating conclusion because the speakers never did figure out that they were entering with different understandings of a core concept, a central word. Witness social debates on "poverty" and "development" – let alone "the economy" or "freedom" or "war". Earlier in this book we presented "truth" as one of those hot words variously understood, and we could easily add "knowledge". When a simple word such as "rock" can slide around as we operate with it,

An abstract ideology such as nationalism, for example... is scarcely imaginable without the information technology of writing, which enables members of society to disseminate ideas over a vast area, thus creating bonds of solidarity between millions of individuals who will never know each other personally.[9]

*Thomas Hylland Eriksen*

---

7   Eriksen, T.H. 2010. *Small Places, Large Issues: An Introduction to Social and Cultural Anthropology.* 3rd edition. London and New York. Pluto Press. Pp 250–3.

8   Early writing tablet, "A History of the World in 100 Objects", contributed by The British Museum, British Broadcasting Company, http://www.bbc.co.uk/ahistoryoftheworld/objects/TnAQ0B8bQkSJzKZFWo6F-g, accessed 5 May 2012.

9   Eriksen, T.H. 2010. *Small Places, Large Issues: An Introduction to Social and Cultural Anthropology*, 3rd edition. London and New York. Pluto Press. P 253.

**Braille book**

Among the many scripts of the world, Braille is distinct for appealing not to the sense of sight but the sense of touch. It was developed in 1825 by Louis Braille, himself blind, and has been used to make writing accessible to the blind. Further technology, such as computer programs to read text aloud, now supplement Braille.

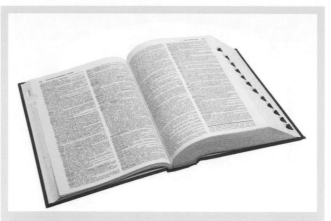

**The Dictionary**

What is the role of a dictionary? Is it *descriptive*, recording the changes in language as they happen? Or is it *prescriptive*, legislating what changes in language are acceptable? In language, new words and usages are generated almost constantly, in response to changing need and creative impulse. Why do you think that some languages (French, Spanish, Icelandic) have official institutes which regulate what new ones are accepted? What are the arguments for and against preserving a language in a particular form?

Make sure you know what the following words mean: ambiguity, denotation, connotation, bias (noun) and biased (adjective).

what slippery territory we enter when we want to talk about the larger concepts that shape our understanding of the world!

When we define our terms, we are trying to use the symbols of our language to make another specific symbol precise. Definitions are statements within the system of symbols, rather like moves in a large language game, with each piece depending upon the others. We call the core definitional meaning the "denotation" of the word, or in cases of multiple core meanings ("rock" is a noun or a verb, with unlike meanings), the "denotations". We call the overtones of meaning, the nuances that arise as we use the word in particular contexts, its "connotations". It is the connotations of a word that give it its "flavour" or its "halo" of meaning.

How we deal with the ambiguity of language – its imprecision in meaning and its connotations – depends on what the nature of our communication is and the kind of knowledge we are exchanging. In some fields, precision is crucial. The sciences take care to define terms tightly in order to use exactly the right word, or leave language behind and instead opt in favour of using numbers or other sets of symbols. In other fields, finding exactly the right word may depend on *deliberately*

*using* the ambiguity. Diplomacy and negotiation, for example, sometimes depend on indirection and subtle suggestion, and literature often depends for its expressive power on language whose connotations stir subjective associations of meaning. In yet other areas of our lives, we may not even care much about what the words we are using actually mean, since the communication of friendly chat is carried largely by the tone and accompanying body movement, and simply by the fact that we are making mouth noise companionably together. Altogether, the kind of knowledge we want to communicate affects our expectations of language and the ways we use it.

## Further meaning: metaphor

The ambiguities and connotative overtones of language certainly shade its meanings. More deeply conceptual, though, may be our idiomatic metaphors: we tend to speak of one thing in terms of another ("Life is a journey."). Certainly, this argument has been made: that conceptual

---

[10] George Lakoff and Mark Johnson, Metaphors We Live By, 1980

### For Reflection

## What's in a name?

Shakespeare wrote, "What's in a name? That which we call a rose by any other name would smell as sweet." (Romeo & Juliet, Act II, Sc. II) Not everyone agrees.

Would it have made a difference to the story had Romeo fallen in love with "Harriet" or "Susan", not "Juliet"?

Does your name (first name, last name) mean anything? Is it easy to imagine exchanging it for any other name?

In your society, are there more common and less common last names? Do certain names have certain socio-economic, political, religious, ethnic or other connotations?

How might your preconceptions about names influence your perception of the people you meet? How might others have preconceptions of your name (or nationality, religion, skin colour, etc.) that affect how they perceive you?

metaphors of our language reveal that we think in certain ways, and encourage us along certain pathways of thought. George Lakoff and Mark Johnson[10]. have so argued, suggesting that we think in terms of correspondences between a source (the conceptual domain from which we take our expressions) and a target (the conceptual domain that we are representing). They have analyzed the structures of English to conclude that embedded in the language are equivalents that reveal how we think systematically. For instance, they identify the metaphors of "time is money" (we save time, waste time, budget time, etc.) and "argument is war" (we win or lose arguments), and maintain that such metaphorical equivalence is indicative of how we conceive of time or argument. It is intrinsic to our conceptual systems.

Whether such use of metaphor truly does indicate something fundamental about how the mind works, or whether the particular metaphors may go no deeper than cultural influences on the development of language, remains a matter of debate. We are surely not *compelled* by language to think of time in terms of money – and metaphors can change. Yet the recognition that metaphor is part of the pervasive idiom of language does point to a further influence of language on thinking.

We pause to clarify the words "metaphor" and "symbol" as we have been using them here, to prevent potential confusion with usage in literary analysis. *Metaphors* in literature are not necessarily deeply conceptual (though they may be), but function rather as part of the imagery of poetry to present one thing in terms of another for the particular effect sought within the poem – for instance, vivid conceptualization or evocative associations. *Symbols*, likewise, are a particular literary usage of language to build associations, sometimes to try to reach beyond the limits of what we can say in language. When a symbol is developed in literature by our finest poets, it gains suggestive power: it is no longer, as in the metaphor, an "equation" of parts but a fused unit echoing with resonance that cannot be rationally explained.

## Perspectives in language

As is evident by now, language does not simply record the world neutrally but largely creates the meaning we associate with it. Our symbolic system separates us from raw experience as we process it, and allows us instead to construct meaning and understanding. Just as our sense perception of the world is not neutral and complete (chapter 5), neither is our language. Our use of both ways of knowing is influenced by the perspectives – cultural, political, religious, professional, and so forth – from which we use them.

The quality of our knowledge exchanges depends on our becoming critically aware of the influence of perspective on what is said and how it is expressed – by ourselves and by others. If we are to disentangle statements of observation from value judgments, for instance, or to pick up the connotations of words and sentences, we need to be aware and analytical. Being critical in this way does not involve being suspicious of everything "subjective"; our emotions and values give purpose and content to our communication. However, to understand the knowledge communicated to us, and to be able to assess it appropriately, we do need to distinguish between facts and interpretations. We want to be able to recognize perspectives (see page 28) and understand how they shape communication.

> " Explicitness... is fatal to the glamour of all artistic work, robbing it of all suggestiveness, destroying all illusion... nothing is more clear than the utter insignificance of explicit statement and also its power to call attention away from things that matter in the region of art.[11]
>
> *Joseph Conrad* "

The term often applied for the influence of perspectives on communication is "bias" – but it is one to consider fully before using. "Bias" is a leaning towards one perspective or another at the cost of impartiality, an ideal in many contexts. It is the presence of perspectives when we judge them to colour the presentation *inappropriately*.

But when do the assumptions, values, and selection of perspectives affect our language inappropriately? Surely, complete neutrality in describing events, even if it were possible, would yield accounts that do not tell us what we want to know: we want to know what happened, but we also want to know *why* it happened and what the *important* features are for understanding its implications. Any communication, whether in conversation, research, or newspapers demands some degree of interpretation.

Outside the research of areas of knowledge, it is probably in news reporting that we are most concerned to distinguish between factual reports and interpretation. The media have been widely criticized, with the common complaint that "they are all biased". However, in throwing all news media into one pot labeled "not neutral", we can fail to make distinctions critical to our understanding

## Discussion Activity

### Metaphor in knowledge

by Julian Kitching[12]

Metaphors play different roles when we use them.

a) They can have an explanatory role: for example, your biology text might portray the nervous, immune and endocrine systems as components in a telephone or communications network. As a result this metaphor helps you think immediately of connections and relations, not isolated parts.

b) They can serve to challenge orthodox thinking, as Darwin's "natural selection" did in his day, and Richard Dawkins's "selfish gene" has done more recently.

c) They can condition our thoughts and actions, such as in the case of the "war on terror", where a geopolitical situation has been portrayed in one particular manner. Perhaps even more pervasive is the way we associate environmental factors (e.g. light and dark) and basic orientations (up and down) with connotative words of values. Consider the values suggested by The Dark Ages as opposed to The Enlightenment, or "feeling high" as opposed to "feeling low".

A case has been made for metaphor being a basic mode of thought. If this is anywhere near the truth, it has far-reaching implications for our approaches to knowledge. It would support the contention that we function within systematic conceptual frameworks constructed largely through comparison, which guide our sense perception and thinking.

Knowledge itself has also been subject to extended metaphorical treatment, being regarded, for example, as a building or a ship at sea...

### Activity

Now, in small groups, take on one of the following metaphors, prepare a short presentation showing how you might develop it, and then defend it as the best of all the metaphors for knowledge:

- Knowledge **is** a web
- Knowledge **is** a map
- Knowledge **is** a collection of stories
- Knowledge **is** a mirror
- Knowledge **is** a crossword
- Knowledge **is** a chain
- Knowledge **is** a window into an aquarium

---

[11] Conrad, J. 2005. *The Collected Letters of Joseph Conrad, Volume 7, 1920–1922*, ed. Laurence Davies and J. H. Stape. Cambridge, UK. Cambridge University Press. P 457.

[12] Julian Kitching, teacher and examiner of theory of knowledge (2012: Chief Assessor). SOS Hermann Gmeiner International College, Ghana.

## Discussion Activity

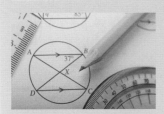

### Other symbolic representation

Language is our primary form of symbolic communication, but it is not our only one. Although none of the others provides a complete symbolic system that would allow it to replace language as a "mother tongue", all of them complement language:

- Mathematics
- Scientific models
- Maps
- Photographs
- Film
- Painting
- Music

Does any of the other forms of symbolism operate as a system, as the combination of words and grammar does in language to create meaning? What similarities and differences do you find?

What, would you say, is the role that each of the others plays most effectively? Is any of the others more effective than language for communicating certain things?

Try this quick drawing exercise. Place the forms of symbolism listed above on a scale: *at one end,*

maximum precision of meaning and convergence of shared understanding and *at the other end,* maximum ambiguity and divergence into personal understanding. What are your reasons for placing particular forms of symbolism in their positions?

With what other ways of knowing do you most closely associate each of these forms of symbolism?

With what areas of knowledge do you most closely associate each of them?

Notice how you have been discussing symbolism and language – through language. Could any of the other forms of symbolism have been used in this way? Notice how familiar it is for us to compare and contrast, group and make distinctions, using language.

> We humans are a musical species no less than a linguistic one. This takes many different forms. All of us (with very few exceptions) can perceive music, perceive tones, timbre, pitch intervals, melodic contours, harmony, and (perhaps most elementally) rhythm. We integrate all of these and "construct" music in our minds using many different parts of the brain. And to this largely unconscious structural appreciation of music is added an often intense and profound emotional reaction to music. "The inexpressible depth of music," Schopenhauer wrote, "so easy to understand and yet so inexplicable, is due to the fact that it reproduces all the emotions of our innermost being, but entirely without reality and remote from its pain…. Music expresses only the quintessence of life and of its events, never these themselves." [13]
>
> *Oliver Sacks*

(remember the danger of generalizations where we use "all"). Bias is a matter of degree, for one thing: accuracy and balance continue to be journalistic ideals, achieved variously across media. Some sources are much better in this regard than others.

Bias is also a matter of placement: in editorials, opinion columns with bylines, and blogs we *expect*

an expression of a perspective that interprets for us the passing events, and we *appreciate* knowledgeable commentary. In accounts that are openly identified as views, we accept the active expression of perspectives as providing an angle on events – though we still remain on guard against any extreme bias that blinds a writer to counter-claims and counter-arguments.

---

[13] Sacks, O. 2007. *Musicophilia: Tales of Music and the Brain.* New York and Toronto. Alfred A. Knopf. P xi.

In aiming to consume media critically, we can't expect sources of information to be totally neutral and "unbiased". We need to take an active role ourselves to find sources that are more consistently reliable for our regular fare, to complement them with others for alternative coverage, and to distinguish facts from expressions of emotion and values so that we can evaluate these interlacing threads.

To take on an active role in dealing with perspectives, first try the activity "Slanted writing". Then extend your range to the activities in critical thinking given at the end of this chapter in "Representation and perspectives". You will play with and analyse not only language but maps, photographs, and statistics, recognizing the way perspectives affect different features of symbolic representation.

# Cultural perspectives in language

As languages die out in face of globalization, we have a particular impetus to consider the relationship between language, culture, and knowledge. When we turn to the perspectives of culture entwined with particular languages, we are entering the diverse worldviews of our world.

Language is the primary means by which the knowledge of one generation is passed on to the next, so the impact of language loss is grave. "Every 14 days a language dies," says the website of the National Geographic project Enduring Voices. "By 2100, more than half of the more than 7,000 languages spoken on Earth – many of them not yet recorded – may disappear, taking with them a wealth of knowledge about history, culture, the natural environment, and the human brain."[14] The loss, clearly, is not only of an archive of knowledge: as languages disappear they also take

## Discussion Activity

### Slanted writing

In order to appreciate how perspective influences language even at the level of fairly simple description, try a bit of "slanted" or biased writing yourself. Choose one incident from your own life, ideally something also familiar to your classmates so that you can share your writing afterwards with their recognition (and perhaps amusement). Write a list of five to ten pieces of information about your chosen incident. Then write two descriptions of it which do not contradict each other factually but which communicate different values and emotions through your selection of information, the emphasis you place on some information, and your word choice. Below is a sample description by a past TOK student. When you have finished, exchange with classmates to appreciate each other's and consider the question: are "true" and "false" tidy categories? What is the role of perspective in telling the truth?

### Home in the Negev Desert 1

In the center of the vast Negev desert lies a small spot of green. That miraculously green dot in the endless yellow is my home. It lies on the edge of a gorgeous valley where the view is breathtaking and the peace and quiet feel like divine magic. The air is so clear and pure, so different from the city. On most days the weather is very good: the sun is shining and the sky is blue. Everyone knows each other in my village, and smiles when they say hello. It is a wonderful place to grow up in – no commotion, traffic, drugs, or violence.

### Home in the Negev Desert 2

In the center of the dry and harsh Negev desert lies an almost unnoticeable spot of green. That small spot in the endless nothingness is where I reside. It is situated on the edge of an arid valley where everything is so quiet that one can almost hear the sound of death. The air is so clear that it has no special fragrance, maybe because there is nothing out there to smell of anything, apart from sand and half dead bushes. Most of the time the sun is shining full blast so that it gets so hot breathing becomes hard. Everyone in the village knows everything about each other because there is nothing better to do than gossip. Nothing ever happens in the village. Even thieves don't bother making the trip out into the middle of nowhere.

*By Gal Pinshow*

---

[14] http://travel.nationalgeographic.com/travel/enduring-voices/ accessed 5 May 2011.

> **"** Every language is an old-growth forest of the mind.[15]
>
> *Wade Davis* **"**

> **"** Translation is always a shift not between two languages but between two cultures.[16]
>
> *Umberto Eco* **"**

with them different understandings of how to live in the world, and the record of human variability in all the ways we talk and think. We lose some of the record of the creative range of our own species.

How deep, though, do the differences go between the ways we see the world because we speak different languages? The relationship between our particular languages and thought has long been a topic of speculative interest, and attracted considerable attention in the first half of the twentieth century. During the 1930s Benjamin Lee Whorf, a student of linguist Edward Sapir, lived with the native American group the Hopi and learned their language. His analysis of differences between Hopi and European languages led him to put forth the idea of "linguistic relativity" – that the particular language we speak leads us to think in significantly different ways about the world.[17]

It is easy to see why this idea has attracted fascination and debate, even beyond linguistic circles. After all, people learning foreign languages often have the sense of entering another reality. Yet Whorf's evidence was insufficient for the reach of his conclusions. Moreover, he had no way of separating language and culture to say which caused which!

Still, the relationship between language and culture, and the influence of their combination on thought, continue to generate numerous questions of knowledge. To what extent do the cultural differences reflected and created by language influence our perspectives on the

world? To what extent is it necessary to learn the language of a group to understand its perspective fully? Examples abound of very different ways of interpreting experience linguistically.

The Aymara people of Peru, Bolivia and northern Chile, for instance, do not speak of the future with the metaphors common to other languages. For most of us, the future is ahead of us as we face into it. According to linguistic studies, however, in the Aymara culture and language a very different set of spatial metaphors operate. The Aymara situate themselves in time as if seated in a rowboat, travelling into the future (at their back) while facing the past from where they have come. In Aymara "q'ipa nia marana" means next year; when literally translated the expression means "in the year behind" or "at our back". In Aymara "ancha mayna pachan" means a long time ago; literally translated it means "a long time in front of you". Such a difference in metaphor both reflects and reinforces a difference in understanding of how people live in the world. It does not, however, mean that people cannot think otherwise; the young Aymara, it seems, now gesture in front of them as they talk of the future.[18]

Differences in languages, tied with differences in cultures, come to the fore in challenges faced by translation. To what extent can we, through translation, come to know how people of other language communities think about the world from their cultural perspectives? It is not surprising that languages spoken only in the tropics do not abound in words for ice and snow, nor that languages spoken only in the far north do not feature words for mangoes or monkeys. That level of difficulty of translation is easily predictable. But to what extent does that geographical context of the language community – with its plants and animals, and its particular difficulties and solutions as its people survive in that world – then penetrate its way of thinking? How can one translate entire social organization that is based on regional animals, for instance, clans associated with the eagle or the bear? How can we translate all of the significance attributed to them culturally – even metaphysically? How, further, can one even begin to translate a sense

---

[15]  Wade Davis, TED. http://www.ted.com/speakers/wade_davis.html, accessed 5 May 2011.

[16]  Eco, U. *Experiences in Translation*, translated by A. McEwen. Toronto, Ontario, Canada. University of Toronto Press. P 17.

[17]  Benjamin Whorf, "The Relation of Habitual Thought and Behaviour to Language", reprinted from pp. 75–93, *Language, culture, and personality, essays in memory of Edward Sapir*, edited by Leslie Spier (Menasha, Wis.: Sapir Memorial Publication Fund, 1941) http://sloan.stanford.edu/mousesite/Secondary/Whorfframe2.html, accessed 6 May 2012.

[18]  Studies by linguist Eve Sweetser and cognitive scientist Rafael Nunez. described in Inga Kiderra, "Backs to the Future: Aymara Language and Gesture Point to Mirror-Image View of Time". 12 June 2006. http://ucsdnews.ucsd.edu/thisweek/2006/june/06_12_backs.asp.

**Voices**

"In Dhivehi, which we speak in the Maldives, we have many words for coconuts or the coconut tree. There's a word for the coconut palm tree itself and another for its edible tip. There are several words for the stages of ripeness of the coconut, and others for the leaves, trunk, and roots. I think that's because we use the tree in so many different ways for food, building materials, fuel, or decoration."

*Mohamed Shakir, Maldives*

"In Thai the value we place on politeness is reflected in our language. There are several levels of formality that affect the structure of our language, so that we do not use the same forms in interactions between the common people as we would if we spoke to a monk. There is also a special language form for the Monarch. We also greet very respectfully. The literal translation of "Hello, King" would be "May the power of the glow of the dust under your majesty's foot bless me." So it's quite obvious that we honour the monarch."

*Phiriyaphong Chaengchenwet, Thailand*

"In Finnish we have no "he" or "she" even for people. We use "han" which is both and gives us a gender-neutral language. It's not confusing because we add extra words in a context where it's relevant to know whether someone is male or female."

*Kati Temonen, Finland*

"We can't translate the Koran to any other language. The Arabic is perfect, given by God—Allah—to Mohamed, and if we translated it, it would lose its perfection."

*Isaac Sadaquah, Jordan*

of time, or of group identity, or of hierarchy to a language which speaks and thinks quite differently?

As languages are lost, knowledge is also lost. We lose with that knowledge entire perspectives on what it is to live as human beings in the world.

## Language: roles in our lives

At the beginning of this chapter, we asked you to think about all the roles that you give language in your life, focusing on a single day. What did you come up with?

How does the list below compare with the one you made? In including the last role, we might be cheating a bit, because major rituals like a wedding are not part of our ordinary single day.

- We think, using the symbols of language as tools for thought.
- We interact socially, connecting with others through greeting and conversation.

- We share information of all kinds – news passed between friends, knowledge in the classroom, reports in the media, research of academic and professional conferences and journals.
- We persuade others, and are persuaded by others, as we exchange our views on how things are and how they ought to be.
- We express our emotions, possibly by speaking of them directly or possibly by using emotionally connotative language.
- We create. We use language imaginatively in storytelling and literature. We play with language as we joke. We shade it with irony, innuendo, or other subtle tonal variations. We make it into lyrics of a song. We take pleasure in language for its own sake.
- We affect the actions around us and our own part in them: we give instructions, make requests, offer to do things, make promises.
- We perform words in ritual contexts, such as in courts, ceremonies, or religious rites.

These words have the power to change our lives: we say "I do" and in pronouncing wedding vows change our personal and social lives thereafter.

## Overcoming limitations

When we look at all the ways we use language, it is hard to think about ways in which language is limited or has its problems. Just as we commented regarding sense perception, language is what it is – and the *idea of limitation* is something that we develop ourselves as we set goals and imagine what else our language might be.

What, then, are the problems we face with language as a way of knowing?

- Is the ambiguity of language a problem? Is precision equally important in all functions of language, all areas of knowledge, and all professions?
- To what extent and in what ways does the variety of languages create problems in communication? What problems does translation face? Would it be better for knowledge if everyone spoke the same language worldwide?
- What kinds of experiences elude language altogether? Do we have alternative means of communication?

You may find that, in dealing with these questions about the apparent limitations of language, you have pulled together many of the threads of discussion woven through this chapter. You may also find that the limitations of language are woven tightly together with some of the very characteristics that make it splendidly human and variable. We have to use this way of knowing with care, recognizing how we can go wrong, but also with appreciation, seeing how far we go right.

### For Reflection

If you speak more than one language, do you find that you cannot easily translate from your own language such things as cultural events, relationships, or ways of thinking?

In learning another language, do you find that it has words, expressions, or constructions that you begin to miss in your own language?

## Language: a TOK way of knowing

Language is surely one of our most influential ways of knowing. It is our primary means of building bridges between personal knowledge and shared knowledge, for passage in both directions. With language, we are not isolated and solitary in our thoughts, but socially and culturally connected with others – including others in the past through oral histories and the written archive, both of which language makes possible. The particular language communities in which we grow up, with their fusion of culture and language, influence how we make sense of the world.

In the exchange that language facilitates, it affects and is affected by all of the other ways of knowing – our memories and emotions, our intuitions and faith, our observations and imaginations, and our process of reasoning. Yet in the interaction of ways of knowing, it is often language which gives us the best access to understanding the others. It is, after all, an indicator of our assumptions and values, and the other features of our perspectives on the world.

Moreover, language is a necessary part of one of our three kinds of knowledge. Although experiential knowledge and skills are both affected by language, knowledge claims ("I know that...") in particular depend entirely on language: it is a necessary characteristic of a claim that it be expressed in words. And then the fun begins! With our knowledge claims and all of our other uses of language in our lives, we step into that zone of exchange. There, in the babble of billions of voices and the copious production of text, we communicate, exchange, and create the knowledge of the world. Thank you, language.

# Fallacies of argument 2: tactics of language

Below we identify just four common devices of persuasion which can subvert an argument and lead to conclusions on grounds other than good justification.

## 1. Repeated affirmation

Effective communication sometimes repeats key points; teaching certainly does. Repeated affirmation, though, is a device designed not to teach or clarify but to drum ideas deep into our minds through catchy slogans or emotionally powerful key words. The repetition of memorable phrasing threatens to replace analysis, evidence, or thoughtful argument as an influence on the conclusions we reach or the actions we take. In our era of glib communication and media sound bites, we are vulnerable to having our thinking packaged and polished into turns of phrase that serve the interests of their creators.

> "
>
> ### Repeated affirmation: Hitler
>
> from Adolf Hitler in Mein Kampf, 1925
>
> "[Propaganda's] effect for the most part must be aimed at the emotions and only to a very limited degree at the so-called intellect. We must avoid excessive intellectual demands on our public. The receptivity of the great masses is very limited, their intelligence is small, but their power of forgetting is enormous. In consequence of these facts, all effective propaganda must be limited to a very few points and must harp on these slogans until the last member of the public understands what you want him to understand by your slogan.[19]
>
> "

## 2. Jargon

The specialized vocabulary of any field is its jargon. It becomes a fallacy only when it is lifted out of its appropriate context and used not to communicate but to impress. Numbing and incomprehensible, it gives the audience the illusion that the speaker is an expert and stuns into silence their capacity to ask critical questions.

## 3. Innuendo

This device of indirect suggestion is sometimes used to imply faults in an opponent or a target without the risk of direct assertion or accusation. (Have you ever encountered Iago in Shakespeare's *Othello*?) Reading "between the lines", the audience picks up the inference without necessarily noticing that no knowledge claim has explicitly been made: "Is it possible that he is a racist? I would be sorry to think so."

---

[19] Hitler, A. 1925. *Mein Kampf*. Boston, USA, Houghton Mifflin. P 176. Cited in Pratkanis, A. and Aronson, E. 2001. *Age of Propaganda: The Everyday Use and Abuse of Persuasion*. New York, USA. W. H. Freeman and Company. Pp 318–9.

## 4. Persuasive metaphors

Although it can be argued that common idioms of language are already metaphorical (such as the way many European languages speak of saving, wasting, and budgeting time as though it were money), the deliberate use of analogy in argument should snap a critical thinker to attention. How is that metaphor being used?

Analogies between unlike things can often help to clarify points in an argument. They can help us think of something unfamiliar and difficult to grasp it in terms of something familiar and comprehensible. Huge stretches of time are sometimes pictured in this way so that our own lifetimes can be measured as fragments of seconds on a clock (whose face represents the time that humans have lived on the earth), or given as fragments of millimeters on a rope (whose length in metres we can comprehend).

However, metaphors can also be used to trick us to think and interpret in a certain way. For example, if a political leader presents his enemy or a situation he opposes as a cancer, and represents himself as being prepared to remove the cancer, he takes by extension of the metaphor the role of a surgeon, with the goal of saving and healing. Wouldn't you support him? The opponent, in political rhetoric, is often associated in metaphor with disease or rot. Historically, one of the most persuasive analogies used to justify violence has been "you can't make an omelet without breaking eggs".

Any one thing always has something in common with any other one thing, so it is not difficult to draw on selected likenesses to suggest others, and to use metaphor to replace the reasoned steps of an argument with the associations of an image – to reach whatever conclusion the speaker desires:

- "The mind is like a knife, cutting through difficult problems; just as too much cutting dulls a knife, so too much studying dulls the mind."
- "The mind is like a knife, cutting through difficult problems; just as being buffed on a whetstone sharpens a knife, so studying hard sharpens the mind."

Metaphors plant an image, already interpreted, in the audience's minds. Witness arguments for sticking to traditions or welcoming changes:

- "A house without strong foundations will collapse; our country without the traditions on which it was built will have no foundations at all."
- "Instead of trying to repair a poorly designed, decaying house on shaky foundations, we have the space and imagination to build a new."

### Discussion Activity

#### Make your own metaphors

#### Round 1

Place yourself in the role of a promoter, persuading others to favour your product.

*Suggestions for your product:* A luxury product such as diamonds or furs, a cosmetic product such as hair dye or lipstick, an electronic device for communication, any team or group, or any ideology. Then choose one metaphor to present it positively and persuasively.

*Suggestions for your image:* Nature is a good source of images. You might use the waxing and waning moon, the changing seasons, life-giving rain, interdependent species of an ecosystem, a beautiful bird, a river thundering powerfully between its banks or flooding the plains, or the shine of the moon upon the ocean.

*Suggestions for the structure*: Comparisons involving your product's special qualities, its abundant uses, its growing popularity, its "natural" place in the consumer's life. Try: "Just as X does this, so too does Y."

#### Round 2

Change your metaphor now to counter the persuasion you attempted in round 1, in order to get the feel of how an image can be used from different perspectives. For example, if you used rising ocean tides as a metaphor for the growing popularity of your product, you might re-interpret the rising tides as growing public realization that the product is a scam. Similarly, you might use falling tides or currents as a metaphor for the product's dropping popularity. Do not expect to shape the perfect poetic metaphor. Just play with this feature of language, which can so powerfully affect how we think.

# Representation and perspectives

## Language and perspectives

Exchanging knowledge is an active process, in which our symbolic systems carry much of the communication. But what perspectives give shape to that communication? We can often recognize them by reading critically. (Did you do the activity on slanted writing on page 144?)

## 1. Selection

Out of all possible events or details that could have been reported, what has been selected? Can you even tell whether you are getting the whole picture or just a small slice? Whose voice is reported and whose is left out?

> Who or what organization owns or controls the report that you are reading? Are you familiar with the biases of the author, newspaper, magazine, radio or television programme where you find an account? (Media generally have some sort of default bias, and most are well known.) Is it possible to compare the account with another from another source?

> Is a topic presented from a particular "angle" that alerts you to other versions that have been left out? Is a hotly disputed area of forested land spoken of as "natural habitat" for animals, "recreational parkland" for people, or "resources" for the economy? Is a complex situation presented through a single lens? For instance, how is the nuclear accident at Fukushima in 2011 presented? It can be portrayed in different lights: a tragedy with deep human dimensions, a warning of the dangers of nuclear power generators, an example of failed governmental policies and safety controls, a story of courage and creativity in coping with disaster. What else?

## 2. Emphasis

Out of all the events or details reported, what has been stressed as most important, and what do the guiding values or criteria seem to be for this emphasis?

> How has the emphasis been achieved: through placement at the beginning of an article rather than its end, through more detailed or vivid treatment of some details rather than others, through quoting an "expert" or particular eyewitness, through placement of ideas in emphasized positions in sentences (main clause) or in very short sentences that stand out (sub clauses)?

## 3. Colouring: emotion and values

What connotations of emotion or values colour the use of language? The choice of words and expressions in the description may tell you more about the writer's perspective than about the thing being described.

> To what extent is the language connotative and suggestive? Are emotions and values expressed explicitly, or do they colour the choice of language? Is a person described as "courageous" or "reckless", as "relaxed" or "lazy", as "curious" or "nosy", as "assertive" or "pushy", as an "environmentalist" or an "extremist"?

> What is *implied* by key words as they are used, calculatedly, in political context: consider, for example, the variable connotations of much used

words such as "reform", "stability", "flexibility", or "junk science"? "Skeptic", for example, can be employed as a respectful term for a critical thinker who considers all evidence objectively, or a derogatory term for someone who cynically refuses evidence. Political factions often compete to make the public speak and think in particular terms or slogans, with the connotations created through their publicity.

## 4. Relationship of parts

Are the parts of a news account sequenced as an argument that is *stated*, with linear presentation, logical connections and verbal transitions? Or are they presented as a juxtaposition of descriptions or images placed together so that, in their association, the meaning is *implied*?

Poetry often uses a method of juxtaposition – placing images side by side to stir meaning in the reader's mind by the association of one with another, in the space between. So does photography in assembling isolated moments, and film through its editing. So does journalism that cuts from anecdotal story to anecdotal story. Are the anecdotes used to imply the general situation, or are they used to illustrate a general situation established otherwise, through evidence-based generalization?

## 5. Framing in context

In what context has the account been placed and how is it identified with headlines and accompanying images? How might this framing affect the overall meaning of the passage? What does its purpose seem to be? "Troops Abandon War-Gutted Iraq" creates a different effect from "Troops Arrive Home to Joyous Families", especially if the former is accompanied by photographs of destroyed buildings and the latter by hugging families.

# Maps and perspectives

In the following two games, be as subtle or as flagrant as you wish as you use maps of the world to support your point of view. Use the same five basic characteristics of representation we outlined above, but apply them now to maps. Selection and emphasis can be given by choice of projection and centring, while emotional colouring can be given by choice of colours, naming, and overlaid graphics. To refresh your memory on projections and framing, flip back to chapter 1.

Divide into groups of four to six people. Your group should plan together both parts A and B of one of the persuasion exercises, then divide into two smaller groups to design the two maps in detail. When you are ready, present your results and identify your tactics of persuasion.

## Round 1: nuclear testing

**A** You are the president of a European country. You want to test nuclear weapons in a region in the South Pacific despite the protests of much of your own population and many other countries. You want to persuade Europeans that the faraway nuclear testing does little damage and certainly will not hurt Europe. What kind of map do you use to persuade them? Design it.

**B** You are a leader in a worldwide environmental organization. You are distressed that the president of a European country is testing nuclear weapons in the South Pacific and want to communicate the damaging impact of the blasts on both the immediate region and the rest of the planet. You want to support the protests that are already coming from many countries. What kind of map do you use to persuade them to protest more strongly? Design it.

## Round 2: threatened invasion

**A** You are the leader of a small country threatened by the strength of a neighbouring one which has recently been showing far too much interest in your natural resources, and is looming large all around you. You want to persuade the rest of the world to pay attention to your problem and to side with you in case of threatened invasion. What map do you use to show yourself as threatened and awaken sympathy? Design it.

**B** You are the leader of a large country with a great need of natural resources. A neighbouring country, fairly small and militarily insignificant, has a concentration of exactly the resources you need. You are considering various ways to gain them – through trade or possibly through invasion. You want to prepare your own population and the rest of the world for a "merger" of your country with your neighbour. What map will you use? Design it.

# Photos and perspectives

## Activity 1: photographs and communication

Choose one photograph that you find particularly powerful in communication or pleasing to look at, taken from any source (possibly your own work). National Geographic and the International League of Conservation Photographers, for example, have some superb photos on their websites, and news sources such as Reuters have online galleries of their best recent photos. Everyone in your class must choose one photograph. Then in groups of four or five, discuss your own and others' chosen images.

1. Describe your own response to each image (What is it "saying"? Why do you like it?) and consider how some of the following might affect that response: centring, angle, focus, colour, moment in time, and shapes in composition. If anyone in your group is taking IB art courses or doing CAS activity in visual arts, use that person's training to extend what you might notice yourself about skills in technique and expression.

2. Then discuss the following questions:

   - A photograph corresponds to the world in taking a "copy" of it through technology. Does it therefore satisfy the truth check of correspondence as giving a true representation of the world? What problems arise in taking a photograph as a simple copy of reality?
   - A photograph does not make explicit statements. To what extent can a photographic record be judged true or false as statements in language can be?

## Activity 2: photo and persuasion

If you have access to digital cameras and computers for enhancing images, plan with your class photographic coverage of a selected event that many in the class will be attending. Divide your class into small groups, and adopt different perspectives on the event for this activity. From what story angle are you viewing it? For a school event, for instance, what is the emphasis for your story: young leaders for tomorrow, people of different ethnic backgrounds working well together, teenage alienation from school experience, teachers as inspiring role models, or institutional and authoritarian oppression of the young? These are merely suggestions! Each group should plan the kind of photos to take to demonstrate the perspective it has chosen to adopt.

Before taking pictures, consider whether your group should ask anyone's permission to take and use them. In taking the photos, freeze your selected moments in time and space into images, considering the photo frame and focus. Select three photos to tell your story. In enhancing them on the computer, consider cropping, lighting, saturation, and any other effects you can achieve with the programme you are using – all to make your point more effectively. In presenting them to the rest of the class thereafter, plan their order and visual relationship to imply the meaning that connects them. Write the headline that would best communicate your story.

### Follow-up discussion

Present your images as "evidence" for the perspective you have chosen to take on the event, and explain to the rest of the class the choices you made. Look closely at the versions of the same event created by other groups from the class.

- Are all your versions equally true – simply different angles on the same event? To what extent did the angle you chose tempt you to exclude counter-views that would have been relevant? At what point would you say that your story stopped being true?
- If you enhanced or manipulated your photographs, do they still legitimately record the moment? In the sliding scale between brightening a dark photo and digitally modifying the image, where do you draw the line and say, "That's not a photograph anymore"?
- In what ways is your treatment of photographs like – or unlike – the treatment that could be given in language? (If your group is ambitious, you might want to write the story as well and create a newspaper page.)

152

## Statistics and perspectives

Enter imaginatively into the following scenario. The government of your country, trying to encourage equal employment opportunities for the Red group and the Blue group, has promised a financial bonus to any company that demonstrates that it treats the two groups equally. Use the data provided to present two contrasting responses.

## Round 1: from the Red perspective

You are the Red owner of a company hiring from both the Reds and the Blues. You want to demonstrate that you give equal employee benefit to each group in order to gain the government bonus. You claim: "I treat Reds and Blues equally. In fact, if I have any leaning *at all* it is towards giving greater benefit to the Blues." Present and justify your argument as persuasively as possible.

## Round 2: from the Blue perspective

You are a Blue worker who wants to demonstrate that the company does not treat employees equally, and does not deserve the bonus. Your claim: "Reds and Blues are not treated equally in this company, with its Red owner. Reds have much greater job opportunity." Present and justify your argument as persuasively as possible.

You may want to take into account any of the following:

- your definition of "job opportunity" and "equal treatment"
- the average salary calculated as the mean (the sum of all the salaries, divided by the number of wage earners), the median (the mid-point salary), or the mode (the most commonly occurring salary). Be aware that these averages can be used differently to illustrate different things!
- the mean average salary for Reds and for Blues separately
- inclusion or exclusion of the owner's income in averages
- the number of workers of each group, and their distribution across the hierarchy
- the ratio of salaries to each other between individuals and groups.

### Company incomes: data

Income and distribution, owner and employees

| 100,000 | Red (owner) |
| 50,000 | Red, Red, Blue |
| 40,000 | Red, Red, Blue |
| 30,000 | Red, Red, Blue, Blue |
| 20,000 | Red, Red, Blue, Blue, Blue |
| 10,000 | Red, Red, Blue, Blue, Blue, Blue, Blue, Blue, Blue, Blue |

## Conclusion

Is persuasion towards a way of seeing and thinking – whether achieved through language, maps, or images – something necessarily to be treated with suspicion? What is the role of effective persuasion in the exchange of knowledge? Why are some methods of persuasion treated as fallacies and some treated as reasonable justifications for an argument? What is the essential difference?

# 9. Emotion as a way of knowing

## Language: defining emotion

Our emotions accompany us throughout our lives so thoroughly and profoundly that we can scarcely consider any of the other ways of knowing without their interwoven emotions. Certainly our sense perceptions, imagination, and memories are affected, surely our faith, and definitely the shadings of our language. We have learned recently how significant emotion is, too, to the intuitions and reasoning of our cognitive processing. Yet for all the colour they give our lives – or all the extreme joy, grief, and turbulence – we find it difficult to pin down what emotions are and why they affect us. Do we know our emotions? Is emotion a way of knowing anything beyond the emotion itself?

The derivation of the word "emotion", like "motivation", is from the Latin *movere*, meaning "to move". We know that emotions can be activated by external causes (being chased by a snarling dog causes fear) and internal causes (one may wake up feeling sad one morning but not know why). We know, too, that different cultures and languages catalogue the emotions in different ways. We know, further, that practitioners in all areas of knowledge are motivated by emotion in their search for or creation of knowledge, and in some areas treat it also as subject matter (notably the arts and psychology). Moreover, the relationship between the emotions and our cognitive (intellectual) apparatus – that is, what we know, think, believe, desire, and value – continues to be the subject of academic discussion and debate among philosophers, artists and writers, psychologists, and neuroscientists. Still, for all the millennia of preoccupation with this "moving" aspect of our lives, there is no universally agreed-upon definition and categorization of emotion, or agreement about the boundaries between emotions and thought.

This lack of a clear common understanding, distilled into a definition, is considered a challenge in many fields that study emotion.

---

## Discussion Activity

### Emotion and IB subjects

In which of the IB subjects taught in your school do you think emotion is most significant as a factor in knowing – knowing your own emotions and those of others? To what extent is emotion part of the *subject matter* of these courses or the *methods* of the subject that lead to the content you are learning?

- What is the role of emotional response, imaginative engagement, and empathy in treating the literature in your IB course? To what extent does literature take emotional and subjective experiences as its *subject matter* and its *method*? To what extent is emotional engagement an important part of the reader's *response* and critical *evaluation*?
- What role do emotions play in your subject from group 3 individuals and societies? Are they part of what you study in the human *subject matter*? Do they have a place in the *methods* of study of the subject? Have you ever been encouraged *not* to become emotional in your response to the subject matter so that you would know it more truly – or the opposite?
- In your group 4 science course and in the mathematics of group 5, have you entered an emotion-free zone in either *subject matter* or *method* of study? Do you think that becoming passionate about an aspect of mathematics or science can affect how well you know it?
- In your group 6 subject of art, music, theatre, film, or dance, what is the role of emotion in *subject matter*, *method of creation*, and *evaluation*? Do you have to know the artist/composer's emotion in order to know the work? If you feel no emotional response yourself to a piece of music or art, can you know it? Conversely, if you want to evaluate a work of art, do you have to be dispassionate and rational?

## Discussion Activity

### What do they feel?

1. For each of these pictures, identify the emotion felt. Write a caption: what do you think the people are thinking or saying?

2. Compare with your classmates. Did you all interpret the emotion in the same way? What features did you emphasize in your caption?

In psychological research, a common understanding is essential to being able to share and build on ideas. Klaus Sherer, a psychologist researching emotion, comments that definitions "need to be consensually considered as useful by a research community". The purpose of a common understanding of emotion, he explains, is "in order to guide research, make research comparable across laboratories and disciplines, and allow some degree of cumulativeness". He comments further on the usefulness of definitions: "they are quite central for the development of instruments and measurement operations – as well as for the communication of results and the discussion between scientists."[1] How, after all, can the sharing of knowledge work if the researchers are talking about different things, with no common concept or model?

The importance of a definition of emotion finds an echo in philosophy, though a good definition there does not serve the same purposes of research and measurement. "There is no widely accepted taxonomy of the inner life," acknowledges professor of religious ethics Diana Fritz Cates:

The philosophical task is…to propose a definition of "emotions" that helps those who ponder it to make better sense of some features of their own and other people's experience and behavior. The task is to offer a conception that may differ from those that readers bring to the inquiry, but a conception that has greater power than other conceptions to promote self-understanding and the understanding of other human beings, to enhance interpersonal communication, and in other ways to improve the quality of personal and communal life.[2]

The absence of a single concept of what emotions even *are* is an immediate indication of the complexity of the topic we are approaching here.

> "
> One of the pitfalls of childhood is that one doesn't have to understand something to feel it. By the time the mind is able to comprehend what has happened, the wounds of the heart are already too deep.[3]
>
> *Carlos Ruiz Zafón*
> "

---

1 Shere, K. "What are emotions? And how can they be measured?" *Social Science Information*. Vol 44, number 4. P 724.
2 Fritz Cates, D. June 2003. "Conceiving Emotions: Martha Nussbaum's Upheaval of Thought," *Journal of Religious Ethics*, Volume 32, issue 2. P 327.
3 Zafón, C.R. 2004. *The Shadow of the Wind*. trans. L. Graves, London, UK. Penguin Books. P 35.

**Identifying emotion**

1 Freeze the class for a moment or two of silent reflection on these two questions:

   a. What are you feeling right now, at this moment? How do you know?

   b. Why do you think you're feeling this way?

Then share your thoughts. Do any difficulties come up in knowing, naming, or explaining your own emotions of the moment?

2 Do you think that some people are more emotionally "knowable" than others? Look around your class. Think of your friends and family. What would make you nominate one or two people in your life as "most knowable" emotionally?

3 To what extent do you think knowing your own feelings is dependent on knowing the feelings of others, and knowing the feelings of others depends on knowing your own? To what extent is knowing emotion entirely personal knowledge, and to what extent can it be shared knowledge?

## Knowing our emotions

It is likely that our emotions have prompted us to reflection more frequently than other ways of knowing. We may be more likely to ask ourselves, "Why am I feeling this way?" than "Why am I hearing this way?" or "Why am I speaking this way?" The perceptual sweetness of honey has provoked fewer songs than the emotional "sweetness" of love.

Yet how do we know our emotions? Before we go on, push your own reflection further with the activity "Identifying emotion". It is likely that by focusing on the few questions in this activity, you will have identified key topics that are being actively researched by psychologists and neuroscientists right now.

To an extent, though, one answer seems very straightforward. You know your emotions because you feel them. Just as only you know your own sense experience of the world "from inside", only *you* know your own emotions directly, as something felt inside *yourself*. If you say, "Right now, I know I am happy," (or depressed or in love) you mean that your direct experiential knowledge leads you to this conclusion.

But can you be *wrong* when you identify your own feelings? Those who know you well may give you, at times, some indication that you seem to be feeling something that you had not yet noticed yourself. You might realize through others, for example, that you are under stress, excited, jealous, or falling in love. Many people have benefited from counseling, which has helped them to recognize their emotions and be able to deal with them better when they are troubling.

Indeed, as soon as you think about what you are feeling and try to identify it, you are already moving beyond direct personal experience into the reflection characteristic of experiential knowledge. You are, even as you name your emotion, moving into shared knowledge of *language*, and if you try to explain how you know and why you feel this way, you are probably involving further knowledge through *sense perception* and *reason*. Knowing our *own* emotions, as personal knowledge, involves the knowledge we share with others.

Perhaps it is not surprising, then, that some of the ways of identifying our emotions include language, observation (using sense perception), and reasoning. All three provide highly interconnected ways of associating the emotions we experience with those that other people experience, and allow us to emerge from solitary introspective awareness into some degree of shared knowledge.

### For Reflection

What kinds of jobs or social roles do you think most demand "emotional intelligence"? Can you think of many jobs or social roles that do not require it, to a degree?

In what parts of your own life do you find yourself most needing this kind of interpersonal and intrapersonal awareness?

Understanding emotion – our own and others' – has been spoken of in many discussions of recent years as "emotional intelligence". Howard Gardner put forward in his book *Frames of Mind* in 1983 a theory of multiple intelligences, including *inter*personal intelligence and *intra*personal intelligence.

These two kinds of intelligences are related, and both indicate that emotion acts as a way of knowing some of what we probably value as crucial knowledge in life:

- *inter*personal intelligence means understanding other people and their motivations and implies being able to work well in cooperation and collaboration. All sorts of people successful in working with others display these skills to a high degree.
- *intra*personal intelligence involves similar abilities turned inwards towards oneself to be able to recognize one's own emotions and be able to control them appropriately.[4]

## Can we know emotion through language?

Our ability to give names to emotions and speak of them with others indicates an emotional life shared with others. This sense of shared human experience is essential to our bonding with others as social creatures. However, how do we know that what we experience ourselves is the same as someone else has experienced and means by a word?

When we considered sense perception as a way of knowing in an earlier chapter, we wondered whether we all mean the same thing when we call an object "red". The ambiguity of our words increases significantly when we call an emotion "love" or "sadness", since we are no longer dealing with objects. We can point to a red object and say, "This thing, this is red" but cannot point to the feeling of sadness, "Look, this is sadness." Although you do understand when a friend tells you she is "sad", you have to accept ambiguity in the communication: our words refer only roughly to the emotional experiences and bring them into shared communication in an approximate way.

The imprecision in naming emotions is increased because they do not stay still. The emotion that

you felt five minutes ago may have changed, or it may have changed even as you reflected upon it and named it. This shifting reality is at least acknowledged by our use of different categories for our emotional experiences. Your "feelings" of the moment that you are aware of through reflection may shift quickly, but your longer term "mood", such as cheerful or gloomy, might remain as your emotional background, and your overall "temperament" might incline you towards holding some kinds of emotions as part of your personality.

Emotions are even more difficult to classify because they may mix together. An emotion can, metaphorically, be experienced as red and yellow simultaneously without being orange, in a way which reasoning would condemn as contradictory. It is, arguably, possible to be sad and happy at the same time, for example, at a wedding, or to feel love's "sweet sorrow" as Juliet does in parting from Romeo. Arguably, too, it is possible to feel love and

Degas *Absinthe (1876, France)*

### Ways of knowing and the arts

What is your reaction to this painting, and why? Is it affected by *sense perception* and interpretation – your "reading" of the body language of the woman? Is it affected by *language* – by the name of the painting? Absinthe is a liquor that in Degas' time was a matter of social concern. How is the emotional effect of depression and isolation created by the composition of the painting, a *reasoned* formal decision by the painter? The arts often communicate emotion, but often use other ways of knowing to do so.

---

[4] Goleman, D. 1995. *Emotional Intelligence*, Toronto and New York. Bantam. Appendix A.

# The Man, His Wife and the Other Woman: A Very, Very, Very Short Novel

## Chapter I

"I'll be back soon, dear." With a quick squeeze of his hand, his wife was gone, and he was left an opportunity to sit down and rest his weary feet.

The fresh aroma of the famous house coffee filled his nostrils, and he decided upon a cappuccino with just a light dusting of cinnamon, and, of course, the chocolate torte. From the shade of the umbrella over his small table he soaked in the warmth of the summer and noticed the gentle breeze that stirred his hair and rustled his newspaper. He was aware of the glorious colour of the blossoms among the greenery of the park across the street and the laughter of children at play.

He glanced at the clock. Still plenty of time to relax! He turned to the sports page.

*What emotion do you think the character is experiencing? How can emotion affect our sense perceptions of our surroundings? How can our sense perceptions of our surroundings affect our emotions?*

## Chapter 2

Someone, he realized, had approached his table. He looked up, then froze. A woman in blue stood absolutely still less than a metre away, looking directly at his face.

"It's been a long time," she said.

"Yes. A long time."

"I saw her leave. Your wife."

"Yes, my wife. My wife."

A waiter approaching with a menu hesitated, and then retreated to leave them alone.

"I didn't think," he faltered, "that I would ever see you again."

*This text doesn't give the feelings of the characters, just actions and dialogue. If you were the director of this film, what emotions would you tell the actors to play and how, in their actions, should they suggest them to the audience? Is there more than one interpretation of this scene?*

## Chapter 3

"I'll be in the bookstore by the church at 10:00 tomorrow morning. If you joined me, we could go somewhere...and talk," she offered, her eyes shining. "Maybe we could even...even go back to my place. For...some lunch."

"Oh yes!" he gasped. "But what if HE found out? You mustn't put yourself at risk!"

"I don't care! I can't bear being separated from you forever! I can't let him rule my life."

"Even if it means being thrown out—cast out without a penny?"

"Yes! Yes!" she cried. "I am able now to take care of myself, and I must make my own choices."

*You may have an opinion as to whether or not what is going on in this scene is moral or not. But stop now to concentrate on the emotions involved. If this scene is a plan for a romantic rendez-vous, with both characters married to other people, what is your moral judgment not on their actions but on their feelings?*

## Chapter 4

"You know that Papa really will disinherit and reject you if he finds out," he countered, "just as he did me! He said he never wanted to see me again!"

"I tell you, I don't care!" she retorted. "I've missed you so much these past four years. We all have. At times I'm sure Papa misses you terribly, too, but he doesn't know how to admit it or apologize."

"Not a day goes by that I don't think of you, miss you all. It's hard to hide my feelings from Marie. I don't ever want her to feel that I regret marrying her."

"You should never have had to choose between her and your family," responded Violet firmly. "It's not her fault or yours that Papa is so prejudiced and has such a temper."

*What connotations does the title of this story encourage? Is the existence of the "romantic triangle" a generalization, a stereotype or a cliché? What's the difference?*

*The story now twists the conventions of the "other woman", as she turns out to be Paul's sister. The twist is also a convention of plot – the surprise revelation in comedy. If you were fooled and then surprised, what is your reaction to being tricked?*

*If you come from a culture where a father's wishes are to be respected at all costs, discuss your interpretation of the story with others from a more "liberal" country.*

## Chapter 5

They both looked up as a woman in white, carrying a tennis racket, approached swiftly.

"Marie!" he exclaimed joyfully, jumping up and scooping her into the curve of his arm. "Let me introduce my sister Violet."

"Violet! What a pleasure!" exclaimed Marie, smiling warmly at her. "You know, he misses you terribly – the whole family, but especially you."

"I didn't think you knew," stammered Paul.

"You never told me – in words," she smiled. "You didn't have to."

*Marie says she does not have to be told how Paul feels in order to know. She understands without words. In your experience, do some people seem to understand particularly well the feelings of others? Is empathy something you value in others, and in yourself? Is it a capacity you are born with or a skill that can be developed or even trained? To what extent is it emotion in action as a way of knowing?*

## Chapter 6

"I'm so sorry about the way my family has behaved," said Violet, "I was afraid to meet you because I thought you'd be hostile. But if you'll accept me, I'd like to welcome you as a sister."

Marie glanced from her sister-in-law to her husband, and smiled. "Of course I always hoped that someday Paul would have his family back."

Paul beamed at both of them, his wife and his sister standing together at last.

"You've made me so happy, both of you," he exclaimed from the heart.

"I'm so very happy, too," his sister cried. "I never want to be parted from you again."

"I'm very happy for both of you," said Marie softly, "but also for myself. Now I have a sister."

And this is the end of our story. It's a happy, happy, happy ending.

*They're all so happy – so they say. Does the fact that all three of them declare themselves to be "happy" mean that they are having identical emotional experiences?*

*Some cultures value expression of emotion in language more than others. From the perspective of your own cultural background, do these characters seem "normal" in their degree of emotional expression?*

*If I say that this is a "novel", does that make it a novel? What more, or what else, would you expect to fulfill the definition of a "novel"? Is it important to have a shared understanding of our concepts?*

Eileen Dombrowski

## Voices

Once I was speaking Persian on the phone with my sister and I was trying to explain to her how frustrated I was about something. In Persian we don't have a specific word for frustration so by the time I had tried to explain my emotion the meaning of what I was saying had slightly changed from what I really meant. My knowledge (of language in this case) became a tool for distinguishing the difference in my emotions, but its limitation was that I could only express it properly in the very same language that I had learnt it in.

*Nakhshab Farhikhtah*

hatred mixed together (in jealousy), or feel joy at the end of a trip at being reunited with your family at the same time as you feel sadness over leaving behind your friends.

However, if you suggested earlier that you can know emotion through naming feelings as you reflect on them, you are on the same track as many psychological researchers who are trying

## Voices

In Japan, we like to keep communication a little fuzzy. We prefer being able to understand from a hint and not being so precise. We have so many ways of suggesting and saying things indirectly that a foreigner couldn't catch.

Emotions are not shown as openly as in North America, though in our generation we do show more than our parents did. In terms of love, we're really shy. Parents don't say, "I love you" to their children and children don't say it to their parents. But we can still see it. The scale is just different.

We also have to be sensitive to relationships and circumstances as we speak politely, so that we choose a more respectful level of language when speaking to elders. In most schools in secondary education, we have to use the words giving respect to the older students, even if they are just a grade ahead.

But it's not as simple as having different levels of formality or politeness, because so many different factors are involved. There are more than ten ways of saying "you" depending on your respect for the person, a combination of your age and their age,

*Kohei Noda*

and their sex. Some choices sound a bit feminine but they are still okay for men, depending on the situation and the relationship. We can sound more loving, more hostile, more formal, more casual. The right choice of words communicates feelings for them.

to gain understanding of people's emotions by asking them to name them in context of psychological testing. Researchers immediately face choices of methods, all with their attendant difficulties. In response to scenarios, do they choose to ask respondents to name emotions freely – using whatever words they consider appropriate? They thereby gather words that fit emotions from the point of view of respondents, but their findings are obscured by hugely variable use of language. Or do they choose to give respondents categories in advance, and thereby force them to answer in pre-decided terms that might not quite be a match?

Have a look at the Geneva Emotion Wheel, used by psychological researchers at the Geneva Emotion Research Group.[5] It uses pairs of words to indicate a family of emotions, and uses different sizes of circles so that respondents can identify the intensity of the emotion. It is the result of considerable research in the spectrum of emotions. Does it seem to you to capture the family of emotions that you experience yourself? This

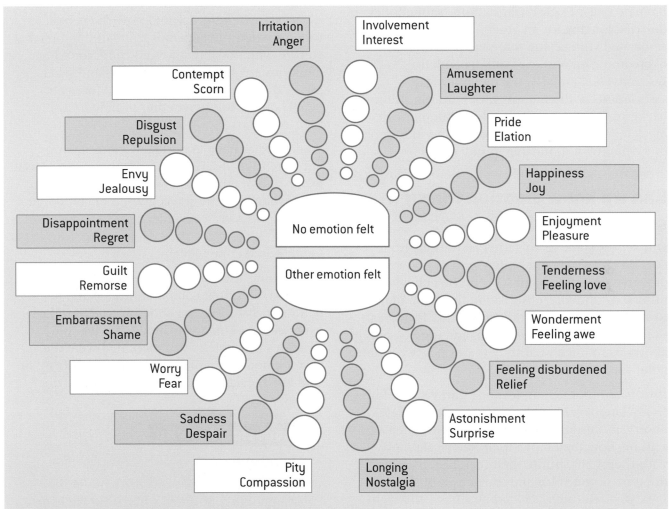

**The Geneva Emotion Wheel from the Geneva Emotion Research Group**

This diagrammatic presentation of basic emotions is used in psychological testing, so that participants in studies can respond to questions by identifying emotions elicited in specific circumstances. They can also identify the intensity of the emotion by the size of the circle along the lines that radiate out from the core. The emotion wheel is a thus a tool that enables emotional research to be done through language and naming.

---

[5]   Geneva Emotion Research Group, University of Geneva. http://www.unige.ch/cisa/gerg.html

research group translates the wheel to use it with respondents from different language groups. What is it thereby assuming or asserting about the universality of these families of emotions?

It is probably unsurprising, given the variability of ways of classifying and thinking about emotions, that different languages reflect, and possibly reinforce, particular feelings. The words that different cultures use to describe the emotional worlds of their members give us a clue about the way different structures may mould the emotional experiences of their people, according to David Matsumoto.[6] He reports, for example, that the Japanese words *itoshii, ijirashii,* and *amae* have no exact English translations, though they describe longing for an absent loved one, a feeling associated with seeing someone praiseworthy overcoming an obstacle, and dependence, respectively. Similarly, the metaphorical associations with emotion vary with the cultural background of the speakers, for example with black being associated with mourning in Europe but white with mourning in India.

## Can we know emotion through sense perception?

Our senses allow us to gather sensations from outside and inside our bodies, and to observe both our own physical responses and the behaviour of others. Admittedly, observation does not allow us to see the emotions of others directly. However, our senses allow us to observe, and our reasoning allows us to infer, according to our past experience, what the emotions must be.

How is another person feeling? Can you read his "body language"? When people communicate, observers gain information from seeing their actions: how they move their hands, sigh, play with their hair, shuffle their feet. Listeners catch the tone of the voice and the pauses of silence. We can often catch very subtle clues – the slight constriction of the lips or forehead, for instance, or the involuntary dilation of the pupils of the eyes. Highly acute observers, often not even conscious of their swift reading of tiny signals, are often

considered intuitive in their capacity to "sense" how someone else is feeling.

In observing a particular pattern of actions or gestures, we come to associate it with a particular emotion (with the help of other ways of knowing: the naming of language and generalizing of reasoning). Observation of others' actions can then give us a context for recognizing our own (and vice versa). You can realize that you are angry as you notice that you are sounding and acting like an angry person.

Attempts to know an emotion based on such observation, though, do encounter some evident problems. Misinterpretation is a constant danger, especially when we do not know the person very well, or when the person is from an unfamiliar culture with possibly different codes for what emotions are acceptable to express and what physical gestures are appropriate. Moreover, people often choose whether to hide or display their emotions.

Some studies have undertaken more rigorous and extensive observation, such as those on facial expression of emotion. Researcher Paul Ekman, internationally testing recognition of emotional facial expressions, concluded that four specific emotions were recognized everywhere: fear, anger, sadness, and enjoyment.[7]

The naming and classifying of these emotional responses and their combinations has not been without debate. Having done his studies of facial expressions, Ekman concluded that the four emotions his subjects had identified were the "core" emotions, rather like primary colours that could be the basis for shades and blends. Other

### Discussion Activity

#### Act and guess

Ask for a volunteer or two to go out of the room and then re-enter, simulating the body language of a particular emotion. The rest of the group tries to guess what emotion has been acted. Is there general agreement?

---

[6]  Matsumoto, D. 1996. *"The Diversity of Human Feeling", Culture and Psychology.* Florence, KY, USA. Brooks/Cole. Pp 247–251.

[7]  Evans, D. 2001. *Joy (some say "happiness"), distress (or "sadness"), anger, fear, surprise and disgust. Emotions.* Oxford, UK. Oxford University Press, P 7. You may also wish to look into Ekman's research into core emotions, and ongoing investigation into facial clues for lying. http://www.paulekman.com/.

psychologists, however, have argued for different sets of basic emotions, from Weiner and Graham's simple opposition of happiness and sadness to Tomkins' set of nine: anger, interest, contempt, disgust, distress, fear, joy, shame, and surprise.[8]

Attempts to identify emotion by recognizing facial expressions have recently led researchers to ask respondents in studies to indicate their own reactions to scenarios by pointing to cards showing expressions and gestures[9] or to animations that include sound.[10] The respondents identify their *own* emotional states by analogy to the observable behaviour of *others*. This method has been developed in part to assess emotional responses to new products before they are marketed.

## Is emotion physical?

Observation has also taken the form of biological study of the human body to tell us more closely what is going on "inside". Physiological changes in the body (heart rate, sweaty palms, and so forth) can be monitored as evidence of certain emotional states. In language we distinguish between the "physical" and the "emotional", but mounting medical findings indicate that this distinction cannot be made neatly. Emotions are affected by (or created by) our physical state, such as our biochemical balance, and our physical state, even our health, is affected by our emotions. Indeed, it has been argued that the biological condition is not just the *cause* of the emotion but *is* the emotion itself as we sense it.

Research into the chemical causes or components of emotion has led to better understanding of the physiology of emotion. This understanding has been extensively applied in the development of drugs to modify emotion, giving a medical solution to people suffering from troubling or debilitating emotional conditions. The extent to which a pharmaceutical solution has become prevalent in some countries, though, has caused concerns of its own. As one scholar at a 2009 Harvard conference on the topic declared: "In 1979, shyness had no

medical status, but by 1993, it had been elevated to the third-most-common mental disorder in the United States after depression and alcoholism. And the treatment? Antidepressants – for which 200 million prescriptions are written every year, earning drug companies over $10 billion annually…. Before you sell a drug you have to sell an illness."[11]

5 December 2009. A large march though central London called on world leaders to take action against climate change. What is the role of emotion in a protest like this one? What perspectives give rise to the emotions? (Consult the guiding questions page 28.) To what extent is empathy involved – imaginative and emotional concern for others?

When something outrages you, as Nazism did me, that is when you become a militant, strong and engaged. You join the movement of history, and the great current of history continues to flow only thanks to each and every one of us.[12]

*Stéphane Hessel*

8   Lancaster, J. 27 February 2006. "Pursuing Happiness," *The New Yorker*. http://www.newyorker.com/archive/2006/02/27/060227crbo_books accessed 20 November 2006.

9   European Network of Living Labs, http://knowledgecenter.openlivinglabs.eu/learn/techniques/emocards, accessed 11 May 2012.

10  Pieter Desmet, ID Studio Lab, http://studiolab.ide.tudelft.nl/studiolab/desmet/premo/, accessed 11 May 2012.

11  Ireland, C. 28 April 2009. "Scholars discuss 'medicalization' of formerly normal characteristics", *Harvard Gazette*, http://news.harvard.edu/gazette/ story/2009/04/scholars-discuss-'medicalization'-of-formerly-normal-characteristics/ accessed 10 May 2012.

12  Stéphane Hessel, French Resistance hero, author of *Time for Outrage*…and much more! We recommend that you look up his life story. He is quoted in Elaine Sciolino, "A Resistance Hero Fires Up the French," *The New York Times*, 9 March 2011. http://www.nytimes.com/2011/03/10/books/ stephane-hessel-93-calls-for-time-of-outrage-in-france.html?_r=1&pagewanted=all accessed 8 May 2012.

> "
>
> Emotions are not just the fuel that powers the psychological mechanism of a reasoning creature, they are parts, highly complex and messy parts, of this creature's reasoning itself.[13]
>
> *Martha Nussbaum*
>
> "

> "
>
> Not long ago people thought of emotions as old stuff, as just feelings – feelings that had little to do with rational decision making, or that got in the way of it. Now that position has reversed. We understand emotions as practical action programs that work to solve a problem, often before we're conscious of it. These processes are at work continually, in pilots, leaders of expeditions, parents, all of us.[14]
>
> *Antonio Damasio*
>
> "

The way we categorize emotions has implications for how we judge and how we act. The significance of the date of 1979 in the example just cited is that the following year saw the publication of a new edition of the *Diagnostic and Statistical Manual of Mental Disorders,* which American psychiatrists consult when diagnosing patients. It included for the first time several anxiety-related problems, such as "avoidant personality disorder", possibly traits that were admired as demureness and modesty in a different era. Did the creation of the new categories recognizing emotional problems afflicting many people – perhaps not truly equivalent to "shyness" – lead to them being taken seriously, and to sufferers being offered some relief at last? Or, from a different perspective, did the creation of the category create expectations and diagnoses of the disorder – and sell the drugs?

## Is emotion in opposition to reason?

A common belief that reason is far superior to emotion has come down to many of us influenced by the western philosophical tradition, along with the belief that they are equal-and-opposite. Have a glance back to the European medieval worldview in chapter 3 (page 61) to see the values placed on reason and emotion at the time. Emotion has not historically been considered a way of knowing at all, but instead a problem to be overcome in order to exercise reason.

To some extent, emotion does oppose reasoning in our responses to many situations. Emotions have a reputation for "clouding" our reasoning, preventing us from "clear" thinking when they "flood" over us. To reason clearly is to be able, potentially, to exercise control and restraint in our responses, in opposition to being "taken over" by the storm of uncontrolled emotions. Like laughter in the cinema, hatred and fear can spread to transform a crowd into a dangerous mob, anger can unleash violence and make a person a murderer, and even happy, uplifting emotions can be worked up to a crazed frenzy.

Many group excesses of emotion are stirred by *language* powerfully delivered by a demagogue, or the ideological manipulation of a leader who has "washed" people's minds. (Notice some of the metaphors for emotional or rational responses that we have mixed together here. Can you think of more? Are they neutral?)

Many of our swift emotional responses are also associated with *intuition*, understood as the rapid processing by our brains before we are even aware of thinking. (See the chapter on reason, "Intuitive system 1 and rational system 2" page 110.) The clearest case is our response to danger. There are neural pathways to the brain that allow certain stimuli, such as those that are perceived as dangerous, to shortcut the parts of the brain that think and go directly to the evolutionarily much more primitive parts of the brain, triggering an immediate fear response. That instant reaction can save us as we leap back from a threat, but may also cause us to misjudge the danger of the stimulus and to lash out – irrationally.

Certainly, the slower, more deliberate processing of reason does help us to appraise emotions and the actions that they could well prompt. It can help us to judge whether an emotional reaction "makes sense" in its context – or is in excess of the

---

[13] Nussbaum, M.C. 2003. *Upheavals of Thought: The Intelligence of Emotions*. Cambridge, UK. Cambridge University Press. P 3.

[14] Antonio Damasio, Director of the Brain and Creativity Institute at the University of Southern California, cited in Benedict Carey, "In Battle, Hunches Prove to Be Valuable", *The New York Times*, 27 July 2009. http://www.nytimes.com/2009/07/28/health/research/28brain.html?_r=1&pagewanted=1 &ref=todayspaper accessed 9 May 2012.

provocation. It can help us to evaluate potential consequences of responding to emotion, and even combine risk assessment with moral evaluation to check impulsive action that we might later regret.

A focus exclusively on swift and passionate reactions to situations, however, can yield an inaccurate view of the interaction of emotion and reason, and an imbalanced one. In fact, recent research indicates that reason and emotion are much more complementary than has often been thought. The classical case of Phineas Gage is often cited to demonstrate the close connection between our emotional and reasoning centres. In 1848 Cage suffered brain damage to his frontal lobes, which prevented him from both feeling any emotion and making any decisions.[15] Indeed, when people have suffered some kinds of brain damage, research has shown, "they see dozens of choices but lack immediate internal feelings of like or dislike. They must examine the pros and cons of every choice with their reasoning, but in the absence of feeling they see little reason to pick one or the other."[16]

Recent studies[17] also indicate that many of our normal decision-making capabilities – from choosing food to solving mathematical problems, from forming grammatical phrases to making

ethical choices – are affected by the emotional pleasure responses in our brains.

Indeed, studies in the cognitive sciences have indicated how deeply intertwined reason and emotion appear to be, at a pre-thinking intuitive level. They show that confirmation bias – our tendency to reinforce what we already believe – seems to blend our ways of knowing before we are conscious of thinking. What we already think affects what we feel; what we feel affects what we think.

The implications are intriguing for the way that reason and emotion act together as ways of knowing. They seem not only to allow us to build our beliefs and their justifications, but also to reinforce our beliefs. And those beliefs have a reciprocal effect on what we perceive through our *senses*, feel with our *emotions*, think with our *intuition* and *reason*, hold with our *faith*, entertain as possible with our *imaginations*, and shape with our *language*.

At least some (and according to some psychologists, all) emotions are cognitively dependent; that is, they depend on our thinking. For example, feeling indignation about something depends on our beliefs about what is and what is not a fair or just treatment of others. If two people's beliefs about what is fair in a certain

## For Reflection

**In your life, is it reason or emotion that guides?**

Would you agree with the assertion that reasoning can guide emotion?

a) Recall a few instances when you were really scared or really angry. In any one of these times, did your fear or anger subside when you got more information about what was happening? (For example, you were angry because your friend did not show up for a meeting, then found out he'd had a car accident on his way.)

b) Have you ever been madly in love with someone you were very attracted to, but upon spending more time with him and getting to know him, you concluded that you were better off without him – or her?

Would you agree with the assertion that emotion can guide reasoning?

a) What are the criteria you are applying to choose your path after you earn your IB diploma? You might face questions such as, "Which university should I attend?" Are all of the criteria you use for making the decision rational or are you also bringing in inclinations such as "like", "dislike", "passion", "interest", "motivation", or "enjoy" or even just "I have a feeling…"?

b) Imagine that you're not pressed for time and are working on a project. At some point, however, you decide that what you've done is good enough. Is this always a rational conclusion, or is there a feeling that tells you when to stop?

[15] Ratey, J.J. 2001. A User's Guide to the Brain: Perception, Attention, and the Four Theatres of the Brain. New York, USA. Pantheon Books. P 231

[16] Haidt, J. The Happiness Hypothesis, New York, USA. Basic Books. P 12.

[17] Philips, H. 11 October 2003. "The Pleasure Seekers." New Scientist. http://www.wireheading.com/pleasure.html accessed 20 November 2006.

> "Feelings are not substances to be discovered in our blood but social practices organized by stories that we both enact and tell.[18]
>
> *Michelle Rosaldo*

## For Reflection

### Emotion and collective beliefs

- What are your feelings about and towards your country? If you now live in a place where you were not born, how do you feel about your "new" country and about your parents' country or countries of origin?
- Do the words you used to describe these feelings have positive or negative connotations?
- Are these *your* feelings, which you developed independently? Or have you learned them (as you have learned the customs, manners and language of your community)?
- To what extent are your beliefs and emotions dependent on each other?

situation are very different from each other's they will most certainly have very different emotional responses. For example, think of a slave owner, an abolitionist, and a slave, faced with the slave being whipped for defiance. Their different responses will be influenced by their perspectives, with their components of assumptions, values, selected or familiar information, processes of validation, and implications (See page 28). Emotion, even though it often appears somehow raw and "natural", is quite evidently affected by what we believe and what situations we occupy in our lives. What we think and what we feel are deeply intertwined.

## Emotion and cultural self

To what extent, then, are our emotions cognitively and socially constructed? As always in the nature/nurture debate, there are people inclined to

emphasize what is *innate* in their arguments and investigation, and others inclined to emphasize what is *learned*. As you will recall from the chapter on language, it currently seems that our capacity for language is innate, but that, of course, the *particular* language we speak depends on the community in which we grow up. Nature first – and then nurture! It would seem that with emotion, too, the community at least influences how some of our emotions develop.

Even our sense of self, some researchers argue, is influenced by our cultures, and that our way of conceptualizing ourselves affects our experience of emotions.

This argument is put forward strongly by researchers Hazel Rose Markus and Shinobu Kitayama.[19] Although they acknowledge that their generalizations cannot apply to *all* members of a culture, they claim that the self in American and other Western societies is conceived of as an *independent*, separate unit, while the self in Asian and some other non-Western societies is conceived of as *interdependent* with others, adapting within different sets of relationships.

These basic cultural assumptions develop and are developed by the accompanying values. In fostering *in*dependence, a society values uniqueness, self-expression, development of personal potential, personal goal setting and personal achievement; members are encouraged to say what they think in a direct way. In fostering *inter*dependence, a society values fitting in with others, occupying a proper social place, acting appropriately for the particular context and its relationships, and promoting the goals and achievements of the group; members are encouraged to express themselves indirectly with sensitivity to the feelings of others. The comparison drawn by Markus and Kitayama echoes the dimensions of culture that we considered in chapter 1, as the sense of the self develops within a culture with its degree of power distance or its relative emphasis on individualism or collectivism.

How, then, do these cultural assumptions and values affect emotion, according to this view? For one thing, different emotions may be

---

[18] Rosaldo's study of the Ilongot of the Philippines, in P. Lauritzen, *Religious Belief and Emotional Transformation: A Light in the Heart*. 1992. Cranbury, NJ, USA. Associated University Presses. P 59.

[19] Markus, H R. and Kitayama, S. "Culture and the Self: Implications for Cognition, Emotion, and Motivation", *Psychological Review*. Vol 98, number 2. Pp 224–53. http://www.iacmr.org/v2/Conferences/WS2011/Submission_XM/Participant/Readings/Lecture8A_JiaLin/Markus%20et%20al%20(1991)%20Culture%20and%20Self%20-%20Implications%20for%20Cognition%20Emotion%20and%20Motivation-8a.pdf accessed 8 May 2012.

stirred. The independent person is more likely to experience anger, frustration, or pride, which are based in a sense of the individual self, while the interdependent person is more likely to experience sympathy and shame, which are based in the relationship with others. Thereafter, the independent person is more likely to express his emotions, in a culture where one does not suppress the authentic inner self, while the interdependent person is more likely to inhibit expression, in a culture where personal emotions should not intrude on social harmony.

For another thing, specific emotions are experienced, expressed, and regarded differently. Whether one should express anger is controversial in Western cultures, but is clearly inappropriate in interdependent ones, since it disrupts good feeling between people. Expression of anger may even be considered childish.[20] More significantly, anger is less likely even to be *experienced* in an interdependent culture: it would be dysfunctional to the self and incongruent with a social emphasis on being aware of the perspectives of others. Anthropologist Michelle Rosaldo has suggested that in a group she studied in the Philippines, there is no private sphere of the emotions in which anger can build up.[21]

In contrast, in interdependent cultures people may develop emotions that attach to relationships, such as a deep feeling of trusting dependence or a greater pain in loneliness. In the latter regard, a Japanese anthropologist has claimed that "the Japanese nightmare is exclusion, meaning that one is failing at the normative goal of connecting with others. This is in sharp contrast to the American nightmare, which is to fail at separating from others, as can occur when one is unduly influenced by others, or does not stand up for what one believes, or when one goes unnoticed or undistinguished."[22]

The degree to which emotions are innate or socially constructed remains a question of

## Discussion Activity

### Perspectives and emotions

It seems to be the perspectives that people hold that, to a large extent, stimulate and give direction to their emotions. Knowing the perspectives in each of the situations below, can you suggest what emotions the person is likely to feel?

*Situation 1:* Within an international committee assigned to consider claims to fishing rights in offshore waters, one member disagrees with the committee leader and puts forward strong arguments in support of his own point of view.

a. If another member of the group believes that good group decisions are best made and tested through exchanging counter-arguments and disagreements, even when they are voiced passionately, what is her reaction likely to be?

b. If a different member of the group believes that group harmony is supremely important and that people of higher rank such as the leader should be treated with deference, what is his emotional reaction likely to be?

*Situation 2:* The only jobs available for young people involve going far away and leaving the family.

a. If the young work seeker believes that everyone should "leave the nest" and be independent on reaching young adulthood, and possibly go out seeking adventure, what is his emotional reaction likely to be?

b. If the young work seeker believes that being together with family in interdependent relationships is extremely important, what is his emotional reaction likely to be?

To name any of these likely emotions, you might find the Geneva Emotion Wheel very useful. Notice that it provides not only paired names of emotions but also degrees of intensity. A situation that creates intense emotion in one person might pass unnoticed by another.

---

[20] Markus and Kitayama. P 236.

[21] Rosaldo's study of the Ilongot of the Philippines, in P. Lauritzen, *Religious Belief and Emotional Transformation: A Light in the Heart*. 1992. Cranbury, NJ, USA. Associated University Presses. P 59.

[22] Lebra (1976) referred to in Markus and Kitayama. P 237.

## Discussion Activity

### Knowing emotion: shame

>  The person who feels shame desires to speak and say he is imprisoned by a silent language made up of the story he tells himself in his inner world. But he dare not utter it for fear of your gaze. He believes saying it would make him die of shame. So instead, he tells the story of someone else just like him who has suffered this very same shattering experience.[22]
>
> *Boris Cyrulnik*

Embarrassment and shame are given as companion terms to identify a family of emotions on the Geneva Emotion Wheel. This is an emotion we hand to you for your own thought and class discussion.

- How do you know if you are experiencing this emotion? How do you know if others are experiencing this emotion?
- What circumstances make you feel this emotion? Can you be embarrassed over something even if no one else knows about it, or is it necessarily a social emotion?
- If you change the way you *think* of embarrassing circumstances, can you change the emotion itself?
- To what extent do you think that the capacity to feel embarrassment in young adulthood is an aspect of growing maturity and a growing social self-awareness?
- Does a feeling of shame depend on caring about others – their feelings and their judgments? If you cared nothing for others, would you never feel shame?
- Is someone from an independent and individualistic culture likely to experience and express this emotion in the same way as someone from an interdependent and collectivist culture?
- Can a group of people or a nation experience collective shame?
- Taking embarrassment/shame as your example for reference, how is emotion involved in knowledge? Is it a way of knowing something other than the emotion itself?

debate for theorists in the disciplines associated with cognitive science. It does seem apparent, though, that our experience of emotion is influenced to a significant extent by cultural and other perspectives, and that we are educated by our societies towards certain norms of emotional expression and behaviour.

## Empathy: Can it be taught?

Like a culture, many an educational system treats behaviour that is grounded in emotion and possibly the emotions themselves as educable – as being able to be shaped according to ideas of what is socially appropriate, morally right, and desirable.

The idea of directing or training the emotions necessitates some degree of removal from the raw experience of emotion, into reflective awareness at the very least. The Dalai Lama, the Tibetan Buddhist spiritual leader, for example, speaks of achieving happiness through "training the mind" but both *happiness* and the *mind* are set within broad concepts and perspectives: happiness involves a "loving kindness" and letting go of attachment to things of the world, and the mind involves much more than rational thinking:

> I believe that happiness can be achieved through training the mind…When I say "training the mind" in this context I'm not referring to "mind" merely as one's cognitive

[22] Cyrulnik, B. 2011. *Morirse de verguenza: El miedo a la mirada del otro*. Translated by Mimi Bick. Buenos Aires. Random House. P 12.

ability or intellect. Rather, I'm using the term in the sense of the Tibetan word *Sem*, which has a much broader meaning, closer to "psyche" or "spirit"; it includes intellect and feeling, heart and mind. By bringing about a certain inner discipline, we can undergo a transformation of our attitude, or entire outlook and approach to living.[23]

Much spiritual teaching regarding emotions has at its core a loving kindness to others, for example, the teaching of Jesus to "love your neighbour as yourself".[24] In spiritual teaching, as in cultural upbringing, emotions held towards others and appropriate behaviour towards others are extremely important.

In the IB educational system, the IB learner profile describes ideal IB learners as "caring" and frames the development of emotion within education with attitudes and goals:

> IB learners strive to be *caring*. They show empathy, compassion and respect towards the needs and feelings of others. They have a personal commitment to service, and act to make a positive difference to the lives of others and to the environment.[25]

One of the key qualities identified as a goal is "empathy" – a capacity to stand imaginatively in someone else's shoes, to see as if through their eyes, or to feel as if with their feelings. It demands a sense of common humanity and belief in the equal value of the other person ("respect"), and is associated with heartfelt concern for others if they are facing difficulties ("compassion").

Yet, even though empathy is significant in developing compassion and a moral response, it is only the starting point for effective and ethical action. Arguably, what is necessary thereafter is understanding of how others think and feel, as they may not respond emotionally exactly as you do yourself. Effective action on a worldwide scale, as in relief and development work, requires knowledge such as provided by history, the human sciences, and ethics.

Whether you go for gut feeling and naive empathy – or whether you make an effort to learn more about others *from their own perspectives* – can affect whether you are effective or not in working with others. Many a well-meant friendly action, service project, or aid scheme has gone very badly awry because it was quite simply ill informed.

## Emotion: a TOK way of knowing

How, then, does emotion work as a way of knowing? We put this question back to you, but turned around backwards. What would you NOT know WITHOUT emotion? Think personally. If you yourself suddenly did not feel any emotions, what difference would it make? Reflect for a moment on the role of emotion in everyday knowledge:

---

### Discussion Activity

#### Creativity, action, service (CAS): Can emotions be educated?

In small groups in your TOK class, choose one of the following questions and discuss it in the context of your school's CAS programme and your own personal experience to date.

- In what ways have your emotions affected (positively and negatively) your ability to perform and to make decisions in this activity? Conversely, how have your decisions affected how you feel?

- Have your emotions changed during the time you have been involved in this activity? Have your ideas and beliefs about the people you are working with also changed, and if so, in what ways?
- In what ways might you have developed more fully the attributes of "caring" identified in the IB learner profile – showing "empathy, compassion, and respect towards the needs and feelings of others"?
- In your experience of CAS, do you think emotion is a way of knowing?

---

[23] The Dalai Lama and Cutler, H. 1998. *The Art of Happiness: A Handbook for Living*. London, UK. Penguin Group. P 14.

[24] Mark 12:31, The Bible http://bible.cc/mark/12–31.htm accessed 15 May 2012.

[25] IB learner profile

- How would your personal relationships with others be affected? What knowledge would escape you?
- How would your understanding of events in your community and the world be affected? What knowledge of human beings and their behaviour would have to be learned in a very different way? What would that knowledge lack?
- How would your other ways of knowing be affected? In what ways might they give you diminished knowledge?
- How would areas of knowledge be affected? For instance, would you work as effectively on a research team, or play music as well in a band? Would you find the developments in knowledge in any field as interesting or see their relevance?

Think through just a single day of your life, subtract emotion, and consider how different it might be. What would you reply, then, to the question of emotion as a way of knowing? (Note that we are asking you to use the way of knowing of *imagination*. Any conclusions you reach are not factual and testable. And yet – by imagining what is not, we can often recognize more fully what is.)

We can readily see some of the roles of emotion in the threads of ideas we have raised in this chapter – connecting us with others in ways affected by cognition and culture (compare with language!), motivating us to think and act in the world, or complementing reason as we make decisions. Equally we can readily note the interdependence of our ways of knowing: we use the other ways of knowing to understand our emotions, and recognize in the other ways the influence of emotion. Our ways of knowing interact, each providing us with a different path to knowledge and all of them providing much greater knowledge as they work together.

It could be argued that emotion has a special role in that interaction of ways of knowing. You will recall that the word is derived from a root meaning "to move". Could it be seen, perhaps, as a vital force that motivates us to learn and know? We are compelled to yield to our inclination towards metaphor: suddenly we can imagine emotion as a river whose currents we ride, or a melody that lifts us to our feet to dance. Are you familiar with the longstanding metaphor for emotion as the heart – often placed in opposition to reason as the head? Emotion, of course, does not literally reside in the heart. But there is still something captivating about the image of emotion as the heart – the animating force, steadily pumping our life essence, and sometimes grabbing our full attention as it pounds in fear or joy.

## For Reflection

How can we know how others feel? Is it enough just to work by analogy to ourselves, believing that all people are basically the same? If others might not respond as we do, then how can we learn more about what affects their emotions and perspectives?

# Fallacies of argument 3: misleading appeals to emotion

A deep distrust of emotion within the western philosophical tradition is understandable in view of the way emotions can derail calm consideration of a line of reasoning. Indeed, in some areas of knowledge the exclusion of emotion is held as an ideal. Papers in scientific journals lay out their reasoning and justifications without including the feelings of the writers. Their relationships with colleagues, their excitement over their work, and their anxieties over the next research grant are relevant to their process of working but not to the quality of their conclusions or the criteria according to which their work will be evaluated by peers.

However, in the major arguments within social groups, emotion cannot be excluded: the goals often are to maximize well-being and happiness. The process of achieving those goals depends on communicating wholly, taking into account deep emotions as much as logic. Issues such as education, unemployment, elections, child care, nutrition and health, public transportation, communication systems, or emergency services all involve people's feelings. The goal for a critical thinker following discussions, then, is to notice *how* emotion enters an argument:

- Is it part of the *subject matter* under discussion (e.g. making people feel more secure, raising happier children, alleviating depression or addiction in segments of the society)?
- Is it part of the *process of decision-making*? Is emotion offered as *justification* for a decision (e.g. compassion, fear and need for security, desire to build community pride)? Or is it used as a *tactic of diversion* from other (perhaps better) justifications for conclusions?
- Is it part of the *style of communication* and persuasion?

Emotional content and emotional appeals are not necessarily inappropriate in an argument. A critical thinker will not reject emotion outright. Indeed, it is often necessary to insist on the relevance to decision-making of compassion or people's happiness as basic premises for logical argument, or as justifications in themselves for conclusions. It is sometimes important to take a stand against those who claim that only those things that are quantifiable (such as profit) should be taken into consideration, and that only logic has value.

Nevertheless, we do need to be on guard against the use of emotion to persuade us to conclusions that are against our "better judgment", often by sweeping aside all consideration of justifications to carry us towards a conclusion based solely on emotion.

Indeed, in influencing the conclusions we accept, little could be more powerful than a direct appeal to our emotions. Advertisers, for example, promote their products by playing on some of our deep desires – for love, security, status, sexual pleasure, or eternal youth. Some political leaders gain their power by igniting fear and hostility, emotions that tend to undermine clear thought. Pity and fear, the grand emotions of tragedy, can be tapped to peddle mouthwash or margarine, or to sell the public on a political agenda.

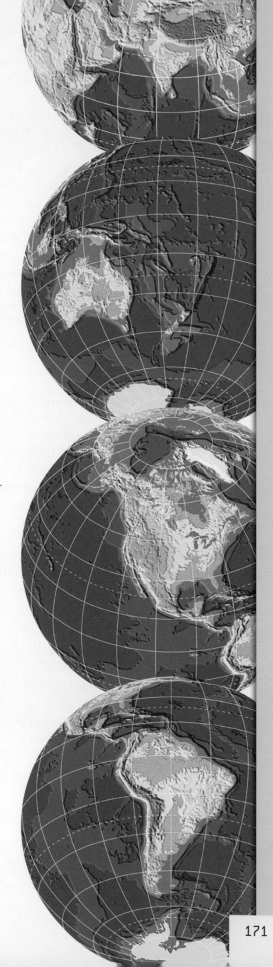

## 1. Appeal to pity

How can compassion, that concern for others that motivates kindness and generosity, ever be used as a mere gimmick for persuasion? Unfortunately, sometimes our most admirable feelings can be exploited in persuasion, deflecting our attention from fact and argument. The embezzler, caught with his hand in the piggy bank, wells up with tears over the bad news just given him by his doctor; he tries to make himself a more pitiable figure in order to divert attention from the stolen money in his fist. The political leader, caught in wrongdoing, presents himself as pitiably under stress. If the appeal to our pity seems to have some genuine basis, we may soften our judgment of the person. But the question to be resolved first depends not on feelings but on facts: did he do what he is accused of doing? In many judicial systems, the verdict (innocent or guilty) is separated from the sentencing (the degree of punishment).

More complex is the appeal to pity on the part of those who present themselves as victims. Pity may be an appropriate response to their distress. But is it a sound basis to conclude that they have, in truth, been wronged by the boss, the family, a divorcing spouse, or another ethnic group? In many conflicts, both sides compete to present themselves as victims rather than perpetrators in order to gain support. When the hardship is demonstrated with evidence, the appeal to pity becomes a thread in complex ethical and political arguments. If a group is partly or wholly to blame for their own misfortune (or if their leaders or their parents are to blame), do they no longer "deserve" compassion?

The emotion of pity is not itself fallacious. What a bleak world this would be if caring for others, and compassion for those suffering hardship, were to be minimized as justifications for conclusions and actions! What makes this appeal a fallacy in some contexts is its use to "prove" innocence or to distract attention from other justifications more legitimate for reaching a sound conclusion.

## 2. Appeal to anxiety or fear

Fear, we are told, is one of the most basic and primitive of our feelings, going back to the fight-or-flight response for survival. Indeed, we are legitimately afraid of many people and forces in our world, and perhaps even insufficiently afraid in the face of some global threats such as climate change. Fear or anxiety is not in itself necessarily irrationally experienced, and can motivate societies towards prevention of problems and preparation of systems for emergency and security.

It is also, however, an emotion easily exploited for less constructive persuasion. The appeal to fear may come as an implied threat: "Are you really planning to expose the Minister of the Public Purse? Doesn't she own the bank which holds the mortgage on your house?" Or it may take the form of generating and nurturing anxieties, anxieties about our personal appearance that persuade us to buy innumerable products, for example. Many businesses thrive on selling us peace of mind by first nurturing and directing our anxieties.

Similarly, some political leaders gain their power or hold onto it by presenting themselves as saviours of the people. But first they create the fear that gives them that role. Historically, leaders of many countries have secured their positions in part by focusing the attention of their people on a common enemy and exaggerating the threat. Think back to recent elections or other campaigns for political support in your country. How much did the candidates or political parties appeal to fear – fear of terrorists, moral decadence, or economic collapse?

Whether an appeal to fear is a fallacy, in the end, is a matter of evaluation and judgment. Is fear an appropriate emotional response to an evidence-based conclusion – or is it being used as a tactic of persuasion, influencing people to respond in a way that suits the writer or speaker?

## 3. Appeal to belonging

Surely almost as basic as pity and fear is the deep human desire to belong to a group and to be accepted. Advertisers encourage us to believe that by buying certain brands or fashions we will gain that elusive acceptability. By buying a particular brand of jeans or mobile phone, for instance, we can achieve a desired and admired identity, perhaps membership of an elite group. In some forms, the appeal to belonging is only marginally different from an appeal to fear – the fear of rejection.

This device also uses the confident voice of the insider calling to other insiders, emphasizing a bond that creates a sense of trust on the part of the people to be influenced: "We Serbians/Americans/ workers/Christians/Muslims/women can no longer tolerate this affront to our rights/dignity/religion/ way of life. We must take the following action …" Conversely, it can appeal equally forcefully to class, caste, religion, nationality or other forms of belonging to arouse suspicion of the outsider and to incite and justify hostile action. Us – and *them!*

## 4. Appeal to the speaker or source

Citing a particular person, publication, or organization as a source can be one of our major ways of justifying knowledge claims. Unable to gain all knowledge first hand, we have to depend to a large extent on the reported knowledge of others. We seek out reliable experts in many areas of our lives, and consult those we trust. As a justification for a conclusion, then, an appeal to the source may be entirely sound.

The appeal becomes dubious, however, when the *only* justification given for a claim is the source. This appeal can take a positive form as an appeal to authority: "He said it, so it must be true." It can also take the negative form of an attack: "He said it, so it must be false." We are encouraged to accept or reject a belief based solely on the basis of the source without being given further evidence or the possibility of checking the claim.

Historically, a major thrust of ideological persuasion has been to create not simply a reputation for a source but also a positive emotional allegiance or a negative hostility. Propaganda has been used to create the image of a leader with wisdom and infallible authority, or the image of a vile enemy whose every word is to be doubted.

## 5. Borrowed associations

This tactic depends on creating an emotional association in our minds between the product – the commercial goods or services, the person aspiring to a position of leadership or dominance, the perspective or the party – and something desirable. Naming and quoting respected figures introduces fine sentiment into a campaign and creates the impression of trustworthiness; using carefully selected music in the background of an advertisement suggests quality, particular status or emotions such as joy; using celebrities to endorse products or campaigns, even ones whose talents are irrelevant to what is promoted, both attracts attention and borrows something of their allure. Indeed, in contemporary television advertising, it is sometimes a guessing game to figure out what product is actually being promoted when the emphasis falls upon a tender family moment, a beautiful woman, or the glorious freedom of the wilderness.

Borrowed associations are also used to discredit an undertaking, a group, or an ideology, often working in combination with other devices such as innuendo or the appeal to fear. The figures quoted are ones regarded with fear or loathing, the music is discordant, the shadows in the photograph deepen.

Whether used in a positive or a negative version, though, borrowed associations employ a frequent tactic of all emotional fallacies: they try to persuade us not on the basis of argument at all, but on the basis of an emotion that replaces argument altogether.

# 10. Faith

Of all of our ways of knowing, faith is probably the one which will most awaken differences of perspective and stimulate exploration of both your own ideas and those of other people. The meaning of "faith" remains ambiguous and its role in people's lives varies significantly between individuals and communities. Yet in many long-standing traditions, the cluster of attitudes most call "faith" has been given a prime spot among ways of gaining knowledge, one more highly regarded in many traditions than any of the other seven we deal with in this book. Consequently, exploration of faith as a way of knowing offers some particular benefits: it invites further inquiry into different perspectives and the relationship between knowledge and belief.

## "Faith": concepts

Ambiguities in words can truly sabotage discussions if we do not recognize them. We can end up talking about slightly different concepts and never connecting in communication. However, if we *do* recognize the variable core of a word and its shades of meaning and connotations, we can end up with discussion that gains from either deliberately including variations or consciously laying them aside as irrelevant. "Faith" is one such word: it has more than one denotative definition, and carries a variety of connotations. Most of these variations are relevant to how we accept knowledge claims.

Although we make no claims to be comprehensive in our survey of language, we can identify at least four slightly different concepts of faith, at least in English. You may be able to identify more.

1. In the first thread of meaning, faith is associated with *trust* – having *faith in* someone, or *placing faith* in a person, a group, or a supernatural being. The security and confidence we gain from this kind of faith can be fundamental to our sense of self and the status we give others as reliable sources of knowledge. It could also be simply a habit of mind influenced by upbringing and culture.

2. Faith, in a second thread of meaning, is associated with *keeping promises* – with pledging one's word, "keeping the faith", and loyalty. This concept, as we cluster ideas, also involves ideas of honour and honesty, such as those involved with people being "in good faith" as they work out problems together.

3. In a third thread of meaning, "taking things on faith" is allied with ideas of *accepting assumptions or appearances* without further questioning for the moment – possibly in pragmatically taking features of the world as "givens", at least for the moment. This practical and provisional acceptance, when adopted in the sciences, is open to change if another set of assumptions proves more accurate, more consistent with

↑Illustration 1: Hands

↑Illustration 2: Pledge of allegiance

other findings or more useful for practical exploration (our truth checks). This is, at least, the scientific ideal. Outside the sciences, we may take a similar approach of accepting certain assumptions or "givens". If they are integral to our worldviews, though, we are less likely to treat them as open to change, and less likely to think that we should.

4. In a fourth and final thread of meaning, faith is subjective: in two interpretations, it is either *belief that rejects the need for justification* that could convince people who doubt, or a *justification that is based on other justifications*. In the latter case, it is a commitment of belief after having taken the merits of other justifications into account. Although those other justifications may not convince everyone, they are persuasive for the believer.

It is the last thread of meaning that is most complex and debatable, but all are relevant to how we define and construct knowledge. To use our ideas as a springboard for reflection on and articulation of your own, give thought to the questions in the activity "Roles we give to faith".

In the fourth of the threads of definition we have offered – both above and for your own discussion

↑ Illustration 3: Ben Kingsley portraying Gandhi

in the activity – faith is acceptance without the justification that is demonstrable or convincing to someone who does not possess the belief. For many people who "have faith", little could be so self-evidently right as their own beliefs and the process of accepting them. In the case of many subjective commitments, such as some forms of patriotism or religious belief, their belief taken on faith may be fundamental to their worldviews. However, for many people who do not share this approach to believing, little could be as irrational, baffling, and sometimes even threatening. As we raise a few more questions for you to think about, we are taking religious faith and patriotism as the main examples, anticipating that you will not consider them equivalent.

## Faith and culture

As we have considered ways of knowing in this book, we have been doing so primarily in terms of gaining knowledge and justifying knowledge claims. Faith, however, raises some further intriguing issues about knowledge claims accepted not singly but in bodies, and about the relationship between personal knowledge and shared knowledge. In a sense, faith leads only to *personal knowledge* as it is a subjective commitment of belief without the evidence that would compel universally shared agreement. In another sense, though, faith can be seen as significantly *shared knowledge*: it is shared not in a scientific way with research and testing in which people of all backgrounds take part, but it is certainly shared within "faith communities" which provide both a body of beliefs and a cultural connection with other people.

↑ Illustration 4: Trusting friends

## Discussion Activity

### Roles we give to faith

Gather your ideas on the following questions in advance of discussion with classmates, so that you have a chance to reflect personally and find words to convey your ideas. In discussion, refer to the seven images provided in this chapter to help communicate your ideas. If languages other than English are spoken by students in your class, you might consider how faith would be defined and discussed in other languages.

### 1  Faith as trust

Reflect on the people or organizations in your own life in which you most place your faith, in the sense that you feel you can trust them. You might find the following list useful in stirring your thoughts: a family member, a friend, a teacher, a political leader, a religious leader, a media figure. You may prefer to keep this part of your thinking private, or may want to draw on it selectively to provide examples as you discuss with classmates the following questions:

- How important is it to you to be able to trust others? How do you decide *how much* to trust them?
- Do any of the seven images in this chapter represent in your mind the kinds of faith you have in others, or in particular others?
- What does it mean to "have faith in yourself"?
- If you trust someone emotionally, are you more likely to accept knowledge claims that he or she makes? Does critical thinking feel uncomfortable or inappropriate in a personal relationship?

### 2  Faith as pledge and commitment

Pledges of loyalty can have a significant cultural and social role: Vikings "pledging their troth" to their leader, serfs pledging fealty to their lord, social groups forming sworn allegiances, citizens pledging allegiance to their monarch or country, marriage partners taking vows. People swearing loyalty (even if doing so is not a free choice) are expected to be "faithful" to their country or their spouses.

What do you have to believe *first* in order to make a pledge? What influence do you think a pledge of allegiance – such as to a flag – can have on what knowledge claims you are inclined to accept thereafter? Does any of the seven

↑ Illustration 6: Life hanging by a rope

images in this chapter represent, for you, a pledge or commitment?

### 3  Faith as acceptance of assumptions

We sometimes accept knowledge claims pragmatically, when we cannot prove them, because they are *useful* – for example, accepting the world really exists outside our sense experience of it, or accepting within a scientific model "all things being equal and neglecting friction", or accepting the axioms at the base of a mathematical system. (See chapter 3 on pragmatic truth.) Do you think that this pragmatic acceptance, which is open to change, is a kind of faith?

When we affirm basic assumptions – our foundational beliefs that we offer as the premises of further argument, as in the Universal Declaration of Human Rights – are we asserting principles of faith? From the Preamble of the Universal Declaration of Human Rights (1948): "the peoples of the United Nations have in the Charter reaffirmed their faith in fundamental human rights, in the dignity and worth of the human person and in the equal rights of men and women…"

Can you pick out an assumption that you take on faith yourself? Does any of the seven images in this chapter represent, for you, this kind of faith?

### 4 Faith as subjective commitment of belief

a. Faith, in a first interpretation, is *belief that rejects the need for justification*. This subjective commitment to believing is sometimes called the "leap of (or *to*) faith". Christian philosopher Kierkegaard, speaking of religious faith, insisted that objective uncertainty increased the significance and value of the personal commitment necessary for belief. From this point of view, to have indisputable evidence in the existence of God would destroy meaningful *faith*.

b. Faith, in a second interpretation, is a *conclusion based on other justifications*. For religious faith, those justifications might include mystic experience, revelation, sacred text, and the authority of religious leaders and institutions. Faith based on them, in a hierarchy of justification, then acts as justification for further beliefs.

If you have religious faith, which of these two interpretations better describes it? If the second, on what do you base your own faith? Do you have a different way of describing the relationship between faith, justification, and belief? Use this opportunity to put into words what you think yourself, phrasing it in terms of what kinds of justifications you find persuasive, or unpersuasive, and why. Does any of the seven images in this chapter represent, for you, a subjective commitment of belief? If you do not claim a religious faith, explore instead your thoughts on *either* patriotic faith (that is, commitment to your country) *or* secular humanism (a worldview focused on human beings, and reason, justice, and ethics).

Use this opportunity to learn about what others think, pushing aside any impulse to tell them

> Without risk there is no faith. Faith is precisely the contradiction between the infinite passion of inwardness and objective uncertainty. If I can grasp God objectively, I do not believe, but because I cannot know God objectively, I must have faith, and if I will preserve myself in faith, I must constantly be determined to hold fast to the objective uncertainty...[1]
>
> *Søren Kierkegaard*

that they are wrong and you are right. Are the justifications that others advance for their faith similar to what you advance for yours, even if you believe somewhat different things?

### 5. Faith and other ways of knowing

What would you say is the relationship between faith and other ways of knowing? Is a subjective commitment of belief primarily *emotional?* If so, what emotions are involved? Does it involve *reason* in evaluating other justifications? In what ways might *sense perception, intuition, memory,* and *imagination* be involved? Is *language* essential? What is the role of sacred text in informing or directing religious faith?

↑Illustration 7: Prayer book

---

1 Kierkegaard, S. *Concluding Unscientific Postscript taken from Philosophical Skepticism.* 2003. Edited by Charles Landesman and Roblin Meeks. Malden, USA. Blackwell Publishing. P 267.

↑Illustration 5: Stars and galaxy

**For Reflection**

Have you noticed our care to avoid "all" statements, using "generally", "sometimes", "often", "possibly", or similar qualifiers when commenting on faith, religion, patriotism, and culture? Do you think that this care is more important with some topics than with others?

Are you able to describe your own religion, if you have one, in terms of a perspective, with its assumptions and other characteristics as above? What importance does your religious perspective have in your own life?

How would you define "true patriotism" – as unquestioning support ("My country, right or wrong!") *or* as support that involves critical questioning and possibly opposition?

Religious beliefs, accepted on the basis of faith, are generally woven into the whole of a believer's perspective on life. Although the primary knowledge claims accepted might be *metaphysical knowledge claims* – belief in a spiritual reality or a god or gods – much else follows. A religion teaches *value judgments*, most significantly about good and evil, and about living a good life, and gives *predictions* about what will happen as the result of actions taken in the present (for example, karma, or an afterlife in heaven). It also sometimes prescribes ways of eating, dressing, and forming relationships with other people, and involves believers in traditions and customs of the particular faith community.

As a result, inquiry into faith and belief can be overly restrictive when the questions are *only* about accepting knowledge claims. "Do you believe there is a God?" or "What is the nature of the spiritual reality you accept?" is a question about the basic metaphysical premise for all of the rest of the beliefs, but even then it can miss the point of what else matters to people: a sense of identity and life purpose, a community to which they belong, and memories and expectations concerning customs and relationships. It is possible that interested inquiry regarding someone's religious faith might *not* centre most usefully on questions about belief in knowledge claims. Instead it might centre on the questions we have posed about *recognizing perspectives* from the beginning of this book.

- What are the basic *assumptions* of this faith or religion?
- What are the *values* associated with this set of beliefs?
- What are held to be important facts according to this religion?
- What are the *processes of validation* for knowledge claims and settling differences of interpretations or views within the group? What councils of authority or leaders make final decisions on matters of doctrine?
- What are the *implications* of the body of beliefs for personal behaviour or other actions?

For patriotic belief in one's country, it might similarly be most fruitful to examine it in terms of perspectives. The foundational beliefs taken on faith sometimes involve metaphysical ones – a state may have an official religion, for instance, or may be seen as a theocracy. However, basic beliefs usually assume the inherent value of one's own country or the principles according to which it is, or should be, run – democracy and human rights, for example, or obedience to leaders. Other beliefs, passed on within the political body, concern the country's status, relationship with neighbours, and future. "True patriotism", it has been argued, demands unquestioning support for the country and the decisions of the leaders. However, "true patriotism", it has equally been counter-argued, demands *not* taking on faith the country's value and its policies, but giving vigilant critical attention to its ideals and actions, and being ready to oppose the decisions of leaders when they are faulty.

## Faith and subjectivity

Regardless of whether faith is considered to be a justification in itself, or whether it is considered to be a conclusion based on other justifications, many would argue that it leads to belief that is *subjective*. Faith as a justification for subjective conclusions is not demonstrable in the way that evidence, testing, or reasoning can be for *objective* conclusions.

That is not to say that evidence and reasoning do not play a supporting role in belief – especially once the belief has been accepted. If you want

evidence, religious believers can say, just look at the order and complexity of the universe! However, non-believers can look and not be convinced; the ordered universe is evidence only through the eyes of belief.

Calling a belief "subjective", however, does not mean that it is of lesser value than beliefs grounded more "objectively". We need both subjective and objective elements in our lives. The objective side of our knowledge gives us factual understanding of our world and logical systems. But it is the subjective side – varying with all the personalities and perspectives of the world – that gives it emotional value, cultural meaning, and, for believers, spiritual significance. The subjective side

### Voices

### Shahla Kanji, IB Diploma graduate 1983

*Shahla Kanji is a Canadian Ismaili Muslim living in Vancouver, British Columbia. Her passion is Personal Development—helping people connect more deeply with themselves and each other.*

### What does faith mean to me as a way of knowing?

Through my faith I know how to be human. My faith is a way of knowing myself, knowing the other, and knowing the world around me. As a Muslim, I do not divide faith and life. Faith informs and infuses my entire existence.

Through my faith, I know how to *be* in the world. Generosity, understanding, forgiveness, kindness; these are ethics of Islam. The Holy Qur'an emphasizes the unity of humankind, that despite our differences, we are all born from one soul. From this, I know that my connection to others is

profound. You are part of me, and I am part of you. If you hurt or suffer, so do I.

Everything in life is a gift, even the most difficult challenges. This I know through my faith. We all experience adversity. It is part of being human. Faith tells me the response to adversity is accepting what has come, facing that challenge, doing my best, and surrendering to Allah's will with gratitude, hope, and joy. Faith tells me that above all, Allah is Loving Compassion. He is all Merciful. He is Kind. "The place where you are right now, God circled on a map for you" (Hafiz).[2]

Faith is a way of life. Through faith, I know that my purpose is to tend the divine spark that is in me, to connect with the Divine through prayer and remembrance, to seek to be close to God, to do His work in the world, and to love. When I'm participating in quiet communication with God, thanking Him for the beauty of His creation, when I forget the self to care for another, when my intention is love and I act lovingly, in those moments, the mundane becomes suffused with the spiritual and I am given the gift of knowing the very heart of happiness.

[2] The Gift, Poems by Hafiz the Great Sufi Master, translations by Daniel Ladinsky. Penguin Books, Middlesex, England, 1999. p.207

## What is the role in science, if any, of faith as a way of knowing?

*Below is a selection taken from a discussion on Facebook. Your author asked scientist Maarten Jongsma for his thoughts. But he went further: he posted some opening thoughts for his former IB Diploma classmates from more than 30 years ago, and precipitated a wide-ranging discussion. As you formulate your thoughts yourself on what "faith" means and what its role is in knowledge, you may want to consider the ideas exchanged here. What would you post yourself, if you were joining this conversation?*

### Maarten Jongsma, IB Diploma graduate, 1980

*Maarten Jongsma is a senior researcher at Plant Research International in Wageningen, Netherlands, working on the interaction of plant chemistry with the living environment. He leads numerous research projects, including some cooperations with China and North Korea.*

Faith (as a way of knowing) in science and religion has different roles. In science it links to knowledge obtained by scientific methods, which represent a rational reconstruction of reality. It is acceptable that the reconstruction will change in the light of better evidence: the initial belief (from personal observation and common sense) that the earth was flat was eventually replaced by knowledge (from experiments) that the earth was a sphere. In good science the conditions that determine the basis of beliefs are made as explicit as possible: they should be falsifiable, and importantly the observer should play no role – we are not the centre of the world.

Religious faith is different in that it is, on the contrary, intended especially to shape one's personal role in the world. In that sense religious and scientific faiths can exist side by side and are complementary.

**Janice Brown:** Personally, I've always been quite uncomfortable with the stark line drawn between scientific and religious truths. Scientific truths can be challenged of course but, once accepted, they can be astonishingly difficult to displace.

**Sissel Gørrissen:** Please, can we avoid using the word "faith" for anything other than religious faith? It just seems to cloud understanding!

**Barbara Drosten:** Sissel, the German translation of "faith" means as much "believe " as "trust" – a reminder of the etymological background. For the sake of Maarten's purpose, I think we should keep it for a while – until we sort it out a bit more, I mean. Science and religion are both very much interconnected.

**Anne Maree Vogt:** Seems to me that there is a danger of falling into the trap of treating religious and so-called scientific faith as *equivalent* when we adopt the term "faith" in relation to one's acceptance of, reliance upon or even "belief" in scientific knowledge *at all*. Accepting scientific knowledge depends on assessing physical evidence and yes, certainly trusting in the scientific method and the honesty of scientists, all of which can be tested. This is not the same as having faith, in my opinion. Faith does not require evidence, I have always thought. Science is all about evidence. It is not helpful and it muddies our thinking, I think, if we start to talk about two "faiths". In that sense, I think there is no "faith" in science, although I readily acknowledge that many people who have faith are also scientists.

**Maarten Jongsma:** I think we agree (do you?). When I say scientific faiths and religious faiths are *complementary* I mean that to be the opposite of *equivalent*. I just think that science doesn't cover all.

**Janice Brown:** No time to respond properly today. But to play devil's advocate, let's consider economics, which has as one of its basic tenets an (in my view) entirely unreasonable faith in the existence of rational consumers and markets and "proves" its theories using models that assume away huge chunks of reality. I think it is important to recognize when any assertion, whether religious or scientific, is essentially a matter of faith – that is, it is something that is as yet unproven and may not be provable – so that we may recognize its limitations and continue to test it.

**Marc Patry:** You are such a devil's advocate! I think economists would say that they "assume" that consumers are rational, and that very few believe this to be fact. Assumptions are not faith. By assuming, you recognize there are missing elements, but you allow yourself to venture something forth, recognizing that you are open to modifying it if your assumptions are proved not quite accurate.

**Geert Jan van Oldenborgh:** Janice, I agree completely, but would argue that every branch of science has unprovable assumptions, ranging from Lorentz invariance in theoretical physics to the Big Bang in cosmology to life being based on carbon-chemistry in biology. The trick seems to be *not* to have faith in them, but check again and again if results based on these assumptions explain the world. If not, it is back to the drawing board, as indeed many economists are doing right now as far as I understand. This latter feedback loop is absent in faith in the religious sense, where questioning the assumptions is often explicitly forbidden.

**Janice Brown:** Seriously, I HAVE to get back to work, but can't resist one quick comment. I'm no theologian but, from my own experience, I don't think it's correct to say all religion forbids the questioning of assumptions.

**Geert Jan van Oldenborgh:** A few days of travel and jetlag and I am far behind on the discussion.

One more point that underlies this all is the faith, in science, that the natural world can be explained by simple rules underlying the rich diversity of phenomena around us. I know of no way to justify this other than "it seems to work well up to now". At the deepest level there is no other justification for science than the claim "it works". You cannot logically prove that the sun will rise tomorrow. You can only blend past experience and the laws of physics as far as we know them into a Bayesian probability that is very close to one. Therefore I would argue that any claim that faith in science and faith in religion (or other dogmatic philosophies appealing to absolute truth) are *equivalent* can be shown to be false *only* by referring to the success of science in explaining many aspects of the world and making useful predictions based on that knowledge. The *basis* of science cannot be shown to be different but the *results* are. Does this make sense?

**Janice Brown:** At an emotional and psychological level, it seems to me religion may offer an explanation for beauty, love and other mysteries of our universe that is more compelling and satisfying than those science has, to this point, at least, been able offer. So where does that leave me? Do I agree there are fundamental differences between religious and scientific faith? Yes, I guess I do, but I don't think those differences can or should be reduced to the simple assessment of which is more rational or evidence-based.

To my mind the difference has more to do with the questions each asks, and the extent to which those questions are provable using existing scientific methods. Perhaps one day science and our understanding of the universe will have progressed to the point that we can begin to address the kinds of questions with which religion grapples (why are we here, what is our purpose, what are our moral and ethical obligations to one another and the world in which we live?) but I don't think they're there yet.

of our knowledge cannot be proved, but we may feel proof to be irrelevant.

This distinction between *subjective* and *objective*, however, could be seen by some believers as simply obtuse – as a failure to recognize the role of faith as going "beyond reason" into higher justification of a transcendent category all its own. If God tells us what to believe and what to do – through Holy Books, Prophets, infallible theological leaders, for instance – then they could argue that human subjectivity and objectivity in building knowledge are totally beside the point. God gives the truth, and it is for us to try to understand.

We remind you of the two different scales of certainty we considered way back in chapter 2. Knowledge is never "certain" objectively, based on evidence and reasoning: it can always be revised as we find new evidence, or think differently about what we know already. However, belief, the psychological component of knowledge, can indeed be "certain": it can be held in the mind without any doubt whatsoever over a lifetime, and through generations.

## Faith and certainty

Faith often attracts critical attention when it is held with total psychological conviction – appearing impervious to counter-claims – and when it becomes damaging either to believers or to others. Some of the problems caused when the "faithful" believe beyond doubt can be demonstrated by beliefs that lie firmly outside of the mainstream.

The Heaven's Gate cult, for instance, believed that as the Hale-Bopp comet passed the Earth in 1997 it was being trailed by an alien spaceship that would take them away to the Next Level of spiritual existence. Thirty-nine members committed ritualized suicide in order to be taken aboard the spaceship as it passed. They had faith – and we cannot *prove* that they were wrong.

Similarly, doomsday cults of various kinds have followed leaders prophesying the end of the world. Sometimes they have committed suicide or taken violent action against others. Sometimes they have just been quietly disappointed when the world carried on as usual. One group was disappointed first in 1994, when leader Harold Camping had calculated the time of the end based on coded

messages in Biblical text and his own mathematical calculation. When the world did not end, he declared a mathematical error, and recalculated for 2011.[3]

When again the world did not end, did he abandon his belief? Why should he? With faith unshaken, such a cult can provide plenty of possible explanations: the math was (again) incorrect; God relented because of their faith; God changed His mind; the End Times really did happen, but only True Believers can tell. They can retain their faith, and nothing can prove them wrong.

Millions of people worldwide who hold religious beliefs could understandably object to our illustrating faith here by examples drawn from the "fringe". We pause to point out – as so often – the difference between "all" and "some" statements. All believers are not outliers to standard conceptions of sanity. These people do, however, embody a problem that most people, religious or not, would acknowledge – that there are strains of bizarre belief and fanaticism that use the same justification of faith as do teachings of love and kindness to others.

Yet it is almost impossible to shake people's beliefs with evidence or argument if they reject the need for either. Faith can bypass further justification and go straight to belief. Consequently, if someone is completely *certain* that God wants him to leap from a mountain top or kill all non-believers, no counter-arguments can be relied on to convince him otherwise.

## Faith and doubt

Utter psychological certainty is not a necessary feature of faith, however. Faith can be mild as well as fierce – and it can be moderated or even replaced by doubt. What, then, is the role of doubt as a counter to faith – or even as an integral part of faith?

Within the variable religious communities of the world, doubt, along with its accompanying counter-claims, has been regarded in very different ways. In some religious traditions, faith is sometimes described as an active struggle with doubt – a will to believe *despite* lack of objective evidence, and *despite* some much-debated problems such as the existence of evil. Indeed,

---

3   Eileen Dombrowski, "Disappointing the doomsday cult," Triple A Learning blogs, 21 May 2010. http://blogs.triplealearning.com/2011/05/diploma/dp_tokglobal/disappointing-the-doomsday-cult-prediction.

in some religious contexts the dynamic struggle of faith is what makes the commitment of belief significant; the believer has to *achieve* belief through personal thought and emotion and not accept on "blind faith".

In other contexts, doubt, with its counter-claims, has been seen as failure or betrayal. Consult for a moment your own knowledge of history, current events, and institutionalized religion to consider the reactions of some religious institutions to those who have deviated in their beliefs or put forth counter-claims. What, for example, is a "heretic" or an "apostate", and how have religious leaders and communities dealt with them?

The variability of faith communities, and institutions of faith, makes all-inclusive generalizations about them nearly impossible. The sheer diversity of concepts, experiences, and expressions of faith makes it elusive and subjective, as do the emotional ways in which it gives interpretation and significance to people's lives.

## Faith: a TOK way of knowing

The ambiguity of what is meant by "faith", the different ways of interpreting it as a justification, and the immense range of knowledge claims that use it as a justification make it highly unlikely that everyone reading these recent pages will agree with everything on them. There is no need for you to agree – and we encourage you to use what we give here to formulate your own views and your own arguments for them. Our goal is entirely to give you a way into reflections on the role of faith in knowledge, and, we hope, some good exchanges of perspectives with your classmates.

Faith, and religious faith in particular, does come with long traditions of being asserted as a way of knowing – that is, a way of knowing a metaphysical reality beyond the ordinary one of our world, and thereby knowing much more that is important for our human lives. Faith has also been a powerful social force in binding people into communities, to the point that it has been conjectured that "the urge to worship sparked civilization".[4] Certainly, civilization has benefitted in many ways from this urge, and works of music, art, and architecture inspired by faith are among the finest of human achievements. Among the finest achievements, too, must surely rank organizations of community support and international development inspired by living the principles of love and charity. At the same time, however, faith has also been a powerful force of division among people, a force of bigotry and murderous destruction – especially when people have not moderated their own psychological certainty with respect for the lives and welfare of others.

In this chapter, we have led up to some major questions about knowledge, and now we pass them to you to answer yourself, possibly in discussion with others in your class.

### For Reflection

Do you consider faith to be a way of knowing? Would it be more accurate – or clearer – to call it a way of *believing?* To what extent can this same question be applied to other ways of knowing? Compare faith in this regard with, for instance, emotion, memory, and sense perception.

What is the relationship between knowledge and belief?

---

4 Mann, C.C. June 2011. "Dawn of Civilization". *National Geographic.* P 35.

# 11. Imagination

> "
>
> I have always been fascinated to imagine the uncertain circumstances in which our ancestors – still barely different from animals, the language that allowed them to communicate with one another just recently born – in caves, around fires, on nights seething with the menace of lightning bolts, thunder claps, and growling beasts, began to invent and tell stories...From the time they began to dream collectively, to share their dreams, instigated by storytellers, they ceased to be tied to the treadmill of survival, a vortex of brutalizing tasks, and their life became dream, pleasure, fantasy, and a revolutionary plan: to break out of confinement and change and improve, a struggle to appease the desires and ambitions that stirred imagined lives in them, and the curiosity to clear away the mysteries that filled their surroundings. [1]
>
> *Mario Vargas Llosa*
>
> "

When Mario Vargas Llosa accepted the Nobel Prize for Literature in 2010, he used his own imagination to picture the transformative human moment of starting to tell stories. He spoke of imagination as liberating humans from the confines of reality to "dream collectively" – to enter the fantasy of the story, to change and improve reality, and to follow their curiosities to discover the mysteries of their world. He is not offering this story of transformation as a factual account of human history, and we do not take it that way; we simply follow him with our own imaginations and understand what he is saying. How is it that we suspend our own immediate realities so readily to enter the fiction? What is this capacity called "imagination"? And is it appropriately called a "way of knowing"?

No single concept of the human imagination has emerged from long centuries of fascination with our ability to picture to ourselves scenes or events – our images and our stories – that we are neither receiving through our sense perceptions nor recalling through our memories. One of

several concepts is imagination as a means of metaphysical apprehension. In the Vedic tradition within Hinduism, for example, it is a transcendent power, through which the gods "create and sustain the harmony of the universe", and through which human beings grasp this harmony. [2] Greek philosopher Plato also attributed to imagination the metaphysical role of allowing human beings to bring to mind eternal forms beyond the world of the senses. English Romantic poet Samuel Taylor Coleridge had a different version of the metaphysical, within which he gave what he called "primary imagination" the role of echoing divine creation as human beings bring the world of their sense perceptions into existence for themselves. Other thinkers have assigned to imagination functions that are more psychological than metaphysical, often giving it a bridging role – bringing together thought and feeling, or the world of the senses and ideals. Often, too, the creative power of the imagination has been given the role of highest importance as it transforms the materials of experience into new forms and meanings. All of these treatments of the imagination are grounded in culture and traditions of thought, and prompt rich and complex questions on how the imagination actually works – if, indeed, there is a single, unified part of consciousness we can call "the imagination".

Altogether, would we *expect* universal consensus on what experiences belong within the category "imagination", and would we *expect* it to be assigned the same role in our minds within all the different perspectives of the world? Although ambiguity can often create difficulties for exchange of views, in this case we suggest that it is liberating – and splendidly appropriate for a human capacity that does not close and confine but opens and appeals to understanding beyond the facts of our immediate reality.

We could move in many directions to consider imagination, but we will choose paths that take us most directly to consider the central knowledge question: can imagination give us knowledge of ourselves and our world?

---

1   Mario Vargas Llosa, Nobel Prize for Literature acceptance speech, http://www.nobelprize.org/nobel_prizes/literature/laureates/2010/vargas_llosa-lecture_en.html, accessed 24 May 2012.

2   "Imagination, non-western traditions". http://science.jrank.org/pages/9769/Imagination-Non-Western-Traditions.html accessed 5 June 2012.

## Foolish flights and dangerous delusions

Not all accounts of the imagination are enthusiastic. It is easy to see how fantasies and daydreams might be regarded with disapproval within some contexts and how making things up might be seen as next door to lying. Probably all of us, too, have found that imagining scenarios has overtaken us at points when it interferes with what we feel we should be doing, and we have told ourselves to "snap out of it!" Of greater concern for imagination's role in knowledge, though, is the way people deal with the borderline between fact and fiction.

For children, the borderline can be very blurry as they play, lost in worlds of their own imagining, engaging with the experiences and impressions of a world still new to them. Although they can "snap out of it" fairly readily, it can sometimes have a frightening grip on them as, terrified by the monsters in the shadows, they have not yet developed the means to dispel them as imaginary.

As adults, we expect the borderline to be clear. Although some people do suffer from delusions, we usually place their difficulty in telling the difference between the real and the unreal in the category of medical problems. Such delusion is not

---

### Discussion Activity

#### Imagination: Where does it take us?

Theo Dombrowski, *Imagine*.

#### Activity 1: Images of imagination

- The painting above is by Theo Dombrowski, longtime teacher of IB English literature. He calls it "Imagination". Why do you think he did so?
- Find a visual image that, for you personally, captures your associations with imagination. In class, share your images with each other and explain why you picked the one you did. Are there any ideas about imagination that most of you have in common?

#### Activity 2: imagination in different fields of knowledge

Read the "voices" of professionals in many fields pictured in this chapter or elsewhere in this book, who use imagination as they create and apply their knowledge. Then discuss with others in your class the questions below.

- Oded Rose, entrepreneur
- Carlos Anciano Granadillo, doctor, surgeon
- Todd Waite, actor, director, teacher
- Heidi Li, performer of traditional Chinese opera
- Jane Clarke, psychotherapist and poet (chapter 6)
- Manini Chatterjee, journalist, writer, editor (chapter 13)
- James Cavers, professor and engineer (chapter 19)
- Patrick Decowski, nuclear physicist (chapter 19)
- As these professionals in different fields comment on the role of imagination in their own present work, what similarities do you find between them? What differences do you find as imagination is tapped for different purposes?
- In what ways do these contributors present imagination as working interactively with other ways of knowing? Compare, for instance, Todd Waite's account of theatre with Carlos Anciano Granadillo's account of medicine.
- In several of the contributions, imagination is associated with understanding other people. Why might working well with other people demand a degree of imagination?
- Pick *one* of your IB higher level subjects and *one* non-academic activity that you do. In what ways do you use imagination to gain, evaluate, understand, apply, or enjoy knowledge in each of these two cases? Without imagination, would your knowledge be diminished?

the result of an active imagination, something we can "snap out of".

When the term "delusion" is used not to indicate a biological disorder but a skewed belief about the world, then concern focuses on knowledge. We have to raise questions about the justifications for belief that people accept, the counter-claims that

>
> You can't depend on your eyes when your imagination is out of focus.[3]
>
> *Mark Twain*

they ignore, and the implications for accepting beliefs that are so far from grounded interpretation that they can be rejected as false. Of course, as we have considered earlier (chapter 3), it is often difficult to draw a clear line between "true" and "false" on a scale of degrees of justification. Moreover, sometimes very new ideas are regarded at first as delusional. (And politicians are sometimes given to calling their opponents "delusional"!) However, even given some of the fuzziness in line-drawing, some knowledge claims simply lie beyond any reasonable belief. When people accept conspiracy theories and alien abductions, for instance, they make themselves vulnerable to taking ill-founded actions, sometimes

## Voices

### Oded Rose, IB Diploma graduate 1982

*Oded Rose holds graduate degrees in Medicine, Business and International Relations. Other than raising five children, he runs a company that innovates in the water and energy markets and also leads a project to establish an international school in Israel.*

### Imagination in entrepreneurship

I once read that people can be divided to two types. This assertion, of course, is simplistic from the outset, but it helps to illustrate something about a human gift we call imagination. The short article I read went on to suggest that you either have imagination or you don't and gave as a test case buying a house. There are those who when they first walk in see the house for *what it is* and there are those who see it for *what it could become*.

I fundamentally believe that everyone has imagination. It is one of a few things that make us human. I also believe that imagination can be developed especially at a young age. I see it with my own children. When my 3-year-old puts a puzzle together or my 6-year-old builds a Lego structure, then they use this something that is hard to describe, but allows them to see "into the future" and know where they want to get to. Kids have the best imagination. It is not yet spoiled by "reality" and by rules and laws of physics. When we imagine, in a way we become kids again.

I am an entrepreneur. I have always been one. Entrepreneurship's biggest asset is imagination, the ability to create in your mind a situation, whether it is a product, or a service, or a project that does not exist today, but that could exist in the future – and then "fuse" it with the reality of today in a timeline. Since this is something new, you use imagination to create a pathway in your mind first, and then follow it by creating the necessary steps to get from now to then in the real world.

---

[3] Mark Twain, *A Connecticut Yankee in King Arthur's Court*, chapter 43. http://www.literature.org/authors/twain-mark/connecticut/chapter-43.html

## Voices

### Carlos Anciano Granadillo, IB Diploma graduate 1995

*Carlos Anciano Granadillo, originally from Venezuela, trained in medicine in the United States. He is a physician and surgeon in a hospital in Pittsburgh, Pennsylvania.*

### Imagination in medicine

On my way out of medical school I spent some months in the Venezuelan Amazon. I quickly learned that I need much more than just reason and medical knowledge to act effectively. On a single day up or down the Rio Negro I encountered at least three to four different local languages, along with their cultural idiosyncrasies. Without a common language to identify pain, discomfort, and other symptoms, I found *non-verbal communication* and *sense perception* – linked to *imagination* and *intuition* – vital in reaching a diagnosis. Malaria is evident not just in the "fever and chills every third day" one reads in books, but may be sensed more subtly in the woman sitting withdrawn on a separate rock by the river shore, or in the girl not running energetically with the others to meet the strange white guy that just jumped out of the boat.

We are taught human anatomy from sets of diagrams, online visuals, models, and textbooks. We memorize the nerves heading to the arm, the arteries in order branching to the body, and the veins travelling back to our hearts. In the present, as I work as a surgeon in a tertiary care reference center, these pieces of knowledge are just the Lego pieces I use in my head to *imagine* what I'll find each day in every chest I go into. Every pulmonary artery branches with a similar pattern – but differently from person to person. Preparing a lung resection takes more than seeing a patient's CT scan image and reviewing diagrams. It requires *imagining* the "en-vivo" paths these living trees of vessels take, and *picturing* where three or four 5mm incisions will allow you to reach them, control them, and take them. Perceiving the trends and patterns in the patient's lung anatomy allows you to search *intuitively* for the critical areas of dissection to safely remove a lung cancer.

A baggage of concepts and sound technique take you only so far. The mental construct in my head paves the way to constantly readapting it on the go. Two plus two is never four in medicine, and minimally invasive surgery is more than just small incisions. In the hospital where I work, I still hear that voice I heard long ago by the jungle river, telling me to watch for subtle clues and use my imagination.

with damaging implications for their lives and those around them. It is no accident that the term "overactive imagination" has negative implications, suggesting as it does that one has been *overtaken* by a mental process beyond reasonable control.

When there are potentially dangerous implications for how we deal with reality, we need to screen imaginative possibilities for those that are logically and physically possible.

If something is imaginatively possible, that does not mean that it is real. Have you had any experiences where the opposite has been claimed? (Do you recall the role of constructive doubt and the checks for truth from chapter 2?)

## Imagination and creativity

If we are too quick to discard imagined possibilities, however, we may lose out both on our imagined worlds and on fresh insights into our real one. For one thing, the untrammeled imagination, not checked or confined, is often held to be of value in itself – putting us in touch with aspects of our own humanity, even giving a kind of transcendent vision. For another, the imagination can be prized as the creative spring from which fresh understanding flows.[4] English poet Samuel Taylor Coleridge called imagination (secondary imagination, in his distinction) "essentially vital" and claimed that it "dissolves, diffuses, dissipates, in order to re-create".[5]

This "vital" force of imagination may lead us to draw on all we have seen and felt, all we have thought and wondered, to recombine it in new ways, and to take it beyond the bounds of the familiar and known. As we create our imaginary images and stories, we let our minds wander in the world. As scientist Peter Medawar points out, this creative capacity to "dissipate" and "re-create" the world is part of the genesis of both scientific and artistic achievements:

> Scientific theories…begin as imaginative constructions. They begin, if you like, as stories, and the purpose of the critical or rectifying episode in scientific reasoning is precisely to find out whether or not these stories are stories about real life…. The scientific and poetic or imaginative accounts of the world are not distinguishable in their origins. They start in parallel, but diverge from one another at some later stage. We all tell stories, but the stories differ in the purposes we expect them to fulfil and in the kinds of evaluations to which they are exposed.[6]

Medawar's comparison of "imaginative constructions" is an appealing one – though he does not specify what features of stories the scientific and imaginative accounts of the world have in common in their genesis. What raw materials of sense perception and thought do they use, and what kinds of connections of association, sequence, or cause do they draw between them? As we have considered already in treating the role of the hypothesis and testing, science does need to constraint its imagination of possibilities, in the end, by the facts.

The rub between imagined possibilities and the constraint of factual truth is characteristic, too, of areas of knowledge that deal with human beings. In telling the story of the past, historian Tom Griffiths comments below on the "creative friction" between the documented past and the gaps to be filled by conjecture grounded in likelihood:

> Imagination must work in creative friction with a given world, there are rules as well as freedoms, there are hard edges of reality one must respect. There is a world out there that humbles one, disciplines one. There are silences not of our making. These silences and this uncertainty are the historian's creative opportunity – and should be part of any story we tell.[7]

In the arts, the imagination is rarely constrained in the same way by this "creative friction" of history, and the stories certainly do differ from the science "in the purposes we expect them to fulfil and in the kinds of evaluations to which they are exposed". Yet the free range of the imagination in the arts also has its confines of various kinds – sometimes in content, sometimes in medium, sometimes in form.

## Knowing through fiction

Where scientists try to find the regularities and patterns in the world (objectively), storytellers and visual artists use the raw materials of the world – including patterns they perceive – to create patterns of their own (subjectively). They discipline their imaginative invention with the demands of form and structure. The result is work that is (ideally!) coherent aesthetically, and, in the extended stories of novels and plays, also coherent for its internal psychology and sequence. We can enter an imaginative world, while still recognizing the one we left behind. In other words, we enter, as Coleridge says, with "the willing suspension of disbelief".[8]

---

4 Lehrer, J. 5 June 2012. "The Virtues of Daydreaming," *The New Yorker*. http://www.newyorker.com/online/blogs/frontal-cortex/2012/06/the-virtues-of-daydreaming.html?printable=true&currentPage=all, accessed 11 June 2012.

5 Coleridge, S.T. 1817. *Biographia Literaria Chapter XIII, part 1.* P 304.

6 Medawar, P. Reprinted 1987, first published 1982. "*Science and Literature*," *Pluto's Republic*. Oxford and New York. Oxford University Press. P 53.

7 Griffiths, T. 2009. "History and the Creative Imagination". *History Australia*. Vol 6, number 3. http://journals.publishing.monash.edu/ojs/index.php/ha/article/view/ha090074.

8 Coleridge, 1987. *Biographia Literaria.* Chapter XIV.

## Voices

### Todd Waite, IB Diploma graduate 1979

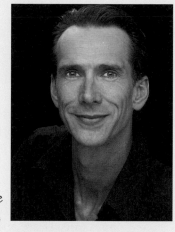

*Actor/Director/ Teacher and recipient of the Lunt-Fontanne Fellowship for contribution to American theatre through acting and teaching, Todd Waite was a member of Canada's Shaw Theatre Festival, before moving to America in 2000 to join The Alley Theatre in Houston Texas where he currently resides.*

### Imagination in theatre

Theatre offers a knowledge that is fueled not by fact and arguments, but by imagination. Theatre is a fiction which reveals truth. By the end of a good play the dance between the imagination of the playwright and the willing belief of the audience allows understanding into the huge range of our shared or conflicting motivations, values, fears, joys, God(s), and societal assumptions and expectations. This knowledge deeply affects our lives because our understanding of them, and the decisions we make as to whether we conform or resist these assumptions, make us who we are in relation to the world.

The knowledge gained in viewing any art is not a series of facts, but rather a complex knowing that encompasses empathy, intuition, philosophy, and spiritual belief.... all influenced by memory (both individual and collective past experience) and expectations regarding the future.

There is no fact-based, purely rational way to traverse society's thicket of irrational, personal, social "realities", because they are constructs... countless constructs, and changing ones at that. And yet understanding them is essential to our happiness, and essential to creating a context for determining how we will use scientific knowledge (because we relate to them based on our needs and beliefs).

At its best theatre of the imagination appeals to the subconscious; it insinuates past our pre-determined opinions and reflexive defensiveness and joins us to a collective memory; and it intimates our collective future. In this way it not only helps us to perceive truths, but reveals and even creates new ones.

A reader's imaginative engagement in fictional worlds has fairly recently caught the attention of cognitive scientists and been dubbed "propositional imagining" or "imagining that…". We accept within the fictional frame that Othello loved but murdered Desdemona or that Harry Potter had magic powers as he used his wand. When we accept the fiction until the moment we "snap out of it" are we using imagination as a *way of knowing*?

We direct you to the discussion activity on "Imaginative fiction" (page 192) to consider the role of imagination in developing empathy and furthering human understanding – drawing on some of the finest of our subjectivity.

> "
> Imagine no possessions
> I wonder if you can
> No need for greed or hunger
> A brotherhood of man
> Imagine all the people sharing all the world
>
> You, you may say
> I'm a dreamer, but I'm not the only one
> I hope some day you'll join us
> And the world will live as one.
>
> *John Lennon, musician.*
> "

## Imagination: a TOK way of knowing

For all that imagination can stimulate us to create new knowledge in factual areas or open us to new "human-scapes" in fiction, probably one of its greatest gifts is to carry us into visions of worlds beyond our present reality. For many of the seven billion inhabitants of this planet, the present reality is one of hardship. For the planet itself, the present reality is steadily growing worse. A world of poverty, environmental degradation, and conflict, however, is not the only possibility for our human future. The world does not have to be this way. *Another world is possible!*

Imagination can certainly take us into grim dystopias of the future or apocalyptic finales – but it can equally give us visions of hope to inspire us. We can imagine people putting down their guns, sharing resources so that everyone has enough, and caring for their fields and forests, sustainably. Through the power of imagination, aided by knowledge gained through other ways, we can project the results of much better present choices beyond a far horizon. Imagination certainly does give us images and stories of things that are not. However, in many cases it also gives us stories of what *could be*, if we *will* it so – and if we act towards making it real. Imagination has the power, if we will fly with it, to give us hope, create alternatives, find solutions, and bring into reality the world that in the present is only in our dreams.

Counter-factual and unreal, imagination does not perform the same role in knowing as perception, reason, or language. Nevertheless, it may be the spark that ignites the others to create the warming, dancing fire around which we tell our stories. Imagination contributes to our discovery and invention, our images of the world dissolved and recreated, and our potent visions of possible futures.

### For Reflection

In many contexts, being "subjective" is something to avoid. In what contexts is the subjective power of the imagination something to celebrate?

**Storyteller in Egypt, wood engraving, circa 1894**

With what storytelling traditions are you familiar yourself? In our day, who takes the role of the storyteller? Where do you go yourself to be told stories, and what, for you, counts as a *really good story*? To what extent do you enter a fiction with what Coleridge calls "the willing suspension of disbelief"?

## Heidi Li, IB Diploma graduate 2005

*Heidi Li, born in Hong Kong, has been a Chinese opera singer from a young age. After living in Canada, the UK and France, she is now living in Italy, pursuing her artistic career as a Jazz singer and songwriter while continuing to promote the traditional art abroad. http://www.heidili.com*

### Imagination and knowledge of conventions in Chinese opera

It can be tricky to turn a new spectator, whether foreign or Chinese, into a long-term Chinese opera fan due to its complexity. Despite its vibrant acrobatic scenes and extravagant costumes, its long-hour performances, acute vocals and unfamiliar stage movements can be demanding for the audience. To truly appreciate the traditional art, it requires patience to put one's imagination into reading all the stylized symbolic stage actions, and to get a deeper understanding of the complex art form through careful observation.

Chinese opera once was a popular entertainment, long before movies, TV and pop music came along.

It was an art for the people, the rich and the poor, the educated and the illiterate. It acted as a medium of oral education, narrating shared history, myths and legends to the majority population. For this purpose, stage space is limited; scenography is kept to the minimal. So, how is it possible to narrate all sorts of Chinese traditional tales and folklore – which can also involve supernatural characters? The symbolic stage movements of Chinese opera actors and actresses, sometimes with the help of their costumes and a few props, are the key to bringing onto the stage scenes that can be meaningfully played in a confined space.

There are no random moves or gestures invented by the actors themselves; all the movements are highly schematized, guided by opera acting conventions and the principle of beauty. A professional Chinese opera actor is often trained from a young age in order to acquire all the essential skills, from walking to singing, from speech delivery to gymnastic skills. All actors or actresses specialize to interpret stock roles, each of which follows distinct rules on how to act, move and sing in a specific manner. The stage movements are also symbolic. For example, walking in fast paces in large circles or in the form of the number eight is the standard representation of travelling in long distances; the swinging of ponytails in a circular motion expresses a character's frustration or extreme grief.

As soon as one grips the logic of Chinese opera acting principles, such understanding can then be applied across all performances. *Imagination* eventually plays a lesser role for an experienced spectator as *knowledge of the conventions* becomes the main tool for appreciating Chinese opera performances.

## Discussion Activity

### Imaginative fiction

There is no point in undertaking the following discussion activity if you simply float around in abstractions. Ground your responses in your own personal experience of imaginative fiction, whether of novels, plays or movies. You might also find relevant your experience of songs and other music, the visual arts, or even imaginary play using the Internet and video games. Do *not* in the process of sharing examples, though, forget about the general questions to which you are responding. Being able to walk the line between too-general-and-floaty-abstract and too-specific-wandering-off-the-topic-into-retelling-stories is a skill to develop not just for TOK but also for your other IB subjects.

### 1   Imagination as a means toward empathy

> When you visualized a man or a woman carefully, you could always begin to feel pity . . . that was a quality God's image carried with it . . . when you saw the lines at the corners of the eyes, the shape of the mouth, how the hair grew, it was impossible to hate. Hate was just a failure of imagination. [9]
>
> *Graham Greene*

First read the quotation above from novelist Graham Greene and then prepare your ideas for discussion of the following questions:

- What is the role of imagination in the development of empathy for others? Can you give examples?

- What is the role of literature, film, and other works of the imagination in developing empathy? Can you give examples from your recent experience of these creative forms?

### 2   Imagination as a means towards further understanding

> Narrative has never been merely entertainment for me. It is, I believe, one of the principal ways in which we absorb knowledge. [10]
>
> *Toni Morrison*

First read the quotation above from novelist Toni Morrison, and then think about specific novels, movies, or visual works that have affected you. Prepare your ideas for discussion of the following questions:

- What knowledge do you gain of history, psychology, culture, ethics, or any other discipline through fiction? If you read a work of literature, do you know more at the end? Do movies set elsewhere in the world give you any kind of knowledge? Give examples.

- Quite aside from factual information, do you gain any sense of insight or wisdom from a good novel, film, or painting? Do you gain any further understanding of the human condition – that is, what it is to be a human being in the fullest, most complex sense? Give examples.

---

[9]   Greene, G. 1940. *The Power and the Glory.* P 102.

[10]   Toni Morrison. 1993. "The Bird in our Hand: Is it Living or Dead?" Nobel Prize acceptance speech. *Azerbaijan International*, Autumn 1998 (6.3), http://www.azer.com/aiweb/categories/magazine/63_folder/63_articles/63_morrison_nobel.html accessed 24 May 2012.

# 12. Intuition

*A full silver moon has risen high in the sky. Through the swaying trees it casts shifting light on the narrow road ahead. Walking alone in this early summer night, you pocket your flashlight and let your eyes adjust to the soft and romantic darkness, dreaming as you wander about the person you wish you had at your side. Suddenly, a chill sweeps over you. Hairs prickle on your neck. With incandescent certainty, you know that you are not alone. There, exactly there – in the bushes! You leap back, stumbling, heart pounding. Just in time! Hurtling past your ear is a…*

On a dark night in a spooky movie, a mysterious sixth sense saves our protagonist. How did he know that danger lurked in those shadows? His own experience is that he *just knew*, accountably. This mysterious "sixth sense" is known as intuition. Intuition, appropriately enough, comes from a root meaning "knowledge from within".

How do we possess this knowledge from within? Accounts vary. Some have claimed that some knowledge is instinctive or innate: we are born with it. They might call all instinctive capacities of our human species "intuitive" in that we gain knowledge of sorts without understanding quite how we do. This interpretation of intuition is relevant to our abilities to use our bodies, including our brains. It is specifically relevant to our inborn capacity to use language, a capacity that develops in response to the particular language communities within which we grow up. Some have argued that we also have an inborn moral sense of right and wrong – or at least an instinct for forms of cooperation that can be interpreted as moral.

A contemporary explanation for the intuition that danger is lurking in the bushes is much less spooky and exciting than the dramatic sixth sense, and much less limited than an interpretation of intuition as instinctive knowledge. However, it is no less mysterious in its own way, for it lies within the way our brains process our sense impressions and make swift connections – so swift that we don't even know that we are noticing and thinking. With rapid cognition, we make judgments and act before we are consciously aware. Just in time!

You have already met intuition as a way of knowing interpreted in this way, at least briefly. You will recall that when we considered *reason* in an earlier chapter (page 110), we brought in Daniel Kahneman's "psycho-drama between two fictitious characters": System 1, the swift storyteller, "interprets the past, interprets the present, and prepares for the future, all of this happening within a fraction of a second and without your *intending* to do anything".[1] This is intuition! It gives us a fast grasp of the world – quick identification of patterns, swift association of patterns with meaning. Meanwhile System 2, with its more deliberative and analytical thinking, remains lazily disengaged. We have to make an effort to employ reason as a way of knowing, while intuition has already leapt into action!

## Does intuition really exist?

Some people argue that intuition does not really exist. They suggest that our other ways of knowing simply act more quickly and unconsciously than we have thought, and that "intuition" is an unnecessary additional category. What arguments might you make in support of their view?

On the other hand, what are the benefits of naming rapid cognition "intuition"? What arguments might you make for having a category and a name?

Recognizing the influence of language and naming on how we think about intuition, we are pushed to further knowledge questions: How do our conceptual categories affect the development of our thinking? *or* How does naming affect theories in research? *or*, broadest of all, How does language affect knowledge?

---

[1] Kahneman, D. "The Machinery of the Mind", audio podcast Big Ideas. 30 March 2012. http://itunes.apple.com/ca/podcast/daniel-kahneman-on-machinery/id129166905?i=112461861

**What's the story?**

Our intuitions give us swift interpretation of the world around us, before we are aware of thinking. They give us interpretations, sometimes with entire narratives, before our slower, more rational thinking kicks in. In looking at this photo, did you find yourself immediately connecting the information in it into an explanation or a story?

In the explanation of social psychologists Jonathan Haidt and Craig Joseph, "Intuitions are the judgments, solutions, and ideas that pop into consciousness without our being aware of the mental processes that led to them. When you suddenly know the answer to a problem you've been mulling, or when you know that you like someone but can't tell why, your knowledge is intuitive."[2]

## Interactive ways of knowing

Intuition certainly compels us to recognize anew the interdependence of ways of knowing that we have noted time and time again in our journey through them. Our eighth and final way of knowing, it does not stand alone.

If we accept the interpretation of cognitive psychology that intuition is rapid cognition, the speedy working of the brain without our being consciously aware, then we have to ask *what* the brain is processing so quickly. Certainly, it grabs our sense perceptions and creates connections of sequence and cause as it tells stories. It gives instant emotional associations and draws on our memories. Altogether, as intuition simplifies complexity to give us quick versions of the world, it works with the other ways of knowing and the knowledge and beliefs we already possess.

It is no accident that we have placed intuition last in our sequence of ways of knowing: recognizing the

role of intuition forces us to look more closely at the ideas of building knowledge and offering justifications that we introduced in chapter 4. Accepting the idea of "dual processing" by the brain – rapid intuition and the slower conscious thought of reason – raises questions about how we actually do come to the knowledge claims we make, even when we think we might reach them otherwise. Further, exploring intuition as a way of knowing pushes us to consider self-knowledge more centrally, and to realize that the IB ideals of the open and critical mind may be more challenging to achieve than at first they seem.

Given its impact on our interpretations and actions, intuition has understandably attracted research, discussion, and controversy in recent decades as the cognitive sciences have illuminated for us many aspects of our thinking. In the chapter

---

[2] Haidt, J. and Joseph, C. 2004. *Intuitive ethics: how innately prepared intutions generate culturally variable virtues*. Daeddalus Fall. P 56.

ahead, we will touch on some of the major threads of discussion of this fascinating and illusive way of knowing: its role in unconscious processing, its function within decision-making, its gut level sense of beauty or goodness, its employment in shortcuts of thinking, and its role in cognitive biases that affect how we use all of our ways of knowing. Finally, we follow its implications for ourselves as we attempt to use our ways of knowing most effectively to construct our knowledge.

## Unconscious skills

We can be quite grateful at moments to our intuitions, and the degree to which we can observe, think, or perform actions without actually having to pay conscious attention. As we become adept at skills, for instance, we no longer need to reach conclusions consciously or make ourselves move in the right way. Drivers, for example, do not have to pay conscious attention to turning the wheel ("Hands, grip and turn to the left!"), or typists to fingertips on the keyboard ("Pointer finger, press the "u" key!") The familiar actions seem "just to happen" in the right circumstances.

It could be argued that these automatic skills are stored in our procedural memory, and it is not intuition but memory that is allowing us to ride the bicycle or file our papers without attention. If intuition is considered to be pre-conscious processing, though, then we can regard it as drawing on procedural how-to memory in retrieval and activation of skills. Our ways of knowing work together. Indeed, even language, which seems so deliberate, is affected by its interplay with intuition as we often produce strings of words without planning in advance what to say. The words "just come".

### For Reflection

What skills do you possess that you can do without conscious thought? Do your hands, for instance, seem to do something all by themselves while your mind is far away? Would you consider yourself to be enacting this how-to knowledge through intuition, through memory, or through both?

>
> The key to successful decision-making, we believe, is knowing when to trust your intuition and when to be wary of it and do the hard work of thinking things through.[3]
>
> *Christopher Chabris and Daniel Simons*

## Making decisions

Often, too, we have to "go with the gut" – making judgments and decisions based on intuition. It would be ideal as we build our knowledge to have plenty of time to evaluate all justifications offered by our ways of knowing – time to consider current evidence, seek more by inquiring further, consult all perspectives, and make a fully considered judgment. Yet in many cases of decision-making, we use our intuition, swift in its conclusions and rough in its judgments.

Some of our intuitive decisions are matters of preferences and taste. Which option is better? Rational weighing of pros and cons can take us to lists of advantages and disadvantages – but rationality is not good at quantifying emotional reactions such as liking or disliking in order to put them on the list along with other factors such as cost or distance. (You may recall the case of Phineas Cage page 165.) In the end, we might choose to push aside our purely rational weighing of pros and cons to buy a pair of shoes that we *like*, or choose to attend the university that feels more *appealing*. We might realize that we'd *already made* the choice – intuitively, with access to emotional factors that we'd rationally neglected.

In other forms of establishing preferences, too, we might reach conclusions without quite knowing how. How do we balance the colours and shapes of a painting so that it's "right"? When do we know when to put down the brush and say, "This is finished"? Could intuition be our way of knowing? When treating emotion, we considered its important role in decision-making. If we accept intuition as a companion way of knowing, then we could well see it as making the leap to judgment by reaching conclusions that integrate emotion.

Similarly, we could see intuition as processing our sense perceptions quickly in some aspects of creativity. In the sciences, for instance, how do we

3  Chabris, C. and Simons, D. 2010. *The Invisible Gorilla: And Other Ways Our Intuitions Deceive Us*. Crown, New York. P 235.

## Voices

*Photo by Boomer Jerritt.*

"Intuition takes us beyond the limits."

*David Pinel, IB graduate 1987*

David Pinel has an MSc in Rural Planning and Development and has worked as a community and strategic planning consultant. He is a college instructor in outdoor education and a guide trainer, and runs his own adventure company, West Coast Expeditions.

Whether in adventure activities or in strategic planning discussions, listening to something deep down inside – a gut feeling – allows us to perform on a line of optimal tension that is safe, exciting, appropriate, and responsive to many rapidly changing variables. Intuition takes us beyond the confines and paradoxical risk of acting only on what we can rationally explain. When is that tingling "spider sense" actually all of the "knowing" that you need?

Despite a forecast for a calm afternoon, we're now paddling into winds that have rapidly picked up to above 30 km/h and seem to be increasing. The waves are building in height from the wind and against the outflowing current from dropping tides. Glancing over my shoulder I notice that the other kayakers with me have replaced smiles and banter with more focused looks in the face of more

challenging conditions that will require more effort. Everyone is instinctively paddling a little closer together and in a steady rhythm – this is good.

Ahead lies a choice: with our campsite and best landing option only 2 km ahead, should we take a short cut into steepening waves through a shallow swell-filled gap (with some rocks) between two islets? This is the most direct route. Or should we add another 20 minutes by going wide around the islets, avoiding a reef-strewn point by choosing deeper water, and then paddling back along the windward side of a rocky shoreline with rebounding waves from beam seas?

Each set of waves brings changing conditions to both options. And each minute brings potentially worsening conditions from the wind and falling tide level. We will lose momentum if we stop to observe further and discuss the options, and waiting will close the window of opportunity for the shorter option through the swell-filled gap, while making the more exposed longer route more challenging.

There is no dress rehearsal – we need to decide then "go for it" and act with organized commitment and no hesitation. Am I ready? Is the group ready? What instructions should I give?

We're taught and encouraged to prudently "gather all of the information" before "evaluating the data and options" then deciding and acting. In the discipline of professional planning, this is described as a "rational comprehensive" approach. For some, "professional" means methodical and therefore accountable.

But is it? Unfortunately, during the time it takes to find supposedly comprehensive information, the conditions and variables tend to change and the information that was originally gathered becomes insufficient or dated. At some point, responsible and responsive planning benefits from our intuition flagging that we have enough information (or skill, or experience) to make and act on a decision – that more information won't necessarily lead to a better result. The "professional" advantage can come from consciously recognizing and acting on your somewhat less explainable intuition that comes from experience and enhances trained responses.

Ironically, though we use it all of the time, intuition is rarely taught or encouraged as a sufficient justification for actions, or as a reliable way of knowing what's best. Though intuition doesn't guarantee the best or optimal outcome, neither do the other tools for knowing and acting. Learning to find, listen to, and respect intuition adds a powerful tool to your kit.

I slowed my forward momentum long enough for everyone to hear the instruction to follow my exact path single file through the gap, leaving a boat length between each kayak and turning where I turn. "Any questions? All good?" A quick round of nods and an "OK" signal from my co-leader at the rear indicated everyone was ready to go.

Within a few strokes, each kayak jockeyed into a line much like cars merging smoothly onto a busy highway – no discussion or negotiations. We were through the gap within 90 seconds and could now see the sheltered calm of our destination ahead. Several spontaneous hoots rapidly widened all smiles and energized the pace and chatter for the final stretch.

catch the first impressions of an emerging pattern in our sense perceptions of the world, and let imagination carry us to a hypothesis for a possible cause? Could it be intuition? Yes, we really should give the other ways of knowing their share of the credit, but intuition just might be the fastest and the first to tap into our awareness of pattern.

Socially, too, it seems that we often make judgments at an intuitive level, strongly affected by our first impressions. Says one social psychologist, "Many psychologists now believe that most social cognition occurs rapidly, automatically, and effortlessly – in a word, intuitively – as our minds appraise the people we encounter on such features as attractiveness, threat, gender, and status."[4] Some psychologists suggest an evolutionary basis to such intuition, harking back to encountering strangers and having to decide in a flash whether they were friends or enemies. Those with accurate intuitions were likely to survive longer!

Other kinds of decisions more clearly demand the capacity of intuition to do fast calculation for us, especially when we are under pressure. And sometimes that intuition does appear to be

fairly trustworthy. When it can draw on deeply familiar knowledge, such as expert skill, it seems that it can take over fairly reliably. Chess players, for example, can rely on their skilled pattern recognition, so that they do not have to think through all the possible consequences of a single move but instead recognize familiar sequences.

The greater the expertise, it seems, the more reliable the intuition – and the more valuable in situations demanding instant decisions. Professor Hodgkinson of Leeds University tells the story of a Formula One racing car driver who suddenly braked sharply when nearing a hairpin bend, even though it was speed that would win him the race. He could not explain why he abruptly put on the brakes. Later, when shown a video, "he realised that the crowd, which would have normally been cheering him on, wasn't looking at him coming up to the bend but was looking the other way in a frozen, static way. That was the cue. He didn't consciously process this, but he knew something was wrong and stopped in time." He thereby avoided hitting a pile-up of cars on the track ahead. His intuition had saved his life.[5]

---

[4] Haidt, J. 2012. Moral Psychology. http://people.virginia.edu/~jdh6n/moraljudgment.html
[5] "Go With Your Gut – Intuition is More Than Just a Hunch, Says New Research", Science Daily, March 6, 2008.

Similarly, outstanding athletes develop skill in reading patterns and intuitively anticipating plays. The great hockey player Wayne Gretsky, for instance, has described sending passes into what looks to the rest of us like empty ice, anticipating that teammate will be there.[6] In a contribution to this chapter, David Pinel, experienced kayak guide and outdoor leader, describes trusting to his intuition – what he calls his "spider sense" – as he judges risks in a complex situation, while variables change all around him.

Intuition based on expertise, though, is specific to its particular domain; an intuitively brilliant chess player is not an intuitively dependable outdoor leader, nor does he have any special insights into the stock market. It seems that there is no such thing as a generically intuitive person.[7]

However, even for those us with no particular expertise, there may be moments when we have to rely on our intuitions – for instance, as we decide in a flash whether to trust a stranger, to turn down one dark street rather than another, to believe one person rather than another, or to call for help. In overwhelmingly complex situations most particularly, we can hope our intuitions have picked up more information than we are conscious of taking in, and have made the right connections!

## Making moral judgments

In addition to being seen as a way of swift cognitive processing of external patterns, connections, and people, intuition has also been suggested to be a source of our moral judgments.

Haidt and Joseph suggest that we make our moral decisions at a gut level, and then rationalize them afterwards:

> Moral intuitions are a sub-class of intuitions, in which feelings of approval or disapproval pop into awareness as we see or hear about something someone did, or as we consider choices for ourselves.[8]

Among the reactions they call moral intuitions are "flashes of feeling" on seeing people suffer, particularly while others cause their suffering, or seeing people cheat or fail to return favours. Haidt has theorized that people possess "moral foundations", and that social liberals and social conservatives intuitively place emphasis on different combinations of moral values.

## Jumping into error

Although our swift pre-conscious processing helps us make quick decisions and judgments, it can also lead us into ridiculous mistakes, and possibly dangers of sorts that do not growl and rustle the grass. Warning us about the impact of following our flawed everyday intuitions are Christopher Chabris and Daniel Simons, the researchers who set up the experiment with the invisible gorilla (page 86):

> What we intuitively accept and believe is derived from what we collectively assume and understand, and intuition influences our decision automatically and without reflection. Intuition tells us that we pay attention to more than we do, that our memories are more detailed and robust than they are,

### Quick math question

How quickly can you do the following computation?

A bat and a ball together cost one dollar and ten cents ($1.10). The bat costs one dollar ($1) more than the ball. How much does the ball cost?[8]

Did you come up with the answer 10 cents? If so, you have made the same error as most university students surveyed by cognitive psychologists. Pause for a moment to move out of intuitive thinking into more conscious rational thinking. Now try again.

6    Malcolm Gladwell, "The Physical Genius", New Yorker, August 2, 1999. http://www.gladwell.com/1999/1999_08_02_a_genius.htm

7    Massimo Pigliucci and Julia Galef. Podcast "Rationally Speaking: Exploring the Borderlands between Reason and Nonsense". New York City Skeptics. 8 April 2012. http://itunes.apple.com/ca/podcast/rationally-speaking-58-intuition/id351953012?i=112896936

8    Haidt, J. and Joseph, C. 2004. *Intuitive ethics: how innately prepared intuitions generate culturally variable virtues*. Daeddalus Fall. P 56.

that confident people are competent people, that we know more than we really do, that coincidences and correlations demonstrate causation, and that our brains have vast reserves of power that are easy to unlock. But in all these cases, our intuitions are wrong, and they can cost us our fortunes, our health, and even our lives if we follow them blindly.[9]

Intuition, after all, gives us only rough judgments of patterns in the world. It is a way of knowing that we must treat with awareness and care. Its swift connection of events in a narrative, instant inferences of cause, lightning grasp of pattern, unconscious processing of practised skills, and rapid attribution of meaning can all enable us to make quick decisions in situations of uncertainty and to manage some of the complexities of the world. At the same time, however, they can block our better judgment and plunge us into error. If we want to build our knowledge reliably, we need to look more closely at intuition as a way of knowing.

## Heuristics and cognitive biases

Some of the common shortcuts in thinking taken by intuition are known as "heuristics", strategies in decision-making and problem-solving that serve us well under many circumstances, especially when information is incomplete or problems are complex. They provide "rules of thumb" for making judgments and decisions by using the swift and associative cognitive system 1 of the brain – intuition as a way of knowing.

The slower, conscious and reflective cognitive system 2 of the brain – reason as way of knowing – may not check, fully or at all, the accuracy of the quick judgments. Kahneman and Frederick explain: "System 1 quickly proposes intuitive answers to judgment problems as they arise, and System 2 monitors the quality of those proposals, which it may endorse, correct, or override. The judgments that are eventually expressed are called intuitive if they retain the hypothesized initial proposal without much modification."[10]

When reason does not override and correct our shortcut heuristics, we commonly demonstrate "cognitive biases", systematic errors in thinking. People have long recognized, of course, the human inclination toward snap judgments, preconceived ideas, and stubborn clinging to what they thought already. The term "cognitive bias" is a newly coined word for a very old human characteristic, studied in our times with the new scientific tools of the cognitive sciences.

Although there are numerous patterns of thinking that carry the label "cognitive bias", a handful of them are particularly illuminating as we try to attain our ideals of open-minded, critical thinking. So far in this book, we have already treated the first four, which we give below in quick summary. We have not previously raised the remaining six, but predict that you will recognize the kind of thinking – in others, and possibly within yourself.

## Four biases you've met

One of the things that is truly appealing about these cognitive biases is that we probably recognize most of them. Cognitive scientists, with all their contemporary methods of investigation, are illuminating on the level of the brain some of the foibles that have long attracted satirists, and which we have surely observed, to a degree, ourselves – at least in *other* people!

> "
> A man convinced against his will
> is of the same opinion still.
>
> *Traditional saying*
> "

> "
> Some valuing those of their own Side or Mind,
> Still make themselves the measure of Mankind;
> Fondly we think we honour Merit then,
> When we but praise Our selves in Other Men.[11]
>
> *Alexander Pope, 1711*
> "

9   Chabris, C. and Simons, D. 2010. *The Invisible Gorilla: And Other Ways Our Intuitions Deceive Us.* Crown, New York. P 231.

10  Kahneman and Frederick (2002), p. 51. cited in Lockton, D (2012), 'Cognitive biases, heuristics and decision-making in design for behaviour change', working paper, available at http://danlockton.co.uk

11  Alexander Pope, "Essay on Criticism", 1711. http://poetry.eserver.org/essay-on-criticism.html, accessed 17 June 2012.

## 1. Confirmation bias

Confirmation bias, our tendency to notice and interpret in terms of what we already think, should be familiar to you by now. Do you recall the problems it poses for a coherence check for truth? (See page 57) If we judge the truth of a claim based only on whether or not it "makes sense", or is consistent with what we know already, we may be inclined to reinforce what we already believe and screen out the knowledge claims that would throw parts of our current body of beliefs into question. Confirmation bias works that way, in a pre-conscious way: it makes us notice what agrees with our beliefs and not notice or reject what does not. Do you recall the difficulties, which we considered for sense perception, of suspending expectations to see what is actually there? This is a major cognitive bias, a generic tendency that takes a number of different more specific forms.

## 2. Inattentional blindness

Cognitive scientists tell us that we are biased in a way that is the negative version of confirmation bias: we do *not* notice what we do *not* expect to see. Remember the experiment with the invisible gorilla (chapter 5)?

## 3. Hindsight bias

This is the "I knew it all along" bias, which you met in the chapter on memory. Hindsight bias is confirmation bias turned to the past: what we know in the present affects what we recall ourselves as having noticed in the past, and how we recall ourselves as having interpreted it. We often think, in *hindsight*, that we had more *foresight* than we exhibited at the time, or wonder why other people could *not* have foreseen what later became obvious: for instance, how could American authorities *not* have recognized danger signals before the terrorist attacks known as 9/11?

## 4. Availability heuristic

Do you remember that you met this one, too, in the chapter on memory? (You don't?) Intuitively, we treat the events that pop to mind most readily as being common or representative ones. Yet the reason they come quickly to mind may be that they stand out as dramatic – because they are unusual. We are inclined, it seems, to be overly impressed and influenced by anecdotal evidence – stories or examples that lodge themselves in our memories.

## Six more worth meeting

### 5. Affect heuristic

The affect heuristic is particularly recognizable, perhaps, to those of us aware that we simply do not like to make rational, even mathematical, calculations to weigh pros and cons or likelihoods. Intuitions are notoriously bad at dealing with statistics and calculation of probability, but we are nevertheless inclined to accept them.

In judging probable risks and benefits, the affect heuristic categorizes risks in an oversimplified way as either good or bad – based on the *emotions* associated with each of the alternatives. As advertisers have discovered, tying a pleasant feeling with an option actually encourages us to believe that the risks in choosing it are low. Conversely, associating the option with fearful language or imagery will make us consider it riskier and see fewer benefits. We do not think analytically when we depend on our shortcuts, and we do not grasp the big picture. The result can be the rather entertaining inconsistencies described by writer David McRaney:

> Stories make sense on an emotional level, so anything that conjures fear, empathy, or pride will trump confusing statistics…. It makes you carry pepper spray while you clog your arteries with burritos. It installs metal detectors in schools but leaves french fries on the menu. It creates vegetarian smokers. Well-known, primal dangers are easy to see, easy to guard against, even when greater dangers loom.[12]

An evolutionary basis is suggested for some of the heuristics, and their simplification of the world could surely be useful for survival. It's easy to conjecture a possible basis for the affect heuristic in the positive or negative emotional associations that might gather around safe or dangerous places. But it is also easy to see the limitations of this shortcut thinking in more complex situations.

---

[12] McRaney, D. 2011. *You Are Not So Smart: Why You Have Too Many Friends on Facebook, Why Your Memory is Mostly Fiction, and 46 Other Ways You're Deluding Yourself*. New York. Gotham Books. P 145.

## 6. Halo effect

Similarly, intuitions can recognize patterns and connections – but cannot be depended on to do so accurately. The "halo effect", for example, persuades us that someone very good at one thing is likely to be very good at something else; the good judgment of a neighbour's character, for instance, is carried over to an assessment of his intelligence, or the good judgment of an employee's competence at one task is generalized to an appraisal that she is good at her whole job. Similarly, attractive people were assumed in studies to be more likeable and to have a greater probability of leading happy and satisfying lives; they were already "winners" in one domain so assumed to be so in all.

A more delicious example of the halo effect is the carryover of positive qualities of food in a way that encourages us to ignore their negative qualities. Health psychologist Kelly McGonigal reports, "Research shows that dieters significantly underestimate the calories in a food that is labeled healthy or organic. Dieters also perceive it as being more appropriate to eat every day, even if it is obviously an indulgence…".[13] It is sad to recognize that even organic foods, or ones packed with nutrients, can completely sabotage a restricted diet if they are also sweet and fatty.

## 7. Sunk cost fallacy

The "sunk cost fallacy" seems at first to be quite different from the halo effect, but has in common with it a way of thinking that ignores complexities and discourages us from changing our minds. Once

---

### Discussion Activity

#### Adopt a bias

Choose just one of the cognitive biases given here and adopt it for a week. Watch out for it in your own thinking and try to notice its effect on what you see and hear around you. When the week is done, bring to your TOK class any examples of it that you have noticed. If everyone in the class also takes on a cognitive bias, trade your best examples.

---

we have put time or money into a choice, we are likely to stick to it rather than lose what we have invested: we will go to a film when we actually want to stay home because we have already paid for the ticket, and will usually not walk out of the film when it proves to be boring because we made the effort of going to it. Similarly, a manager of a company, having made an investment in equipment, might learn of a different model that could do the same thing more cheaply and save money overall, but does not make the change because he does not want to waste the money he has already spent.[14]

In a more serious example, a country may add to its military forces even when a conflict is not going well because withdrawing would be difficult when so many lives have already been lost in the cause. Withdrawal may seem a betrayal of dead heroes, making their sacrifice futile. The emotional investment of loss and grief can thus give momentum to conflict and render peace-making more difficult.

## 8. The just-world fallacy

This cognitive bias depends on believing that the world is fair, and that people *deserve* their fortune or misfortune. We would like the world to work this way. If we feel the world is fair, then we gain a sense of greater control of our own lives and a greater sense of security: since we do not deserve misfortune, it is not going to happen to us. The intuitive belief that the world really does work this way is the just-world fallacy.

This fallacy, unfortunately, leads to a tendency to blame the victims of misfortune for their own victimization. Has a woman been raped? She must have been doing something that provoked the attack! Despite all information about actual circumstances of rapes (the rapist is usually someone familiar to the victim, and what the victim was wearing is irrelevant), this message continues to be common – with the blame and shame often assigned to the woman. A similar reaction is sometimes voiced about people who have been bullied. Couldn't she stand up for herself? Couldn't he fight back? What is wrong – *with the victims?*

---

[13] McGonigal, K. 2012. "The Halo Effect: An Example of Marketing Genius that Can Derail Diets", The Science of Willpower. Psychology Today. http://www.psychologytoday.com/blog/the-science-willpower/201202/the-halo-effect-example-marketing-genius-can-derail-diets

[14] Kanodia, C., Bushman, R., and Dickhaust, D. 1989. "Escalation Errors and the Sunk Cost Effect: An Explanation Based on Reputation and Information Asymmetries". *Journal of Accounting Research*. Vol. 27. No. 1. P 59.

While good fortune and bad do often come from personal qualities and effort, often they do not. In the real world, people do not have equal chances from the beginning or equal control of their lives. In the real world, the bad guys do often thrive while the good guys get crushed. Rationally, we know this. Yet we are inclined to feel otherwise. In one study, participants observing two men solve puzzles were told that one of the men was given a large amount of money at the end – and that it was awarded randomly. Yet even though they knew the reward was random, the observers still evaluated more highly the person who was given it, deciding that he was "smarter, more talented, and more productive."[15]

What is your first reaction to this photograph? Do you wonder what he did to be put behind bars? Do you assume that he must have *deserved* to be put in prison? The just-world fallacy reduces a world of complex social causes to a version of the world where people "get what's coming to them" – whether fortune or misfortune.

Like other cognitive biases, this one cuts out all the complexities of causation to affirm a simple pattern of the world – in this case with a sense of how the world *should* be as a secure place in which to live. The social implications of this cognitive bias are evident. It generates a belief that the poor *deserve* to be poor and that the wealthy *deserve* their wealth. The further implications for action are also clear: the belief that people deserve what they get can undermine compassion and reduce a sense of responsibility to take action on behalf of the unfortunate. The just-world fallacy turns our eyes away from examining the complex psychological and social causes of misery that befalls individuals or groups.

## 9. Attribution bias

In the attribution bias, we assign much better causes to our own actions and much better reasons to our own beliefs than we do to other people's. If we are successful ourselves, for instance, we might attribute our success to our ability and hard work (our own characteristics), while we might attribute someone else's success to their connections and pure luck (situational circumstances). If we trip and fall ourselves, we might attribute our fall to a crack in the pavement (situational circumstances), while if someone else trips and falls, we might consider him clumsy (his own characteristics).

Particularly interesting about this bias is recent recognition of the influence of culture: Asians are more likely to take the situational circumstances into account for other people as well as themselves and not fall into this bias. This difference fits with other findings about cultural differences in how we see and think: studies indicate that where Americans focus on particular details, Asians take in more of the context; and that where American news emphasizes personal attributes, Asian news focuses more on situational factors.[16]

The attribution bias is recognizable within western public discussion where perspectives conflict; people often present themselves as rational and clear thinking, while they claim that their opponents are emotionally driven and muddled. According to psychologists, the attribution comes

---

[15] McRaney, D. 2001. *You Are Not So Smart: Why You Have Too Many Friends on Facebook, Why Your Memory is Mostly Fiction, and 46 Other Ways You're Deluding Yourself*. New York. Gotham Books. Pp 108–9

[16] Winerman, L. February 2006. "The culture-cognition connection", *Monitor, American Psychological Association*. Vol 37, number 2. P 64. http://www.apa.org/monitor/feb06/connection.aspx accessed 3 June 2012.

## For Reflection

Much of the cognitive study on these biases seems to have been conducted in the United States. What difference would it make if instant cognitive reactions were studied in a culture that put less emphasis on the individual and individual choice? We can expect to learn more in upcoming years, as this is a fairly new area of study, and is being carried out in other parts of the world as well.

Add to your Life List of Interesting Issues, to explore when you can, the religious framing of ideas of the "just world" and human deserving. Think about heaven and hell, karma, and reincarnation, about ideas of divine punishment (plagues and pestilence), about the difference between determinism and fate in approach to the question of free will, about the "problem of evil" in philosophy, and about the whole idea of causation.

as a swift and intuitive bias of judgment, with justifications and arguments added later to confirm the instant judgment. One social psychologist gives a striking example from studies of attitudes toward gun control in the United States:

> …you will hear someone attribute their own position to reasoned intellectual choice ("I am for gun control because statistics show that crime decreases when gun ownership decreases" or "I'm against gun control because studies show that more guns means less crime"), and attribute the other person's opinion on the same subject to emotional need ("He's for gun control because he is a bleeding-heart liberal who needs to identify with the victim" or "He's against gun control because he's a heartless conservative who needs to feel emboldened by a weapon")[17]

As is evident in this example, the actual presentation of arguments to support the intuitive judgments can be deliberate and developed. Here, the treatment of the opposing point of view uses a form of the straw man fallacy of argument (page 129) to caricature opponents, the more readily to dismiss what they say.

This particular cognitive bias certainly stands in the way of the exchange of knowledge; it suggests that, in some contexts, people do not enter into knowledge exchange at all. Even though they contribute their own thinking to the common pool, they do not take from it the thinking of others. Instead, they stand outside the "zone of exchange" and verbally throw stones at each other.

When we come to evaluate conflicting perspectives, then, we certainly need to look at how insiders present their ideas, and not just at what outsiders claim their ideas to be! Recognition of attribution bias also hands to all of us who want to become fair thinkers, with critical and open minds, the challenge of looking at our own tendencies when we evaluate knowledge claims and perspectives.

### 10. Bias blind spot

We saved for the end the cognitive bias that we think you will like the most. "Bias blind spot" is our tendency to notice how others are affected by cognitive biases but to be blind to how we might be biased ourselves. In response to this one, what can we do but laugh? What funny creatures we are!

## Which comes first – belief or justification?

Clearly, to consider knowledge fully, we have to consider *people*. People are the ones doing the knowing – people with all their ways of knowing, all the beliefs they build from them, and all their biases. No matter how much we insist that people *should* weigh the evidence before reaching conclusions, we have to accept that human beings are not evidence-weighing machines.

Science commentator Michael Shermer goes so far as to suggest that our ideal model of knowing that we presented in chapter 4 – examining justification and *then* deciding what to accept – is backwards from what people actually do:

> We form our beliefs for a variety of subjective, personal, emotional, and psychological reasons in the context of environments created by family, friends, colleagues, culture, and society at large; after forming our beliefs we then defend, justify, and rationalize them with a

17  Shermer, M. 2011. *The Believing Brain*. New York. Times Books, Henry Holt and Company. P 265.
18  Shermer, M. 2011. *The Believing Brain*. New York. Times Books, Henry Holt and Company. P 5.

host of intellectual reasons, cogent arguments, and rational explanations. Beliefs come first, explanations for beliefs follow.[18]

Confirmation bias seems to rule out thoughts! If we aspire to be critical thinkers with open minds ourselves, we obviously need to look considerably more closely at some of our human tendencies. When we are considering how our minds deal with justifications, we need to gain knowledge of our own selves and the way we exchange ideas with others.

## Overcoming problems of intuition

How, then, can we learn about ourselves and learn to think more clearly, taking our intuitive judgments into account? Just as we did in treating sense perception as a way of knowing far back in chapter 5, we propose *not* becoming distressed over human imperfection *but instead* working as thoughtfully as we can with the ways of knowing we have.

Back then, we gave four suggestions for overcoming limitations of sense perception: pay attention, suspend expectations, disentangle observation from interpretation, and check your own observations. At this point, having examined other ways of knowing, do you see even more clearly how challenging these goals can be?

Would you agree that an exploration of knowledge is, in effect, an exploration of our own humanity? That is, in our view, one of the things that makes it so interesting!

So here are some ideas on getting the most from intuition as a way of knowing.

### a.  Learn about cognitive biases.

We are not doomed forever to leap into the same errors. The very awareness that we are inclined toward particular cognitive biases is a step toward recognizing them, moving to a deliberate and rational response, and correcting our thinking.

### b.  Try to activate rational thinking.

When we reach a conclusion intuitively, we may be right, especially in situations where our swift judgments have considerable experience and background knowledge to draw on. Yet we may be wrong. The quick hunch or the "funny feeling" ideally should not conclude our inquiry

but launch it! As cognitive scientist David Myers says, "Smart thinking, critical thinking, often begins with self-reliant hunches, but continues as one examines assumptions, evaluates evidence, invites critique, and tests conclusions."[19] The role of intuition in the methods of the sciences, for example, is exactly that: to generate hunches and hypotheses. Then reason, the companion system in our dual-system cognition, can take us the next step.

### c.  Practise counter-arguing and shifting perspectives.

To break free of some of the influence of confirmation bias, we can try to develop flexible habits of mind. When we reach a conclusion, we can ask ourselves: what could be said against it, or from another point of view? When we find ourselves facing opposing perspectives, we can ask ourselves: what differing assumptions are we starting with, and do we have different values that affect the information we consider important? What do we have in common? (As ever, see page 28.) Demonstrating these thinking skills is built right into the criteria for assessment for the TOK course. Being able to think flexibly is likely to make you a better researcher in any area of knowledge and probably a more effective member of your various communities.

### d.  Think about people, not just points of view.

Understanding how intuitions work can illuminate what is going on in some polarized knowledge exchanges. Australian scientists John Cook and Stephan Lewandowsky, having investigated why many people reject the science of climate change, identify three "backfire effects" when people encounter strong arguments opposed to their own views.

- Oppositional argument often entrenches confirmation bias; when they feel fundamental beliefs to be threatened, people strengthen their views in resistance.
- Complex factual explanations in support of an argument can provoke people to accept instead an argument that is simpler and intuitively easier to grasp, even if it is inaccurate.

---

19  David G. Myers, ""Do What You Feel, Maybe – the power and peril of relying on intuition", In Character, January 1, 2007. http://incharacter.org/ archives/self-reliance/do-what-you-feel-maybe-the-power-and-perils-of-relying-on-intuition/

- Repeating a false but familiar account in order to refute it simply makes it more likely to be remembered, uncritically.

Their overriding point is that communicating knowledge (and not just on a particular topic or from a particular perspective) has to take into account not just the facts but also the people: "It's not just *what* people think that matters, but *how* they think."[20]

We would go further to suggest that, in exchanging knowledge claims and justifications, the quality of the connection with people may in many contexts be as important as the quality of the information. The counter-arguing that we suggest above does not have to follow the "argument is war" conceptual metaphor identified in English idiom! We are probably more effective in communication of knowledge if we treat others with respect, move exchange of ideas out of a confrontational arena if possible, and develop our patience, capacity for empathy, and self-knowledge.

## Intuition: a TOK way of knowing

And so, we conclude with one last suggestion on getting the most out of our intuitions.

### e. Appreciate the power of intuition well used.

Although intuition does create some problems as we try to build knowledge reliably, it can also help us greatly in grasping patterns and relationships, and in making quick judgments and decisions. As a way of knowing, it draws on all of the others to give us swift access to our experience, skills and knowledge.

When we have a "funny feeling" that something is wrong with a friend, an "inkling" that the person we've just met is not fully trustworthy, or a "hunch" that it might be useful to take our research in a particular direction, we might well listen to our intuitions. They may not be enough in themselves for a sound conclusion, but they can alert us to situations that our more rational processing has entirely missed.

They might, too, jolt us to action that saves our lives. *There, exactly there – in the bushes! You leap back, stumbling, heart pounding. Just in time!*

> "
> Intuition is bigger than we realize. It feeds our expertise, creativity, love and spirituality. It is a wonder. But it's also perilous. Today's cognitive science aims not to destroy intuition but to fortify it, to sharpen our thinking and deepen our wisdom.... In realms from sports to business to spirituality, we now understand how perilous intuitions often go before a fall, and how we can therefore think smarter, even while listening to the creative whispers of our unseen mind.[21]
>
> *David G. Myers*
> "

### For Reflection

Do you trust your own intuitions? Why or why not? If your answer is, "It depends", then on what does it depend?

Is additional experience, reflection, and critical thinking likely to affect the nature or quality of your intuitions?

Is intuition a convincing justification for shared knowledge?

---

[20] Cook, J., Lewandowsky, S. (2011), The Debunking Handbook. St. Lucia, Australia: University of Queensland. November 5, 2011. http:/sks.to/debunk

[21] David G. Myers, "The Powers and Perils of Intuition", Psychology Today, November 1, 2002. http://www.psychologytoday.com/articles/200212/the-powers-and-perils-intuition

# 13. Ways of Knowing, Areas of Knowledge

## Discussion Activity

### Interpret the picture

You cannot look at this picture without some degree of interpretation, even in recognizing what the lines represent – a man, woman, and child. But what do you think is going on, and why do you think so? Take a moment to write down your interpretation before moving on in this book. You will see and interpret another picture at the end of the chapter.

We return, after eight chapters, to the same spot on the map. Do you recall that at the end of chapter 4 we promised we would do so – that we would take a giant loop to visit each of the eight ways of knowing in turn, but return to the questions we had been discussing at that point? Again, we are back on the high hill, looking out across the broad contours of knowledge – but you bring with you increased awareness of our different ways of knowing and many human factors involved in the knowledge exchange.

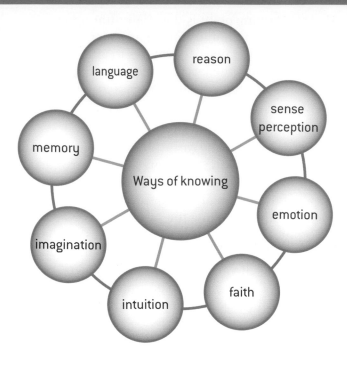

At the end of chapter 4, we were introducing huge knowledge questions that we have been exploring in different ways ever since:

- How do ways of knowing contribute to personal knowledge and shared knowledge?
- How do ways of knowing provide justifications for knowledge claims?

These same questions, accompanied by others, will take us into the next phase of our journey, into the areas of knowledge that we have constructed.

With all the thinking and discussing you've been doing of ways of knowing, it's time to drop some formality and call them by more familiar names. Surely, by now it's culturally appropriate for us all to do so! So, just as we refer to Theory of Knowledge as TOK, in this chapter we will refer to "ways of knowing" as WOK. In anticipation of even greater intimacy to come, we will call "areas of knowing" as (you guessed it!) AOK. So in our present chapter of transition, we will make sure that WOK and AOK interact in a friendly fashion, so that your onward journey will be an amicable one.

First, we'll look back on how we've seen them connecting already, as a summary and review. Then we'll look ahead to the different forms of relationships they enter in different forms of shared knowledge. From our high hill, we'll look out over the busy landscape below:

1. WOK interact with each other

2. WOK interact within a context, within a perspective

3. AOK give us knowledge of WOK

4. WOK build AOK: classification and concepts

5. WOK build AOK: methodology

6. WOK and AOK interact within a context, within a perspective.

## 1. WOK interact with each other

As we introduced you to the ways of knowing in chapter 4, we presented the list of eight to you as a useful simplification. Taking these eight as distinct "ways of knowing" is immensely helpful for identifying significant components of our process of knowing and for disentangling them to consider their characteristic features. Every one of them individually presents us with knowledge questions valuable to explore. Together, they provide a set of excellent pathways into the central question, "How do we know?"

As we will see increasingly as we enter areas of knowledge, it is extremely useful to identify specific paths into topics of complexity and to establish a common vocabulary. *First* we pin down where we want to go and what we mean, and *then* we can put our ideas more effectively into play! By now, you will be able to talk together as a class with a shared understanding of what you mean when you say "sense perception", or "intuition", or "faith", and will be able to use these concepts for further discussion of knowledge questions – as you will be doing as you treat the TOK areas of knowledge.

By now, too, you will appreciate more fully certain features of the model of the WOK wheel that we have been using. The perimeter of the circle and the crossbars of the wheel join up every way of knowing to every other, with a large zone of exchange in the centre where all of them can meet. This idea is certainly familiar to you by now: that our ways of knowing intersect with each other, and interact. You will also recognize that a wheel can be held still for examination, but that its features blur together when it spins in active use.

The WOK wheel is not static but dynamic. Even while we have disentangled the ways of knowing as much as we could for separate consideration, we have also recognized, time and time again, how they interact. Simply think back to the small child trying to recognize and name "doggies" early in the chapter on reason, with numerous ways of knowing in play, or to the role of sense perception and language in trying to pin down exactly what "emotion" is as a way of knowing. Recall the dual-system cognition of intuition and reason and how it affects sense perception and memory. Do you remember, too, the uncertainties that surround eyewitness reports, involving sense perception, memory, and emotion – at the very least? How did you respond to questions on the intersection of faith with all of our other ways of knowing, or to the questions on imagination as it draws on other ways of knowing to create a new connection or fusion? Before moving on, we suggest that you undertake the activity "Just a minute! Talk WOK." for a quick review – and for fun.

## 2. WOK interact within a context, within a perspective

When we use our ways of knowing, we use them somewhere in the world, in a real context alive with different perspectives. We use them interactively, yes, but in different blends and balances within different circumstances and different cultural backgrounds.

Again, this idea should be familiar to you. Think of the concept of "perspectives" that we raised in chapter 1 particularly for cultural and political views, and have been using ever since, with references back to our guide to analysis (page 28). The cultural, political, religious, and other perspectives that make up our worldviews affect how we use all of our ways of knowing. Do you remember from the chapter on sense perception, for instance, the little story of Mrs. Ngo and the cultural choice of stairs, or the discussions involving the Deaf community on medical and cultural models of deafness? You are likely to recall the strong suggestions, as we treated emotion, that what emotions we feel in particular situations, and how we act on those feelings, are affected by our cultures. You are aware, too, of the convergence of sense perception and emotions with memory, and how deeply affected that blend can be by personal and collective experience of the world, hugely influenced by our social contexts.

### Discussion Activity

### Just a minute! Talk WOK.

1 Divide your class into small groups of 3–4 students. Each group needs two sheets of heavy paper, different colours.

2 Within your group, cut each sheet into eight equal rectangles, to create two sets of "cards". For each set, write the names of the eight TOK ways of knowing. Place both stacks with the names face down and sit in a circle around them.

3 You will be playing several rounds. For each round, you will have a **timekeeper**, a **speaker**, and a **judge**, with each role moving each turn to the person on the left.

4 To play, pick your first speaker. He or she will pull one card from each stack and turn it over – to hold two ways of knowing. (If the same WOK comes up from both piles, put one of them back and pull again.)

**Timekeeper**, be ready! You will be counting seconds. A timing device like a watch or mobile phone is useful.

**Speaker**, you have only 20 seconds of preparation time, and must speak for ONE MINUTE on how your two ways of knowing interact.

Goals:

- Speak clearly and *non-stop!*
- Give as many ways as you can in which your two ways are interconnected in knowing, not just listing them but explaining what you mean (e.g. how one influences the other, opposes or helps the other, explains the other – in either direction – or how they work together toward particular goal).
- Give at least one example of their interaction from an area of knowledge (e.g. one of your IB subjects).
- Give at least one example of their interaction from personal observation of everyday life.

**Judge**, you must listen closely and be ready to give a score out of a maximum of 10:

- 2 points for each connection the speaker makes between the ways of knowing if it is distinct and clear
- 2 points for each of the examples if they are clear
- 1 point for speaking non-stop, with pauses no longer than about 5 seconds
- 1 bonus point if you think the speaker has been lively or funny.

You must award your score within 20 seconds of the end of the speaker's turn. Do not hesitate to give the full 10 if the conditions are met.

**Scramble:** Everyone in the group should now quickly add any further ideas that come to mind on the speaker's WOK combination.

Then the cards are shuffled back into the others and play moves on to the left. Who wins? Everyone!

Language, of all ways of knowing, is probably most obviously rooted in culture, but so, too, may be faith – how we conceptualize this way of knowing and what role we give it in our lives. Similarly, even the interaction of emotion and imagination in empathy – that capacity that in turn motivates how we use our ways of knowing further – is affected by how we develop within our home and educational contexts in different places around the world. (Indeed, a consideration of the impact of context on how we develop and use our ways of knowing often confronts us with a significant ongoing question of research and theory: To what extent are we as human beings affected by nature/heredity, and to what extent by nurture/environment?)

Before moving on, read the "Voices" contribution here from Sylla Cousineau, a multi-lingual IB Diploma history teacher, speaking of first learning Japanese as a young man. In it, he is sharing his personal experience of entering a language and a culture. But when you've read what he says of the experience, consider the following questions:

- What ways of knowing does he seem to be using as he learns the language in Japan? What more is necessary for speaking the language than simply knowing how to position and utter the words? From your own experience learning languages that are not your mother tongue, what ways of knowing have you found interacting when you are speaking it within a living context?

## Voices

### Japanese: "I found that it mediated my thinking"

I was a grown individual, aged 21, when I learned Japanese, but even acquiring the language at that point of relative maturity, as an outsider, I found that it did over time end up mediating my thinking. Perhaps it has not changed the filters

*Sylla Cousineau*

through which I see reality, but it has modified them.

In Japan traditionally one was never determined by the self as an individual, but always as a member of a group, and the language has been shaped by that. In learning Japanese, I had to come to a new understanding of myself, and of hierarchy and group, and the language forced me to internalize this new understanding, partly intellectually, partly organically. Japanese is constructed in a way that often makes it difficult to know what might be expressed until the very end of the sentence. This structural aspect as well as the fact that it is a supremely situational language has made me a much better listener than I used to be, more attuned to what others might mean, and less prompt to project my understanding onto their expressed meaning.

I had previously assumed that sincerity was something that one saw on someone's face, that truth could and should be read into someone's

eyes. Not anymore. In Japan, the prescribed body language is such that insistent personal expression makes one feel quirky. It is rough, confrontational. In Japanese society, truer feelings are not displayed but intimated; it is traditionally not a culture of representation of the self but of representation by consent. In Japan, one generally deals with people completely in their social roles, where everything is codified, and smooth, with the support of the expected: one always knows what to do or to say.

For these reasons, the Japanese have often been thought of in the West as hypocritical, but in a certain way, they are less so than people in the West, because no one is fooling anyone else. I find this more honest. The mask is a lie—but it is a socially true lie. In the west we also wear masks, but we pretend it is our real self. In fact, we have a "representational neurosis"—enhanced by television, movies and other media with their emphasis on faces—whereby people are acting their own lives. "I feel joy. I feel anger. Can't you see it on my face?"

This being said, with the advent of mobile phones first and smart phones later, there has been a sea change in attitudes in Japan over the last few years. Japanese society has become more atomized and the old codes are being eroded by the prevalence of mobile electronic communication (especially texting) that have led to a breakdown of conventions and have forced their users into linguistic idiosyncrasy.

*Sylla Cousineau*[1]

---

[1] Sylla Cousineau, IB Diploma teacher of History, is currently at the Li Po Chun United World College in Hong Kong.

- What background knowledge does Sylla Cousineau bring to the experience of language learning, and what does he take out of it? From your own experience, what areas of knowledge contribute to your gaining the most from your experience? Is an understanding of sociology, politics, psychology, history, or any other area valuable?

## 3. AOK give us knowledge of WOK

We have learned a great deal about how our ways of knowing work through studies within our AOK, many of which actively investigate them. You may have noticed in the recent chapters how often we have brought in recent research.

Even the basic understanding of our key concepts that weave through our discussion of the WOK relies on what others have learned before us. If you glance back, you'll recognize that the treatment of perspectives in chapter 1, for instance, owes much to the fields of cultural studies and political science, and that the treatment of truth in chapter 3 owes much to philosophy. Most of the fallacies of argument that we have presented in the "Thinking Critically" interchapters also have a long history, and

### Senses and Anthropological Sensibilities

*by Thomas Hylland Eriksen*

…how does the use of the senses differ cross-culturally, how can smell, touch and sound be explored ethnographically, and what methodological problems arise from the variations?

A certain visual bias is evident in many – probably most – ethnographic writings. Descriptions of field settings usually concentrate on spatial organisation, buildings, plants and generally what meets the eye. Sounds, tastes and smells tend to be conspicuously absent, as noted by Mary Louise Pratt (1986). Constance Classen (1993) remarks that the Ongee of the Andaman Islands live in a world ordered by smell, and links the "olfactory decline of the West" with the growth of scientific rationalism. Whereas a rose was associated with smell in antiquity and in medieval times, by the eighteenth century its main purpose had become "to divert the eye and thereby divert the mind" (Classen 1993, p. 27). Paul Stoller has argued along similar lines (1989), indicating that the senses have been subject to a lot of scattered attention, but little systematic treatment, in anthropology. Stoller's work on the senses in society and culture range from embodied memories to the classification of smell, while David Howes (2003, 2004) is concerned equally with cross-cultural comparisons and the cultural specificity of the senses as social and cultural phenomena in particular societies.

In the pioneering monograph Sound and Sentiment, Steven Feld (1982) describes a people in New Guinea, the Kaluli, for whom sound and music are central cosmological categories. The Kaluli classify birds not only according to their appearance, but also according to their song. Indeed, Feld shows how sounds function as a symbolic system of meaning in Kaluli society. Song and music, thus, are considered highly important among the Kaluli. Speaking more generally, Walter Ong (1969; see also Stoller 1997) argues that oral societies, unlike literate ones, tend not to "picture" the world and thus do not, in a strict sense, have a "world-view", but rather "cast up actuality in comprehensive auditory terms, such as voice and harmony". Classen, comparing three oral societies, the Tzotzil of Mexico, the Ongee of the Andaman Island and the Desana of Colombia, finds that they all have distinct ways of making sense of the world: "the Tzotzil order the cosmos by heat, the Ongee by smell, and the Desana by colour" (Classen 1993, p. 122). In other words, the visual/aural dichotomy is too simple, but at least it points out the importance of studying the social use of the senses – and of reflecting critically on ethnography's over-reliance on sight and visual metaphors (Salmond 1982).[2]

---

[2]　Eriksen, TH. 2010. *Small Places, Large Issues: An Introduction to Social and Cultural Anthropology*, 3rd edition. London and New York. Pluto Press. Pp 50–1.

versions of most of them also bear, in other contexts, Latin names two millennia old. As we develop *personal knowledge* of concepts central to TOK, we are drawing on the *shared knowledge* from times past.

Our contemporary understanding of *how we know* has been influenced considerably by research in the cognitive sciences – an interdisciplinary study of how the mind works. We have encountered the cognitive sciences again and again, for instance in the debates on how language is learned (chapter 8), or in current ideas of the dual-system cognition of intuition and reason (particularly chapters 7 and 12), or in the heuristics and cognitive biases that affect how we reach conclusions through ways such as sense perception and memory. Included within the cognitive sciences are neuroscience (biology, chemistry, and others), psychology, linguistics, anthropology, philosophy, and artificial intelligence. They share knowledge on the very process of thinking and knowing.

Clearly, our AOK give us greater understanding of our WOK. Before moving on, we suggest that you pause to read one example of AOK doing so, in the extract presented here entitled "Senses and anthropological sensibilities". When you have read it, consider the questions below:

- What do we learn about cultural influences on human use of sense perception from studies mentioned in Eriksen's summary – even though he makes no generalizations universally applicable to all societies?
- Did you notice Eriksen's extensive use of other anthropologists as he surveys the literature? To what extent does his point in this short piece depend on anthropology being not *personal knowledge* but *knowledge shared* through publication?
- Eriksen expresses concern about what he sees as a bias in "ethnographies" – that is, the records that anthropologists write of cultures. Why is the method of study – the *methodology* of a discipline – important in making and recording observations? What is the role in any AOK of critical reflection on shortcomings in methodology?

## 4. WOK build AOK: classification and concepts

The relationship between WOK and AOK goes much further, though. We *construct* our areas of knowledge using our ways of knowing. Our observations of the world, our emotions, our intuitions and reasoning, our faith, memories, imaginations, and our languages all provide the ways through which we gain knowledge. The areas of knowledge accepted in academic contexts are specializations of our everyday knowledge, using WOK as they take certain subject matter within their scope and develop appropriate methods of study.

One of the most important elements of knowledge, everyday or academic, is the way we classify our world and our thoughts. We generalize and name, and in the process lay down the paths that much of the rest of our knowledge will follow. This idea is already familiar to you – perhaps notably from the chapters on reason (generalization), language (naming), and emotion and faith (importance of defining concepts). As we will increasingly see throughout Part 3, how we classify our ideas in language -- that is, how we establish our concepts -- has a major impact on how we build our different areas of knowledge.

> "
> Categorization is not a matter to be taken lightly. There is nothing more basic than categorization to our thought, perception, action and speech. Every time we see something as a kind of thing, for example, a tree, we are categorizing. Whenever we reason about kinds of things – chairs, nations, illnesses, emotions, any kind of thing at all – we are employing categories … And any time we either produce or understand any utterance of a reasonable length, we are employing dozens if not hundreds of categories: categories of speech sounds, of words, of phrases and clauses, as well as conceptual categories. Without the ability to categorize, we could not function at all, either in the physical world or in our social and intellectual lives. An understanding of how we categorize is central to an understanding of what makes us human."[3]
>
> *George Lakoff*
> "

---

[3]  Lakoff, G. 1987. *Women, Fire and Dangerous Things. Chicago.* University of Chicago Press. Pp 5–6

## Discussion Activity

### Classification game

In advance, designate one person to collect 12 objects with as much diversity as possible. These should be placed on a surface so that everyone can see them. Get into groups of 3–4 people. Each group's mission is to classify those 12 objects into categories. These are the rules:

**Rule 1:** Create three or four categories that will accommodate all the objects. Describe each category with the label "Things that are […]".

**Rule 2:** Each category must have two or more objects (no orphans or empty categories!).

**Rule 3:** Each object must belong to one, and only one category.

**Rule 4:** Be as creative as you can. Groups are encouraged to handle the objects in order to get creativity flowing.

When ready (probably 15–20 minutes of discussion), each group should describe their classification scheme to the rest of the class. The class then critiques each group's scheme. Among the schemes that survive close scrutiny, the scheme that best satisfies rule 4 is deemed to be the winner.

### Follow-up questions:

- What TOK ways of knowing did you use in establishing categories?
- What different criteria of classification did your class as a whole consider, regardless of whether they worked or not? For what purposes would each set of criteria be useful?
- What difficulties did you encounter in creating your categories? If rule 3 was the most difficult, why do you think that would that be? Is this rule necessary for a useful classification scheme? As you put objects and people into categories in everyday life, do you often find that they do not fit neatly into categories?
- In what ways can you be categorized yourself? How might you be classified by your school's database, your doctor's office, your country's military, or manufacturers of products such as jeans or mobile phones – just as examples? In each of these categories, does rule 3 apply?

Here, we turn some closer attention to classifying, and to tracing some of the implications of how we do it. We recommend that you start by playing the classification game we provide here, and discussing with your class the follow-up questions. In playing this game, you deal directly with some of the features of classification schemes.

But how certain are the categories we construct? If they are based on *observation*, are they accurate knowledge statements about the world? If they are based on *social convention*, are they useful – and if so, *for what and whose purposes*? If they based on *value judgments*, or have values attributed to them, on what are those judgments based and who holds them? If they are *definitional* statements, how clear and useful are they?

Classification *based on observation* is basic to our being able to tell a rock from a tree, or more finely a tree from a bush. Some major undertakings in knowledge have tried to classify our world following the inclusive rule 1 and the exclusive rule 3 of our game. Take, for example, Carl Linnaeus in the 1730s, starting to develop his impressive *Species Plantarum and Systema Naturae* (kingdom/phylum/class/order/family/genus/species). He aimed to classify all the elements of the natural world. But what should his criterion of classification be? Weight, colour, density, texture, shape, symmetry, or even smell – any of these could have qualified as important distinguishing features of the vast array of elements he meant to classify. Over a period of 35 years, Linnaeus continually revised his system, including new plant and animal species. He had a significant insight about what features were important when, in the 10th edition, he decided to classify whales as mammals instead of as fish.[4]

---

4  Uppsala Universitet. *Systema Naturae—an epoch-making book.* http://www.linnaeus.uu.se/online/animal/1_1.html

## Discussion Activity

### Implications of classifications

Although some of our categorizations are fairly trivial, others carry significant implications for understanding and action. Consider the following examples with your class. What are the implications for how the categories are applied?

- What is meant by "triage" and how was it established? What are the implications for action of this classification scheme?
- What is the Integrated Food Security Phase Classification and how was it established? What does "famine" mean? Does designating a crisis by this word place any responsibility on the world community?
- When is a fetus classified as a human being? What are the possible implications of this classification?
- When is a person living in a society classified as an "illegal alien", "refugee", "immigrant", or "citizen"? What comes with being placed in each category?
- Can you think of classifications within your own society, and possibly your own life, that carry significance for attitudes or actions?

His *Species Plantarum* (1753) listed approximately 8,000 plant species from around the world, while his *Systema Naturae* (12th ed., 1758) includes some 4,378 animal species.[5]

Significant to the classification that Linnaeus constructed is how he used the ways of knowing. We can conjecture that he used imagination – how could he not have done so? It's likely that intuition took him to some of his categories, and that emotion, memory, and faith were all involved in the process. Yet, as we regard his classification scheme, the backstory disappears. In his scientific results, what we recognize are sense perception (observation), reason, and (in sophisticated binomial nomenclature) language.

Significant, too, is the way that Linnaeus' classification scheme was open to change. Not only did he revise it himself as he worked, but others since him have modified the classification

as they did further investigation. Does a virus, for instance, belong in a category of living things? It was demoted in 1935 to a "package of complex biochemicals".[6]

When their subject matter seems to have fewer observable regularities than the natural world, areas of knowledge construct classifications that may not be able to follow inclusive rule 1 of the game (accommodate all in a category) or exclusive rule 3 (place in only one category). Complex material often eludes precise categorization in the human sciences and history as they deal with human thought and behaviour (present or past), the arts as they deal with products of creativity, and ethics as it deals with morality.

The human sciences and history, moreover, study the way that human beings construct their categories. These areas of knowledge often deal with our "social constructs" – that is, the classifications that we do not observe in the world but instead invent socially or culturally. We don't usually give such categories much thought if we fit the systems, and they benefit us. But, have you ever had to fill out a form, only to find that you didn't fit its categories in a way that enabled you to answer the questions? Do names always have one "surname" and more than one "given name"? Are the given names (sometimes called "first names") customarily placed first in use? We have

### For Reflection

What are the roles played in classification by hasty generalization and confirmation bias?

What are the differences between a generalization, a stereotype, and a caricature? How does each influence how we think?

---

5 Hunt Institute. *Order from Chaos: Linnaeus Disposes. The search for a natural classification scheme.* http://huntbot.andrew.cmu.edu/HIBD/Exhibitions/OrderFromChaos/pages/02Linnaeus/scientific.shtml

6 Villarreal, L.P. December 2004. "Are Viruses Alive?"*Scientific American* http://www.scientificamerican.com/article.cfm?id=are-viruses-alive-2004

multitudes of cultural systems and conventions of classification like this one – along with scores of ways of categorizing people (e.g. class or caste, gender roles) and measuring the world (e.g. distance, size, direction).

To the question *"Is this classification accurate?"* that we applied to observations of the natural world, then, we have to add, *"Who developed this classification?"* and *"For what purpose and for whose benefit?"* After all, our categories carry implications for how we think and possibly how we act in the world. Classifications of gender and race are particularly socially potent, since the way they are imposed and interpreted involves social power. What we claim that we *know* about categories of people affects their destinies. Scientific study of race, for instance, tells us that it has no biological reality, and that racist categorization has fixed on certain human variables among many and attached to them value judgments and emotions.[7] And yet – this social construction of meaning and value has significantly affected the history of the world.

This kind of classification often resists change, as it is entrenched in the prejudices of society. As social analysts Ella Shohat and Robert Stam remark, "Racism often travels in gangs, accompanied by its buddies sexism, classism, and homophobia. Systems of social stratification thus get superimposed on one another…"[8] In classification, clearly, we are dealing not just with objects but with *concepts*. As we build our knowledge, we need to examine closely the concepts we use, for what we assume or accept along with them. In treating areas of knowledge ahead, we will have reason to give attention to the categories they use for analysis, and the kinds of language they employ.

We leave this topic with a final question of how we categorize our concepts, through using other concepts: *"Is the definition clear?"* As anyone following debates over "multi-culturalism" will be keenly aware, little knowledge is exchanged when the participants in discussion are talking about entirely different things![9] As we will see regarding AOK, how we classify our ideas in language - that is, how we name and define our

concepts - has a significant impact on the way we investigate and exchange ideas. Indeed, as we turn to the *knowledge framework* that will structure our discussions, you will find *language and concepts* to be a major conceptual category itself!

## 5. WOK build AOK: methodology

Clearly, our ways of knowing interact to give us much of our everyday knowledge as we classify, and give us much of our academic knowledge as we develop conscious classifications systems or study socially constructed ones in the different areas of knowledge. As we grow aware of how those categories affect us, and try not to be drawn into errors or pre-judgments, we are exercising our capacity to think critically. We are taking a giant step down the road toward conscious and careful methods of study.

How we use our ways of knowing in the different areas of knowledge is dependent upon their subject matter and their goals. What are these areas all about, and what do they want to do? The arts will not use the same balance or blend of WOK as the natural sciences, nor will either of them use WOK in the same manner as in religious knowledge. These AOK talk about different things, for different purposes, and therefore employ their WOK differently in their methods.

Our AOK may lie along a spectrum in their goals, from *subjectivity* to *objectivity* (Overview p108). As you will see increasingly through Part 3 of this book, such a spectrum allows only fuzzy categorization; all areas involve subjectivity, so differences are a matter of its role and degree. Moreover, the WOK used in the *creation* of knowledge are not necessarily the same ones as are evident in its *communication* (as we noted with Linnaeus) or its *evaluation*.

Yet, despite the fuzziness and patchiness of this spectrum, we can see its usefulness in drawing distinctions between the goals and methods of different AOK. The works of art that we celebrate across our histories do tend to stir our sense perceptions, emotions, and imaginations, as well as ideas in our minds. They lie towards the subjective end of our spectrum. And the works of science

---

[7]  "Interview with Jonathan Marks", Race, the Power of an Illusion. PBS. http://www.pbs.org/race/000_About/002_04-background-01-08.htm

[8]  Shohat, E. and Stam, R. 1994. *Unthinking Eurocentrism*. London and New York. Routledge. P 22.

[9]  Inglis, C. 1995. *"Multiculturalism: New Policy Responses to Diversity"* Management of Social Transformations (MOST) - UNESCO. Policy Paper No. 4. Available online at: http://www.unesco.org/most/pp4.htm#clarification

## Discussion Activity

### Sunlight on the Garden: language in sciences and poetry

#### The Sunlight on the Garden

The sunlight on the garden
Hardens and grows cold,
We cannot cage the minute
Within its nets of gold,
When all is told
We cannot beg for pardon.

Our freedom as free lances
Advances towards its end;
The Earth compels, upon it
Sonnets and birds descend;
And soon, my friend,
We shall have no time for dances.

The sky was good for flying
Defying the church bells
And every evil iron
Siren and what it tells:
The Earth compels,
We are dying, Egypt, dying

And not expecting pardon,
Hardened in heart anew,
But glad to have sat under
Thunder and rain with you,
And grateful too
For sunlight on the garden.

*Louis MacNeice*

### Language in the sciences

- Physics students, what is *light?* How would you describe it in physics?
- Chemistry students, how would you describe *gold?* What is it on the periodic table?
- Biology and environmental systems students, what is a *garden* – or an ecosystem? What is the reaction of plants to light in the process of photosynthesis? Can you give a formula?

Why is it important to classify our concepts using language, and to share a common definition in naming? What is the attitude in the sciences towards ambiguity in definitions?

### Everyday denotations and connotations

Now take the words not for their denotations but for their connotations, their shades of meaning.

- What are your associations with "sunlight"? Does "sunlight" mean something other than "light"?
- What are your associations with "gold"? What stories or legends do you know in which gold is important? What sports or social events?
- What are your associations with a "garden"? Do you have personal memories, or cultural or religious associations?

### Language in poetry

- Does sunlight literally "harden and grow cold"? Would you try literally to cage a minute? Is MacNeice, in the poem as a whole, actually talking about a garden and sunlight?
- Does "beg for pardon" mean (a) apologize, or (b) petition to cancel a punishment such as execution? How can you tell? Is every interpretation in poetry equally valid?
- "We are dying, Egypt, dying" is a modification of the dying words of Mark Anthony of Rome to his beloved Cleopatra of Egypt in Shakespeare's *Anthony and Cleopatra*, IV, xv, 41. The lovers can't escape their public roles and the forces of empire. Why does MacNeice use Shakespeare's line here? Would borrowing someone else's work without acknowledgment be acceptable in science?
- Would you expect scientific language to use rhythm, rhyme, alliteration, assonance, and words seemingly selected for their sound? What is their effect in this poem?
- Why does MacNeice repeat himself? Was he not able to make his point the first time?
- Is your interpretation of the poem affected if we tell you it was written in 1937, when MacNeice foresaw war in Europe? Did you realize that the "iron sirens" are air raid warnings?
- A poem, like a song, can gather personal associations which add to its meaning for you personally. Does it surprise you that past IB Diploma Programme students have written songs with this poem as the lyrics?

**Knowledge question:** How do the subject matter and goals of an area of knowledge affect the kind of language it uses and the ways in which it draws on subjectivity and objectivity?

What is going on in this picture? On what do you base your interpretation? First write down what you think, and then compare your impressions with those of classmates.

Refresh your memory on how you and your classmates interpreted the picture at the beginning of the chapter. As the visual perspective on the three people shifts, do you gain any new information relevant to an interpretation?

What is the role of intuition in this activity? What is the role of other ways of knowing? What does the activity of interpreting both pictures suggest metaphorically about perspectives in the context of TOK?

What do variable interpretations suggest about the role and value of methodologies of observation in the human sciences?

that we value – and have not discarded so far in the development of the discipline – are ones that demonstrate close observation and reasoning, shared in a particular kind of language. They lie towards the objective end of our spectrum. Take a moment here to discuss "Sunlight on the Garden" and to consider how the subject matter and goals

of an AOK affect the language it uses and the ways in which it draws on subjectivity and objectivity.

Clearly, our AOK are characterized by features of their own: they consider different subject matter and do not always take the same goals. They use their ways of knowing in dissimilar balances, as a result, drawing variably on subjectivity and objectivity. After all, *how* we study depends on *what* we study: AOK have to construct appropriate methods of gaining knowledge. As they develop as disciplines, they are typified, to a great extent, by their *methodologies*. We will return to this point more fully in the *knowledge framework* in the next chapter.

## 6. WOK and AOK interact within a context, within a perspective

As we recognize how ways of knowing actually create our areas of knowledge, the relationship between WOK and AOK becomes downright intimate! How can we even separate them?

Indeed, placing WOK and AOK into categories – deciding what the categories will be, and how many – is simply another kind of classification. It is one that we have constructed, and one that could be done otherwise. WOK and AOK don't exist as physical entities in reality; they are *concepts*. Indeed, "ways of knowing" and "areas of knowledge" gain their meaning as concepts only within a particular approach to discussing knowledge, and within TOK what is included within WOK and AOK has changed with shifts in the course. Our classification of WOK and AOK is a tool for thought, nothing more. But, significantly, it is *nothing less*. Conceptual tools help us to share our thoughts and to build and reflect upon knowledge together.

And who uses these tools? In talking of "ways of knowing" and "areas of knowledge", we are abstracting them artificially from the people who create and exchange knowledge in all the living contexts of this world. Let us, as we conclude this section of our exploration of knowledge, step back into the social world. We will end with the comments of journalist Manini Chatterjee as she both uses ways of knowing and observes others also doing so, within a cultural context with which she is deeply familiar. Read "Journalism in cultural context" and consider how the WOK and the AOK of our TOK classifications interact in knowledge.

## Interview

## Journalism in cultural context

## Manini Chatterjee, IB Diploma graduate 1981.

*Manini Chatterjee is a writer and journalist based in New Delhi. She is author of* Do and Die, The Chittagong Uprising 1930–34 *(Penguin India 1999; Picador 2010). She is currently Editor, National Affairs, of The Telegraph, a newspaper published from Calcutta.*

➔ **As a journalist, you work with language as a way of gaining and communicating knowledge. But to what extent do you have to be aware of other "ways of knowing" in order to work effectively with language?**

As a journalist, I use words to tell a story. But that is only the last link in the chain, so to speak. In order to tell a story, one has to first understand its various dimensions, many of which fall outside the domain of language, strictly speaking.

Most good stories are about ordinary people – what they think and feel, what moves them to anger or despair, to hope or joy. And these emotions are not always conveyed in clear-cut sentences. Often, the tone of what is said is important; the pauses and silences and sighs convey volumes; and the use of idiom draws on lived experience, inherited memories, historical tradition and folklore.

In India, particularly, where we have a multiplicity of languages, cultures, and histories, a journalist has to be acutely aware of "context" that goes beyond the verbal in order to understand a situation and then convey it through words. I write in English, but the people I speak to seldom know the language. So we are translating from spoken Hindi (or Bengali or any of the many "vernacular" languages) in our reports. But a literal translation does not always work. Moreover, in India, where literacy levels are still very low, people often refer to myth and legend, to characters and situations in our two great mythological epics – the Ramayana and Mahabharata – to convey something seemingly quotidian but actually quite profound.

What I am saying is that we often use language without being aware of how embedded it is in so many different ways of knowing and communicating. This is much more explicit in non-western cultures where the oral tradition – or the non-literal tradition to be precise – till recently, was the principal mode of transmission of knowledge from one generation to another. Under the Indian caste system, only the upper castes were allowed to read and write and regarded themselves as the sole custodian of "knowledge and culture". But though the rest of the population may have been illiterate, they were not devoid of knowledge. Weavers and potters, wandering bards and folk singers, actors and artists were also both gatherers and disseminators of knowledge, using their mediums to tell stories from the past and about the present.

As a journalist, I am – as indeed we all are – aware of how words are only one way of giving expression to the world around us and how inadequate they can be. It is a constant struggle to convey the myriad shades of experience and meaning and knowledge through the written word.

➔ **What kinds of background knowledge do you find important for interpreting what you observe as a journalist?**

Let me give you one example of the need for background knowledge. I have done all kinds of writing and reportage as a newspaper journalist but I am essentially a political journalist and have covered Indian politics for decades now. But more than meeting the country's top politicians and reporting on Parliament proceedings, what I enjoy most is field reporting during elections – that is, travelling to remote villages in India at election time to talk to the ordinary voter to find out which way the political wind is blowing.

In the state of Bihar, one of India's biggest and most backward provinces, the local ruling party headed by a charismatic leader had been ruling for 15 years. His primary political base was among a caste called the Yadavs. Members of this caste traditionally rear cows, buffaloes and sundry cattle. The election symbol of this ruling party was a lantern. (In rural India, where many villages still don't have electricity, kerosene oil lanterns are used extensively as the only source of light after sunset.)

When I was covering the elections in this state in 2005, I came across a man sitting atop a buffalo, and he confirmed that he belonged to the Yadav caste. I asked him whether the lantern was shining brightly this time. His cryptic reply was: "When kerosene is selling at more than Rs 30 a litre, how do you expect me to light a lantern?" On the face of it, it was a simple reply to a simple question. But it was redolent with political meaning because the lantern denoted both a political party and the state of the people's wellbeing. Since my interlocutor belonged to the caste that usually voted for the local party, his answer indicated that the party was in bad trouble this time. When the results came out, I was proved right. The party lost the election. An outsider, who did not know the layers of meaning behind a simple set of words, would not have caught the nuances of what was said or what was actually happening on the ground. ■

**Questions for discussion: "Journalism in cultural context"**

- In this interview, Manini Chatterjee speaks of gaining and communicating knowledge. What ways of knowing, other than language, does she comment on using? Would you add any others that she seems to use but does not mention?
- What background knowledge is evident in Ms Chatterjee's responses to the interview questions? Which of the following might be relevant to her observations and interpretation, even in her brief comments: knowledge of folklore, culture, languages, the arts, psychology, sociology, politics, and history?

# WOK, AOK, and TOK

As we look out across the landscape of knowledge for the last time in this part of the book, we offer you these final questions. In the chapters ahead we will be using extensively the concepts that we have established in our model:

- What are the advantages to discussion of knowledge gained by identifying and using eight "ways of knowing" and eight "areas of knowledge"?
- What are the advantages to discussion of knowledge gained by recognizing that our WOK and AOK are simplified models?

# Should I believe it? A guide to evaluating knowledge claims

| The three S's: source, statements, self | | |
|---|---|---|
| *Source* | *Statements* | *Self* |
| As we gain knowledge from a range of different sources – people, books, Internet sites, media – what general critical questions should we ask about them? | What critical questions should we pose about the knowledge claims themselves – what they say, how they say it, and what justification they provide in support? | What critical questions should we ask ourselves about our own perspectives, blind spots, skills in evaluation, and responsibility for action? |

## 1. Source

- To what extent does this source provide credible authority? What are the speaker's, writer's or organization's qualifications and experience? Are they relevant to the claims being made?

- If the source is claiming to be an expert, has he actually had work published in peer-reviewed journals respected in the relevant field? If you are reading on the web, what kind of website hosts the article (check "about" and "home")? Is it a credible source, such as a university website or a peer-reviewed journal?

- Are there any "red flags" that instantly suggest a dubious source? For example, is the source claiming to be a lone genius, unappreciated and suppressed by the establishment?

- Does the source acknowledge counter-claims or limitations of its own knowledge – as you are expected to do in your own TOK essays?

- Has your understanding of this source been influenced by other sources, such as friends, speakers, bloggers, or other media? If the source has been controversial, is the controversy relevant to the topic and the source's credibility? Is it well-founded criticism, or is it a fallacy of appeal to the speaker or source? (See fallacies p173)

- Does the source give information from an identifiable perspective (See perspectives chapter 1)? Could it have a motive for deception? Is your source consistent with other credible sources? Does it conflict or complement? (See coherence check for truth p57.)

- Does the source provide ways of checking accuracy – references to professional or social organizations, or footnotes to further sources that can be readily traced? Do you judge the sources of your source to be reliable?

- If the source is an eyewitness, how reliable? Are or were his senses working normally, free of drugs or other substances? Did he have good viewing conditions, over adequate time? Was he in a situation of stress at the time of observation? What factors of race, sex, ethnic group, etc. could generate confirmation bias

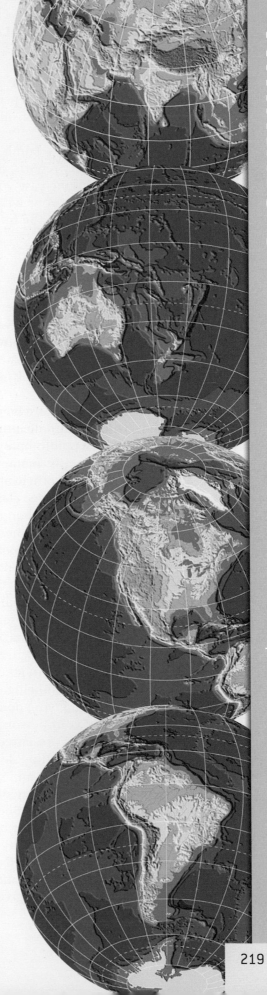

(p62, 93, 199)? What degree of memory decay is likely with the passage of time? (See eyewitness memory in chapter 6.)

- If the source is a collective one, such as Wikipedia, what degree of dependence will you place on it? Will you consult it at first but read further?
- If the sources are friends, familiar authority figures, or community reports, does personal trust in relationships increase your trust – or possibly undermine your willingness to evaluate the accuracy of the information?

## 2. Statements

- Why is the particular topic being discussed at this time, and why from this perspective? Is the article contributing to a larger discussion or debate within an area of knowledge, a professional body, or the media? Do the conclusions have implications for any current social issues?
- What knowledge claims are being made by this source? Are they implicit or explicit? What kinds of claims dominate – observational claims, value judgments, metaphysical claims, definitions, hypothetical statements, predictions? (See knowledge claims p45)
- Can you sum up the central arguments the source is making? (See argument p125)
- Can you identify any fallacies of argument? Do they seem to be momentary failures or part of a strategy of communication?
- What seems to be the main goal of this speech, article, blog, or video – to present facts, narrate background, explain ideas, make causal connections, recommend a cure, persuade to a point of view, encourage to take action? If the last, what action are you being encouraged to take, such as buying, giving political support, making changes in your personal life?
- When conclusions are presented, is any account given of the methodology used to gather information, test it, and reach results?
- Are the knowledge claims free of contradictions and supported by evidence? (See coherence and correspondence checks for truth chapter 3) What is the quality and quantity of evidence? Is the support given to knowledge claims based on general surveys or merely anecdotal stories? What other justifications are given?

- If the knowledge claims are accompanied by statistics, maps, graphs, or photographs, are they relevant? Are they factual or emotionally affecting, or both? (See Representation and perspectives interchapter p150.)
- Are there any "red flags" that signal possibly questionable claims: for example, extraordinary claims, conspiracy theories, "secret" information or ingredients, promises of "guaranteed" results, generic all-purpose cures, or claims that are too good to be true?
- Is a particular perspective identifiable through analysis of features of representation: selection of facts, emphasis, colouring of emotions and values, relation of parts, and framing in context? (See Representation and perspectives interchapter p150.)
- Can you further identify broad features of that perspective – the assumptions, values, selected facts, processes for validation, and implications? (See Exploring different perspectives p28)

## 3. Self

- What features of my own perspective might influence my understanding of the source or the statements – limiting it, biasing it, or deepening it? (See own perspective p26)
- Do I recognize in myself an inclination in advance to believe or reject particular knowledge claims? Is this inclination based on thoughtful evaluation in the past or is it a reaction of bias? (See cognitive biases p199)
- Can I push myself to keep an open mind and apply critical thinking to all sources and topics?
- If I use my own past experience and understanding as a basis on which to judge the plausibility of new statements, how extensive and relevant is that past experience?
- Am I affected by features of a particular source that are irrelevant to the arguments and justification – a speaker's attractiveness, age, sex, racial or ethnic heritage, manner of dressing and speaking, accent, self-confidence?
- Do I have a responsibility to know about some topics? Do I have a responsibility for taking action on the basis of my knowledge?

## 14. Shared Knowledge: Taking Compass Bearings

At the beginning of this book, we promised to explore the landscape of knowledge by following different routes and paths of thought. Tangled woods open up with handy deployment of ever-ready questions – even though the responses to those questions might sometimes tempt us to scatter off in different directions. On such a journey, we have to remember to keep coming back together purposefully, to understand *why* we're exploring knowledge in this way. Increasingly, though, we are expecting that the sense of purpose is *your own* and that, while heading in the right direction, you will take responsibility for reading the map and anticipating the next steps.

When we set out, we referred to the IB learner profile for the overriding sense of direction and to the table of contents of this book for the immediate map bearings. At this point, many chapters later, you have already achieved some significant exploration: you have investigated key concepts of the course such as perspectives, truth, justification, and the shared exchange of knowledge; you have explored ways of knowing in a broad loop through them all; and you've added analytical approaches to your critical tool kit, ready for practical application to academic knowledge and the world.

We're now on the top of a high hill, with a splendid view out over the territory and a rest break to think not just about your next footsteps but the goals of this whole knowledge expedition.

Pause now to read the TOK aims as set out in the IB subject guide (next page). At this point, you will find them entirely recognizable. You will also find the objectives for assessment, the qualities for which your work will be evaluated, entirely familiar. If you want more detail on what you'll have to do for assessment, do feel free to turn ahead to the final chapter.

In this next part of the book, then, we will certainly continue to guide you with broad concepts and thinking skills, but you should increasingly be taking the lead yourself.

### Shared knowledge

The areas of knowledge ahead are all shared knowledge. But *shared knowledge* is a concept we must revisit and refresh before moving on.

Although not every personal experience is communicated to others, the knowledge that we exchange and shape communally makes up a large part of what we know in our lives. We learn our ways of communicating from others – most centrally our languages – and are brought, through communication, into our cultural, social, and academic knowledge.

The realization that knowledge is shared, however, does not in itself take us far into exploring it. Knowledge is shared by groups large and small, on any topic imaginable, at any level of generality, with any methods of communication or justification. Football players, gardeners, Buddhists, glass blowers, Arctic explorers, Fijians, web designers, women, Superman comic book

## Aims

The overall aim of TOK is to encourage students to formulate answers to the question "how do you know?" in a variety of contexts, and to see the value of that question. This allows students to develop an enduring fascination with the richness of knowledge.

Specifically, the aims of the TOK course are for students to:

- make connections between a critical approach to the construction of knowledge, the academic disciplines and the wider world
- develop an awareness of how individuals and communities construct knowledge and how this is critically examined
- develop an interest in the diversity and richness of cultural perspectives and an awareness of personal and ideological assumptions
- critically reflect on their own beliefs and assumptions, leading to more thoughtful, responsible and purposeful lives
- understand that knowledge brings responsibility which leads to commitment and action.[1]

## Assessment objectives

It is expected that by the end of the TOK course, students will be able to:

- identify and analyse the various kinds of justifications used to support knowledge claims
- formulate, evaluate and attempt to answer knowledge questions
- examine how academic disciplines/areas of knowledge generate and shape knowledge
- understand the roles played by ways of knowing in the construction of shared and personal knowledge
- explore links between knowledge claims, knowledge questions, ways of knowing and areas of knowledge
- demonstrate an awareness and understanding of different perspectives and be able to relate these to one's own perspective
- in the presentation, explore a real-life/contemporary situation from a TOK perspective.[2]

fans, and oncologists all possess knowledge that is shared with at least *some* others. But what impact does recognition of communities of shared knowledge have on our inquiry?

What is relevant to us, in an inquiry into knowledge, is not primarily *how many people* share the interest or the beliefs nor, in some areas of knowledge, *who they are*. Most relevant for our onward inquiry is the *nature of the knowledge* shared, and the *methods by which it is constructed* – that is, created, communicated, and evaluated.

## Flashback: knowledge exchange

Time for a quick look back at where we've already been! Do you recall the questions we raised, long ago, about the *exchange* of

knowledge? In chapter 2 we stressed the *dynamic nature of knowledge* in creation, as individuals take in shared knowledge to build their own personal knowledge, and contribute their own personal knowledge to further the knowledge creation in the shared pool:

> It is *exchange* … that stimulates questioning and exploration, debate and testing, and active acceptance or rejection. As others give us their knowledge, we do not, if we are active thinkers, simply accept it and passively join those who share it already. We want to understand why this knowledge has persuaded so many other people and why it would be reasonable to accept it ourselves. (page 34 )

Do you also recall the issues we raised in chapter 4 when we introduced *ways of knowing* and their relationship with *justifications* in the knowledge exchange?

---

[1] *Theory of knowledge guide* (first assessment 2015), International Baccalaureate, page 15.
[2] *Theory of knowledge guide* (first assessment 2015), International Baccalaureate, page 15.

## For Reflection

- Your education: What do you consider to be the most important goals of your education as a whole – both in and out of school? What knowledge do you think is most important for you to gain?
- Your International Baccalaureate education: What is the place, in your own life, of your own IB learning? Do you have a sense at this point of where you want to go in life, and how the thinking and the knowledge of the IB – with its subjects, CAS, and TOK – contribute to the person that you would like to be?
- The theory of knowledge course: This course is very unusual. It is holistic in overview rather than specialist, and it is much more demanding than most other courses in its breadth of thinking, from panoramic concepts to close-up application of critical skills. In what ways do you think this course contributes to your personal development and your life ahead?

As we exchange knowledge claims in a thoughtful and critical manner, we exchange right along with them accounts of the ways of knowing that took us to them, and the justifications that convinced us to accept particular conclusions. Knowledge, as we construct it and exchange it, constantly involves assertion, inquiry and response. (page 77)

In examining fallacies of argument (in the Thinking Critically interchapters) and cognitive biases

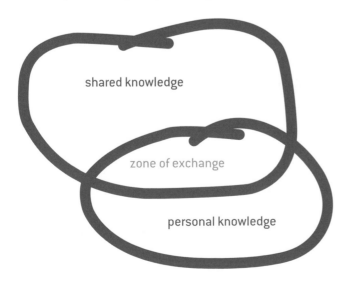

(chapter 12), we also stressed the need to recognize errors and biases that pose challenges to developing an open and critical mind. The challenges can be particularly acute when communication involves differing perspectives. Developing the qualities of the IB learner profile significantly improves the quality of the knowledge exchange.

## Areas of knowledge

How knowledge is created and shared, then, will be the central investigation of the next section of this book. We will be raising the core question "how do we know?" for knowledge of different areas of inquiry. You have the chance, in TOK, to stand back from much that you have been learning in school and the rest of your life to think about how the different parts fit together holistically as knowledge.

What those areas of knowledge are, though, and how they are distinct from each other is a knowledge question of its own: on what basis is knowledge categorized into areas?

In TOK we classify areas of knowledge primarily by their subject matter, as does most academic education. We will want to question some of the lines we draw between interrelated areas but at the same time to consider the arguments for this criterion of classification.

## Knowledge Framework

To facilitate the discussion of areas of knowledge, the TOK guide provides a structure that identifies five components of areas of knowledge. Approaching each area using the knowledge framework ensures that major features that characterize its knowledge are raised for attention and discussion.

The framework also immediately invites comparisons between areas and thereby leads to the larger overview of knowledge towards which the course is directed. How does the use of language in *this* area of knowledge compare with the use of language in *that other one?* How does the method of investigation in *this one* resemble *that other,* and in what ways does it differ?

The framework does not specify *all* the key concepts of TOK that can be treated, and the key concepts and vocabulary of the course as a whole are *understood* to thread through the treatment of areas of knowledge. We do not leave behind anything that we have built up so far.

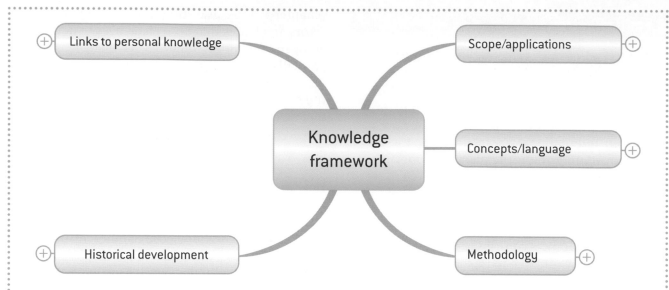

## Knowledge framework

### 1. Scope/applications

This component of the knowledge framework involves identification of what distinguishes each area of knowledge in terms of its subject matter, goals of inquiry, outside boundaries (possibly determined ethically), and practical applications. What is this area of knowledge all about?

### 2. Concepts/language

This component gives attention to the central concepts, named and shared through language, that characterize the knowledge in each area and provide building blocks for thought. It deals with language as a way of knowing in the form taken in the particular area of knowledge.

### 3. Methodology

*What* an area studies and *why* (its scope) affect *how* it inquires and builds knowledge. The

methodology of an area is its means of creating, exchanging, and evaluating knowledge. Areas of knowledge vary in what they value most highly in their processes, and how they use the TOK ways of knowing.

### 4. Historical development

This component highlights the development of the area of knowledge around the world and across time, seeing it as a human construction that could have been otherwise. It touches key points of development as they have led to its current form.

### 5. Links to personal knowledge

This component deals with the exchange of personal and shared knowledge in the form characteristic of the particular area. It also considers what the area contributes to our own personal knowledge.

## Inquiry

In the chapters ahead, we'll be dealing with the knowledge questions raised within the framework. True to the spirit of inquiry, we will certainly not be handing you lists of "answers" to the knowledge questions we raise. We want to give you not a tidy list of points to be memorized, but a much more nuanced understanding and confidence in discussion.

As a result, we've designed activities to get you thinking and talking to each other. We've also gathered some interesting interviews with experts in particular areas of knowledge – mainly experts who were once IB Diploma students themselves. And, of course, we offer you some thought-provoking extracts and questions for personal reflection.

So that you'll have some clear background on each area of knowledge, we sketch in some major ideas on each area of knowledge ourselves in the ongoing chapter text, with some examples and stories.

After you've had a chance to consider how the knowledge questions connect with your personal knowledge, you'll be able to read and consider what we say for a broad overview of how knowledge works. We'll encourage you to think about the general characteristics of each area of knowledge, and how it compares with the others.

We have chosen not to follow the order of the framework in all cases. The different activities we have suggested to launch discussion influence the route thereafter through the ideas, as do some of the particularly appealing features of each area.

## Order of ideas ahead

You've been gathering concepts and skills cumulatively ever since we started this book. In our sustained metaphor, we've been exploring the territory, circling back from different angles to the same central knowledge question: "How do I/we know?" In this metaphor, we left you on top of a mountaintop looking out over the whole terrain. You are ready now to take compass bearings on the aims of the TOK course – and then head out to enter the eight areas of knowledge. Where, then, will we begin?

### Chapter 15 The Arts

### Chapter 16 Ethics

We will enter through the arts and ethics, areas that stimulate discussion and make an evident connection between shared knowledge and personal knowledge. Multiple perspectives animate these areas and give rise to questions about balancing subjectivity and objectivity. The ethical perspectives raised in chapter 16 are relevant to considering the implications of pursuing and possessing knowledge in all of the other areas.

### Chapter 17 History

### Chapter 18 The Human Sciences

### Chapter 19 The Natural Sciences

These three areas have much in common. They aim to construct *true descriptions* of the world, *interpretations* of that world, and *explanations* for how and why the world works (or worked) that way. We will consider the ways in which their respective subject matter – human beings (past or present) or the natural world – influences the appropriate methodologies that they develop and the degree to which differing perspectives are brought into agreement. The degree to which they generalize about their subject matter shifts across their spectrum, as does the balance between subjectivity and objectivity.

### Chapter 20 Mathematics

Mathematics demonstrates, most transparently, many of the ideas that run through this book about basic assumptions and what is built upon them. It deals rationally with abstract ideas, but at the same time contributes to almost all the other areas of knowledge a "language" for talking about patterns in the real world.

### Chapter 21 Indigenous Knowledge

### Chapter 22 Religious Knowledge

These final chapters are a culmination of the process of thoughtful inquiry into perspectives that we opened in the first chapter of this book. Both topics probably demand greater sensitivity and cultural awareness than the earlier areas of knowledge. We place them at the end of the sequence, expecting that discussion will benefit from the experience you have accumulated of considering alternative views and communicating effectively. In these two last chapters, even more than in earlier ones, we pass the active exploration to you.

Does this order make sense to you? We hope so. Your rest break is over and we are heading out on the final huge loop of this exploration, heading first toward the arts.

# Knowledge Framework with Knowledge Questions

## SCOPE/APPLICATION

- What is the SUBJECT MATTER of this area of knowledge: what does it talk about and what knowledge questions does it ask? What determines its outside boundary?
- What does it take as its broad GOALS in constructing knowledge? Are there any important contemporary goals?
- What important CONTRIBUTION does it make to our knowledge as a whole?

## CONCEPTS/LANGUAGE

- What central CONCEPTS characterize the subject matter of this area? (see "scope")
- How does the naming of concepts – classifying ideas in LANGUAGE – affect the way knowledge is created in this area?
- How does this particular WAY OF KNOWING otherwise affect its knowledge? (see "methodology")

## METHODOLOGY

- How does the combination of subject matter and goals (see "scope") affect this area's methods of inquiry? How do *What* and *Why* influence *How*?
- How are the eight TOK WAYS OF KNOWING combined interactively to gain, exchange, and evaluate knowledge in the area? How are they used, more specifically, to justify its knowledge claims?
- What, if any, are the ETHICAL CONSTRAINTS on the methods of this area?
- Do practitioners in this area use a DIVERSITY OF METHODS or do they follow METHODS IN COMMON?
- How does this area balance in its methods between the PARTICULAR and the GENERAL: treating particular instances (observations, stories, cases studies etc.) and making generalizations?
- What is the role in this area, if any, of THEORIES and MODELS?
- In what ways do cultural, theoretical or other PERSPECTIVES influence the methods of gaining knowledge and the conclusions that therefore result? What are the roles of the following components of perspectives: assumptions, values, selected facts, processes of validation, and implications?
- How does this area's construction of knowledge in the present build on its knowledge constructed in the PAST?

## DEVELOPMENT

- In what ways has knowledge in this area been a product of its human and historical circumstances? Have particular unique events or KEY CONTRIBUTIONS significantly affected its development?

## LINKS TO PERSONAL KNOWLEDGE

- How do people, as individuals or groups, contribute PERSONAL KNOWLEDGE to the development of this area? How do they gain from its SHARED KNOWLEDGE? (see "methodology" and "development")
- In what ways does this area contribute to your own personal knowledge? Are there ways in which you contribute yourself to this area, or hope to do so in the future?
- Is it important to be aware of your own personal perspective, including its implications for how you think and act? Does your knowledge bring responsibility?

# 15. The Arts

## Discussion Activity

### Scope: What are "the arts"?

- Do you accept all of these images as representing fields of "the arts"? Are there any you would exclude? If so, why?

- What do these examples of the arts have in common? Is there a single feature that defines them as "arts" – or perhaps two or three broadly shared characteristics? If your definition is not precise, why might that be so?

- What other arts would you add to the ones we have represented here? List as many as come to your mind. How would you draw the "outside boundary" of what you would *include* in the category of the arts, and what you would *exclude* from that category? Can you think of new forms developed within the past century that have extended the outside boundary as they joined the group already inside?

Creative representations come down to us as some of the earliest artifacts of human existence, with cave paintings in northern Spain now dated as at least 40,800 years old.[1] Almost unimaginably long ago, our ancestors had the urge towards symbolic representation, essential for the development of language and the arts across the millennia. From the civilizations that have flourished and died out since that time, evidence remains of the urge to communicate and to create, to make life not only more functional but more beautiful. Although we do not know fully the significance to the people of the time of their sculptures, wall decorations, or jewelry, we can recognize in them the drive behind our arts as they enter the records of history.

---

[1] Pike, A.W.G., Hoffman, D.L., Garciá-Diez, M., Pettit, P.B., Alcolea, J., Deb Balbín, R. González-Sainz, C., de las Heras, C., Lasheras, J.A., Montes, R. and Zilhão, J. "U-Series Dating of Paleolithic Art in 11 Caves in Spain". *Science.* Vol 336, number 6087. Pp 1409–13.

> "
> Not everything assumes a name. Some things lead beyond words. Art inflames even a frozen, darkened soul to a high spiritual experience. Through art we are sometimes visited - dimly, briefly - by revelations such as cannot be produced by rational thinking. [2]
>
> *Alexandr Solzhenitsyn, Nobel Prize for Literature 1970*
> "

## Scope of the arts

What do all of these forms, across all of that time, have in common to group them together as "the arts"? It may not surprise you that not all languages do cluster them together. In Balinese, for instance, the arts are so integrated with the rest of life that there is no single word that picks them out as a separate category of endeavour.[2] And yet most of us, speaking most languages, do seem to cluster together creative undertakings of particular kinds into the conceptual category "the arts". What, then, are the arts all about?

Do they deal with a particular kind of subject matter, perhaps? The natural sciences, after all, deal with the natural world, the human sciences with the human mind and behaviour, and history with the past. Ethics studies morality, and religious knowledge deals with spiritual beliefs and practices. They have areas of study to which they lay claim.

But what about the arts? What is distinctive of the subject matter of the arts, possibly paradoxically, is sheer inclusiveness. Although particular art forms in particular cultural contexts are often focused on specific topics and often have distinct bounds, *as a whole* the arts embrace the world and people, morality and religious belief. They even overlap with the subject matter of mathematics, if it is taken to be a study of abstracted pattern.

Within this inclusive subject matter, do the arts at least pursue specific kinds of knowledge questions as the other areas of knowledge do? After all, ethics and history also treat immensely diverse human thought and activity, but have their own kinds of inquiry, their own sorts of distinctive knowledge questions. Do the arts have characteristic knowledge goals?

Again, the answer can be "yes" regarding particular art works within particular contexts. But the answer has to be "no" in terms of the arts as a whole. Admittedly, the arts represent, convey, or elicit a multitude of thoughts and feelings, many of them on recurring human issues that *could* be entered through knowledge questions. For instance, they often treat a metaphysical realm, human relationships and society, and individual thoughts and feelings – and sometimes they do pose questions or give kinds of answers. Yet posing and investigating a distinctive set knowledge questions held in common is simply not what the arts as a whole undertake to do.

### Discussion Activity

#### Language and concepts in the arts

Which arts use language as their medium of expression?

Which arts include language, not as their primary medium of expression but sometimes as part of their work?

Which arts are affected by language in the way they are taught or promoted?

Which arts have the concepts and categories through which artists approach their work affected by language? Can you name concepts important in music?

To what extent can the arts be considered to be "language" themselves, metaphorically speaking? To what extent do you think that some of the arts gain their communicative power by being free of language and its confines?

Are there concepts, named in language, that you think are extremely important – perhaps even essential – in discussing and evaluating the arts? Are there terms that are essential in teaching and learning within the arts?

---

[2]   Savannah Hughes, "Exploring Balinese Art and Color", Her Royal Majesty: A Paris-based Literary Arts Journal. Nov.7, 2011 http://www.heroyalmajesty.ca/exploring-balinese-art-color-rough-guide/

Can the scope of the arts, then, at least be characterized by the nature of their contribution to our knowledge as a whole? Here we may be drawing closer to identifying features-for instance, their immense contribution to our pleasure, our awareness and understanding of many topics, and our aesthetic enjoyment of beauty. In the chapter ahead, we ask you to consider what the arts give us, and what methods they use to do so.

## What ways of knowing do the arts use?

The arts, viewed broadly across their multiple forms, exclude no ways of knowing. In some popular stereotypes of the arts, however, one way of knowing is treated as though it were excluded: reason. The arts, according to this version, draw almost entirely on emotion, imagination, and intuition, escaping the clutches of "cold rationality".

What a misrepresentation! Simply in subject matter alone, how could novelists capture a general understanding of human psychology or society – distilled into particular characters and setting – without reasoning? Similarly, how could artists in any medium *even begin* to make those compositional choices that are thought-out, even calculated, without reasoning? In conscious planning, they apply background knowledge and skill in their medium of expression to the new work. (Admittedly, they may not be consciously reasoning

as they use their skills. Some thinking, you will recall, is done quickly and intuitively, drawing on procedural memory, especially in those areas where people have gained expertise.)

Furthermore, if as a critical audience we are to understand the arts, we need some rational detachment from our experiences of works of art in order to study or analyse them – even to identify common features from which generalizations can be drawn. Regardless of the immense variability within the arts, reasoning helps us recognize broad patterns and the place of the arts in our knowledge.

Emphasizing the role of reason, however, does not suggest that it is the major way of knowing for the arts. We are merely trying to correct a common misapprehension. You will probably recognize that chapter 11 on imagination was in many ways a preamble to the arts, and that sense perception, emotion, memory, and intuition are probably inseparable from the creation of works of art. Even in non-literary arts, moreover, language may still be involved in learning their skills, conceptualizing their creation and performance, and evaluating them critically.

As the audience appreciating the work of art, we use many of the same ways of knowing that the artist used in creating it, and we can be taken, through them, beyond our own horizons. Being emotionally moved by music or responding with imaginative identification to characters in literature can sometimes create a startling awareness of sharing our experience as human beings.

## Discussion Activity

### Sharing personal knowledge

If you participate in the arts, would you be willing to share with others in your class a sample of what you do, and talk about it with them? Ideally, several volunteers from your class will bring their paintings or poetry, for example, or an instrument to play. If you do not feel comfortable sharing your work, feel free in any case to join in discussion about what actually *doing* an art means to you.

Thinking of yourself as an active participant in the arts, consider the following questions.

- What motivates you to do it? Do you have particular goals?
- What do you get out of participating actively in your form of the arts?
- To what extent do you use your art as a way of communicating with others?
- Do you think someone from a different culture or another epoch would understand what you are communicating?

- What ways of knowing do you think you are using?
- What kind of knowledge is most involved in your participation in the arts: personal experience with reflection; the skills of "knowing how"; or knowledge claims ("I know that...")? Glance back to chapter 2 if you need to refresh this distinction.
- Have you gained any further knowledge through doing it – perhaps greater self-knowledge or knowledge of others? Do you see yourself differently because of your participation in the arts?

Think of yourself now not as participant but as audience.

- What do you get out of the music you listen to, the literature you read, the dances or theatre you watch, or any of the other arts that are part of your life?
- Do they influence your view of the world? If so, in what ways do they affect it?

## Voices

*Nathan Bowman, Kentucky, USA*

The banjo is the most obnoxious instrument in the world. It's loud and twangy and addictive. You just can't quit playing.

I grew up playing traditional blue grass with my whole family, including all my cousins, with all of us playing several instruments. The banjo is my eleventh instrument. For me, music is like another language. I can't legitimately claim to be bilingual, or to be fluent in music, but that's how I think of it.

I don't play because I want to express things. I don't play my angst out into my songs! But I can get lost sometimes and realize that four or five hours have passed on the clock and I have holes in my fingers. I have to consciously limit myself to an hour and a half a day.

## Voices

*Mona Aditya, Nepal*

My dance talks about the ironies of life so it's a bit sad, but the rhythm makes me jump and keeps me happy. I have to balance between the rhythm and the meaning.

The gestures and steps have meaning. Some of the steps are obvious, but others are more like a non-verbal language. Since the language is not known to people in Canada where I'm now studying, I try to make my movements very clear. In the dance I put on a bindi to be beautiful as I do make-up in the mirror, but the dance says that life is as fragile as the image on the mirror.

I can't say that the dance represents Nepal because we are so diverse, with 70 dialects and 36 ethnicities. But it reflects a part of Nepal. Dances are an important part of our culture. We learn them originally in school and put on performances on occasions such as Parents' Day.

## Personal and shared knowledge

If you *participate* in the arts, you probably find yourself drawing on your own feelings, thoughts, personal taste, training, cultural background, and so forth as you create or perform. If you *evaluate* what you have done, you will be trying to take an outside perspective – trying to see your work as someone else (or several different people) would see it and trying to put your own performance in context of expectations of form, technique, or expression. The outside critical perspective, difficult though it may be to achieve, can be illuminating and influential for your continuing work.

If you are the *audience* of the arts, you may be interested *solely* in having your own personal

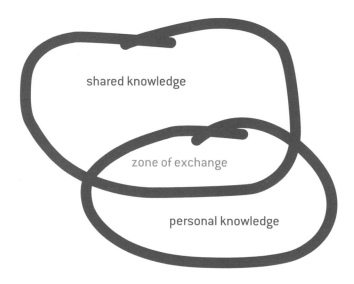

shared knowledge

zone of exchange

personal knowledge

response. It can be one of the great pleasures of the arts that you are able simply to enjoy them or to be affected, and not to have to explain. If, however, you wish to gain a greater understanding of your experience, you will try to see your own response to the artwork in a larger context of critical judgment. When you learn more about dance, music, theatre, painting, or literature, for instance, your own response is likely to deepen and become more nuanced. When you consider what a professional dancer says about dance, for instance, you are likely to gain greater appreciation of the form. You are moving toward a critical goal – informed judgment.

 Interview
## Choreographer, dancer, and critic: roles in the arts

### Fearghus O'Conchuir
### IB graduate 1988

*Brought up in Ireland, Fearghus completed degrees in English and European Literature at Magdalen College Oxford, before training at London Contemporary Dance School. Recent work includes Tabernacle – a major new work in the Dublin Dance Festival 2011 that has toured Europe – and If the Invader Comes, an installation in the Martello Tower at Jaywick on England's east coast. He was the first Ireland Fellow on the Clore Leadership Programme and continues to contribute to the programme as a facilitator and speaker.*

→ **As a choreographer, what are your main goals as you compose or design a dance? Is a dance in any way a statement or expression of knowledge?**

Dance is a body of knowledge, an exploration of the knowledge within and between our bodies. When we learn a new language, when we learn to play an instrument, when we learn to love, our bodies grow and change: neural pathways are extended, specific coordinations of muscle – strength and flexibility – are established and the physical sensations of a particular emotion are stored. The processes are not secondary to knowledge acquisition; they are the process of learning. However, many people are oblivious to this physical aspect of knowledge. In a Western culture in which a strand of religious thinking regards the body as animal and reprehensibly distanced from the divine, and in which a Cartesian separation of mind and body privileges mind as the site of selfhood and consciousness, the ignorance of body knowledge is as unsurprising as it is unhelpful.

In choreographing I am trying to understand, express and extend the knowledge in my body and in the bodies of the dancers with whom I collaborate. When I share my work with an audience, I want to model for them the possibility of growth and understanding which they may not have experienced. Such growth is a moral imperative for me. If Socrates says that the unexamined life is not worth living, I suggest that the examination should start in our mindful bodies, in our embodied minds. Dance, among a range of mind and body practices such as yoga or tai chi, provides me with a framework for that study.

→ **As both a dancer and a choreographer, you practise, in a sense, two different art forms. What, for you, is the relationship between the two?**

There are similarities in the relationship between the composer and the musician and that between the choreographer and dancer. The composer decides what notes go where but when he writes a symphony he is not in a position to deliver all the notes. The distinction is usually drawn between the composer/choreographer as a creative artist and the musician/dancer as an interpretive artist. In much current choreographic practice, however, the dancer is expected to have a great deal of creative input, contributing movement ideas that a choreographer uses and shapes. Unlike the composer who may compose complex scores in the privacy of his or her room before ever encountering the musicians who will deliver the work, choreography takes place most often in a studio, evolving over time in relationship with the dancers who will perform the work. In these situations the dancers are more than interpreters of the work, they can be creative partners too. This creative contribution can be overlooked, however, because of the circumstantial power-differential which often exists between those titled "choreographer" and those called "dancers".

When I choreograph, I take responsibility for the work and by doing so hope to facilitate the free and creative exploration of the dancers. In my case, the environment I create and the atmosphere I foster is my greatest contribution to the choreographic process. The rest is open to chance, to discovery, to the inspiration of others. Instead of fleshing out something I already know, this is the way I learn something new.

I have danced for other choreographers and choreographed often for other performers, but at the moment I derive greatest satisfaction from performing my own work. This is not the case for many choreographers, some of whom would argue that it is impossible to consider how a work is taking shape, how it looks, when one is inside it. But for me there are a number of reasons for wanting to be inside the performance, even if I use video technology in the choreographic process to allow me to see and shape the work from the outside: if I expect an audience to learn something from my work, in particular if I want them to better comprehend a way of being, I think it is my responsibility to face that challenge myself, to lead by example. I also want to be a direct part of the encounter with an audience, not simply authoring the work and abandoning it but learning from experience how an audience reacts to what I have made. The challenge to grow is two-way. It's a demand I make of myself as much as it is an invitation to the audience.

→ What do you see as the relationship between the dance creator and the dance critic? Do they have to possess different kinds of knowledge?

I think I've always wanted to be an artist or whatever I understood an artist to be, but it took

me a while to find that dance could provide me with a form for artistic investigation and expression. I studied literature at university, was good at words and thought writing might be my art form. However, whenever I tried to write, I felt hampered by my critical knowledge. I was aware of my shortcomings, aware of how derivative my "voice" was. Later, when I began choreographing, I had no such direct critical knowledge and felt free to acknowledge the validity of the movement that came from me. Of course, the movement was derivative, unconsciously influenced by a lifetime of exposure to a variety of physicalities (Ukrainian dance, MGM musicals, sports, kayaking). Of course, I wasn't entirely without critical knowledge either, since the years of studying literature taught me many ideas about aesthetics, about form and structure, which I could apply indirectly to my new art form. The prerequisite for my creative process, however, is that critical knowledge doesn't precede and consequently dampen the creative spark that I need to ignite my work. Once that spark has been allowed to express itself, once it is outside of me and I can observe it, then all my critical and analytical faculties can kick in. The artist needs to be creator and first critic of his/her work, but without the moment of creativity, the critic's work cannot begin.

→ In general, what do you consider the relationship to be between the creator and the critic? What is the role of critical theory in an understanding of the arts?

The burgeoning of critical theories (psychoanalytical, feminist, new-historicist, post-colonial, queer, deconstructive, Marxist etc.) has provided new ways of reading and seeing and in doing so has altered how we experience the world. These ways of seeing seek to replace existing filters on our perception that have become so familiar as to be invisible. However, these radical theories very quickly become new orthodoxy. The danger with orthodoxies is that in allowing us to see some stories, they are blind to others. The artist's job is to keep exploring and expressing the widest range and deepest extent of stories possible. Attentive, informed and adventurous theory can help those stories be perceived; theory that has atrophied into dogma can hide them. But the stories exist in the art, waiting to be acknowledged. ■

## Discussion Activity

### Interview with Fearghus O'Conchuir

1   In what ways is the "body knowledge" of which Fearghus O'Conchuir speaks related to the three forms of knowing identified in this book: knowing by experience, knowing how (skills), and knowing that… (knowledge claims)? Is it a blend of these, or is it something else entirely, and largely neglected in this book?

2   Fearghus likens the choreographer to the composer. Are there other art forms in which this distinction between composer and performer is also relevant? What, do you think, is the difference in the kind of knowledge that each role demands?

3   On the basis of this interview, what ways of knowing would you say are involved in dance? What would you add from your own experience?

4   Fearghus speaks of wanting the audience to learn through his dance, but also growing himself in his relationship with the audience. What do you think you yourself learn from watching dance performance, theatre, live music, or any other form of performance arts?

## Critical judgment: opinion – or *informed* opinion?

More than any other field, the arts may foster a resistance to critical analysis – perhaps because the experience of creating and enjoying the arts can be so personal. Even those who expect close scrutiny to be given to *works of science* have been heard to protest regarding *works of art*, "I just know whether I like it, and that's enough. Why do we have to tear it apart?"

What, then, is the role of background knowledge about the arts – familiarity with artwork of the past, and with the visual arts, performance arts, and literature of the present? What is the role of awareness of goals and techniques in making critical judgment? Certainly, we would not expect to evaluate the knowledge created in history, the

**Aurora Zinc Oxide**

2nd place winner, Science as Art Competition, 2010 Materials Research Society Fall Meeting. "This picture was created from the convergence of a high-resolution cross-sectional and a plan view SEM image of a zinc oxide 'nanowall structure' synthesized by a metal-organic chemical vapor deposition technique. Color was added to the original image." Dong Chan Kim, Sungkyunkwan University[3]

The original of this artwork is not visible to the naked eye. It requires a scanning electron microscope (SEM). It does "hang" in a gallery, though – the photo gallery of images on the Materials Research Society website. The human imagination, it seems, will find materials to be shaped into art, give them significance in framing and naming, and share them with others – no matter where our observations take us.

You might find it keenly interesting to consider further the crossover between scientific discovery and the arts. We would suggest investigating the impact of the development of chemistry on the pigments and palette of the nineteenth century French Impressionist painters, or the impact of the technological development of the camera and the computer on the visual arts. We see again how our areas of knowledge (in this case, the sciences and the arts) do not exist in isolation from each other.

[3]   http://www.mrs.org/f10-science-as-art-winners/.

The artist...speaks to our capacity for delight and wonder, to that sense of mystery surrounding our lives; to our sense of pity, and beauty, and pain; to the latent feeling of fellowship with all creation—and to the subtle but invincible conviction of solidarity that knits together the loneliness of innumerable hearts...which binds together all humanity—the dead to the living and the living to the unborn.[4]

*Joseph Conrad 1897*

sciences, or mathematics without having some training in that subject. In most other areas of knowledge the need for specialized knowledge before evaluating works is evident: the works may be incomprehensible to those of us who are not creators or peers within that particular field.

Our contention here is that being appropriately critical is a way of getting more out of the knowledge of *any area*. As we move to thinking further about the arts, we will use critical thinking just as we would in any other area of knowledge, not destructively but as a means to appreciate fully by penetrating beyond surface impressions.

## Methods: knowledge questions

If we aim to extend ourselves beyond immediate personal response, then, we will want to inform ourselves about the arts. Although the arts do not follow a universal methodology, they do share some common features in how they work. Keep the following knowledge questions in mind as we treat the methods and development of the arts:

- What characteristics do the arts share in common in their ways of working?
- To what extent is it important to base generalization about the arts on a sample from different historical and cultural contexts?
- When the arts represent the world at all (as some don't), how do they balance particular cases and general conclusions ?
- How do the arts of the present use the arts of the past? Is there "progress" in the arts?
- To what extent do the arts make knowledge claims? Is the line clear between art and propaganda?
- According to what criteria are works of art evaluated? How do critical perspectives influence judgments in this area of knowledge?

## Methods: Diversity and subjectivity

As we have seen, one of the distinguishing features of the arts within areas of knowledge is their sheer scope, their immense diversity and range: broadly inclusive *subject matter*, variety of *forms* (from songs to architecture!), engagement with all *ways of knowing*, and (as you will explore in the activity on arts from around the world p236) *multiple roles* in our lives.

This diversity and inclusivity extends yet further into the abundance of different *perspectives* which give impetus to communication in the arts. The arts, after all, are infused with our perspectives on the world and our lives within it: cultural perspectives and individual perspectives. Such perspectives embrace (page 28) assumptions, values, emphasis on certain aspects of the world, conventions of expression and methods of challenging them, and implications for further thought and behaviour.

Furthermore, despite all the perspectives on the world that have emerged in the arts over the history of our civilizations, *none of them proves others false*. In logic, a claim that "A" is true and a claim that "not-A" is also true create a serious contradiction in reasoning. In mathematics and the sciences, opposing claims present problems to be solved. In the arts, however, multiple opposing views add to the rich variety of human concepts and expression and do not negate or falsify each other.

Admittedly, no *single* place or time welcomes all visions and all styles. When we drop from an overview survey of the arts to a close-up examination of particular places, single perspectives with their conventions generally

4   Conrad, J. 1897. Preface to "The Nigger of the 'Narcissus'". Penguin Books.

## Discussion Activity

↑ Shadow puppet of Bima, Indonesia. 1800–16.

↑ Throne of Weapons by Kester. Mozambique. 2001

↑ Guernica by Pablo Picasso. Spain. 1937.

↑ Terracotta Warriors. China. 3rd century BC.

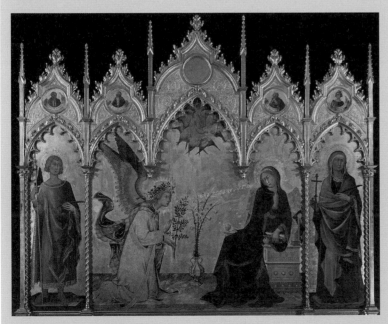

↑ "Annunciation with St. Margaret and St. Asano" by Simone Martini. Italy. 1333.

↑ Raven and the First Men by Bill Reid Haida. Vancouver UBC Museum of Anthropology.

## Arts from around the world.

Divide your class into teams, one for each of the six artworks pictured here. Try to choose the artwork least familiar to you. Your goal initially will be to find out about it, to share the information you have gained with the rest of your class, and to stay aware of how growing knowledge may affect your response.

## Team activity

Step 1. **Reflect.** Before you begin to talk with your team, write down your own **immediate** response to the work you will examine. What is your understanding of what it represents? What do you like or dislike about it?

Step 2. **Discuss.** Get together with your team and exchange your reactions. Do other people's thoughts change your own response?

Step 3. **Research.** As a team, find out as much about the artwork as you possibly can in the time you have. Prepare a *short, clear* report to deliver to the rest of the class, which deals with the following questions. Note any that seem not to apply well to your particular artwork:

a. **The artist.** Who was/were the artist(s)? Can you find any information on what motivated them, and within what circumstances they were working? If there is no apparent artist whose name you can find out, why not? How much of the artist's personality or feelings can you see expressed in the work?

b. **The audience.** Who was or is the audience? What impact might the artwork have in their lives? Can you find out anything about audience reaction to it at the time it was created? What are reactions today?

c. **The meaning.** What is the meaning of your artwork within its cultural background? In trying to answer this broad question, consider the relationship between the image and relevant cultural stories, cultural practices, or historical events.

d. **The form.** Look at the work itself. How are the shapes balanced structurally, for example, or space handled? Is there any special significance associated with its form?

e. **Art?** Do you consider this work to be a work of art? Why or why not?

Step 4. **Report.** Return to your full class group and give a brief report on your chosen artwork. More details on it will probably emerge in the follow-up discussions.

## Follow-up class discussion 1: What roles do the arts play in our lives?

As you discuss the question above, appoint a class scribe to take notes on the various ideas that teams raise and to ensure that everyone gets a copy. As you collectively contribute to a growing list of what functions the arts play in our lives, keep in mind *all* the artworks you have just examined and make sure that their apparent roles are reflected in your notes.

## Follow-up class discussion 2: What knowledge should precede value judgment or opinion?

To discuss the question above, divide your class into two groups according to who is inclined to support each of the following two points of view. Break into your contrary groups for roughly 10 minutes to prepare your supporting arguments, referring to all six of the examples. Then move back into teacher-moderated discussion. This is not a debate with a winner and a loser, but an exploration of two viable points of view.

1 Surely, a response that is based on some understanding of the meaning of a work within its context – the context of the culture and the context of expectations of that particular form of art – is a fuller response. In evaluation of a work of art, an informed opinion should be taken more seriously than an uninformed one.

2 Surely, on the other hand, one of the characteristics of the arts is that they are able to make us respond and understand to some extent, even if the particular art form is unfamiliar or if we know very little indeed about its context. In evaluation of a work of art, an immediate response is sufficient justification for a value judgment.

Finally, is there a possible compromise position between these two views?

prevail. For example, Christian paintings showing the Virgin Mary and Jesus to illustrate teachings in a church would be unacceptable in a Muslim mosque where no human figures should be depicted, creation of the human image being exclusively the work of Allah. Look ahead to the chapter on mathematics for the patterns, abstract and contemplative, that are used in mosques. Even artists working within their own traditions have often provoked storms of outrage, with their novels or paintings being condemned as "immoral" or "obscene" or their music as "grotesque".

When we comment on the arts being diverse and embracing plural perspectives, then, we are speaking of the arts at a high level of generalization. It is from this vantage point that we can most effectively recognize perspectives as intrinsic to artistic expression, frame the frictions between perspectives as probably inevitable and often energizing, and affirm a core characteristic of the arts: they are essentially *subjective*. Look back to the Overview following chapter 6 to ensure that you do not misunderstand what we mean. Subjectivity is not a weakness in knowledge. It is an essential ingredient, operating in different ways across the areas of knowledge.

Subjectivity in the arts does not imply an arbitrary way of working or a lack of rigour in learning and applying the appropriate skills and discipline of the art form. It *does* imply that the arts are not aiming to get outside our human experience to make factual, testable statements about it. Instead, they are tapping into our human experience, excluding no ways of knowing, and giving us a powerful means to communicate what we think and feel about experience, and how we would abstract from that experience to create pattern or aesthetic form.

## Methods in the arts: common characteristics

Although subjectivity is a major characteristic of the arts, not all subjective expression is art. What, then, distinguishes the arts in their methods of working?

We will offer you our own view here, pared down to what we consider to be essential features. We are giving you not testable statements of fact but an informed opinion that we hope will spur you on in your own thinking.

1. The arts *create something accessible to the senses*, for instance, a piece of music, pages of writing, a

### Discussion activity

#### My hat writes poems or "What is art?"

This activity raises the question (for class discussion) "What is a poem?" More broadly, as the discussion comes to a close, the question becomes "What are the essential features of a work of art?"

Here's how. The teacher, wearing a distinctive hat, hands a small piece of blank paper to every student. Each student writes a single word and hands the paper back. The word can be anything, with two restrictions: it must be in English and it must not be offensive. The teacher places all the pieces of paper in the hat, shuffles them, and utters a few magic words to inspire the hat. She then pulls out the words and lays them in order, one at a time, on a surface that all students can see. Her claim: "My hat writes poems. This is a poem."

Is it? Students, what do you think? Read it, and read it again. What features do you expect a "poem" to possess? If you agree that it is a poem, then why do you think so? If you disagree, give your reasons. Don't be surprised if you end up liking your poem and wanting to sign it, collectively.

And as imagination bodies forth
The forms of things unknown, the poet's pen
Turns them to shapes and gives to airy nothing
A local habitation and a name.[5]

*William Shakespeare*

sculpture, a film, a dance, a drawing. Often they give us tremendous pleasure through our senses.

2. In the creative process, the arts *deliberately shape* the raw material of human experience together with the medium used to communicate it (whether it be clay, sound, words, graphic images etc.). Artists make *aesthetic choices* to create an effective composition. Arguably, the beauty of art lies not in its subject matter but rather in the way that the chaos of experience has been given *aesthetic form or pattern*, and thereby given impact and meaning. It has even been argued that the aesthetic form can lift the arts out of the transient world by creating a state of contemplation and detachment.

3. The arts *communicate*, though what is communicated and to whom is immensely variable. Usually the communication is from the artist (composer, writer etc.) to an audience. The communication has a purpose, and is set within a perspective. We would venture to say that the arts are our most powerful means of subjective communication, affecting us deeply through their appeal to our senses, our emotions, our recognition of a world given form, our imaginations, our sense of rhythm and pattern, and our accompanying appreciation of beauty.

In all three of these characteristics, the arts draw on our human subjectivity: our imaginations, our creativity, our aesthetic judgments, and our capacity to communicate the diversity and range of our human experience.

## Methods in the arts: the general and the particular

In the sciences, particular work done by particular scientists feeds into the general enterprise of science. The same is true of the arts. In fact, some

of the features of outstanding contributions are very similar in both the arts and the sciences: they inspire fresh ways of seeing the world or thinking about it, or they invent creative methods to handle ideas and materials in order to make something new. Individuals – or often groups – are celebrated for their creativity.

When it comes to the actual work, the sciences and the arts differ significantly. In the sciences, personal knowledge feeds into the shared knowledge being created in the field, and loses its identity within the public and communal undertaking. Others use it, build on it, change it, or refute it, and at the point when it is no longer useful, discard it. Individual work is mixed or blended with the work of others, as science works collectively.

In the arts, though, individual work does not lose its particularity, and different perspectives and their expressions are not mixed or blended for a general picture. We do not average different depictions of mothers or kings or gods, as though they were data points, to get closer to what is "really there" objectively in motherhood, or kingship, or godliness. Nor do we refute musical compositions or epic poems with "more accurate" ones. Indeed, we do not always leave old art behind as we do old science; often we take individual and particular pieces with us, cumulatively and appreciatively, through our histories, even if the meaning we give to the work changes over time with our changing perspectives.

Even as we preserve particular artworks, though, we do generalize about their characteristics as we construct knowledge about the arts. As we learn, we can make broader and broader generalizations, for

### For Reflection

To what extent do you think you gain understanding of human psychology *in general*, or society's dynamics *in general*, from the *particular* version in the particular novel?

To what extent is your response to music without words particular to the specific piece, and to what extent do you feel that the music resonates beyond the particular notes into more general, even timeless response?

---

[5] Shakespeare, *A Midsummer Night's Dream*, V, I, 15–19.

example, about a particular novelist's whole body of work, or more broadly about novels from the writer's historical period, or about novel form itself as it developed across centuries in some parts of the world. We look more broadly still at characteristics of whole forms of literature developed in different historical periods or in different cultures. And, still more broadly, we can place the whole of literature comparatively within the context of the other arts, choosing to compare according to numerous different criteria. The generalizations we can make are not the universal "all" generalizations that apply to every example in a category, but they are broad tendencies that give us greater understanding of a specific work within its context.

We apply that general knowledge to particular cases as we respond to the arts and interpret them. Simply in recognizing a sculpture as ancient Mayan rather than ancient Greek, for instance, or a song as Andean rather than African, we show our familiarity with general categories. We recognize the characteristic forms and possibly something of the cultures within which they were created.

Clearly, we can generalize about the arts, to an extent. *But can the arts generalize about us?* This question applies particularly to literature and film as representational arts – and has a firm answer. Yes, writers often do *explicitly make huge generalizations* about life in authorial exposition, and often do *imply a general condition* of society through a particular character or slice of society depicted: the life of the poor, the role of women in a particular society, the impact of racism, the struggle for life within totalitarian regimes, the alienation of modern life, the ravages of war and so forth. A writer creates a *particular* character in a *particular* setting with a *particular* conflict and very *particular* relationships and dialogue. The writer can suggest through that portrait much larger human patterns within real life. He can give universal features of humanity, in Shakespeare's words, "a local habitation and a name".[6]

*But why should we believe* the generalizations directly stated or implied? Well, we shouldn't. We should not take them as factual or believe them literally. We should not base our knowledge of cultures and societies entirely on films, novels, plays, and

poetry. However, when an author is writing of a world he knows intimately through experience, he can often portray a vivid and authoritative picture of society that is backed up by findings made in the human sciences: how they live in a society (anthropology, sociology, political science).

When the representative arts give us a jolt of recognition or "ring true", we can also recognize a subjective version of the correspondence check for truth (chapter 3): we speak of "realism" or "verisimilitude", and may find the representation convincing. The work is fiction, a product of the observation shaped by the imagination, but it might well hold "the mirror up to nature".[7] When we have entered into the imaginative construction of a fiction (chapter 11), we might find characters "realistic" even when we have never met such people and or their societies. A subjective version of the coherence truth checks also quickly comes into play: we enter a fictional construction with Coleridge's "willing suspension of disbelief" (chapter 11), but would be troubled if there were internal inconsistencies in the story.

We would suggest that this is one strong element of the knowledge that literature gives us: it enlarges our sense of human experience beyond the narrow limits within which we live our own lives, it takes us imaginatively into lives and parts of the world far different from our own. It can give us understanding of others unlike ourselves, and possibly opens us to caring.

## Development in the arts: tradition and the individual talent

"No poet, no artist of any art, has his complete meaning alone," writes poet T.S. Eliot. "His significance, his appreciation is the appreciation of his relation to the dead poets and artists. You cannot value him alone; you must set him, for contrast and comparison, among the dead. I mean this as a principle of aesthetic, not merely historical, criticism."[8]

Few artists have ever been as critically conscious as T.S. Eliot, whose famous essay "Tradition and the Individual Talent" argues that the artwork of the past is still living in the present, and that the poet

---

6   Shakespeare, A Midsummer Night's Dream, V, I, 15–19.
7   Shakespeare, Hamlet, III, ii, 22
8   Eliot, T.S. 1921. "Tradition and the Individual Talent," *The Sacred Wood; essays on poetry and criticism.* New York. Alfred A. Knopf.

For Reflection

## For Reflection

If an artist makes a copy of a great painting that is so well done that he can deceive most experts, is he as great an artist as the original painter?

In the works of literature you are reading in your courses, do the authors make allusions to iconic works of their culture or build their works showing awareness of literary tradition?

In your own society at present, who are the musicians, writers, or visual artists who are challenging established tradition?

should be aware of the tradition even as he renews it with his own work. "The poet must be very conscious of the main current, which does not at all flow invariably through the most distinguished reputations. He must be quite aware of the obvious fact that art never improves, but that the material of art is never quite the same."

This relationship between the artist and the tradition – the legacy of great work of the past – is a central issue for the arts. To what extent should artists follow the tradition, and to what extent should they create work that is *new* in its vision or handling of its medium – even if using traditional forms and techniques? Does creativity demand *novelty*?

Not every age or every artist has dealt with this question in the same way. European neo-classicists looked back to the arts of antiquity to formulate rules for themselves to follow (though their own work was distinctive) while, in contrast, European and American visual artists of the twentieth century were remarkable for their iconoclastic treatment of the past and venture into new expression. Development in the arts, however, generally works largely in bursts, with the contributions of prominent artists or their groups setting the lead for new directions. Often historical events or shifts in cultural perspectives in a society set off new waves of creativity across the arts as a whole, as artists respond to new issues, and then affect each other. Collectively, the arts of a society thereby come to convey "the mind of the times".

Yet the arts do not "progress" as the sciences expect to do. Although artists may use increasingly advanced tools and technologies, the

artistic undertaking itself has no shared goal or measurable steps toward reaching it. The arts shift as the times shift, and as personal knowledge of individuals and groups interacts with the shared knowledge of the artistic tradition.

## The arts and knowledge claims

We've already considered that writers, because they use language, can readily make broad knowledge claims. As we lay aside many works of literature, or turn away from many a painting, there is little doubt that the artist has engaged us imaginatively in order to make us see through his eyes and accept his ideas. Have you noticed in your own reading that some writers make almost editorial assertions? That characters are shown to be products or victims of society? That some characters comment directly on their society or argue with others? That some writers employ powerfully symbolic or allegorical criticism? Or, that biting satire ridicules injustice or abuse of power?

As we consider how dictatorial regimes have imprisoned or executed artists, such as the Kenyan writer Ngũgĩ wa Thiong'o or the Russian writer Alexandr Solzhenitsyn, one thing is clear: it is not only critics of the arts who recognize that artists are making knowledge claims and passing judgments about the societies in which we live.

## Arts and propaganda

Indeed, regimes have often tried to make sure that artists are on their side. They have often enlisted artists to glorify leaders, create images of the ideal worker, inspire the citizenry to work hard or support the war effort, convey moral messages or slogans, or target scapegoat groups within the population. Harnessing the power of music, leaders have complemented explicit knowledge claims in language with emotionally stirring compositions of glorification or triumph.

It is not always easy, however, to draw the line between art that promotes a *particular perspective*, on the one hand, and *propaganda*, on the other. The Roman Catholic Church of the seventeenth century in Europe, for example, attempted to counter the growing influence of Protestantism by employing architects, artists, and musicians to glorify God, in part by creating splendid churches

>
>
> I think I am fortunate in that my relationship to politics is resolved very simply: I come from a country that is so highly politicized that there is no act, even the most private you can think of, which does not resonate politically...
>
> Art has a role. Art is at work in South Africa. But art works subterraneanly. It's never the striking, superficial cause and effect people would like to see. Art goes underground into people's dreams and surfaces months later in strange, unexpected actions. People bring a sort of instant-coffee expectation to art; they'd like the results to be immediate. It doesn't work that way. I like that image of art dropping down through the various layers of the individual's psyche, into dreams, stirring around there and then surfacing later in action.[9]
>
> *Athol Fugard, 1989 South Africa*

to attract worshippers away from the opposition. Would you treat the arts sponsored in this way as expressions of a perspective – or would you cross the line to call it propaganda? Currently, businesses commission art for advertising, trying to persuade us to buy their products or convince us that they are acting in the public good. Is this propaganda?

## Taking critical perspectives

In the arts, as in other areas, creators may often become critics, and peers may often evaluate each other's work. More than in other areas, however, the role of the creator and the role of the critic may be taken by different groups of people; critics are not always creators, and creators are not always critics. "Peer review", so important in the sciences with equivalent colleagues, does not operate in the arts with the knowledge producers critiquing each other's work toward a communal, shared result. And more than in other areas, too, you are involved in the role of critic yourself as a member of the general public.

In order to go further into critical perspectives on the arts, you may need to think back to the opening feature of the knowledge framework – the scope of the arts, considering their goals as knowledge. In order to be able to evaluate

any work of knowledge (such as a piece of art or a mathematical discovery), it is important to identify the goals of that particular piece of creation – what it is that they are aiming to achieve – in order to measure them according to their own appropriate criteria. We do not evaluate the results of scientific research according to the expectations of mathematics, nor historical articles according to the expectations of music. For evaluating art, then, what are its goals?

As you will have noticed already, *there is no single goal for the arts*. Yet several identifiable goals do exist, each of them centred in a different aspect of a work of art: the *artist* and the creative process, the *artwork* itself for its compositional and technical features, and the *audience* for the impact of the work. The *society* within which the creation and exchange are set also introduces expectations and criteria of evaluation. Similarly, the *natural world* often plays a role as setting, subject matter, or a force of its own. These different centres of interest and attention provide different critical perspectives on art.

---

[9]  Lloyd Richards interviewer. Summer 1989. "Athol Fugard, the Art of Theater No. 8". *The Paris Review.* Number 111.

Although artists and critics themselves often argue for one critical perspective over another, it might well be that each is rather like a spotlight illuminating a different part of the whole. We will now give some explanation of each one in turn, hoping to add something to that illumination. As you read each of the following critical perspectives, consider the extent to which you accept it as relevant or useful to your understanding. You might find it useful throughout to refer back to the activity "Arts from around the world".

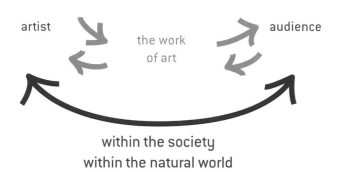

artist — the work of art — audience

within the society
within the natural world

## Four critical perspectives

In the opening chapter of this book, we outlined for you some theoretical perspectives on culture and some broadly identifiable perspectives within politics, and followed the chapter by a guide to exploring perspectives in general. We recommend that you glance back to refresh your memory on the role of perspectives in bringing attention to selected features of our lives and our world, based largely on our assumptions and values. This concept of perspectives runs right through areas of knowledge – that where you stand influences what you notice and consider important. Here, it is crucial in dealing with central knowledge questions of the arts:

- What are the goals of the arts?
- Is there a common "method" in the arts?
- What knowledge do we gain or exchange through the arts?

## 1. Do you evaluate the artwork with emphasis on the artist?

*Critical attention focuses on the biography of the artist, the artist's intentions, the creative process, and the artist's views in the work. This attention acknowledges the* **expressive goal of the arts.**

Some critics emphasize the artist's role – the imagination, inspiration, and mysterious creativity that energizes the arts. They emphasize the intentions of the artist at work, and the frustrations, pleasures, and growth of the process. Psychoanalytic critical theory is particularly concerned with examining works, especially literature, as reflective of human psychology.

From a perspective centring on the artist, some critics further argue that the essential criterion for a work to be considered "art" is that the creator must have *intended* it to be so. The implications of this particular argument are that we cannot be sure that a work is "art" unless we are sure of the artist's intentions. A further implication is that creative products made with a practical or social purpose, or products from cultures with no general concept of art, are eliminated because their creators did not have the intention of creating art.

You are not unfamiliar with this criterion at work if you have been involved in the arts. For many participants in the arts personal development in skill and expressive power may be the only goals that matter. Their audience, similarly, may seek the artist in the work.

### Goal and evaluation

From this perspective, are any of the six works from your class activity "Arts from around the world" either disqualified or strongly confirmed as art?

From this perspective, what constitutes a particularly good work of art?

Can you find an example – perhaps a particular poem, piece of music, or painting – that you consider to excel according to this criterion?

## 2. Do you evaluate the artwork with emphasis on the artwork itself?

*Critical attention focuses on the formal features of the work, its composition and technique. This attention acknowledges the* **aesthetic goal of the arts.**

Many critics stress above all the work of art itself and its formal and technical features. For example, in photography, a critic might examine the composition, focus and centring, depth of field, balance of tone and colour. In dance, a critic might scrutinize the body lines and movements in space, the technical skill, the integration with music. Every field of the arts has its own compositional rules, to be followed or broken, and its own expectations of composer and performer skill – and they are specific to the field. Yet the analysis of a raga in Indian music for its ascending and descending structure, its modal structure, its movements and so on has something in common, in this regard, with an analysis of a painting for its structure (often using geometric forms or mathematical ratios), its balance of tone and colour, the way it leads the eye into the picture space and so forth. (Try examining a raga played by Ravi Shankar and a dramatic painting by Caravaggio.)

Many critics argue that aesthetic form is the *only* essential criterion for a work to be considered art at all. It must be beautiful.

Whether it treats ugly or troubling subject matter, as do many works of literature, film, and painting, is often argued to be irrelevant to its aesthetic value. A work is aesthetically successful if it is effectively composed and has mastery of technique. Picasso's Guernica, for example, with its grotesque and distorted figures, possesses a triangular composition that holds the tormented individual images within a strong overall structure. In the reproduction in this book (page 234), notice the strong sense of form and pattern that underlies the work, and the balance of light and dark.

The aesthetic approach to the arts is often held to be contrary to any that involve the emotions, as a formal response is frequently described as contemplative, even rational. Interestingly, in works that people from many different cultures find aesthetically pleasing, certain mathematical ratios recur, for example, the proportions called the golden ratio or the golden section, or sometimes called "divine proportion".

The approach of structuralist criticism, most relevant to literature, also looks closely at features of the work itself, identifying features of construction, for example, pairs of oppositions such as binary contrasts in characterization.

You are not unfamiliar with this criterion at work. In your literature course, the commentary stresses the formal aspects of text – the form of the work, and the way technical devices, handled skillfully, create their meaning and their effect. You look at authorial point of view, structure of ideas, tone, imagery, sentence pattern, word choice, rhythm,

## Interview
## Novelist's perspective: knowing through fiction

### Anne Enright
### IB graduate 1980

*Anne Enright is an Irish novelist, living and writing in Dublin. She won the prestigious Man Booker Prize in 2007 for The Gathering and published The Forgotten Waltz in 2011.*

→ When your readers put down *The Gathering* or *The Forgotten Waltz*, is there anything they might know that they did not know before they read it?

*The Gathering* and *The Forgotten Waltz* ask questions about the way we construct the story of our lives, not for other people, but for ourselves. Veronica and Gina find it difficult to tell the truth, although neither sets out to lie. The books push the limits of a first person point of view. *The Gathering* looks inwards, testing the lines where memory shades into imagination or turns into "history". *The Forgotten Waltz* looks outwards to break (I hope) from solipsism into empathy. If the reader knows anything at the end of the books, I hope it is that being certain and being right are two different things: often the proper response is to be unsure.

*Critical comment on The Forgotten Waltz:*
*"Enright gets the why of love."*
*"Each of her sentences has a stand-alone beauty, spring-triggered with wit."*[10] ■

---

[10]  Lisa Moore. 3 June 2011. "Desire and its wreckage". *The Globe and Mail.*

and devices for sound, examining them for their creation and support of ideas and mood. The context of the author's work or historical time period are not relevant in the way they would be from another perspective.

### Goal and evaluation

From this perspective, is any of the six works from your class activity "Arts from around the world" either disqualified or strongly confirmed as art?

From this perspective, what constitutes a particularly good work of art?

Can you find an example – perhaps a particular poem, piece of music, or painting – that you consider to excel according to this criterion?

## 3. Do you evaluate the artwork with emphasis on the audience?

*Critical attention focuses on the effect the work of art has on the audience. This attention acknowledges the **didactic goal of the arts** (to teach) and, like the first, the **expressive goal – but in terms of stirring of audience emotions.***

Many critics argue that the intention of an artist (our first critical perspective) is totally irrelevant to evaluating an artwork, and that what is of primary or even exclusive importance is the impact the work has upon its audience – the peers affected in their own work, the public moved to rapture or rage. Some critics, proponents of reader response

theory, argue that art exists *only* within this response – that art is brought into being only as the reader or viewer responds to it.

This perspective highlights, for example, the way a piece of music may make people sing along with pleasure, or the way its experimental features may challenge audience familiarity and current taste. It brings attention to the popularity of certain forms, and the continued popularity of many works that pass the "test of time" and continue to "speak" to people long after their creator has gone. It is also the perspective that most emphasizes ethical issues over what should or should not be treated in art, because of the consequences – predicted and debated – on the public's values and behaviour.

It is from this point of view, too, that we most fully appreciate the didactic impact of a work of art (though we might also appreciate didactic *intentions* of the artist). A didactic goal might include: to reach and teach the audience, inspire an audience to embrace ideals or beliefs, satirize foolishness, or expose social problems and wrongdoing. This goal is strong in some schools of painting, for instance, and is particularly strong in literature.

### Goal and evaluation

From this perspective, is any of the six works from your class activity "Arts from around the world" either disqualified or strongly confirmed as art?

From this perspective, what constitutes a particularly good work of art?

*Richard Underhill*
*IB graduate 1979*

Richard is an award-winning jazz composer and performer, based in Toronto, Canada. From the time

he was an IB student, he has electrified his audiences with his alto saxophone and stage presence.

"During my IB, my exposure to the concepts of international understanding, service to the community and social justice definitely affected my musical and personal life in a positive way. I have consciously and lovingly opened myself up to music and cultures of the world, playing Salsa, African, Klezmer, Reggae, Blues, Jazz, Funk and many other styles of music with equal love and respect. I always have time to do benefits for worthy causes, and often bring my saxophone to anti-war rallies and peace marches."

Can you find an example – perhaps a particular poem, piece of music, or painting – that you consider to excel according to this criterion?

## 4. Do you evaluate the artwork with emphasis on the context of society or the natural world?

*Critical attention focuses on the effectiveness of the work in representation of society or the world, its role within tradition, and its role as a social and historical document or artifact. This attention acknowledges the* **representational goal of the arts** *(to hold the mirror up to nature), and the* **social roles** *given to the arts.*

Many critics give attention – above all – to the way the arts can give a vivid portrayal of the world, one that we often call "realistic". A piece of literature, for example, may reflect keenly observed details of psychological and social interactions; it may capture the turn of phrase of conversation, or represent societies with all their interplays of power. A painting may catch light as it shimmers across water or a woman's face, or pick out revealing moments of people in action. It is from this perspective that we recognize what much art has in common with the human and natural sciences – a keen eye and ear for details, and a capacity to record them with clarity and accuracy. The work has, metaphorically speaking, "[held] the mirror up to nature".[11]

In capturing a record of people, places, and times, the artwork can also provide a kind of historical evidence of their tastes, values, and experiences; paintings and literature of today become artifacts and documents for sociologists of the present and historians of the future.

It is also from this perspective (in combination with that of the third, the reaction of the reader or audience) that we most appreciate the capacity of the arts to take us imaginatively into the lives of other individuals and other societies – people and places that are true to life, that we "recognize" without ever having seen them before.

Particular critical theories emphasize different aspects of the society pictured: feminist criticism stresses representation of women and gender relations; Marxist criticism stresses class relations; postcolonial criticism stresses issues of ethnicity, race, power, and injustice, particularly in former colonies; criticism centred in cultural studies stresses the values and practices of the period in which the work is set.

Placing an artwork within its society also raises questions about the relationship of the individual artist and the artistic tradition, with all of its expectations of what art should be and do, and the conventions of expression it should follow.

Finally, putting the artwork in its social context gives attention to its social functions and uses – whether for display and status, public gatherings or ceremonies, religious veneration or invocation, entertainment, decoration, affirmation of beliefs, or any of the other roles we give the arts in our societies.

You are not unfamiliar with this criterion at work. In your literature course, the works you read take you into the lives of people and societies, some of them crossing cultures in the process. This perspective on the arts is fairly strong in the west at the moment – an interest in examining music, dance, literature, or the visual arts for their relationship with their social background, as part of cultural studies.

### Goal and evaluation

From this perspective, is any of the six works from your class activity "Arts from around the world" either disqualified or strongly confirmed as art?

From this perspective, what constitutes a particularly good work of art?

Can you find an example – perhaps a particular poem, piece of music, or painting – that you consider to excel according to this criterion?

## Critics and evaluation

With rare exceptions, these four perspectives on the arts, each placing emphasis on one major aspect of the artistic creation and communication, do not operate independently. Just as the artist affects the audience through his work, the response of the audience affects the artist and thereby often influences work the artist does in

---

[11] Shakespeare, *Hamlet*, III, ii, 22.

the future. The reciprocal influence of the artist and the audience is most immediately evident in performance arts, where, for instance, actors can sense the audience reaction. However, novelists working all alone with a pen or keyboard, or

**How much is a painting worth?**

In 2011, a painting by Paul Cezanne called The Card Players sold for more than $250 million.[12] Leonardo Da Vinci's Mona Lisa (above) currently holds the record for having the highest insurance value of a painting in history, but will never top The Card Players' price tag because the Louvre in Paris would never sell it. It is "priceless" in all senses of the word. It is not only a great painting, but an icon of painting of the Great Masters, familiar from calendars, chocolate boxes, tee-shirts, and advertising.

Can you explain the fascination with the Mona Lisa? Is it a better painting than any other? Can you give any explanation of the social forces that have led to its "pricelessness" and The Card Players' record price? (You might like to think more broadly on how we put a monetary value on anything.)

painters working in studios, can also be affected in their confidence and productivity by the criticism their work is given – buoyed up by recognition (and grants) or crushed by bad reviews.

But how can we *judge* the arts in order to buoy up the best practitioners with recognition?

Certainly, judgment in the arts brings to life a range of opinions. It is one of the wonderful qualities of the arts that they are accessible to *anyone* to understand, to an extent without study, and to *like* and *dislike* according to personal taste and personal knowledge, without needing to agree with anyone else. Saying "I like this music" is comment on *your own response*.

However, when it comes to comment on *the work itself*, not all criticism is equally justified. As we commented earlier, the arts are subjective – and so, to a large extent, is criticism. However, "subjective" does not mean arbitrary or unjustified. Four hundred years ago, poet Alexander Pope went so far as to claim that skill in criticism could rival the importance of skill in writing:

> 'Tis hard to say, if greater Want of Skill
> Appear in Writing or in Judging ill,
> But, of the two, less dang'rous is th' Offence,
>
> To tire our Patience, than mis-lead our Sense.[13]

A good critic, in our view, possesses many of the same qualities in any area of knowledge. Already in this chapter, we have considered two of them: *background knowledge* sufficient to understand the particular work produced (the genre, the cultural "language", technical features, and so forth) and *awareness of different critical perspectives*.

Moreover, critics, we suggest, should have some *familiarity with accepted standards*. They might contest the accepted standards rather than accepting them – and even campaign, for instance, to break the hold on the arts of an established canon of Good Work – but they will be *aware* of expectations and current debates as they distinguish exceptional work from the mundane. Moreover, critics are likely to agree on some standards, for instance, rejecting as insignificant art that is formulaic, sentimental, clichéd, manipulative, or trite.

---

[12] Alexandra Peers. 2 February 2012. "Qatar Purchases Cézanne's *The Card Players* for More Than $250 Million, Highest Price Ever for a Work of Art". *Vanity Fair.* 2 February 2012.

[13] Pope, A. 1711. "Essay on Criticism".

## For Reflection

Above, we have proposed four major qualities that, in our view, good critics should possess. Do you think any of them are unnecessary, and if so why? Would you propose others? To what extent should critics in other areas of knowledge possess these, or similar, qualities?

In treating criticism here, we have distinguished between liking a work of art and being able to give a good criticism of it. To what extent do you accept this distinction?

Thereafter, *discernment and taste* play a significant role. Subjective qualities both, they can be developed through exposure and experience: the eye notices more, the ear hears more, and the mind applies more assuredly the growing general understanding to particular cases. If critics have to explain and justify their views, their skills draw on an increasing number of ways of knowing! In the end, they may disagree with each other, or even hotly defend differing interpretations and evaluations – but if they are informed and articulate, they contribute opinions that are likely to illuminate different features of the work on which they comment.

Evaluation and criticism in the arts is never devoid of this element of personal response and debate – and it is an element that, far from being a weakness of this area of knowledge, contributes to its strength. The communication *around* the arts – the exchange of knowledge and views – is part of the life of the field. Tastes change, goals shift, different media come into play, and artists and the public interact in the process of change. Neither creation nor criticism is fixed and static.

## Arts and ethics

One of the most controversial issues in the arts is what should *not* be treated as art in its representation of the world. Different places and times have had their own kinds of prohibitions – whether it would be shocking to break the conventions of iconography in the representation of Christian saints in the European medieval period, or whether it would be inappropriate to represent the human body at all, as in much Islamic art. In the twentieth century, visual arts in the west have particularly pushed the barriers of acceptability, sometimes provoking cries of "grotesque!" or "obscene" or "huh? Is that supposed to be *art?*"

The hottest controversies lie along the line where the arts meet ethics, in arguments against representation of what, from particular perspectives, is considered "indecency" or "immorality". In treating ethical controversies in the arts in TOK, it is important not just to describe what one group and another think, but to analyse them (as ever!) in terms of their framing perspectives, and to bring in different ways of evaluating within ethics. You may wish to turn ahead to the chapter on ethics, to the section on "Theoretical persepctives in normative ethics".

## A comment on TOK essays on the arts...

And now, having raised numerous ideas for you to consider regarding the arts, we want to ensure that you do not forget them all and fall back into stereotypes if you choose to write about the arts in your assessment essay. Alas, in TOK essays on the arts, students commonly make only two comments, both of them so limited that they distort the area of knowledge as a whole:

**(a)** the purpose of art is to express the emotions of the artist

**(b)** art must be beautiful (with beauty being in the eye of the beholder, so who can say what's good?).

In their essays, these same students tend to take their examples only from visual arts of twentieth century Europe and North America, and only from those that challenge concepts of art (for example, urinals or rotting meat). While this approach does pick out some important features of the arts, its narrow focus demonstrates little understanding of this area of knowledge. It is sometimes also accompanied by a dismissive attitude towards art as something a monkey with a paintbrush could do (and fool all the silly critics).

It is our hope that this sad comment on TOK essays on the arts will very quickly go out of date – and that it does not apply to you and your inclinations in any case!

Just in case you are inclined to sum up the arts in two points *on reflex,* here comes a stretching exercise for your mind. Apply your understanding of perspectives on the arts as you consider

## Discussion Activity

### Sniffy the Rat: art and ethics

In Vancouver, Canada, performance artist Rick Gibson announced his intention to drop a 25-kilogram concrete block on a rat in public. It would be squashed on impact between two canvasses, which would take the imprint of its body. The result would be a diptych, a double image in art.[14]

The rat was dubbed "Sniffy" in the Vancouver media, and its scheduled execution on 6 January 1990 provoked an outpouring of horrified condemnation. Animal rights activists were outraged. They stole the concrete block, suspended and ready for the squashing. When artist Rick Gibson appeared at the appointed time, he told an angry crowd that he had returned Sniffy to the pet store from which he had rented him, and declared that being

squashed was a better way to die than being fed to a snake, the likely fate of a pet store rat. Gibson fled from the swarming protestors. Sniffy was purchased from the pet store by an activist and taken home to live out his days.

**Our question for you:**

Is squashing a rat in "performance" art moral or not? You must give your reasons.

---

"Parades, Parades" written by Derek Walcott, from St. Lucia in the Caribbean, who won the Nobel Prize for Literature in 1992. Our accompanying questions will give you a push.

## The arts as an area of knowledge

For all that the arts give us, what is the nature of their knowledge? According to the criteria of history, the human sciences, and the natural sciences, what the arts give us, at least for the most part, would not be accepted as knowledge at all.

Certainly, if an essential ingredient in knowledge is considered to be knowledge claims asserted in language, the arts would not qualify. As we considered earlier, most arts do not use language. Even those that do have language as their medium do not necessarily communicate through assertion, preferring depiction and suggestion. Nor do they gain their value as art through whether those assertions that they do make are literally, factually true. The knowledge that the arts give us is not in the form of objectively testable statements.

But what form, then, does it take? We would venture to suggest that what the arts give is *subjective understanding*: exposure to multitudes of perspectives and ideas, some grasp of human beings and society astutely observed in ways that may take us far beyond our own limited experience, some challenge to our ideas and provocation to think further, a sense of significance created through the shaping of the chaos of sensory experience and our lives into meaningful pattern, and a lift of the mind to a "still point" of aesthetic beauty in experiencing and contemplating shape and form.

To the extent that the arts are shared knowledge, they share a rich and varied humanity. They give us, surely, immense pleasure, increased awareness, and often insight into our common humanity. Their diversity and subjectivity, qualities that some other areas of knowledge attempt to overcome, are for the arts quite possibly the very qualities that give them power to stir us and connect us, and to contribute splendidly to our lives.

---

14 "Sniffy the rat saved from squishing", CBC digital archives. http://www.cbc.ca/archives/categories/arts-entertainment/visual-arts/artists-busted-censorship-in-canada/squishing-sniffy.html.

## Discussion Activity

### Parades, Parades

Read the poem through two or three times, and then pull together your thoughts on it in response to these questions. Notice that we do not ignore the two comments that we claim students make to excess, but try to get to grips with *expressing emotions* and *being beautiful* more technically, and add further goals of the arts for your consideration.

1    How does Walcott express his emotions? *Note that this question is no more than an introduction.* Does the poem seem written to express the author's personal feelings for his own sake while we as readers eavesdrop, or does it seem that the personal voice is used as a *strategy* to reach others and engage them – to ultimately provoke them to thought? Where does the first person point of view ("I") enter the poem? Does Walcott actually express any emotion *directly* ("I feel Y")? How do you know what his attitudes and feelings are? To what extent is the attitude he conveys the point of the poem?

2    Is the poem beautiful? *Let us, going further, rephrase the question* to stress aesthetic beauty of form rather than an implicit assumption that poems should be about love and flowers. Is the poem *effectively shaped* in its overall structure and *technically adept* in its use of language and poetic devices? Does the way that it is written support (or create) the ideas it conveys – form and content working together?

These two questions raise two of our critical perspectives – the *expressive goal* of the arts (attention given to the artist) and the *aesthetic goal* of the arts (attention given to the work itself). Now push on.

3    Thinking in terms of the audience (yourself), what is the impact of the work on its readers? Does it comment on its society, stir thought, and challenge your ideas – the *didactic goal* of the arts? Does it affect your feelings? In communication between the poet and the audience, several goals of the arts come into play.

### Parades, Parades

*by Derek Walcott (1971)*

There's the wide desert, but no one marches
except in the pads of old caravans,
there is the ocean, but the keels incise
the precise, old parallels,
there's the blue sea above the mountains
but they scratch the same lines
in the jet trails–
so the politicians plod
without imagination, circling
the same sombre garden
with its fountain dry in the forecourt,
the gri-gri palms desiccating
dung pods like goats,
the same lines rule the White Papers,
the same steps ascend Whitehall,
and only the name of the fool changes
under the plumed white cork-hat
for the Independence Parades,
revolving around, in calypso,
to the brazen joy of the tubas.

Why are the eyes of the beautiful
and unmarked children
in the uniforms of the country
bewildered and shy,
why do they widen in terror
of the pride drummed into their minds?
Were they truer, the old songs,
when the law lived far away,
when the veiled queen, her girth
as comfortable as cushions,
upheld the orb with its stern admonitions?
We wait for the changing of statues,
for the change of parades.

Here he comes now, here he comes!
Papa! Papa! With his crowd,
the sleek, waddling seals of his Cabinet,
trundling up to the dais,
as the wind puts its tail between
the cleft of the mountain, and a wave
coughs once, abruptly.
Who will name this silence
respect? Those forced, hoarse hosannas
awe? That tin-ringing tune

from the pumping, circling horns
the New World?  Find a name
for that look on the faces
of the electorate.  Tell me
how it all happened, and why
I said nothing.

4    Does the poem "hold the mirror up to
     nature" as in the *representational goal* of the
     arts? Do the words conjure up images in your
     own mind, vividly?

5    In what ways does the poem stand as a *social
     document* itself? What is Walcott saying about
     the transfer of power in a former colony
     which has gained its independence? If you
     were interested above all in postcolonial
     issues, what might you say about the poem?

6    Do you *believe* the poet, and accept him as an
     authority on problems in the Caribbean? Are
     you inclined, when an author presents a point of
     view personally and vividly, to accept the point
     of view presented? If so, you might wish to
     reflect on the limitations of anecdotal evidence –
     *and* the persuasive power of literature.

7    Look back now to the other poem to
     which you have been introduced in
     this book, "Sunlight on the Garden" by
     Louis MacNeice (Chapter 13). Although
     both poems deal with very particular
     experiences and are quite obviously
     subjective, do they give or imply any
     general understanding relevant to
     broader human experience? Does the
     *particular* imply the *general*?

## The knowledge framework, the arts

In this chapter, we have aimed to stir up your own thinking about the arts and to supplement it with further understanding of this area of knowledge. Before you leave this chapter, gather up your present ideas in summary, using the knowledge framework below.  For more detailed guidance, look back to the Overview following chapter 14. As you move through areas of knowledge, you will find that using the framework for summaries gives you very helpful terms for comparisons, toward your own overview understanding of knowledge.

### Discussion Activity

#### Knowledge framework: arts

First summarize your responses to these questions in your own words. Then exchange ideas with others in your class.

1.  **Scope:** What are the arts all about? What do they take as their subject matter and their goals? Is anything excluded, and if so why?

2.  **Language:** How does language affect the production of knowledge in the arts? To what extent are the naming and defining of central concepts significant in this area?

3.  **Methodology:** What ways of knowing are used in the methods of the arts? Are the arts characterized more by diversity of methods or more by methods held in common? Within diversity, are there common features?

4.  **Historical development:** In what ways do the arts of today use the arts of the past? What social or technological factors have given particular directions to development of the arts? Have there been remarkable turning points or changes in direction punctuating the development of this field?

5.  **Links to personal knowledge:** What do individuals gain from the shared knowledge of the arts, and how do they contribute to the field themselves? How do the arts affect your own knowledge?

251

## What is "cause"?

The arts, scooping up nearly the whole of human experience within their subject matter, often deal centrally with the question "why?" as part of their subject matter. In literature particularly, the psychological motivation of characters is crucial to novels and plays, and is often keenly observed to the point that great fictional characters can crystallize for us major characteristics of human thought and feeling. Why does Othello kill Desdemona, or Hamlet almost fail to kill Claudius? Why does Elizabeth first refuse Darcy so vehemently, and then later accept to marry him? Similarly, in handling the larger "why?" of social forces of the background setting, novels can show us the dynamics of race and gender relations, for instance, or the building causes of violence and war.

Paintings, too, can show us "why", even if they do not make the knowledge claims in language. Grand church paintings of the Last Judgment, for example, leave us in little doubt about cause and effect, as good people are taken up into the clouds by angels, while bad people are hurled down into the flames of hell. Come to think of it, such a painting depicts only the effect; we are left, standing in the church, to think about the cause!

As we leave the arts behind us, we do not leave behind the question "why?" Ethics, which we enter next, considers *motivations* and *consequences* as it treats moral thought and conduct, and the moral choices that we make. The areas of knowledge we deal with thereafter – history, the human sciences, and the natural sciences – aim not only for factual description of *what* there is but also *why*. In interpretations and theories, they aim for *explanation*.

We invite you to plunge into these ideas yourself – probably not for the first time! No one is likely to have reached the age of maturity of the IB Diploma Programme without having reflected on the questions in the discussion activity below.

### Discussion Activity

#### Why?

Take time now to ask yourself the question, "Why am I here in this particular place at this particular time?" Consider all the possible answers you might give and select for discussion those that you think give the best explanation.

You may have stories to tell of how you happened to end up in this place or how things might easily have been otherwise. You might recall "turning point" moments in your own life, involving personal decisions or the actions of others. ("If it weren't for X, I wouldn't be here.") You might consider, too, what background situations had to exist for the particular events to have happened as they did. Do you feel that your being *here*, *now* is chance, or do you consider there to be some purpose or plan for your life?

## "Why?" How do we explain?

Please read the questions below only after you have completed the discussion activity on the previous page on why you are *here, now*. Use them to reflect on your own answers and the answers that emerged from discussion with your class group.

1.  Did your explanation involve or even emphasize *your own decisions?* Did you feel it relevant to give the factors that in turn affected the choices you made, and to explain why they were important to you? Do your expectations of the future affect your decisions in the present?

2.  Did your explanation involve *actions by other people?* If so, did you think mainly of the effect those people had on you in terms of their actions, or also in terms of their intentions?

3.  Did your explanation involve *negative causes,* things that did *not* happen to prevent the present? Many people have stories of times when they (or their parents before their conception and birth) might have died from illness, accident, or violence, for example, but did not.

4.  *How far "back"* in time did explanations within your group go? Did they move back in time to the lives of your parents and grandparents? How did your mother meet your father? Is their story part of your own? Did you go further back into the lives of your ancestors? Did you assume that cause was a linear sequence, metaphorically going back and back to a beginning, perhaps the Big Bang theory and/or a First Cause as God/Allah?

5.  *How far "out"* did explanations within your group go? How many background details did you find it necessary to include? Did you feel it relevant, for example, to include the existence of the International Baccalaureate or your school, or the political, economic, and cultural background of your region that affects the educational context?

6.  What did you consider "cause" to be?
    *   Was it the *largest influence* (even if it is in the background)?
    *   Was it the event or influence that stands out as *most unusual*?

*   Or was it perhaps the one that *happened last,* to provoke your being in the particular place at the particular time?

7.  Did your explanation include *metaphysical influence* in any form? Does your personal understanding of cause and effect involve, for example, destiny, karma, or God?

In the knowledge fields of history, the human sciences, and the natural sciences – which seek to give explanations for different aspects of the world – questions of which events *cause* other events are central. We do not, after all, *see* cause. We observe many events in the world, but it is with our own reasoning that we join the dots to conclude, among all the possible variables and connections, which one (or which ones) caused a particular situation or event.

## Metaphysical explanation

An atheist, a Buddhist, a Jew, a Christian, and a Muslim can work together on the same research team, converging in their knowledge: they may have the same level of doubt or questioning regarding the knowledge claims of their field and the same skills of investigation. Each *knows* the same thing. However, each may integrate that knowledge into the coherent whole of all his beliefs and *understand* the knowledge differently.

For the Jew, Christian, and Muslim, the explanation may fit into a conception of the world where God/Allah is the cause of all – He is the Creator, the causal force behind the events of the world, and a force that may intervene in life in response to prayer. For the Buddhist, the explanation may be part of an understanding of a universe where cause and effect are of central significance, where all actions create good or bad karma that will come back to affect the doer and others. For the atheist, the scientific explanation has no additional spiritual explanation – none, at least, in the form of a god.

The five researchers do not differ in their knowledge. They differ in the meaning they attribute to it and the place they give it in their larger worldview. An examination of where we converge in our *knowledge* may be incomplete without a complementary recognition of what we have in common and where we differ in the broader *worldviews* of our perspectives.

## Discussion Activity

### What counts as *cause*?

A man has a heart attack while jogging. The following pieces of information are available. On a sheet of paper, diagram the causes: draw an arrow from each fact back to its cause. Then answer the question: What is the cause of his heart attack?

1   He was given a new pair of jogging shoes for his birthday and wanted to try them.

2   He had eaten far too much (far, far too much) during the previous week.

3   He has always loved chocolate cake, and cannot resist second, third, or fourth helpings.

4   As a child, he had associated his mother's chocolate cake with approval, since she had rewarded him with extra pieces if he had done well.

5   He loves his mother.

6   Poor jogging shoes have in the past made his shins ache.

7   He frequently makes new starts, with fresh resolutions for the future.

8   He likes a sporty image.

9   He would like his wife to think of him as a thwarted athlete who, under other circumstances, might have been of Olympic quality!

10   He was pleased that his wife had given him a sporty present for his birthday.

11   The road he was jogging on was hilly.

12   He is 57 years old.

13   Although basically fit, he has not jogged for six weeks because of an injury to his Achilles tendon.

14   When he was 13, he had won a trophy for being the best runner in his age group in the surrounding region, and still thinks of that prize as a special achievement.

15   His father had been admired for his skill in tennis.

16   His mother admired athletic ability.

17   His mother married his father.

18   He was born.

19   He had jogged 12 kilometres when he had his heart attack.

20   He had decided to go jogging at that particular moment because his wife and son were fiercely arguing politics.

# 16. Ethics

As we examine ethics in TOK, we will not be *studying* ethics any more than we *study* sciences or the arts when we discuss them as areas of knowledge; we will not be making or arguing for the knowledge claims of the field except to see how arguments are made and how they are justified, and to consider their implications for other knowledge and potential action.

The moral judgments you may reach yourself are only the raw material here for your further reflection. We ask you to bring your views into discussion but notice above all what reasons you give in their support. Thinking and talking about this area of knowledge demands a lot from you in terms of reflection on your own ideas, willingness to exchange views with others, and readiness, even if your own views are firm, to listen for what justifications persuade others. What touches us most deeply can be contestable.

## Scope: What is ethics all about?

If ethics seems at moments to be messy and confusing, that is not a weakness in ethics but instead a characteristic of what it takes as its subject. It deals with human thoughts and actions, to give an understanding of goodness and moral choice. Where the human sciences and history deal with how people *are* or *were* in their thoughts and conduct, ethics deals with how people *should be*.

Ethics surveys all that human beings do and persistently asks knowledge questions: "What does it mean to be good?" "What should I/we do (or not do)?" "How do we justify our moral decisions?" And then it explores possible ways of thinking about the questions and possible ways to answer.

We often use the words "moral" and "ethical" interchangeably in everyday language. Here, for clarity, we consider morality to be our sense of right and wrong and ethics to be the area of knowledge that examines that sense of morality and the moral codes we develop from it. We treat moral decisions and choices as the material for ethical reflection and ethical decision-making.

### For Reflection

Why be moral?

How did you gain your own sense of right and wrong?

Have you (except, of course, when you were very young) ever been close to doing anything you "knew" to be immoral? If you stopped, what stopped you? Why did you think what you were about to do was immoral?

With what others do you share this sense of right and wrong? Is it linked to any kind of community to which you belong – locally, nationally, or internationally?

Since all of us are involved throughout our lives in moral decision-making, ethics is an area of knowledge whose subject matter concerns us personally. And it is to your own thoughts that we turn next – in the reflection above and your response to the questions that come with the opening activity "How should people treat each other?" They ask you to consider some of your own moral responses, and where they come from.

## Shared knowledge and the "knowledge community" for ethics

Since all of us deal with ideas of morality in our lives, we are *all* part of the knowledge community for ethics. It is shared knowledge of the broadest sort, including everyone in the world and affecting numerous aspects of our lives. Like the arts, it pervades our everyday lives – though possibly with a greater need to respond and make decisions.

In the arts, you will recall, we considered the way our personal knowledge intersected with shared knowledge. We are all able to respond to and understand the arts, to a large extent, without formal training. Yet some people have taken in greater shared knowledge on the background of the arts and the topics in the field. Artists, musicians, and writers, for instance, or critics knowledgeable in particular forms, can illuminate for us many ideas that we could have missed. While we can all formulate opinions, we gain from the shared knowledge of *informed opinion*.

In ethics, similarly, some people specialize in understanding what the major knowledge questions are, how they have been answered in the past, and how they could be answered freshly. These people are philosophers, with some of them also being religious scholars. They exchange ideas and views much as in other academic areas, with discussion and debate in peer-reviewed journals and conferences, and sometimes with public talks that raise important issues for society. Their *informed opinion* develops ethics as an area of knowledge.

Ethics, indeed, is an area of knowledge that consists almost exclusively of critical argument,

akin to the critical and theoretical side of the arts. Unlike the arts, though, it does not create works of its own to critique: it does not produce anything equivalent to novels or symphonies. What it examines and evaluates is thought, choice, and action that take place in other areas of knowledge and in the whole of life.

## For Reflection

To what extent is evaluation of ideas in all areas of knowledge, not just the arts and ethics, dependent on "informed opinion"?

What is involved in being "informed" in the different areas of knowledge? How "informed" do you have to be to understand and evaluate?

## Discussion Activity

### How should human beings treat each other?

Kofi Annan, then Secretary General of the United Nations, looked back in 1998 at a century for which Guernica stands as an icon:

> The world has changed since Picasso painted that first political masterpiece, but it has not necessarily grown easier. We are near the end of a tumultuous century that has witnessed both the best and worst of human endeavour. Peace spreads in one region as genocidal fury rages in another. Unprecedented wealth coexists with terrible deprivation, as a quarter of the world's people remain mired in poverty.[1]

**Question for discussion:** What are the moral values that Kofi Annan is either stating or implying for how people should treat each other? Can you pick out from his comments any moral values that you, too, accept?

Look again at Picasso's Guernica. The emotional outcry against violence and the pain of war need not be confined just to the bombed civilians of the village of Guernica.

Can any moral values be inferred from Picasso's painting regarding how human beings should or should not treat each other? Can you identify any moral values that you, too, accept?

Entering a discussion on ethics, we will be considering both what people should do and what people should not do, and the various perspectives on telling the difference between them. Many of the ethical issues of our times have profound implications for people's lives, and people's interconnected lives, all around the world.

---

1   Kofi Annan on Guernica, speaking 3 November 1998. In G. van Hensberngen. 2004. *Guernica. The Biography of a Twentieth Century Icon*. London. Bloomsbury, P. 1.

## What kind of choices are *moral* choices?

Ethics deals with moral choices – choices we make that reflect our values of good and bad, right and wrong.

Let us pause to clarify some language! The choices themselves are called "moral choices". In everyday language, choices that meet with approval are called "moral" and those that meet with condemnation are called "immoral". Choices that do not involve morality, such as a choice between seeing one Bollywood film or another, or choosing chocolate ice cream rather than strawberry, are called "amoral" or "morally neutral".

Almost any choice, however, has the potential to be a moral choice within a particular context: what we wear may be merely a matter of style but can also come accompanied by religious and social values; what we eat may be a matter of taste, but can also be grounded in religious prohibitions against certain foods or values placed upon animal life; how we greet someone else may be a matter of custom, but can also reflect the value of respect for others. Whether we wear white or red could become a moral issue for what it symbolizes, and how the symbolism is used in the particular context of a wedding or a street protest. How we vote could be seen as matter of preferring one leader over another, but also seen as a moral choice that affects human welfare and the environment. To consider what criteria you think characterize choices that are specifically moral ones, turn to the discussion activity "What makes a choice a 'moral choice'?"

## Levels of generality

In dealing with living a good life and making the right choices, ethics deals with knowledge questions at different levels of generality from the broadest overview questions to the most focused and applied. The area of knowledge has become conventionally divided, as a result, into three broad fields. We will touch on each briefly

### Discussion Activity

#### Concepts and language: "moral choice"

a. Is eating meat a moral issue, involving moral choice? Can you identify different perspectives and present their arguments?

b. Is the degree to which people expose parts of their body a moral issue, involving moral choice? Can you identify different perspectives and present their arguments?

c. Are poverty and ways of dealing with it moral issues on the part of the society, with moral choices to be made? Can you identify different perspectives and present their arguments?

d. Is the death penalty a moral issue in society, with moral choices to be made? Can you identify different perspectives and present their arguments?

Can you point out any issues in your own social context which appear to be moral choices in the eyes of some people but amoral in the eyes of others?

here, in order to give you the Big Picture of what ethics takes within its scope.

1. **Meta-ethics**: What is the nature of ethical knowledge?

2. **Normative ethics**: How do we know whether we are doing the right thing?

3. **Applied ethics**: How do we apply ethical thinking to particular topics under social debate, or to conduct in particular professional fields?

## 1. Meta-ethics

*What is the nature of ethical knowledge?*

This overview field of ethics deals with hugely general questions. Are ethical values independent from human beings with a metaphysical existence of their own in the universe, or are they a product of human thought? Psychologically, what motivates people to act morally – and is morality part of human nature? Do moral truths exist?

One meta-ethical debate centres on whether moral principles are universal. Can ethics present "all" statements and generalize on universal moral choices, or is it restricted to making "some" statements that are confined to some people or some circumstances? Ethical relativism and ethical absolutism take contrary perspectives on this issue.

*Ethical relativism* argues that there is no such thing as right and wrong outside the values of the particular individual or the values of the society. It points observationally to moral variability from person to person and society to society and places emphasis on divergences. It also counter-argues any justifications for ethical judgments that transcend individual or group values.

The weakness of relativism in logical terms is that it is self-defeating: if all claims are just relative to the particular person or group, then so is relativism itself. Many would also find weakness in practical and emotional terms in that its implications are repugnant: it nullifies all general moral judgments

## Ethical absolutes and human rights

Arguments that some moral principles are absolute and universally applicable lie behind the concept of human rights. These rights are the basic entitlements of all human beings. Politically, they have been accepted internationally in documents such as the Universal Declaration of Human Rights,[2] signed in 1948 at the United Nations by all countries of the world.

The document opens with this initial founding statement, the basic assumption or premise on which rests all the subsequent assertions: "recognition of the inherent dignity and of the equal and inalienable rights of all members of the human family is the foundation of freedom, justice and peace in the world."

We give just the first articles out of the full 30 articles here and encourage you to find them online and read them all, thoughtfully and critically, as a political endorsement of ethical principles. Although human rights are often violated, the Universal Declaration of Human Rights provides the moral standards by which such actions can be judged:

Article 1: All human beings are born free and equal in dignity and rights. They are endowed with reason and conscience and should act towards one another in a spirit of brotherhood.

Article 2: Everyone is entitled to all the rights and freedoms set forth in this Declaration, without distinction of any kind, such as race, colour, sex, language, religion, political or other opinion, national or social origin, property, birth or other status...

Article 3: Everyone has the right to life, liberty, and security of person.

Article 4: No one shall be held in slavery or servitude; slavery and the slave trade shall be prohibited in all their forms.

Article 5: No one shall be subjected to torture or to cruel, inhuman or degrading treatment or punishment.

Article 6: Everyone has the right to recognition everywhere as a person before the law.

---

2  Universal Declaration of Human Rights, United Nations, http://www.un.org/en/documents/udhr/

and allows no possible grounds for general condemnation of any actions, including slavery, infanticide, rape, torture, or genocide.

What relativism contributes to ethical debate, by rejecting any moral absolutes, is an emphasis on responsiveness to particular circumstances. It also may *possibly* result in its adherents thinking through personal values and tolerating those of other people.

*Ethical absolutism* (or ethical objectism), at the other end of the spectrum, argues that there is such a thing as right and wrong applicable universally. It uses arguments from moral principles that do not vary with the situation, the society, or the individual.

Its weakness is that, in reality, there appear to be no moral judgments accepted by every society worldwide. Thus, it cannot be justified by observation that there are values on which all societies agree, without exception. Since ethics argues for how people *should* act rather than solely observing how people *do* act, however, it can still be argued that they ought to agree, or would if they really knew! Its greater weakness, in practical and emotional terms, lies at the other extreme from relativism's: it opposes the arbitrariness of relativism, but argues for inflexibility.

Absolutism contributes a lot to ethical debate. It challenges all other systems to try to rise above immediate circumstances and establish a guide that would be applicable worldwide. It also challenges traditional codes of morality to be open to change.

The two positions, extremes in the ethical spectrum, remind us that ethics is not an area of knowledge where the conclusions are based on describing how the world *is*. Instead, it deals with how it *ought* to be. Neither is it an area of knowledge with methods of proof that can be expected to command universal assent.

And yet ... people do come to a considerable level of agreement. They are often in accord

## The golden rule in world religions[3]

| | |
|---|---|
| **Christianity** | All things whatsoever ye would that men should do to you, do ye so to them; for this is the law and the prophets. *Matthew 7:1* |
| **Confucianism** | Do not do to others what you would not like yourself. Then there will be no resentment against you, either in the family or in the state. *Analects 12:2* |
| **Buddhism** | Hurt not others in ways that you yourself would find hurtful. *Udana-Varga 5,1* |
| **Hinduism** | This is the sum of duty; do naught unto others that you would not have them do unto you. *Mahabharata 5,1517* |
| **Islam** | No one of you is a believer until he desires for his brother that which he desires for himself. *Sunnah [or 40 Hadith of an-Nawawi 13]* |
| **Judaism** | What is hateful to you, do not do to your fellowman. This is the entire Law; all the rest is commentary. *Talmud, Shabbat 3id* |
| **Taoism** | Regard your neighbor's gain as your gain, and your neighbor's loss as your own loss. *Tai Shang Kan Yin P'ien* |
| **Zoroastrianism** | That nature alone is good which refrains from doing to another whatsoever is not good for itself. *Dadisten-I-dinik, 94,5* |

---

3   Teaching Values, http://www.teachingvalues.com/goldenrule.html, accessed 30 July 2012.

on convincing arguments – ones that make assumptions that seem acceptable, provide clarity in the reasoning, and put forward justifications that seem compelling. Cogent ethical arguments can provide ways of thinking about topics that seem, rather like models in other areas of knowledge, to capture the essential features and clear away the clutter.

Moreover, despite the arguments of relativism that ethics can be considered only in terms of *particular cases*, we continue as individuals and societies to seek the *generalizations* that can provide useful guidance. We cannot establish them in the way that the natural sciences establish scientific laws or the human sciences establish general trends; ethics is not dealing with the physical, material world. But as we seek guides to moral action we look for *generalized ideas* in ethics, in order to be able to apply them to our own particular circumstances.

## 2. Normative ethics

*How do we know whether we are doing the right thing?*

Normative ethics deals with choices and actions, asking the question "What should I (or we) do?" Answers to this question involve values of right and wrong, and are often phrased as sentences using "should" or "ought". "You should do X" is a normative ethical statement.

More broadly, normative ethics attempts to provide answers using general approaches that act as guides to thought and action. There is more than one general approach, however, with its own assumptions and ways of arguing. The coherent

---

### "Acting out of concern for others' well-being"

*by His Holiness the Dalai Lama*

"Actually, I believe there is an important distinction to be made between religion and spirituality. Religion I take to be concerned with faith in the claims to salvation of one faith tradition or another, an aspect of which is acceptance of some form of metaphysical or supernatural reality, including perhaps an idea of heaven or nirvana. Connected with this are religious teachings or dogma, ritual, prayer, and so on. Spirituality I take to be concerned with those qualities of the human spirit – such as love and compassion, patience, tolerance, forgiveness, contentment, a sense of responsibility, a sense of harmony – which bring happiness to both self and others. While ritual and prayer, along with the questions of nirvana and salvation, are directly connected to religious faith, these inner qualities need not be, however. There is thus no reason why the individual should not develop them, even to a high degree, without recourse to any religious or metaphysical belief system. This is why I sometimes say that religion is something we can perhaps do without. What we cannot do without are these basic spiritual qualities."

"The unifying characteristic of the qualities I have described as "spiritual" may be said to be some level of concern for others' well-being. In Tibetan, we speak of *shen pen kyi sem* meaning "the thought to be of help to others". And when we think about them, we see that each of the qualities noted is defined by an implicit concern for others' well-being. Moreover, the one who is compassionate, loving, patient, tolerant, forgiving, and so on to some extent recognizes the potential impact of their actions on others and orders their conduct accordingly. Thus spiritual practice according to this description involves, on the one hand, acting out of concern for others' well-being. On the other, it entails transforming ourselves so that we become more readily disposed to do so. To speak of spiritual practice in any terms other than these is meaningless."[4]

---

[4]  His Holiness the Dalai Lama. 1999. *Ethics for the New Millennium*. New York. Riverhead. pp. 21–4.

perspectives within normative ethics are known as "ethical theories" – just as the perspectives on the arts (page) are known as "critical theories". (We will have reason later to consider the different shades of meaning given to the word "theory" in different areas of knowledge.) What are these different ethical perspectives, or ethical theories? Below is an activity in which you can identify them yourself.

## 3. Applied ethics

*How does ethical thinking apply to situations in society?*

Where meta-ethics hovers above moral choices looking at their nature, and where normative ethics moves closer to consider how to make those choices and to decide what we *should do*, applied ethics gets right into specific topics, bringing normative ethics to bear on moral issues controversial in a society. It deals with such topic areas as bio-medical ethics, environmental ethics, organizational ethics, business ethics, and sexual ethics.[5] It is at this level of informed debate that decisions are recommended, as ethical ideas become operative in social policy and law, and in writing ethical codes for professionals in various fields to follow. It is at this level that real doctors apply ethical frameworks to decisions with real patients. It is at this level that ethical frameworks of thinking help make debate on controversial topics in society into *informed* debate, with clearer thinking.

## The ethical dilemma

Although ethics is often characterized as an area of conflicting conclusions and controversy, we venture to suggest that people tend to be much in

---

### Discussion Activity

### Ethical dilemma: IB examination hall

A teacher, while supervising an IB examination, sees someone indisputably cheating. (Note that the issue here is not one of sense perception and possible error. It is a *given* in this question that the student really is cheating.) Read all pieces of information carefully, and then decide what you think the right action is for the teacher to take. The conclusion you reach is less important than your reasons for reaching it, so we encourage you to think from different perspectives.

- The student needs to pass the exam in order to get his IB diploma.
- The student is predicted to pass the exam.
- The student is very popular, so his friends will be upset over the incident if his cheating is exposed.
- The teacher really likes the student.
- No one else sees the student cheating, and at this moment he is not aware that the teacher has seen him.
- No one else writing the exam is cheating.
- The teacher has undertaken invigilation, or the prevention of exam irregularities of any kind, as part of her professional responsibility.

- The student is under pressure to succeed from his family and his community, who expect him to bring them pride.
- The teacher has heard it said that the student has cheated in the past in minor ways, but cannot recall the details.
- The IB system of examinations is a means of comparing student performance worldwide with identical examination conditions.

Now describe what you think is the right course of action for the teacher to take.

---

5  Internet Encyclopedia of Philosophy: http://www.iep.utm.edu/ethics/#H1. This is a good resource if you want to know more. It is clearly written and presented, and describes itself as a peer-reviewed academic resource.

agreement in moral decision-making. It is when we face *dilemmas,* however, that we are most often pushed to look at our values consciously and, in ethical argument, try to resolve what the moral action would be and why.

We ask you to engage in this kind of thinking yourself, in order to recognize some of the major lines of argument in normative ethics. To give you the chance to discover what you think yourself and how you would argue, we give you a single example of a dilemma, one in an IB examination hall. In discussing it, treat disagreements as valuable and consider the case that can be made for any point of view.

## Theoretical Critical perspectives in normative ethics

The situation of the IB examination hall provides an example deliberately simpler than many situations we find in life in order to start you off with a focus on major lines of argument. It is likely that a good class discussion will bring to the surface different perspectives, ones centred on each of the elements of the diagram provided: the moral agent (the person making the choice), the moral choice, the others affected, and the background society and world. Our ensuing comments here assume that you have already thought about and discussed the dilemma yourself.

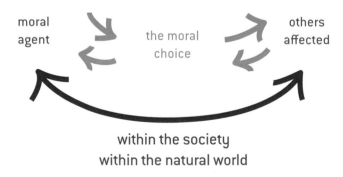

moral agent    the moral choice    others affected

within the society
within the natural world

### 1. Did you evaluate with emphasis on the moral agent and intentions?

The "moral agent" is the person making the choice. The teacher is the moral agent of this dilemma as it is written, but did you also consider the student as a moral agent making a choice?

When we focus attention on the moral agent, we are likely to approach ethics from one of two

directions – to emphasize either the person's *intentions* or the person's *moral character.*

It is the first one that is most relevant to case studies of specific choices – *intentions.* As this case is written, the student intends to cheat; there is nothing accidental about his action. What does the teacher *intend* to do if she ignores the cheating? Is she aiming to protect a student she likes? What does she *intend* if she exposes the cheating: retribution to the student, justice for other students, or protection of her own job? In this particular case, do her motives affect your evaluation of her possible choices?

We often take people's intentions into account. If someone injures you, you are likely to judge the hurt and damage quite differently depending on whether the injury was completely accidental or whether it was deliberately inflicted.

Even in a court of law where the codes are formalized, the apparent motives of a lawbreaker are often taken into account in the sentence. In at least some legal systems, premeditated murder, for example, brings a harsher judgment than a killing considered to be an unplanned crime of passion.

When intentions lie in complex human psychology, intertwined with beliefs and emotions, however, they can be quite elusive to pin down. As we considered regarding emotion as a way of knowing, it is difficult to *know* the feelings of others and it is possible to lack *self-knowledge* about our own. How can we be sure that a person's intentions are what they claim them to be, or that we are identifying even our own intentions accurately?

A further issue to be considered is whether the person could have reasonably expected the damaging outcome or have taken precautions to avoid it. A drunk driver can claim, "I didn't *mean* to kill the pedestrian". However, he does have the responsibility, most would argue, to be driving with care and not to be driving drunk.

The second ethical approach that centres on the moral agent is focused on *moral character.* It is less likely to have come up through this case study, but we mention it briefly here by way of introduction: virtue ethics. Virtue ethics emphasizes someone's moral character as a whole – not looking at isolated choices or even specific fine moral qualities. A person of virtue

## For Reflection

What is the relationship between ethics and the laws of a society? Can there be an unjust law?

What is the relationship between ethics and the customs of a society?

What is the relationship between ethics and religions?

What are the advantages of dissociating ethics from all three of these for separate consideration?

embodies virtues and, although philosophers have debated what those are, they are often given to include honesty, prudence, courage, wisdom, justice, and generosity. A person's actions are a reflection of inner morality. We do not apply this approach to this case study because virtue ethics is holistic rather than centred in specific choices and actions.

## 2. Did you evaluate with emphasis on the choice itself, and moral rules of right and wrong?

When we focus attention on the choice itself, we are generally assessing its compliance with rules or principles.

The teacher's choice in the examination hall has the potential to raise several moral principles. Did you take into account, for instance, the obligations of the teacher as an invigilator to report cheating, or the obligation of the student not to cheat in the examination? These obligations, or duties, involve making promises to act in a particular way as you take on particular roles, and then telling the truth as you claim to fulfil them.

Principles and duties can be derived in different ways. Religious teaching gives rules to follow, such as the Ten Commandments of the Abrahamic Old Testament telling followers not to lie, steal, or desire what other people have. Someone who believes in God and accepts moral imperatives asserted in sacred text or scriptures is likely to consider them absolute rules to follow. Interpretation of what those imperatives mean and how they should be applied, however, can be contentious.

Reasoning, quite a different source of justification, may also lead to rules and duties. Philosopher Immanuel Kant, presenting rule-based ethics of deontology, argued that moral duties can be recognized through reason, and that they are *absolute*. That is, the duty must be followed regardless of the circumstances.

Kant's principle of *respect for persons* is a fundamental one in this regard, rather like an ethical premise – an identified and articulated assumption on which all further reasoning rests. He argued that human beings, as free rational beings, possess status and worth in themselves. All persons are owed respect.

This approach to ethics attempts to establish universal moral principles, even in face of the cultural and individual variability of human societies over what is considered right and wrong. It lies behind the concept of human rights, for instance, which identifies basic entitlements of all human beings, such as freedom of speech, freedom of religion, or freedom from being tortured.

Sometimes rule-based ethics are established in a more limited way, though, for particular spheres of action. In applied ethics, principles are developed to guide the specific circumstances within which the moral agents will be working. Some organizations formalize their rules in this way, as the International Baccalaureate does for the examination system of our example. Professional bodies, for example those for doctors or engineers, often set out codes of conduct for their own members to follow. These codes of ethics remove the stress of moral dilemmas from their members by clarifying appropriate choice, and contribute towards more predictable and consistent professional action.

Dilemmas arise within this approach to ethics, though, when principles that *must* be obeyed come into conflict with each other and result in a problem with no solution. Suppose that you promised a friend that you would keep her secret, but then what she tells you fills you with fear that she is in danger. Both keeping a promise and preserving life are your duties, but you cannot fulfil either one without failing to fulfil the other. In response, philosopher W.D. Ross has ranked duties so that some override others: you would be right to save your friend, not because breaking a promise is morally acceptable in itself but because saving your friend takes moral priority.

## 3. Did you evaluate with emphasis on the effect on others – the consequences of the choice?

When we focus attention on the consequences of a choice or an action, we are following moral guidance broadly familiar. "Think about others!" Utilitarian ethics judges the right action to take based on looking for the maximum happiness or benefit for the greatest number of people.

If you did think in terms of the consequences of the teacher's choice, what impact did you take into account?

- The immediate consequences on the teacher, the cheating student and the others in the exam hall?
- The longer term consequences on the student's reputation, education and character, or the teacher's reputation and character?
- The broader possible consequences on the examination results of other students or the evaluation of the school as a reliable IB examination centre?

If others also argued on the basis of consequences, did you all agree? It is entirely possible to use the same way of arguing and reach different conclusions – for example, that the consequences are worse if the teacher reports the cheating because the student's IB results will be compromised, or that the consequences are better if the teacher reports it because the student will learn not to cheat. Even long-term consequences are relevant: "Would you want to go to a doctor who had cheated his way through medical school?"

Some difficulties of evaluating ethically according to consequences, though, become evident in this small story of the examination hall:

- How accurately can we predict the consequences of an action? Accurate prediction is a challenge even with measurable data in the sciences, and extremely problematic with people involved. How can we tell in advance what the consequences will really be for either the student or the teacher? Will the student become haunted by guilt and never cheat again or, quite the opposite, go on to a career of cheating?
- What importance do we give each of the possible consequences, and how do we weigh them up against each other? We cannot quantify harm

and benefit in grams and place them physically on a scale to compare them. Is preserving the student's IB diploma more important than preserving the system's fairness to all?

What this ethical perspective of evaluating according to consequences cannot do, in the end, is to make ethics into a science. It does use observation, prediction, and attempts at quantifying and weighing results, but it is not dealing with the material world. It is dealing with immaterial value judgments and unpredictable people.

Utilitarianism faces further criticisms. As it argues for the greatest happiness for the greatest number of people, it could possibly permit great harm to a minority if the majority is benefited. Is it morally acceptable to kill off a very small tribe of people if a very large tribe would benefit? Utilitarianism has also been criticized for being so dependent on the particular situation that it produces unpredictable decisions.

Objections to ethical ways of thinking, though, can be dealt with by further thinking. In deontological ethics, as we saw, the problem of absolute duties in conflict was resolved by giving priority to some over others. In utilitarian ethics, the problem of not having any absolutes at all has been dealt with by a move towards generalizing the thinking. "Act utilitarianism" looks only at the specific case, for example, whether the particular teacher in our examination story should report the particular student for cheating. "Rule utilitarianism", however, looks at the effect on everyone, extending to similar circumstances. Whereas the act utilitarian will expect that the teacher could decide either way depending on her understanding of the consequences she is weighing, the rule utilitarian is likely to insist that the teacher report the student, as the consequence of all teachers ignoring all cheating would be to destroy the examination system – a consequence probably held to be undesirable for its further effects on local education. (If it is seen as a desirable consequence, though, the conclusion could be different.)

Utilitarian ethics does not lead to the firm decisions, independent of circumstances, that deontological, rule-based ethics can reach. However, it does allow us to take into account the complexities of situations in which ethical decisions so often have to be made, and does encourage consideration beyond the immediate moral choice into future effects. It also gives a moral guide to practical decision-making: when resources of time, money, or equipment, for example, are scarce, utilitarian thinking directs them to where they can provide the greatest happiness for the most people.

## 4. Did you evaluate with emphasis on the moral code of the surrounding society?

When we focus attention on the context of the moral choice, we might take one of two different viewpoints: one stresses obeying or conforming with the expectations of the social context, and the other stresses caring responses within a network of relationships.

From the first viewpoint, the *expectations of the social context*, the moral agent may not be making a conscious choice at all, but simply obeying or conforming. He might, though, accept values in a conscious way, such as those involving loyalty to a group. For example, some IB students of the past, considering not the teacher's choice but the student's, have argued that in their home context it would be considered immoral *not* to cheat, on the basis that friends should help each other and that it would be selfish of one student to succeed and allow friends to fail.

A society or culture is rarely homogeneous, and it is entirely possible that in different parts of the social networks that surround you, you would find quite varied responses to this dilemma. When ethics are considered to be relative to the context, there can be no universal guide to moral choice.

From the second viewpoint, *caring responses to relationships*, the moral agent is part of the social situation, in which interconnected individuals should act caringly towards others. The details of context are important, and those who are vulnerable, as young students may be considered to be, require extra support. This approach to ethics rejects the detached and rational stance of deontology and utilitarianism for a more emotionally engaged and spontaneous response, based on safeguarding and promoting the welfare of everyone involved. This approach to ethics is fairly recent, coming out of feminist thought of the 1980s.

Taking this approach, the teacher will be concerned not primarily about the momentary decision to apprehend the student, but about how she and others manage the whole situation. Concerns may include giving counselling support to the student for the choices he now faces and communicating effectively and caringly with any friends who learn about the event and are distressed.

| Perspectives in normative ethics | |
|---|---|
| **Emphasis is on the moral agent.** | **Emphasis is on features of the choice.** |
| **Intentions**: The intentions of the moral agent are significant: did the person intend good or harm to others? | **Moral principles**: The moral agent recognizes duties or obligations, formulated as rules to follow. |
| Or **character**: Is the person of good character – for instance, a wise, honest, generous person? In philosophy, this approach is called **virtue ethics**. (It applies not to specific choices but to overall conduct.) | They can be based on reason. In philosophy, this approach is called **deontology**. |
| | They can also be based on **authority** such as religious teaching, accepted through faith. |
| **Emphasis is on the people affected by the choice.** | **Emphasis is on the social context.** |
| **Consequences**: The moral agent chooses the action that will give the greatest happiness to the greatest number of people. This approach is based on observation, imagining consequences, and reasoning to make predictions. In philosophy, it is called **utilitarianism**. | **Conformity/loyalty**: The moral agent acts as expected in the **social context**. |
| | Or **caring**: The moral agent acts out of concern for the welfare of others within networks of relationships. The personal and emotional are included as well as reason. In philosophy, this is called **ethics of care**. |

**What makes a choice "moral"?: practising argument and counter-argument**

Two criteria are often advanced to characterize moral choices.

1    The moral agent (the person making the choice) has to make the choice consciously and deliberately.

2    The action has to affect someone else, other than the moral agent himself.

Take each of these criteria in turn, and formulate as many arguments as you can to *support* them.

Then take the other side, and formulate as many arguments as you can against them. You may want to divide your class into opposing groups or pairs, each taking either the affirmative or the negative stand.

Exchange your arguments with the rest of the class. The purpose is not to "win" a debate, but to consider arguments on both sides. What benefits does the process of arguing and counter-arguing contribute to the treatment of a topic?

## Methods of ethics

If you've entered into the dilemma we just gave you, you've already tried the methods of ethics. They require no expensive equipment and no special lab or studio! You use your mind.

You ask, "How do I know what the right thing is to do?" And then you think carefully to reach conclusions. The quality of your conclusions will depend on how sound your assumptions and assertions are and how coherently and reasonably you have combined them. If you've given a line of argument and justified it with good reasons, then you've taken a giant step into the ethical method: *thought and argument*. The goal is to create clear guides to moral action, generated and tested by thoughtful analysis.

The knowledge base for ethics is centuries of such thought and argument, examined and counter-argued to develop greater consistency and usefulness in application. The ethical perspectives we've summed up on the dilemma of the dining hall have all been developed within nuanced philosophical discussion and debate.

The reflective and argumentative method of normative ethics can appear at times to detach this area of knowledge from the real world into a largely hypothetical one. Yes, it's the hypothetical imagination at work: "Supposing such-and-such were the case, then what follows from it?" Stories are often used to focus abstract ideas: "Imagine this situation. What should you do?" A preferred form of the hypothetical situation is the dilemma such as the one you've just analysed, whose choices

of alternatives help to refine arguments. Indeed, ethics goes even further into storytelling and abstraction with thought experiments, in which the variables of a dilemma are systematically changed to elicit new reactions and consider new arguments. We will return shortly to this method.

Yet all of the hypothetical thinking is developed in preparation for application to the real world, which provides dilemmas which are often complicated and in which variables cannot readily be controlled. Abstraction and argument have to deal with human anger and despair, violence and blood, and situations that sometimes appear hopeless in their tangled complexity. Applied ethics works with abundant real-life case studies – in clinical research, in doctor-patient relationships, in situations faced by social workers, business people, teachers, elected politicians, and numerous other subgroups in society. When normative ethical theory is applied to real life, does it provide guidance that leads coherently to resolution? Does the guidance work in pragmatic terms in an observable world of human beings? If not, then the real-life dilemmas are handed back to philosophical theorists to consider further.

The methods of ethics thus negotiate between abstraction and application, and between specific cases or stories and general lines of argument on what we should do in the world.

Recently, a new field of experimental ethics has bypassed the traditional methods of ethics of thought and argument to investigate morality in a laboratory. Cognitive psychologists use questionnaires and brain scans of people as they react to hypothetical dilemmas to find out what kind of *moral intuitions* they have in their pre-logical "gut" response. They observe where activity takes place in the brain and how intensely. They can also experiment with what prior stimuli (towards reason, towards emotion) affect how people react intuitively. "Maybe by understanding how people think," says Joshua Knobe of Yale University, "we can get more insight into what really is the right answer to these questions."[6] Clearly, researchers in the cognitive sciences are not "doing ethics" – that is, they are not arguing for how people *should* act. Nevertheless, they are inquiring into our intuitions and responses in a way that could lead to further understanding of moral decision-making.

## Discussion Activity

### Moral choices at scale

In the question sets and discussion below, treat the first set fully before moving on to the second.

### Set 1

The following are not trick questions. The important thing is to give *reasons* for your response.

1   Your friend has a beautiful and valuable ring. You want it. Is it right for you to take it? Why or why not?

2   You have accidentally broken your mother's favourite plate. She sees the broken pieces and, quite upset, asks you if you did it. What is the right thing for you to answer? Why?

3   You told your teacher that you would prepare a presentation for tomorrow's class. However, tonight you would rather watch television. What is the right action for you to take? Why?

### Follow-up discussion questions

Did your responses in each of these three cases require you to acknowledge the difference between what you would like to do and what you feel you should do?

What do we mean by "conscience"? Do you think that it is something that you are born with, or do you think that it develops with maturity and awareness? Conscience is sometimes spoken of as something that "pricks" you or as a little voice in your ear. How do you experience it (if you do)?

### Set 2

In each of the following cases, give reasons for your response.

1   You are the leader of a country. A neighbouring country has territory with valuable oil fields that they are not developing and seem not to need. You want them. Is it right for you to invade and take them? Why or why not?

2   You are the director of a company that has accidentally spilled harmful chemicals into a river. The government environmental agency detects the spill, assesses the damage, and decides that you are responsible. You want to deny that you caused it. What is the right thing for you to do?

3   You are the leader of a country that has signed a world agreement not to develop nuclear weapons. You are inclined, however, to do otherwise because possessing the weapons is in the interests of your country. What is the right thing for you to do and why?

### Follow-up discussion questions

Do you find that the questions in the second trio are similar to the original three? The difference is the scale! From your own experience and your knowledge of world politics, do you think that human beings adopt different moral behaviour on the large scale from on the small scale?

What are the constraints on human actions to compel moral behaviour? Are they different at a small scale in your own home or community from what they are on a large scale, international level?

---

6   "Joshua Knobe on Experimental Philosophy". Podcast Rationally Speaking: exploring the borderlands between reason and nonsense. Minute 18:55. 7 November 2010. http://www.rationallyspeakingpodcast.org/show/rs21-joshua-knobe-on-experimental-philosophy.html

## For Reflection

### Ways of knowing

Where does a moral sense come from? What ways of knowing seem to be involved in gaining a sense of morality?

What ways of knowing do the different approaches of normative ethics use? Look back to the four perspectives we treated earlier in order to respond to the following questions:

- Which perspective of the four we treated earlier uses reason most centrally, to establish or apply general rules? Do all perspectives involve the use of reason?
- Which perspectives might use faith as a way of knowing, and religious belief?
- Which one applies reasoning to observation (sense perception) and prediction? To what extent is it using the methods of science as it does so?
- Which ones draw most on emotion and imagination? In what different ways? Do all perspectives involve emotion and imagination to a degree?
- What is the role of language in all of the ethical perspectives? To what extent do the methods of ethics depend on language?

What ways of knowing are involved when we shift from normative ethics to applied ethics? Does the application of ethical thinking to real people and their problems change the ways of knowing used, such as sense perception and imagination?

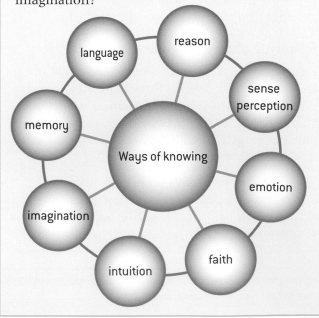

## Thought experiments

Of the methods we have just considered, it may be the "thought experiment" that most demands further explanation. In an experiment in a laboratory, a researcher will run the test again and again to check it and possibly, with control, change variables that contribute to what happens. Ethics does not deal with beakers and bunsen burners, but does take an approach that is similar, at least metaphorically.

In a thought experiment, the irrelevant details of background life are cleared away to help us see more clearly the essential ethical features – much as in a model in the sciences. The thought experiment may use simplified stories, then change features of the fictional circumstances to see whether they make a difference to the ethical conclusions that people might reach. Using the imagination, it can follow the implications of changing circumstances and different lines of argument.

We will take as an example fictional dilemmas that have generated considerable discussion since the 1960s – the "trolley problems".

The most entertaining challenge they initially present is to know what a trolley is, since vocabulary in English is used slightly differently in different countries. A trolley, in these problems, is a trolley car, a bus-like vehicle that moves on tracks. It is roughly equivalent to a tram. It is not a shopping cart (though the lethal potential of a shopping cart is not to be underestimated). Armed with these definitions, you are prepared to tackle the discussion activity "Trolley problems".

These trolley problems are a development of the philosophical principle of the Double Effect: a harmful action might be permissible if it also promotes a good effect.[7] They have been developed extensively to add one variable or another to the hypothetical story in what one commentator has wryly called "the ever-expanding universe of trolley problems"[8]. Suppose that the person standing on the tracks was your mother. Suppose that the large man you could push onto the tracks was a villain, who was

---

[7] "Doctrine of Double Effect," Stanford Encyclopedia of Philosophy. http://plato.stanford.edu/entries/double-effect/

[8] Massimo Pigliucci, "Rationally Speaking," Podcast. 7 November 2010. http://www.rationallyspeakingpodcast.org/show/rs21-joshua-knobe-on-experimental-philosophy.html

↑ England, this is a trolley.

↑ San Francisco, this is a trolley.

responding to trolley problems and their variations, cognitive scientists are gaining knowledge on our moral intuitions – or quick pre-logical responses.

It is not clear, however, whether intuitive responses to dilemmas in experiments carry over to the real world. After all, the participants in the experiment are using their intuitions and hypothetical imaginations in an artificial situation (under a brain scan) removed from consequences. Can we extrapolate to the real world, and assume that they really would react that way if faced with an equivalent real-life choice (if there is such a thing)?

Moreover, an important distinction remains. Cognitive science is not ethics: it is not yet clear how conclusions can be drawn, from experiments on the brain, on how people *should* behave.

## Methods and their assumptions

If the runaway trolleys (or any other dilemmas) are used for traditional ethical argument rather than experiment on moral intuitions, they have to be recognized for the way in which they direct thinking down particular paths. Ethical theories and their mind-models do share this feature with theories in other areas of knowledge – that they

responsible somehow for the five people in front of the trolley being in danger. Suppose …

These stories can be used to focus some forms of normative ethical thinking, such as utilitarian thinking and deontological thinking, on what the right action is.

Part of their use, however, has most recently been in the experiments of cognitive science we mentioned earlier in connection with the methods of ethics. By doing brain scans of people

---

### Discussion Activity

#### Trolley problems

These dilemmas focus ethical thinking on specific choices we make in our moral decision-making. Discuss the first one before moving on to the second. Is there a difference in your decision as the details change?

The following summary is given by ethicist Peter Singer:[9]

#### Version 1

"You are standing by a railroad track when you notice that a trolley, with no one aboard, is rolling down the track, heading for a group of five people. If the trolley continues on its present track, they will all be killed. The only thing you can do to prevent this tragedy is throw a switch that will divert the trolley onto a sidetrack. But

there is one person on this sidetrack, and he will be killed. Should you throw the switch?"

#### Version 2

"In another version of this dilemma, the trolley is again rolling down the track, heading for a group of five people. This time, however, there is no switch or sidetrack. Instead, you are on a footbridge above the track. You consider jumping off the bridge, in front of the trolley, thus sacrificing yourself to save the five people in danger, but you realize that you are far too light to stop the trolley. Standing next to you, however, is a very large stranger. The only way you can stop the trolley killing five people is by pushing this large stranger in front of the trolley. He will be killed, but you will save the other five. Should you push the stranger?"

---

9   Peter Singer, "Putting Practice into Ethics" *The New York Sun*. 16 January 2008. http://www.nysun.com/arts/putting-practice-into-ethics/69595/ See also: Josh Clark, "How the Trolley Problem Works", How Stuff Works, http://people.howstuffworks.com/trolley-problem.htm

draw attention to some characteristics and not others of what they study.

Many dilemmas, in this way, focus ethics on situations of individual choice rather than group decisions, and isolated moments of choice within the web of variables. How could they do otherwise, you might wonder, and still be able to use focused, rational argument? Perhaps they couldn't. Yet the focus on *individuals*, *choices*, and *moments* is not necessarily the only possible centring for ethics, and *rational argument* not necessarily the only possible method. The dominant ethical theories that adopt this centre and method – deontology (duty ethics) and utilitarianism (consequentialism) – have been argued to be predominantly western and even argued, in some feminist thought, to be predominantly male.

By the very nature of how they think about morality and living a good life, other ethical theories apply less well to the dilemmas or thought experiments set up for analysis. *Virtue ethics* and *ethics of care* emphasize more holistic or systemic human qualities. They do not *contradict* deontology or utilitarianism; differing theories in ethics do not prove each other false! Instead, they provide alternative internally consistent perspectives to illuminate different ideas within the study of what it means to be moral.

## Ethics and controversy

Dilemmas and controversies – yes, these do to a large extent characterize ethics in the minds of many people. For one thing, moral controversy often catches attention in society, and it is in moral controversies that people often call for ethics to help find resolutions. For another, the methods of ethics do not always allow a tidy solution: there is not just one single line of thinking on which everyone is sure to agree. It may be one of the delicious ironies of knowledge that the questions that are most important to ask of ourselves as human beings might be the ones which least yield clear and certain answers.

Yet we would venture to say that ethics does, in fact, give many very clear answers. Regardless of what line of argument you take, you can end up with considerable agreement: it is wrong that in a world of plenty, millions of children die of hunger; it is wrong that nations still go to war against

> ## For Reflection
>
> To what extent do you find each of the ethical perspectives offered here a useful or insightful way of thinking about morality? Do you find one or other of them fits better with your own mind and feelings?
>
> How do you react to trolley problems and other mind experiments? Do you personally find it interesting to consider hypothetical dilemmas and the different ways of thinking that can be brought to them? Or do you find yourself impatient with hypothetical problems when so many real ones surround you in the world?

each other as a result of greed. What is missing from the world is not agreement that some things are morally unacceptable. What is missing is the collective determination, worldwide, to act on that ethical awareness and make a change.

## Ethics and responsibility

Ethical conclusions deal with "should" and "ought". They prescribe how we should act in the world – and they carry, as a result, implications for action. They carry, in short, responsibility.

But what specific actions should we take in order to "be responsible" or "fulfill responsibilities"? It is at this point that TOK begins to bow out. In TOK, we aim to introduce you to the kind of knowledge questions that are posed in ethics and the nature of the knowledge in that area: the perspectives that animate the area, the methods that are used, and the justifications given. We point out that ideas of "should" and "ought" point towards action, and we can follow the implications for action of any particular ethical stand you take. But when we come to the practical "how" of taking action, or the specific issues on which you *should* act, we refer you to other parts of your IB Diploma Programme and other parts of your life.

## CAS and the concept of service

Acting morally and taking responsibility are clearly part of the whole of your life. Yet within your IB studies there is one programme that is explicitly directed towards ethical education. It picks up where TOK leaves off, and moves thought into action. The IB subject guide for creativity, action, service (CAS) is very clear on its aim to provide students with opportunities for moral growth and reflection: "Because it involves real activities with significant outcomes, CAS provides a major opportunity for ethical education, understood as involving principles, attitudes and behaviour."[10]

"Principles, attitudes and behaviour": the *principles* could be seen as those derived within a system of duties, obligations, and rights (a deontological system); the *attitudes* could be seen as those that arise from developing character (virtue ethics) and fostering relationships (ethics of care); the *behaviour* could be seen as arising from any of the normative theories, but certainly guided by concern for the effects of actions on others (utilitarianism) – and as adding the crucial element of action.

The overriding idea in CAS, though present in all the ethical perspectives we have examined, is that we owe something to other people, and that we should act on it in the form of "service". The idea of service to others takes its root in the most basic of ethical concepts. Ethical theories take as their starting point – as their most basic assumption – the worth and dignity of every human being, and the need to treat every person with respect. The logical results, following on from that premise, include the following principles of a duty-based ethical theory:

- respect for autonomy: we should recognize people's choices over their own lives

- non-maleficence (least harm): we should not harm others
- beneficence: we should act to benefit others
- justice: we should be fair in giving everyone what is due to them (different interpretations dispute what is meant by "justice")
- fidelity: we should keep our promises
- veracity: we should tell the truth.

In one way or another, all of these principles are involved in how we act with others in all circumstances. In the concept of service, what stands out is the *principle of beneficence:* we should act to benefit others.

The actual form of benefitting others depends on you, your context, and the stage of your life. Indeed, acting to support and benefit others may be so much part of your life that thinking of it as "service" may even seem strange. Isn't it *just what one does?* Yet the conscious recognition of a principle of beneficence may open up reflections on why you might accept it, and whether you might extend its application beyond the communities within which you usually move.

## How large is your circle of caring?

Certainly, one of the recurring knowledge claims in ethics is that as human individuals we owe something to others – attitudes of respect, concern, or even love, and actions that promote their welfare along with our own. Ethical systems based on consequences aim for the maximum of human

---

### Discussion Activity

#### Service to others

In CAS, doing service reflects ethical ideas on what we owe to others. With your own service activities in mind, exchange your thoughts with the rest of your class on the following questions.

1  In your own service activities within CAS, have you ever encountered moral dilemmas? If so, how have you thought about them, resolved them, or learned from them?

2  Consider the following questions taken from the IB CAS subject guide. They are questions asked by both CAS and TOK. Exchange ideas with classmates on what "ethical education" involves, and what "obligation" means – especially as it comes not from outside yourself, but within.

- In what ways might CAS be said to promote ethical education?
- Is service to others, in whatever form, a moral obligation?
- If so, on what might the obligation be based? If not, why not?

---

[10] *Creativity, action, service guide.* 2007. International Baccalaureate. Page 4.

happiness. Ethical systems based on principles present doing good for others as an obligation. Furthermore, ethical systems based on care stress nurturing relationships as important. All of these ethical systems agree that we should care for others. Religions of the world teach variations on the golden rule – to treat others as you would like to be treated yourself. Together, they lead to concern, caring, and compassion.

Within your IB studies, you have encountered the idea of owing something to others within our TOK treatment of ethics as an area of knowledge and within the service activities of CAS. The idea of contributing actively to making the world a better place opens the list of qualities in the IB learner profile: "The aim of all IB programmes is to develop internationally minded people who, recognizing their common humanity and shared guardianship of the planet, help to create a better and more peaceful world."

As we conclude this chapter on ethics, we leave you with another question for further thought. If you are concerned for the welfare of others, how far do you extend your concern? Do you care about your family and friends and act to give them help and support? Do you also feel concern for

the well-being of others in your society, such as to those in some form of need, and others unlike yourself? Do you think beyond to the world, to "think globally" while you "act locally"? How large is your circle of caring?

---

## For Reflection

Do I have any ethical responsibility to inform myself about topics that affect my community or my world? Is there knowledge that I should gain, or should not gain, for ethical reasons?

Do I have a responsibility to gain any *skills* that could be used to help others?

Do I have a responsibility to act on my knowledge? If I am aware of situations where I could act to improve them, am I obligated to act to the best of my ability?

We sometimes hear people say, "It's just not ME to be a Mother Teresa! I believe my main responsibility is to be true to myself." Would you accept such an argument? Or do you think that everyone on this planet has a responsibility to act for the good of others?

---

## Discussion Activity

### Knowledge framework: ethics

First summarize your responses to these questions in your own words. Then exchange ideas with others in your class.

1. **Scope:** What is ethics all about? What does it take as its subject matter and its goals? What contribution does it make to knowledge overall, and to other areas of knowledge?

2. **Language/concepts:** Why is it significant to name and define central concepts in ethics? What central concepts characterize this area of knowledge?

3. **Methodology:** How are ways of knowing (including language) used in creating, exchanging, and evaluating knowledge claims

in ethics? To what extent does ethics use a diversity of methods, and to what extent a general methodology shared in common? How do different perspectives illuminate different aspects of ethics?

4. **Historical development:** How does ethics of today build on ethics of the past? Have individual, social, or technological factors given particular directions to ethics?

5. **Links to personal knowledge:** How do people contribute personal knowledge to this area, and what do they gain from its shared knowledge? How does ethics affect your own knowledge? What are the main responsibilities that you think you have in the world?

**Ethics into action**

Do I have a responsibility for
gaining knowledge? If so, why? And what?

**SKILLS**
knowing how

**KNOWLEDGE CLAIMS**
knowing that . . .

practical
skills

photo courtesy of NASA

information
and
explanations
on issues
that affect
our world

skills of
research
and critical
thinking

**EXPERIENTIAL
KNOWLEDGE**

exposure and
personal experience

Does knowledge bring responsibility?
If so, why?

# 17.  History

## Scope and methods: What is history all about?

### The Lewis Chessmen, British Museum, London, England

These chess pieces were almost certainly made in Norway in the 12th century. They were fashioned from walrus tusks. They were discovered buried in sand in the early nineteenth century in the Scottish Western Isles. Two parts of the total find have since then been on display in Scottish and English museums. You may want to look online for close-up pictures and further information as you respond to the questions below.

**1   What is the subject matter of history?**

These chess pieces of a king and queen, with advisors and an army, represent much of what history tells us about figures of power and war. The decorated stones that flank the

king and queen in this picture are the pawns: undifferentiated foot soldiers given no human form or face.

To what extent is history "about" major power struggles and rulers? Is the life of the individual pawns equally as important in the study of history? What other features of these chess pieces raise, in your mind, topics that you consider appropriate subject matter of history?

## 2 How can we know about the past? What are the methods of history?

Which of the following methods of gaining knowledge would you NOT do if you were trying to find out more about the Lewis chessmen? Why not?

- Directly observe traders passing through the Western Isles during the twelfth century.
- Interview the Norwegian craftsmen who are believed to have made them.
- Break the chess pieces open to examine the materials they are made of.

Surely, there must be better methods! What are – and have been – the appropriate methods of history to find out as much as we now know about these figures? In what ways are the materials and representative features (details of dress, social categories, idiosyncrasies of actions) of the chess pieces clues to where they were made? In what ways does the location in which they were found (the Western Isles, at that time part of the kingdom of Norway) give us more information? How does it help our understanding of these figures to know about the background of the times: political relationships, trade routes, and fashionable recreation?

## 3 What counts as historical evidence? What is the role of the historian?

In themselves, the chess pieces are no more than bits of walrus tusk, and "tell" us nothing. They become "artifacts" only when we recognize the cultural modification of natural materials and they become "evidence" only when we use them to argue for an interpretation of the past.

The same artifacts can become evidence for many different lines of investigation. Since a historian cannot simply research the whole past, he takes a particular focus to narrow his research and to be able to trace a connection between events and ideas in the past. These chessmen, then, could become evidence within many different stories that could be told.

Can you suggest four different stories that would use the four different pieces of information below? To what broad research topics might these facts be relevant?

1: The figure on the right, biting down on his shield, is interpreted as a "beserker", a fierce warrior from Norse mythology who goes into a frenzy before battle.[1]

2: The Isle of Lewis, in the Western Isles, was on a trade route between Norway and Ireland. It is speculated that a merchant buried them for safekeeping.[2]

3: Chess originated in India in the sixth century AD, spread through Persia westward, and by the end of the eleventh century was a popular game among the medieval European aristocracy. It was considered a game of skill and intellect.[3]

4: The figures of the chessmen are not the same as those in original Indian or Islamic chess games. The Lewis Chessmen of the European medieval period are among the earliest examples in which both a queen and Christian bishops are found.[4]

## 4 What is historical "fact"?

Historians base their accounts of the past – that is, their descriptions and causal explanations – on facts, such as the facts of different kinds listed above. In what way do historical facts differ from the facts of biology and physics?

[1] James Robinson. 15 November 2011. "Going beserk: the Lewis chessmen in New York", British Museum blogsite. http://blog.britishmuseum.org/2011/11/15/going-berserk-the-lewis-chessmen-in-new-york/

[2] "The Lewis Chessmen", The British Museum. January 2008. http://www.britishmuseum.org/about_us/news_and_press/statements/the_lewis_chessmen.aspx

[3] James Robinson, Lewis Chessmen, British Museum, http://www.bbc.co.uk/ahistoryoftheworld/objects/LcdERPxmQ_a2npYst0wVkA

[4] "The Game of Kings: Medieval Ivory Chessmen from the Isle of Lewis." Metropolitan Museum of Art. http://www.metmuseum.org/about-the-museum/press-room/exhibitions/2011/the-game-of-kings-medieval-ivory-chessmen-from-the-isle-of-lewis

## A note to history students

As we enter history as an area of knowledge, we remind you that our exploration of knowledge is not primarily something *we* are doing; it's something *you* are doing. Who should be your guides?

If you are a student of IB history, you are splendidly placed to take a strongly contributive role yourself, bringing what you are learning in your history class into your TOK class. You may be able to explain, amplify, dispute, or illustrate the ideas that we give you in this chapter in your double role as both history student and TOK student. You may also have valuable input into the three activities we suggest: the first a broad introduction to history (Lewis Chessmen), the second a closer look at historical documents (Eyewitness to history), and the third a short research activity (the Oba and Europeans) to apply the ideas. As you deal with topics of this chapter, moreover, you might also be able to pick out, from your own history course, examples to share with your classmates.

## Ways of knowing and methods of history

As you move into this part of the book, you are not leaving behind any of the ideas you considered earlier. As we've said frequently, using our metaphor of exploring territory with map

> " What his imagination is to the poet, facts are to the historian. His exercise of judgment comes in their selection, his art in their arrangement. His method is narrative. His subject is the story of man's past. His function is to make it known.[5]
>
> *Barbara Tuchman*
> "

and compass, we do keep returning to the same central ideas, but we just approach them from different paths. Consider the next points we raise to be refreshers – reminders of the ideas relevant to history that you are familiar with already from earlier in this book. We will not repeat everything here, but instead encourage you to pick up threads from earlier and carry them forward into this area of knowledge.

## 1. The events of the past: sense perception and memory

You are likely to have left chapter 5 on sense perception with a heightened awareness of the variable, actively selective, and interpretive nature of sense perception. If someone was a participant in an event of the past, how much of it is he likely to have observed, and how accurately? Could he have been affected by cognitive biases, introduced in chapter 5 and further developed in chapter 12?

And memory? How good is an eyewitness's memory? Do you recall some of the uncertainties raised in chapter 6?

Only very recent history, however, deals with living people's sense perceptions and memories. Despite the uncertainties that surround observation and memory, we do gain first-hand information from eyewitnesses and a chance

### For Reflection

We cannot repeat observations of the past. How does the nature of what history studies – the past – affect the methods of study historians use?

5   Tuchman, B.W. 1982. *Practicing History: Selected Essays.* New York. Random House. P 32.

to ask questions. Especially when many people experienced an event and remember it, we tend to take their reports collectively as justifications for believing accounts of what happened in the past.

The past, though, is gone. Where scientists can replicate experiments to repeat observations, historians cannot rerun the past in order to take better notes. This is the most distinct feature of history as an area of knowledge: it deals with the past, trying to find out what happened from the echoes that remain. (But echoes do repeat.)

## 2. Evaluating sources: language as a way of knowing, with photographs and other representations

You will also want to bring back to mind all we considered regarding language as a way of knowing. Language is the major means for eyewitnesses to give us their personal knowledge while they are alive, and language is the major way that they leave records behind them – letters, diaries, articles, books, ledgers of trade deals, treaties, and many other forms of writing. Do you recall the early record carved in cuneiform writing from the chapter on language, an account of beer rations?

The archive of the human experience, built up through our accounts in language, is skimpy for the distant past but vast for the recent past – especially since the development of computer technology. In what ways do both pose challenges for historians – having too few records, or having too many?

Do you recall the numerous characteristics we considered of language as a way of knowing in chapter 8, as symbolic and interpretive, as linked to culture and other perspectives? You might find it useful to look back to "Representations and perspectives" (page 150) to refresh your memory on some features of representation that are relevant in considering historical records:

- selection of information
- emphasis placed on some information
- emotional colouring of words and expressions
- relationship of parts – linear argument or juxtaposition
- framing in context – interpretive headings, apparent purpose.

Any records left require interpretation, keeping in mind these principles. History students, what are you learning about understanding historical documents? Can you amplify what is given here, and even give examples from your own course?

For numerous factors that affect judgment of the reliability of sources, you will probably also want to flip back to "A guide to evaluating knowledge claims" with which we closed Part 2, to refresh your memory on the "three S's": the source, the statements, and the self.

## 3. "Historical event": language and reasoning as ways of knowing

By now, you are likely to be highly aware of the assumptions, values, and intentions that are active in our process of classifying. Right from the beginning of this book, we have raised this topic – at the beginning classifying knowledge claims to identify different kinds of knowledge, and just recently dealing with the rather elastic category "the arts". How we cluster and group our observations and concepts, how we emphasize their common characteristics and name them, these can have serious implications, as we considered in the chapter 13. Our categories – "famine" or "citizen" – can affect how we think, what options we consider to be open to us, and how we act.

One of the most significant knowledge questions of history is one that has to be decided before the historian can even begin work: "What counts as a historical event?" or, even more broadly, "What falls into the category of appropriate subject matter of history?" The decision has implications for the

### For Reflection

What understanding of documents – what critical literacy – is essential to the methods of studying history?

### For Reflection

What makes an event of the past historically significant?

## Discussion Activity

### Eyewitness to history

### A. The eyewitness: you!

A team of researchers has suddenly taken a profound interest in your school. They want to compile an historical record, and seek from you, as eyewitness and participant, first-hand information about the past year.

Before you respond individually to their questions, identify as a class a public event in your school that occurred within recent weeks. It could be a school meeting, a performance or dance, an event involving the public, or anything that most of you were present for.

Then write individual answers to the following questions in section B. After everyone has finished, compare your replies and use the questions in section C as a prompt for further discussion.

### B. Eyewitness questionnaire

1   List the most striking characteristics of the public event that your TOK class identified.

2   What would you consider the five most important events for your school during this past year?

3   What do you consider to be the three most important things that the students from your year group have gained from its time so far at the school?

4   One of the researchers asks you how you think he can best gain information on the events, culture, and ambience of 1999/2000 within the school. What would you recommend?

5   Who do you think is best qualified to write a history of your school: a graduate, a teacher, a member of the school board, a parent, or a local journalist? Why? Would someone else be better? Why?

6   At what point do you think the past events of your school become "history"? Why?

### C. Follow-up discussion

1   In identifying the **most striking characteristics** of the event, what do you think affected what you noticed with your *sense perception* and later recalled with your *memory*? How would a historian, for whom you are a primary source, try to overcome the limitations of your eyewitness memory?

2   In picking out the **five most important events** for the school, on what criteria did you base your *selection* and *emphasis*? Do all of you in your class share the same set of *value judgments* on what is important?

   Did you define "school" as the institution, or as the current school population, or something else? Does the definition affect the events you picked? Is your principal or school head likely to have a different definition and selection of events?

3   In picking out the **most important things gained** so far, the question shifts from events to abstractions. Are the value judgments that you made within your group more varied than in the previous questions? Why?

4   What **sources of information** did you recommend? Do you expect researchers to look only at the factual records such as attendance numbers, lists of names, and budgets? Or do you expect them to check more subjective materials such as yearbooks or newspapers, or even personal artifacts such as school rings or jackets? Would they interview past students or staff? What kinds of documents and artifacts do you expect historians to examine? Why? How do "primary sources" and "secondary sources" differ?

5   Who should be **the historian?** What perspectives and skills should historians have?

6   **What would be a good history?** At what point do current events of your school become "history"? What is the difference between sources and a "history"? What are the qualities you consider most important in a history book?

direction of research and the conclusions that are drawn from the artifacts and documents of the past.

Historians, after all, cannot describe everything. They must select information relevant to the stories they want to tell, in response to the questions they want to ask, in the context of an audience of their particular place and time. What, then, do we want to know about the past?

Our interests shift with our times, so that, paradoxically, history frequently needs to be brought "up to date". During the twentieth century, for example, many historians researched the lives of people marginalized in previous histories, contributing new perspectives on the past through, for example, black histories or women's histories of the United States.

## 4. Conjectures about the past: imagination as a way of knowing

What would you consider to be the essential difference between the fictional form of literature – that often uses fact – and the factual form of history that has to fill the gaps with plausible fictions? What is the role of imagination in the writing of history?

Do you recall (from chapter 11 on the imagination) the "creative friction" of the historian between facts and interpretation, and the need to respect, as historian Tom Griffiths put it, "the hard edges of reality"? Since that time, we have considered the arts as an area of knowledge, and the possibility that literature, a fictional form, often uses keen observation and fact in its creation of character, setting, and interpretations of societies. Where does literature leave off and history begin, in the "creative friction"?

Griffiths comments on "history's commitment to verifiable truth – to evidence that can be revisited", but suggests that in some regards historians have more freedoms than novelists:

### For Reflection

Within what constraints do historians work? What comparisons would you draw with literature?

> Events happen; but to become history they must be communicated and understood. For that, history needs writers – preferably great writers…[6]
>
> *Barbara Tuchman*

Historians, like novelists, are producing literary texts that have their own internal demands of consistency, plausibility and integrity, their own organic rationale derived from decisions about where to begin and end, about which characters to foreground, about what relationships to map. And this internal, textual, literary dynamic wrestles with hard external reality. But historians also have some greater freedoms available to them. Some fiction writers will tell you that historians have a broader canvas to paint on than they do, because truth really is stranger than fiction.[7]

This claim is an appealing one – that historians "have some greater freedoms available to them" than fiction writers do, that "truth really is stranger than fiction".

## 5. "Neutrality" in history: emotion and imagination as ways of knowing

In a history that accepts Griffiths' "commitment to verifiable fact", is the writing necessarily neutral – denotative rather than connotative – and free of emotion? The facts place constraints on the exercise of imagination. Do they preclude, with an aim of objectivity, any role for emotion in the

### For Reflection

To what extent do you think the historian should try to preserve an emotional neutrality to his human subject matter, and write in denotative, dispassionate language? Does "neutral" language increase or decrease the reader's understanding or even emotional response to the events the writer is talking about?

---

6  Tuchman, B.W. 1982. *Practicing History: Selected Essays.* New York. Random House. P 64.

7  Griffiths, T. 2009. "History and the Creative Imagination". History in Practice. *History Australia.* Vol 6, number 3. Monash University Epress.

writing of history? Glance back to the interchapter on Subjectivity and Objectivity (page 108).

In some regards, emotion is inevitably part of the *subject matter* of human experience that history treats. Primary sources such as letters and diaries from the time include expressions of the emotions of the writers, and that written expression becomes potential material for the historian. Expressions of love and fear in letters written home by soldiers in war zones form part of the historical record – and perhaps not just as a means to other informative ends. Maybe such emotions are, in and of themselves, what we want to know about.

Our response to history *as readers* is likely to be emotional as well, as our interest is caught and we sympathize with the people long gone. Indeed, it could well be our emotional response and imaginative engagement that draws us to history in a way similar to literature.

But the real question is whether the *historian* should attempt not to let his emotions affect his writing. Should he remain detached? Should he write about atrocities and oppression without expressing a feeling or a view? It could be argued that an effective presentation of the facts should be enough to convey the significance of the past event for the people at the time. Yet it could equally be argued that to write unemotionally about genocide would be to miss the point of communicating about the topic.

## 6. Causal connections: reason as a way of knowing, and possibly intuition

We do not *observe* cause; we *infer* cause through reasoning as we make connections between variables. This point is an extremely important one for history as an area of knowledge that aims not simply to describe what happened in the past but to explain why it happened as it did.

In the interchapter "What is 'cause'?" (page 252), we raised some knowledge questions about causation, with significant implications for how we deal with it in our different areas of knowledge. Within the vast conceptual space of what ideas are involved in "cause", the historian has to make constant choices. How far "back" and "out" should she go to capture enough detail to explain, but not so much that the connections she draws are confused by details? Should she emphasize causes that lie in peoples' wills and intentions, or in background circumstances? Is the cause of a

war the *largest influence* (even if it is a background situation not sufficient in itself), or the event that stands out as *most unusual*, or the one that *happened last* – the proverbial "straw that broke the camel's back"? The historian's reasoning that causally connects situations and events is set within her own interpretations of the nature of cause, and perhaps broader perspectives on how she sees the larger patterns of history.

You might want to turn back, too, to the interchapter "Fallacies of argument 1: Errors in the reasoning process", to refresh your memory on the difference between correlation and cause, and the error known as *post hoc* that confuses a sequence in time (B follows A) with a causal connection (A causes B). The historian by training is aware of both fallacies, but, as she deals constantly with connection and cause, she has particular reason to be on guard.

Human interactions create a massively complex web, within which historians follow particular causal strands. Different historians follow somewhat different connections, and as a result many different historical accounts of the same event emerge. These sometimes contradict each other, but often they complement each other and add to our fuller understanding.

An emphasis on reasoning for causal connections would be incomplete, however, without at least some consideration of an intuitive grasp of patterns, especially when the historian is experienced. You

### For Reflection

To what extent do you accept Berlin's argument on the next page for subjective "understanding" as a justification for writing about human *motivation* in the past? To what extent can we assume universal ways of thinking and acting, and universal motivations for action? What hesitations might you have?

Is this "understanding" of cause closer to ideas of cause and motivation in literature, or closer to ideas of cause and motivation in the human sciences?

Among histories that trace different threads through the causal web, why are some acclaimed and others neglected? What do we look for in good historical explanation?

will recall, from the chapter on intuition, the fast thinking of the brain (System 1) that allows us to recognize large patterns – not always reliably, but roughly. It may be that, in all of the immense detail of historical records, the historian may grasp relationships and causes not by conscious reasoning through all the facts but by intuition.

According to one eminent historian, the historian's grasp of causal connections in history may depend less on rational judgment than on a more holistic understanding of human subject matter. Sir Isaiah Berlin (in 1960) so argues:

> If someone tells us "X forgave Y because he loved him", or "X killed Y because he hated him", we accept these propositions easily, because they, and the propositions into which they can be generalized, fit in with our experience, because we claim to know what men are like…because we claim to know (not always justifiably) what – in essentials – a human being is, in particular a human being who belongs to a civilization not too unlike our own, and consequently one who thinks, wills, feels, acts in a manner which (rightly or wrongly) we assume to be intelligible to us because it sufficiently resembles our own or those of other human beings whose lives are intertwined with our own. This sort of "because" is the "because" neither of induction nor of deduction, but the "because" of understanding – *Verstehen* – of recognition…[8]

Berlin's argument here for the "verstehen" position of *understanding* draws on coherence within the human experience such that we, today, can *understand* human motivation of the past.

## 7. The balance of particular and general: reason and language

Where does history stand in the balance between treating unique events and trying to identify broad generalizations in the human record of the past? Certainly, the same people will never do or experience the same thing in the same place ever again: the Partition of India in 1947 was a single event; the first landing on the moon in 1969 could never happen again; the earthquake in Chile in 2010 hit hard at particular places and people. The events that history records stand out as distinct for all of the journalistic questions we could apply: who, what, when, where, why, how?

Yet in the very fact of naming major historical events we are compelled to categorize in order to apply language, and therefore to identify features that one event has in common with another event. We are forced, to some extent, to generalize. Despite all the differences between armed conflicts, we group many of them into the one category "war". Despite the difficulties of definition, observation, and ideological interpretation, we cluster attitudes and actions into the term "nationalism". Even though no two events or situations are the same, we find the similarities in the very process of naming and communicating. Admittedly, the very process of identifying similarities is interpretive, as historians choose between, say, "civil unrest" or "revolution".

But can history go further in identifying repeating patterns through the past into the present? Can it generalize on all – or at least some – of the particular events, using inductive reasoning to justify knowledge claims regarding broad trends and tendencies? These are major knowledge questions of history. They affect whether we

### For Reflection

To the extent that the study of the past illuminates recurrent human patterns, what can we learn from history lessons that will help us to manage our affairs better in the present and future? Without any knowledge of history, are we likely to manage worse?

History teaches us about human nature and our future best choices by teaching us about *possibilities* rather than *regularities*.[9]

*Michael Scriven*

8   Berlin, I. 1966. "The Concept of Scientific History", *Philosophical Analysis and History*. Ed. William H. Dray. New York and London. Harper and Row. Pp 34–5.

9   Scriven, M. 1966. "Causes, Connections, and Conditions in History". *Philosophical Analysis and History*. Ed. William H. Dray. New York and London. Harper and Row. P 250.

believe that we can learn from the past, and take its lessons as help in doing better next time! Different perspectives on the historical record, as we will consider soon, affect the degree to which we expect history to repeat itself, and how.

## Interview

### Knowing the past
### Interview with historian Charles Freeman

*Historian Charles Freeman has written extensively about the history of European culture and thought, particularly on the ancient classical world, early Christianity, and their legacy. He was for many years an IB history teacher (St. Clare's, Oxford) and examiner for the IB in both history and theory of knowledge. He also acts as a consultant, writer, and guide for historical tours. In 2003, he was elected a Fellow of the Royal Society of the Arts.*

→ In your study of ancient Egypt, Greece, and Rome, you are dealing with eras for which, surely, most of the records have been lost. What is the nature of evidence when studying times so long ago?

Traditionally scholars studied the surviving texts in Greek, Latin and, following the decipherment of hieroglyphics in the 1820s, Egyptian. There is an excellent range of writings but naturally they represent the voices of the literate elite. There are very few women's voices and none of slaves. In the past twenty years, there has been far greater interest in, and effective use of, material remains, statues, pottery, buildings and the traces of human activity in the landscape. Balancing and assessing these sources is not easy but a much fuller picture of the ancient Mediterranean is emerging and the subject is academically a very lively one.

→ When information is missing, how do you close the gaps?

One of the most important attributes for the historian of any era is common sense. You must understand what humans are and are not capable of and how the natural world conditions human activity. So the story you create must, in the first instance, reflect what is humanly possible. Next you cannot make any assertions which contradict reliable evidence.

There is a mass of interlocking evidence, for instance, that the major pyramids at Gizeh in Egypt were built about 2400 BC. There are some pseudo-historians who claim they were built in 12000 BC by a superhuman race who aligned them with star patterns. These historians appeal to the credulous. In the last resort the historian must tell a plausible tale, one which realistically reflects the evidence. Obviously there is room for creative imagination here and history comes alive when there is debate between different possible interpretations of an event.

→ History is sometimes described as being mid-way between science and literature. Do you follow the methods of a scientist as you reconstruct the past?

Science, in the traditional sense of the word, is increasingly used in the study of the ancient world. For instance, there was an important volcanic eruption of the island of Thera in the Greek Mediterranean which was probably followed by a tsunami which must have done a lot of damage to coastal cities and may even have temporarily destroyed the Minoan civilization in Crete. For decades there was controversy over the date but now an exact one, of 1628 BC, has been proposed on the basis of the analysis of wood samples and other debris. Once a date has been securely fixed, a lot of archeological sites which suffered destruction at the same time can also be dated. This is laboratory work.

In a broader sense, a scientific approach is useful in proposing hypotheses from the existing evidence and testing new discoveries against the hypothesis, although, unfortunately, one cannot carry out experiments by rerunning the past. In short, one has to be aware of what science can achieve in analysing material remains and also be ready to apply deductive logic to evidence.

→ To what extent do you agree that history resembles literature?

History is about the activity of human beings, as individuals and within societies. They have stories to tell of themselves and we can suggest our own stories of their lives. The great historians are those who can convey the motivations of those who created the past and allow us to empathize with them. This is, in essence, a literary skill and it is essential if history is to be communicated in an effective way.

→ You say that history deals with causes and motivations. Is explanation the major goal for historians?

For me personally, the excitement of history lies in trying to offer explanations for developments. The greatest satisfaction comes from reviewing the evidence and realizing that it can be rearranged to produce a fresh interpretation of an event. For instance, in my study of the fourth century AD, *The Closing of the Western Mind*, I found a lot of texts which denigrated reason in favour of a commitment to faith. When I put these together, I was able to offer a new approach to the decline of intellectual life in the late Roman empire. I found it absorbing, especially when I found other historians supporting my thesis.

→ In your study of the role of reason and faith, have you found it difficult to put aside your own beliefs as you researched and wrote?

We all have our beliefs and no historian achieves complete neutrality. (Could one write a history of the Holocaust which is free of all emotion?) Myself, I am committed to the idea that a society which enjoys freedom of speech is not only a much healthier society in itself but achieves a much higher standard of intellectual activity. That is why a lot of my work recently has concentrated on times when freedom of speech has been eroded by governments or religious dogmatism.

This does not mean I am against religion per se – it obviously fulfils important human needs – but in my latest book, *381 AD, The Turning Point that Time Forgot,* I am arguing that spiritual life was also diminished by the imposition of religious orthodoxy in the fourth century by the emperor Theodosius. Everyone, religious and non-religious alike, suffered by not being able to enter into free discussion.

→ In our era, are there perhaps too many records? How do you suppose historians in the future will be able to make sense of our era?

Every era has its own problems of interpretation and it is often only in hindsight that we can begin to spot the important trends. The present day is similar to that of antiquity in that the vast majority of voices go unrecorded, despite the many paper and electronic records the elite produce. However, one does feel that there are more fragmented societies today, societies split apart by globalization, deteriorating environments and the lure of the west. It will surely be hard for historians to reflect the totality of any modern society.

→ What advice would you offer a student of history?

Firstly, don't stick to one single period. Ideas, knowledge, and skills learned from the study of one era can often be transferred to help provide a fresh approach to another. The best historians, such as Simon Schama, have written on a wide variety of subjects. In Schama's case he has written of seventeenth century Holland, the French Revolution, slavery, and a history of Britain.

Second, realize that evidence does not come only from texts. I have learnt a lot from looking at the art and architecture of the periods I have been studying. It tells you a great deal about how a society presents itself and what it considers important to spend resources on. One of the most important moments in the history of Christianity came, for instance, when the emperor Constantine transferred the pagan custom of spending a lot of money on temples into Christianity so that the religion of the poor became the religion of the big builders. Every major European city was transformed as a result! Always be ready to see everything from coins to the writings of philosophers as potential evidence. A broader approach makes the subject more interesting and will help deepen your understanding of a period. ■

## Discussion Activity

### Interview with Charles Freeman: Follow-up questions

1   Charles Freeman says that "there is room for creative imagination" in history. What two or three things does he suggest, on the other hand, that restrict the creative imagination?

2   Charles Freeman presents emotion as a way of knowing that is not excluded from history – that is unavoidable in treating subject matter of atrocity and possibly a means of achieving a connection between people of the past and readers today. As he says, "The great historians are those who can convey the motivations of those who created the past and allow us to empathize with them." What is your own expectation of the role of emotion in the *content* of the historical records, the *process* of selecting and filtering the evidence, and the *writing* of the resultant history? In what way is emotion relevant in the *response* and understanding of the reader?

3   What are the relative advantages to the historian of studying the recent past or studying the more remote past?

4   Charles Freeman says that today, still, "the vast majority of voices go unrecorded, despite the many paper and electronic records the elite produce". Why would this be so? In what ways might it be important to future historians that we have extensive electronic records – and in what ways does the issue of representation remain unchanged?

5   "Realize that evidence does not come only from texts", he reminds us. What other sources does he suggest? What further sources of information would you add to his list? Are there others, unimaginable to historians of the past, now made possible by contemporary science?

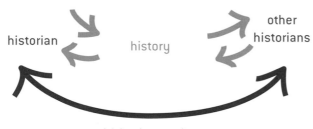

within the society
within the natural world

## Perspectives and facts

For history, we must ride the arrows that connect the components of this now-familiar diagram, to stress a point that needs no emphasis in the arts: that knowledge is created from different perspectives, and that *shared* knowledge is built up by the movement back and forth of ideas. Research, writing, critique and debate – these keep the past alive in the present as we take from it what we find relevant and illuminating for the continuity of the present with the past. The uniting idea through the rest of this chapter is a familiar one: perspectives.

## Evaluation: checks for truth

You may be beginning to wonder: is every topic raised in the earlier part of the book relevant to history? For an area of knowledge that deals with all the complexities of human beings, and then with the added challenge of studying such beings in the context of the past, how could it be otherwise?

We point you back, just briefly, to the truth checks we raised in chapter 3, and the different forms of justification they push us on to seek. The *correspondence check for truth* expects that we go and check the world to see if the statements we make about it actually do correspond to reality; it demands evidence. The past, however, is gone. We cannot go and check it, so the evidence in history is of a different sort from much in the sciences.

The *coherence check*, as a result, is more relevant, as historians compare documents to find points of agreement and overlap, and attempt to piece together a picture of the past in which all the parts fit together harmoniously. To a large extent we evaluate artifacts and documents as

## For Reflection

Is a history that is rationally consistent necessarily true? Could more than one version of the past, even contradictory ones, each be internally consistent?

"evidence" for an interpretation by finding rational consistency among the pieces. This approach to truth as internal consistency is significant in what we consider next: appreciating different perspectives but not allowing them to dissolve external evidence into the fog of relativism.

## Historians, perspectives and historical fact

Perspectives. You must have suspected we would end up bringing you back to a major theme of this book, which is grounded right back in the first chapter. As this point the early framework "Exploring differing perspectives" (page 28) should be very familiar to you, along with the components identified there: assumptions, values, facts selected as important, processes of validation or resolution of competing views, and implications.

Historians approach their study from different perspectives depending on their personal backgrounds, the contexts in which they live and work, and the theoretical emphases within their professional training. They do not park their humanity outside on the street as they enter an archive. Their training in critical literacy and study of the practice of history give them conceptual tools to recognize many of the influences upon their thinking. However, that training is likely also to give them a particular theory in the investigation.

These days, few would claim that historians could possibly be completely neutral as they work with human records; personal, cultural, ideological, and theoretical interpretations inevitably take part in their understanding of the human record. We could lament that lack of complete neutrality as a big problem. But why? What else would we expect of the human subject matter, the removal into the past, and the need for someone to make sense of it for us? The communication between the historian and the reader has to acknowledge and work with that element of subjectivity.

### For Reflection

How does the historian combine objectivity and subjectivity in researching, identifying facts, and using facts as evidence within an interpretive argument?

**"Criticize the old world and build a new world with Mao Zedong Thought as a weapon"**

The Great Proletarian Cultural Revolution (1966–76) in China stands as an historical attempt at social transformation that sought its ends, in part, by changing the value placed on knowledge. Consolidating his power base, Mao Zedong mobilized rejection of the Four Olds all of which was knowledge prized in the past – Old Customs, Old Culture, Old Habits, and Old Ideas. He caused cultural treasures such as literature, historical records, and artworks to be destroyed and teachers and intellectuals to be persecuted or killed, all for the ideological purpose of eliminating a gap between social classes. Closing schools, he enlisted students of ages roughly 12 to 17 as Red Guards to enforce his revolutionary principles with youthful zeal. In large population shifts, he had youth sent from urban centres to learn, instead, from farmers and workers. Throughout the revolution, campaigns including posters such as the one pictured here aimed to educate the public on Maoist thought. The social upheaval left much culturally precious knowledge destroyed and millions dead. It would misrepresent the Chinese Cultural Revolution to suggest that it was caused by differing perspectives on knowledge, but Mao's revision of the knowledge that was deemed important certainly played an ideological and tactical role.

Major social shifts all around the world are very often driven by people gaining and holding power not just through force but also through ideology and persuasion. Often, too, they are catalysed by ideas catching hold of a population. What people believe, or are intimidated into seemingly accepting, has implications for how they act in the world. Believing and knowing – these can be personal and intimate issues, but for a society they can be essentially political.

## Perspectives and postmodern thought

All the areas of knowledge take their shape from the various ways of knowing we considered earlier. From them, they develop methodologies to fit their own subject matter and build their own traditions of research and scholarship. They also develop their own successive topics for critical discussion. It is in context of such discussion that we dwell a bit longer on the relationship between the historian, his perspective, and the nature of historical fact.

In successive historical periods in thought, or with successive theories, different dominant ideas are contributed to academic and public discussion – as historians can tell us. Relevant to our consideration of the historian and his facts, for example, is a broad current of thought known as "postmodernism" which gained considerable influence on academic discussion in the arts, human sciences, and philosophy particularly in the second half of the twentieth century. It has given considerable recognition to the degree to which we construct our own sense of reality within our own perspectives.

As a movement in thought, it emphasized the variability of perspectives, with none of them absolute, and the way in which many social "realities" are social "constructs"– products of the mind that people tend to treat as though they had an existence independent of ourselves. It emphasized, above all, that rather than simply recording or mirroring the world, we build our realities through our own interpretations of what we see in the world.

### *The influence of perspective*

We will take one example here to illustrate the way in which a perspective influences the way that history is told. We turn to Ella Shohat and Robert Stam, authors of *Unthinking Eurocentricism: Multiculturalism and the Media*. They trace the impact of a western perspective in particular.

> "
> The story and study of the past, both recent and distant, will not reveal the future, but it flashes beacon lights along the way and it is a useful nostrum against despair.[10]
>
> *Barbara Tuchman*
> "

The dominant perspectives that shape historical and social narratives, the authors argue, are embedded in relationships of power. Their focus is on the way the West has created a version of history and contemporary society that places itself at the centre of consciousness. They call this dominant perspective "Eurocentrism" and argue that people holding a Eurocentric perspective are largely unaware that they do so, or that an alternative exists. If you bring to mind the maps of the world and cultural perspectives we considered in chapter 1 of this book, you will readily understand their central point:

> Eurocentric thinking attributes to the "West" an almost providential sense of historical destiny. Eurocentrism, like Renaissance perspectives in painting, envisions the world from a single privileged point. It maps the world in a cartography that centralizes and augments Europe while literally "belittling" Africa. The "East" is divided into "Near", "Middle", and "Far", making Europe the arbiter of spatial evaluation, just as the establishment of Greenwich Mean Time produces England as the regulating center of temporal measurement.

> Eurocentrism bifurcates the world into the "West and the Rest" and organizes everyday language into binaristic hierarchies implicitly flattering to Europe: *our* "nations", *their* "tribes"; *our* "religions", *their* "superstitions"; *our* "culture", *their* "folklore"; *our* "art", *their* "artifacts"; *our* "demonstrations", *their* "riots"; *our* "defense", *their* "terrorism."[11]

Shohat and Stam suggest that a Eurocentric perspective has a profound impact on the telling of history in the West. For example, Eurocentric narrative treats the West's oppressive practices such as colonialism, imperialism, and slave-trading as exceptions and not as an integral causal part of the West's power; it traces from classical Greece a linear trajectory with itself as the driving force; it presents itself as progressing towards democratic institutions, treating as aberrations the Inquisition, Mussolini, and Hitler, and "masking the West's part in subverting democracies abroad".

The authors further argue that a flattering presentation of themselves is accompanied by an unflattering presentation of others: "Eurocentrism

---

[10]  Tuchman, B.W. 1982. *Practicing History: Selected Essays*. New York. Random House. P 55.

[11]  Shohat, E. and Stam, R. 1995. *Unthinking Eurocentrism: Multiculturalism and the Media*. London and New York. Routledge.

sanitizes Western history while patronizing and even demonizing the non-West; it thinks of itself in terms of its noblest achievement – science, progress, humanism – but of the non-West in terms of its deficiencies, real or imagined."[12]

At the same time, though, these authors warn against swinging to the other extreme of blaming Europe for all the ills of its former colonies.

This critique of a perspective whose features are largely invisible to those who hold it contributes to understanding events of the past, the histories written about them, and the contemporary society that inherits and interacts with the dominant historical versions.

Shohat and Stam's analysis is a critical perspective on historical perspectives!

Their analysis, moreover, falls within a broader trend of thought within academic scholarship. Postmodern thought has encouraged a far greater awareness and understanding of the influence of perspectives on the way in which we shape knowledge.

### But if everything is a matter of perspective, then...

However, it could be argued that a postmodernist intellectual climate fostered *excessive* awareness of perspective, to the point of treating "truth" as if *entirely* constructed from particular viewpoints without any external check in reality. That is, it treated reality as entirely what we *think* it to be.

If all historians, working within their own perspectives, are selecting and shaping material in accordance with their own assumptions, values, and worldviews, then can we know what "really happened"? Is there no such thing as fact, and no appeal to any check for truth outside a point of view?

One of the most riveting treatments of this problem of truth and perspective in history that we have encountered is an essay by Jane Tompkins, writing on trying to pin down what "really happened" between American Indians of the seventeenth century and the settlers of New England. The facts were significant, she felt, because "the result of that encounter was virtual genocide". The essay is the story of trying to find out the truth, in spite of the multiple perspectives she encounters.

First, the conflicting versions of events lead her to conclude that she must evaluate the credibility of the writers. As she reads on, however, she is drawn more and more deeply into versions and interpretations that have no common features that would even allow comparison. Turning then to primary sources, original documents, she finds the same problem. At this point, not only can she not decide what versions to accept, but she can *no longer even see how such a decision can be made.*

And yet, she balks at accepting a relativist position that there is no truth independent of a perspective:

> The historian can never escape the limitations of his or her own position in history and so inevitably gives an account that is an extension of the circumstances from which it springs. But it seems to me that when one is confronted with this particular succession of stories, cultural and historical relativism is not a position that one can comfortably assume. The phenomena to which these histories testify – conquest, massacre, and genocide, on the one hand; torture, slavery and murder on the other – cry out for judgment.[13]

And then she sees her own contradiction. How can she say that events "cry out for judgment"? How can she judge – when she has *no facts*? Her awareness of so many different perspectives had disqualified *all of them* from being true; all facts were facts *only* within a perspective.

But then she questions that conclusion in turn. Wasn't it the poststructuralist theory in her own educational background that was encouraging her to accept the conclusion that the multiple perspectives rendered all facts unbelievable? And wasn't poststructuralist theory *also just a perspective*, to be taken no more seriously than any of the others?

Tompkins reaches a conclusion. Rather than discarding all versions, she has to piece together bits from here and there that seemed most reasonable and plausible, as to some extent she found she had already done:

> If the accounts don't fit together neatly, that is not a reason for rejecting them all in favor of a metadiscourse about epistemology; on the

---

12  Shohat, E. and Stam, R. 1995. *Unthinking Eurocentrism: Multiculturalism and the Media.* London and New York. Routledge. P 3.

13  Tompkins, J. 1993. "'Indians': Textualism, Morality, and the Problem of History". *Ways of Reading*, ed. David Bartholomae and Anthony Petrosky. Boston. Bedford Books. P 597.

contrary, one encounters contradictory facts and divergent points of view in practically every phase of life, from deciding whom to marry to choosing the right brand of cat food, and one decides as best one can given the evidence available.

Her ultimate realization is that by diverting attention from the problems in the world onto the construction of the mind, such an approach to knowledge "once again ignores what happened and still is happening to American Indians".[14] There are real-life implications to the version of history accepted, and to the versions of history ignored.

### Perspectives and shared knowledge

In conclusion, we suggest that it is essential in a critical approach to knowledge to recognize and critique perspectives, particularly when doing so brings to attention ways in which the shaping of knowledge reflects and entrenches relationships of power.

> ## For Reflection
>
> Should historians be largely in accord on what they pick out as significant causal connections through the past? What differences could be argued to be weaknesses in history and what differences could be argued to be strengths?
>
> What puts a version of history "out of bounds" for being considered legitimate work?

In recognizing competing perspectives and dominant voices, however, we equally suggest that we cannot legitimately embrace relativism – to throw up our hands and declare the past to be unknowable and all versions of it to be equally true and solely a matter of interpretation. Yes, historical accounts are written within a range of uncertainty, depending on the extent of the

**Josef Stalin. Poster, USSR, 1944**

"Forwards, let us destroy the German Occupiers and drive them beyond the borders of our homeland!"

Is history driven (metaphorically) by individuals – or do individuals rise to power on a (metaphorical) tide of the times?

We may be drawn with greater urgency to explain the events of the past when they appear unbelievable. We may fear that, if we do not understand them, we increase the possibility of something similar happening in the future. "How could this have happened?" we ask ourselves. One example is what happened in the Soviet Union under Stalin. There are extremely divergent accounts of the number of people who died during Stalin's regime as a result of his purges, executions, gulags, war, or policy-induced famine. The count depends on what is included and whether archival records are treated as complete. Originally estimating a much higher total, for instance, historian Robert Conquest settled on a victim count of roughly 20 million people after the Soviet archives were opened.

How could this have happened? Don't we *need* an explanation? Don't we even have a *responsibility* to understand how this event – like too many other equivalent ones – was possible, so that we can heed warning signs in our own present?

History students in your class may be able to tell you about the cult of personality that glorified Stalin's image at the time. They are likely to be able to describe Stalin's own rewriting of history, and the revision of history since his death in the "de-Stalinization" of the Soviet Union.

---

14 "'Indians': Textualism, Morality, and the Problem of History" an essay by Jane Tompkins, from journal *Critical Inquiry*, [C1 Vol.13, No 1 (Autumn, 1986), pp.101-119] published by the University of Chicago Press.

records available and the nature of the facts. But that does not mean that "anything goes". Some interpretations have considerably more justification than others – and we must use critical judgment to create (if we are historians) or to accept (if we are readers) the best version possible.

## Development of history: perspectives on patterns

As they research and write, historians are working within concepts of larger patterns of time and history. These kinds of large patterns, whether historians *assume them to exist* or *argue them to exist,* can provide conceptual frameworks for the particular stories set within them, and influence the interpretation these stories are given. Indeed, it is not only historians but also their entire societies that may embrace particular patterns of history to validate their own visions of themselves and give a positive interpretation to purposes that could be construed otherwise.

As they develop their interpretations, then, historians may be influenced by concepts of the past such as the following ones that have been embraced at different times:

- Is history a cycle, with events repeating in an identifiable sequence or rhythm, like the rise and fall of dynasties and empires? Is it a story of repeating Ages, with rise to the Golden Age and then decline, or possibly an alternation of Dark and Golden Ages (ancient Greek and Hindu thought)?
- Is history linear? If so, is it progressing towards a better time in the future? Or is it moving from beginning to end in accordance with the will of God (as in eschatology)?
- Is history the story of individuals who influence its overall course (Carlyle's idea that history was the biography of great men)?
- Is history continually shaped by opposing forces which fuse together, only to be opposed in turn by a new force that arises (Hegel's dialectic materialism, Marx's class struggle)?
- Is history characterized (as Freud suggests) by the constant conflict between the life drive and the death drive?

Not only do they work within large frameworks of time, historians also work within theories that influence how they think about the basic units of their human subject matter.

- Will they treat human beings as individuals, as do classic liberals, with an emphasis on *individual* motivation and assumption of universal characteristics of human nature such as "rationality" and "self-interest", or as *social groups*, as do Marxists, with an emphasis on relations between groups with contradicting interests and differential power (such as the class struggle)?
- Will they classify societies into abstracted types with specific characteristics, such as democracies, and use these types for historical analysis?
- Will they treat forms of social relations, such as barter and trade or gender relations, as historically grounded in a time and place, or will they treat them as universal?

Clearly, writing history is not simply a matter of neutrally investigating records and recording what happened. It is an investigative, interpretive discipline that depends greatly on the personal and theoretical perspectives of the historian (and her skills). It is a challenge for the historian to become self-aware and, with the training of the discipline, recognize and acknowledge her perspectives. And then it is up to her readers to apply to her writing the same skill she practised herself – skill of critically evaluating each source.

↑ How big is your history? What does it include? When you think of the history with which you are familiar, how large a frame of time do you place around yourself? What factors in your life have affected your personal knowledge of history and your own personal sense of its scope and scale?

## Discussion Activity

### Learning from history

In this 1938 photograph, Adolf Hitler ascends the steps in one of the Nuremberg Rallies. The Nuremberg Rallies were massive annual events that inspired fervent dedication to the German Nazi party and glorified its leader. The contemporary account included here of the 1936 rally conveys some of the atmosphere.

1.  What ways of knowing seem to be employed in this rally in exciting patriotism and fervour? How is sense perception used? What emotions are stimulated, and how? What is the role of faith – and which of the definitions we treated in chapter 10 is most relevant? What kind of language is used, and why in unison?

2.  If you know what happened in Nazi Germany under Hitler, then you will surely hope that nothing like this happens again. What is the role of thinking critically in preventing propaganda from taking hold of people? To what events or situations should awareness and analysis be applied? What is the role of media, and alternative media?

3.  Do we learn from history? If so, in what ways? If not, why not?

"

"Attention! The Führer is here!" The shouts that always accompany the Führer resound from the Dutzendteich train station. The colonnade slowly circles the field, then suddenly – as the shouts of those on the other side of the platform announce the Führer's arrival – 180,000 people look to the heavens. 150 blue spotlights surge upward hundreds of meters, forming overhead the most powerful cathedral that mortals have ever seen.

There, at the entrance, we see the Führer. He too stands for several moments looking upward, then turns and walks, followed by his aides, past the long, long columns, 20 deep, of the fighters for his idea. An ocean of Heil-shouts and jubilation surrounds him.

Several stars shine through the deep blue curtain of the cathedral of light, and the flags of the German nation flutter in the soft wind…

Finally, finally, as the masses gaze as if transfixed, the flood of flags comes to a rest. Fanfares sound into the night, and 500 pupils from the school at Burg Vogelsang take the oath for us all, for all Germans:

We have come
For the good
And to renew the holy oath.
Blazing flames hold us together
Into eternity…
No one shall take this faith
From those who are dedicated to Germany…

… Turning toward the Führer, Reich Organization Leader Dr. Ley speaks the words of the oath to the gathered formation:

My Führer! The political leaders of the party stand before you. Millions more of them throughout the country join us in this festive hour and listen with us…

No one but you, My Führer, can take the credit for having saved Germany. You alone saved Germany. (Jubilant agreement.)[15]

"

---

[15] "The Oath under the Cathedral of Light at the 1936 Nuremberg Party Rally", German Propaganda Archive, http://www.calvin.edu/academic/cas/gpa/pt36dom.htm, accessed 10 June 2012.

# History and personal knowledge

The past is gone, but its effects live on in the present in both the finest of our achievements and the worst of our conflicts. We live within borders we did not draw ourselves, and with identities that we inherit, with poverty or wealth, with war or peace, all of which influence the possibilities of our lives. For better or for worse, the place we occupy in the world from the first moment we open our eyes upon it has been a convergence of causal sequences of the past.

If you have thought about the questions we raised before this chapter regarding the question "why?" you will be aware of many different ways of thinking about causation, including beliefs about chance or purpose. If you have also thought about the way we give shape to our representations of reality – our use of framing and selection, for instance – you will also be aware that there are many different possible histories of your own life that you could write. How we see the past, and how we place ourselves within the present, can affect what records and historical interpretations we value.

Cultural attitudes vary, for instance, in the value they place on tradition and in their orientation towards the past, present, or future. People in some groups can trace their ancestry far back or venerate their ancestors, while others have no such ties. People in some groups are grounded by a feeling of belonging to a particular place, perhaps given to them through their own religious beliefs, while others move through a globalized world with an easy transference of the idea of home.

People vary, too, in the scope of their histories. In some cultures, a sense of history relevant to their own lives stretches back to long ago moments of a religious or mythological account of the past. In some places, ancient architecture and historical monuments are part of the daily street scene, while in others the landscape is forest and fields, with no human ties to the past. For some groups, relevant history goes back to ancient dynasties or

## For Reflection

What is your own orientation to the past, present, or future? (cultural perspectives, chapter 1) Do you think it influences how you read and understand history?

## For Reflection

Do you belong to a community that expresses a sense of a collective "we" continuous with the past? What role does that community identity have in your personal sense of identity? Does it affect the historical accounts that you consider important?

ancestors, while for others the sense of history begins most significantly with stories of refugees and immigrants starting over in a new land.

Groups vary, similarly, in the extent to which they gain a sense of identity from stories of a collective "we" that is continuous with family, clan, or nation in the past. The version of history told within families and communities is part of the cultural identity of the group. The stories told may be of shared blood that makes events of the past belong to a group in the present as their heritage. They may also be of group entitlement, destiny or mystic connection with a particular piece of land, and carry implications for appropriate action in the present:

> "We have been victims in the past and are therefore owed _____."

> "Many of us have died for this cause/this land and we owe it to them to _____."

> "We have always lived on this land and so _____."

The stories of a living past may also emphasize the characteristics in which the group takes particular pride, perhaps their honesty, or their capacity to endure hardship, or their sense of responsibility:

> "We are the kind of people who have always _____ and therefore we must _____."

The assumption of a continuous collective "we" may also carry further assumptions regarding the acceptability of change of various kinds, for instance, changes in culture, relationship to the land, or relationship with other groups of people.

In many nation states, the creation of a sense of the collective "we" is closely bound up with the national narrative, the shared story of the country in the past with implications for citizen identity and obligations in the present. In the words of Benedict Arnold, a nation is an "imagined community" within whose boundaries members conceive of themselves as sharing a significant comradeship, even though they have never

## Example: history as a story of progress

We choose one example here to demonstrate the way that a version of history can be integrated coherently into a much larger ideological worldview. Take the picture of history as linear, with human life improving as it goes. Much of western history from the nineteenth into the twentieth century is enmeshed with this idea of progress, tied in with colonialism, industrialization and technological development.

In the nineteenth century, the idea of progress was tied to European colonialism and the development of empires. Europeans thought of themselves as carrying "enlightenment" and the true religion of Christianity to dark places of the world, and as nobly taking on the "white man's burden" of civilizing "primitive peoples". In their own eyes, they were contributing to progress.

Even scientific theories, such as Charles Darwin's theory of evolution (*On the Origin of Species*, 1859), were drawn into the large story of progress, with meanings attributed to it that were not present in Darwin's ideas at all. White Europeans justified their dominance through a distortion of science: they saw darker races as less evolved biologically, and as having inferior civilizations.

Ideas of progress associated with industrialism and economic competition similarly used a distorted idea of the theory of evolution to claim scientific justification. Charles Darwin had used the term "natural selection" for the survival of organisms better adapted to their environment. Herbert Spencer adopted the idea of natural selection for his economic theories, and coined the term "survival of the fittest" for the success of individuals within competitive society.

"Social Darwinism" was never a coherently advanced theory, but a name given retrospectively to attitudes regarding competition, struggle, and individual advancement within the ruthless capitalism of the turn of the nineteenth century. Some industrialists who made a fortune declared themselves to be "fitter" than the poor, who had simply lost in a "natural" struggle. Wealthy American businessman John D. Rockefeller, for instance, declared, "The growth of a large business is merely a survival of the fittest...the working out of a law of nature".[16]

By the mid-twentieth century, the fusion between evolution and concepts of purposeful advance was distilled into the image of the march of progress. "The march of progress", says biologist Stephen Jay Gould, "is the canonical representation of evolution – the one picture immediately grasped and viscerally understood by all."[17] He argues that the idea of "progress" in evolution is a concept that people impose in hindsight on a sequence of events that happened to lead – of course! – to them.

The idea of progress continues to have impact on the world today. Are human beings and their societies really getting better and better? What constitutes "progress"? Is it industrialism and growth? Do "developed" countries represent an ideal of progress to which "lesser developed" countries should aspire? History, although it is all about the past, continues to reinterpret the records in terms of what we want to know in the present.

↑   The march of progress

---

[16] Jerry Bergman, "Darwin's Influence on Ruthless Laissez Fair Capitalism", Institute for Critical Research. http://www.icr.org/article/454/ accessed 5 August 2012.

[17] Gould, S.J. 1990. *Wonderful Life: The Burgess Shale and the Nature of History.* New York and London. W.W. Norton. P 31.

## Discussion Activity

### History and ethics

> History and justice come too late for the dead.[18]
>
> *John Caputo*

History deals with the past, gone. Do ethical issues still apply when we speak of the past? Do we owe anything to the dead?

> The fundamental obligation of historians is to the maximal telling of truth, maximally keyed to the weight of the available evidence. Here is where the only ethics of history worthy of the name is to be found.[19]
>
> *Allan Megill*

Megill places history within the ethical imperative of telling the truth. On what grounds – that is, on the basis of what ethical perspectives – could denial or misrepresentation of the past be judged to be unethical? What differing issues arise depending on whether you argue ethically in accordance with each of intentions, principles, consequences, or social codes?

> Truth commissions stand out as a brave attempt to recover factuality, narrate history in the light of testimonial memories, and construct a historically-informed ethical vision… Yet, their dependence on political endorsement and support leaves them with little room for creating a novel space in the midst of existing political arrangements.[20]
>
> *Onur Bakiner*

Attempts to deal ethically with the past – and the relationship between acknowledging the past, having a truthful historical record, and affecting the present – have led to various national commissions of truth and reconciliation and state official apologies for the way groups in their population, such as aboriginal peoples, have been treated in the past. What do you see as the ethical merits of official acknowledgment and apology?

## For Reflection

What history have you learned in school? Does it centre on your own country? Does it include both moments of pride and moments of shame? Do you think that most people in your country know roughly the same story? What role do you think it plays in a sense of collective identity?

## Knowledge framework

Consider the knowledge framework for history: its scope, central concepts, methods (including use of ways of knowing), development as a discipline, and links with your own knowledge. We suggest you then wait until you've treated the human sciences and discuss these two areas together, comparatively.

met. The creation of "imagined communities" is achieved to some large extent through the teaching of history, unofficially in community stories and media, and officially in schools. Students from parts of the world in conflict have often been surprised, meeting in international schools outside them, to find how different are the versions of history they learned in school.

History as an area of shared knowledge can contribute significantly to our own personal knowledge – our sense of who we are in the world and how we are placed between the past and the future. It could be argued, further, that our conception of our place within the unrolling story affects our sense of our own responsibility to our society and the world.

---

18  Cited in John Zammito. 2004. *Review of The Ethics of History*, ed. David Carr, Thomas R. Flynn, and Rudolf Makkreel. Northwestern University Press.

19  Cited in John Zammito. 2004. *Review of The Ethics of History*, ed. David Carr, Thomas R. Flynn, and Rudolf Makkreel. Northwestern University Press.

20  Bakiner, O. 30 August 2010. "History, Ethics, Politics: Rethinking the Legacy of Truth Commissions". *Social Science Research Network*.

## Discussion Activity

### Research activity:
### Benin plaque of the Oba with Europeans

This final activity offers a chance to look closely at artwork of historical significance. Information is readily available online. We start you off with a few questions, but expect that you will generate your own as you find out more. "It is more rewarding", writes historian Barbara Tuchman, "to assemble the facts first and, in the process of arranging them in narrative form, to discover a theory or a historical generalization emerging of its own accord. This to me is the excitement, the built-in treasure hunt, of writing history."[21]

- The plaque represents contact between the Oba, ruler of Benin (in present-day Nigeria), and Portuguese traders in the sixteenth century. Why was that contact considered important enough for artists of Benin to commemorate it?
- Where is this plaque presently located? Why? Is the location historically significant?

- "It need scarcely be said that at the first sight of these remarkable works of art we were at once astounded at such an unexpected find, and puzzled to account for so highly developed an art among a race so entirely barbarous", said a British museum curator, 1890s.[22] As you research the Benin plaques, be alert to numerous different perspectives on their significance.

**Your mission:** Write a short history, not more than a page, of the Benin plaques, or of this one in particular. Then summarize in a few sentences what you think influenced your choices in the history you wrote. Find a way of sharing, on paper or online, the different histories written within your class group. We close the chapter here, leaving our instructions quite loose, to give you a chance to apply the ideas raised in this chapter to your own writing. This activity might also prompt reflection on why the histories that we write of our past actually matter.

---

[21] Tuchman, B.W. 1982. *Practicing History: Selected Essays*. New York. Random House. P 34.

[22] http://hotw.cgb.im/mobile/77#/index.php/mobile/77/transcript

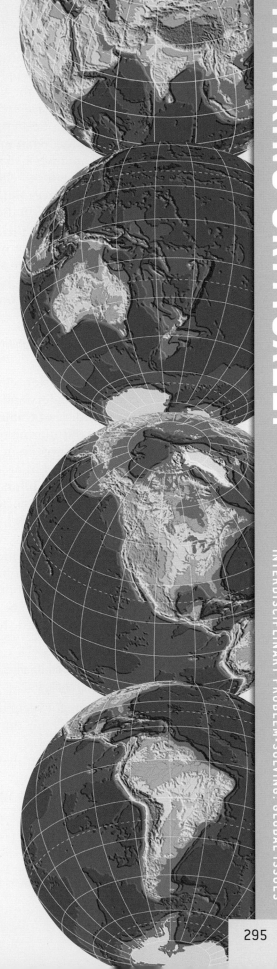

# Interdisciplinary problem-solving: global issues

It is a common misconception that studying academic knowledge removes one from the "real world". It doesn't. The real world – past and present, society and nature, what is and what *should be* – is exactly what academic areas of knowledge study. We need the knowledge they contribute to understand the problems our real world is facing, and to find possible solutions. As we examine areas of knowledge in TOK, we give attention to how they work together in any holistic grasp of global issues.

 Interview

## Causes and Solutions

**Michael Watson**
**IB graduate 1995**

*Michael Watson is an IB graduate and an IB teacher of geography and economics. He is also a development professional, formerly Director of Programmes for the Institute of Cultural Affairs International and more recently an advisor working with the Red Cross in Haiti, Madagascar, Côte d'Ivoire, and Niger.*

→ In development work, what areas of knowledge are most relevant?

In the areas of both disaster relief and longer-term human development, an awareness and appreciation for multiple areas of knowledge is key to effectiveness. For example, in Niger, we know that a central problem is food insecurity; vast numbers of people suffer from food shortages or the threat of food shortages. Potential solutions are many (food distribution, better farming techniques, new crop varieties, encouragement of small businesses, population relocation, etc.) but not all will work, and some may make things worse.

Thus an effective response depends on an appreciation and understanding of multiple areas of knowledge: knowing the historical antecedents and whether something has been tried or not in the past (history); listening to people to gain their wisdom and knowledge about the local ecosystem, how it responds to different stresses and how it has changed through time (local and indigenous knowledge); understanding what matters to and motivates people, and what shapes their worldviews (psychology, ethics, religion, faith); understanding the major forces shaping climate patterns and changing climate in the region (natural sciences); appreciating the importance and nuance of gender relations and power dynamics within a village or society (human sciences). To approach a human development challenge such as hunger from within the silo of one area of knowledge is to invite failure.

→ Why is the analysis of causes significant in development work?

Arguably, in the field of disaster relief, it is not always necessary to understand complex underlying issues in order to be able to provide some temporary relief of suffering (one could make the analogy of the surgeon not needing to know why the heart failed in order to be able to replace it). However, if our ultimate goal is to prevent humanitarian emergencies and help individuals and communities develop resiliency and improve their lives in the long-term, then a clear understanding of issues is critical. Indeed, unless we have a clear understanding of the various dimensions and causes of problems our efforts and resources may at best be wasted, or, at worst, may work against our basic humanitarian or development goals.

→ What are the benefits and limitations of using the problem tree for causal analysis?

A problem that at first might seem overwhelming in its complexity might become, once represented through a problem tree analysis, more manageable. However, while it can help identify key underlying causes and consequences, it is only as good as the information and insight on which it is based. Incorrect assumptions, biases and false or misleading information can all find their way into problem trees (and they may be given increased legitimacy once enshrined in the analysis). Also, it can be a highly reductionist exercise, where it is assumed that each problem can necessarily be reduced to a handful of key, identifiable causes. Moreover, it doesn't always identify the relative importance of specific causes (and can make some contributing factors seem more important than they are) nor does it necessarily allow for clear identification of threshold effects (when a particular problem only becomes significant once it surpasses a certain threshold) or interaction effects (the effect of two or more 'independent' causes working together, where the effect is 'greater' than the sum of its parts).

Nevertheless, it provides a structured and visually appealing way to methodically consider a problem. A well-conceived problem analysis can point toward solutions and concrete actions. Moreover, it can be an extremely useful way for analyzing problems as a group, where perspectives may differ and where establishing shared understanding and finding common ground is important. ■

> "
>
> In spite of what you majored in, or what the textbooks say, or what you think you're an expert at, follow a system wherever it leads. It will be sure to lead across traditional disciplinary lines....
>
> Seeing systems whole requires more than being "interdisciplinary," if that word means, as it usually does, putting together people from different disciplines only if there is a real problem to be solved, and if representatives from the various disciplines are more committed to solving the problem than to being academically correct. They will have to go into learning mode. They will have to admit ignorance and be willing to be taught, by each other and by the  system.
>
> It can be done. It's very exciting when it happens.[23]
>
> *Donella Meadows*
>
> "

[23] Meadows, D.H. 2008. *Thinking in Systems: A Primer*, ed Diana Wright, Sustainability Institute. Chelsea Green Publishing. White River Junction, Vermont. P 183.

consequences

problem

causes

## Problem tree, solution tree: Activity

In the problem tree image, the trunk is the problem itself. The causes of the problem lie below ground, with numerous secondary roots joining into primary ones to feed the tree. The consequences of the problem are the branches, forking into more and more effects.

Use this image to focus a TOK class discussion in which you give attention to an issue of global concern and ideas of causation. Refer back to pages 249–251 for concepts of cause and to page 126 for recognition of fallacies.

**Step 1:** Choose a global issue (or a more local issue if you wish). Possible topics:

- global: the AIDS pandemic, climate change, poverty, hunger, refugees, terrorism
- more local: bullying in communities, prejudice against a specific group.

Brainstorm in small groups to pin down causes and consequences of your chosen issue, to the best of

your present knowledge. Draw and label the roots with the causes of the problems as you understand them. Identify the major causes as main roots, and their contributory causes as secondary roots. For instance, a major cause of malnutrition in children could be insufficient food, whose causes in turn could be numerous (e.g. poverty or crop failure – each of which has causes of its own), or lack of parental education on nutrition, whose causes could likewise be numerous. Identify the effects of the problem in the branches of the tree. (You can find further examples of problem trees on the Internet.)

When you are finished, propose solutions to counter each of the causes, with the aim of producing positive effects in the branches above.

**Step 2:** Now add further TOK analysis to your problem tree.

*concepts and language:* How have you conceived of "cause"? How does the way you named and defined the problem affect your analysis? Does it matter, for instance, whether you treat "global warming" or "climate change"? Do you emphasize one element of a complex situation by picking it out as the problem, for instance "civil war in country X" or "refugees"?

*scope of different areas of knowledge:* To what extent and in what ways does knowledge about your chosen global issue fall within the scope of each TOK area of knowledge, with its sub-disciplines? What kind of knowledge does each contribute in terms of information, explanation, and perspectives, or possibly ways of representing and communicating ideas on the issue?

*methodology:* To what disciplines do you turn most extensively for trying to pin down causal connections in your particular issue? What are their methods of establishing cause? What counts as evidence in each discipline, and how is it found? What cultural, political, religious, theoretical or other perspectives come into play in trying to understand the causes and their effects?

*Links to personal knowledge*: In what ways does knowledge of this global issue affect you personally? Do you feel any responsibility to learn more, or to take action? (See page 271.)

**Step 3:** Remember the problem and solution trees you were able to build at this point, and continue to learn more in years to come.

# 18. The Human Sciences

As we leave history as an area of knowledge and enter the human sciences – more commonly known as the "social sciences" – we have not left behind the essential questions that we considered in the chapter about history:

- What is an accurate *description*, based on evidence, of how human beings *are* as individuals and as societies?
- What *interpretations* and *explanations* can be given of their social structures and actions?

It could well be argued that the understanding we gain from history and the human sciences is essential for anyone who accepts *to any extent at all* the aim expressed in the IB mission statement "to develop internationally minded people who,

recognizing their common humanity and shared guardianship of the planet, help to create a better and more peaceful world". Areas of knowledge that study human beings have the potential to shed some light on what the nature might be of our "common humanity" and what perspectives comment on the "shared guardianship of the planet". The sheer complexity of the human subject matter does not make study easy or the conclusions tidy. Yet surely little could be more central to our understanding of how the world works than a basic understanding of the human sciences.

The human sciences take in a considerable range of disciplines – though perhaps not as diverse a group as those categorized as the arts.

## Discussion Activity

### Scope: What do the human sciences study?

First, working on your own, write the following words, widely spaced, on a page: *psychology, anthropology, sociology, economics, psychology, political science, human geography.* Join them up in ways that show the interconnections you think they have. Then exchange ideas with the rest of your class.

- What does each one study? Do some of them overlap in what they study? Are any of them specialized subcategories of others?
- What general characteristics do these disciplines share?
- Do you consider there to be any significant omissions to the human sciences in this list? What characteristics does a discipline *have to possess* in order to be considered a member of the group?
- What general features do the human sciences share with history, on the one hand, and with the natural sciences, on the other?
- To what extent do you think the following claim applies to the human sciences?

Frequently, the way to understand a complicated system is to understand its component parts, but that's probably not the case for the most interesting complicated systems—like us.[1]

*Robert Sapolsky, biologist and professor of neurology, Stanford University.*

---

[1] Robert Sapolsky. 20 April 2012. "Starting Over". Seed. http://seedmagazine.com/content/article/starting_over/

> "
> The facts of contemporary history are also facts about the success and the failure of individual men and women. When a society is industrialized, a peasant becomes a worker; a feudal lord is liquidated or becomes a businessman. When classes rise or fall, a man is employed or unemployed; when the rate of investment goes up or down, a man takes new heart or goes broke. When wars happen, an insurance salesman becomes a rocket launcher; a store clerk, a radar man; a wife lives alone; a child grows up without a father. Neither the life of an individual nor the history of a society can be understood without understanding both. [2]
>
> *C. Wright Mills*
> "

It is far easier here than in the arts to talk about common goals and generally identifiable methods. Nevertheless, the field remains characterized by multiple perspectives that illuminate different aspects of the human subject matter.

The IB subject guides for the respective human sciences offer these descriptions of them:

"Psychology is the systematic study of behaviour and mental processes."

"The study of economics is essentially about dealing with scarcity, resource allocation and the methods and processes by which choices are made in the satisfaction of human wants."

"Social and cultural anthropology is the comparative study of culture and human societies."

"Geography is a dynamic subject that is firmly grounded in the real world and focuses on the interactions between individuals, societies and the physical environment in both time and space."

Although these four descriptions are just introductory indications of their disciplines, you can see in them instantly a collective emphasis on human beings and methods of study: "systematic study", "methods and processes by which choices are made",

"comparative study", "firmly grounded in the real world". Although all of these disciplines have ways of working appropriate to their specific subject matter, they possess broad features in common.

>
> We cannot possibly reach the final Socratic wisdom of knowing ourselves if we never leave the narrow confinement of the customs, beliefs and prejudices into which every man [sic] is born. Nothing can teach us a better lesson in this matter of ultimate importance than the habit of mind which allows us to treat the beliefs and values of another man from his point of view… The science of man in its most refined and deepest version should lead us to such knowledge and tolerance, and generosity, based on the understanding of other men's point of view.[3]
>
> *Bronislaw Malinowski, 1922*
>

---

[2]  Wright Mills, C. 1959, 2000. *The Sociological Imagination*. New York. Oxford University Press. P 3.

[3]  Malinowski, B. 1922. *Argonauts of the Western Pacific*.

## Studying human beings

Not accidentally, we have placed this chapter on the human sciences between history, with which it is usually grouped as "human-ities" in university departments, and the sciences, with which it shares the other half of its name.

The human sciences are distinct from these other areas of knowledge in ways significant to the methods they can employ. Unlike history, they can make direct observations of human actions. Unlike the natural sciences, they can talk with their data.

Nevertheless, the human sciences have much in common with these other two areas of knowledge. Like the natural sciences, they aim to make generalizations about their subject matter which can be well justified by careful observation. Like them, too, human sciences seek to identify broad regularities within their subject matter, for instance, *trends* in social or economic activity, *common features* to be compared across all cultures, or *kinds* of psychological behaviour or thought. They do not make claims about "all" people (chapter 7), but about "many" or "most". Their goals include both providing an accurate *description* of what human beings are like across large populations and *explanation* of why they are that way. In identifying correlations and testing for causes, they are guided, as are the natural sciences, by theories and models. These provide a shared frame of reference for their investigation and exchange of knowledge.

The human sciences also possess many of the features of history, with its tension between *particular* events and *general* understanding. History records *unique* events set in particular places and times, that pass with the era. At the same time, though, it interprets the human past in causal terms, providing insights into broad patterns and connections that stand to make it valuable for understanding the present. The human sciences can usually go further than history in identifying regularities, since they can repeat their observations of the same or similar events.

Knowledge in the human sciences shares characteristics of *map making* and characteristics of *storytelling*. Within the metaphor of maps and stories, maps zoom back from the territory to represent a generalized overview in which particular features of the landscape lose their distinct identity. The natural sciences are characteristically map-knowledge. Stories, though,

move close up to describe particular geographical spots and narrate the lives of particular individuals. Literature and history, within this metaphor, are characteristically story-knowledge. The human sciences are map-knowledge to the extent that they can generalize, and story-knowledge to the extent that they remain anchored in specific cases.

The characteristics of the human sciences are affected greatly by their combination of goals and subject matter – a combination that shapes the methods of this area of knowledge. Human scientists have developed their methods largely over the past century or so, gaining increasing understanding of both the limitations created by their human subject matter and the appropriate methods for gaining knowledge as reliably as possible within those limits.

## Complexities and challenges

As they seek the regularities in human action and thought, human scientists have to take into account a number of factors:

- Individuals are not identical in how they behave or think, and no two societies are the same. Moreover, both individuals and societies change over time: they are not static, but shift in many features such as choices they consider desirable to make. Broad generalizations on individuals and societies, therefore, will not apply to all members of the group generalized. Researchers in the social sciences vary in the

### For Reflection

What are your thoughts about the metaphor of stories and maps? Does this metaphor illuminate features of knowledge, or distort them?

Which of the following statements makes most sense to you?

1. Stories and maps represent different kinds of knowledge.

2. Stories and maps represent the same kind of knowledge, but at different scales of generality.

3. All areas of knowledge combine stories and maps, so that to separate them as we've done in this metaphor is misleading.

degree to which they emphasize the general case and look for universal features, or emphasize the particular case and examine the local and contingent nature of societies.

- Individuals and groups are enmeshed in complex webs of causal variables, just as we considered for history. Trying to trace particular causes within an interconnected society is difficult; human scientists cannot control all other variables while they test their hypotheses. They have to take this complexity into account in constructing their methods and offering their explanations.

- What or how human beings think is not directly observable. Human scientists have to devise methods to find out what people think, recognizing that *asking* them demands awareness of features of the questioning that affect the responses. Recent developments in cognitive science have extended the methods of study through imaging of the brain, as the human sciences overlap with the natural sciences.

- People react to being observed, changing their behaviour in numerous possible ways, and even changing their attitudes. Wouldn't you? Suppose that someone is entering your home or workplace to observe how you act, wouldn't you behave just a bit differently? Suppose that someone is asking you questions about your habits as a consumer, wouldn't you present yourself as being just a bit better?

- Human scientists involved in empirical research or fieldwork have to take into account their own humanity as they construct their methods in order to be on guard against their own personal responses, the personal responses they could induce in their human subject matter, and all manner of biases. They have to devise methods – such as blind studies and long-term observation – to try to minimize *themselves* as variables that influence the observation. Anthropologists also often make known their own cultural and theoretical background to readers, so that readers are able to take it into account.

- Although ethical issues arise in every area of knowledge, human scientists most particularly have to take into account the effect of their methods of investigations on their subject matter, with some kinds of testing deemed unacceptable: "Let's remove their altars and see what they'll do." "Let's declare a massive stock market crash and see if it fulfills our hypothesis about the effect on trading." Indeed, a sense of ethical responsibility is expected as a guide to research on human beings – respect for their rights, such as informed consent, and concern for the effect of the investigation upon them.

## Concepts: reliability, validity, generalizability

In both the human and natural sciences, experiments are designed seeking to maximize their reliability, validity, and generalizability.

"Is the experiment reliable?" is asking the question, "Will we get the same results if the experiment is repeated?"

- Internal reliability refers to results being consistent among different random samples, or the same random sample measured over a period of time.
- External reliability refers to other scientists being able to replicate the experiment in their own labs.

"Is the experiment valid?" is asking the question, "Is the experiment measuring what it claims to measure?"

"Are the results generalizable?" is asking the question, "Can the results obtained with a sample population be applied to the whole of the population?" In quantitative studies, such as surveys that collect countable data that can be treated statistically, random sampling ensures that the results can be generalized. In qualitative studies, such as ethnographies and focus groups, the question of generalizability is not at all simple.

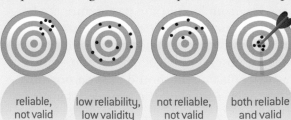

reliable, not valid    low reliability, low validity    not reliable, not valid    both reliable and valid

## Constructing appropriate methods

At moments, human scientists might well envy natural scientists, who do not have to take into account the sense of humour of their microbes, figure out ways to find out what their plankton is *really* thinking, or try to infer cultural meaning from the behaviour of gases. Having to be conscious of the humanity of their subject matter, human scientists construct methodologies appropriate to their particular disciplines – participant observation, for instance, for cultural anthropology, questionnaires and experiments for psychology, statistical analysis and construction of models for economics. The methods, as in every other area of knowledge, are ones suited to the subject matter being studied.

Just as the research methods fit the subject matter, so do the kinds of results, for instance the nature of the explanations that an area of knowledge can provide. In the chapter on history, we placed emphasis on *perspectives* in the writing of different histories – perspectives of historians and those of their societies on the record of the past. We will not be leaving this idea behind. In the human sciences, the interpretations lean towards the more general explanations of human behaviour and thinking provided by *theories*.

In both the human sciences and the natural sciences, theories have a central function of bringing together individual researchers in such a way that they can contribute their small pieces to a larger shared inquiry. Theories give a shared direction for investigation, shared concepts and vocabulary for exchange of findings, and a shared way to interpret and understand the results.

## Learning how to learn

Admittedly, people have been interested in individual psychology and social organization for as long as we have records – for what could be more interesting than ourselves? Literature and history from long in the past demonstrate interest in human motivation and behaviour, and philosophy gives us a long tradition of considered observation, reflection, and argument on how people do and should act and organize their societies. However, the human sciences,

> …we see the lives of others through lenses of our own grinding and … they look back on ours through ones of their own.[4]
>
> *Clifford Geertz*

applying the methods of the sciences to human beings, are a relative newcomer as an area of knowledge.

Although important antecedents can be found looking back across centuries, the area of knowledge of the human sciences has developed largely since the nineteenth century. Much of its development has involved the process of learning how to learn – developing research methods and a body of research results to draw upon as evidence. Debates have centred on the most significant questions to ask, the appropriate methods of investigation, and the most fruitful theories for giving direction to research and interpretation of results. The shifts in methods and theories in the human sciences across the twentieth century make an extremely interesting story within knowledge.

## Cultural anthropology: development as human science

The development of social and cultural anthropology is a particularly interesting story of an emerging discipline. It tells us a great deal about the influence on knowledge of currents of thought in the background and a great deal about the construction of methodologies of study.

Anthropology of the nineteenth century was still "armchair anthropology" based on missionaries' stories and travellers' stories. This information was gathered without any systematic investigation. Although early anthropologists contributed ideas that are still significant, such as the importance of kinship structures and questions regarding universal patterns of thinking,[5] their work was largely framed by a belief in social evolution – that is, that humans advance from primitive civilizations to advanced civilizations (like their own).

---

4   Geertz, C. 2000. *Available Light: Anthropological Reflections on Philosophical Topics*. Princeton. Princeton University Press. P 65.

5   Eriksen, T.H. 2010. *Small Places, Large Issues*. London and New York. Pluto Press. Pp 12–14.

## Ethics and anthropology

What ethical restraints do we recognize as we seek knowledge? This running question found a particular focus recently in the discovery of an "uncontacted" tribe in Peru. When they have been seen or encountered, the Mashco-Piro tribe makes it clear that they want no intruders. Is it unethical to try to find out more about these people? Although they live in a national park, they are threatened by illegal logging and oil projects. Contact usually brings disaster for remote tribes in the form of disease or violence. You can learn more on the website of *Survival International: the movement for tribal peoples.*

Both their methods and their framing concept of social evolution were later replaced with the advent of more investigative and theoretical grounding to gaining knowledge. Franz Boas, a major founder of contemporary anthropology at the opening of the twentieth century, insisted on the need for a more particularizing perspective on societies. He insisted on meticulous collection of data and the need to understand each culture in its own terms (cultural relativism). He applied his ideas in doing significant research in the 1890s with the North American Inuit and Kwakiutl Indians. A second major founder, Bronislaw Malinowski, developed his ideas while doing fieldwork over four years (1914–18) with the Trobiand Islanders of the South Pacific. He developed standards for participant observation and for writing ethnographies, the field reports that still form the basis for anthropology. These are holistic descriptions of cultures that synthesize the information gathered through observation, field notes, interviews (often filmed in recent years), and questionnaires. These give anthropology its grounding as a discipline, and provide detailed evidence on particular cultures for comparative conclusions about features of cultures in general.

In the second half of the twentieth century, after the Second World War, anthropology developed further in major ways. For one thing, theoretical debate increasingly pulled anthropology between generalizing and particularizing perspectives: to what extent are societies similar, and to what extent unique?

Attempts to find universal cross-cultural characteristics fostered several different approaches, including:

- "structural-functionalism (all societies operate according to the same general principles),
- structuralism (the human mind has a common architecture expressed through myth, kinship and other cultural phenomena),
- transactionalism (the logic of human action is the same everywhere) and
- materialist approaches (culture and society are determined by ecological and/or technological factors)."[6]

At the same time, these attempts to generalize were countered by insistence on focusing on the individual and particular nature of cultures. Indeed, anthropologists looking more closely at sub-groups within societies questioned the very concept of "culture" as a coherent unit for analysis, stressing the diverse components that make up the whole. These contrary pulls between the general and the particular have been behind further changes in anthropological thought in the late twentieth century.

One change was in the relationship between the observed and observer. Colonized peoples, who had earlier been studied as subject matter for investigations, began to assert their own interpretations of their own societies: they were no longer just the *observed* but also *observers*

---

6  Eriksen, T.H. 2010. *Small Places, Large Issues*. London and New York. Pluto Press. P 6.

> "
> Just as there is a biological web of life, there is also a cultural and spiritual web of life—what we at the National Geographic have taken to calling the 'ethnosphere.' It's really the sum total of all the thoughts, beliefs, myths, and institutions brought into being by the human imagination. It is humanity's greatest legacy, embodying everything we have produced as a curious and amazingly adaptive species.[7]
>
> *Wade Davis*
> "

themselves. As a growing diversity of voices joined a growing field, the "etic" or *outside* perspective of the anthropologist was complemented by the "emic" or *inside* perspective of the observer commenting on his own society, with the terms coined in the 1950s.

Another change has been in the understanding of the central concept of *culture*. By the 1980s, even the emic/etic distinction was thrown into question, with increased recognition that cultural groups do not really have boundaries that would justify the distinction between insider and outsider, and that people have multiple identity groups. Anthropologists are presently giving increased attention to subcultures within their own heterogeneous societies. Anthropology has never, in any case, taken the study of remote societies as its goal, but rather the study of humanity across all space and time, with previously remote cultures providing case studies for structured comparisons.

In its development over more than a century, anthropology has contributed to revealing *ourselves* to *ourselves*. The discipline started in the nineteenth century with a mode of thinking that was pervasive in European society. It was profoundly *ethnocentric* – that is, Europeans evaluated all other cultures in terms of their own and found them, as a result, inferior. Anthropology has changed to illuminate the very nature of ethnocentric thinking. As Clifford Geertz has asserted:

> We [cultural anthropologists] have been the first to insist on a number of things: that the world does not divide into the pious and the superstitious; that there are sculptures in

jungles and paintings in deserts; that political order is possible without centralized power and principled justice without codified rules; that the norms of reason were not fixed in Greece, the evolution of morality not consummated in England. Most important, we were the first to insist that we see the lives of others through lenses of our own grinding and that they look back on ours through ones of their own.[8]

Cultural anthropology, to which Geertz is referring, belongs within a wider discipline of anthropology that includes three other fields: archeology, biological anthropology, and linguistic anthropology. Though psychologists and economists might have other views, anthropologist Eric Wolf places the whole of anthropology interestingly within a knowledge spectrum:

> [Anthropology] is less a subject matter than a bond between subject matters. It is in part history, part literature; in part natural science, part social science; it strives to study men both from within and from without; it represents both a manner of looking at man and a vision of man – the most scientific of the humanities, the most humanist of the sciences.[9]

## Cultural anthropology: methods of study

Given the challenges of their subject matter, what methods do the human sciences use? We will first stay with anthropology, taking a quick look, and then move on to the rather different methods of psychology and economics.

---

[7]   Parsell, D. 28 June 2002. "Explorer Wade Davis on Vanishing Cultures," National Geographic.

[8]   Geertz, C. 2000. *Available Light: Anthropological Reflections on Philosophical Topics*. Princeton. Princeton University Press. P 65.

[9]   Eric Wolf cited in T.H. Eriksen. 2010. *Small Places, Large Issues*. London and New York. Pluto Press. P 1.

## For Reflection

Consider further Eric Wolf's placement of anthropology within a spectrum of areas of knowledge. In what ways do you see his description as appropriate for anthropology? Are there some features of his placement in the spectrum that you might question? Why?

Cultural anthropology faces some challenging knowledge questions:

- What is culture? How does the definition affect what is studied and how?
- How can we know how people in other cultures behave and think? What methods of study are appropriate to the subject matter?
- In what terms can we compare different cultures for meaningful knowledge of universals or the range of human possibility?

The major method of anthropology is *participant observation*: the anthropologist does fieldwork by living with a group over a period of time, usually around a year, but possibly more and possibly with return visits for comparisons over time. Present during daily life, he forms a relationship with people such that he can participate and talk with them, if possible learning the language, but otherwise using a translator. Not only does he observe behaviour, then, but he can also interview people and possibly use questionnaires, gaining information on facets of current life, life histories, and genealogies. Although a pen and a journal were the tools of the early anthropologists, more recent audio and visual technology have generated new kinds of records and made it easier to discuss the recorded material with members of the group. Ultimately, though, the anthropologist tries to do something yet more difficult: to try to understand the meaning that people attach to their actions and their world.

Theory plays an important role. The anthropologist enters a culture with a theoretical framework for focusing observation on particular features of a society, giving attention to features of a culture such as kinship structure, gender relations, power relations, symbolism, social change, or

exchange. This theoretical framework allows anthropologists to compare different cultures in the same terms and evaluate the different meanings attached to each of these features across different cultures

At the end of the period of observation, the participant anthropologist produces his observations in the form of an ethnography – a written profile of the society at the particular time. Every ethnography provides material for anthropologists sharing knowledge and drawing comparisons. (See "Senses and Anthropological Sensibilities" chapter 13.)

As human beings ourselves, thinking about human beings researching human beings, we can probably foresee some of the challenges of this research. It is one thing to recognize that ethnocentrism exists, for example, and quite another to overcome it! With background study in different cultural possibilities, anthropologists try to lay aside the values of their own cultures to understand the societies they are studying in their own terms. They call this stance "cultural relativism" – an attempt to see "from the inside" what the members of the cultures mean by their behaviour, and how they view the world. (By the way, the open-minded stance of *cultural relativism*, consciousness of personal cultural biases and suspension of judgment for the purposes of study, is not equivalent to *ethical relativism*, the belief that all morality is a matter of perspective and that there can be no absolutes.)

Altogether, the greatest challenge for the anthropologist is one he shares with researchers in all areas of knowledge – to use his *ways of knowing* with consciousness and care. Interpretation is an integral part of our sense perception, as we considered earlier in this book. We receive the sights and sounds of a typical street in our own town, for instance, with learned cultural

> " …other cultures are not failed attempts to be us; they are unique manifestations of the spirit—other options, other visions of life itself.[10]
>
> *Wade Davis*

---

[10] Parsell, D. 28 June 2002. "Explorer Wade Davis on Vanishing Cultures," National Geographic.

understanding. We see or hear, and instantly interpret our surroundings: the traffic light that changes and its relationship with the flow of traffic, the post that is marked "bus stop" with the people gathering at it, the calls of a street vendor, the shops that may be open or closed depending on the time, the men passing in suits, the woman sitting on the sidewalk with a begging bowl in front of her, or a wailing siren coming closer. Is it even possible to describe what we see in a way that does not presuppose a particular way of understanding, especially when that understanding affects the language that we use, our very word choice and phrasing?

To give you some sense of anthropological thinking, we offer you the activity "You are

> "
> Culture is not an exotic notion studied by a select group of anthropologists in the South Seas. It is a mold in which we are all cast, and it controls our daily lives in many unsuspected ways.[11]
>
> *Edward Hall*
> "

the anthropologist". We leave anthropology as a discipline within the human sciences, then, with a final question regarding shared knowledge: What can the shared knowledge of cultural anthropology contribute to our own personal knowledge? It might be a great deal!

## Discussion Activity

### You are the anthropologist

What are the challenges that an anthropologist faces in studying human beings, and what awareness and method does he need? The following activity will give you a small taste of anthropology. We recommend doing it in class while working in pairs, but coming together at the end for group discussion.

1   Choose one picture here that represents something familiar to you. (Feel free to

substitute an image of your own as long as it requires cultural knowledge for accurate interpretation.) Partner with someone choosing a different image.

2   First try to lay aside your understanding of what the photo represents. Describe what you see using language as neutral as you can make it. Try not to make judgments about what is important in the picture, about what the purpose is

---

[11]  Hall, E.T. 1959, reprinted 1981. *The Silent Language*. Toronto. Anchor Books. P 29.

of actions, or about what people intend or think. Then exchange your writing with your classmate to check each other's work for any cultural interpretations or judgments that may have slipped in. Discuss the following questions.

- What factors make it difficult to write completely neutrally?
- In what ways is knowledge gained by observation from a distance (as if people were flocks of birds) beneficial to understanding human culture? What are its limitations?
- How long would you have to observe to be able to infer the meanings of actions reliably?

3   Now imagine that you are a very bad observer – someone with no inside knowledge of the culture, no anthropological training, and no hesitancy over judging what you see. Use your imagination (and possibly your sense of humour) and have fun here. How could the photo you chose be described by someone who imposes interpretations that sound plausible but are *completely incorrect?* Write your interpretation and again exchange with your partner. Discuss the following questions.

- What is ethnocentrism?
- Why do anthropologists adopt a position of cultural relativism in their fieldwork? (Do not confuse this term with moral relativism.)
- In what ways can trying to think in terms of this anthropological approach affect our own personal experiences of contact with people of different cultures?

4   Now imagine that you are a trained anthropologist investigating the culture shown in the photograph you chose. Not only can you observe your data, but you can also communicate with it! All the same…you might foresee some difficulties with being able to communicate effectively and find out what you want to know. Again, work with your partner and study the two photographs that you chose. Make a list of difficulties to acknowledge and/or overcome. For example:

- Do you need an interpreter? How dependable is translation?
- Can you think of any of your own personal characteristics that might affect what information you are able to gain?

Remember, the observer and the observed are both human beings. Put yourself imaginatively in both roles: the anthropologist who wants to know and the people who are revealing their lives and their thinking.

5   Last, move to a full class group for further discussion.

What difficulties did each pair identify in question 4? Collectively, generate a shared list, along with suggestions of ways of dealing most effectively with problems that come up.

What personal qualities and skills would the ideal anthropologist possess? Which of these is not necessary for an historian or a natural scientist? What personal qualities should the anthropologist *not* have, such as a bad temper and tactlessness?

Like natural scientists and other human scientists, cultural anthropologists observe with theory and hypotheses that could be modified by observations. Even without having the theoretical background yourself, what kinds of themes or areas of study do you think emerge from these photographs and the human behaviour they display?

6   Follow-up questions:

- *concepts and language:* How does the definition you adopt of "culture" affect what you look for as you observe?
- *links to personal knowledge:* What do you think you gain through recognizing what anthropology studies? What do you think you would gain if you studied it yourself?

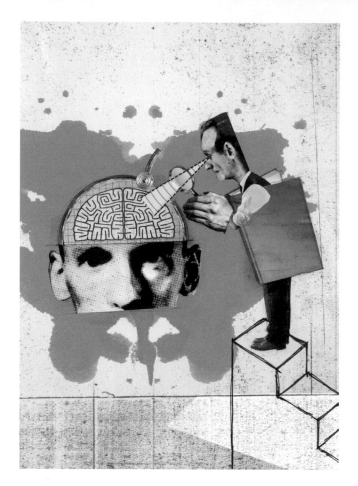

## Psychology: development as a human science

Psychology has its roots in ancient thought in many cultural traditions, with ideas of human nature, relationships between the body and the mind, inner feelings and the spirit or soul. Interest in what we can conceive of as *the mind* was developed within philosophy, the precursor to many contemporary areas of knowledge. Philosophy's reservoir of observation, introspection, reflection, and argumentation influenced many threads of psychology as it developed as a human science. Although it is impossible to specify exactly when a discipline begins within currents of thought and multiple contributions that provide antecedents for later theory and study, psychology as a human science could be argued to emerge in the late nineteenth century and to develop extensively in the twentieth century.

In combining interest in the mind with methods of experiment, psychology began in Europe and the United States. Wilhelm Wundt in Germany established the first psychology lab in 1879 as well as a journal of psychology, and applied the method of experiment to study how people responded to external stimuli through sensation and perception. His results were replicable and thus Wundt is credited with establishing psychology as a science.

Numerous other individuals also made significant personal contributions to the growing shared knowledge within psychology. Sigmund Freud in Austria developed his approach of psychoanalysis, analysing patient case studies in terms of the unconscious mind and the mechanism of repression, while Carl Jung developed ideas of archetypes, the collective unconsciousness, and personality types of the extrovert and introvert. In the United States, William James opened a laboratory for demonstration to support courses he was teaching at Harvard, and contributed the textbook *Principles of Psychology* that influenced the questions psychology asked long into the following century. He explored his own mind through introspection, reporting on what caught his attention, on how he experienced emotions, and on his own "stream of thought".

At the end of the nineteenth century, debates in Germany over preferable methods of introspection set the stage for the rejection of introspection as an experimental method altogether.

## Behaviourism and cognitive psychology: theories

The twentieth century in psychology was dominated by two major successive theories – behaviourism and cognitivism. Behaviourism in the first half of the century reacted against the subjectivity of introspective methods and aimed to model the study of consciousness on the methods of the natural sciences, through observation of external behaviour without introspection for mental states.

Behaviourism succeeded in providing experimental justification for its conclusions, and thereby moved psychology out of the speculation of philosophy into the sciences. For example, it recast the long-standing philosophical debate between free will and predestination by God in empirical terms. Do individuals choose freely how they act? Psychology looked for the answer not in metaphysical concepts but instead in the effect of experience and the environment.

Behaviourists gave their attention, as a result, to the effect of *conditioning* on human behaviour. They studied positive and negative reinforcement of actions. Two key figures were John Watson, who founded behaviourism, and B.F. Skinner, who investigated through experiments the role of reward and punishment in affecting behaviour. Many behaviourist experiments involved tests run in laboratories with animals (such as white mice running through mazes) with extrapolation to human beings (a form of reasoning often argued to be problematic). Although the theory and its methods are no longer current, behaviourism succeeded in bringing attention to the impact of the environment on how human beings act, with implications for arguments for social change. It also contributed to ideas on conditioning that still affect marketing campaigns today.

In a similar manner, behaviourist psychology recast in experimental terms the philosophical idea that human beings are born as "blank slates" on which their experience from birth writes all their knowledge. It assumed no mental states or innate knowledge and experimented entirely with external influences. This rejection of mental states, which at first enabled behaviourist psychology to establish its scientific credibility and its methods, in the end proved to be its limitation.

You may recall the story of B.F. Skinner and Noam Chomsky that we recounted in chapter 8 on language, and their debate at the end of the 1950s over how we learn language. Since that time, behaviourism has been left behind as psychology has joined with other disciplines in the cognitive sciences.

Psychology no longer focuses only on observable behaviour but also on internal mental states, and uses empirical research methods to study how people perceive, think, remember, and learn. To the methods of study available to earlier generations, it has added direct imaging of the brain. It is not surprising that the section of this book on ways of knowing was influenced by findings in cognitive psychology; it is now a discipline that tells us a great deal about knowledge and the process of knowing. Indeed, cognitive psychology courses are often offered to future teachers so that they can learn how best to present knowledge in ways their students can apply and retain it.

## Methods and metaphors

A distinction has often been made between "outside" methods of the human sciences in observation and "inside" methods of asking the data under observation what they think. That distinction becomes increasingly fuzzy with the development of cognitive sciences. We raise it here simply to highlight that the outside/inside distinction is, after all, *a metaphor*. It can be used to apply to different kinds of distinctions, and always stands to be questioned.

The metaphor of an "inside" approach to knowing human beings has sometimes been used to represent a leap to believing that we understand others, through our being human beings ourselves. This approach to knowing is appropriate to literature and, argues Isaiah Berlin, also to history in the "verstehen" approach. It involves emotional engagement of empathy and imaginative identification with how other people would feel in particular circumstances, based on one's own experience and understanding of people.

In the human sciences, however, anthropology has exposed our ethnocentrism and raised some serious questions regarding the degree to which we really can assume that others think and feel as we do. Experiments in cognitive psychology have also suggested that we often believe erroneously that others must think as we do. This approach of "understanding", then, is problematic when applied beyond literature to the real world. Although it could lead to empathetic attitudes towards other people, in the end it can also lead to faulty interpretation of other people's actions.

## Method: experiments in psychology

Experiments in psychology have demonstrated both the complexity of studying human beings and the ingenuity of psychologists in setting up tests that tell us something significant about how human beings respond and think. We select a few examples here, which are spread across the last century, to illustrate different features of this human science.

### Experiment and the Hawthorne effect

One early set of psychological experiments ended up revealing a great deal about human behaviour in the *failure* of their hypothesis, and the reasons given for that failure. The experiments at the Hawthorne Electric Company attempted to study human behaviour in its natural setting, in this case, women working on factory assembly lines in the 1920s in the United States. Researchers hypothesized that improved lighting would increase worker productivity.

They tested in different ways – by raising and lowering lighting on control groups, and then changing lightbulbs in the sight of the women and telling them that the new bulbs were brighter (though they were identical). Regardless of whether the lighting improved, worsened, or stayed the same, however, the productivity continued to rise. The researchers concluded that the women under observation were affected by the very fact of being given the attention of the study.

These experiments and others at the Hawthorne Electric Company have recently come under criticism for their reliability, as data lost from that time has been recovered and seriously questioned.[12] However, the phenomenon of human response to being studied has been well documented since then, and is still often

## Discussion Activity

### Argument and evidence

The following two graphs display results for a university entrance examination run in Chile until a few years ago. On the vertical axis of each are the examination points scored, and on the horizontal axis are the years of examinations (1996–2001). Both graphs represent the same school's results over the same period of time.

Which graph would be used by the school's Director to demonstrate to the Board of the school how well the students have been doing? Why?

Which graph would be used by an angry parent demanding an explanation for the school's terrible examination results in 2001? Why?[13]

Now choose an area of your own life which can be quantified and expressed as data (how many hours you spend studying, how much money or time you spend unproductively, how often you are particularly helpful, how often you are in conflict with someone else, or so forth). Present the data twice – once in the way most flattering to yourself, and once in a way much less flattering. Do not change the data. Change only the way in which it is represented. The graphs below may give you ideas, but you may also have ideas of your own.

Share results with the rest of your class. Then discuss together the expression "Let the data speak for itself." What does it mean? Can the data ever "speak for itself"? Is data informative without interpretation – without people doing the speaking?

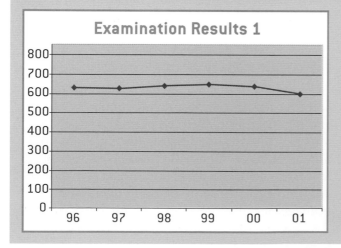

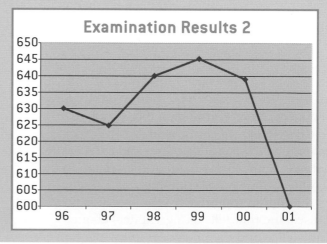

---

[12] "Light work: Being watched may not affect behaviour, after all". *The Economist*, 4 June 2009. http://www.economist.com/node/13788427 accessed 5 July 2012.

[13] Ministry of Education, Chile. 2003. "Filosofía y Psciología: Problemas de Conocimiento". Programa de Estudio de Educación Media. Pp. 129–130.

## A "blind" study?

What is a "blind study"? The expression sounds a bit like a self-contradiction, doesn't it? If you don't know already, find out what a *double*-blind study is as well as a *triple*-blind study. Blind studies are a splendid example of the development of methodology so that researchers can overcome biases in their study participants – and biases in themselves. Studying human beings does demand self-awareness and ingenuity!

referred to as the *Hawthorne effect*. Recognition of it has contributed to continued development of methodology: psychologists take into account the *placebo effect* and have developed *blind testing*, in which participants, and often even the experimenter, are denied information that might affect their responses and interaction.

## Milgram and Zimbardo: two renowned experiments

Unlike the Hawthorne experiments, the next two we consider here involved simulation or testing under controlled conditions. Typically in such experiments, participants are asked to do tests or respond to situations, while all the time under observation.

Milgram's famous experiment on obedience (1961), for example, gave participants the role of "teachers" administering electric shocks to an unseen "learner" (an actor) whenever he answered a question incorrectly. Despite the screams of pain from the learner, the majority of participants in their role as "teachers" continued to administer shocks in increasing voltage when the experimenter in charge insisted that they should do so. Obedience to the authority figure wearing the white coat overrode their moral objections and compassion. The tests, run while Adolf Eichmann was on trial for war crimes, posed questions on why Nazis acted as they did in the Holocaust. The results continue to be unsettling.

Zimbardo's Stanford Prison experiment (1971)[14] similarly used role play to investigate how the situations in which people were put might

## The placebo effect

One of the most fascinating ways our minds deal with justifications and belief is brought to light in cases where it seems that it is the *belief itself* that causes certain effects: for instance, people in pain (or exhibiting certain other symptoms of illness) given tablets or rituals that they believe will help them sometimes do indeed feel pain relief (or other improvement). This is called the "placebo effect". How we *think* about what we feel can affect what we *actually experience*.

This effect of belief on biological reality is immensely controversial. Many proponents of folk or alternative medicines claim that their products give direct biological cures. Their critics, however, insist that it is the belief in the cure that produces the effect. In the mind of the person cured, the cure becomes a further justification for the belief: it worked. (And what more could they want?) Yet, when many alternative remedies are tested in systemized studies, they are shown to make no difference at all. Critics of placebo-based medicines express concern that they deflect people from seeking real cures of illness in evidence-based medicine.

As a method of gaining knowledge, a placebo is often used in medical trials to create control groups to test the efficacy of particular treatments. In a common procedure, two groups of patients are given pills. One group is given the real pill and the other group is given an inert pill, a placebo, without the patients knowing which pill they have. All are then tracked to see whether the real pill does produce measurably better biological effects.

This kind of testing straddles the sometimes artificial divide between the natural sciences and the human sciences. Where does biology stop and psychology begin? Can we really separate the body and the mind?

change their behaviour. The participants, university students, were given roles to play as guards or prisoners in a "prison" in the

---

14 Zimbardo and Associates: The Stanford Prison Experiment. PsychExchange

basement of a building at Stanford University. As they became absorbed into their roles, the boundary blurred between reality and fiction, and increasingly they took on the social norms they associated with their assigned roles. The guards degraded, harassed, and intimidated the prisoners, and the prisoners acted fearfully with obedience and then group rebellion. Zimbardo himself reported that he became

involved in running the "prison" and lost sight temporarily of his role as the experimenter. The experiment, planned for fourteen days, was terminated after six. Hardly surprisingly, it has been criticized as being unethical (though with the knowledge of hindsight) and as insufficiently rigorous (small sample size, no repeated trials, duration of few days) for reliable conclusions to be drawn.

## Discussion Activity

### What makes a really bad questionnaire?

Imagine that you graduated 10 years ago with your International Baccalaureate diploma. A group of student researchers, trying to find out about the impact of international education, has decided to survey IB students of your graduation year. They have contacted those students for whom their schools have up-to-date contact information. You receive via email a link to a website, on which you are asked to fill in a questionnaire. What problems do you face in trying to do so?

**Questionnaire:**
**Your International Education**

1   **International Education:** How much of your IB education was international?

  ☐ all of it          ☐ a satisfactory amount
  ☐ none               ☐ not enough

2   **Creativity, action, service (CAS) in your IB Diploma Programme**

  **(a)** How many hours a week of service did you do during your IB Diploma Programme?

   ☐ 0–60 minutes     ☐ 2–3 hours
   ☐ 3 or more hours

  **(b)** How many hours a week have you contributed to doing service within the past year?

   ☐ 0–60 minutes     ☐ 2–3 hours
   ☐ 3 or more hours

  **(c)** How much money have you donated to international charities within the past year?

   ☐ 0          ☐ 1000       ☐ 3000
   ☐ 5000       ☐ more

**(d)** Are you satisfied with the number of hours and amount of money you have contributed?

  ☐ yes                    ☐ no

3   **International Outlook:** Do you believe that IB graduates have a more international outlook than non-IB graduates?

  ☐ yes                    ☐ no

4   **International Outlook:** On a scale of 1 to 7, rate how much more international your outlook is, having taken an IB diploma, than it would have been if you had not done so.

  ☐ 1   ☐ 2   ☐ 3   ☐ 4   ☐ 5   ☐ 6   ☐ 7

Several months later, you are sent a general report on the results of the survey. What difficulties do you face in accepting the researcher's conclusions?

### Questionnaire conclusions

1   Male graduates are more generous than female graduates. They have donated 15 per cent more to charities in the past year than female graduates have.

2   IB graduates contribute on average 15 hours a week to doing service.

3   IB graduates are 17.69 per cent less international in their outlook than are graduates of any other form of international education.

## Questionnaire discussion: round 1

Can you pick out the following?

- at least 10 flaws that make this questionnaire and its following interpretation unlikely to gather accurate and useful information
- at least 5 reasons why the conclusions stated cannot logically follow from information gathered through the questionnaire

## Questionnaire discussion: round 2

What skills must the human scientist possess to find out information through questioning? Perhaps nothing highlights the importance of skills more than their *absence*.

What advice for improvement would you give to the student researcher who sent you the questionnaire on the following features of the questionnaire?

- the method for gaining a sample of graduates
- the representativeness of the sample
- the assumptions seemingly made
- the choice of the particular questions to ask
- the choices of answers offered
- the definitions of terms
- the apparent bias in language
- the scales for evaluation
- the use of a control group (your alternate self without the IB diploma)
- the likelihood of accurate memory in reporting

- the likelihood of accurate answers as people report about themselves
- the precision of the statistics
- the consideration (or not) of alternate explanations of the impact of an international education

## Questionnaire discussion: round 3

If you have students of the human sciences in your class, they may be interested in taking the lead in commenting on general features of survey design and the role of questionnaires in providing evidence in research. Questionnaires are used in psychology, anthropology, sociology, and economics. Consider what you would need to do with care, as a critical thinker, when:

- planning your sampling technique for a large enough and representative sample
- wording the survey questions for clear communication that does not bias the answers
- drawing conclusions: moving from individual answers to statistical results, averaging or establishing correlations, and considering significant sources of error
- representing conclusions in language, numbers, and graphs.[15]

When you have thought about all of these issues, you may become a writer of surveys yourself, unleashed upon the world! Just, *please*, don't *ever* do any survey quite as bad as the one we invented for you for comment here!

---

15 Useful resource online: Centre for Psychology Resources, Research Methods. Athabasca University.

Milgram's experiments on obedience and Zimbardo's Stanford Prison experiment depend on *observation* of reactions and then *inference* to what they mean: we do not observe the minds of the participants directly to see the effect of the situation, but we *infer* conclusions, with an inevitable element of interpretation. These two remain among the most famous of all psychological experiments – largely because what we infer from them about human beings is as disturbing as it is revealing.

## Experiments in cognitive psychology

With the shift from behaviourism to cognitive psychology, experiments likewise shifted to focusing more directly on the process of gaining information. Do you recall the invisible gorilla experiment (1999) which we considered in the chapter on sense perception? The researchers were able to run the experiment repeatedly, in front of different groups of participants, to confirm their original results and reach conclusions on "inattentional blindness". No question arises about the validity of the experiment, as it clearly measures what it sets out to measure.

Another experiment by Chabris and Simon investigated *correlations* between two factors, as does much testing in psychology. Participants took two tests, designed to be of equivalent difficulty, several weeks apart. In each, they were asked to give responses of "true" or "false" to fairly challenging trivia questions, but also to rate their degree of confidence in their answers as a percentage. The results showed that people were overall 75 per cent confident, but that the accuracy of their answers was only 60 per cent. This suggested that most people express overconfidence. Moreover, by knowing how confident someone was on the first test, the researchers could predict how confident they would be on the second test. "Of those people who rated themselves in the top half on confidence in the first test they took, 90 per cent rated themselves in the top half on confidence in the second test."[16] Nevertheless, confident people did not score better on the tests. The researchers were able to conclude that confidence is not an indicator of accuracy.

Do you think you might have *known* this already, simply on the basis of your own observation? But what, then, does it mean to "know"? The conclusion of this experiment is particularly interesting in view of our apparent cognitive bias to believe – intuitively, without conscious analysis – that confident people know what they are talking about! (For further cognitive biases, see chapter 12.)

The Hawthorne experiment, Milgram's, Zimbardo's, and the two run by Chabris and Simon – these five examples, in many ways, catch key moments in the development of psychology. They stop short of the current major development. To recognize what goes on in our minds, psychologists are now able to take MRI scans of the brain to locate activity in response to particular kinds of stimuli, such as reactions to items in a questionnaire. A century ago, the human sciences set out to become more like the natural sciences in reaching conclusions based on evidence. In the present day, some parts of the human sciences are merging with the natural sciences, as psychology does with biology to form "cognitive sciences".

## Method: questionnaires

Just as experiments are a major method of gaining knowledge in psychology, so also is the survey. A survey is a widespread gathering of information through questionnaires. In this method, people are asked directly about themselves: their major leisure activities; their attitudes towards products, political parties, or proposed community activities; their habits as consumers; or their intentions in voting. Through these surveys, information can be gathered and evaluated statistically. The combination of ways of knowing shifts with the method: observation (sense perception) takes a back seat and ever-present language firmly takes the front.

What issues do psychologists have to take into account when designing surveys? We pass the question to you in the activity entitled "What makes a really bad questionnaire?" Be critical. Have fun. Note that it applies not specifically to psychology but more broadly to surveys, a method widely used in the human sciences.

---

[16] Chabris and Simon. P 100.

# Interview

## Economics: assumptions, predictions, and "externalities"

## Susan McDade, IB graduate 1983

*Susan McDade, a development economist, is the United Nations Resident Coordinator for Uruguay and the United Nations Development Programme representative. She was previously in the equivalent position in Cuba for four years, with long-term earlier positions in Guatemala and China. She has also been Manager of the Sustainable Energy Programme at UNDP headquarters in New York.*

→ In economics, dealing with human beings, is it possible to generalize and predict in the manner of the natural sciences?

Economics is not a pure science as its ability to predict price or market outcomes is limited. Moreover, many economic theories and analyses which have been developed to suit western European or North American social and market conditions are not easily transferable to developing countries.

→ What limits the ability of economics to predict?

Most economic theory used in western, or market-based economies, falls into the category of neo-classical economics. These theories have a number of assumptions in common. Although many of the assumptions can be pointed out to be weak or not always true, the line of argument goes that as long as the predictive quality of the theory holds true, or gives good results, it doesn't matter if the assumptions are not 100 per cent true. This is a major weakness and limits economic analysis. We should not be surprised that sometimes the predictive ability of economic analysis is very limited – and this often is linked to the weaknesses in the baseline assumptions.

→ What are these baseline assumptions?

The underlying assumptions include things like: markets will clear when supply and demand are mediated by prices, markets are rational, information flows freely, and people are individual utility maximizers. These assumptions can be major limitations in many places. Information certainly does *not* flow freely, especially if you are illiterate or offline – akin to the same thing as information technology permeates countries around the world. Moreover, consumers do *not* make their purchasing decisions solely based on what is best for them. Many consumers will make decisions that are guided by their community, the religious group that they belong to, or what they think might be best for their children, village or ethnic group in the future. They may in fact maximize some utility function other than their own.

Things that are not easy to measure or which are thought to be outside economic systems are considered "externalities". Until recently, this included environmental inputs like fresh air or extreme storms, but now economists see that these types of things do impact the ability of economies and price systems to function.

A sad but useful example of the limits of economic analysis is how we measure the cost of traditional energy delivery in poor countries. Fuelwood if cut, gathered and transported by a company with a truck has a price determined by the market in which it is sold. It reflects the cost of labour, the cost of the truck, and the fuel for the truck among other things. The same fuelwood collected by women and young girls, transported on their heads and backs and consumed at home is seen to be "free". Economists can compute the "opportunity cost" of that non-traded fuelwood but in this mathematics it is easier to value the transport costs represented by a mule than by an eight-year-old girl.

Similarly, the loss of ecosystems from land degradation caused by over-harvesting that fuelwood is not normally calculated, nor is the cost of illiteracy in the lives of the girls that cannot go to school while they are out collecting wood. So in short, this wood that is "free" may in fact have very high economic, social, and ecological costs that price systems and the market do not reflect at all.

Economic analysis is useful in providing a range of information to policymakers to assist in decision-making, but it is limited in its predictive value and will not capture transactions that cannot be easily observed, measured, or quantified. ■

### Follow-up questions

1.  Susan McDade identifies four "baseline assumptions" of neo-classical economic theory. What is the role of assumption within a theoretical perspective?

2.  McDade refers to "utility function" and says that people are not always "individual utility maximizers". What does this mean? Is neo-classical economic theory making assumptions about human nature?

3.  A theory is accepted, says McDade, if it gives good predictive results. What check for truth is used in this case? What could or should make a theory fail this test? How do we define a "good" result?

4.  What are "externalities"? Is it characteristic of theories in other disciplines that they illuminate only certain features and ignore others?

5.  Is economics neutral or value-free? In what ways do the particular "externalities" that Susan identifies here indicate value judgments within an economic perspective?

## Economics

Perhaps the greatest difference between economics and the other human sciences arises in the way its knowledge is *applied*. Economists are called on to give specific advice to businesses and governments. Decisions *will* be made, for instance, about on what and at what level to tax citizens, how much to spend on what issues, what and how to regulate. And economic theories play a large role in informing these decisions. But why is knowledge in economics applied in this way, and why is it given such influence over our lives? What is this human science all about?

There is a property common to all the moral sciences, and by which they are distinguished from many of the physical; that is, that it is seldom in our power to make experiments in them. In chemistry and natural philosophy [i.e. physics], we can not only observe what happens under all combinations of circumstances which nature brings together, but we may also try an indefinite number of new combinations. This we can seldom do in ethical, and scarcely ever in political science. We cannot try forms of government and systems of national policy on a diminutive scale in our laboratories, shaping our experiments as we think they may most conduce to the advancement of knowledge.[17]

*John Stuart Mill (1836)*

In the IB Course Companion to economics, Jocelyn Blink and Ian Dorton introduce economics as a study of the relationship between human wants and needs and the limited resources of the world.

> Human needs and wants are infinite. Needs are things that we must have to survive, such as food, shelter and clothing. Wants are thing that we would like to have but which are not necessary for our immediate physical survival, such as televisions and mobile phones.
>
> There is a conflict between the finite resources available and infinite needs and want. People cannot have everything that they desire and so there must be some system for rationing the scarce resources. This is where economics comes in.
>
> Economics is a study of rationing systems. It is the study of how scarce resources are allocated to fulfill the infinite wants of consumers.[18]

One of the key ideas in economics, then, is the idea of *scarcity*. We do not and cannot have the means to satisfy *all* our needs and wants, and therefore we must make choices. Our choices are affected by internal factors (such as motivation and desires) and external factors (such as availability of particular goods and services, laws and regulations). As the IB subject guide summarizes it, "The study of economics is essentially about

---

[17]  Mill, J. S. 1836. "On the Definition of Political Economy and the Method of Investigation Proper to It," in *Collected Works of John Stuart Mill*, 1967. Vol. 4. Toronto: University of Toronto Press. P 124

[18]  Blink, J. and Dorton, I. 2007. *Economics: Course Companion*. Oxford and New York. Oxford University Press. P 9.

dealing with scarcity, resource allocation and the methods and processes by which choices are made in the satisfaction of human wants.".

The "methods and processes" of choice are central to economics. Every choice for one thing, though, is a choice to give up alternatives – and economics considers this "opportunity cost" of choices. This concept contributes to goods being seen as relatively scarce and prices being placed on them.

When human choices are involved, it is not possible to make universal generalizations (e.g. "all consumers"); like the other human sciences, economics recognizes that human beings are not identical or entirely predictable. While it is possible to deal fairly precisely with very specific circumstances, generalizing broadly becomes much fuzzier. Like other human sciences and some parts of the natural sciences, economics gives us knowledge not about inevitable causal relationships but about general tendencies and broad trends.

## Assumptions

Basic to economics are concepts of how human beings act – concepts that provide the premises for economic reasoning. Human beings are assumed, first, to seek "utility" in their choices. That is, they make choices that will maximize the benefits they gain. Depending on different perspectives, the factors that increase *utility* might differ: for example, they might include monetary gain, novelty, status or simply enjoyment. The concept of utility also includes the possibility that choices that increase usefulness and personal pleasure could be ones to help other people.

Human beings are assumed, second, to make choices in a rational way, trying to gain the maximum utility. Economics does not look at motivations and feelings as psychology does, so in treating rationality looks not at the people but at the choices they make and treats them *as though* they are made in a process of balancing costs and benefits. For instance, if two shops are selling the same goods at different prices, consumers are likely to buy from the seller offering the lowest price (all other things being equal); it would be irrational to do otherwise.

This latter assumption about rational choice, though, has been questioned in recent years, in large part through the findings of behavioural economics. Behavioural economist and psychologist Dan Ariely, for example,[19] has identified numerous patterns of behaviour that undermine the assumption that people weigh costs and benefits to maximize utility. He has found, for instance, that people will make economic sacrifices themselves in order to get revenge for having their trust broken; they would rather punish the transgressor than make a financial benefit themselves. He has also found that economic incentives can backfire if the incentive is high. People are distracted by thinking about the reward, become stressed, and end up not performing as well. Taking such studies into account, we might be inclined to qualify economic assumptions of rational choice.

## Models

Using their assumptions, economists construct models – representations of the world in simplified terms – created as a tool for thought. They do so in order to be able to pick out particular sets of variables for closer study of the connections between them, such as between rates of unemployment and inflation, between the price of a good or service and the amount of that good or service sold in the market, or between consumer confidence and household expenditure.

Models provide tools for reasoning with a central role in enabling economists to be able to deal with particular features of subject matter otherwise overwhelmingly complex. As economist John Craven comments:

> An attempt to build an explanatory model that reflects every aspect of behaviour leads to a similar problem to that of a geographer who wants to draw a completely accurate map of a city, and finds that she can do so only by using a scale of one metre to one metre. A good explanation, like a useful map, tries to capture the *essential features* without becoming overburdened with detail.[20]

---

[19] Dan Ariely discusses these ideas in his books *Predictably Irrational* and *The Upside of Irrationality*.

[20] Craven, J. 1990. *Economics: An Integrated Approach to Fundamental Principles*. Cambridge, UK. Blackwell. P 11. (Italics added by author.)

## Symbolism and value

This gold coin of King Croesus of Lydia, now western Turkey, is one of the earliest coins ever used. What made it possible, 2600 years ago, to use a chunk of decorated metal as "currency"? What is the basis of the symbolic connection?

Like the coins and currency we use today, this ancient coin derived its worth from an authority with power – in this case, the king. The royal symbols of the lion and bull, and the social meanings of the Lydian silver and gold themselves, represented a social system in which kings held the wealth and power.

Today, the value of currencies is no longer attached to the value of the metal itself – a change that is the outcome of political power and will in modern history. Yet the meaning and the value attributed to them are still inseparable from the social institutions that make money part of organized social relations. As capitalism brings more resources and economic activity into the dynamics of market exchange and valuation, the modern coin – or modern money in all its forms – is given material and social meaning within the market.

### Questions for reflection

- Why do the coins you own have any value at all?
- What is the role of symbolism in your use of money? How does the use of money compare with other forms of symbolism discussed in chapter 8?
- To what extent does the use of money in your society require understanding of mathematics?
- Is having money important to you? If so, why? What gives it value to you?

A major challenge for economics, in a world where a causal web is so interconnected and complex, is to find those "essential features" and to try to account for, or explain away, the "detail". Economists build their models on data available and logical reasoning, drawing a relationship of variables that they will then test.

They usually represent their models numerically and visually, using equations or graphs. The law of supply and demand regarding the price of goods within a market, for example, can be represented by statements in language, however, the variables can be placed in relationship with each other much more clearly using graphs. The following graph shows the relationship between the price (P) and quantity (Q) of a good demanded (D) and supplied (S) within a market. As demand shifts from D1 to D2 (perhaps due to increased wealth) the equilibrium price also shifts (P1 to P2).

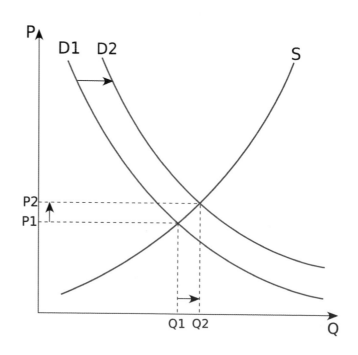

## Testing models

To test models against reality, then, economists work deductively: if the model is correct, then the variables that it places in relationship with each other should be consistently correlated – or else show a variability that can be explained. But how can testing be done in economics, when an entire society – or interconnected national economies – cannot be placed in a laboratory with the variables controlled?

Right from the start, economics accepts a degree of imprecision. In their methodology, economists use the "ceteris paribus" assumption – "all other things being the same" – an acknowledgment of simplification as they rule out factors that, in their judgment, are either not relevant to their particular study, or that are simply too difficult or impossible to measure or control for. They are not expecting a perfect correlation, nor an indisputable causal connection, but are looking, in very pragmatic terms, for what seems to work best.

Then, although they cannot run controlled experiments, they check their models using large data sets – statistics on the behaviour of people in large populations. For instance, they may use government statistical information across the population of a country, check financial institutions for such information as interest rates and loans, or check with firms that routinely gather data on consumer habits. The large data banks they consult may have been the result of tracking consumer behaviour, for example, or the outcome of large surveys equivalent to those done in psychology. In both microeconomics (studying individuals and firms) and macroeconomics (studying national economies), economists try to base their conclusions on data that provides a very large sample.

In a rough sense, it could be said that economists are constantly conducting experiments – or at least observing the effects within society of changes in variables. On the macro scale, a government adjustment to the interest rate could be seen as an experiment with fairly predictable results in most cases. (The *ceteris parabis* pragmatic assumption comes into play here.) On the micro level, if control randomized trials are carried out in enough contexts, they can be generalized and claimed to have "external validity" – that is, they translate to other contexts.

Economists likewise observe what are known as "natural experiments". When major variables have changed, for instance, through war, shifts in political power, discovery of major resources, or technological development, economists gather the data that allow them, in hindsight, to make connections between events that have already happened.

Indeed, current development of the fields of behavioural economics, development economics and a few other subfields do actually allow well-controlled field experiments. The main assumption is that control and treatment groups are large enough and comparable on a set of well-established economic, ethnic, geographic and other variables. A well-designed study or application (such as cash transfer program, introduction of a training, etc.) and a well-carried out statistical analysis lead to causal inference.

It has been argued that the increasing use of "econometrics" – mathematical analysis applied to the statistical data – bestows upon economics an aura of certainty that people associate with mathematics. That sense of exactitude, however, is an illusion, as economics draws all its numbers from human behaviour in complex interaction.

## Theoretical perspectives

In their adoption of models and interpretation of data, economists do not always agree. Just as there are different interpretations in history, and different theories in anthropology and psychology, there are different understandings in economics of what the "essential features" are of a model and how to interpret correlations observed.

A model is affected, inevitably, by the particular perspective within which it sits. In positive terms – that is, in factual terms – how is the market *described* as working, in terms of the central concepts used in analysis? In normative terms – that is in terms of values – how is it *prescribed* to work: that is, how *should* it work ideally?

There are many different perspectives and "strands of thinking" within economics, with some major differences, and other fairly nuanced and detailed differences. Two strands, for example, are neo-classical economics and neo-Keynesian economics: both are macroeconomic theories based on microeconomic principles. Both are concerned with economic growth, but see it differently. Neo-classical economists have greater belief in the ability of unfettered markets to allocate scarce resources most efficiently, where neo-Keynesians consider that markets, when left alone, can fail. Keynesians think that government intervention is important in certain circumstances to stimulate the economy, where classical economists tend to think that government intervention is a problem. When economists are given the role of guiding government decisions, therefore, it is clear that from different perspectives they might give different advice.

Similarly, what roles do different theories, with their models, give to the natural environment? Is the natural environment only to be regarded as a source of inputs ("natural capital") to the production process, or does it play a larger, more complex, and more important role as part of a model of sustainability? Economics has struggled to build more holistic understandings of the role and importance of the natural world, and the existing and growing sub-disciplines of environmental economics and ecological economics show that it is a concern that is not lost to all within the discipline. Questions of how to internalize environmental concerns and realities that were previously ignored, and how to properly assign economic value to environmental services for which there are no markets, are among questions that influence the work of a great number of economists working today.

Within the decision-making of societies, what role is economics given in ideas of achieving a less destructive, more sustainable world? The diagram on this page represents sustainability as a balance between society, the economy, and the environment – or social organization, the market, and the natural world. Economic issues are placed within a larger picture. As Carl Folke of the Stockholm Resilience Centre comments, "Humans have a tendency to fall prey to the illusion that their economy is at the very center of the universe, forgetting that the biosphere is what ultimately sustains all systems, both man-made and natural. In this sense, 'environmental issues' are not about saving the planet – it will always survive and evolve with new combinations of atoms – but about the prosperous development of our own species."[21]

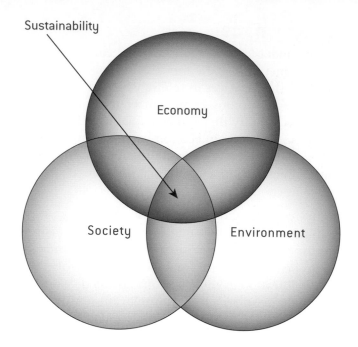

## Poverty: concepts and measures

Economics has always been concerned with wealth (one need look no further than the title of Adam Smith's famous *An Inquiry into the Nature and Causes of the Wealth of Nations*) and with the efficient allocation of resources. Recently, the conceptualization and detailed study of poverty has attracted much greater attention as the subject of major branches of economics, particularly at macroeconomic level. Not surprisingly, given the existence of competing strands of dominant economic thought, different theoretical perspectives conceive of poverty very differently, measure it in different ways, ascribe very different significance to its existence and prescribe very different remedies to its ills. How is "poverty" defined, then, and how does the definition that people accept affect how they measure it?

The activity we offer here on poverty, "What are 'facts' about poverty?", walks the very edge of TOK in that it asks you to do research for *information*. In TOK we emphasize inquiry into the nature of knowledge, not the facts on the ground! Yet, as in earlier activities on international works of art or the Benin plaques, you will find that the information you gain in research will improve your understanding of the knowledge questions that arise.

21  Carl Folke. 2012. Seed Magazine. http://seedmagazine.com/content/article/starting over/

## Discussion Activity

### What are "facts" about poverty?

The purpose of this activity is not centrally to learn more about poverty – though doing so is valuable in applying your critical thinking skills to the world. For TOK, knowledge questions arise when we consider how *what we know* is affected by the perspectives we take: the assumptions we start with, the essential concepts we include in our definitions, the methods of measurement we therefore choose, and the conclusions we draw.

We suggest that you work in small groups for this activity so that you can split the research, pool the results, and discuss information as you find it. If you have economics students in your class, they may well take a leadership role. When your groups have used up the time you can afford to give the research, gather as a full class to discuss the knowledge questions below.

### Research questions

- What is the difference between "absolute poverty" and "relative poverty", and how is each measured?
- What do the following measure and how do they measure it: Gross Domestic Product (GDP) and the Human Development Index (HDI)? What are the implications of accepting each of the methods of measurement for understanding poverty? How could accepting one or other potentially affect government policy decisions?
- How is poverty officially measured in your country? Identify how different measures

of what is "essential" affect statistics on the proportion of the population in poverty, and what segments within it are poor. Can you identify different ways of measuring poverty and wealth on the part of different political parties, such that the "facts" they possess might be different, even before they propose their solutions?

### Knowledge questions for discussion

- Why is the definition of concepts so important in the human sciences? Can you give examples of important definitions in each of the social sciences with which you are familiar? Are they universally accepted, *or* are they ambiguous, *or* defined clearly in different ways, *or* contentious?
- What are the implications of accepting one definition of a social reality rather than another in the human sciences?
- Can disputes regarding social reality be resolved by a simple and straightforward appeal to "the bare facts"?
- "Tell me your measure of who is poor and I will tell you what your values are." To what extent are definitions and measurement of social realities embedded in values, and the values in turn within larger theoretical and social perspectives?

### Useful resources available online

- United Nations Statistics Division. *Handbook on Poverty Statistics: Concepts, Methods and Policy Use.*
- The World Bank. Voices of the Poor.
- www.worldmapper.org. Links statistics to maps. Look for human development, wealth, poverty.
- www.gapminder.org. Presents statistics in dynamic and attractive graphs, with easy access to statistical breakdowns.
- www.odi.org.uk. Overseas Development Institute, UK. Resources include Simon Maxwell, "The Meaning and Measurement of Poverty."
- http://www.un.org/millenniumgoals/UN Millennium Goals
- http://bostonreview.net/BR31.4/contents.php. Banerjee, Abhijit. 2006. "Making Aid Work: How to Fight Global Poverty Effectively", *Boston Review*, July/August 2006.

# Knowledge about human beings

Of all the areas of knowledge that we consider in TOK, it is the human sciences that have developed most recently. They have antecedents in thought that go back centuries, but they have defined themselves as disciplines by the application of scientific methods to the study of human beings (as much as is possible). In developing methodologies of research, most prominently since the nineteenth century, they are able to justify their conclusions on the basis of evidence.

At the same time, the human sciences have exposed the difficulties of investigating human thought and behaviour in a scientific manner and have brought these inherent uncertainties to attention, to acknowledge these difficulties within their methods and the knowledge claims that emerge as their conclusions. As they have encountered shortcomings in their methodologies, they have often adjusted them, as anthropology has done in establishing the professional stance of cultural relativism and psychology has done in developing double-blind studies. Nevertheless, no methodology can remove the humanity from its subject matter, so that this area of knowledge works of necessity with variability and degrees of uncertainty.

In part because of the difficulties in generalizing about human beings, the human sciences are pulled in opposing directions. In one direction, they are pulled to identify broad patterns, universal characteristics of human behaviour, and scientific generalizations – general statements that explain trends, tendencies, and likelihoods (though not universal behaviour as in the laws of the natural sciences). In the other direction, they are pulled towards recognition of the specificity of each case and each context, and of the unwarranted nature of extrapolation from one context to all. Different theorists within the human sciences place emphasis more firmly either on the general patterns or the particular instances.

Anthropology, psychology, economics, sociology, political science, human geography – all of these disciplines studying the immense complexity of human thought and behaviour have their special areas of study. All of them, developing research methods and an archive of knowledge, have contributed greatly to our understanding of what it means to be a human being as an individual, and to be part of a society.

## Discussion Activity

### Knowledge framework: human sciences and history

First summarize your responses to these questions in your own words. Then exchange ideas with others in your class.

1. **Scope:** What are the subject matter and goals of history? What are the subject matter and goals of the human sciences? What do they have in common and how do they differ?

2. **Language/concepts:** What central concepts characterize these areas of knowledge? In what ways are the naming and defining of central concepts significant within both areas? In what ways is language as a way of knowing crucially important in these areas?

3. **Methodology:** What differences exist in the overall combination of ways of knowing used to create, share, and evaluate knowledge in these two areas? What challenges do they face, and what methods do they devise to gain the most reliable knowledge of human beings? How do history and human sciences build on knowledge within their areas in the past?

4. **Historical development:** How do history and the human sciences differ in their development over time?

5. **Links to your personal knowledge:** How do these two areas contribute to your own knowledge, both personal and shared?

In comparing human sciences and history, you will find much in common, as they both aim for factual description and explanation of human behaviour. Universities usually group them together. Yet in looking at them within the knowledge framework, you will also see differences that account for their being separated for attention in TOK.

# 19. The Natural Sciences

photo courtesy of NASA

## The scope of the natural sciences

- What do the sciences study? Don't miss the online videos "The symphony of science". They introduce central ideas in science in an imaginative way.
- What do the sciences study? For beautiful microscopic close-ups that illustrate regularities, mathematically describable patterns, and beauty in nature, have a look at the online galleries of Olympus BioScapes.
- What do the sciences study? For riveting images illustrating sea life and ocean geography have a look at Science Daily's online galleries on oceanography.
- What do the sciences study? NASA (North American Space Agency) has online galleries of particular projects and splendid astronomical images. These pictures bring together sophisticated scientific technology and awe-inspiring beauty.

## A note to students of natural sciences

In dealing with history as an area of knowledge, we suggested that students taking IB history could be a valuable resource for their TOK class in contributing ideas, examples, and skills they were learning in history. In dealing with the natural sciences now, we make the same suggestion: that students studying the natural sciences will contribute valuable ideas to class discussion. In this book, we deal with the natural sciences in very general terms. At all points, though, your whole class would benefit from connecting that general treatment with specific knowledge from your science class.

## Scope and methods

Carl Sagan once declared science to be balanced between seeming opposites in its search for truth: "At the heart of science is an essential balance between two seemingly contradictory attitudes – an openness to new ideas, no matter how bizarre or counterintuitive they may be, and the most ruthless skeptical scrutiny of all ideas, old and new. This is how deep truths are winnowed from deep nonsense."[1] The natural sciences can be argued to share their "openness to new ideas" and "skeptical scrutiny" with other areas knowledge, and even to hold similar central knowledge questions in common. However, they apply them to different subject matter and develop them into a distinctive methodology.

It is not actually the *knowledge questions* themselves that change as we enter this area of knowledge. The natural sciences share with history and the human sciences the same fundamental questions:

- *How* do we know? What methods can we use to investigate, and what justifications can we offer for our knowledge claims?
- *What* constitutes a true description of the world?
- *Why* is the world that way, or why are people that way? What causal interpretations or explanations can we give in this area of knowledge?

What changes is the *subject matter* of study. The natural sciences take within their scope not the human mind and human behaviour (with exceptions such as their part in the cognitive sciences) but instead the natural world and ourselves as a biological species within it. Their range of subject matter is immense: among other things, they study galaxies and subatomic particles, ecosystems and species, evolution and DNA, the movement of continental plates and sedimentary rock. They take on practical projects of all kinds, configuring carbon nanotubes or synthesizing

---

[1] Sagan, C. 1996. *The Demon-Haunted World: Science as a Candle in the Dark*. New York. Balantine Books. P 304.

medicinally effective rainforest products. They leave behind the complexities and challenges of studying human beings and take on complexities and challenges of their own. A whole world full!

With the shift of subject matter comes a shift in methodology. The natural sciences cannot use some methods of investigation; scientists cannot, for instance, interview their DNA or subatomic particles or give them questionnaires. However, they are able to use methods of observation to great effect. Moreover, with many human uncertainties removed, they are able to bring perspectives on knowledge much more into convergence than in history and the human sciences. As a result, knowledge is constructed to an increased degree as a collective endeavour, with scientists contributing within the same models and theories.

It may be the shared methodology that, above all, distinguishes the natural sciences. Admittedly, the knowledge *content* of the natural sciences ("knowing *that*") *also* has its characteristic features: the knowledge claims are observational statements about the world, accompanied by definitions, hypothetical statements, and predictions (page 45). But the specific knowledge claims change as we learn more and more. It is the knowledge *process* ("knowing how") that defines science and remains even when old knowledge is superceded by new.

## Knowledge of the natural world: general patterns

As we considered earlier, both history and the human sciences are pulled in their knowledge claims between particular instances and general tendencies:

- between particular events in history, and general historical patterns into which different perspectives would place them
- between features of particular cultures, and features that might be (or not) universal to all cultures
- between particular psychological experiments, and general tendencies that might be concluded about humanity
- about behaviour of consumers, and generalized economic trends in society.

These areas of knowledge generalize inductively, as far as they can, to identify broad categories,

tendencies, and trends. The degree to which they can generalize, though, depends on the degree of regularity and consistency of what they are observing. How regular, we might ask, are human beings in their behaviour? Well, we human beings share plenty of similarities that allow for broadly applicable knowledge claims, but we do not have identical minds, societies and cultures, or economic behaviour. We escape universal ("all") generalizations!

Similarly, although natural scientists can generalize more extensively than do human scientists, the extent to which they do so depends on what phenomena they are studying and how regular they observe them to be. It might also depend on the present development of knowledge: perhaps we will recognize the regularities that we are missing today only in hindsight tomorrow!

Among the natural sciences, biologists make fewer universal generalizations than do physicists, for instance, simply because of what they study. Certainly, they do make some universal knowledge claims: for instance that all phenomena of life are consistent with the laws of chemistry and physics; or that the cell is the fundamental unit of life; or that life is continuous across generations; or that life evolves.[2] However, dealing with living systems,

## Scales of knowledge

It may be the level of abstraction, rather than features of the basic process of reasoning, that marks the difference between traditional indigenous knowledge and the knowledge of the natural sciences. Or at least such is the argument put forth by Lilian "Na'ia" Alessa in "Scales of Knowledge", which you will find in the chapter on indigenous knowledge.

Alessa refers to contemporary science as "western". To what extent is contemporary science in fact built by *numerous* cultures of the past? Can you suggest why, from a native North American perspective, the natural sciences are called "western"?

As we create maps of knowledge at larger and larger scales of overall generality, what do we gain, and what do we leave out?

---

[2] Akif Uzman. 25 September 2005. Natural Science Department, UHD. Houston Urban Network for Science, Technology, Engineering and Mathematics.

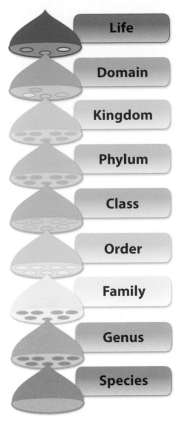

↑ Taxonomic hierarchy

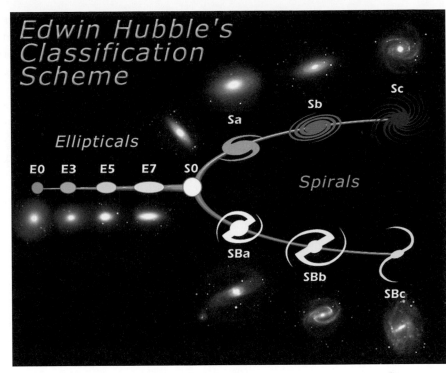

↑ Hubble's classification system for galaxies

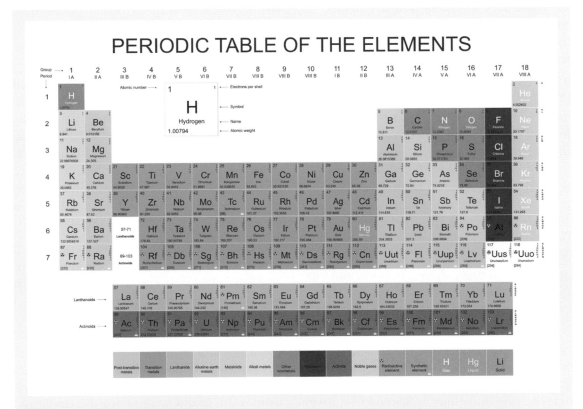

### The periodic table of the elements

The periodic table is a diagrammatic representation of a general pattern that chemistry has found in the world. Does the periodic table *describe* the world, or *explain* the world? What is the difference between these two terms, and what is necessary to qualify for each?

biologists confront enormous complexity. It may be, for instance, that one cause does not have one effect, but that a cluster of causes may produce a range of effects – not a one-to-one relationship but a many-to-many relationship, as in the relationship of genes to their effects. Moreover, scientists face further challenges in dealing with complex systems, which have to be seen for the whole rather than reduced to parts. According to biologists Dhar and Giuliani, "Finding fundamental organizing principles is the current intellectual front end of systems biology".[3] You may want to turn ahead for a moment to the chapter on mathematics, for comments of a biological researcher on organizing principles and mathematical expression in biology.

Whether or not their area of study possesses easily identifiable regularities, natural scientists are out to find them. They attempt to make generalizations about entire categories of things and their causal relations with each other. To the extent that their area of study allows, their goal is to make generalized knowledge claims that are true, universal, necessarily the case (not accidental), and applicable to the world.

At the same time, they recognize that statements that generalize to "all" members of a category cannot be made with certainty, as we considered in the chapter on reason (page 115). They are always on the lookout for that anomalous black swan that falsifies a universal generalization.

The generalizations that scientists make frequently take the form of classification: categorizing all living things into a biological taxonomy, for instance, or categorizing all elements within the periodic table. Clouds are classified as cumulus, stratus, cirrus, and nimbus; rocks are classified as igneous, sedimentary, or metamorphic; galaxies are classified in the Hubble "tuning fork" sequence as elliptical, normal spiral, or barred spiral; subatomic quarks are classified into six flavours: up, down, strange, charm, bottom, and top. Although categorization is always open to challenge, general patterns observed in nature allow knowledge about a whole category, and about all its members.

Of all the general patterns that scientists seek, though, perhaps the most significant in furthering knowledge are universal causal relationships. As relationships of cause and effect withstand extensive testing, over time, they are increasingly accepted into the body of scientific knowledge claims. Ultimately, they may become "laws of science" – generalizations that are based on extensive evidence with no falsifying instances. Scientific laws are expressed as compactly as possible, in simple statements or in mathematical formulae.

As an example, Boyle's law, one of the gas laws in chemistry, places in relationship to each other the volume, temperature, and pressure of a gas in a closed container. When the quantity of any one of the three changes, one or both of the others must change to keep the relationship constant. With the pressure (P), volume (V), temperature (T), and a constant (k) all represented by symbols, the relationship is expressed in a simple equation: $PV = kT$. The universal relationship allows us to predict what will happen as we change any of the variables. Robert Boyle established this law in 1662, and it remains to this day.

"There is…a rhythm and a pattern between the phenomena of nature which is not apparent to the eye, but only to the eye of analysis," commented physicist Richard Feynman, "and it is these rhythms and patterns which we call Physical Laws."[4]

## Natural sciences and religion

It is worth noting here, because of frequent misunderstandings, that the natural sciences neither refute nor support spiritual or religious interpretations of the universe and the human role within it. Although scientists *as people* have beliefs of all kinds, and may personally accept or reject religion, the natural sciences *as an area of knowledge* deal only with the material natural world, and have nothing to say about deities.

Moreover, there is no necessary contradiction between scientific explanations of the universe and religious ones. The sciences describe the world and give material explanation: they talk about "how" and "why" in material terms. Religious explanations place the whole of scientific explanation in a larger envelope, giving accounts of purpose and meaning in terms that lie outside the domain of the sciences. The sciences can tell us that the world began with the Big Bang and that human beings developed on earth through a

3  Dhar, P.K. and Giuliani, A. 2010. "Laws of biology: why so few?" *Systems and Synthetic Biology*. Vol. 4(1), P 7–13.
4  Richard Feynman, 1985. The Character of Physical Law. 1964 Messenger Lectures. Cambridge and London, M.I.T. Press. p. 13.

process of evolution, but they do not and cannot say whether or not the mechanisms of the world they observe are the work of a deity, or whether or not they have a spiritual meaning.

## Shared knowledge

In turning now from the scope and kind of knowledge the natural sciences seek and towards the seekers themselves, we are entering more emotional, imaginative, personal, variable territory. Although scientists make generalizations about the natural world, they can make no equivalently secure generalizations about themselves as human practitioners of the sciences! As soon as our subject matter is the human mind or human behaviour, we are back to the rougher categories of the human sciences, with many human qualities to take into account.

---

## Discussion Activity

### Components of science: your own natural science course

All of you in the class should bring your science textbooks and notes to class. Break your class into groups of four or five. If students in your class are studying different IB sciences, group together the chemistry students, biology students, and so forth so that, in the upcoming activity, you are finding examples within your own science courses, from books, notes, and lab work.

First, answer the following questions within your group. Then, as a class, exchange what you have found. Compare your understanding of scientific knowledge as a *process* of investigation and as a *product* in the form of knowledge claims.

**1 Small group preparation**

From your own science course, find examples of each of the following components of science and prepare to share them with the rest of your class:

**(a)** *A scientific hypothesis:* an informed conjecture of a general pattern or causal relationship, based on evidence, interpretation, and imagination, ready for testing.

**(b)** *A scientific theory:* an explanation based on evidence of relationships found in the world, which accounts for phenomena already observed. Can you identify theories used within the science you are currently studying?

**(c)** *A scientific model:* a conceptual representation of entities, systems or processes that we believe to exist in the world. Representations include diagrams, three-dimensional objects, and formulae, which select essential features and omit details.

**(d)** *A scientific law:* an expression of a universal state or relationship established on the basis of evidence and tested so extensively that it is treated as true.

**(e)** *A scientific prediction:* a statement of what *will* happen if certain conditions are met, based on a scientific law, model, or theory.

**2 General discussion**

Back together as a full class group, share the examples that you have found while a volunteer "scribe" takes notes to circulate later. These notes support the connection you make between your science class and your TOK class, and act as a reservoir for examples to use in your TOK assessment essay. We will be treating all of these five components of science later in the chapter, and it is important that you have anchored the ideas in your own knowledge first.

### Concluding discussion topics:

- What is the importance of each of these five components within science? Does each have a role to play in the *process* of gaining knowledge? Which of the five are part of the *product* of bodies of knowledge claims?
- In describing and explaining, what kind of language is used in your textbooks? What is the role of the following in communicating knowledge: specialized terms defined within the subject, mathematical expression, graphs, and models?

---

> "The first reason for studying astronomy and cosmology is simply exploration, to discover what's out there. The second reason, which is what motivates astrophysicists, is to try to interpret what's out there and understand how the universe evolved, how the complexity of the present universe has emerged from the primordial simplicity. The third reason is that the cosmos is a laboratory that allows us to probe the laws of nature under conditions far more extreme than we could ever simulate in a terrestrial laboratory, and thereby to extend our knowledge of the fundamental laws of nature.[4]"
>
> *Martin Rees*

> "Many people become strongly emotionally committed to their theories and defend them, almost like advocates, against contrary evidence. It's a real trauma for them to have to give their theories up.[5]"
>
> *Martin Rees*

## The variability of scientists

The kinds of pulls that draw scientists into this area of knowledge are as various as the individuals. As biologist Peter Medawar said, surveying his colleagues,

> There is no such thing as a Scientific Mind. Scientists are people of very dissimilar temperaments doing different things in very different ways. Among scientists are collectors, classifiers, and compulsive tidiers-up; many are detectives by temperament and many are explorers; some are artists and others artisans. There are poet-scientists and philosopher-scientists and even a few mystics. What sort of mind or temperament can all these people be supposed to have in common?[6]

The picture of "the scientist" becomes even fuzzier in contemporary science because scientists generally work in teams – teams of physicists, chemists, biologists, environmental scientists, and increasingly, interdisciplinary teams – experimenting in laboratories, observing in the field, or working in offices connected to very powerful computers. Glance through this chapter to see the photographs of scientists at work, no two of them working in the same way.

No fixed "scientific method" of exactly the same sequence of steps unites all of these kinds of natural scientists, all of whom are working in very different ways on very different problems in very different aspects of the natural world. Yet they are all working within the expectations of the natural sciences, so, regardless of the details of their specific research, they are all working within the same broad methodology.

The methodology of sharing knowledge in the natural sciences benefits from the variability of the human beings who take on research. Multitudes of individual scientists, with their own particular strengths, contribute to the collective enterprise. They have their own ideas and insights to bring to the knowledge exchange.

---

5 Rees, M. 1995. "An Ensemble of Universes", *The Third Culture*, ed. John Brockman. New York. Simon & Shuster. P 264.
6 Medawar, P. 25 October 1963. "Hypothesis and Imagination". *Times Literary Supplement*.

I believe in intuition and inspiration. Imagination is more important than knowledge. For knowledge is limited, whereas imagination embraces the entire world, stimulating progress, giving birth to evolution. It is, strictly speaking, a real factor in scientific research.[8]

*Albert Einstein*

Intuition is not something that is given. I've trained my intuition to accept as obvious shapes which were initially rejected as absurd, and I find everyone else can do the same.[9]

*Benoît Mandelbrot*

The methodology of sharing knowledge likewise compensates for the particular weaknesses of the human beings who work within the scientific enterprise. As the journal *Nature* comments, "Science can fall victim to human frailties. One researcher hoards her samples out of fear of competition; another doggedly promotes his hypothesis long after the data have falsified it; negative results are hidden because of competing financial interests. And the most frequent sin of all: questionable results go unchecked because it is in nobody's interest to check them."[7]

Questionable results can certainly derail investigation for a time in the sciences, but the communal nature of research and sharing exercises a corrective influence: where one scientist falls into error, others replicating the work can replace the faulty conclusions with ones that are better justified.

It is to the methodology of the natural sciences that we must now turn in order to understand this area of knowledge. We will next treat two major knowledge questions, applied to the natural sciences:

- **Methodology, ways of knowing:** How do natural scientists use the ways of knowing in a manner characteristic of their area of knowledge?
- **Methodology, the communal nature of science:** How does the collective and corrective method of the natural sciences work to produce knowledge?

## Methods: ways of knowing

In building shared knowledge, natural scientists do not use ways of knowing at all unfamiliar to us. Even in using them with the care demanded by their field, they are still applying the skills of critical thinking that we have been considering since the beginning of this book. "The whole of science", Albert Einstein once commented, "is nothing more than a refinement of everyday thinking".

What distinguishes the natural sciences from most everyday thinking is primarily the methodology within which that thinking is set: the ways of knowing are used with greater consciousness and care, and they are used to build public knowledge subject to intense critical scrutiny.

### 1. Ways of knowing: emotion, intuition, imagination

Emotion as a way of knowing can both benefit and hinder the development of scientific knowledge. On the one hand, it fires the process of investigation with a range of emotions: keen interest, pleasure, pride in work, and sometimes surprise or even awe. What would we *ever* know if not for human involvement in solving problems or longing to find the answer?

[7] "No Shame". 18 April 2012. *Nature*. Vol 484. Pp 287–88. http://www.nature.com/nature/journal/v484/n7394/full/484287b.html.

[8] Einstein, A. 1931. *Cosmic Religion: With Other Opinions and Aphorisms*. Covici-Friede.

[9] Gleick, J. 1987. *A Geometry of Nature, Chaos: Making A New Science*. London. Penguin Books. P 102.

On the other hand, it can interfere with motivation as well in the moments of disappointment over findings, worry over funding, or irritation with colleagues. It is human beings who create science, and their feelings are part of the context in which they work. They start with their own subjectivity, even though they work through a public methodology to leave these feelings behind in the conclusions that they reach.

Intuition and imagination are likewise significant for the creation of science. Intuition is often credited for the first glimpse of patterns emerging from research, and imagination valued for conjecturing beyond the known into other ways of conceptualizing connections. "Suppose that this were so…" As we considered earlier, imagination is significant in creativity. It helps to generate the hypothesis (chapter 7) essential in the hypothetico-deductive reasoning and fosters the fresh explanations of new theories.

## 2. Ways of knowing: sense perception and reasoning

Although we disengaged sense perception and reasoning to consider their separate characteristics as ways of knowing in the earlier part of this book, we would be hard pressed to separate them from each other in the methods of science. They are interconnected in fieldwork and experiments, and they combine to provide the major justification for accepting knowledge claims in the natural sciences: *evidence*. They work together in generalizations and in explanations.

We will not repeat here all we considered in chapter 5 regarding the characteristics of sense perception or the ways we attempt to overcome limitations. Observation, with care in using sense perception, is the very basis of science. We must emphasize here, though, the importance of repeated observations by the initial researcher and replication of work by other scientists.

Replication of observations by other scientists exposes errors in procedures and possible biases, including experimental error and the confirmation bias of interpreting results in terms of prior expectations – seeing what one expects to see. You may want to search out the iconic story of N-rays, a new type of radiation supposedly discovered by physicist René Blondot in 1903, or polywater, a new form of water identified and then rejected in the 1960s. The 2011 to 2012 story of neutrinos

>  I, and probably most physicists, regard reality as a genuine physical reality, a reality influenced by people only insofar as we can reach and move things and so on. Reality exists independent of people. The goal of the physicist is to understand that reality.[10]
>
> *Alan Guth*

seeming to travel faster than light also highlights the importance of peer review and replication.

We refer you back to chapter 7 for scientific reasoning: the inductive reasoning that science uses to make generalizations from particular observations; the deductive reasoning it uses to apply generalizations to new instances; and the hypothetico-deductive reasoning of formulating a hypothesis – an educated guess – and testing it.

We must emphasize here, too, the importance of understanding scientific "truth" and "uncertainty". Do you remember the checks for truth in chapter 3? Scientists work with them all. They look for results that are *coherent* with other findings, without apparent contradictions. They often treat results *pragmatically*, accepting conclusions that seem to work. In addition, they examine evidence, in order to justify their inductively reasoned conclusions. It is this last check for truth, the *correspondence* check, that makes the natural sciences reliable in representing the world – and, at the same time, so open to change.

Do you remember Popper's single black swan, the one counter-example that proves a universal generalization to be false (page 115)? It is not possible to achieve completely certain results based on evidence when further evidence just might overturn current findings. As a result, the natural sciences work always with *provisional* truth, recognizing that there is never enough evidence to reach 100 per cent certainty.

So what do scientists mean when they say, "We can't be certain"? They could be saying that the results are tentative. But they could also be expressing their professional skeptical reservation when, in fact, there is an enormous amount of evidence to support a particular conclusion. When scientists say they are "uncertain", they are not saying just that they *don't know*.

[10] Quoted in Brockman, J. 1996. *The Third Culture*. New York. Touchstone Edition, Simon and Shuster. P 277.

# Interview

## Basic sciences and applied sciences

*Dr. James Cavers*

*Jim Cavers earned a PhD in Electrical Engineering in 1970. Over the next 38 years, he was a faculty member at two universities and a manager and engineer at two companies. He has published about 130 papers and one book, and holds 12 patents. He has received provincial, national and international awards for his research in wireless communication and its practical applications. Now that he is a Professor Emeritus, he does his research in Canada and New Zealand.*

→ How do the applied sciences differ from the basic sciences (formerly called "pure" sciences)?

The terms basic science and applied science refer to the objectives of the work – roughly, whether it's to determine some property of the physical world (I'll stick to the physical sciences here) or to design something for a specific purpose – more than the methodology and activities. But even that distinction is often tenuous. Is an experimental physicist or chemist who is designing the apparatus for the next experiment conducting applied science? Is someone working in quantum computing doing basic or applied science? Is an engineer who develops new ideas in information theory as a detour in designing a communication system doing basic science?

→ Are creativity and imagination required for engineering, which applies scientific knowledge already developed?

Not all the knowledge we need in engineering has been developed! In any advanced design, we'll stumble on (or over) things that just aren't known yet. In that case, the designers or applied researchers will explore the topic themselves, or else buy a coffee for a physicist (or zoologist, or psychologist, or mathematician...) and try to talk them into looking at it. Grants or contracts often have their roots in a cup of good coffee.

But, as for imagination and curiosity, those are the forces driving any engineer or applied researcher. How can you make a mechatronic structure that mimics the locomotion of a lizard? Is it even possible to design a concrete and steel surface to cover this strangely shaped area with enough strength and stability? Can we make a lightweight, inexpensive device with small screen that can give anyone a wireless link to phone and Internet services and do a thousand other things? (Hint: that one has been done.)

And as for creativity – well, it depends on how good you are at this game.

→ It is clear in all your work that you love engineering. Why do you enjoy it so much?

Engineering, applied science and design are always about something new. If it weren't new, we would just buy an existing product. Even a new bridge – not your average product – presents plenty of challenges and opportunities to try something different. And the activities are truly engaging – figuring out what the real problem is, and if it differs from the stated one, drawing on complicated things that you already understand, identifying what you don't understand and whether anyone understands it yet, working out the new bits, trying it in an experimental or prototype version, working through the stress and excitement of getting the final version out by the deadline and within the budget, seeing the happy faces of clients, basking in the (*ahem*) admiration. Who wouldn't love working like that? ■

## 3. Ways of knowing: language

Crucial though other ways of knowing may be, language is clearly also essential to the natural sciences. How else could knowledge be shared and archived? How else could scientists scrutinize other people's work in peer review, or communicate their own replicated findings?

Within the scientific community, language has to be precise and denotative, with as little ambiguity as possible. (You'll recall the discussion on "Sunlight on the Garden".) The need for precision demands clear definition of terms and makes mathematics generally the preferred form of communication – for its precision, compactness and usefulness in both quantifying particulars and abstracting to relationships between phenomena and concepts. If you do the activity we offer here, "Components of science: your own natural science course", do make a point of noticing the role of mathematics, graphs, diagrams, and models in scientific

> We must be clear that when it comes to atoms, language can be used only as in poetry.[11]
>
> *Niels Bohr*

textbooks to supplement languages for precision of communication.

Before we move on to the use of language for building common knowledge in exchange and peer review, however, we should consider some of the difficulties of communicating scientific knowledge to the general public. This communication is extremely important: the findings of science often have serious implications that the people of a society need to consider. And yet this communication often falls into a giant gap between how scientists and non-scientists use language.

## Scientific language and the general public

When scientists communicate beyond their professional communities to the general public, misunderstandings frequently arise. The misunderstanding of climate change among many members of the public has brought to greater attention recently both the gaps in communication and the importance of overcoming them.

"Climate researchers know that the case for human-induced climate change has become stronger, more compelling, and increasingly urgent with each passing year," comment Richard C.J. Somerville and Susan Joy Hassol[12], both of whom work in climate

| Terms that have different meanings for scientists and the general public | | |
|---|---|---|
| word | public meaning | scientific meaning |
| enhance | improve | intensify, increase |
| aerosol | spray can | dispersion of a fine particles of a liquid or solid in a gas |
| positive trend | good trend | upward trend |
| positive feedback | good response, praise | self-reinforcing cycle |
| theory | hunch, speculation | scientific understanding |
| uncertainty | ignorance | range |
| error | mistake, wrong, incorrect | difference from exact true number |
| bias | distortion, political motive | offset from an observation |
| sign | indication, astrological sign | plus or minus sign |
| values | ethics, monetary value | numbers, quantity |
| manipulation | illicit tampering | scientific data processing |
| scheme | devious plot | systematic plan |
| anomaly | abnormal occurrence | change from long-term average |

[11] Quoted by Werner Heisenberg, as translated by Arnold J. Pomerans, in *Physics and Beyond: Encounters and Conversations.* 1971. http://www.todayinsci.com/B/Bohr_Niels/BohrNiels-Quotations.htm

[12] Edited version of Richard C.J. Somerville and Susan Joy Hassol. October 2011. "Communicating the science of climate change". *Physics Today.* Vol 64, issue 10. http://physicstoday.org/resource/1/phtoad/v64/i10/p48_s1?bypassSSO=1

communication. "Yet in some countries, notably the US, the proportion of the public and policymakers who reject the science has grown." They identify numerous barriers to the scientists' communication to the public, including the following:

- Scientists typically communicate ideas in an order that is the reverse of what is most familiar to the public. They open with background, go next to supporting details, and end with their conclusions. However, the public expects to be given the conclusions first, to know why an article is worth reading. (Note that both orders can work in your TOK essay, if used with care. We'll come to that later.)
- Scientists, like any other experts, do not easily simplify enough for the rest of us, often using unfamiliar words and too much detail.
- Scientists tend to emphasize what is important for the development of science rather than what is important to the public. For instance, they tend to stress new science rather than the larger picture, and to start off with what they do not know rather than what they do know.
- Scientists tend not to use simple analogies and metaphors that would help a lay public understand significance.

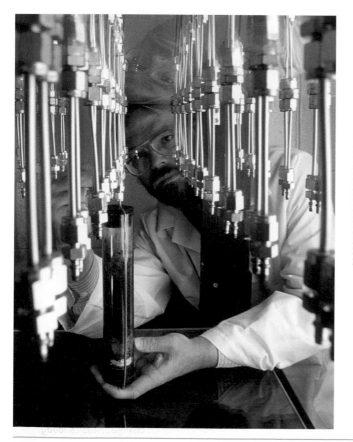

## How to talk to real people

Emory University in Atlanta, Georgia, USA, has introduced a course for graduate students, to teach them how to communicate their academic work to laypeople. Below is a sample of a presentation by a student of chemistry.[13]

*A chemistry student in the "Communicating Science" course explains herself …*

- to peers at an American Chemical Society meeting:
  "Using laser-induced temperature jump techniques I focus on elucidating the kinetics and mechanism of dihydrofolate reductase as a model system to better understand how enzymes work."

- to biologists and mathematicians at an American Association on Advancement of Science meeting:
  "By enhancing our understanding of enzymes we hope to advance many fields—enzyme design, drug discovery and chemical synthesis."

- to neighbours:
  "With this model we will be able to design, optimize and control enzymes to help us perform reactions more cleanly, develop new materials, and enhance our abilities to produce everyday products."

- to third graders:
  "Inside the bodies of every living thing, including you and me, are tiny little machines called enzymes that do a variety of things. They help break down our food, fight diseases, and help our bodies grow. We aren't completely sure how enzymes work, but I am trying to understand them so that one day we can make enzymes to do whatever we want them to do."

- Scientists often use the same words as the public does, but with slightly different meanings that can create confusion. For instance, they use scales of uncertainty (likely, not certain) that convey the impression of lack of knowledge and use the term "consensus" for nearly universal agreement regarding climate change, a word that may sound to the public more like a matter of rough opinion.

---

[13] "How to Talk to Real People," *New York Times*. 22 July 2011. http://www.nytimes.com/2011/07/24/education/edlife/edl-24jargon-t.html?_r=2

In the table earlier, Somerville and Hassol identify words that scientists use in a different way from members of the public, with the potential to confuse communication about climate change.

## Methods: the communal nature of science

Science is shared knowledge, knowledge shared publicly, communally, and internationally. Not only do scientists generally work in research groups, but they contribute their findings to the larger scientific community, so that their evidence and reasoning can be scrutinized and questioned. Their experiments can be replicated to determine whether others reach the same results. If judged sound, their work can contribute to the further research of others.

Results are fed into what we have called "the zone of exchange" in our diagram familiar from earlier. This exchange takes place many times over: scientists exchange their personal understanding within their research team, and the research team exchanges knowledge with multiple research teams

### Discussion Activity

### Metaphors in the sciences and other areas

by Julian Kitching

Metaphors are more than linguistic devices. They can influence they way we think about all sorts of things and, by extension, guide our actions. (The three functions of metaphor identified in the chapter on language are applied below specifically to areas of knowledge.)

**(a) Explaining and understanding**

Metaphors use everyday words or technical terms from another discipline in order to make links that make explaining and understanding easier.

> **Example: Communications in the human body**
> One way of conceptualizing some of the organ systems in the body is to compare them with aspects of a telephone network. The nervous system corresponds to land lines with fixed "cables", cells in the immune system correspond to mobile telephones that move around, picking up signals and responding to them, and the endocrine system corresponds to transmitter stations that broadcast signals. Points of similarity and difference can be easily identified here. By integrating the three specific metaphors into a larger systematic one, a certain kind of understanding is forged that views all these systems as part of a larger dynamic whole. This can help us to see these three systems in a new way – overcoming, for example, the traditional Western biological view that the body can affect the mind much more powerfully than the mind can affect the body.

This traditional view is, of course, built upon the widespread idea that mind and body are somehow separate entities.

**(b) Challenging orthodoxy**

Metaphors provide new and different ways of thinking through their "surprise value".

> **Example: The "selfish gene"**
> Since the British evolutionary biologist Richard Dawkins coined the term "selfish gene" in his book of the same name in 1976, the term has become a stimulus to thinking about the nature of living organisms in a certain way. Dawkins wanted to switch the emphasis in biology from the primacy of organisms to that of genes, and to do that he employed the new term in order not only to help people to understand what he was saying, but also to challenge accepted ways of thinking. The behaviour of genes could best be explained by imagining them showing intentional behaviour, such as being selfish. When the metaphor is extended logically, it is clear that "selfish" genes would put their "interests" ahead of the bodies in which they found themselves, and that therefore bodies could be regarded as merely the vehicles for transmission of genes from one generation to the next. This was a powerful and influential new way of looking at biology. Nevertheless, there have been those who mistook Dawkins's metaphor for literal reality, and mocked his allegedly poor grasp of the subject! Once again, it is important to understand metaphor.

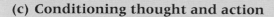

## (c) Conditioning thought and action

Metaphors are powerful as they can be used for deliberate manipulation of thought and action, or simply because they reflect basic aspects of our environment. They help to create structures of thought that are variously described as paradigms, conceptual schemes, or frameworks. Let's consider biological evolution as an example.

### Example: "Natural selection"

When Charles Darwin wrote of "natural selection", he intended the term to build on the more familiar concept of "artificial selection", in which plant and animal breeders influenced the make-up of their stocks by choosing individuals with desirable characteristics for breeding. This metaphor was very successful in emphasizing certain points of similarity, such as the gradual nature of change and the basic importance of individual variation, but has also contributed to 150 years of misunderstandings. "Selection" seems to imply a "selector"; it seems to invoke intelligence, and encourages the thought that the fundamental process involves positive selection of "fit" individuals rather than the elimination of "unfit" ones. It could be argued that Darwin's metaphor has been only partially successful in promoting public understanding of evolution.

## Discussion: metaphors in IB courses

The table given here contains terms that are important in particular IB courses. From which subject(s) does each term come? What is the *source* of the metaphor? What is its *target*?

It may be necessary to know some of the history of the subject disciplines in order to make informed judgments about what was borrowed from where, but, according to what you know, can you tell from which other subject(s) words or terms have been borrowed in order to create an effective metaphor?

| Innate drive | Computer virus | mRNA translation |
|---|---|---|
| Concentration gradient | Electric current | Punctuated equilibrium |
| Monetary inflation | Computer hardware | Big Bang |
| Work done | Regime purge | Natural selection |
| System firewall | Cognitive dissonance | Netiquette |
| Buffer solution | Price elasticity | Selfish gene |
| Radioactive decay | Group pressure | Great Leap Forward |
| Eukaryotic cell | Electrical resistance | Trojan horse |
| Liberation front | Nitrogen fixation | Computer software |
| Lock and key model | Greenhouse effect | Network topology |

- Can you suggest other examples from your studies in various subjects?
- If some disciplines are richer in metaphor than others, is this the result of the subject matter with which it is concerned or more the result of the methods that it uses?
- If different languages use the same metaphor, but with a different meaning, how might this affect the pursuit of knowledge?
- Does geography play a special role here in providing raw material for the construction of metaphor? If so, why might this be the case?

working on related topics worldwide. Within such extensive communal production and scrutiny, the personal element – without which no knowledge would have been generated in the first place – is mixed with the thinking of others to such an extent that it is rarely completely separable. Certainly, some contributors do stand out for the significance of what they add to shared knowledge. However,

their work is much less distinct from the collective enterprise than a novelist's or historian's would be.

How is the exchange achieved in the natural sciences? As you would expect in an area of knowledge that depends on sharing, the channels of communication are well established. Scientists work with others in their university or institute, take part

## Discussion Activity

### Creating science: telling the story

*Class research exercise*: Divide up your group to investigate the following examples of fundamentally different "methods" of creating scientific knowledge. (You may choose another example if another discovery appeals to you.) Do not simply *report* your findings back to the group but instead shape what you have found into a narrative, a true story about discovery in science that brings out its significance. Choose your method of narration: novel form, diary entries, short interview, epic poem, letter to a friend, sung ballad, or another form of your choice.

- Serendipity and methodical work: Roentgen and discovery of X-ray
- Exploration and observation: Von Humboldt and the biogeography of ecosystems
- Hypothetico-deductive method: Edward Jenner and the discovery of smallpox vaccine
- Mathematics and new assumptions: Max Planck and quantum theory
- Luck and observation: Alexander Fleming and discovery of penicillin
- Scrutiny of astrological images: discovery of Eris 2005

in academic seminars, give papers at conferences, contribute papers to journals, and are currently developing more systems of web-based sharing.

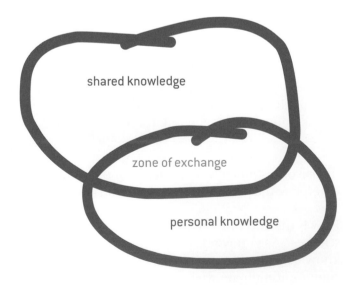

## Peer-reviewed journals

Crucial to this process of exchange is "peer review" – the examination and evaluation of a scientific paper by scientists working in the same or a related field. When scientists submit papers to journals for publication, editors place them with two or three referees, usually confidentially, who read them closely in order to make recommendations to the editor on whether it would be suitable to publish them as is, reject them, or accept them with correction or amplification. The referees are able to strengthen good papers with further advice and give expert critique to weaker ones, with encouragement to submit papers another time. Peer review, taken on voluntarily by scientists as part of their professional responsibility to the whole scientific exchange of knowledge, helps to share the workload of evaluation of new work, bring in appropriate expertise for particular areas of research, and maintain scientific standards in published work.

Particle physicist Patrick Decowski places peer review for journal publication within a larger process of peer evaluation:

> This peer assessment does not mean that the article is factually correct. The process doesn't ensure the truth, but it's another layer, a filter to increase reliability. It's an important process, but not the only process...

> The chief advantage of the peer review process is that you can rely on the editor and the journal. Journal standards can differ, though, depending on the editor and the number and quality of the reviewers. Some journals are highly regarded and rightly so. *Science* and *Nature*, for example, put a lot of effort into maintaining quality...

> You don't have time to read everything. If an article is published in a journal I have never heard of, it does not rank high in my mind for my reading time. It is easy enough to publish if you aim low enough. In a resumé of my own work, I would cite only the papers in prestigious journals.[14]

Peer review does not end when a paper is published, since publication allows other scientists to examine, criticize, and possibly replicate the findings. Publication is just one step in the communal methodology.

---

14 Dombrowski, E. 1 October 2010. "Scientific Informaton Sharing: Interview with a Scientist," blog TOK meets global citizenship, Triple A Learning Blogs.

## Peer Review: the nuts and bolts

The publication "Peer Review: the nuts and bolts" is available online from *Sense about Science*. It is a short, clear, attractive summary of the peer review process, with scientists explaining how it works, some of its limitations, and its role in society.[15]

It includes some interesting results from a survey done in 2009:

"In a survey of over 4000 researchers, most (84%) believed that without peer review there would be no control in scientific communication."

- 90% review because they like playing their part as a member of the academic community
- 85% just enjoy seeing other papers and being able to improve them
- Almost all researchers (91%) believe that their last paper was improved through the peer review process

## Pre-publication servers

Exchange of scientific knowledge does not depend entirely on these journals, however. Already in many scientific fields, papers are posted on websites for comment and criticism, largely for pre-publication review and correction. The process is much faster than publication in a journal, and notes ownership of ideas as they are developed. Decowski gives an example of the speed of response:

> Within six hours of our posting our article on the pre-print server, I got an email from the spokesperson working on a related project. She was asking why we hadn't taken into account the results that her group had posted back in July. And she was right. We really had missed results that are significant to our own. We'll now take them into account and update our article, probably within a week...

In the days when we depended entirely on print publication, it would have taken half a

year to get out our article, then another half a year to publish an update. But this can happen now in a few days. The version currently on the website carries a number ending in v1 for version 1. Version 2 will soon be posted.[16]

It is on these pre-print servers that physicists in Decowski's field can keep track of findings as they develop, with open access that ensures that the exchange of knowledge is not confined only to the richer institutions that can afford the journals.

## Shift towards open access

Indeed, call for open access to scientific exchange has led to protest against the current model of journals: scientists and funders declare that expensive journals lock away knowledge behind a "paywall".[17]

"We have to maximise the public benefit of the research that we publish," says a spokesperson for the funding body Wellcome Trust, "and we only do that by distribution."[18] Open-access journals that cost the users nothing already exist in some fields

[15] "Peer Review: the nuts and bolts," Sense about Science, http://www.senseaboutscience.org/data/files/resources/99/Peer-review_The-nuts-and-bolts.pdf

[16] Dombrowski, E. 2 October 2010. "Scientific Information Exchange: A Follow-up," blog *TOK meets global citizenship*, Triple A Learning Blogs.

[17] http://gowers.files.wordpress.com/2012/02/elsevierstatementfinal.pdf.

[18] Alok Jha. 9 April 2012. "Wellcome Trust joins 'academic spring' to open up science," *The Guardian*. Accessed 11 April 2012. http://www.guardian.co.uk/science/2012/apr/09/wellcome-trust-academic-spring?newsfeed=true.

> In general we look for a new law by the following process. First we guess it. Then we compute the consequences of the guess to see what would be implied if this law that we guessed is right. Then we compare the result of the computation to nature, with experiment or experience, compare it directly with observation, to see if it works. If it disagrees with experiment it is wrong. In that simple statement is the key to science. It does not make any difference how beautiful your guess is. It does not make any difference how smart you are, who made the guess, or what his name is – if it disagrees with experiment it is wrong.[19]
>
> *Richard Feynman*

of science, and this means of communication is likely to develop further in the near future.

An article in *Nature*, one of the most highly regarded journals, acknowledges the current trends, and the challenge of opening access and yet keeping standards high:

> The rise of digital media has revolutionized the management of information and created opportunities for broader involvement in science's production... Such a widening of participation might be liberating, but it also risks lowering standards. Not everyone shares the ideal that intellectual integrity comes before personal gain.[20]

In a collaborative model of "intellectual property", participants in the "creative commons" and "open source" already allow others to copy and adapt their work, on the condition that they credit the source and share their own ideas in turn. Without gatekeepers who screen material and ensure quality, participants rely instead on communal criticism. (You are probably familiar with this issue from discussions on the reliability of Wikipedia.)

As the model for sharing knowledge changes, the four "norms of science" coined in 1942 by sociologist Robert Merton are frequently invoked in debate. They are known by their acronym CUDOS, and sum up ideals in science: communalism (originally "communism"), universalism, disinterestedness, and organized skepticism.

## Ethics: scientific fraud

It is hardly surprising, given the way in which scientists build on each other's work, that reliability in published work should be so highly valued – or that fraud should be condemned as dishonest and as potentially damaging to the work of others.

A striking recent example is that of Andrew Wakefield, whose 1998 findings were partly discredited in 2004 and completely retracted in January 2010 by the prestigious medical journal *The Lancet* in which they were originally published. In January 2011 the British General Medical Council condemned his work as "irresponsible and dishonest" and removed Wakefield from its professional register, while the British Medical Journal denounced it as "elaborate fraud".[21] The significance of this example of fraud is the extensive damage it has done.

Wakefield claimed to have found a connection between one of the most common vaccines given to children (measles-mumps-rubella, MMR) and autism. The impact of his much-publicized study was devastating to public health as parents became fearful of vaccinating their children as protection from childhood diseases, protection which had previously been medically routine. They thereby put their own children at greater risk and decreased the "herd immunity" of the general population.

*The Lancet's* retraction and the later verdict of fraud are enough to rule out *within the scientific community* the link Wakefield claimed to have found, which has not been supported by any further evidence. However, *within the public* doubts over the safety of vaccination remain. Wakefield's claims had seemed to justify anecdotal claims by mothers about their own children, which had been widely disseminated through media,

---

19 From Lecture 7, "Seeking New Laws", delivered by Richard Feynman in 1964 at Cornell University, as part of the Messenger Lectures series. http://www.cosmolearning.com/video-lectures/the-relation-of-mathematics-physics-16-9945

20 Ravetz, J. 5 January 2012. "Sociology of science: Keep standards high". *Nature*. Vol 481, number 25. http://nature.com/nature/journal/v481/n7379/full/481025a.html. Accessed 16 July 2012.

21 "Journal says doctor faked data linking autism to vaccines". 5 January 2011. *The Washington Post* (Reuters). http://www.washingtonpost.com/wp-dyn/content/article/2011/01/05/AR2011010507052.html

including repeated appearances by an actress on a popular talk show.

Wakefield's own response to being found guilty of fraud contained no apology for damage done:[22] "Dr. Wakefield has called the British decision to strike him off the medical register an effort to 'discredit and silence' him. Undaunted, Dr. Wakefield said he would continue his research into the link between vaccines and autism." As we emphasized earlier, the creation of science is a human process, involving different personalities within the communally corrective process.

## Pseudo-science

That communally corrective process is not universally welcomed. Quacks and remedy-mongers of all sorts accuse the "scientific establishment" of being closed-minded and prejudiced in their insistence on the methodological requirements of science. "They're just a closed club." "They won't listen to anything that isn't done their way." "They can't stand anything that challenges their ideas." Although there is an element of truth in such accusations when scientists resist new ideas, eventually knowledge claims justified by rigorous, repeated observation and valid reasoning do make their way through the resistance. But these are the very things that pseudo-scientists cannot provide.

How can we recognize pseudo-science? One commentator, a professor of physics, proposes seven "warning signs" of pseudo-science – while recognizing that "even a claim with several of the signs could be legitimate".[23] His warning signs can be summarized as follows:

1. The discoverer bypasses peer review to go directly to the media.

2. The discoverer claims that the scientific establishment, possibly as part of a larger conspiracy, is trying to suppress his work.

3. The evidence is extremely hard to detect.

4. The evidence takes the form of individual observations or stories, not able to be generalized.

5. The discoverer claims that the knowledge is ancient and hence more credible.

6. The discoverer has worked alone.

7. The discoverer needs to propose modification to the laws of nature in order that his findings be credible.

In trying to distinguish pseudo-scientific claims from the claims of the sciences, we affirm once again a basic principle of this book: that critical thinking requires a mind open to alternatives yet concerned to sift through them for the version that is the best justified. A contemporary emphasis on knowledge as culturally constructed and variable helps us see the significance of different perspectives. However, the fact that there are many perspectives on something does not imply that all of them have equal claim to be accepted.

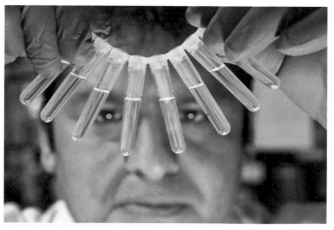

---

22 "Andrew Wakefield". 6 January 2011. *The New York Times*. http://topics.nytimes.com/top/reference/timestopics/people/w/andrew_wakefield/index.html.

23 Park, R.L. 31 Jan 2003. "The Seven Warning Signs of Bogus Science." *Chronicle Review, The Chronicle of Higher Education*.

## 🎤 Interview

### Science, technology, and the sub-atomic world

## Interview with Patrick Decowski
## IB graduate 1991

*Patrick Decowski has an MSc in Nuclear Physics from Utrecht University, the Netherlands, and a PhD in Nuclear Physics from the Massachusetts Institute of Technology. He is currently an Associate Professor at the University of Amsterdam.*

→ Would you please explain what you are researching?

My research focuses on a subatomic particle called the neutrino, one of the particles emitted in radioactive decay. The neutrino does not have electric charge and very little mass. We do not know the exact mass yet, but it is for sure 500,000 times less massive than the electron, the lightest particle of "ordinary matter". The neutrino is copiously emitted by the Sun, but very difficult to stop: more than a hundred billion neutrinos pass unhindered through your thumbnail every second! The neutrino is still one of the least understood subatomic particles and many current and future experiments aim at unravelling its mysteries.

I work on a project called KamLAND. The experiment is located in an old zinc mine in western Japan. The experiment consists of a large 18-metre diameter container filled with 1000 tonnes of liquid scintillator (essentially baby-oil with a fluorescence)

that is viewed by 1800 light sensitive detectors. About 40 times per second particles interact with the liquid scintillator and give off light flashes that are recorded by the light sensitive detectors and stored for later analysis. It turns out that the vast majority of the light flashes we see come from natural radioactivity, uninteresting background events. However, using elaborate computer algorithms, we can identify particle light flashes coming from neutrino interactions with the liquid scintillator. Our project has been very successful; based on our measurements we have gained a much better understanding of the properties of the neutrino.

→ When we discuss the natural sciences in TOK class, we talk about it as a study of the natural world – the physical or material world. If what you are studying is a particle far, far, far too small to see, are you still studying the physical world? Should we change the way we talk about science?

The neutrino (or any other subatomic particle for that matter) is indeed far too small to see directly. We always study these particles through their interactions with other particles, "amplifying" their presence and inferring their existence. Also, once you get to subatomic length scales, you are firmly in the quantum world and you can no longer talk about particles being objects of a defined shape or form.

At the same time, although we do not see these particles, they are part of the physical world. We can make accurate predictions of what we expect to see and then perform the experiment to test the hypothesis. Indeed, one of the great triumphs of particle physics was when the quark model was developed (quarks are the building blocks of protons and neutrons that make up the atomic nucleus). The quark model not only describes how protons and neutrons behave, but it also predicted the existence of a certain short-lived particle. When physicists looked for this particle, they found it. The material world is not limited to entities that we can see or touch. As a matter of fact, the vast majority of our material world turns out to consist of vacuum, with only every now and then a tiny particle that determines the properties of the material. Additionally, in recent years we have discovered that we see only 15 per cent of the total mass of the Universe! Eighty–five per cent of the mass is so-called "Dark Matter". We know it is there because it interacts gravitationally (i.e. the same force that holds the Earth in orbit around the Sun), but we have no idea what Dark Matter is made from.

Besides neutrinos, my other research interest is trying to detect and understand Dark Matter.

→ Models, from what you say, really help you to conceptualize particles and their relationships. Do you have other ways of conceptualizing them, perhaps using metaphors?

It really depends on what questions you want to ask. Different theories work as different metaphors in science. To give an example, when studying properties of a gas, the gas particles (which can be single atoms) can be thought of as being little billiard balls. It is not that they are really little billiard balls, but that metaphor allows us to make certain predictions for the gas that are validated by experiment. But one must not confuse that metaphor with reality. When looking at the gas particles at a smaller scale than the overall gas (such as what I am doing in neutrino physics), the billiard ball metaphor breaks down and we really have to think in quantum-mechanical terms. It turns out that viewing particles as waves is a much better metaphor at those length scales. Even the mathematics that sits underneath all of our theories can be seen as "quantitative metaphors". Just because there is currently a correspondence between these equations and the physical world, does not mean they are one and the same.

→ What is the role of computer modeling in your research? Can you do "experiments" within a computer?

Computer modeling is extremely important in most branches of science nowadays. In subatomic physics it is particularly important. Most experiments cannot be interpreted without a significant amount of modeling, to understand both the behaviour of the detector and the physics being studied.

Doing experiments in computers has also become very popular, because specific hypotheses can be tested relatively quickly for their consequences. A hypothesis with a set of starting conditions can be stepped through in time inside the computer and then tested for violation of specific physical laws (such as energy conservation) and discarded if it does violate some important law or does not match observation. The great advantage is that computer simulations allow us to study theories that are otherwise hard to test. The modeling helps in fleshing out the theory, but the computer predictions have to be compared to real, physical world experiments. Computer simulations are not only used in nuclear physics and meteorology, but also in astrophysics, biophysics, climate studies and so on. Computer modeling really

has revolutionized the way we do research and the current generation of scientists spends considerable time in front of computer screens.

→ Einstein has been quoted as saying that imagination is more important than knowledge. In your kind of scientific research, what is the role of imagination?

I think that what Einstein meant was that you have to have an open mind and think out of the box. It is extremely important to have imagination in physics. When seeing some unexpected effect, you have to use your imagination to try and understand what you are seeing. Is it a detector effect? Is it due to the environment? Could it be new physics? This is usually where we spend most time, in interpreting the data. You try and vary some accessible parameter in the experiment and ask, "Is the effect changing?" The imagination is necessary for coming up with hypotheses, but this is always followed by testing.

→ Why do you find your research so interesting?

I have always had a fascination with how things work. Over time I realized that what is even more amazing is that nature itself works so well and that I wanted to understand it better. Certain "themes" come back in areas that superficially do not have anything to do with each other. Why is it that ocean waves and light rays can behave in similar ways? Why do the same equations describe a mechanical and an electrical oscillator? There are similar "themes" and symmetries at the very smallest particle level. This led me to become interested in subatomic particles and the neutrino is one of the least understood and most fascinating particles.

The fundamental nuclear physics that I do is in some sense similar to what astronomers do when they look at stars. They look upwards at the large scale, whereas I look downwards at the very small scale. My research does not have any direct application – just like knowing how stars shine does not have any obvious application. We are studying it purely for the knowledge and trying to understand what is behind it. This is in many respects similar to the reasons why people enjoy art. Science is captivating. ■

## Questions for discussion

1. Patrick Decowski speaks of "our project" and "our measurements". In a field such as his, would you expect scientists to be working alone or in research groups? Why?

2. What is the role of technology in his group's experiments?

3. What does he say are the roles of imagination, models and metaphors, and testing? Do his comments also apply to the science you are studying for the IB?

4. He describes both the correspondence check for truth and the coherence check for truth (pages 57–65) in action, though without giving them these names. What is the role of each in his experiment? In your most recent experiment for your IB science course, what truth check were you using?

5. From his description, what resemblances do you find between scientific research and detective work?

## Science in action: Faster-than-light neutrinos

Two of the most headline-grabbing stories in recent science are a report that neutrinos had been caught moving faster than light, and an announcement that the elusive Higgs boson had finally been found. When you've read the next section, it will fall to you – be warned! – to answer two questions.

- In what ways do these two stories characterize science?
- What story can you find yourself that represents contemporary science in action?

In September 2011, an international collaboration of scientists announced a startling result. A beam of subatomic neutrinos, sent from a laboratory

> Humans may crave absolute certainty; they may aspire to it; they may pretend, as partisans of certain religions do, to have attained it. But the history of science – by far the most successful claim to knowledge accessible to humans – teaches that the most we can hope for is successive improvement in our understanding, learning from our mistakes…but with the proviso that absolute certainty will always elude us.[24]
>
> *Carl Sagan*

in Switzerland to a laboratory in Italy, had been recorded as *travelling faster than the speed of light*. How could this be possible? Their results were incompatible with well established physics, according to which *nothing* travels faster than the speed of light.

The scientific community was buzzing with the news. This was a major challenge to scientific understanding, by a major research group. The collaboration of scientists, with a project name of OPERA, involved 200 physicists from 36 different institutions and 13 countries,[25] working in the prestigious European Centre for Nuclear Research (CERN) and the Gran Sasso Laboratory in Italy. These were highly trained scientists, using sophisticated equipment.

"If this is proved to be true it would be a massive, massive event," explained Subir Sarkar, head of particle physics at Oxford, as the information hit the press. "It is something nobody was expecting.

Photo courtesy of CERN

[24] Sagan, C. and Druyan, A. 1996. *The Demon Haunted World: Science as a Candle in the Dark*. New York. Ballantine Books. P 28.
[25] OPERA collaboration homepage http://operaweb.lngs.infn.it/spip.php?rubrique33

## Discussion Activity

### Obsolete science: what does NOT appear in your science textbook?

Split up your class for a mini research exercise, for a look at what does NOT appear in your current textbook. Consider the topics listed below, which are now all outdated ideas in science. Work individually or in pairs, preparing a short report for the rest of your class. Your report should give a brief explanation of the outdated science and attempt to answer the following three questions:

1 Why did people accept these interpretations of observations?

2 Why do people no longer accept these interpretations?

3 Which of these obsolete interpretations is now irrelevant to science, and which has led to refined versions currently accepted?

- spontaneous generation
- maternal impression
- miasma theory of disease
- recapitulation theory
- caloric theory
- N-Rays
- Lamarckian inheritance
- phlogiston theory
- anomalous water
- luminiferous aether
- steady state theory of the universe
- Rutherford model of the atom

The constancy of the speed of light essentially underpins our understanding of space and time and causality, which is the fact that cause comes before effect".[26]

By late October, thousands more scientists were involved. More than 1,000 had contacted OPERA to comment on the announcement in immediate peer review, and conferences were organized to discuss the results.[27] Could a law of physics be overturned by the findings? Could this result be the metaphorical black swan – the single counter-example that proved a universal law to be false? Some scientists found the thought exciting, but all waited for further developments.

"We are very much astonished by this result," commented Antonio Ereditato, coordinator of the OPERA collaboration, on first making the announcement, "but a result is never a discovery until other people confirm it."

"When you get such a result you want to make sure you made no mistakes, that there are no nasty things going on you didn't think of. We spent months and months doing checks and we have not been able to find any errors."

While physicists worldwide scrutinized the results for sources of error in peer review, OPERA re-ran its experiment, with the same results. However, as other scientists tried to replicate the experiment, they could not. Other experiments within the same San Grasso Laboratory in Italy (including the ICARUS experiment), alongside the T2K project in Japan, and the MINOS experiment in Illinois, all found that neutrinos moved at the normal speed expected.[28] At the end of March 2012, just six months after their original announcement, the OPERA group announced sources of error in the faulty attachment of a fibre optic cable and flawed timing in the master clock.[29]

Within the OPERA collaboration, the leader and the spokesman both stepped down after a vote of no confidence in their handling of the experimental results and communication – though they affirmed that their voluntary withdrawal was not because of the science but because of internal tensions and media leaks. (The human element does not disappear in large international collaborations.) The journal *Nature* summed up the event:

> Extraordinary claims require extraordinary evidence.[30]
>
> *Carl Sagan*

[26] Ian Sample. Faster than light particles found, claim scientists. *The Guardian*. 22 September 2011.

[27] Eileen Dombrowski, "Following the neutrino story", TOK meets global citizenship, 11 November 2011. http://blogs.triplealearning.com

[28] "Faster-Than-Light Neutrinos Aren't," by Clara Moskowitz and SPACE.com. 8 June 2012. http://www.scientificamerican.com/article.cfm?id=faster-than-light-neutrino. Accessed 19 July 2012.

[29] Reich, E.S. 2 April 2012. "Embattled neutrino project leaders step down". *Nature*. http://www.nature.com/news/embattled-neutrino-project-leaders-step-down-1.10371.

[30] Carl Sagan (writer/host). 14 December 1980. "Encyclopaedia Galactica". *Cosmos*. Episode 12. 01:24 minutes in. PBS.

...scientists should celebrate the way in which the results were disseminated and the findings ultimately refuted. The process was open and deliberate, and it led to the correct scientific result. In an era in which politics, business and celebrity fixate on spin, control and staying 'on message', OPERA's rise and fall make science stand apart. The message here is that scientists

are not afraid to question the big ideas. They are not afraid to open themselves to public scrutiny. And they should not be afraid to be wrong.[31]

In June 2012, Sergio Bertolucci, research director at Switzerland's CERN physics lab, confirmed at an international conference in Japan that neutrinos "respect the cosmic speed limit". "Although this result isn't as exciting as some would have liked," he said, "it is what we all expected deep down."[32]

## Science in action:
## Celebrating the Higgs boson

Whereas the faster-than-light neutrinos set the scientific community buzzing because of *unexpected and challenging* results, the Higgs boson created excitement and celebration for totally opposite reasons: the discovery of the subatomic particle experimentally was a *confirmation of expectations* created by theory.

In July 2012, scientists at CERN (European Centre for Nuclear Research) made a jubilant announcement: it seemed that after two decades of searching they had discovered a new subatomic particle that was likely to be the Higgs boson, the subatomic particle that was the last and extremely important missing piece predicted to exist within the Standard Model of particle physics.

When physicist Joe Incandela announced that the research group held the conclusion "with a 5-sigma certainty" the audience burst into applause. "5-sigma certainty"? On the scale of justification, that rates 99.999 per cent confidence! But is it certain on the scale of justification (epistemological certainty)? It cannot be – not ever!

### For Reflection

What role in scientific knowledge does each of the following play?

In what ways is each one of these interconnected with the others?

- Evidence
- Peer review
- Replication
- Certainty and uncertainty

> We have reached a milestone in our understanding of nature. The discovery of a particle consistent with the Higgs boson opens the way to more detailed studies, requiring larger statistics, which will pin down the new particle's properties, and is likely to shed light on other mysteries of our universe.[33]
>
> *CERN Director General Rolf Heuer*

---

[31] "No Shame," 18 April 2012. *Nature*. http://www.nature.com/nature/journal/v484/n7394/full/484287b.html.

[32] "Faster-Than-Light Neutrinos Aren't," by Clara Moskowitz and SPACE.com. 8 June 2012. http://www.scientificamerican.com/article.cfm?id=faster-than-light-neutrino. Accessed 19 July 2012.

[33] CERN press release. 4 July 2012 http://press.web.cern.ch/press/PressReleases/Releases2012/PR17.12E.html.

Is it certain, though, on the scale of psychological confidence, personal belief? Peter Higgs, who first theorized the existence of the particle, clearly *felt* sure: "I never expected this to happen in my lifetime and shall be asking my family to put some champagne in the fridge." CERN Director General Rolf-Dieter Heuer declared, "As a layman, I would now say, I think we have it. It's a historic milestone today. I think we can all be proud, all be happy." And Joc Incandela explained enthusiastically, "This boson is a very profound thing that we have found. This is not like other ordinary particles. We are reaching into the fabric of the universe like we've never done before. It's a key to the structure of the universe."[34] Personally, they're convinced.

But whose discovery is it? Although Higgs was the one who pointed out in 1964 that the theory required a new particle in nature, six physicists (in three teams) published similar theoretical work at roughly the same time – and all, of course, built on the work of others. At CERN over the past two decades, two teams involving thousands of people did the work of "spotting traces of the particle amid the subatomic debris of more than a thousand trillion collisions inside the Large Hadron Collider". So, who's to be given credit?[35]

Huge collaborations with sophisticated technology and massive budgets have certainly changed the face of science from the time of Galileo dropping objects from a tower to see whether heavier ones were faster in hitting the ground!

## Methods: scientific theories

The common turn of phrase "it's just a theory" suggests that a theory is not to be taken seriously – that it is a conjecture not grounded in fact. In the sciences, however, theories are taken much more seriously as major scientific achievements. Justified by evidence and reasoning, they integrate all information available so far into coherent explanations.

As we have seen already in the human sciences, theories frame scientific understanding and facilitate the communal construction of knowledge. By giving diverse groups of scientists common models and vocabulary for central concepts,

shared theories enable them to communicate and exchange knowledge in terms comprehensible to each other. Theories also point the direction towards new research that would expand and clarify the large overall picture, and allow prediction of what scientists are likely to find.

Theories, clearly, are far more than mere conjecture. They are based on the body of evidence that currently exists (correspondence check) and rationally consistent interpretation (coherence check). They have a practical role (pragmatic check) in providing concepts that work for investigating the world. The theories that we accept open up the world to our directed inquiry.

The best scientific theories have several characteristics.[36] They:

- encompass scientific laws, which are deducible through them
- make factual knowledge claims, such as "electrons exist and have a charge of minus one", or "ideal gases consist of a very large number of atoms with negligible size, in random motion, which collide elastically with one another"
- refer to unobservable entities or properties that stand behind the measurements we make. For example: natural selection, the curvature of space, or strings
- are interrelated in such a way that they explain not only a particular law or phenomenon, but whole ranges of each, such that apparently diverse laws or phenomena can be explained within a common framework

34  Mann, A. 4 July 2012 "Newly Discovered Particle Appears to Be Long-Awaited Higgs Boson", Wired Science. http://www.wired.com/wiredscience/2012/07/higgs-boson-discovery/

35  Ian Sample. 4 July 2012. "Higgs boson's many great minds cause a Nobel prize headache," *The Guardian.* http://www.guardian.co.uk/science/2012/jul/04/higgs-boson-nobel-prize-headache?intcmp=239 accessed 18 July 2012.

36  Klemke, E.D., Hollinger R. and Kline, A.D. 1980. "Introduction to Part 3, Theory and Observation." *Introductory Readings in the Philosophy of Science.* New York. Prometheus Books. PP 142–3.

- provide an enormous predictive power (including phenomena which were previously unknown).

Larger theories can unite smaller ones by bringing them together under the umbrella of a larger understanding. For example, plate tectonics, the explanation of the drift of continents of the earth's crust, is picked out by science writers David Brody and Arnold Brody as one of the seven greatest scientific discoveries in history for exactly this reason: "One sweeping global theory, plate tectonics, has fused broad perspectives and diverse information discovered by geologists, biologists, and physicists. These scientists have now accounted for the mid-oceanic ridges, the world's great mountain ranges, almost all of this planet's earthquakes and volcanoes, the birth and disappearance of oceans, the movement of continents, and an essential chapter in our knowledge of evolution."[37]

It is not surprising that some physicists dream of a grand theory that will unify all physics – nor is it surprising that there is often an ironic or playful edge in referring to a "theory of everything". Although he comments on difficulties, puzzles, and paradoxes, Stephen Hawking treats such a theory as the ultimate aim of science: "Today we still yearn to know why we are here and where we came from. Humanity's deepest desire for knowledge is justification enough for our continuing quest. And our goal is nothing less than a complete description of the universe we live in."[38]

## Changing theories

Given a theory's structural role in providing unified explanation of ideas, it has much in common with other perspectives on the world. Like cultural perspectives, theoretical ones possess their own internally consistent characteristics (page 28). They are likely to start from different assumptions and values, and certainly possess different mechanisms for accepting or rejecting ideas. However, theoretical perspectives have in common with cultural perspectives a way of making sense of the world that, once adopted, influences our vision. We see what the theory picks out as important, and understand it in the theory's terms. We are caught, as ever, in one of the paradoxes

of knowledge: that seeing with the eyes of experience and interpretation simultaneously helps us to understand and makes it more difficult for us to understand *otherwise*.

Given this important role of theory in framing our understanding, a change from one theory to another has a major impact on the natural sciences. The person most credited with bringing to attention the way theories function and change within science is Thomas Kuhn, in his 1962 book The *Structure of Scientific Revolutions*. He emphasized the way that science is not a step-by-step progression, but a dynamic process involving bursts of change – the most significant change being a change in overall theory.

In normal science, according to Kuhn, scientists work within the accepted theory (which Kuhn calls a "paradigm"): they fill in details of the overall pattern of connections it illuminates and use its overview explanation to point the way towards further research. For example, the search for the Higgs boson of our earlier example was experimentation to find a particle predicted to exist within the Standard Model. The teams of thousands of scientists using the immensely sophisticated and expensive technology of the Large Hadron Collider did not work randomly or whimsically. They had an idea of what they were looking for within the conceptual framework of an accepted theory *before* they invested vast resources.

The work of normal science, though, is rarely as spectacular as this example, and the findings rarely

---

[37] Brody, D.E. and Brody, A.R. 1997. *The Science Class You Wish You Had...:The Seven Greatest Scientific Discoveries in History and the People Who Made Them*. New York. Perigree. P 254.

[38] Hawking, S. 1988. *A Brief History of Time: From the Big Bang Theory to Black Holes*. London and New York. Bantam Books. P 13.

make the news. Kuhn calls such science "puzzle solving" and comments that "normal science does not aim at novelties of fact or theory and, when successful, finds none".[39]

However, the work of normal science may accumulate anomalous results that cannot be explained with minor adjustments to accepted models. It may even turn up research results that seem to contradict features of the explanation itself. At this point, the theory is placed under strain as scientists become increasingly critical and discontent.

The stage is set for what Kuhn calls "scientific revolution", a new theory that completely reconceptualizes the relationship of parts held together by the old theory: "a new theory, however special its range of application, is seldom or never just an increment to what is already known. Its assimilation requires the reconstruction of prior theory and the re-evaluation of prior fact, an intrinsically revolutionary process that is seldom completed by a single man and never overnight."[40]

Scientists normally resist the new "paradigm", Kuhn says, because it requires fundamental shifts of thinking to see the old in terms of the new. In the revolutionary shift from Newton's theory to Einstein's, for example, "the whole conceptual web whose strands are space, time, matter, force, and so on, had to be shifted and laid down again on nature whole".[41] Yet the new theory, with better explanatory value than the previous one, eventually becomes the normal one … until the process happens all over again.

As much of his analysis has become mainstream thinking, Thomas Kuhn provides an example of someone whose personal knowledge contributed considerably to shared knowledge; he gained knowledge from the common pool, but his re-interpretation left that shared knowledge changed. Not only did he shed light on the role of theory and changing theories in the way science works, but he also placed science firmly in its human context of scientists as they work within a shared conceptual framework and react in different ways to change.

A common criticism of Kuhn, though, is that he over-emphasized the role of "revolution" in thought, when science tends to work more through incremental change. Moreover, he stressed the

way in which new theories replace the old, when sometimes we continue to use an older theory for its range of applicability. Consider the following two sets of theories, for example, as successive explanations of roughly the same aspect of the natural world.

| Biology | Physics |
|---|---|
| 1. spontaneous generation | 1. Newtonian mechanics |
| 2. Lamarckian evolution | 2. Einstein's theory of special relativity |
| 3. Darwin's theory of evolution | 3. quantum mechanics |

In the biology set, spontaneous generation was shown not to happen; new theories replaced the old. In the physics set, we continue to use Newtonian mechanics most of the time to explain what happens in human size ranges and at speeds at which we usually move.

## Science in action: chaos theory

As an example of scientists learning to "see" in new ways as theories change, we pick chaos theory. It is a riveting example for what it brings together: it crosses boundaries of disciplines in the patterns that it recognizes, and it fuses mathematics, the sciences, and (arguably) the visual arts in the images that epitomize its geometry. Developed during the 1970s and 1980s, chaos theory illustrates many of Thomas Kuhn's arguments regarding paradigm shifts in the natural sciences: the challenge to think differently, the resistance, and the ultimate acceptance, with growing appreciation of what the new theory opens up to view.

Despite its catchy name, this theory is in many ways a theory of order: it reveals a new kind of pattern within the turbulence of nature, with limits on the degree to which it can be predicted. The intuitions of new kinds of relationships in nature are visualized in the Mandelbrot set, fractal images showing self-similarity at larger and smaller scales: you can zoom *in and in* on the image and find that the same pattern is replicated over and over.

The theory, developed by pioneers working in a variety of different fields and coming together during the 1970s, was not immediately welcomed, as James Gleick documents the reactions of

[39] Kuhn, T. 1962. *The Structure of Scientific Revolutions.* P 52.

[40] Kuhn, T. 1962. *The Structure of Scientific Revolutions.* P 7.

[41] Kuhn, T. 1962. *The Structure of Scientific Revolutions.* P 149.

scientists to this new theory: "Uncomprehension; resistance; anger; acceptance. Those who had promoted chaos longest saw all of these."[42] Its early development found no support or funding within established fields, since it crossed disciplines in dealing with such topics as populations in biology, weather patterns, fluid dynamics, and electrical activity of the heart. Moreover, the theoretical models of the time were not compatible with the non-linear systems of chaos. "The phenomenon of chaos could have been discovered long, long ago," commented one of the pioneers. "It wasn't discovered, in part, because this huge body of work on the dynamics of regular motion didn't lead in that direction."

"You have to change gears," commented Feigenbaum on the shift in the way of thinking within physics which sparked the discovery of the chaos theory. "You have to reassemble how you conceive of the important things that are going on… It requires a different way of thinking about the problem."[43]

It required, too, almost a new way of "seeing" pattern. The perfect circles, triangles, and cones of Euclidean geometry turned out to be inapplicable to the patterns of complexity. "The new geometry mirrors a universe that is rough, not rounded, scabrous, not smooth. It is a geometry of the pitted, pocked, and broken up, the twisted, tangled, and intertwined."[44]

It was the development of the computer and its capacity for mathematical calculations that provided the fractal images of chaos theory, and allowed scientists readily to change variables and recalculate. Minute changes in the initial variables, calculated over time, produce very different results.

This realization of sensitive dependence on initial conditions has been called "the butterfly effect". Lorenz, who studied chaotic behaviour in weather systems, coined the term with the theoretical example that the beating of the wings of a butterfly in one part of the world could affect the formation of a hurricane in another part of the world. Tiny variables, in short, can affect major outcomes. Without perfect knowledge of all possible conditions in the present, we cannot perfectly forecast the weather, or any other complex system, into the future, with small imperfections making our predictions more and more inexact as we project them ahead over time.

---

[42] Gleick, J. 1987. *A Geometry of Nature, Chaos: Making A New Science*. London. Penguin Books. P 305.

[43] Gleick, J. 1987. *A Geometry of Nature, Chaos: Making A New Science*. London. Penguin Books. P 185.

[44] Gleick, J. 1987. *A Geometry of Nature, Chaos: Making A New Science*. London. Penguin Books. P 94.

Chaos theory has contributed to a new understanding of patterns in nature. Far from considering those ragged, self-replicating patterns to be ugly aberrations of perfect geometry, scientists and much of the public familiar with fractal images call them "fascinating" and "beautiful". The mathematics of chaos theory yields images of the patterns of our world – branching and forking, swirling, reiterating – and produces works that, with some aesthetic choices, are often considered art. In many ways, the development of chaos theory illustrates the ideas of theory and "paradigm shift" as presented by Thomas Kuhn.

Our models fall far short of representing the world fully. That is why we make mistakes and why we are regularly surprised. In our heads, we can keep track of only a few variables at one time. We often draw illogical conclusions from accurate assumptions, or logical conclusions from inaccurate assumptions. Most of us, for instance, are surprised by the amount of growth an exponential process can generate. Few of us can intuit how to damp oscillations in a complex system.[45]

*Donella H. Meadows*

## Thinking in systems: the web of life

Chaos theory boosted a further paradigm shift, by reinforcing the thinking of some biologists. Through the earlier part of the century, they had been insisting that living things cannot be understood in isolation from each other, but rather as parts of interconnected wholes.

"The new paradigm may be called a holistic worldview seeing the world as an integrated whole rather than a dissociated collection of parts," writes physicist and systems theorist Fritjof Capra. He calls it an "ecological view": "Deep ecological awareness recognizes the fundamental interdependence of all phenomena and the fact that, as individuals and societies, we are all embedded in (and ultimately dependent on) the cyclical processes of nature."[46]

Like chaos theory, systems thinking reaches beyond the natural sciences. It crosses disciplines in giving a greater understanding of complex systems and recognition of processes that work together to make an ecosystem or a social organization stay in balance. It emphasizes the need for a new, holistic understanding of reality "for dealing with our overpopulated, globally interconnected world".[47] This paradigm shift, coming out of biology, has significant social implications for how we understand the problems of our world, and the conceptual framework within which we seek solutions.

## Models

As we noted in the chapter on the human sciences, models are simplified abstractions from the world, selecting features essential to the relationships being emphasized and leaving out other features as irrelevant detail. They are not easy abstractions to construct, given the complexity of the systems that models often represent. But then, the model is not a representation of reality as much as a representation of how we *think about reality* within the framework of a particular theory.

In your own science courses, you will be familiar with models of different kinds, including:

- physical representations of atomic structures
- simplified diagrams of systems in the environment

[45] Meadows, D.H. 2008. *Thinking in Systems: A Primer*. Edited by D. Wright, Sustainability Institute. White River Junction, Vermont. Chelsea Green Publishing. P 86.

[46] Capra, F. 1996. *The Web of Life: A New Scientific Understanding of Living Systems*. New York. Anchor Books. P 6.

[47] Capra, F. 1996. *The Web of Life: A New Scientific Understanding of Living Systems*. New York. Anchor Books. P 4.

- schematic flow charts
- equations describing worlds without friction
- mathematical models developed within a computer.

The general classifications of the natural world that we treated at the beginning of this chapter come with their models to help us imagine them – that is, they bring useful images to our minds. Tools for thought, models allow us to focus on particular features of the world. They work as clarification of the theories within which they are set, to connect observations and possibly allow for prediction. In the activity we suggested earlier in the chapter dealing with your own science courses, we trust that you had no difficulty in identifying examples.

Models, probably even more than the theories they distil, can take on in our minds a sense that somehow they are real – that somehow they really are what nature *looks like* or *acts like*. We have to remember that they are abstractions and simplifications, and, like theories themselves, leave out the background that, for humanly chosen purposes, is not "important".

## Scientific prediction

The models we accept allow us to predict – in both scientific senses of the word "predict". Prediction in science can mean either prediction of *what must be the case* as the logical consequence of accepting

a hypothesis or theory, or *projection into the future* based on knowledge of the present.

Prediction of *what must be the case* is derived through deductive reasoning, as the logical consequence of accepting a hypothesis. If the hypothesis is true, then, deductively, specific situations or events must follow from it. But do they? We test to find out. The Salk vaccine for poliomyelitis, for example, was hypothesized to protect those vaccinated from the disease. In fact, when people were first given the vaccine in 1952, they did not develop polio. So far, so good: tentative confirmation. Vaccination for polio soon became widespread, and incidence of the disease dropped accordingly. In the example we used earlier, the subatomic Higgs boson was predicted to exist according to the Standard Model in physics, so the tests run were to confirm or refute that prediction. Similarly, paleontology is full of "missing links" that have been predicted to exist according to evolutionary theory, and then found in the fossilized remains. Recently, the link between dinosaurs and birds has been confirmed by fossils of dinosaurs with feathers.[48]

In the second use of "prediction", *predicting into the future*, we use our knowledge of the regularities of the world to project what will happen across time. The better justified our present generalizations about the world, the more reliable will be the predictions based on them. We can describe the path that meteors will take, predict eclipses, and draw up tide tables well into the future. As we apply our knowledge to technology, in some areas of science we can achieve considerable accuracy. Just think for a moment of all the calculation of future trajectories that was involved in launching Mars rover *Curiosity* into space and having it land safely on the surface of Mars. When setting up an international space station, then sending people up in a capsule to join it, we need this degree of precision. Astronauts do not want to end up *approximately* near the space station, or *probably* reaching it, and being only *likely* to return home.

Other areas of science deal with rougher predictions, for instance, as they project past and present trends into the future. For example, climate science cannot tell us exactly what will happen in 20 years, but instead can give us most likely scenarios. As variables in the present change – such as the global levels of carbon emissions – predictions of future events change with them. What will, in

48  David Hone. 5 July 2012. "Feathers edge closer to the origins of dinosaurs," *The Guardian*. http://www.guardian.co.uk/science/blog/2012/jul/05/feathers-dinosaurs-fossils accessed 4 August 2012.

## For Reflection

In what ways does the general public – like you and your family – benefit, directly and indirectly, from the products of scientific research? Do you consider there to be effects that are not beneficial? Do the benefits outweigh the risks?

Is the public – that is, you – responsible for keeping abreast of scientific developments? When they affect social and political decisions, what is the nature of your own responsibility? If not the general public, then who should be the gatekeepers?

fact, happen depends very much on human beings, in a world context where we depend on political processes to control the variables.

## Science and society: shared knowledge, shared and personal implications

The natural sciences are an amazing area of knowledge for the understanding they have given us of the world in which we live. They have constructed a methodology that draws on our human subjectivity in aspiration and imagination, but that combines skepticism and openness as they aim for objectivity. Through rigorous testing, peer review and replication, as we have seen, they attempt to make knowledge claims about the world that correspond with how it really is. They work towards communal agreement on the justifications for their knowledge claims regardless of who is doing the observing and reasoning. It would seem that the knowledge is independent of personalities, culture, and social forces – and in certain ways it is.

To a large extent, we have emphasized in this chapter the way that the natural sciences *do* remove their knowledge from any particular context as we aim to examine the features of the knowledge itself. At the same time, though, we have also emphasized the humanity involved in creating the sciences, as an equally important part of the picture of knowledge. We have given you stories of science in process, interviews, and photographs of scientists at work. We have dealt with the creative and imaginative

side of science and the human responses to new discoveries and new theories. As well, we have suggested the human attributes that have to be overcome in an area of knowledge that aims to be cooperative. While we probably do not tend to forget the human beings who create the arts, we can too easily forget the human beings who create the more overtly communal knowledge of the natural sciences.

Those scientists, as we have seen, usually work within collaborative groups, some of them huge collaborations in international teams. How is it that such an extensive enterprise can be constructed and maintained? How does this interconnected community of millions of people function within society as a whole? And how does the way scientific investigation fits into society affect the knowledge that the sciences create?

Dealing with these questions of where the sciences fit within society takes us to other areas of knowledge that provide their own kinds of approaches to answering, and different perspectives within the overall approaches of their disciplines. We could turn, for instance, to history for an explanation of the how the sciences began and have developed, or to sociology for accounts of their internal social structures, networks of communication, mobilization of resources, or impact on other features of society. We could turn, likewise, to sociology, political science, and ethics for illumination of how the sciences work as social institutions, how they fit with other institutions of society, how they affect the lives of individuals within the broader social structures, or what societies *should* do regarding the sciences. Clearly, asking questions about the place of the sciences in society can take us into knowledge as extensive as the knowledge of the sciences themselves. It is at a level of very general overview, then, that we pass you some ideas to think about.

### 1. How is scientific knowledge used by societies?

This first is not a knowledge question but one asking for general information – to establish *what* is before we think about what *should be*. Simply looking around your surroundings and thinking about your own life, can you identify the uses to which we collectively put scientific knowledge and its technological products. Are you aware of how such knowledge is applied in other parts of the world?

## 2. How does funding affect the pursuit of knowledge?

Take a moment to think about the resources given to the pursuit of scientific inquiry: the salaries, the equipment, the buildings, the journals and conferences. Think about not just the economic investment but the social investment in education and decision-making, and in the amount of time and talent given to the sciences.

Where do all the resources come from, and who directs their investment in the sciences? You might look to different components of society such as business and government for their economic or political support for the sciences, or their opposition to them, and the different ways in which they invest financial and human resources.

To what extent, then, do funding agencies of business or government direct how science develops? Large corporations such as pharmaceutical companies or oil companies and large social components such as the military have directions in which they want research to develop, in response to market forces or national interests. It would be hard to generalize about the role of governments within all the political systems of the world, but you might consider within your own society what role the government plays in identifying what research is important to take on, or to avoid. The agencies that fund science affect what kind of knowledge is gained and whose benefit is being sought.

## 3. Who owns knowledge?

This question is not disconnected from the previous one. It looks beyond the funding and process of the sciences, though, to the products of science – the knowledge itself with all of its implications, and the technology to which it leads.

Different interest groups involved in knowledge production have quite different perspectives. Scientists themselves may want to be able to publish their findings in accordance with the communal methodology of science and their own goals of advancing their careers. Business organizations funding the research, in contrast, may want to conceal developments from competitors and ensure that the results are claimed as their own through a system of copyright and patents. Other scientists, organizations and the

general public may want to benefit from the knowledge with an array of different interests from narrow personal gain to broad social benefit.

Tensions between the interest groups have created some large international controversies.

- For example, should communication technology such as the Internet be controlled by governments, by business, by the people, or by no one? Which should be given priority: freedom of speech, freedom of access to information, political or national interests, or business interests? Who should be able to close down what is said on the Internet? (Interesting controversies: government control of the Internet in some countries; the Wikileaks controversy)

- For example, should pharmaceutical companies own the medical knowledge that is the result of research they have funded, or should the knowledge be shared according to the principles of open science? Should lifesaving drugs be made available to those who can pay the highest price in the market, or should the poor and desperate also have access? (Interesting controversy: the accessibility of generic HIV/AIDS drugs to people in Africa.)

## 4. What responsibilities do societies have for understanding and influencing the sciences?

This question is a thorny one, bristling with different perspectives on what kind of development and application of the sciences is desirable, economically feasible, ethical and politically acceptable. How should the sciences be directed, and what should we do with the results?

The answers that societies give to this question can affect the way we bring children into the world and keep them healthy, the way we feed ourselves or the world, the degree to which we live in security, the ways in which we use natural resources, and the impact on the planet of the future on the choices that we make in the present. Although public debate on these topics can be tense, social exchange of ideas is crucial to informed social judgments.

First, do we have a responsibility for informing ourselves on major scientific topics relevant to our lives? If so, how? Although most of us don't have the expertise to understand scientific details, we do have access to commentators who can explain the significant points in language we understand, and help us grasp the implications. Finding reliable explanation and analysis is an issue of critical literacy of evaluating sources (page 219) and building on a basic understanding of science (possibly gained through IB science classes and TOK).

Second, do we have a responsibility for understanding public debates on how scientific research is directed and how the findings are applied? Can we follow the views exchanged (sometimes hotly!) on the impact of climate change, research into sources of energy other than fossil fuels, development and availability of drugs against diseases that ravage the world, development of nuclear or biological weapons, medical extension or termination of life, birth control, genetic modification of crops, use of pesticides and fertilizers in farming – to name just a few? Our best tools for thought may be our grasp of how perspectives work (page 28), how they influence the way information is selected, emphasized, expressed, or used in different ways (page 150), and how different ethical lines of argument contribute useful ideas.

### For Reflection

To what extent do you find in the sciences a refinement of simple curiosity about the world, such as children possess as they ask about the stars or animals?

In what ways do you consider a basic scientific training to be helpful to you in matters of everyday life? Which seems to you more beneficial – a general background in the knowledge claims of science ("I know that...") or an awareness of the process of inquiry and investigation ("I know how...")?

But if we *do* resolve both to inform ourselves on the science and to understand the issues under debate, then what? Does an informed opinion bring a responsibility to act? Does it involve our choices as consumers? Does it affect the directions we take in our future work? Does it involve our actions as citizens? We live in exciting times, with knowledge as never before. What is our world going to do with it, and do we have a part to play?

### Discussion Activity

#### Knowledge Framework: Natural Sciences

First summarize your responses to these questions in your own words. Then exchange ideas with others in your class.

1.  **Scope:** What are the natural sciences all about? What is their subject matter and what are their goals? What is their contribution to knowledge overall?

2.  **Language/concepts:** What central concepts characterize this area of knowledge? In what ways is the naming and defining of central concepts significant within the natural sciences? What is the role of language (and other symbolic systems of representation) in the production of scientific knowledge?

3.  **Methodology:** What ways of knowing (including language) do the natural sciences use, and how? How do scientists create, exchange, and evaluate knowledge? What methods do they use to gain the most reliable knowledge possible of their subject matter (at a given time)? Are the sciences characterized more by their methodology of shared knowledge or by the nature of the knowledge claims they make?

4.  **Historical development:** What social and technological factors have pushed the natural sciences in particular directions? How have significant contributions of individuals or groups changed the way science is done or understood?

5.  **Links personal knowledge:** How do individuals and groups contribute personal knowledge to the natural sciences, and gain from its shared knowledge? How do the natural sciences contribute to your own personal knowledge?

Compare your responses on the natural sciences with those you developed on history and the human sciences. What do the goals and methods have in common, and how do they differ?

# Creation and criticism

## A tale of two dreamers: the poet and the chemist

"The scientific and poetic or imaginative accounts of the world are not distinguishable in their origins. They start in parallel, but diverge from one another at some later stage. We all tell stories, but the stories differ in the purposes we expect them to fulfil and in the kinds of evaluations to which they are exposed."

### Peter Medawar[49]

### How did he know?

In 1797, English poet Samuel Taylor Coleridge (1779–1834) composed a well known poem while dreaming. In poor health, he had taken a medicine containing opium. As he was falling asleep, he was reading a book about the emperor Kubla Khan. In his sleep, he composed "without any sensation or consciousness of effort" what he later recalled as two to three hundred lines of poetry. Waking, he wrote down about 50 lines before he was interrupted.[50]

### How did he know?

German chemist Friedrich August Kekulé (1829–1896) was given to interesting visions while daydreaming. He claimed to have come upon his notion of chemical structure while falling asleep atop a London bus and seeing "atoms gamboling before my eyes." In another such episode he was dozing off when the hexagonal ring structure of the benzene molecule appeared to him in the form of a snake biting its own tail: "I woke up as though I had been struck by lightning."[51]

In Xanadu did Kubla Khan
A stately pleasure-dome decree:
Where Alph, the sacred river, ran
Through caverns measureless to man
Down to a sunless sea.

## Comparison: Methods of the Arts and the Natural Sciences

Coleridge and Kekulé both wake from dreams with new ideas. To what extent is either the poem or the model of the benzene molecule a finished product of knowledge at that point, ready for publication? To what processes of evaluation is each of their works subjected, before and after publication?

49 Medawar, P. Reprinted 1987, first published 1982. *"Science and Literature," Pluto's Republic*. Oxford and New York. Oxford University Press. P 53.
50 Samuel Taylor Coleridge, "Kubla Khan", The Norton Anthology of English Literature: 2. W W Norton and Co. Inc, New York, 1962. page 197
51 Curt Suplee, Milestones of Science, National Geographic Society, Washington, DC, 2000. page 153.

# 20. Mathematics

> The patterns and relationships studied by mathematicians occur everywhere in nature: the symmetrical patterns of flowers, the often complicated patterns of knots, the orbits swept out by planets as they move through the heavens, the patterns of spots on a leopard's skin, the voting pattern of a population, the pattern produced by the random outcomes in a game of dice or roulette, the relationship between the words that make up a sentence, the patterns of sound that we recognize as music… Because it studies such abstract patterns, mathematics often allows us to see – and hence perhaps make use of – similarities between two phenomena that at first appear quite different. Thus, we can think of mathematics as a pair of conceptual spectacles that enable us to see what would otherwise be invisible…[1]
>
> *Keith Devlin*

## Scope: what does mathematics study?

The knowledge questions of history, the human sciences, and the natural sciences share a great deal in common as these areas of knowledge aim to give a true description of the world (natural world or human beings) and, to varying extents, to identify generalized relationships and causal connections. They vary in their methods and the reach of their conclusions primarily because they apply their thinking to different aspects of the world they collectively study.

When we turn to mathematics, though, the nature of the knowledge has changed. It still asks the central questions of all areas of knowledge: *How do we know? What methods can we use to investigate, and what justifications can we offer for our knowledge claims?* It still maintains a relationship with these other areas of knowledge, frequently an intimate one that invites some investigation, but it kicks itself loose from the world in which the others are grounded. Mathematics removes itself into

abstraction, into concepts. And oddly, these abstractions often prove useful as a way of talking about the real world that mathematics seemed to have left behind.

As we enter mathematics, we are going into an area of clarity, abstraction, and, according to many a brilliant mathematician, ultimate beauty.

## Mathematics as the study of pattern

Mathematics is the study of pattern – abstract pattern that places concepts in a systematized relationship to one another, expressed in a symbolic system that we can manipulate using reason alone, with no necessary reference to the world. We open this chapter with a discussion activity looking at *particular* kinds of patterns we can see in the world, but mathematics finds ordered relationships between ideas in almost every aspect of our lives. Mathematician Keith Devlin, quoted on the left, explains further:

> …the patterns studied by the mathematician can be either real or imagined, visual or mental, static or dynamic, qualitative or quantitative, utilitarian or recreational. They arise from the world around us, from the depths of space and time, and from the workings of the human mind. Different kinds of patterns give rise to different branches of mathematics. For example, number theory studies (and arithmetic uses) the patterns of number and counting; geometry studies the patterns of shape; calculus allows us to handle patterns of motion; logic studies patterns of reasoning; probability theory deals with patterns of chance; topology studies patterns of closeness and position.[2]

## Mathematics and the real world

Mathematicians have long posed the question, "Do we discover mathematics in the real world, or do we invent it with our minds?" Across the centuries some have been completely

---

[1] Devlin, K. 2000. *The Math Gene: How Mathematical Thinking Evolved and How Numbers Are Like Gossip.* UK. Basic Books. P 74.

[2] Devlin, K. 2000. *The Math Gene: How Mathematical Thinking Evolved and How Numbers Are Like Gossip.* UK. Basic Books. P 8.

convinced of the answer. For instance, Galileo Galilei firmly declared in the early seventeenth century that the universe was written in mathematical language, and in the twentieth century British mathematician G.H. Hardy agreed: "I believe that mathematical reality lies outside us, that our function is to discover or observe it, and that the theorems which we prove, and which we describe grandiloquently as our 'creations', are simply our notes of our

## Discussion Activity

### Treasure hunt

### The preparation

Ask in advance for two volunteers from the class to prepare and present a short explanation of what each of the following terms means:

- bilateral symmetry, radial symmetry, hexagon, circle, cone, fractal
- Fibonacci series, golden ratio, golden spiral.

### The hunt

On a class field trip into nature or into the Internet, find an example in nature of at least five of the mathematical ideas in the lists above, and at least one example of a mathematically describable shape, sequence, or other relationship not on the list. Work in pairs or small teams, with a time limit. Each team should return ready to share with the class the example that they consider to be the finest mathematical treasure in their collection, with their reasons for considering it so.

### The discussion

Read the quotation from Keith Devlin with which this chapter opens and then turn back to the examples you have collected. As a class, agree on three of the original categories and share examples of each that your team has collected. If you are in doubt, we recommend radial symmetry, fractals, and the Fibonacci series. Then consider the following questions:

- Do the mathematical patterns that you have found show up in natural forms that you would normally classify into different categories – such as animals, plants, and physical geography, or different species? How do the patterns studied in mathematics differ from the patterns studied in the natural sciences?
- Devlin says that "mathematics often allows us to see – and hence perhaps make use of – similarities between two phenomena that at first appear quite different". In what ways does the abstraction of pattern from physical reality allow us to create anything that we can "make use of"? From your list of treasures, can you provide an example of similarity that you did not see at first? How might the abstraction they have in common be something we could "make use of"?

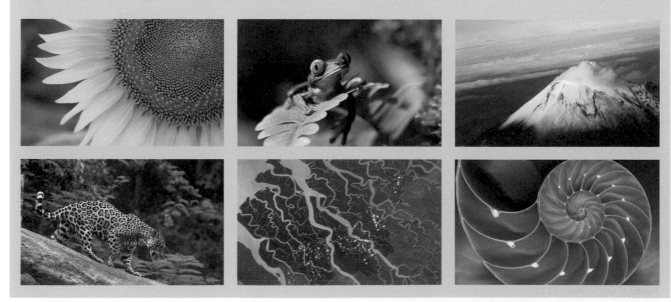

observations."[3] Yet the relationship between mathematics and the world captivated Albert Einstein with a greater sense of wonder: "How can it be that mathematics, being after all a product of human thought which is independent of experience, is so admirably appropriate to the objects of reality? Is human reason, then, without experience, merely by taking thought, able to fathom the properties of real things?"[4]

Regardless of whether we consider mathematics to be part of the structure of the universe or to be a formal system invented by our minds, however, it is undeniable that mathematical equations can describe the physical universe extremely well. We can truly marvel that the area of knowledge which takes us into abstract thought simultaneously provides us, very often, with the symbolic system with which we can talk most precisely about the physical world.

Two very special irrational numbers illustrate this amazing connection between the abstract and the concrete. Pi ($\pi = 3.14159...$) and Euler's constant ($e = 2.71828...$) show up in many equations in the natural and human sciences, and within mathematics itself.

Pi appears when we consider the circular shape, and is defined as the ratio of a circle's circumference to its diameter. It naturally appears whenever knowledge about circles and spheres is invoked, even within physics formulae.

Euler's constant likewise makes frequent and surprising appearances in unlike areas of computation. The formula $e = 1/0! + 1/1! + 1/2! + 1/3! + 1/4! + ...$ (infinite series) provides one way to calculate Euler's constant, and uses factorials (e.g. $5! = 5 \times 4 \times 3 \times 2 \times 1$; $0! = 1$ by definition). As students of calculus learn, the function $e^x$ has very peculiar properties. It also appears naturally in equations describing phenomena such as radioactive decay, the spread of epidemics, compound interest, and population growth.

Perhaps most fascinating of all, though, is an equation that mathematicians marvel over for the way it unites much mathematical thinking in a way that is economical and beautiful. Within

mathematics, many consider Euler's equation $e^{i\pi} + 1 = 0$ to be one of the greatest equations of all time. Not only does it uncannily connect the five most important numbers of mathematics ($e$, $\pi$, 1, 0, and the imaginary number i), but "what could be more mystical than an imaginary number interacting with real numbers to produce nothing?"[5]

## Pure and applied mathematics

As it develops, mathematics moves both towards the abstractions of the mind, and also towards the connection with the world. The main difference between pure and applied mathematics, as some universities classify their departments, is in the application of the knowledge they develop. (The qualifier "pure" to describe one kind doesn't imply that the other kind is impure or inferior; according to one practitioner,[6] a more fitting name might be "theoretical mathematics".) Researchers in pure mathematics – which includes abstract fields such as algebra, analysis, geometry, number theory, and topology – are not concerned with the direct practical applications of their labour. Applied mathematicians, on the other hand, focus on developing mathematical tools to enable and enhance research in other areas of knowledge. Applied fields include numerical analysis, scientific computing, mathematical physics, information theory, control theory, actuarial science, and many others.

As is usual with classification schemes, some of the distinctions between "pure" and "applied" are imprecise. The very establishment of applied

---

[3] Hardy, G.H. 1940. *A Mathematician's Apology.* London. P 35.

[4] Einstein, A. 1920, 2004. *Sidelights on Relativity.* Kessinger Publishing. P 12.

[5] Crease, R.P. 2004. "The greatest equations ever." *Critical Point, Physics World.*

[6] Runde, V. September 2003. "Why I don't like 'Pure Mathematics." *π in the Sky.* Pp 30–1.

mathematics resulted from the successful application of pure mathematics to real-world problems! As Nikolai Lobachevsky once said, "There is no branch of mathematics, however abstract, which may not someday be applied to the phenomena of the real world."[7] In the 1970s his assertion was verified yet again with the application of the fundamental theorem of arithmetic – considered useless for more than 2000 years! – to cryptography, in order to enable secure electronic communications.[8]

A second degree of imprecision in classification occurs when we consider the relationship between applied mathematics and the areas of knowledge they support. For example, many advances in physics – perhaps even most advances – did not result from fitting a mathematical expression to experimental data points. To derive the equation $E=mc^2$, for example, Albert Einstein applied a set of equations called Lorenz transformations to what he believed was true about light and logically deduced, one step following the other, his theory of special relativity. Thus, it is sometimes difficult to distinguish clearly between applied mathematics and theoretical physics. With the pervasiveness of computational techniques applied to modelling and simulation in various fields, today the boundaries have become even more blurred.

Whether we're dealing with pure or applied mathematics, though, both deal solely with ideas, at a level of extreme abstraction.

## Methods: shared knowledge

> "
> Mathematics is not a careful march down a well-cleared highway, but a journey into a strange wilderness, where the explorers often get lost. Rigour should be a signal to the historian that the maps have been made, and the real explorers have gone elsewhere.[9]
>
> *W.S. Anglin*
> "

Mathematics, like the other areas of knowledge, is *shared*. Individual mathematicians contribute their work to a communal pool, where other mathematicians, in a process of peer review, scrutinize it for error. If it is found to be reliable, they build on it themselves in their own further work – which in turn they contribute to the collective pool.

Collective knowledge in mathematics acts differently, though, from collective knowledge in the sciences. Peers in the field examine each other's work to eliminate error, just as in the sciences. However, once the knowledge has been proven, it remains proven forever. Mathematicians build on each other's work differently from in the sciences as a result, expecting no established knowledge claims to be revised or rejected as false. They can use all that has gone before as an irrefutable platform on which to build their own new work.

Nevertheless, the stability of past knowledge in mathematics in no way suggests that mathematicians stick to old paths and troop off, all of them, in the same direction. Mathematical thinking can adventure across the map and into a huge range of topic areas. In its rich past, mathematics developed from the study of numbers by ancient Egyptian, Babylonian, and Chinese mathematicians; it has grown through the development of formal arguments by the ancient Greeks, through further developments particularly in Arabia and China, and then onwards to Europe (calculus), and now into an internationally shared exchange.

Mathematical knowledge increased vastly in the twentieth century. As that century opened, mathematics consisted of roughly 12 subject domains, but as it closed there were 60 to 70. Some are specializations of earlier fields, but some, such as complexity theory and dynamical systems theory, are entirely new.[10]

But who are these mathematicians at work in this community that stretches far back into the past? Well, they do not work in teams as contemporary scientists usually do, and as performance artists do in putting on plays, operas, or dance. And they work more quietly. They do not require the sophisticated technological equipment that some groups of scientists do; they need no Large

[7] Lobachevsky, N. 1988. In *Mathematical Maxims and Minims* by N. Rose. Raleigh, NC. Rome Press Inc.

[8] Runde, V. September 2003. "Why I don't like 'Pure Mathematics'" *π in the Sky*. Pp 30–1.

[9] Quoted in Singh, S. 2002. *Fermat's Enigma. The Epic Quest to Solve the World's Greatest Mathematical Problem*. Penguin Books P 71.

[10] Devlin, K. 2000. *The Math Gene: How Mathematical Thinking Evolved and How Numbers Are Like Gossip*. UK. Basic Books. Pp 6–7.

## Pattern: mathematics, the sciences or the arts?

Would you classify the following fractal images as works of mathematics, the sciences, or the arts? Why?

What is the relationship of each of mathematics, the sciences, and the arts to the concept of pattern? Do mathematics, the sciences, and the arts (a) describe pattern in the world, (b) abstract pattern from the world, or (c) impose pattern on the world? What comparisons would you draw between areas of knowledge when it comes to studying patterns?

Hadron Collider since nothing in their work ever collides physically with anything else. Perhaps mathematicians most resemble poets or novelists in the way that they work with the products of their minds. As we treat some particular developments in mathematics later in this chapter, we hope to create a greater sense of the passions and personalities at work.

## Ways of knowing

As we have commented in the past, it is entirely artificial to separate ways of knowing from the people using them. It is, however, one of those distinctions and classifications that is useful in highlighting central features. As we turn first to sense perception and language as ways of knowing, we consider the ways in which mathematics uses the ways of knowing in its own characteristic balance. In the back of your mind, you might want to be comparing mathematics with the human and natural sciences, with the arts, and with ethics.

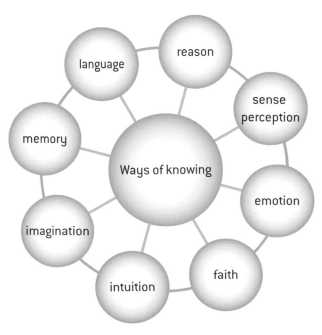

## Mathematics and reality: "dealing exclusively with acts of the mind"

*by Tobias Dantzig*

Between the philosopher's attitude towards the issue of reality and that of the mathematician there is this essential difference: for the philosopher the issue is paramount; the mathematician's love for reality is purely platonic.

The mathematician is only too willing to admit that he is dealing exclusively with acts of the mind. To be sure, he is aware that the ingenious artifices which form his stock in trade had their genesis in the sense impressions which he identifies with crude reality, and he is not surprised to find that at times these artifices fit quite neatly the reality in which they were born. But this neatness the mathematician refuses to recognize as a criterion of his achievement: the value of the beings which spring from his creative imagination shall not be measured by the scope of their application to physical reality. No! Mathematical achievement shall be measured by standards which are peculiar to mathematics. These standards are independent from the crude reality of our senses. They are: freedom from logical contradictions, the generality of the laws governing the created form, the kinship which exists between this new form and those that have preceded it.

The mathematician may be compared to a designer of garments, who is utterly oblivious of the creatures whom his garments may fit. To be sure, his designs originated in the necessity for clothing such creatures, but this was long ago. Nowadays, a creature will occasionally appear who will fit into the garment as if the garment had been made for it, even though he didn't design it for that creature. Then there is no end of surprise and of delight!

There have been quite a few such delightful surprises. The conic sections, invented in an attempt to solve the problem of doubling the altar of an oracle, end by describing the orbits followed by the planets in their courses about the sun. The imaginary magnitudes invented by Cardan and Bombelli describe in some strange way the characteristic features of alternating currents of electricity. The absolute differential calculus, which originated as a fantasy of Riemann, became the mathematical vehicle for Einstein's theory of Relativity. And the matrices which were a complete abstraction in the days of Cayley and Sylvester have become ideal tools for studying the quantum theory of the atom.

Yet, delightful though these surprises may be, their discovery is not the moving force behind the creative work of the mathematician. For him, mathematics is the field in which he can best manifest his personality. Mathematics for mathematics' sake![11]

## Way of knowing: sense perception

> The point of mathematics is that in it we have always got rid of the particular instance, and even of any particular sorts of entities … The certainty of mathematics depends on its complete abstract generality.[12]
>
> *Alfred North Whitehead*

Alfred North Whitehead, in the quotation above, is not simply pointing out the abstraction of mathematics from our sense perceptions of the world. He goes further: it is this separation of mathematics from the world that allows it to be free of all the uncertainties of observation and thus produce results which are true in all cases, without exception.

Degrees of uncertainty, as we considered in the earlier chapter on sense perception, are characteristic of any knowledge of the world based on our human, variable, actively selective, and interpretive senses. In the sciences, much of the methodology is directed to overcoming, through peer review and replication, the limitations of an observational basis to justification. In mathematics, there is no such requirement, because the senses,

[11] Dantzig, T. 1954. *Number: The Language of Science.* New York. The Free Press. Pp 231–2.
[12] Whitehead, A.N. 1926. *Science and the Modern World.* Cambridge University Press. Pp 27–8.

even if they may have originally engendered mathematical concepts, have no place in mathematical development (though again they do in application of mathematics to the world). Although obviously mathematicians use their senses in creating notation and exchanging their work, the *justifications* for mathematical conclusions do not rest on sense perception.

## Way of knowing: language

Neither does *justification* for mathematical conclusions rest on language. But it would not be possible to develop mathematical reasoning into shared knowledge, built up and archived, without it. Language – that is, our everyday spoken language – is the means of learning and teaching mathematical concepts. Mathematical symbolism is a subset of the ideas developed in language. As it has grown, it has taken on many features of a language itself. As a symbolic system, it allows ideas to be manipulated in the mind and communicated with others.

We cannot speak of single or isolated numbers. The essence of number is always relative, not absolute. A single number is only a single place in a general systematic order. It has no being of its own, no self-contained reality. Its meaning is defined by the position it occupies in the whole numerical system.

We conceive it as a new and powerful symbolism which, for all scientific purposes, is infinitely superior to the symbolism of speech. For what we find here are no longer detached words but terms that proceed according to one and the same fundamental plan and that, therefore, show us a clear and definite structural law.[13]

*Ernst Cassirer*

## Characteristics of mathematical "language"

You have learned many mathematical symbols in your lifetime so here we intend simply to guide some reflections on what you know already. Please join us.

First take a few moments to write down 10 mathematical symbols (other than real numbers,

which would be too easy). Note how each symbol has a very precise meaning.

Are you allowed to combine these symbols in any way you wish? No. In the same way that the string of words: "there go pretty me went I" uses English symbols but is not grammatical, a string such as "x + 2 )( = > " is not grammatical in mathematics. It is meaningless.

In being symbolic and able to be manipulated into meaningful statements, mathematics has many characteristics of language. Although it does not have the range of functions of language and depends on being consciously taught through language, mathematics has features which make it far superior to language as a symbolic system for abstract, rational argument:

1.  It is precise and explicit. 3 is always 3, whereas "a couple" can mean two, three, a few… or even many, as in "I just need a couple of minutes!"

2.  It is compact. Considerable thought can fit into a few lines. To see the difference for yourself, explain the Pythagorean theorem, $c^2 = a^2 + b^2$ using English.

3.  It is transformable without loss of meaning. We can say that of 100 students, 25% are male and 75% are female, that there are 50 more females than males, that the ratio of females to males is 3 to 1, that the probability of a student being male is 0.25. And so on.

Now, write down a few of the rules with which you manipulate mathematical symbols and statements. Examples include the commutative property, cross multiplication, not dividing by zero, reducing a fraction, factoring a polynomial, and many others. Note that these rules are general. The introduction of rules leads us to two more features of mathematics as a symbolic system:

4.  It is completely abstract and conceptual. It manipulates its statements solely with its own rules.

5.  It can lead to new conclusions that were not readily apparent. The step-by-step manipulation according to rules can create new knowledge from statements already accepted.

---

[13] Cassirer, E. 1994. *An Essay on Man: An Introduction to a Philosophy of Human Culture*. New Haven and London. Yale University Press. P 128.

## Discussion Activity

### Mathematical "language" and the arts: four class activities

For the following activities, choose the topic that appeals to you most, then work with a partner or in a small group to investigate it and report back to the class. At the end, consider as a whole class the general question on mathematics as a "language".

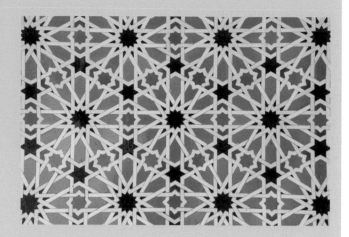

1 To visualize ideas that are mathematical and spiritual through art, investigate tile patterns in Muslim mosques and their significance. Why are there no representations of human beings in mosques? What is the symbolic significance of geometric patterns and arabesques in the decoration that covers the surface of walls and roof? Among other designs, Islamic designers were using quasicrystalline Penrose patterns five centuries before their discovery in the west.[14] (Curious? Find out!)

2 Investigate the artworks of M.C. Escher, many of which tease and puzzle sense perception while they play with mathematical concepts. Images and mathematical commentary can be found on the Internet. Share with the rest of the class what you have found – possibly an increased appreciation of what is involved in mathematical symmetry and increased delight in looking at Escher's art.

3 If you are a musician familiar with compositional analysis, share with the rest of your class some mathematical principles within music. You may wish to work as a small group, and illustrate to the class the connection between mathematics and music with recorded music or live performance. (Bonus: Can you find out about the European medieval "music of the spheres", the significance of the movement of planets in perfect circles and the cosmic significance of harmony?)

4 Write a poem in mathematical language. Concepts of nothingness, difference, union of sets, and infinity, for example, lend themselves to poetry – but they are merely the start. When you have exhausted your capacity to unite mathematics with your poetic imagination, consider whether what you have written is a poem in mathematics or, instead, poetry using mathematical imagery. Choose your means of presenting your work to your class, possibly with dramatized readings or possibly as a small book or web page of poetry assembled by your group.

### General question

With its wide range of applications, what is it that mathematics *cannot* do as a "language"? Why is the IB never likely to offer Mathematics A as a language subject in the Diploma Programme? On the other hand, what can mathematics do particularly well as a "language"? If we call mathematics a language, are we being literal or metaphorical?

---

14 Nell Greenfield Boyce, "Medieval Mosques Illuminated by Math," NPR. 22 February 2007. http://www.npr.org/templates/story/story. php?storyId=7544360 accessed 25 July 2012.

Note that when these abstractions are applied to the world, the meaning of mathematical statements gains concrete dimension: for example, I can abstractly know that the equation $c^2 = a^2 + b^2$ is applicable to every right triangle, but when I'm buying fence for my garden, or calculating the resultant force in a physics problem, a, b and c have very specific meanings.

For mathematicians, this precise, compact, abstract, and transformable symbolic system provides the vocabulary and grammar that enable them to talk about abstract relationships such as symmetry, proportion, sequence, frequency, and iteration. Thus, mathematics simultaneously provides a way of speaking about and analysing not just patterns found in the world by the sciences but also those created from the world by the arts. But then – when you think about it – didn't you know that already?

 Interview

## "Splitters and Lumpers": unifying observation with mathematics

### Miles Davenport
### IB graduate 1986

*Miles Davenport is a Professor in the Faculty of Medicine at the University of New South Wales in Sydney, Australia, where he heads the Complex Systems in Biology Group. It consists of physicists, mathematicians, and computer scientists, all of them working on biological questions.*

→ When we consider ways in which mathematics applies to the world in the natural sciences, I suspect we first think of physics. In your own field of medical research, immunology, do you find mathematics to be likewise applicable?

Physics has come to accept that mathematics is an essential element in describing the world around us, and by the application of a few relatively simple rules, and fairly basic mathematics, we can predict a whole lot of behaviours in our environment. Medical biologists still argue, "Biology is way too complex, we could never make simple rules to understand it". I guess physicists may have felt like that several hundred years ago. "How can we understand the rising of the sun and stars, light and shadow, combustion and freezing? Way too complex for simple rules!" While we maintain the mindset that simple rules won't work, this will be a self-fulfilling prophecy, because we won't make, test and refine these rules.

The general goal in my field (immunology) seems to be one of classification. We define and categorize different cell types, and endlessly discover new cells types. One view of this is that every new "cell type" is like an auxiliary explanation for every new phenomenon [or epiphenomenon] we observe. We are essentially "splitters", who make new categories and new rules for everything we see. What we urgently need are some "lumpers", who search for the overarching rules which help us understand how the different phenomena arose and how they fit together. Occam's razor needs to be applied to cut away all the different and subsidiary rules and classifications we have invoked.

Mathematics, by using a formal (quantitative) language to describe basic "rules" of behaviour, tends to unify our observations. (If it is to be useful at all, it must.)

However, we need to be confident enough to try to predict biological behaviour with simple mathematical rules. We will be wrong at first, but only by making testable, quantitative predictions can we advance the field. The discipline that mathematical analysis imposes on the field is the need to state how different factors will interact, and what outcomes we predict. Because the predictions are quantitative, they can then be rigorously tested, and the models refined. As a result, we learn more about the system in question. At the end of the day, Newtonian physics is a simplification and an abstraction, but those simple rules took us a long way in understanding and predicting the world around us. We have made major leaps in many areas of biology (such as quantitative genetics, and membrane physiology), but there is still a lot of work to do! ■

## Ways of knowing: intuition and imagination

> Of all escapes from reality, mathematics is the most successful ever.[15]
>
> *Giancarlo Rota*

Mathematics certainly shares many characteristics with the other fields of knowledge in how its practitioners use intuition and imagination. The fresh ideas, the new insights – we attribute these across all areas of knowledge to intuition and imagination. Yet it is possible that mathematics may use these ways of knowing somewhat differently.

Intuition – that rapid processing of our brains – gives fast and rough grasp of pattern. In dealing with mathematics when applied to the world, unfortunately, our intuitions appear to be particularly faulty, so cognitive scientists tell us.

A practical example, though, may tell us little about abstract intuitions on the part of mathematicians. Although intuition may give a grasp of patterns or connections as they emerge in thinking, it is equally possible that creative thinking takes counter-intuitive routes, as has been suggested[16] regarding the major recent proof of Fermat's Last Theorem (to which we will soon arrive). In mathematics, it is probably more useful to look to that other way of knowing: imagination.

Imagination – that creative capacity to reassemble familiar components into new ones, or to project beyond them into fresh conceptualization – is as alive in mathematics as in any of the other areas of knowledge, even though it differs markedly from literature! The very nature of mathematical knowledge, with its abstraction from physical reality, may involve the imagination in a somewhat different way. Although mathematicians often speak *as though their mathematical objects and concepts are real*, the subject matter of mathematics is already in a world of "imagination" even before they manipulate it creatively.

*So, what is going on in there?* What is going on in the imagination as employed by mathematicians? The question is a living one, as Arielle Saiber and Henry Turner attest in their introduction to a 2010 special journal exploration of the topic:

> Do mathematicians imagine differently than poets, painters, philosophers, or novelists? Are the cognitive operations necessary for solving problems, writing equations, and engaging in abstract mathematical thought the same as those used in other sorts of creative endeavour? Are the semiotic differences among words, numbers, and diagrams as distinct as they seem? How have accounts of the imagination (philosophical, psychological, physiological, neurological, literary, aesthetic) positioned it in relation to the kind of knowledge that mathematics is thought to provide?[17]

---

[15] Rota, G. 1989. In N. G. Cooper, *From Cardinals to Chaos*. Cambridge. Cambridge University Press. P 26.

[16] Gibson, A. 2003. *Metaphysics and Transcendence*. London. Routledge. P 105.

[17] Arielle Saiber and Henry Turner, "Mathematics and the Imagination: A Brief Introduction". 29 January 2010. P 18. http://www.rci.rutgers.edu/~hsturner/pdfs/config.pdf

Mathematicians can confirm that they use propositional imagining: that is, they *imagine that* a statement is true and trace the implications of considering it to be so, much as scientists do with a hypothesis. However, in mathematics not only the *generating* of the proposed statement but the *testing* of it demands that the imagination be engaged, since the logical implications are not played out in the real world. They are played out only in the mind.

Indeed, the mathematical imagination can do some creative stunts in total abstraction, chasing those logical implications. Just as an example, take Cantor, who invented set theory at the end of the nineteenth century. He was thinking about infinity – which already placed him outside the real world – and then constructed a proof that *there is more than one kind of infinity* – which placed him even further beyond the real world! To top it off, to prove one of his ideas about infinitely small intervals between numbers, he used a totally backward way of thinking, the tactic known as *reductio ad absurdum*. He *assumed to be true* a statement he suspected of being false (that real numbers between 0 and 1 are countable and so could be paired with integers) and demonstrated that the result was a contradiction. (Multiple infinities can be part of the game, but a *contradiction*? Never!) As a result, he could prove that the opposite was true.[18] (True? We'll come to that!)

Clearly, Cantor was being creative in constructing new mathematics, and taking paths in his mind that others had not taken before. Equally clearly, he was working in total abstraction from a world where some of us still sneak a peek at our fingers when counting. What is *not* as clear is whether mathematical imagination works in the same way as imagining in the arts or as hypothetical imagining in the sciences. We use the same word "imagination" to cluster the common features, but in doing so may fail to recognize significant differences. It may be that the cognitive sciences will, in time, tell us more about imagination and creativity as used in different areas of knowledge. Stay tuned. We are likely to know more in a few years than we know now.

## Way of knowing: reason

At last we come to the way of knowing that you have been expecting: reason. We wanted to treat sense perception, language, intuition and imagination first so that they had their moment in the spotlight before we turned that beam on the way of knowing that most characterizes mathematics – *reason* as a way of working and as a way of justifying conclusions. In all of our areas of knowledge, we use reason. In mathematics, though, the reasoning process appears to be freed from sense perception to function independently.

Before we can say a word about how mathematics uses reasoning, however, we have to take you back briefly to chapter 7, which was all about reason as a way of knowing. Do you remember the way that deductive reasoning – logically figuring out fresh conclusions from information you were given already – could lead to solutions of puzzles? Did you try the IB genie puzzle (page 116)? Deductive reasoning uses a process of logical inference to draw out new statements from a combination of old ones, and to yield new knowledge.

Of course, there have to be old statements first in order to draw out those new ones. There has to be something for the reasoning process to process! So, do you also recall the role of *premises* in deductive reasoning? Those premises provide the content, the subject matter, to which reasoning is applied.

Perhaps the most important point to remember, though, as we prepare to launch into a story about mathematics, is the distinction we emphasized then (you may feel we even *over*-emphasized it, as we are about to do again):

> VALIDITY applies to the reasoning process. If the reasoning has been done according to the rules, it is valid. It is free from contradictions.

> TRUTH applies to the content of the statements as checked in different ways (chapter 3).

When we apply deductive reasoning to statements about the world, we can be sure of one thing: that if the original premises are true, and the reasoning is valid, then our conclusions are also true. Beyond doubt. No black swans come flying into the picture in *deductive* reasoning as they often do in *inductive* reasoning, as we generalize from observations of the world.

So here's the trick with mathematics: how can we establish those first true statements, such that all of what we reason from them (validly, of course!) is also true?

---

18 Kasner, E. and Newman, J. 2001. *Mathematics and the Imagination*. New York. Dover Publications. P 50.

## Definitions and playing by the rules

A farmer called an engineer, a physicist, and a mathematician and asked them to fence the largest possible area with the least amount of fence.

The engineer made the fence into a circle, and proclaimed that he had the most efficient design.

The physicist built a long, straight line of fence and proclaimed, "If we were to extend this length around the earth, we would have the largest possible area."

The mathematician just laughed at them. He built a tiny fence around himself and said, "I declare myself to be on the outside."

## Methods: building on foundations

Mathematics is often spoken of as a building, constructed on firm foundations (again, note the use of metaphor in this description). If the foundations are solid and unshakeable, the construction that is built on top rests secure.

This metaphor for mathematics gives a very important role to its original premises – its initial assumptions – because they have to be strong to support the whole of the knowledge that is constructed on their base. They have to be true or, rather, we have to accept them as our opening assumptions *as though they were true.*

So…if we can identify a few true statements and use them as our "foundations", then any valid deductive reasoning we do based on them is like adding new bricks to a growing structure. Each

brick is also true and ready to support more on top (like adding LEGO® building blocks).

In mathematics, these initial premises – these initial assumptions – work much in the way this metaphor suggests to provide foundations. Mathematicians call these foundational assumptions "axioms". On their base, they carefully erect a building through the process of deductive reasoning, step by step, often over a span of many centuries.

## Building on Euclid's axioms: validity and truth

We have to rewind far back into history for the first flash of genius in identifying axioms and using them foundationally. It was Euclid, 2300 years ago, who identified the first known set of only

## Euclid's axioms

### Common notions[19]

1. Things which are equal to the same thing are also equal to one another.

2. If equals be added to equals, the wholes are equal.

3. If equals be subtracted from equals, the remainders are equal.

4. Things which coincide with one another are equal to one another.

5. The whole is greater than the part.

### Postulates[20]

1. A straight line segment can be drawn joining any two points.

2. Any straight line segment can be extended indefinitely in a straight line.

3. Given any straight line segment, a circle can be drawn having the segment as radius and one endpoint as center.

4. All right angles are congruent.

5. If two lines are drawn which intersect a third in such a way that the sum of the inner angles on one side is less than two right angles, then the two lines inevitably must intersect each other on that side if extended far enough. This postulate is equivalent to what is known as the parallel postulate.

---

[19] http://www.sfu.ca/~swartz/euclid.htm

[20] Weisstein, E.W. "Euclid's Postulates." From MathWorld—A Wolfram Web Resource. http://mathworld.wolfram.com/EuclidsPostulates.html

10 axioms (the fewer, the better). He considered these axioms (which he called "postulates" and "common notions") to be true, derived from experience and requiring no proof.

And then he built upon them: he constructed geometrical proofs, one at a time, carefully adding bricks to the walls, and constructions that joined one wall to another to support yet more building. With one proof at a time – some less formal than others, because Euclid "assumed details and relations read from the figure[s] that were not explicitly stated" – Euclid's system of plane geometry was built.

For over 2100 years, Euclidean geometry was considered to be perfect knowledge. The entire system was valid, with the reasoning done flawlessly. It rested on axioms regarded as true, and so the whole system was also considered true. Euclidean geometry, over all those years, was considered to be universally and eternally true.

Moreover, Euclidean geometry, applied to the world, was immensely useful. Countless generations of people benefited, for example, from being able to calculate using right angles, circles, and triangles. They found, in geometry's established truths, easy ways to solve their everyday problems, such as to determine how many bricks they will need to build a wall or how to calculate the area of their fields.

No challenge came to the perfection of Euclid's mathematical system until the nineteenth century, and even then the challenge was not to its validity but to its truth. What if Euclid's axioms, the very foundations of his system, were not true – or what if they were not the *only possible* true axioms?

## Alternative axioms, alternative systems

The first four of Euclid's postulates seemed self-evident because they could be verified by drawing figures in the sand. The first required joining two points with one, and only one, line segment; the second required imagining that this line segment continues forever on the flat ground; the third required constructing a circle centred on a point; and the fourth required only that people compare right angles they could easily draw, and conclude that the angles are congruent.

But the fifth axiom – known as the "parallel postulate" – was more problematic, even for Euclid, who used it himself only upon proving his twenty-ninth theorem.[21] How could anyone ensure that through a point P next to a given line ℓ, only one line parallel to that line can be drawn? Verifying the truth of that axiom would require someone to accompany the line forever, to ensure that it never intersects the first line. Mathematicians tried to prove the fifth postulate as if it were a theorem, and failed.

It was Carl Friedrich Gauss in the early 1800s who first noticed that a geometry could be built *without* including Euclid's fifth postulate. Gauss paved the way for the non-Euclidean geometries of Nikolai Lobachevsky and later that of Bernhard Riemann. Lobachevsky replaced Euclid's fifth postulate with the idea that through a point P next to a given line ℓ, *at least two* lines exist that are parallel to ℓ. Riemann, on the other hand, assumed that *no* parallel lines exist through P, which logically implied that he had to adopt modified versions of Euclid's first and second postulates as well.[22] These non-Euclidean geometries – consistent and valid, though based on different axioms – demanded a re-evaluation of the metaphor of mathematical foundations, and the concept of mathematical truth.

## Mathematical truth

For more than 2000 years, Euclidean geometry had been considered both *valid* as a system (because of its careful deductive reasoning) and *true* with reference to the world. However, if more than one mathematical system could be constructed equally well, but with axioms that replaced Euclid's, then could Euclid's system still be regarded as absolutely certain, as truth beyond doubt? The recognition of alternative systems, equally internally coherent, forced a reassessment of mathematical truth – *as truth within a system.*

In terms of our checks for truth, mathematics was no longer seen in terms of the correspondence check for the accuracy of its statements in reference to the world. Instead, it came to be understood in terms of the coherence check: the Euclidean system or the Riemann system are both internally

21  Weisstein, E. W. "Euclid's Postulates." MathWorld – A Wolfram Web Resource. http://mathworld.wolfram.com/EuclidsPostulates.html accessed 24 July 2012.
22  Loy, J. 1998. Non-Euclidean Geometries. http://www.jimloy.com/geometry/parallel.htm accessed 24 July 2012.

coherent, both with bodies of statements free from contradiction. Both are *valid*. Neither is *true*, however, outside the reasoning of its own system.

We now consider axioms to be not "self-evident truths" but to be the assumptions, premises, definitions, or "givens" at the base of a mathematical system. We still use the metaphor of foundations, but recognize more than one possible building. With this recognition, a vast amount of space opened up for the creativity of mathematicians. Today, they do indeed have the freedom to declare whatever they please, independently of whether their assumptions have anything to do with the real world or not.

As we considered earlier in this chapter, the fact that mathematics is now understood to be working completely in terms of abstractions does not undermine its usefulness in providing a tool for understanding the world and a language for talking about it. And as for Euclid's and Riemann's differing geometrical axioms – well, a cabinetmaker can continue to use Euclid's plane geometry in building kitchen cupboards, while a pilot can use Riemann's spherical geometry when flying an airplane. Indeed, a pilot could be grateful that the "line" he follows hugs the curvature of the earth and does not send him straight out into space.

## Methods: proof and peer review

Euclid and Riemann both created knowledge by means of the characteristic method of justification in mathematics: the proof. In mathematics, proof is the process of carefully reasoned steps that create new knowledge based on the axioms, or based on other proofs which previously have been based on the axioms. However, no mathematical result enters the realm of mathematics until it becomes public

---

### Personal knowledge from mathematics?

*by Eileen Dombrowski*

With a background originally in literature and the arts I had to struggle at one point to understand why mathematicians seemed to have such an aversion to contradictions and paradox. Were they just inflexible and humourless?

However, I quickly came to admire what they attempt to do: to recognize their own assumptions, place them clearly up front, and then figure out all the logical implications of having accepted them. They call them "axioms" and consciously recognize them as assumptions (or sometimes definitions) – though originally Euclid, like the rest of us with many of our cultural and ideological assumptions, did think they were self-evident truths.

None of us normally comes to a set of assumptions about our lives and our loves and our politics in quite the way that Euclid came to his axioms for his geometry. We do not identify all those we possess that we will use, articulate them clearly, restrict ourselves to a limited opening set, and accept them consciously and intentionally. Besides, we do not reach our conclusions based on them through a process of reasoning alone.

But we might recognize, as mathematicians do, that simple assumptions, once accepted, can lead to extensive conclusions down the road.

We might also learn a lot from what they found out as they went along. Admittedly, it was a shock for them about a century and a half ago to discover that more than one set of axioms was possible and that, when a second set was pursued just as rationally and rigorously as the previous set, it led to an alternative, and equally valid, system. However, recovering from the shock of supplanting one absolutely true system with multiple possibilities, mathematicians have never looked back, pursuing them all.

More than one internally consistent, coherent system of thought? Equally applicable to the world? Considering them simultaneously but holding them up to careful scrutiny? Those mathematicians were really onto something big! As we recognize the internally coherent perspectives of culture and politics that bounce about in our world, we could learn a lot from mathematicians. And then – we might look closely at what assumptions provide their axioms![23]

---

23 Eileen Dombrowski, from blog *TOK meets global citizenship*. Triple A Learning. 13 May 2010.

> The mathematician's patterns, like the painter's or the poet's, must be beautiful; the ideas, like the colours or the words, must fit together in a harmonious way. Beauty is the first test: there is no permanent place in the world for ugly mathematics.[24]
>
> *G.H. Hardy*

knowledge: it must undergo peer review, just as do the knowledge claims of the sciences.

The process of peer review is made all the more challenging by the sheer length of some contemporary proofs. In 2003, for example, Russian mathematician Grigory Perelman announced that he had solved a classical problem within the field of topology, the Poincaré conjecture, in a proof that took "three book-length papers with about 1,000 pages of dense mathematics and prose between them". In 2006 Perelman's traditional proof was confirmed after peer review.[25]

Mathematicians, taking pleasure in such abstract creation, are the more delighted if the proof goes beyond merely being valid. It should be, as they say, *elegant*. The elegant or beautiful proof is incisive and ingenious. It is economical in using as few steps as possible and holds a little jolt of surprise as ideas fall neatly into place. A swirl of a cape, a flash of a rapier and – *voilà* – proved! Even the longest and most elaborate of proofs can exhibit this quality, one which mathematicians speak of as *beauty*.

## Mathematics in action: Fermat's Last Theorem

A good example of peer review at work is the rejection, for almost four centuries, of all attempted proofs for what came to be known as Fermat's Last Theorem. And then – finally a jubilant acceptance!

In 1637, Pierre de Fermat, as the story goes, was reading for pleasure a book of ancient mathematics: a French translation of Diophantus' *Arithmetica*. Mathematicians still do not know what was going through his mind when he wrote in the margin of the book the message, "I have a truly marvellous demonstration of this proposition which this margin is too narrow to contain."[26] Without ever sharing his proof, he died. When the proof was published posthumously in 1655, the note remained. Fermat had a solid reputation as a mathematician, so it could not be dismissed lightly. But what was his "marvellous demonstration"? Fermat had left to his successors the most famous unsolved problem in the history of mathematics.

We know from working with right triangles that many trios of integers can satisfy the equation $c^2 = a^2 + b^2$. What Fermat postulated was that no trios of integers exist that can satisfy equations such as $c^3 = a^3 + b^3$, or $c^4 = a^4 + b^4$, and so forth, for powers greater than squares. Many mathematicians tried and failed to find a proof. Even more just turned away to work on problems more likely to be fruitful. Why waste time on Fermat's Last Theorem?

---

### Discussion Activity

**What's wrong with this proof?**

Given: A = B

Multiply both sides by A: $A^2 = AB$

Subtract $B^2$ from both sides: $A^2 - B^2 = AB - B^2$

Factor both sides: $(A + B)(A - B) = B(A - B)$

Divide both sides by $(A - B)$: $A + B = B$

Since A = B, B + B = B

Add the Bs: 2B = B

Divide by B: 2 = 1

When we liken mathematics to a game with its own internal rules, we do not mean that it is trivial. Games can be very serious.

However, mathematicians are not always very serious. What is the trick in this proof?[27]

---

[24] Hardy, G.H. 1940. *A Mathematician's Apology*. London. P 14.

[25] Overby, D. 15 August 2006. "Elusive Proof, Elusive Prover: A New Mathematical Mystery". *New York Times*. http://www.nytimes.com/2006/08/15/science/15math.html accessed 24 July 2012.

[26] Weisstein, E.W. "Fermat's Last Theorem." MathWorld – A Wolfram Web Resource. http://mathworld.wolfram.com/FermatsLastTheorem.html accessed 24 July 2012.

[27] Notice the point at which you divided by (A-B) and recall that if A=B, then you're dividing by 0.

Yet the theorem attracted huge numbers of amateur mathematicians and puzzle-solvers, eager to win a prize that had been offered and to make history as the one who solved the famous FLT! A professor in Germany, responsible for evaluating proofs submitted for the prize, found he could get little of his own work done with all the amateur proofs arriving in the post. His solution was to hand the proofs to his graduate students to check, along with printed cards of rejection:[28]

---

Dear ............................,

Thank you for your manuscript on the proof of Fermat's Last Theorem.

The first mistake is on:

Page….............. Line….…............

This invalidates the proof.

Professor E. M. Landau

............................…............

---

## Methods: peer review

When a proof was finally announced, it caused a sensation. It was in 1993 that mathematician Andrew Wiles first announced proving Fermat's Last Theorem. His proof was international news, making headlines around the world.

Wiles presented his 150-page paper at a conference as a "traditional mathematical proof", which omits routine logical steps and assumes that knowledgeable readers can fill in the gaps. Such proofs rely on intuitive arguments which can be easily translated by trained mathematicians into rigorous deductive chains. Proofs are usually presented this way because too much formality would obscure its main points, much like watching a movie frame by frame would distract the viewer from following its storyline.

When other mathematicians followed the steps closely, though, Wiles' proof was found to have a flaw. In Wiles' own words, "It was an error in a crucial part of the argument, but it was something so subtle that I'd missed it completely until that point. The error is so abstract that it can't really be described in simple terms. Even explaining it to a mathematician would require the mathematician to spend two or three months studying that part of the manuscript in great detail."[29] Clearly, when we talk about "peer review" at this level of mathematics, there are very few peers with the relevant background to be able to evaluate the work.

Wiles went back to work, creating still more mathematics in order to remedy the error. In 1994 Wiles presented his revised proof. Again peer review went to work – and this time the mathematical community accepted the proof! Wiles became a celebrity overnight, surrounded by public excitement over the solution of such a famous and long-standing problem.

It was also the end of a chapter of Andrew Wiles's own life. He had been preoccupied with the problem since childhood, and had worked on it for years before he achieved his proof. He has spoken of the melancholy and sense of loss over losing the problem that was part of what drew him to mathematics to begin with. But he has also spoken of the sense of relief:

> Having solved this problem there's certainly a sense of loss, but at the same time there is this tremendous sense of freedom. I was so obsessed by this problem that for eight years I was thinking about it all the time – when I woke up in the morning to when I went to sleep at night. That's a long time to think about one thing. That particular odyssey is now over. My mind is at rest.[30]

Intriguingly, though, his proof of Fermat's Last Theorem cannot have been Fermat's own, as the twentieth century mathematics on which it is based was unknown back in 1637 to Fermat. Was Fermat wrong? Were mathematicians for three and a half centuries chasing an illusion?

## Development across time

The story of this proof illustrates many characteristics of mathematics as an area of knowledge. For one thing, it shows something of its humanity – the fascination, the

---

[28] Singh, S. 1997. *Fermat's Enigma: The Epic Quest to Solve the World's Greatest Mathematical Problem*. Toronto. Penguin. P 132.

[29] Public Broadcasting Corporation. "Solving Fermat: Andrew Wiles." 2000. Material supplementary to "The Proof", episode of NOVA. http://www.pbs.org/wgbh/nova/proof/wiles.html accessed 24 July 2012.

[30] Singh, S. 1997. *Fermat's Enigma: The Epic Quest to Solve the World's Greatest Mathematical Problem*. Toronto. Penguin. P 132.

challenge, the creativity, the aspiration, the disappointments, the sense of triumph. At the same time, though, it reflects characteristics of more ordinary mathematical endeavour: the level of care and detail demanded, the peer review and its difficulties when the work is new and complex. It also illustrates the respect given to achievement that the lay public does not understand and for which there may be no apparent practical use.

It shows, moreover, the way mathematical knowledge builds across time. The way that mathematical ideas and puzzles were passed from the mathematician Diophantus of ancient Greece, to Pierre de Fermat of seventeenth century France, and then to the contemporary Andrew Wiles highlights certain features of mathematical knowledge. Its challenges and its products can last over centuries. Yet once it is satisfactorily proved, the proof is permanent in all places and all time, and the proven knowledge claim earns its place as yet another brick in the edifice of mathematical knowledge, built across boundaries of time and culture.

Placing the spotlight on the successful proofs, however, may obscure the contributions of the failures. Have their failures really been failures for mathematics? After all, the development of mathematics relies on failed attempts at proof as well as successes. Much new knowledge is generated in attempts to solve problems and, through failed attempts as well as successful ones, many interconnections between mathematical fields are established. As Wiles said about his own effort, "The definition of a good mathematical problem is the mathematics it generates rather than the problem itself."[31]

## Cracks in the foundations: contradiction

With the creation of considerable mathematical knowledge through the past century, mathematics is evidently flourishing. But in the early twentieth century mathematicians reached a shocking conclusion: that mathematical knowledge has flaws and limitations. If mathematical truth depends on coherence of all the statements within a mathematical system, what are the implications for mathematics if it is found to contain contradictions?

Bertrand Russell, working with Alfred North Whitehead, discovered this very thing: a contradiction within mathematics. They had been trying to deduce the entire field of mathematics from the principles of logic alone. They started by attempting to construct the real number system using mathematical sets, which are a product of logic. In 1901 they were disturbed to discover a contradiction regarding those sets which are, or are not, members of themselves.

If the set is a set of cakes, for example, the set is *not* a member of itself. However, if the set is a set of all those things that are *not* cakes, then the set *is* a member of itself. Russell discovered that he could easily create a contradiction, no matter what objects he was including in the set, by creating a set of all sets that are *not* members of themselves. Hence a member of the set would have to be (a) a member of itself, because it is part of the set and (b) not a member of itself, because that is exactly what is the set *is* – a set of things *not* members of themselves.

Russell's paradox had implications for all mathematics: if mathematics is an intellectual game played by its own internal rules, and expected to be complete and free of contradiction, then what claim to knowledge can it have if there is an inconsistency within it? Russell and others, including Gottlob Frege and David Hilbert in the 1920s, attempted without success to eliminate paradox from mathematics.

Verbal analogies to self-reference and paradox may give some sense of what these mathematicians experienced. Self-reference, after all, is not unusual in itself. Singers sing songs about singing songs, poets write poems about writing poetry, and painters have been known to paint paintings of painters painting. Every time you use "I" you are using self-reference. Even reflection on knowing in TOK is often self-referential, as we try to know about knowing. Still more so is the research of cognitive psychologists, who use their brains to think about the thinking of the brain. (If you wore a self-referential T-shirt, what would be the design on it? If you took a self-referential photograph, what would it show?)

---

31 Public Broadcasting Corporation. "Solving Fermat: Andrew Wiles." 2000. Material supplementary to "The Proof", episode of NOVA.

## Discussion Activity

### The water and the wave: mathematics and other areas of knowledge

The Great Wave of Kanagawa, by Katshushika Hokusai, Japan roughly 1830.

What knowledge does each different area give us of the same phenomenon in the world? Divide your class into six groups according to the following categories: the arts, history, human sciences, natural sciences, mathematics and ethics. Appoint a timekeeper.

Each group has just 15 minutes to prepare an answer to these questions:

- How does this area of knowledge, or its component disciplines, talk about water or waves?
- What does it take as its relevant subject matter?
- What kind of language does it use?
- What kind of knowledge does it give?

As a group, report back to the class as a whole, trying to convey the essence of that area of knowledge. Appoint a timekeeper to hold each group to a maximum of four minutes. Aim for the essence!

As a full group, then, consider the following question:

- Are there advantages for knowledge to be gained by looking at something from the perspective of different areas? If not, why not? If so, what are the advantages?
- How would the knowledge change – and possibly which areas of knowledge would have more to contribute – if you were treating not "the water and the wave" but water shortages of severe drought?

A mathematician, like a painter or poet, is a maker of patterns. If his patterns are more permanent that theirs, it is because they are made with *ideas*.[32]

*G.H. Hardy*

When self-reference creates contradiction, the results can be quite witty. The writer Oscar Wilde once quipped, "I can resist everything – except temptation" and on the basis of similar cleverness became a favourite party guest for a time. Depending on your sense of humour, you may find paradox quite entertaining as it jams your mind with contradiction: "Disobey this command." (Just try doing that!) Ancient paradoxes live on to perplex us largely because we enjoy them, including the famous Liar's Paradox: Epimenides,

from ancient Crete, uttered the claim, "All Cretans are liars" or, in another version, "I am lying." Well, if he is telling the truth, does that mean he is lying? If he is lying, does that mean that he is telling the truth? This kind of paradox, many find, is immensely entertaining. But mathematicians did not burst into laughter when Gödel made a similar move in mathematics.

## Incompleteness theorem

In 1931 Kurt Gödel published what is now known as "Gödel's Incompleteness Theorem", which basically states that the dream of having mathematics reach a state of completeness is impossible to achieve. There cannot be a guarantee, within any axiomatic system, that the axioms adopted will not give rise to contradictions. There will always be, in any formal system, statements that are not decidable within it.

---

[32] Hardy, G.H. 1940. *A Mathematician's Apology*. London. P 13.

> A mathematician is a person who can find analogies between theorems; a better mathematician is one who can see analogies between proofs and the best mathematicians can notice analogies between theories. One can imagine that the ultimate mathematician is one who can see analogies between analogies.[33]
>
> *Stefan Banach*

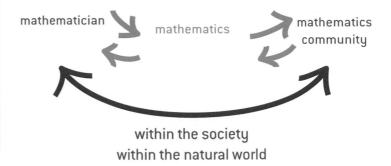

within the society
within the natural world

Gödel intended to do quite the opposite of what he actually achieved. He had originally set out to ground the axiomatic approach to mathematics more firmly on logic. Yet the numbering system he created, which referred to mathematical statements, created the kind of self-reference which was characteristic of the liar's paradox – and he recognized the implications of his reasoning.

Did the philosophical recognition of uncertainty in mathematics undermine the area of knowledge? Not at all! Mathematicians absorbed the realization that their discipline was not certain after all in its very foundations – and then went back to work.

Mathematician G.J. Chaitin[34] looks back on the Incompleteness Theorem as almost inevitable – as a step in mathematical progress now absorbed into further thinking. He feels that, like Alan Turing's work thereafter and Wiles' more recent proof, the Incompleteness Theorem becomes clear in hindsight: "So you see, the way that mathematics progresses is you trivialize everything! The way it progresses is that you take a result that originally required an immense effort, and you reduce it to a trivial corollary of a more general theory!" He speculates that in a century or two, Wiles's proof, hundreds of pages long, will be reduced to a single page and understood readily in context of mathematics developed after its time. "But of course that's the way it works. That's how we progress."[35]

## Mathematics in social context

As we consider mathematics in generalized overview, we turn once again to the diagram of knowledge in the process of development and exchange. As we have seen, mathematics is created by individual mathematicians and reviewed by peers in a methodology of shared knowledge. As we have already considered, it has an intimate relationship with the natural world, even though its methods of justification leave that world behind. But what is its relationship with the social context within which it is generated?

### Universal or cultural?

"Mathematics transcends all cultures and binds us," declares Janna Levin, professor of astronomy and physics. She adds, "Abstract knowledge may seem to have nothing to do with any of us and yet has to do with all of us."[36] Rational and depersonalized, mathematics is knowledge shared universally, true everywhere, known all around the world. As it takes us into abstract thought, it appears to take us out of any possible culture context. But does it?

Certainly, it does appear that mathematical thinking, at least, occurs all around the world, in cultural contexts that could scarcely be more varied. Alan Bishop, who has specialized in mathematics and cultural values, has identified six forms of recurring mathematical ideas spanning vastly different cultures.[37]

[33] http://math.wikia.com/wiki/Stefan_Banach

[34] Chaitin, G.J. 1975. "Randomness and Mathematical Proof," *Scientific American*. Vol 232, number 5. Pp 47–52.

[35] Chaitlin, G.J. 2000. "A Century of Controversy over the Foundations of Mathematics." in C. Calude and G. Paun. *Finite vs Infinite.* London, UK. Springer-Verlag. Pp 75–100.

[36] Janna Levin, The Sound the Universe Makes, TED talk, March 2011. http://www.ted.com/talks/janna_levin_the_sound_the_universe_makes.html, accessed 10 August 2011.

[37] Bishop, A.J. 1993. "Culturalizing Mathematics Teaching," *The Multicultural Dimension of the National Curriculum*, ed. Anna King and Michael J. Reiss. London. Falmer Press. P 37.

## Discussion Activity

### Development of mathematical knowledge

*by Manjula Salomon*

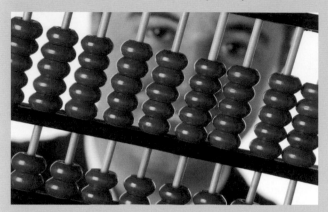

In the following activity, you will take on a research topic, find out about it, and share your findings with the rest of the class. Be prepared to identify your findings according to historical time and place of origin.

Divide your group so that someone is investigating each of the following topics. Allow at least 20 minutes for the investigation using the library or the Internet.

| | | |
|---|---|---|
| abacus | Pythagoras' Theorem | algebra |
| decimal system | Omar Khayyam | Euclid |
| Ramanujan | chaos theory | algorithm |
| probability | geometry | trigonometry |
| calculus | zero | infinity |

In your class group, create a timeline on the board or a large poster. Each person or group should report the information obtained to the class and place the relevant information on the shared timeline.

### Questions for discussion

1 What inter-developments do you see between the various topics?

2 To what extent does your research suggest that mathematics is an international area of knowledge? How would you compare it in this regard with other areas of knowledge?

3 Does your research challenge any of your previous assumptions?

4 The development of mathematical knowledge is often illustrated by a tree diagram (that is, roots labelled as arithmetic, the trunk labelled as calculus, etc.). Mathematical scholars often select the banyan tree as the best tree for such an illustration. Why might this be so?

*Note: Conventional division of the mathematical history timeline separates it into periods: earlier times to ancient Bablyonia and Egypt, the Greek contribution, the Far-Eastern and Semitic contribution, and the European contribution from the Renaissance onward.*

- Counting ("How many?"): Thousands of counting systems exist.
- Locating: Navigating and placing things in relation to one another, with compass directions, give rise to many geometrical ideas.
- Measuring ("How much?"): Units of measure include parts of the body, pots, baskets, string, beads, and coins.
- Designing: Geometrical shapes appear in decoration on objects from household utensils to temples.
- Playing: Many games involve such features as puzzles, paradoxes, rules and gambling.

- Explaining: People find a reason for why things happen through mathematical ideas, such as number patterns, geometrical shapes that fit together, and mathematical laws in the natural world.

Bishop emphasizes the rich variety of mathematical thinking worldwide:

Anthropological and historical research, for example, is revealing more and more of the rich tapestry of mathematical knowledge existing in the world. We can find literally hundreds of different counting systems, using different symbols, objects and materials and varying with the cycles, or bases, used to deal with large numbers. We can find very different conceptions of space from Euclidean notions of points, lines and regions. The Navajos, for example, assume that objects are always in motion (some more slowly than others) and that space cannot be subdivided. The symbolic and religious properties of geometric figures are of more interest in some societies than in others, as are the predictive powers of certain numerological practices.[38]

As an advisor to UNESCO, Bishop has contributed to the growing awareness of ethnomathematics:

> From the Incas with their *quipus* to help with their accounting (Ascher and Ascher, 1981), to the Chinese with their detailed geomantic knowledge for designing cities (Ronan, 1981), or from the Igbo's sophisticated counting system (Zaslavsky, 1973) to the Aboriginal Australian's supreme spatial and locational sense (Lewis, 1976) the known world is full of examples of rich and varied indigenous mathematical knowledge systems.[39]

## Cultural dominance of "western" mathematics

Why, then, has one system of mathematics dominated the world's mathematical education? Bishop argues that the imposition of western mathematics – which he points out is not really "western" in its merge of traditions – was largely through colonialism. Not only was the particular system of symbolization spread through the administration of trade and taught through educational systems set up in European colonies, but the values that came with it were also taught. Above all, those values are rationalism and objectivism – "a way of perceiving the world as if it were composed of discrete objects, about to be removed and abstracted...from their context." Further values are associated with the application of mathematical and related technological ideas to

controlling the physical and social environment. "From those colonial times through to today," he argues, "the power of this mathematico-technological culture has grown apace – so much so that western mathematics is taught nowadays in every country in the world. Once again, it is mainly taught with the assumption of universality and cultural neutrality".[40]

As ethnomathematics has become a field of knowledge, educators from many parts of the world are revising the teaching of mathematics of their regions to make it more culturally relevant to their students. Mathematics professor Claudette Englobm-Bradley (Schaghtiocoke), for example, describes her realization, working on a beadwork loom, that "beading was like graphing! I was placing colorful beads in the loom to create a design; it was like plotting points on graph paper."[41] Subsequently, she designed lessons in mathematics and computer programs through beadwork in a college near Boston with mainly Mic Mac students. She added weaving rugs and coil baskets when working with Navajo students in Utah, and extended to navigation with Yup'ik students on the tundra in Alaska.

So is mathematics cultural rather than universal? Or...could it, like language, be considered both – universal as a way of thinking, and cultural in the specific forms that it takes? Are rationality and abstraction from context (two of the features that Bishop points out as cultural) also able to be applicable beyond cultural boundaries? Could Levin *also* be right, that, at a level of abstraction, "Mathematics transcends all cultures and binds us"?

## Social attitudes toward mathematics

Education is frequently a topic of social debate, with competing views on what a society should expect its young people to learn. Mathematics, often regarded as intellectually challenging, comes in for its share of controversy. Concerned discussion has focused on the status of mathematics in society, the relevance of specific national

[38] Bishop, A.J. "Culturalizing Mathematics Teaching," *The Multicultural Dimension of the National Curriculum*, ed. Anna King and Michael J. Reiss. London. Falmer Press. P 37.

[39] Bishop, A.J. 1993. "Influences from Society," Science and Technology Education Document Series No.47. Significant Influences on Children's Learning of Mathematics. UNESCO Paris. P 6. http://www.unesco.org/education/pdf/323_47.pdf accessed 20 July 2012.

[40] Bishop, A.J. 1995. "Western Mathematics: The Secret Weapon of Cultural Imperialism", *The Post Colonial Studies Reader*, ed. Ashcroft, Griffiths, and Tiffin. London and New York. Routledge. Pp 74–5.

[41] Englobm-Bradley (Schaghticoke), C. 2009. "Seeing Mathematics with Indian Eyes". *The Alaska Native Reader: History, Culture, Politics*. ed. Maria Shaa Tláa Wiliams. Durham and London. Duke University Press. P 238.

## Discussion Activity

### Statistics: representing the world

We opened this chapter with the relationship of mathematics to the world, and we return at the end to a variation on the same topic. This time, though, we pose a question about applied mathematics and the kind of understanding we gain through statistical representation in a world filled with sensory experience and emotions.

In the quotation to the right, the authors argue that we cannot grasp the enormity and significance of world hunger through its statistical representation: quantitative representation of human misery does not reach our understanding. First, read what they are telling us.

In response to the quotation, we pass you two clusters of knowledge questions, at different levels of generality, for your reflection and discussion.

### Discussion questions

#### 1 World hunger and numbers

Do you agree with the authors that we need to use the ways of knowing of imagination and emotion (combined in empathy) in order to "understand" hunger and the sense of powerlessness? Do these ways of knowing give us a *better* understanding than observations generalized in mathematical terms? In what ways does reason, developed mathematically into the numbers they deplore, contribute understanding of hunger that might be just as important?

**World hunger**

Numbers can numb. They can distance us from what is actually very close to us. So we asked ourselves, what really is hunger?

...how we understand hunger determines what we think are its solutions. If we think of hunger only as numbers — number of people with too few calories — the solution also appears to us in numbers — numbers of tons of food aid, or numbers of dollars in economic assistance. But once we begin to understand hunger as real people coping with the most painful of human emotions, we can perceive its roots. We need only ask, When have we experienced any of these emotions ourselves? Hasn't it been when we have felt out of control of our lives — powerless to protect ourselves and those we love?

Hunger has thus become for us the ultimate symbol of powerlessness.[42]

*Frances Moore Lappé, Joseph Collins, Peter Rosset, with Luis Esparza*

#### 2 Statistical knowledge of the world

What knowledge of the world can statistics give us? How does it differ from the understanding given by images or the arts? What would be the effect on our knowledge of choosing one or the other, rather than seeking both?

educational systems to the needs of students and the society, and the effect on both students and society of using mathematical testing as a measure of ability and a filter for access to higher education. These topics, though, are hard to consider on an international level, given the variability of mathematical education around the world.

On a national level, where at least commentators are likely to be speaking of the same course content and teaching practices, debates often

centre on *what* mathematics should be taught. Commentators may argue in favour of either basic calculating skills or the process of logical thinking that is involved in these and other operations. Discussions are intensified by the role that mathematics examinations are sometimes given as a gate through which applicants must pass to gain further education.

American professor Andrew Hacker, for one, argues that mathematics has the status of

---

[42] Moore Lappé, F., Collins, J., Rosset, P. with Esparza, L. 1998. *World Hunger: 12 Myths*, The Institute for Food and Development Policy. Canada and the United States. Pages 1 and 3.

a difficult subject, so that some universities and medical schools use it as an entrance requirement simply in order to look rigorous: "mathematics is used as a hoop, a badge, a totem to impress outsiders and elevate a profession's status."[43] Many graduates, he says, never use the mathematics they learn in any case in their later work. He argues for removing a mathematics requirement where it is not relevant to the student's future profession and shifting to teaching "quantitative literacy" that is directly useful to citizens and consumers for understanding practical and political issues.

Although Hacker's arguments are directed towards his own educational system, they raise more general issues regarding what role mathematics *should* play in an education. They also place centrally the idea of "usefulness" as a criterion of the value of studying an area of knowledge.

In what ways is knowledge useful? What does each area contribute to our lives? Mathematics – completely abstract and yet everywhere applicable to our knowledge of the world – prompts such questions of knowledge. We pass to you for reflection the questions below. What is the place of mathematics in your life, and what value do you give your own growing knowledge?

## For Reflection

- In what ways does mathematical knowledge prove useful in your own life and the lives of your family members? Can you identify areas of everyday life where you apply mathematical skills? Does usefulness include benefit to your thinking skills? (Can you apply these questions also to other areas of knowledge?)

- Are you developing "quantitative literacy" – understanding the way statistics, graphs, and other numerical knowledge claims are used in argument on social and political issues? If so, are you learning through your course in mathematics, other courses, or everyday life? Why is this knowledge important?

## Discussion Activity

### Knowledge framework: mathematics

First summarize your responses to these questions in your own words. Then exchange ideas with others in your class.

1  **Scope:** What is mathematics all about? What are its subject matter and goals? What does it contribute to our knowledge overall?

2  **Language/concepts:** What central concepts characterize this area of knowledge? In what ways are the naming and defining of central concepts significant? What is the role of language (and other symbolic systems of representation) in the production of mathematical knowledge?

3  **Methodology:** What ways of knowing does mathematics use, and how? How

do mathematicians create, exchange, and evaluate knowledge? What methods do they use to gain the most reliable knowledge possible of their subject matter? In what ways do mathematicians use knowledge already gained in the past within their fields?

4  **Historical development:** What individual, social, and technological factors have pushed mathematics in particular directions?

5  **Links to personal knowledge:** How do individuals and groups contribute personal knowledge to mathematics, and how do they gain from its shared knowledge? How does mathematics contribute to your own knowledge?

---

[43] Andrew Hacker, 28 July 2012. "Is Algebra Necessary?" *New York Times.* http://www.nytimes.com/2012/07/29/opinion/sunday/is-algebra-necessary.html?pagewanted=1

# 21. Indigenous Knowledge

Students will no doubt encounter those, including some indigenous people themselves, who are surprised to see indigenous knowledge placed in a separate category in TOK. They might also encounter those who ask why this loose category of different cultural worldviews is selected for attention rather than any other, such as Asian knowledge, for instance. These puzzled questioners might ask, too, why indigenous knowledge is treated as a TOK category equivalent to history or mathematics rather than presented as a synthetic category more roughly equivalent to women's knowledge or farmers' knowledge. The category "indigenous knowledge" prompts knowledge questions of classification, with many social, political, and economic implications for how those questions are answered.

Indeed, any consideration of indigenous knowledge must also challenge another system of classification: the categories into which TOK divides knowledge for examination and discussion. Among the characteristics most commonly accepted for indigenous knowledge is a holistic worldview that does not conceive of literature, ethics, history, social understanding, the sciences, or mathematics as separate, or separable.

It is these differences, however, that stands to make an exploration of indigenous knowledge enriching in TOK. Can those of us who are not indigenous enter into another way of conceptualizing knowledge that can help us realize some of the assumptions that we make ourselves? Can we recognize more fully some of the implications that come with thinking about the world and ourselves in a particular way? Gaining some understanding of indigenous knowledge is valuable in taking an outside perspective on our own ways of constructing and using knowledge.

But there is a problem. Did you notice that we spoke about *enriching ourselves* by understanding? Many indigenous people and indigenous scholars might well object to an approach that is based on treating knowledge as a resource to be plundered, taking selectively what we want, interpreting it in our own terms, and using it in ways that fit our own goals. Is this approach appropriate to

>
> In all regions of the world are found local communities who have long histories of interaction with the natural environment. Associated with many of these communities is a cumulative body of knowledge, know-how, practices and representations. These sophisticated sets of understandings, interpretations and meanings are part and parcel of a cultural complex that encompasses language, naming and classification systems, resource use practices, ritual, spirituality and worldview.[1]
>
> *UNESCO (United Nations Educational, Scientific and Cultural Organization)*

knowledge that is culturally developed, specific to groups of people, shared within cultural groups with codes of communication and ownership particular to the group, and surrounded by issues of identity and relationships with other human beings and the cosmos? Does cultural knowledge rightly become part of our own "shared knowledge" if it is not offered but taken without consent, or offered to varying degrees but then misunderstood or misrepresented by its recipients?

Before we attempt to explore indigenous knowledge we must acknowledge some of the problems raised by these questions and set our own goals accordingly. We must acknowledge that cultural knowledge is best understood in its own terms and within its own frames of reference. You might think back to the position of cultural relativism adopted for study by anthropologists (chapter 18).

At the same time, however, the goal of understanding how others see the world has been one that has guided this book from the opening chapter on perspectives. We have treated understanding always as *inquiry and exploration*. Recognizing that we have perspectives ourselves, we attempt to learn about the perspectives of others with interest and respect, regardless of whether we can easily place ourselves within the terms of their worldviews or whether we are in accord with the conclusions that arise from them.

---

1   http://portal.unesco.org/en/ev.php-URL_ID=5065&URL_DO=DO_TOPIC&URL_SECTION=201.html

We do face limitations: a movement from one perspective to another is almost always incomplete and characterized by difficulties of communication to be overcome. Yet if we do not try, we shut down our own flexibility for problem-solving and generating new ideas, close ourselves off from much of the human intellectual and cultural heritage, and accept a world where people live in their isolated bubbles of understanding and have difficulty in coming together in cooperation. To some extent, a grasp of other perspectives is a magnetic goal in itself for anyone who wants to understand knowledge in its human context. To some extent, too, it is the *implications* of gaining understanding that make it important in practical terms – as is surely the case with indigenous knowledge.

You will notice that we did not enter a discussion of the natural sciences or mathematics with an acknowledgment of problems or a declaration of values and goals in approaching perspectives. Why might that be? We give you the following knowledge questions to consider in the back of your mind during this chapter:

- What is "shared knowledge"? How does the sharing within academic areas of knowledge compare with the sharing of knowledge within cultures and societies?
- On what basis do we classify knowledge into different areas?
- What is the difference between knowledge and wisdom?

## What does it mean to be "indigenous"?

It is difficult to pin down with precision the concept of being "indigenous". The peoples and their cultures are so particular to the land on which they live that developing a working definition of "indigenous communities, peoples and nations" was a major challenge for UNESCO (United Nations Educational, Scientific and Cultural Organization). The one achieved in 2004 read as follows:

> Indigenous communities, peoples and nations are those which, having a historical continuity with pre-invasion and pre-colonial societies that developed on their territories, consider themselves distinct from other sectors of the societies now prevailing on those territories, or parts of them. They form at present non-dominant sectors of society and are determined to preserve, develop and transmit to future generations their ancestral territories, and their ethnic identity, as the basis of their continued existence as peoples, in accordance with their own cultural patterns, social institutions and legal system.[2]

This definition, you will notice, does not use their cultures as the common feature to identify indigenous people. It would not be possible to do so: indigenous peoples represent more than 5000 languages and cultures, spanning over 70 countries of the world, with a diversity that escapes generalization to the level of definition. Instead, the UNESCO working definition groups these cultures, and the 350 million individuals within them, according to their shared history, including their marginalization within the societies that have occupied their traditional lands. "Despite their important contribution to the world's cultural diversity and to the sustainable development of our planet," UNESCO reports, "many of them live on the fringes of society and are deprived of basic human rights."[3]

> "
> If you turn the boat the wrong way, you die; if you don't catch fish, you starve; if you do not build a shelter properly, you freeze. Those were very hard lessons. School was very easy after that.[4]
>
> *Dr. Evan Adams, IB graduate 1984.*
> *Physician and actor. Sliammon First Nation, Coast Salish.*
> "

[2] "The Concept of Indigenous Peoples." Background paper prepared by the Secretariat of the Permanent Forum on Indigenous Issues. Workshop on Data Collection and Disaggregation from Indigenous Peoples. New York, 19–21 January 2004.

[3] "UNESCO and Indigenous Peoples: Partnership for Cultural Diversity", UNESCO http://portal.unesco.org/culture/en/ev.php-URL_ID=35393&URL_DO=DO_TOPIC&URL_SECTION=201.html

[4] Robert Matas. 16 April 2012. Native actor and doctor takes on new role championing health in B.C. *The Globe and Mail*. http://www.theglobeandmail.com/news/british-columbia/native-actor-and-doctor-takes-on-new-role-championing-health-in-bc/article4239401/

*Maori carving*

The Maori of New Zealand have a rich tradition of creating intricate patterns in carving, tattoos, building, sculpture, jewellery, and other forms. But what do the forms mean? In what ways do the images connect the knowledge of the people today with the knowledge of their ancestors? For instance, you might like to investigate the symbolic significance of the architectural design of the *wharenui*, or meeting house. In what ways does the structure often represent the body of an ancestor through the carved vertical posts, ridgepost, and rafters?

Apparently, then, the definition that groups these cultures into the collective of "indigenous" is historically based, placing them together for the impact on them of colonialism and globalization. They are defined, in large part, by a history that is predominantly told not from their perspective.

## Scope: What is "indigenous knowledge"?

Across a collection of unlike cultures classified by a roughly common experience of conquest and domination, can we find common features of their knowledge? Drawing boundaries around cultures is inherently problematic (chapter 18), and making assertions about their knowledge, especially as it changes over time, can be even more so. However, the use of the category of "indigenous knowledge" (in academic scholarship particularly since the

1960s) has directed attention to the common threads of worldviews woven through this diversity. These commonalities are what we refer to as indigenous knowledge.

Again, UNESCO is able to offer some very broad features.[5] Indigenous knowledge is:

- locally bound; indigenous to a specific area
- culture-specific and context-specific
- non-formal
- orally transmitted, and generally not documented
- dynamic and adaptive
- holistic in nature
- closely related to survival.

This description of commonalities serves as a very rough definition and enables us to use the concept.

## 1. Culture-specific

The generalizations that we make about indigenous knowledge must be seen in terms of broadly applicable features, with awareness of possible exceptions to every statement.

## 2. Locally bound, context-specific

Indigenous knowledge is grounded in a specific area, and rich in close observation of details of the surrounding environment:

> A tribal person in New Guinea can still identify 70 species of birds by their songs; a shaman in the Amazon can identify hundreds of species of plants and which preparations will enhance their chemical potency in the human body; a traditional Polynesian navigator can detect an island miles beyond the horizon by a pattern in the waves and the behavior of birds. This kind of knowledge seems almost supernatural to a modern person stumbling noisily through the forest; but it's not supernatural. It is human intelligence honed over millennia, through unimaginably vast numbers of individual observations, experiments, reflections, intuitions, refinements of art and experience and communication.[6]

---

5    Best Practices on Indigenous Knowledge, UNESCO http://www.unesco.org/most/bpindi.htm

6    Carol Black. 13 January 2012. Occupy your Brain. On Power, Knowledge, and the Re-Occupation of Common Sense. Blog http://schoolingtheworld.org/blog/

## Going and gone

In the time it takes you to read a few pages on indigenous knowledge, another language has died. A language disappears every 14 minutes.[7]

The Polynesian navigator and the tribal person in New Guinea, in these examples, possess entirely different bodies of knowledge, specific to their surrounding environments. For both, though, the knowledge is detailed, almost encyclopedic, with survival depending on precise reading of winds and currents or unambiguous distinctions between plants that heal and plants that kill. "On some of our visits together to the forest," a researcher says of eight and nine year olds from the Baiga tribe in northern India, "they named over 60 plants with medicinal properties, and many more that bore fruits that could be eaten or were useful. They stopped their list out of consideration for me because I could no longer keep track…"[8]

Increasingly, indigenous knowledge is being recognized as understanding the processes and relationships of the environment. Recently it has been given the term "traditional ecological knowledge", with acknowledgment of the observation and reasoning that makes it akin to contemporary currents in scientific thinking.

It would appear, at first glance, that nomadic peoples, who live in no fixed place but move in a pattern often determined by the seasons and the hunt, have no such connection with a particular piece of land. Indeed, nomads have sometimes been misrepresented as though they moved randomly or aimlessly, rather than purposefully across larger territory. Such a representation reinforces the notion of "terra nullius", land belonging to no one because no one constantly occupied it, and has been used to contest indigenous claims to land or hunting rights.[9]

The phrases "traditional ecological knowledge," "traditional local knowledge," and "folk knowledge" are often associated with "fuzzy knowledge," the kind that comes from funneling information through a human instrument, whereas "Western science" suggests an absolute objectivity, immune from human bias. In order to discern between the two, one must understand how different cultures, including the "knowledge seekers" of both, come to exist, survive, and thrive in their worlds. The bottom line is that both address knowing the world using different, yet ultimately similar, approaches. Western science excels at unraveling the unseen—our medical technology a testament to this precision—while traditional knowledge reveals the dynamics of larger systems, particularly animals, plants, and habitats, and the wisdom of our place among them.[10]

*Lilian Na'ia Alessa, biologist of Salish ancestry (Canadian west coast)*

## 3. Non-formal and orally transmitted

An indigenous worldview is characteristically passed on informally and orally, through language, songs, and dance, through demonstration and shared work, through all of the rituals and customs of everyday life. Because indigenous cultures depend on oral transmission

## Appropriate language

Acceptable terminology for indigenous groups varies with the region. Before dealing with the knowledge of a particular group, try to find out what they prefer to be called. Various possibilities include: indigenous, aboriginal, native, Indian, First Nations. Consider being specific and referring to the name of the particular group, in their own language.

---

7   Disappearing Languages, *National Geographic*. http://travel.nationalgeographic.com/travel/enduring-voices/

8   Sarangapani, P.M. 2003. "Indigenising Curriculum: questions posed by Baiga vidya". *Comparative Education*. Vol. 39. No. 2. P 203.

9   "'Doctrine of Discovery', used for centuries to justify seizure of indigenous land, subjugate peoples, must be repudiated by United Nations, permanent forum told", Economic and Social Council HR/5088, United Nations. http://www.un.org/News/Press/docs//2012/hr5088.doc.htm

10  Lilian Na'ia Alessa, "What is Truth?" *The Alaska Native Reader: History, Culture, Politics*, ed. Maria Sháa Tláa Williams, Duke University Press, 2009. Pp 247–48

*The medicine wheel or sacred hoop*

The teachings of the medicine wheel span numerous indigenous groups in North America, and bring together a huge range of cultural teachings. We recommend here investigating the sacred hoop of the Sioux or Lakota Nation for gaining a sense of the holistic nature of an indigenous worldview. The four directions of the crossed bars in the centre all have significance, but even though the directions are opposite they are still held together within the circle.

For whatever particular indigenous group you consider in your own TOK class, it is immensely rewarding to find out about the songs, dances, stories, clothing, building styles, sources of food, ways of cooking, and so forth. It is important, though, not to see cultural actions simply as decorative. It is possible that they might have significant meaning for the people themselves. It is the symbolic meaning that takes you into their knowledge.

of knowledge and rarely written language, storytelling is a significant means of passing down the whole body of cultural teachings from one generation to the next. As one educational

philosopher explains, stories were far more than simply entertaining tales:

> Oral cultures long ago invented techniques to ensure that the young would efficiently learn and remember the social group's store of knowledge and would also take on the values that sustain the structure of the society and establish the sense of identity of its individual members.

> Prominent among those techniques was the use of rhyme, rhythm, meter, and vivid images. Perhaps the most powerful technique invented, and the greatest of all social inventions, was the "coding" of lore into stories. This had the dual effect of making the contents more easily remembered – crucial in cultures where all knowledge had to be preserved in living memories – and of shaping the hearers' emotional commitment to those contents. One could ensure greater cohesiveness within the social group by coding the lore that was vital to one's society into stories – be it proper kinship relationships and appropriate behaviour, economic activities, property rights, class status, or medical knowledge and its application.[11]

Some indigenous cultures developed extensive cycles of stories for passing on the accumulated knowledge of countless generations. Oral transmission, however, depends on communal memory and language, and thus continuous contact between generations as the elders educate the young. If that connection is broken, as has often been the case when people have been colonialized, so too is the chain of knowledge.

Many indigenous peoples of today no longer work within the traditional oral tradition but depend on written language to preserve and develop their cultures. Indeed, vital and dynamic works of literature, history, and memoir, all closely clinked to traditional cultures, have resulted from indigenous people using not oral but written language.

## 4. Holistic

Indigenous people do not generally place their close observation of the natural world into a separate category of knowledge: their knowledge is holistic. There is scant echo in indigenous

---

[11] Egan, K. 1991. *The Educated Mind: How Cognitive Tools Shape Our Understanding*. Chicago and London. University of Chicago Press. P 10.

**Traditional Native Knowledge**

- holistic

- includes physical & metaphysical world linked to moral code

- emphasis on practical application of skills and knowledge

- trust for inherited wisdom
- respect for all things

- practical experimentation
- qualitative oral record
- local verification
- communication of metaphor & story connected to life, values, and proper behavior
- integrated and applied to daily living and traditional subsistence practices

**Common Ground**

**Organizing Principles**

- universe is unified
- body of knowledge stable but subject to modification

**Habits of Mind**

- honesty, inquisitiveness
- perseverance
- open-mindedness

**Skills and Procedures**

- empirical observation in natural settings
- pattern recognition
- verification through repetition
- inference and prediction

**Knowledge**

- plant and animal behavior, cycles, habitat needs, interdependence;
- properties of objects and materials;
- position and motion of objects;
- cycles and changes in earth and sky

**Western Science**

- part to whole
- limited to evidence and explanation within physical world
- emphasis on understanding how

- skepticism

- tools expand scale of direct and indirect observation & measurement
- hypothesis falsification
- global verification
- quantitative written record
- communication of procedures, evidence and theory
- discipline-based
- micro and macro theory (e.g. cell biology & physiology, atomic theory, plate tectonics, etc.)
- mathematical models

↑   Qualities Associated with Traditional Knowledge and Western Science[12]

cultures of the distinct classifications that most contemporary societies construct of science, literature, history, ethics, and religion.

Typically, holistic knowledge places human beings within the world not as observers but as part of its processes. A metaphysical worldview in which human beings live in accord with other beings and the cycles of nature stands to influence not only how indigenous people think about the world but how they act towards it.

For instance, the natural world, for many indigenous peoples, is not seen exclusively in terms of "resources" for human use – though certainly they do depend on the land. The geographical landscape is often considered sentient – alive and conscious – and the animals are often considered as kin to human beings. As a result, many groups understand their own history in a way that does not separate human beings and the natural world.

12   Barnhardt, R., & Kawagley, A. 0. 2005. Indigenous Knowledge Systems and Alaska Native Ways of Knowing. *Anthropology and Education Quarterly,* Vol 36, number 1. Pp 8–23. http://www.ankn.uaf.edu/curriculum/Articles/BarnhardtKawagley/Indigenous_Knowledge.html

"It is not that indigenous approaches to the past do not have categories of explanation for events and meanings," explains Michael Marker regarding the way the stories of the cultural past are conceived in some North American aboriginal groups. "It is that these categories do not necessarily correspond to Western intellectual frameworks and purposes."

The historic view conveyed by the stories places the people not as separate from the world but as part of it:

> Indigenous historical narratives place human beings in a landscape that is understood to have mythic forms converging with everyday forms of experience. Many Aboriginal communities are familiar with hearing the past narrated in this seamless fashion, which places mythic and moral understandings alongside genealogies that include animals and culturally important places on the landscape. Histories include moral teachings from encounters with animals such as Owl, Raven, Wolf, and Bear.[13]

## 5. Dynamic and adaptive, closely related to survival

Concerned with survival in a particular place, indigenous knowledge keeps a sharp focus on the particular features of the landscape and its life. It does, as it must, adapt to changing conditions that affect the group's survival. It is knowledge renewed with the experience of each generation, incorporating shifts in environmental or social conditions. For instance, the work and creative achievements of some indigenous groups took new forms after contact with Europeans, as they applied newly acquired metal tools for their own purposes, such as hunting or carving.

In speaking of the knowledge of any particular group, as a result, we have to take into consideration whether we are thinking of hundreds of years ago, the recent past, or the present. If much traditional knowledge has been lost to people in a present generation, the cause generally lies in part in the adaptations groups have made and even more in the destruction of enforced assimilation.

## Indigenous and "western" knowledge: methods

At first glance, indigenous knowledge differs most notably from those areas of knowledge such as the natural sciences, which are shared and constructed by *decontextualizing* and *depersonalizing* knowledge.

Certainly, the natural sciences predominantly take the *decontextualizing* of knowledge as a goal. They leave behind the particular forest plants or rainy seasons to construct statements at high levels of generality, with the extreme being scientific laws that fit all places at all times. The knowledge of a *particular* landscape, with its geographical features and its plant and animal life, is lost within the generalizing process of inductive reasoning as it takes a larger and larger overview.

However, the gulf between decontextualized scientific knowledge and indigenous knowledge grounded in context could too easily be exaggerated. For one thing, contemporary understanding in the natural sciences includes growing ecological awareness, with recognition of the complexities of living systems and the interconnectedness of living things. Within the academic sciences, indigenous knowledge has increasingly been given respect as traditional ecological knowledge and understood to complement scientific understanding. (See extract "Traditional Ecological Knowledge" later in this chapter.)

For another thing, the natural sciences and indigenous knowledge have been argued not to differ fundamentally in how they use ways of knowing for observing and learning about the natural world. Like the natural sciences, indigenous knowledge generalizes in order to classify and name, draw correlations between natural phenomena, make causal connections, and predict. As biologist Lilian Na'ia Alessa suggests in the extract "Scales of Knowledge", the difference may be primarily one of scale, in response to the needs of the people seeking the knowledge.

Thus, for example, scientists far removed from the local context may be able to isolate medicinally active substances from certain plants grown in laboratory conditions; their general knowledge of biology and chemistry serves them well. Certain

---

13   Marker, M. 2011. "Teaching History from an Indigenous Perspective. Four Winding Paths up the Mountain". in Clark, P. [Ed.]. *New Possibilities for the past: Shaping history education in Canada*. Vancouver, BC. UBC Press. P 102.

## "Scales of Knowledge": The Natural Sciences and Traditional Knowledge

*by Lilian "Na'ia" Alessa, a biologist of Salish ancestry, from the Pacific Northwest of North America*

It is my opinion that an important distinction must be made between scales of knowledge with respect to the scientific method and traditional knowledge. Technologies such as microscopes and antibodies have given us insights into the unseen worlds of micro-scale processes that we would otherwise never have acquired. As you increase the level of space (for example a cell in the body) and time, you increase the level of complexity, or how many things interact with each other at any given time. By the time you arrive at ecosystems, the interactions of organisms and their habitats, you have accumulated an enormous amount of complexity. As you can imagine, it becomes increasingly difficult to resolve what is causing which effect. As a consequence, the scientific method and the Western approach to "understanding" is more tenuous, and it is at this intersection of time and space that traditional knowledge is most apparent as another approach.

By necessity, western science must simplify things to develop testable hypotheses about how they work, which is both precise and useful at smaller scales. In the process, however, and as you increase in scales of complexity, it eliminates details, many of which are considered "descriptive" and either not important to understanding or too confounding. A hallmark of traditional knowledge is that details are exquisitely noted and communicated in such a way that the user can detect small changes and respond accordingly.

Having said that, traditional knowledge has developed around the processes which sustained indigenous peoples and historically all our ancestors: primarily interactions of plants and animals with their environments, whereas western science has enticed us to explore the range of existence, from the way the mind works to the quantum physics of northern lights, a reflection of some of the luxuries of time afforded certain societies as they secured reliable food and shelter.

Much evidence, never mind common sense, suggests that traditional knowledge has existed as long as we have as a species…. The act of residing, surviving, and thriving in a place means that the resident must "know" her environment in such a way as to repeatedly have a high likelihood of regularly acquiring necessary resources, whether they are physical or not, on a regular basis. The consequence of failure is not the ridicule of one's peers or the failure to get a research grant; it is sickness, suffering, and death.

One could say that the stakes in traditional knowledge are much higher, and hence so is the precision. Traditional knowledge requires something that, with few exceptions, western science has failed to accomplish: long periods of observation in the same place and the transmission of these observations to others in that place so that they can use them practically and often, from a young age.

Some western schools of thought romanticize traditional knowledge and perceive that somehow possessing it brings ultimate harmony of the user with his world. No mistakes will be made because there exists a magical link where all things are known. This is part of the devalidation of traditional knowledge because it fails to acknowledge that it, like the scientific method, is a process where information is accepted or rejected based on receiving knowledge continuously, both directly from the system and from one's colleagues, friends, family, and mentors, usually to benefit the community and future generations. The same can rarely be said for western science.[14]

---

[14]  Lilian Na'ia Alessa, "What is Truth?" *The Alaska Native Reader: History, Culture, Politics*, ed. Maria Sháa Tláa Williams, Duke University Press, 2009. Pp 50–1.

## Traditional Ecological Knowledge

*by Milton M. R. Freeman*

Increasingly, the published scientific literature and the convening of conferences and workshops reflect the growing awareness that there is a legitimate field of environmental expertise known as traditional ecological knowledge. For about a half century anthropologists and some animal and plant taxonomists (e.g., Mayr et al. 1953:5) have recognized the accuracy with which various non-western peoples have identified different species; indeed, such "folk-taxonomies" include more than just those food or medicinal species having obvious practical utility. The comprehensiveness of the taxonomic system suggests that the extent of traditional knowledge may be quite profound, and that, indeed, taxonomy is important (as in the biological sciences) as the basis for building extensive systems of knowing about nature.

More recently, many scientists have begun to understand that such traditional knowledge extends far beyond what in western science would be called descriptive biology, beyond knowing how to identify different species of animals, or describe their feeding, reproduction, or migratory behaviour. The knowledge possessed by such tradition-based, non-industrial societies is essentially of an "ecological" nature, that is to say, it seeks to understand and explain the workings of ecosystems, or at the very least biological communities, containing many interacting species of animals and often plants, and the determinative role played by certain key biological and physical parameters in influencing the behaviour of the total biological community...

Expressed another way, traditional ecological knowledge is more than merely esoteric; it is directed toward gaining a useful understanding of how ecological systems generally work, to how many of the key components of the total ecosystem interrelate, and how predictive outcomes in respect to matters of practical concern can best be effected. This is precisely what ecological scientists or wildlife and fisheries attempt to do...[15]

indigenous people, on the other hand, may understand that those plants best used for medicine can be found growing in specific locations and can be harvested in certain ways or at particular times. Both construct knowledge using fundamentally the same ways of knowing, but at different scales or different degrees of removal from the landscape. Yet even this distinction of difference of scale can break down as some sciences, biology in particular, emphasize unique adaptations of a subspecies to a very small ecological niche, for example, Darwin's finches in the Galapagos.

Perhaps a more marked difference between indigenous knowledge and the areas of knowledge we have been studying is the degree to which the latter *depersonalize* knowledge – though this difference certainly applies less to the arts than to the sciences. The mechanisms for sharing knowledge in the sciences make it public across a "knowledge community" where people may never meet each other, and where the conventions of exchange and ownership of knowledge are formalized, impersonal systems. In these areas of knowledge we speak appropriately about a "methodology", a conscious, formal, impersonal, and deliberately adopted system of investigation, exchange, criticism, and revision.

Indigenous knowledge, however, is set within cultures and real communities that affect the exchange and ownership of knowledge. Within them, there are certainly mechanisms for sharing knowledge, as we have noted already. Yet the transfer of knowledge is not between research groups pursuing new information and explanations but between generations respecting traditional understanding.

Within indigenous communities, there are also conventions of ownership of knowledge that bear a resemblance to concepts of "intellectual property". Yet that resemblance is entirely superficial: ownership does not go to the first who registers the copyright or patent within a competitive system. The restrictions on the knowledge exchange are

---

[15] Freeman, M.R.M. "The Nature and Utility of Traditional Ecological Knowledge," *Northern Perspectives*, Vol 20, no. 1, summer 1992. Published by the Canadian Arctic Resources Committee. http://www.carc.org/pubs/v20no1/utility.htm

particular to their communities and embedded in specific cultural traditions: some knowledge may be women's knowledge, and some men's knowledge; some knowledge belongs to certain families or clans, including performance of some songs or dances; some knowledge is sacred and should not be uttered in inappropriate circumstances.

Clearly, there can be no shared "methodology" identified in a general overview of indigenous knowledge without a considerable departure from the common understanding of the word. It is crucial to recognize differences between how knowledge is shared in a formalized way in depersonalized academic communities and how knowledge is shared as part of the cultural life of a particular and personalized community. Knowledge is not separated from the people who possess it.

## Historical development: colonialism, globalization

The fact that indigenous knowledge is particular to cultures and to peoples means that we do have to treat it differently in discussion from the way we deal with public, depersonalized knowledge of the areas of knowledge. We have to be cautious with generalizations, particularly those applied to human groups (chapter 13). However, there is a further need for awareness as we deal specifically with indigenous knowledge.

Colonialism and globalization have often fostered insulting versions of indigenous people and their knowledge. Native peoples have been notoriously misrepresented – romanticized as stoic and noble or denigrated as lazy and ignorant. The claim that they were "savages" has been used to justify killing them, confining them, destroying their cultures, and taking their lands. As a result, many indigenous people are often understandably sensitive about how they and their knowledge are represented.

Indeed, much of the colonial conquest of indigenous groups was managed through stamping out their knowledge and imposing upon them the knowledge of their conquerors. From the perspective of European colonial powers of the nineteenth century, education was a means of saving and "enlightening" primitive peoples by making them more like their conquerors. How better could

colonial powers take up their "white man's burden", their heavy self-assigned responsibility of civilizing the "savages", than to teach them, giving them Christian religion and literacy? Or so they thought.

At the time of European colonial expansion across Australia and North America, many aboriginal peoples were conquered by force and then educated to forget their cultures. Educational systems were commonly set up by the state but run by religious societies. In Canada, the residential schools were started in the middle of the nineteenth century, with attendance compulsory until the middle of the twentieth century. Children were forcibly taken from their families and villages in order to educate them collectively. In residential schools, they were forbidden to speak their own languages, taught to despise their own cultures, and often treated harshly, even abusively. The cultural knowledge of generations past, dependent on the connection between elders and children in an oral tradition, was largely extinguished.

*Film Recommendation: The documentary film Schooling the World: The White Man's Last Burden treats the impact of contemporary education on indigenous cultures. Filmed on location in the Indian Himalayas, it features interviews with the Ladakhi people, anthropologists and educators. Using beautiful images and glimpses into other ways of thinking, the film challenges notions of cultural superiority, as sustainable ancient cultures are educated out of existence. Its website provides a discussion guide that stimulates questions of what knowledge should be passed on from one generation to the next, and in what ways. "We've moved from wisdom to knowledge, and now we're moving from knowledge to information, and that information is so partial – that we're creating incomplete human beings." – Vandana Shiva[16]*

---

[16] http://schoolingtheworld.org/

The official apology of the Canadian government in 2008 to former students of the Indian Residential Schools for this "sad chapter in our history" acknowledges the aims of the imposed schooling:

> Two primary objectives of the Residential Schools system were to remove and isolate children from the influence of their homes, families, traditions and cultures, and to assimilate them into the dominant culture. These objectives were based on the assumption that Aboriginal cultures and spiritual beliefs were inferior and unequal. Indeed, some sought, as it was infamously said, "to kill the Indian in the child". Today, we recognize that this policy of assimilation was wrong, has caused great harm, and has no place in our country.[17]

In Canada, the adults who experienced this system call themselves "residential school survivors". In Australia, they are called "the stolen generations".

Many indigenous people have little left. They have lost their traditional lands and to a large extent control of their lives. It is worthwhile reading the United Nations Declaration on the Rights of Indigenous Peoples (2007),[18] and to consider why it was considered necessary to create a document beyond the generic Universal Declaration of Human Rights (1948).

What indigenous people have left, in many cases, is their cultural knowledge, or the parts of it that have not been destroyed. And at present, many of their languages and cultures are dying. "By 2100, more than half of the more than 7,000 languages spoken on Earth – many of them not yet recorded – may disappear," notes the Disappearing Languages Project of National Geographic, "taking with them a wealth of knowledge about history, culture, the natural environment, and the human brain."[19]

## Accuracy and respect: guidelines

A history of conquest gives us an intensified reason, then, for trying to make sure that we are not disrespectful in our own treatment of indigenous knowledge. One could argue that it is urgently important for us to recognize and talk about aboriginal cultural achievements so that they be more widely recognized and appreciated. However, as we suggested at the beginning of this chapter, talking about peoples and their knowledge without their consent – in effect, taking all they have left – can, for some groups, be an additional offence or theft.

Faced with this dilemma, what should we do in TOK to discuss indigenous knowledge?

First, we suggest that at least those of us who are not ourselves indigenous might start with our own perspectives and try to pin down what we think we already know about indigenous knowledge. We could start by identifying any stereotypes or values that we may have encountered associated with the people and their culture. We may have no choice but to start with ourselves as we reach out to learn about other cultures, and it helps to recognize consciously, to the extent we can, what beliefs we carry. Exploration might justify those beliefs, but might also change them.

Second, we can be aware of the need for respect and listening, and interest in learning. In considering indigenous knowledge in TOK, we recommend that, as much as possible, you find peer-reviewed resources in which trained anthropologists, sociologists, historians, or art historians write or film with understanding of surrounding issues. (That "informed judgment" again!)

In many cases, it is possible to find such resources on indigenous cultures produced by indigenous people themselves. Many First Nations groups have their own journals, radio stations, books and plays, websites, or online videos – though the knowledge they deal with may not be exclusively indigenous. Consistently directed towards cultural preservation is a current project on the part of UNESCO which supports the undertakings of indigenous peoples around the world to create their own media. (For resources, keep an eye on the materials developing on the UNESCO website.) When the knowledge of culture has moved into the public zone in this way, you can be reasonably confident that you are gaining reliable knowledge, selected to be shared and framed with the relevant worldview.

---

[17] "Statement of Apology,", Government of Canada website, 11 June 2008. http://www.aadnc-aandc.gc.ca/eng/1100100015644

[18] United Nations Declaration on the Rights of Indigenous Peoples, http://www.un.org/esa/socdev/unpfii/documents/DRIPS_en.pdf

[19] Disappearing Languages, National Geographichttp://travel.nationalgeographic.com/travel/enduring-voices/

One useful set of guidelines to treating aboriginal people and their knowledge with accuracy and respect is available on the University of Saskatchewan website,[20] from which we distil the following points in terms relevant to our own context of TOK:

- It is important not to "translate" cultural views into each other, probably distorting them, but to try to see them in their own terms.
- Acknowledge diversity and do not treat aboriginal people as though they were all the same.
- Acknowledge the source and ownership of knowledge, and the permission we have to use or describe the knowledge.
- Clarify what "traditional" means when you use it, giving traditional knowledge a historic time or date. Recognize that culture changes over time.

- Take care with the tense of verbs for what is past and what continues to be present as knowledge useful to people now.
- Remember that aboriginal knowledge is not something "accumulated and possessed", but instead a process or a journey.
- Acknowledge the interconnected, holistic nature of aboriginal knowledge.

We recommend that TOK classes treating indigenous knowledge consider the broad characteristics of indigenous knowledge such as we have introduced here, but use the topic to learn more about very specific cultures, perhaps in the region where the school is located. It might thereby be possible to visit cultural sites or to invite guest speakers from the local indigenous communities to talk about their own cultures.

## Voices

### Changing culture, changing knowledge

In Nunavut, knowledge has changed a lot from my grandparents' generation. They lived on the land, hunting, fishing, following animals. They didn't need a GPS [global positioning system via satellite] to know their way around because they navigated by the stars. My grandmother was a teacher in traditional skills like preparing skins and beading. We still learn about the land, and there's a school programme on learning traditional skills.

But this kind of knowledge is not the most important now because going to school and finding out about the world around us is what we need. We depend on the internet in a big way because the population is so small and so spread out that we can't have a large library anywhere. The solution is having the legislative library and the territorial newspaper online. We depend a lot on technology, including radio and satellite TV, for education. When I was around 3 or 4 I remember our computer

*Lindsay Lloyd, Nunavut, Canada*

arriving. It was frozen so we had to let it thaw out before we could use it.

Yes, we're losing our culture. It's an oral culture so very fragile. With no trees we had no paper to write things on and no photos—no archive—and with the land frozen we have no large archeological remains. We're losing our culture, but we're making a new one.

---

[20] http://www.usask.ca/education/ccstu/guiding_documents/guidelines_for_representing_kn.html

*Réal Carrière is Cree from the Northern Saskatchewan village of Cumberland House. He is currently a Ph.D. student in Public Policy and Administration at Ryerson University.*

*Réal Carrière*
*IB graduate 2002*

### Indigenous perspective

I am Cree and if I am around other Cree speakers I may even further define myself as "Apeetogosan", which is Cree for "halfman", similar to Métis. I find it hard to characterize "indigenous knowledge" because of the varying indigenous traditions around the world. In the Canadian context you may be able to point towards some very general shared "knowledge" practices such as the use of oral history, the interpretation of dreams, respect for nature, and the role elders play in the transmission of knowledge from one generation to the next.

My father has a saying that he was taught to respect as an important piece of traditional knowledge: "In the hierarchy of life man is least important because he depends on other living things to survive." This teaching is the foundation of my philosophy and it is a philosophy that has been passed down for generations. If I have children I would like them to

see how important maintaining a relationship to the land is, and that relationship has to be more than a summer vacation.

My own experience with living off the land has been in northern Saskatchewan, in Canada. My family has been living in that area for generations. Daily life includes no power, running water, and no road access, with the nearest neighbour 50 kilometres away. To get to my home in the summer we have to travel 50 kilometres by river and in the winter we have to travel across country by dog sled. We have a seasonal lifestyle. In the summer we fish, in the fall we hunt, and in the winter we trap. We try to keep a garden when we are around during the summer.

Now as someone that is working on a Ph.D, I have to situate myself within the knowledge production world. Within that context I have realized that I am an Indigenous researcher. This means that "thinking critically" is now a tool that I use from my position outwards. As an Indigenous academic, I am taking a particular stance and as such "critique" has become a tool that I use to challenge the other types of knowledge.

## Knowledge questions

The knowledge that we try to gain in TOK is inescapably comparative, as we try to see how knowledge fits together from a high-in-the-sky overview. Yet how is comparison to be handled when we are counseled not to impose our own ways of understanding on the indigenous knowledge of particular peoples?

Again, we have to acknowledge the problem and trust that our TOK inquiry skills will lead us to appropriate investigation. We might think in our own terms as we enter the inquiry – and then try to think more holistically as we exit.

Because of the vast diversity of indigenous cultures, we cannot treat here any specific indigenous cultures. However, we can try to identify some knowledge questions that might be useful to you in your own investigation.

### 1. How do perspectives affect knowledge?

Indigenous knowledge is imbued with a perspective on life. Since this is the only group of cultures specifically singled out for treatment in the TOK subject guide, treating them in terms of characteristics as perspectives could provide a fuller understanding of how people make sense of the world in ways that are coherent, or internally consistent. An indigenous perspective as a whole, with its comprehensive vision of life, might well stimulate discussion on the differences between "knowledge" and "wisdom".

"Cultural characteristics: worldviews" (page 18) gives general characteristics of cultures as identified by theorists. Of particular interest could be Kluckhohn and Strodtbeck's values orientations relevant to indigenous concepts of: time, relationships between human beings and nature that involve harmony and respect, collective culture with individuals in cooperation, and a sense of living and growing as a journey. (A good resource to consider would be "Our Responsibility to the Seventh Generation" from the International Institute for Sustainable Development.)[21] See also "Thinking critically: Exploring different perspectives" (page 28): this outline for analysis has been foundational for this book.

## 2. What forms does knowledge take?

Indigenous knowledge is strongly characterized by knowledge seen as skills, developed through experience. For an emphasis on skills (knowing how) and teaching through demonstration, see the extract in this chapter "Knowing how: learning to be a successful hunter", in which the father tells his sons to watch as he hunts caribou. One of the sons remembers this lesson, conveyed not through language but through demonstration, for the rest of his life. The implications of mastering hunting skills are significant: failing to learn could mean dying of starvation.

As you read the passage, notice the cultural perspective that framed the skills. The relationship between the hunter and the hunted, although eroded since that time, was "intimate", the hunting skills were set within a worldview integrating human beings and nature, and the hunter took no more than he needed. Within his village, the father was a "highly respected hunter" not only because he brought food home but also because he "shared it with others in the village". His skill was certainly personal, but set within shared knowledge as he

learned it and taught it, and as he understood it in cultural terms.

Indigenous knowledge is also characterized by knowledge claims and, as we noted earlier, often ones particular to the geographical location. Although many of those claims are observable and testable in the context – as they must be for survival – as a body they cannot readily be separated into observational claims as distinct from value judgments or metaphysical claims. (It could be argued that the same could be said of the claims of any cultural worldview.)

## 3. How is knowledge affected by structures of power?

In treating indigenous knowledge, the people and their history of contact and colonization are extremely important, including residential schools and attempts to replace indigenous knowledge with that of the dominant culture. We have introduced this topic already in this chapter, but must emphasize that the situation of particular indigenous groups can vary from the generalizations we have made here.

In considering the suppression of indigenous knowledge, you might want to pay particular attention to the loss of language and to current systems of preserving or reviving language.

## 4. How do we classify knowledge?

TOK looks at knowledge in overview, but also gives attention to areas of knowledge that are common to the structuring of academic knowledge worldwide. By treating them comparatively and questioning the classification itself, TOK encourages thinking "outside the box". But from an indigenous perspective, there isn't even a "box" to "think outside of"! Consideration of the holistic nature of indigenous knowledge – where ethics, religion, literature, history, the sciences, and mathematics are all integrated – can help in TOK to develop a broad understanding of not just indigenous knowledge but of cultural and historical forces in our own classification system.

---

21  Linda Clarkson, Vern Morrissette and Gabriel Régallet, "Our Responsibility to the Seventh Generation: Indigenous Peoples and Sustainable Development," International Institute for Sustainable Development, Winnipeg, 1992. http://www.iisd.org/pdf/seventh_gen.pdf

## Knowing how: learning to be a successful hunter

*by Ray Barnhardt and Angayuqaq Oscar Kawagley*

An Inupiaq elder stood up and explained through an interpreter that he was going to describe how he and his brother were taught to hunt caribou by their father, before guns were commonplace in the upper Kobuk River area of northern Alaska.

"The elder described how his father had been a highly respected hunter who always brought food home when he went out on hunting trips and shared it with others in the village. One day when he and his brother were coming of age, their father told them to prepare to go with him to check out a herd of caribou that was migrating through a valley a few miles away. They eagerly assembled their clothing and equipment and joined their father for their first caribou hunt. When they reached a ridge overlooking the nearby valley, they could see a large herd grazing and moving slowly across a grassy plain below. Their father told his sons to lay quietly up on the ridge and watch as he went down with his bow and arrows to intercept the caribou.

"The boys watched as their father proceeded to walk directly toward the caribou herd, which as he approached began to move away from him in a file behind the lead bulls, yet he just kept walking openly toward them. This had the two brothers scratching their heads wondering why their father was chasing the caribou away from him. Once the father reached the area where the caribou had been grazing, he stopped and put his bow and arrows down on the ground. As the (now) elder told the story, he demonstrated how his father then got into a crouching position and slowly began to move his arms up and down, slapping them against his legs as though he were mimicking a giant bird about to take off. The two brothers watched intently as the lead bulls in the caribou herd stopped and looked back curiously at their father's movements. Slowly at first, the caribou began to circle back in a wide arc watching the figure flapping its wings out on the tundra, and then they began running, encircling their father in a closing spiral until eventually they were close enough that he reached down, picked up his bow and arrows and methodically culled out the choice caribou one at a time until he had what he needed. He then motioned for his sons to come down and help prepare the meat to be taken back to the village.

"As the elder completed the story of how he and his brother were taught the accrued knowledge associated with hunting caribou, he explained that in those days the relationship between the hunter and the hunted was much more intimate than it is now. With the intervention of modern forms of technology, the knowledge associated with that symbiotic relationship is slowly being eroded. But for the elder, the lessons he and his brother had learned from their father out on the tundra that day were just as vivid when he shared them with us as they had been the day he learned them, and he would have little difficulty passing a graduation qualifying exam on the subject 70 years later. The knowledge, skills and standards of attainment required to be a successful hunter were self-evident, and what a young hunter needed to know and be able to do was both implicit and explicit in the lesson the father provided."[22]

The following resources could be useful in understanding the holistic picture of some indigenous knowledge:

- Consult the *Four Directions Teachings,* a resource for learning about indigenous knowledge from five First Nations in Canada.[23]
- Consider the medicine wheel or sacred hoop of the Lakota or Sioux people of North America. All areas of known experience fit into a circle, which also serves as a model of the universe.[24]
- The Australian aboriginals have possibly the oldest living culture in the world. An entry point is the website on Australian Indigenous cultural heritage of the Australian government. Learn about the Dreaming and songlines.[25]

---

[22] Barnhardt, R and Kawagley, AO. 2005. "Indigenous Knowledge Systems and Alaska Native Ways of Knowing." *Anthropology and Education Quarterly*, Vol 36, number 1. Pp 8–23.

[23] You will find some informative online interactive videos: http://www.fourdirectionsteachings.com/index.html

[24] On YouTube you will find some good introductions to the medicine wheel. Search for *medicine wheel* or *Lakota medicine wheel* or *Sioux medicine wheel.*

[25] http://australia.gov.au/about-australia/australian-story/austn-indigenous-cultural-heritage. See also the website First Australians.

## 5. How does indigenous knowledge intersect with TOK areas?

Within this book, we have already touched on particular indigenous experiences and knowledge. It may be useful to you to recall these moments and build on them.

**a.** The arts

We selected a sculpture "Raven and the First Men" by Haida carver Bill Reid as one of the works of international art to investigate (chapter 17). Representing a moment in a creation story, it introduces indigenous visual arts, storytelling, and spiritual views of the interconnected human and animal worlds. The stories belong to the Haida people, who live on Haida Gwaii, islands off the west coast of Canada, formerly called the Queen Charlotte Islands within a colonial naming system. The visual arts make a very good gateway into an indigenous worldview, as does postcolonial literature by indigenous writers.

**b.** Ethics

Although generalizing on the ethical codes held by indigenous peoples would be nearly impossible, certain values seem to recur. Indigenous cultures generally give respect to elders and to their traditional knowledge. They also respect the earth on which they live, often considering it to be living. Admittedly, the idea that all indigenous people have always lived sustainably with the environment would be a romantic overgeneralization; the story of Easter Island and the extinction of numerous species of New Zealand birds provide ready counter-examples.[26] However, many indigenous cultures have long embodied a principle of responsibility to the earth and to future generations.

The concept of living sustainably is well summed up in the idea of the "seventh generation", attributed to the Iroquois Nations: that every decision we make today should benefit the children of the future that we will never see and know, the children of the seventh generation hence. The Great Law of the Iroquois gave this responsibility to its leaders:

"Look and listen for the welfare of the whole people and have always in view not only the present but also the coming generations, even those whose faces are yet beneath the surface of the ground – the unborn of the future Nation."[27] We could all learn from this wisdom.

**c.** History

We have illustrated the influence of postmodern thinking on perspectives and knowledge with a commentary on native North American history (chapter 15) in which the writer points out some of the implications of relativism in obscuring real-world injustices. The topic of aboriginal perspectives could be developed much more fully in treating history, to consider why some stories are told and not others in dominant versions of the past in books, films, and educational systems. The "winning of the west" in American history, for instance, would be strikingly different from the perspectives of settlers and indigenous people.

Treating history from an indigenous perspective, however, involves more than simply telling versions of a shared story differently. It may require some understanding of a different conception of time, not as linear progression but as circular, with a spiraling of events that reappear within the circles of the seasons.[28]

Moreover, it may demand that stories of resource exploitation, such as the beaver trade or buffalo hunting, be reconceptualized so that the animals are recognized for their place in a concept of life:

Indigenous systems of knowledge and understandings of the past are different from these approaches in that they place animals as unsegmented from human beings. Many indigenous traditions recognize the animals as having been created first and therefore as being older and wiser than humans. From an indigenous perspective, much of the knowledge of the past came from the relationships that human beings developed with animals. The histories of tribal people are filled with stories of how particular animals sacrificed and taught the human

[26] New Zealand Ecology: Extinct Birds, http://terranature.org/extinctBirds.htm and John Cairns Jr. 2004. *Sustainability ethics: tales of two cultures. Ethics in Science and Environmental Policies.* Pp 39–43.

[27] The Constitution of the Iroquois Nations: The Great Binding Law, article 28. Indigenous Peoples Literature. http://www.indigenouspeople.net/iroqcon.htm

[28] Marker, M. 2011. "Teaching History from an Indigenous Perspective. Four Winding Paths up the Mountain". in Clark, P. (Ed.). *New Possibilities for the past: Shaping history education in Canada.* Vancouver, BC. UBC Press. P 100.

communities. In these narratives, the sacred ecology of animals and humans and the sustaining cycles of life are explained.[29]

Similarly, the earth itself may well take on a living role in the narratives of the past and the sacred geography of earth and sky.

**d.** Human sciences

As we have already commented, anthropology and sociology give insight into indigenous cultures, and how to learn about them in their own terms. Moreover, in postcolonial developments in these human sciences, it is often indigenous people themselves who provide the commentary. This shift in the position of the observer is part of the historical development of the human sciences (chapter 18). From that position, it is easy to see that indigenous peoples, though not practising the human sciences as we know them, have had their own approaches to psychology, economic exchange, and politics.

**e.** Natural sciences

Indigenous science is characterized by generalizations that preserve the particular cases, and by ecological knowledge, as we have considered earlier in this chapter. Note the extracts we have included in this chapter: "Scales of Knowledge: The Natural Sciences and Traditional Knowledge", the diagram "Qualities Associated with Traditional Knowledge and Western Science," and "Traditional Ecological Knowledge". Consider that "most of the world's staple crops, feeding billions, were developed by tribal peoples. Many of the principal drugs used in 'modern' medicine originate with them."[30]

**f.** Mathematics

Indigenous mathematics involves forms of universal mathematical skills often demonstrated in art, technology and sophisticated skills of navigation (chapter 20).

Altogether, in entering indigenous knowledge through our own structures of areas of knowledge, we are thinking of it in our own terms. Although we acknowledge the disadvantages of doing so, we could

*Aboriginal elder, Tiwi Islands, Australia*  *Aboriginal boy playing didgeridoo, Kuranda, Australia*

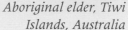
↑ Passing on traditions

also insist that we do end up with an appreciation of some aspects of the knowledge and a good entry point for learning more about particular cultures.

## "Indigenous Knowledge"

Certainly, the classification "indigenous knowledge" was not one created by indigenous people themselves from within their own traditional understanding of the world. With localized knowledge, they could not have stood outside their own traditions to see themselves in the same category as some of their enemies, or as unlike people in unlike environments on the other side of the world. As we saw earlier, the category was created first by recognition of the impact of colonialism and globalization on many peoples of the world, and then elaborated by features held loosely in common. Since the 1960s, the term "indigenous knowledge" has come increasingly into use, "connected with initiatives to promote socioeconomic development and environmental conservation".[31]

The category is a loose one: the UNESCO features of indigenous knowledge identified in this chapter are neither *inclusive* in applying to the knowledge of all groups nor *exclusive* in applying only to them.

---

[29] Marker, M. 2011. "Teaching History from an Indigenous Perspective. Four Winding Paths up the Mountain". in Clark, P. (Ed.). *New Possibilities for the past: Shaping history education in Canada*. Vancouver, BC. UBC Press. P 103.

[30] Survival International, http://www.survivalinternational.org/info

[31] Van der Velden, M. 2012. "Designing for Culture: An Ecological Perspective on Indigenous Knowledge and Database Design". in P. H. Cheong, J. Martin & L. P. Macfadyen (Eds.), *New Media and Intercultural Communication: Identity, Community and Politics*. New York. Peter Lang. P 24.

## Owning and sharing cultural knowledge: songlines

When cultures change, what measures should be taken to preserve knowledge that is vulnerable to being lost? The answer depends on specific cultural groups and sometimes specific individuals.

Australian Aboriginal songlines, from the Dreaming of creation, connect the people with the land, carry cultural heritage, and act as a non-visual map to the territory. The Australian Aboriginal culture is the longest living culture in the world, dating back 70,000 years and covering an estimated 2,000 generations. Yet a culture successful for millennia is being eroded as songlines have been broken by colonization and stories lost.[32]

Nevertheless, a project to record the Australian Western Desert's most important creation stories demonstrates the sensitivities that often accompany preserving knowledge that is deeply cultural and deeply personal. Although the Songlines project was initiated by Anangu elders and is backed by Australian and aboriginal cultural organizations, a respected figure in the Anangu community protested in May 2012 that the project is unethical.[33] A traditional owner of the Ngintaka creation story of the giant lizard, he has declared his aim to block the project from entering his homeland, where the story begins.

Yami Lester accuses women of "meddling in men's law" and the Australian National University of "attempting to remove the sacredness and essence from our culture and fling it before the eyes of the material world." "Exposing the most sacred of Aboriginal men's law to unready women and children, let alone the entire world, will further weaken our culture and humiliate traditional Anangu men."

Dr. Diana James, project co-ordinator, insists that the protest is based on a misunderstanding. "It has always been very clear this is an Anangu-led project and the men are protecting their law and the women protect their secret law."

A senior owner of the Ngintaka story, Robert Stevens, declares, "Men's business is separate, we are following the track, telling the story that we all understand, men and women. Everyone tells this story to their grandsons and granddaughters so the Tjukurpa [Dreaming] will still remain. I think this project is very important, not only for Anangu people now, but for the future, our kids and their kids."

When we talk of "shared knowledge" of indigenous peoples, we are clearly not speaking of the same thing as depersonalized, decontextualized shared knowledge in the sciences. It is passed on in different ways, with different restrictions, and with different purposes. The meaning of the knowledge is cultural, as is the traditional way of sharing. The knowledge is owned, and personal – with deep emotional connection with identity. As outsiders, we cannot treat it as we would a proof in mathematics or or a theory in physics.

The category is also an important one, we would argue. For one thing, through learning more about *other* ways of building knowledge and using it, we gain awareness also of our *own* ways and a potential to do things differently. We also gain some sense of our larger human heritage – what it means to be human, living and learning in the world, and making sense of our experience. And, if we will, we might even learn from the wisdom many groups have embodied of living sustainably with nature.

For another thing, indigenous peoples themselves may benefit from our learning more. As Survival International declares regarding tribal peoples in particular, "The more tribal peoples are understood, the more they'll be respected and the less they'll be mistreated."[34] Although not all indigenous groups are as vulnerable as tribal peoples, this same need for understanding applies.

Moreover, the exploration of indigenous knowledge adds a rich cultural dimension to

---

[32] See the website First Australians. See also "The Songlines", National Film and Sound Archives, http://dl.nfsa.gov.au/module/1539/.

[33] Stuart Rintoul, "Songlline at heart of secret men's business", *The Australian*. 19 May 2012

[34] Survival International http://www.survivalinternational.org/info

knowledge questions that we have posed and considered throughout this book. We return, as we conclude, to the questions we offered you for thought at the beginning of this chapter:

- What is "shared knowledge"? How does the sharing within academic areas of knowledge compare with the sharing of knowledge within cultures and societies?
- On what basis do we classify knowledge into different areas?
- What is the difference between knowledge and wisdom?

## Differences or similarities?

In this course, you are frequently asked to make comparisons. What will you emphasize as you do so: the differences or the similarities? Will your choice depend on the point you want to make?

Notice that in treating the cultural context of knowledge in many places in this book, we have chosen to stress differences in order to think more about the variability of contexts that affect what we know. In doing so, though, do we end up at the same time with an exaggerated impression of human difference?

We might heed the words of Xwĕ lī qwĕl tĕl, honoured as Grand Chief by the Stó:l⁻o Tribal Council. He is also His Honour, The Honourable Steven Point, appointed Lieutenant Governor (the Queen's representative) of the Province of British Columbia, Canada in 2007. As a leader in both his First Nations community and his provincial one, he speaks of change he would like to see:

> Our values and our systems are not European. However, the more I study Europeans and the more I learn about my own history, the more I find that in fact we are the same. You love your Elders, you love your God, you cherish your young people, and you have a strong sense of justice, just as we do. In fact, if you look long and hard enough, you will find that there are probably more similarities than there are differences.... We have both paid too much attention to the differences between us, and I want to see that change. I hope that you do, too.[35]

---

35  Stephen L. Point, "Getting Back Our Dignity", 2 October 2007. http://thetyee.ca/Views/2007/10/02/Dignity/

# 22 Religious Knowledge

## Exploring perspectives: sensitivities

Many people hesitate to discuss religious beliefs outside their own faith communities because of their own sensitivities, or their desire not to trespass on other people's sensitivities; beliefs in religion can be held with more emotion than those, for instance, in mathematics or the sciences – for most people! A TOK class, however, should give a secure and trusting atmosphere and one with the habit of sincerely interested inquiry. It can be a very comfortable place for talking about religion, to reflect on your own worldview and understand more about someone else's. We bring back here the advice we gave right at the beginning of the book, regarding exploring perspectives.

1. **Listen open-mindedly.** Listen to others who hold views unlike your own with a desire to learn, not blocked by eagerness to find fault and refute.

2. **Inquire.** Unfamiliar perspectives are not always easy to understand at first, especially if they are different from your own. If you are puzzled, activate your curiosity and (tactfully) try to learn more.

3. **Try to see from the other point of view.** Empathy and imagination help in entering into a different worldview. The challenge is to grasp the perspective not as described by an outsider but as held by an insider.

When we speak of "religious knowledge", we are referring in large part to the bodies of beliefs held by the followers of different religions. Religions draw together beliefs on the origin and purpose of life, teachings on moral and social conduct, a sense of the sacred and holy, and usually concepts of metaphysical deities. Religions interpret for their followers the meaning of life and give guidance on living it well.

Religious knowledge, more loosely, encompasses familiarity with the customs and practices of religious communities, and the place they give in their lives to their beliefs. Few would dispute that religious perspectives have a significant influence on the way societies run in the world today, and how they interact. We would argue that knowledge about religion, and some understanding of the perspectives on the world of major world religions, is an essential part of education for anyone wanting to take part in the communication and knowledge exchange of a diverse world.

## Religious communities and methods of sharing knowledge

Although we speak of "knowledge communities" when we refer to groups of physicists and psychologists, for example, with their shared

## Concepts and language

Check the meanings of any of the following words unfamiliar to you: theism, monotheism, polytheism, pantheism, atheism, religious pluralism, agnosticism, humanism.

methods of gaining, exchanging, and evaluating knowledge, we mean something different when we refer to "knowledge communities" of religion, as we think of the cultural component of religion and both informal and formal ways of passing on knowledge.

Certainly, most major religions are set within cultures. After considering social anthropology earlier, you will recognize that "culture" is a complex concept, such that we can reasonably speak of a culture for academic communities as well, and for many other groups with their shared knowledge and practices. Yet religion is accepted by families and societies in ways that make it, arguably, more significant for group identity and perspectives on the world. You may have identified membership of a religious community as part of your identity in the "personal profile" early in this book and may wish to do the activity here on "Personal memories and associations".

A deeply personal part of identity for many people, religion can often be associated with childhood memories of eating special meals with the extended family, exchanging gifts, taking part in public ceremonies, and listening to the stories told again and again of deities, great teachers and leaders, and important events of the community's past. The observances of religion may also shape a sense of time, possibly with prayers that mark the day, holy days that mark the week, and rituals or festivals that pattern the year.

Part of life, the observances of religion gather associations that affect all ways of knowing – *faith* as trust and a justification for belief, *memory* as it recalls and re-shapes the past, and *sense perception* in what is taken in through senses and how it is interpreted – with some religions using the arts and sense appeal to heighten teaching, and some avoiding them for more austere contemplation. *Intuition* and *reasoning* affect how conclusions are drawn from experience. *Imagination* and *emotion* are both stirred by the stories, public ceremonies, accompanying arts such as music, and teachings of a religion. Indeed, religion is entwined with the whole of its followers' ways of knowing, and can influence the whole of their worldview.

It is not, however, the whole of the worldview – and it is important to distinguish between what a religion teaches and the beliefs and practices of the people who follow it. The same religion may be interpreted and applied differently in different parts of the world as it overlaps and is integrated with the culture of the region, with all of its particular traditions, history, and economic and political attitudes and interests. Similarly, it is important not to infer the teachings of a religion entirely from the conduct of its followers, as few would claim to live fully according to the ethical ideals or spiritual teachings.

It may also be significant to distinguish between passing on knowledge informally in culture and teaching it formally within the social structures of religion. In most religions, there are teachers who formally introduce children to the beliefs and practices, instruct the adults, and organize and lead the rituals. In most, too, there are institutions, with their hierarchies, which not only pass on teachings but, in matters of controversy, decide what beliefs and practices are correct.

## For Reflection

In what ways does personal knowledge interact with shared knowledge in religion? The personal religious knowledge of individuals is drawn from the shared knowledge of their family and surrounding culture: one can predict with some likelihood the religion that will be followed by a child growing up in a Hindu family in India or a child growing up in a Christian family in Lesotho.

To what extent would you consider religion to be entirely *shared knowledge*, with a new generation accepting communal knowledge into their own personal knowledge? Is the "knowledge exchange" a one-way communication, possibly involving respect for authority and personal humility?

To what extent, on the other hand, would you consider religious beliefs to be essentially *personal knowledge*, even if people hold them in common with others in their societies? What is the importance of the personal, even private, element of religions with which you are familiar? Conversely, is there an element of nullifying anything personal or even social when contemplating something transcendent?

Many individuals and families do not hold any religious beliefs. If you have no religious beliefs yourself, are you affected in any way by the religious culture of your surrounding society? Without religious beliefs yourself, do you think it is easier for you to inquire into the religious beliefs of others with an open mind, or harder?

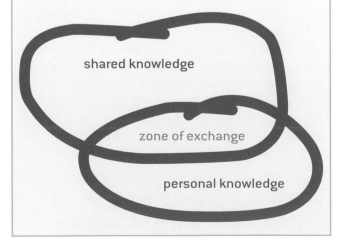

shared knowledge

zone of exchange

personal knowledge

## Discussion Activity

### Personal memories and associations

If you belong to a religious community, pick out one association with its ceremonies or religious acts that you consider special in some way. It could be with any ritual or any celebration, and could be special for its sense of relationships, its aura of mystery, or any special memories or personal stories that you have. Share this association with others in the class.

### Follow-up questions for discussion

What knowledge about religion is gained by the exchange of personal associations and stories? To what extent does understanding religious knowledge depend on gaining a sense not just of what beliefs people hold, descriptively, but what they *mean* to them in their cultural associations and influences on their worldviews?

## Voices

### Personal memories associations

The Torah is the Jewish sacred text. It is believed to have been written by Moses, and is read on a yearly basis. Each (Jewish calendar) week of the year has a section of the Torah assigned to it, and every week's section is read aloud and discussed by the group. My uncle says that it's quite interesting to revisit the same

*Lena Rotenberg, Brazil and USA*

section over the years, even if with the same group. The text is always the same but the people reading the text are not. Their interpretations change, what stands out for them each year changes, and thus the conversation is different each year. Reading the Torah together is a way to reflect together, to learn together, and to grow and form community together. Individually, each weekly reading serves as a marker, as an organizer in each person's memory of what was happening in their lives and in the world when they read that same text a year ago, 5 years ago, or 50 years ago.

Clearly, across the varying religions of the world, there is no shared methodology for developing their knowledge, no shared body of knowledge claims, and no shared way of questioning and revising knowledge claims – that is, in situations where questioning is permitted at all. Like indigenous knowledge, religious knowledge is specific to the groups who hold it. Yet, also like indigenous knowledge, on the other hand, there are numerous commonalities that make the conceptual category "religious knowledge" meaningful. The upcoming activity "Exploring world religions" may well bring many of these to forward for you to think about and discuss.

For formal methods of knowledge exchange *about* religion, however, many universities have academic departments that function just as other academic departments do. Religious knowledge

in this context – knowledge about religions – is a discipline with research, debate, conferences and publications using the means of communication conventional to all fields of academic study. Within this area of knowledge, scholars study the nature of religious knowledge, the meaning it holds for its followers, and its influence upon the world. Their subject matter of investigation overlaps with that of several other areas of knowledge, perhaps most notably history in study of the past, the human sciences in study of individual and social thought and behaviour, and ethics in the study of morality.

## Knowledge claims

When we shift emphasis from *religious communities* to the *beliefs* themselves, we again see differences and commonalities between religions – with the differences more apparent up close and commonalities perhaps more evident from a distance. Generalizations about what beliefs are held and what knowledge claims are made have to be taken as very broad, not necessarily applicable to all religions. Nevertheless, we will attempt here first to identify, as well as we can, the *kinds* of knowledge claims that are made within religions, and then to consider the kinds of justifications that are persuasive to followers of religions.

For the different categories of knowledge claims, you may refresh your memory by turning back to the end of chapter 2.

**Metaphysical knowledge claims:** To a large extent, what distinguishes religious assertions from other knowledge claims is the statements that go beyond the material world. Most religions make claims, for instance, about the existence of a spiritual reality, or the existence and nature of the soul, or the existence and nature of deities. They make claims about life after death and often before birth. The acceptance of metaphysical knowledge claims is perhaps what distinguishes religious knowledge most markedly from history, the human sciences, and the natural sciences. Unlike the knowledge claims of these fields, metaphysical ones cannot be proved false on the basis of evidence. They are not testable assertions, open to being discarded and replaced as part of the process of building knowledge.

**Value judgments:** Religions make claims about the nature of goodness or morality, and teach attitudes and ways of acting held to be good. Often, too, they prescribe codes of conduct for their followers. In some religions, what and how its followers eat and dress also come within the scope of moral judgment. These value judgments and directives are sometimes interpreted differently by different subgroups of the same religion, occasionally leading to deep rifts between these groups. And yet religious leaders can sometimes find much in common: the extract at the end of the chapter from the Parliament of the World's Religions takes a stand on "the moral foundation for a better individual and global order".

**Definitions (concepts and language):** Religions deal with metaphysical concepts beyond physical observation, so use language to establish concepts that may not be common in non-religious contexts. Clarifying exactly what is meant by a particular concept such as the "soul" or "reincarnation" or "heaven" or "nirvana" can involve extensive religious scholarship and debate, and may result in groups accepting one concept splitting from groups that accept another.

**Observational claims:** Religions provide many statements of observation, statements of how things *are* or *were*, with some of them overlapping with documented histories.

When the statements in sacred text are held to be *literally* true, they can conflict with knowledge claims established in other areas of knowledge, to the extent that religious followers have to choose whether scientific evidence or sacred text takes priority as justification for belief. When the statements in sacred text are interpreted *metaphorically*, as poetic language suggesting not testable fact but more subjective understanding, then assertions in holy books have the potential to be entirely compatible with the sciences, history and other academic areas of knowledge.

**Predictions:** In placing a metaphysical framework around life, religions often predict what will happen in the future: what will happen to an individual after death as a result of beliefs and actions within life, what will happen to the universe in the future if and when it is ended by a metaphysical process or a deity. Like the metaphysical knowledge claims on which they are based, these predictions are not testable. And like them, they have a very different significance for religious believers from observational statements about the material world.

Religions vary in the extent to which they use all of these kinds of knowledge claims, and certainly in the content of the particular claims they make. Looking at what different religions say – that is, looking at the beliefs themselves – is an fascinating way to enter comparatively into different worldviews.

Information about beliefs in different religions is easy to gather: the facts about what a group believes, when it was founded, when one group split with another over historic controversy, and so forth. Information of this sort is important as an introduction to a religion and can act as a gateway to understanding a perspective on the world. It is important to remember, though, that the beliefs themselves are only part of the religion – and they can so easily be over-emphasized as if they make up the whole of the religion.

Perhaps more important than the particular beliefs – the particular knowledge claims accepted – is the meaning they have for people within their communities and their lives. Arguably, more important than the *beliefs* is the *believing* – what persuades people, how they feel about their beliefs, and what role they give the beliefs within their knowledge as a whole.

## Methods of justification: faith

If we look not at the *beliefs* themselves but the process and meaning of *believing*, we shift attention from knowledge claims to justifications. Here we can offer some ideas on what justifications different people accept, but encourage you to understand our comments to be very broad and open to exceptions.

What are the justifications for accepting knowledge claims? In this book, we have considered this question for all areas of knowledge and for everyday life, urging an approach of an open and critical mind. In different areas of knowledge and in our lives, we have slightly different expectations of the ways in which we apply our critical thinking: accepting a conclusion in mathematics does not involve the same kind of evaluation of justifications as does accepting a conclusion in history. When we turn to religion, the nature of justifications that persuade people changes with the nature of the subject matter.

In religion, a major justification for belief is faith. Since chapter 10 was entirely on faith, we will not repeat here all of the comments we made or questions we raised for discussion there. We refresh your memory, though, on the four strands of definition we proposed for "faith":

1. faith as trust ("having faith in someone")

2. faith as pledge and commitment (making promises and being "faithful" to them)

3. faith as acceptance (sometimes pragmatic) of assumptions ("taking on faith")

4. faith as subjective commitment of belief (faith as a justification for belief).

The first two strands of definition could be applied to the communal context of religious beliefs: the trust in the religious community of family, neighbours, and religious leaders with which one grew up, and the sense of commitment to a whole cultural way of life and its knowledge claims.

Faith, in the third strand, might also be an *assumption* that the metaphysical beliefs are so. Pragmatically, we might push aside endless philosophical argument over whether we exist or not, or whether the world really exists or not, to *assume* that we exist and so does the world. For some people, a metaphysical reality could be accepted in the same way, as a pragmatic but totally basic assumption of a religious worldview.

The fourth and final strand of the definition leads to questions about justifications for beliefs. What we suggested in chapter 10 was that faith as a justification for belief could take two forms. One is fundamentally a rejection of the need for justification altogether – a leap of belief totally subjectively, with commitment, holding that it is the faith itself that is of greatest importance. The other is a treatment of faith as a justification based on other justifications. Either of these might characterize religious believing, for billions of believers.

## Other justifications

Other justifications for belief, we would argue, are mainly supports to faith, and likely to convince believers but not necessarily others. The knowledge claims cannot consequently be held with *certainty* on the scale of justification, but they can be held with *certainty* on the psychological scale of belief (page 66). Believers may be convinced by justifications – convinced without doubt.

Among the most personally persuasive reasons for believing could be a *personal intuition* of a metaphysical reality, or an experience described as religious or *mystical experience*. Mystical experiences are sometimes described as a state of consciousness or feeling that cannot be communicated to someone who has not experienced it, accompanied by a sense of timelessness, transcendence beyond the bounds of the self, and the Oneness of everything[1]. Although these experiences are not provable in material terms to skeptics, neither are they disprovable in material terms (though some neuroscientists claim that mystical experiences can be triggered by or linked to stimulation of parts of the brain)[2]. They remain personal and subjective.

---

1  Happold, F.C. 1963. *Mysticism: A Study and an Anthology*. UK. Pelican.

2  John Horgan, "Spirit Tech: how to wire your brain for religious ecstacy," Slate. 26 April 2007. http://www.slate.com/articles/life/brains/2007/04/spirit_tech.html accessed 16 August 2012.

## Discussion Activity

### Exploring world religions

We offer this activity as stimulation to think beyond dominant local religions to consider religion more broadly, as a system of beliefs and practices set in different cultural contexts. The activity is an exploration of ways of thinking that may be unfamiliar to you, and possibly an introduction to other conceptions of knowledge.

As in all activities involving research in TOK, you will be finding out information not as an end in itself but as a means to provide more knowledgeable responses to knowledge questions. As you examine each aspect of the religion in turn, pay attention to the questions you are being asked regarding ways of knowing, justifications for accepting knowledge claims as true, influence of some beliefs on other beliefs (including non-religious ones), and their cultural and spiritual meaning for the followers of the religion.

### Instructions: research and report back

Break your class into five smaller groups according to the major world religions, with flexibility to modify this list depending on the interest of the class and location of the school:

**a.** Hinduism    **b.** Buddhism

**c.** Judaism    **d.** Christianity

**e.** Islam

Others could include, for instance, Baha'i, Confucianism, Sikhism, Taoism, Jainism, Zoroastrianism, Mormonism, or native spiritualities.

As you allot class time to this activity, bear in mind that any of these questions could take a lifetime to answer. You have to accept that you are doing a fairly simple overview of major points, and need not stop learning when class time runs out.

When groups report to the rest of the class, appoint a timekeeper to ensure that each group has equal time to present their findings. We recommend taking each question in turn and having all groups contribute what they have found. That way, commonalities and contrasts are likely to emerge for immediate discussion. When you are unsure about information, note questions for later investigation.

1 **Metaphysical beliefs.** Briefly, what central beliefs are held about the creation of the world and life after death? Do these metaphysical beliefs affect other beliefs, such as about how and why to live a good life? Do they provide explanation of the purpose of life?

2 **Deities.** Are there deities within this religion? Is it a single deity or many? Does it (or they) have a single name? What is the nature of the deity? What is the nature of its contact with human beings? What knowledge does the deity possess, and what knowledge do human beings have of it?

3 **Spiritual leaders.** Are there any major spiritual leaders in the founding or development of the religion? What status are their teachings given – possibly as revelation of metaphysical reality, prophesy, or wise guidance for living life? What status are the leaders themselves given – as human teachers, or as supernatural figures themselves? How wide is the diversity of opinion among believers about the divine or human qualities of the leader? Are their words accepted as indisputably true information, or considered to be wise advice and guidance?

4 **Sacred text.** Does this religion have sacred text? How did the holy books or other sacred writing come into being? Is the writing believed to be human, supernatural, or a combination? What

status is the written text given – possibly as revelation of metaphysical reality, prophesy, or guidance for living life? What is the role of translation in the history of this text? Is it considered important for followers of this religion to be familiar with the sacred text, or to memorize parts?

5 **Prayer or meditation.** Does this religion use prayers? Are they private or public, and  are they silent, spoken, or sung aloud? What is their role? Does this religion use meditation? If so, what is its role? Are prayer and meditation an expression of feelings and ideas, a means of communication, or a means towards knowledge? Does the religion have a tradition of mystics and mystical experience?

6 **Religious events.** Are there any major events regularly celebrated within the  calendar year? What is the role of rituals or sacred ceremonies? What is the role of symbolism? Are the events linked with a version of history significant to the members of this religion? Are the events linked with reflection and learning?

7 **Sacred space.** What is the role of religious spaces (e.g. church, temple, synagogue,  mosque) in the belief system and in the social and cultural context of the religion? Are there also holy places in other parts of the world? What do they mean to people of this religion? Is there a tradition of pilgrimage to sacred places? If so, what is gained by this pilgrimage?

8 **Social structures.** Does the religion you are investigating have an institution with a social structure and hierarchy? If so, who are the supreme leaders of the organization, and what is their role and authority? What is the process by which they are identified or elevated to a position in the hierarchy? What are the means for resolving disputes or declaring official views on religious beliefs or practices? Is this religion the official state religion of any government?

9 **Religion and ethics.** Is there any central statement in this religion of what it means to live a moral life? What are the core ethical beliefs of this religion? What are the roles in this religion of impurity or sin on the one hand and, on the other, possibilities and processes of purification and redemption? What is the process of dealing with those who do not comply with these ethical practices or rewarding those who do? How much does this religion emphasize the relative roles of faith and good works in achieving blessedness? How much does it emphasize engagement with the world of suffering or detachment from it?

10 **Attitudes towards dissent.** How does this religion deal with those who question the religious teachings or leave the religion? Does it ever expel followers? If so, what are the implications of the expulsion for the followers? If it is a religion that attempts to spread its beliefs, what process does it use? What is the attitude in this religion towards other religions and their believers? (More vocabulary for you to understand: apostasy, apostate, heresy, dissenter, excommunicate.)

## Follow-up questions for discussion

- What major points in common between religions did you particularly notice in your class investigation and report? What major points of difference?
- In general, on what grounds do religious adherents seem to hold their beliefs? Are there *justifications* that most of the religions you examined would put forward for their beliefs – the same kind of justifications, even if the beliefs themselves are different?
- When you think of a religion, do you think about *both* its beliefs and its culture of practices, rituals, events, use of sacred space, and institutional structures? How would you rank the relative importance of these in your general impression of a religion other than your own?

403

Out of the personal intuitions, experiences, and insights of some religious leaders, however, might come a sense of having achieved wisdom, even enlightenment, so that their teachings become central to the way followers live their lives.

Some particular moments of personal experience become central within the justifications of religions, or even their founding. Adherents of some theistic religions – that is, religions in which there is a god or gods – believe that the deity gave knowledge to a chosen human being, a prophet, in the form of direct *revelation* – such that a manifestation of the deity was accessible to his senses. In Judaism, Christianity, and Islam, for instance, followers believe that God revealed Himself to the prophet Moses and gave him the Ten Commandments. In Islam, followers believe that the Quran (or Koran) is the direct word of Allah, transcribed by Muhammad, the last of the prophets.

What justifies this belief, in monotheistic religions, that Jehovah, God, or Allah revealed Himself to a prophet who reports the experience? Faith comes back into play – faith as trust in the prophet, and faith as subjective acceptance without further evidence. There is also the existence of the *sacred text* that puts into language the revealed knowledge.

The sacred text or *holy books* of a religion may in themselves give followers of religion persuasive reasons to believe, even though they are not justifications in a logical sense. Logically, a holy book cannot *prove* anything about a god: it would be a circular argument, for instance, to say that the Bible proves God, if at the same time it is God who gives the Bible its authority. A belief in the deity would logically come first, as a prerequisite for taking the book as the truth revealed from the deity to human beings. Yet adherents of a religion may find qualities within their holy books that persuade them to believe or confirm their belief, such as significant teachings or inspiration.

Between the revelation and the understanding comes an extremely important process: *interpretation of the language*. Problematic issues abound. The words themselves may be believed to come from the deity through direct revelation, or through divinely guided human report of events. But can language ever capture the essence of a metaphysical realm beyond human experience? Moreover, is the language of an ancient original – such as the Sanskrit of the Hindu Vedas or the Hebrew of the Christian Bible – still fully understood? How is it to be translated, if at all, from a sacred original to a version accessible to contemporary believers? Who is qualified to interpret what the words mean, and teach others what is being said in the holy book? Subgroups within religions can differ significantly in their understanding of sacred text.

Once the divine nature of the holy book has been accepted as a basic premise, and the *authority* accepted of those within the religious institution who interpret it for followers, its content leads to many further beliefs. Followers of the Abrahamic religions (Judaism, Christianity, and Islam) have identified themselves as "people of the book" and hold their books with reverence. Other religions, too, have sacred text.

Beyond personal experience and holy books, some people have looked for justification for belief in *reasoned arguments*, such as those put forth in philosophy. For example, Christian theologians – philosophers of religion within the church – have given arguments for the existence of God. You may find interesting a simplified version of the three main arguments:

- ontological argument. God is *defined* as existing, as a Being greater than which it is impossible to conceive. Since it is greater to exist in reality than to exist only in the mind, God must exist in reality. If you are thinking of a God that does not exist, you are not thinking of God.
- cosmological argument (First Cause argument). This argument depends on tracing a causal sequence back and back into the past, and deciding that it cannot go back forever in an "infinite regress". So there has to be a first cause, the one that started the causal sequence. And that is God.
- teleological argument (argument from design). The universe is complex. It must have been designed, and with a purpose. The Designer is God.

Predictably enough, all of these arguments within western philosophy have their counter-arguments, simplified here:

- ontological argument, countered: Anything can be argued to exist in this way.
- cosmological argument, countered: 1. If the First Cause is itself infinite, why not accept the idea of infinity in an infinite regress of causes?

2. What caused the First Cause? Why stop the chain of causation there?

- teleological argument, countered: 1. If there were a Designer, it does not have to be the Christian God, or even a single deity. 2. Complexity could have an alternative explanation (e.g. chance, evolution).

Within such argument back and forth many people may find reasons that persuade them to believe that God exists and therefore offer "reasoned argument" as a justification for belief. Yet it is likely that this kind of argument is persuasive primarily to those who believe in God already, and not to those whose religions have no Supreme Being or to those who do not have religious beliefs.

In religion, the justifications cannot be demonstrated in a way to convince everyone, using material evidence accessible to the senses, or reasoning from universally agreed premises. It could be argued that the very nature of the subject matter necessitates justifications of a different kind from those applicable within areas of knowledge that study the material world. It could also be argued that none of the other justifications is convincing without the essential element of faith.

## Agnosticism and atheism

We must not neglect two further positions on religious belief – agnosticism and atheism. People holding either of these views do not accept the metaphysical knowledge claims of any religion.

Agnosticism is the view that it is impossible to know whether metaphysical knowledge claims are true. Agnostics neither believe religious claims nor disbelieve them, and take this position consciously.

Atheism (from the root "without god") covers a wider spectrum of absence of belief in religious knowledge claims. In some current usage, an

### For Reflection

What do *you* think? We have offered some comments here on different forms of justification for religious beliefs, offering you ideas to consider. Would you describe such justifications differently? Would you offer other justifications that we have not included?

atheist is assumed to be someone who rejects belief in a deity or deities, or even argues against believing. An atheist, however, need not engage in any debate or even give attention to the question of the existence of a deity; an atheist may simply not possess a belief that one exists.

Indeed, some have argued that the category of "atheist" is not a meaningful one for many atheists, who do not define themselves by what is *not* present in their worldview. The term is constructed from within a religious belief system, specifically one that includes a deity, to designate those who do not share their belief. Thus some atheists, wishing to define themselves by what they *do* believe in rather than by what they do *not* believe in, have accepted the philosophical attitudes of "humanism" and call themselves "humanists."

Atheists and strongly religious people may have to make a particular effort if they are to understand each other's perspectives on the world. For an atheist, it could seem strange that people believe in invisible gods who control the universe. Isn't this, from the point of view of many atheists, just "fantasy and superstition"? For a theist, it could seem equally strange that people believe in a universe empty of a deity or purpose. How can they be "so blind"? How can they be moral people and not "heathens" who offend the deity? From each perspective, life and the universe make sense, and from each perspective it may take effort to enter imaginatively into the other perspective. As we have emphasized throughout this book, however, it is not necessary to agree with a perspective in order to attempt to see how the world and life appear when seen through its eyes.

## Religious perspectives

When we consider the range of beliefs and variety of their cultural contexts, we are clearly in a world where the passing events are viewed and thought about in a diversity of different ways. What religions give, finally, is perspectives on the world. Once again – and for the last time – we return to an idea that has run through this book: that trying to understand what people see when they look is basic to being able to understand and communicate well with each other. And, for the last time, we give you the same questions on perspectives for your own exploration:

- What are the basic *assumptions* of this faith or religion? Are there "givens" taken as indisputably true?

- What are the *values* associated with this set of beliefs? How do you know what they are?

- What are held to be *important facts* according to this religion or the particular religious community?

- What are the *processes of validation* for knowledge claims and settling differences of interpretations or views within the group? What councils of authority or leaders make final decisions on matters of doctrine?

- What are the *implications* for personal behaviour or other actions of the body of beliefs?

Religious perspectives are often difficult to disentangle from other views held within a society, including politics and the traditions of the surrounding culture. As you explore religious perspectives, you may find that generalizations are difficult to make in any but the roughest of terms. *Increasing* the degree of accuracy depends on *decreasing* the level of generality, so that you are not talking about "all Muslims" but "most Muslims in a particular country" – and then "some Muslims in a particular region" – and then finally "my Muslim friend Abdul".

When we identify perspectives that belong to particular communities, it is well worth remembering that we are always walking a line of generalization – between the group *in general* and members in *particular*. Constant awareness of problematic issues of categorizing will help us walk that line better.

Such awareness often shifts us away from *stating*, and towards *inquiring*. In any genuine inquiry with the aim of gaining understanding, a few common features are perpetually present: keeping an open mind, asking sincere and tactful questions, trying to grasp the ideas that come up, and then thinking critically to filter them for the most reliable contributions to your own growing knowledge.

You have heard all of these views before, throughout this book, in many contexts. We must emphasize them here, though, because of the importance of inquiry into religious perspectives. These are sometimes willfully misrepresented for political and ideological purposes. They are also often understood *exclusively in terms of differences* rather than similarities in the way that people frame their lives with meaning. In fact, the sense of difference can be so strong that people sometimes hold their own perspectives with passionate conviction that they alone have knowledge that is true and pure, and that others are a defilement and a threat.

## Discussion Activity

### Knowledge framework: religious knowledge

First summarize your responses to these questions in your own words. Then exchange ideas with others in your class.

1 **Scope:** What is the subject matter of religious knowledge? What are its goals? What does it contribute to knowledge overall?

2 **Language/concepts:** What is the role of language in religious knowledge? In what ways are the naming and defining of central concepts significant? What difficulties arise in using language?

3 **Methods:** What ways of knowing does religious knowledge use, and how? What methods does it use to gain and claim knowledge? Is it an area characterized by a methodology held in common, or a diversity of different methods? In what ways does religious knowledge build on knowledge established in the past?

4 **Historical development:** What individual and social factors have pushed the development of religion in particular directions?

5 **Links to personal knowledge:** How do individuals contribute to, and gain from, the shared knowledge of religion? How does religion contribute, if it does, to your own knowledge?

Compare your class responses on religious knowledge to those on the arts, ethics, and indigenous knowledge. What is their relative balance, within shared knowledge, towards academic sharing or cultural sharing? What similarities and differences do you find?

And yet, even apparently large gulfs between communities of people can often be bridged by genuine inquiry. Learning about other perspectives to try to understand them from inside is enriching for the understanding it gives of the people with whom we live, work, and share the planet. This is knowledge that we need. And perhaps only through this knowledge can we learn to live together in cooperation and peace.

## Declaration toward a global ethic

In 1993, the Parliament of the World's Religions, bringing together 8,000 people from around the world, approved the "Declaration Toward a Global Ethic" as a statement of ethical common ground among the world's religious traditions. It was prepared by roughly 200 leaders from all of the world's major faiths, and has been signed by thousands more people since that time. We give some excerpts below.

## Principles of a global ethic

"Our world is experiencing a *fundamental crisis:* A crisis in global economy, global ecology, and global politics. The lack of a grand vision, the tangle of unresolved problems, political paralysis, mediocre political leadership with little insight or foresight, and in general too little sense for the commonweal are seen everywhere: Too many old answers to new challenges.

"Hundreds of millions of human beings on our planet increasingly suffer from unemployment, poverty, hunger, and the destruction of their families. Hope for a lasting peace among nations slips away from us. More and more countries are shaken by corruption in politics and business. It is increasingly difficult to live together peacefully in our cities because of social, racial, and ethnic conflicts, the abuse of drugs, organized crime, and even anarchy. Even neighbors often live in fear of one another. Our planet continues to be ruthlessly plundered. A collapse of the ecosystem threatens us.

"Time and again we see leaders and members of *religions* incite aggression, fanaticism, hate, and xenophobia – even inspire and legitimize violent and bloody conflicts. Religion often is misused for purely power-political goals, including war. We are filled with disgust.

"We condemn these blights and declare that they need not be. An *ethic* already exists within the religious teachings of the world which can counter the global distress. Of course this ethic provides no direct solution for all the immense problems of the world, but it does supply the moral foundation for a better individual and global order: a *vision* which can lead women and men away from despair, and society away from chaos".

*The Declaration identifies as its fundamental demand that "Every human being must be treated humanely", and identifies four "Irrevocable Directives".*

## Irrevocable directives

1. Commitment to a Culture of Non-violence and Respect for Life

2. Commitment to a Culture of Solidarity and a Just Economic Order

3. Commitment to a Culture of Tolerance and a Life of Truthfulness

4. Commitment to a Culture of Equal Rights and Partnership Between Men and Women

## A transformation of consciousness!

"In conclusion, we appeal to all the inhabitants of this planet. Earth cannot be changed for the better unless the consciousness of individuals is changed. We pledge to work for such transformation in individual and collective consciousness, for the awakening of our spiritual powers through reflection, mediation, prayer, or positive thinking, for a conversion of the heart... we commit ourselves to a common global ethic, to better mutual understanding, as well as to socially beneficial, peace-fostering, and Earth-friendly ways of life".[3]

---

[3]  Declaration Toward a Global Ethic. Council for the Parliament of the World's Religions. 4 September 1993.

## What do you take away from TOK?

Our guiding role is nearly done, and you are ready to venture forward on your own. May the ideas you have gained in our TOK journey serve you well in dealing with the multitudes of further knowledge questions you will encounter hereafter. May you forever find purpose and pleasure in exploring the enticing – but challenging – territory of knowledge.

## Seeing knowledge more holistically

You take with you, surely, an overview of knowledge. We've considered core concepts, looped through eight ways of knowing, and then connected those ways with everyday knowledge and eight particular areas of knowledge. You are likely to feel comfortable now with many distinctions and comparisons as you recognize characteristic features of areas of knowledge: what they take as their goals, how they use different methods for fulfilling them, and what kinds of understanding they contribute to our knowledge as a whole. The overview you've gained helps to counter the fragmentation of knowledge that comes with specialization, and may give you a greater understanding of purposes and connections in further learning.

## Understanding perspectives

By now, you're oh-so-familiar with one of the central themes of this book, the importance of recognizing other perspectives – cultural, political, religious, and theoretical perspectives among them. Take with you an appreciation of how different individuals and groups make sense of the world, and develop your understanding further in your future studies, workplace, and community. If you can put into practice the goals of open-mindedness and critical thinking, you may be able to resolve misunderstandings between people and contribute to more effective communication in any group.

Your critical awareness of perspectives is fundamental, too, to your being able to evaluate the knowledge claims that swirl through societies and the media. By now, you'll know better than to expect human beings to be neutral recording machines, and may respect those who demonstrate an astute capacity to interpret the events of the world for their significance. Yet, always, you will want to evaluate the sources of information for their reliability and relevance to a topic, and assess their statements for their supporting justifications, accuracy, and insight. We hope you will always have the reflex to listen to many voices for the larger chorus of meaning.

## Thinking more critically

Don't let these skills die out, but foster them in your further learning and engagement in the world! Take with you, for further development, your present capacity to: analyse features of perspectives, apply different concepts of truth to raise further questions, distinguish different kinds of knowledge claims within the exchange of knowledge, identify and assess justifications, recognize fallacies of argument and cognitive biases, read critically for the influence of assumptions and values on how issues are represented in language and other symbolic systems, evaluate the reliability of sources and knowledge claims, critically appreciate the goals and methodologies of different disciplines, and draw comparisons that demonstrate your larger grasp of knowledge. May your capacity for critical thinking grow throughout your life!

## Understanding why classifying is important

By now, you are fully aware that naming and connecting objects and ideas can be done in more than one way. You're aware that categories in language carry implications for how we think about the natural world, how we treat other people, how we construct our theories to explain natural and social realities, and how we therefore decide and act. Categories of race, gender, class, and nationality – of political friends or enemies – of acceptable or unacceptable environmental risk – of moral or immoral actions – these are merely examples of categories that affect our thinking far beyond the classifications themselves. Stereotypes and prejudices, hasty generalizations, and confirmation bias all trouble our judgments when we classify our world. Keep your ear tuned for how thoughts are placed in boxes – and be ready to question whether they might be packaged otherwise!

## Recognizing complexities of "cause"

By now, you have considered the follies and fallacies of attributing causal connections to what are, in reality, no more than swiftly glimpsed associations. Little could be more important for our lives and our societies than grasping genuine cause and effect. To be knowledgeable and effective, we need to recognize the best justified explanations of our world, rightly trace the factors from the past that contribute to our present, evaluate problems and proposed solutions within the interconnected variables of our lives and our societies, and even arrive at a sense of purpose in our personal lives. Take with you from TOK your awareness of the complexities raised by the question "Why?" and of the methodologies of different disciplines for contributing their responses. Stay alert, and no matter where you go you will learn more!

## Considering ethical imperatives towards action

Last, we hope that you take with you this living question: "What can I do to help in the world?" If you have agreed with the values that have guided this book, you will feel the importance of keeping an open mind and thinking critically for a base of knowledge and understanding, and of responding ethically and effectively in face of need. These responsibilities resonate far beyond TOK as you take your onward journey. Where are you going? With a clear mind and a compassionate heart, you'll always find your way to where you can contribute!

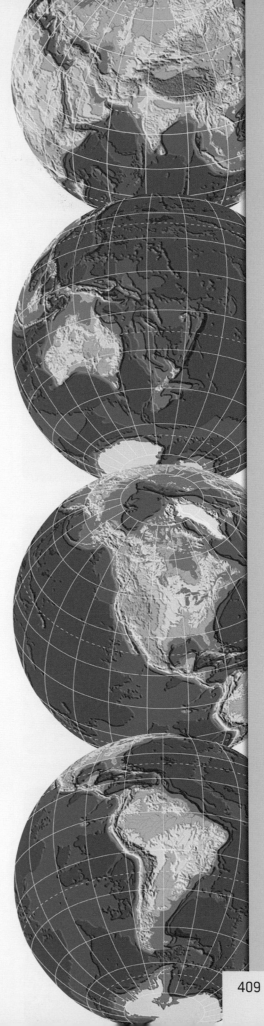

## "Taking the stars"

This ancient and beautiful object is an astrolabe – a "star-taker".[1]
People centuries ago used it for placing themselves *in time* by
positioning themselves *in space*, using the sun and stars.

Why did people want such knowledge, and how did they use it?
In this medieval astrolabe, we can see much of what motivates
human beings to seek knowledge: curiosity, practical benefit, desire
to position themselves in context of the universe, or even to reach
beyond it in the spirit. Astronomers used it to predict positions of
heavenly bodies, astrologers used it to cast horoscopes, surveyors
used it for marking boundaries, Muslims used it to calculate times for
prayers, navigators used it as a directional aid, mathematicians used
it for trigonometry. In this sophisticated and lovely instrument, we
can see a blend of science, technology, and intricate artistic design.

We can also witness, in small, knowledge exchanged and shared
across centuries and cultures. The astrolabe was invented over
2,000 years ago in Greece, developed by Islamic scholars, and used
in medieval Europe. This particular astrolabe, inscribed with both

---

[1] You can see this astrolabe in more of its exquisite detail on the website of the British Museum,
*History of the World in 100 objects (#62)* and find out more about its cross-cultural background.

Hebrew and Arabic markings, was a product of Jewish, Christian, and Muslim shared knowledge.

In all that long history, all individuals turning the astrolabe to their own purposes brought knowledge shared with many before them into their own personal knowledge. Applying it, they could sight the stars in only one way – from the spot on which they stood. They built their knowledge outward, from their own places on the planet. And so do we.

We opened this book with the metaphor of a journey, an archetypal image of experience and reflection contributing to knowledge. We invited you to come with us to explore knowledge. As we have journeyed from section to section of the book, we have given you regular "locators" of where we are in the map of ideas. As we conclude the book, then, where are you, and where do we part?

## Navigating knowledge, homeward

From the beginning, we have guided you out from your own home centre to look at the very idea of "centrism" within knowledge. Do you recall the very first activity, where we recognized the positioning and choices within maps of the world? Do you recall a later activity on *ethnocentrism*, to recognize some of the assumptions of culture as you look at the world? The capacity to "shift your centre" and to see from multiple perspectives develops with greater understanding of knowledge, and of all the historical, cultural, political, religious, and theoretical influences that go into its creation and interpretation.

Finally, however, you need a centre of your own within the knowledge you are constructing; you need to shape your own perspective as you integrate your own experience and what you are learning in a way that makes sense to you. We have guided you around loops and over viewpoints on this metaphorical journey, but now return home to where we met you. It's a good place, home. We hope that this book leaves you with fuller understanding and heightened appreciation of your own place in the world, the place you stand yourself as you "take the stars".

## Final reflection: personal knowledge

- Near the beginning of the book (page 26), we asked you to reflect on features of your own identity that affect your knowledge. Is there anything you would modify now, or add?
- What do you value most about the knowledge given you by your own language, your own culture or cultures, its arts, your own religion, your own history?
- What do you value most about your own IB education?
- What do you hope to contribute yourself to the communication and exchange of knowledge in the years to come?

## 23. Assessment

> **The capacity to shuttle between levels of abstraction, with ease and with clarity, is a signal mark of the imaginative and systematic thinker.[1]**
>
> *C. Wright Mills*

Throughout your theory of knowledge course, you have been developing your skills of inquiry and thoughtful analysis, and your capacity to see from other perspectives and recognize the implications of holding them. These are skills that will benefit you all your life, as you work and communicate with other people, and as you attempt to deal with the complex issues that arise in your community and your world. These are skills, too, that you will consciously develop and refine as you undertake your two "assessment tasks" for the theory of knowledge course.

The *class presentation* and the *essay* both give you a chance to show your own mind at work, engaging with knowledge questions in a mature and thoughtful way. They push you to show yourself at your best – at your *present* best, as you continue to learn and grow. If you tackle them with a genuine interest in exploring ideas and the TOK course behind you, you are likely to do them with pleasure and gain the reward of a good grade.

After all, what you do for your mark is just a distillation of what you've been doing the whole time in the course – flying high above knowledge, dipping low to see the close-up, and frequently landing securely on the ground. You've been learning to navigate through levels of abstraction, learning concepts and skills that make the steering easier, and more fun.

By now, you've practically qualified for a pilot's license! You've been up, up, up into the stratosphere, asking, "How do we know?" You've zoomed closer to earth to examine areas of knowledge, and you've flown with some of the questions there. For instance, "What difference does the subject matter of study make to the methods of gaining knowledge?" (We don't investigate human beings with a Large Hadron Collider! We don't stage and appreciate a musical performance with the methods of a mathematical proof – or, at least, not entirely!) Cruising over knowledge, you've seen its broad contours and how the parts all fit together.

Closer to earth, you've recognized from above the humming groups of busy people – sharing ideas, critiquing them, and using them to explain our world, our societies past and present, our moral codes, our varied and vibrant arts, and the meanings we give to life.

And you've landed. Right there on the ground, you've met real people creating and applying knowledge – a dancer, for instance, or a historian, or a physicist. You've met individuals personally, and found out a lot about their colleagues and what they're engaged in doing, why and how.

Here, in a recognizable world of people observing, creating, writing, and arguing, you've brought your experience of the high-flying overview to your everyday life and the subjects you're studying. Here in your own life, you can apply those concepts – "knowledge", "perspectives", "justification", "implications" – and use those skills of thinking critically to figure out what you're being told, evaluate it for its justifications, apply your filters to allow in the most reliable knowledge

---

[1]  Wright Mills, C. 1959, 2000. *The Sociological Imagination.* New York. Oxford University Press. P 34.

claims, and appreciate their contributions to your own understanding.

If you can demonstrate for assessment the concepts and skills you've gained between the stratosphere and the ground, then you're likely to do well. The real reason for learning to navigate is the pleasure and value of the flight (and its landing!) but if you can get a mark for it, well, that's a fine bonus!

## The two assessment tasks

For your mark, you have to do two things: an oral class presentation and an essay. The presentation starts on the ground with a particular situation you've noticed in the world, picks out one of the knowledge questions that make it interesting, and travels skyward to look down upon the situation and comment on how it distills many of the questions of the TOK course. In contrast, the essay starts high in the sky at an overview level of knowledge questions, but dips to cruise over particular areas of the territory below. To show the territory better, it includes plenty of examples of what the people are doing on the ground. Both of these tasks you can do!

**AND SO**...here are the practical details.

The class presentation is oral. It will be on a topic you propose, with guidance from your teacher. Your teacher will grade it out of 10 and keep a record of all documentation that goes with it, since the IB moderates a number of schools each year – that is, it checks for appropriate work, procedures, and

documentation. The security of your mark depends on your fulfilling the expectations. The mark contributes to 33 per cent of your final TOK mark.

The essay (maximum 1,600 words) will be a written piece of work on a topic you choose from a list of six provided by the IB. Your essay is sent to an external marker appointed by the IB, and marked out of 10. The mark contributes to 67 per cent of your final TOK mark.

Your final grade will take the form not of a number but of a letter, as the mark for TOK is combined with the mark for the extended essay in a single outcome for these core requirements of the IB Diploma Programme.

## Refreshing core concepts

Before we go into detail on the assessment tasks, we'll briefly go over the key concepts that are used in the evaluation of both. In this book, we've been dealing right from the beginning with the key concepts and skills, so they're familiar to you. Still, before doing the assessment tasks, you should refresh your memory on terminology and set your sights very clearly on the concepts and qualities relevant to doing well.

What should you re-read from this book? Well, certainly you should go back to chapter 14 to look again at the *aims* and *objectives* of theory of knowledge. You might also benefit from the transitional chapter 4 on exchanging knowledge, since it introduced the ways of knowing as means towards building knowledge, sharing it, and justifying it.

The central concepts of TOK have run right through this book. But to pull them to the front of your mind, you might want to look back at a few parts in particular:

**1. knowledge questions**

See the overview on inquiry (page 68). Look also at the conclusion to chapter 2 on gaining knowledge, re-reading the final sections on knowledge questions, broad and narrow.

**2. perspectives**

Review the touchstone pages to which we have referred so often during this book: the early reflection "Your own personal perspective" (page 26) and "Exploring different perspectives" (page 28). In all of the areas of knowledge, watch for variations on the basic diagram that often gives a structure to shifting perspectives:

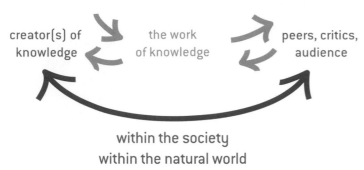

creator(s) of knowledge — the work of knowledge — peers, critics, audience

within the society
within the natural world

### 3. implications

Seeing implications of different conclusions – that is, what follows in logic and in action from accepting them – is part of understanding perspectives. To refresh the definition of "implications", see the chapter on reason, and for an example of implications see the discussion activity on different measurements of poverty at the end of chapter 18. For the implications of classification and concepts, see chapter 13.

### 4. exploration and analysis

Although an approach to inquiry should be so familiar as to need no conceptual review, do look back through all of the pages identified as "Thinking critically", including the summary that concludes Part 2, "Should I believe it? A guide to evaluating knowledge claims". The table of contents is also likely to be useful to you in identifying pages for spot-review.

### 5. argument and counter-claims

Review the final pages of chapter 7 on reason on the nature of arguments. If you feel the need for further practice and advice on tracing or building arguments, do the discussion activity later in this chapter entitled "Follow an argument".

### 6. real-life situations and examples

There is no point to the TOK course unless you can apply the awareness and thinking skills to the world you live in. We have tried to keep the book grounded throughout in examples from the real world. To refresh a general way of thinking, though, you might look back through all of the interchapters marked "Thinking critically" for the kind of examples we gave. You might also have a quick look at how each of the chapters on areas of knowledge concludes: the arts with commenting on society, history with an activity including colonial attitudes towards African art, human sciences with concepts of poverty, natural sciences with social responsibility, mathematics with the role of statistical measures in understanding a world issue, ethics with ideas of service to others, and indigenous knowledge and religious knowledge with extracts on treating other people respectfully and ethically. TOK does fly high in the sky with its abstractions and general overviews, but it is not helpful to your everyday thinking unless you also bring it down to the ground.

## How to do a really good class presentation

During your TOK course, you must do at least one oral class presentation in which you demonstrate your ability to apply your thinking skills to the world around you. You have a lot of flexibility in what you choose as a topic, whether you do it solo or with others, and how you bring your ideas to life. With plenty of choice and a world full of situations alive with knowledge questions, surely you will be able to shape the presentation to be a good experience for yourself and for the rest of your class.

**Know what's expected**
You cannot score in basketball if you're demonstrating the skills appropriate for tennis or golf, or following the rules for football. You cannot score in a class presentation if you don't meet the expectations of the form. In planning your presentation, set yourself appropriate goals.

**TOK presentation assessment instrument**

## Do(es) the presenter(s) succeed in showing how TOK concepts can have practical application?

| Level 5 Excellent 9–10 | Level 4 Very good 7–8 | Level 3 Satisfactory 5–6 | Level 2 Basic 3–4 | Level 1 Elementary 1–2 | Irrelevant 0 |
|---|---|---|---|---|---|
| | | **Typical characteristics** | | | |
| The presentation is focused on *well-formulated* **knowledge question** that is *clearly connected* to *specified real-life situation*. The knowledge question is *effectively explored* in the context of the real-life situation, using *convincing* **arguments**, with *investigation of different* **perspectives**. The **outcomes of the analysis** are shown *to be significant to the chosen real-life situation and to others.* | The presentation is focused on a **knowledge question** that is *connected* to a *specified real-life situation*. The knowledge question is *explored* in the context of the real-life situation, using *clear* **arguments**, with *acknowledgement of different* **perspectives**. The **outcomes of the analysis** are shown *to be significant to the real-life situation.* | The presentation identifies a **knowledge question** that has *some connection* to a specified **real-life situation**. the knowledge question is *explored* in the context of the real-life situation, using *some adequate* **arguments**. There *is some awareness of the significance* of the **outcomes of the analysis.** | The presentation identifies a **knowledge question** and a **real-life situation**, although the *connection between them may not be convincing.* There *is some attempt* to explore the knowledge question. There *is limited awareness of the significance* of the **outcomes of the analysis.** | The presentation describes a **real-life situation without reference to any knowledge question**, or treats an abstract knowledge question **without connecting it to any specific real-life situation.** | There is *no evidence* that the requirements of the TOK presentation have been understood. |
| | | **Some possible characteristics** | | | |
| Sophisticated Discerning Insightful Compelling Lucid | Credible Analytical Organized Pertinent Coherent | Relevant Adequate Acceptable Predictable Ordinary | Underdeveloped Basic Unbalanced Superficial Derivative Rudimentary | Ineffective Unconnected Incoherent Formless Elementary | |

Your presentation is going to be evaluated according to criteria that emerge from the single summary question:

Do(es) the presenter(s) succeed in showing how TOK concepts can have practical application?[2]

The answer, if you plan well, will be "yes" – and the grade will reward you.

Think of the presentation as a performance in which you demonstrate particular skills that will be evaluated according to particular criteria – rather like any competition for dance, music, or sports. Perhaps think of yourself as playing basketball, and aiming to dunk the ball in the hoop, using the appropriate set of skills. And then dunk it!

## STEP 1: Know what is expected

You're expected to choose a real-life situation of interest to you, identify a knowledge question that arises from it, and explore that knowledge question analytically. You should demonstrate your skills of critical thinking as you identify and investigate different perspectives on your chosen situation, including the implications of taking particular perspectives. You should also indicate how the investigation of the particular real-life situation is broadly relevant to other such situations. In short, you're getting right into the way that knowledge is constructed by real people in the real world – on a topic you care about.

You have to do at least one class presentation. Whether you are permitted to do more than one – and to have the best mark submitted to the IB – depends on your teacher's overall plan for class time. If you do more than one, you can't treat the same knowledge question again, or deal again with the same real-life situation. No repeats! Move on!

## STEP 2: Decide whether to go solo or as part of a team

There are advantages to either way of doing your presentation – on your own or with others, up to a maximum of three in a group.

A major factor to take into consideration is the effect of the timing on the breadth of ideas. Approximately 10 minutes of class time is allowed

### Criteria

#### What are the criteria for an excellent presentation?

The presentation is focused on a *well-formulated* **knowledge question** that is *clearly connected* to a *specified* **real-life situation**. The knowledge question is *effectively explored* in the context of the real-life situation, using *convincing* **arguments**, with *investigation* of *different* **perspectives**. The **outcomes of the analysis** are shown to be *significant to the chosen real-life situation and to others*.

for each presenter, so that two people will have roughly 20 minutes and three people roughly 30 minutes. If you decide to work on your own, then, you'll have to choose a narrower topic in order to manage it in a short time. If you work with others, you'll want to choose a topic with a wider focus and develop ideas more fully.

Another major factor to consider is whether you can get together with others easily for the planning process. If you don't have opportunities to meet and discuss ideas – face to face or electronically – it is probably more practical to work on your own.

If you do work with others, though, you have some advantages in the variety of ways in which you will be able to present the ideas. A pair or trio can more easily dramatize different perspectives, run mock interviews, and so forth. If you can compose a group where individuals genuinely bring different perspectives – such as from their cultures or religions – you might find the planning all the more interesting. (It is not necessary for individuals to speak from their own perspectives in dramatizing ideas. They could speak from each other's.)

## STEP 3: Choose your topic

For your presentation, you can pick a situation that really interests you – one that seems to involve lively knowledge questions on a topic that you'd enjoy investigating. It's possible that you will see situations all around you and will launch yourself easily into thinking and talking about it. It's also possible that…suddenly…not a single

---

situation leaps into your field of vision! Oh no! Where can you find ideas?

Make your shopping list! You are looking for a topic for your presentation that seems to offer three ingredients:

- a real-life situation that interests you
- knowledge questions appealing to pose and consider
- different perspectives on the knowledge question(s).

You could start with any one of the three and use it to find the others. Interesting incidents, enticing questions, and different ways of answering them are often found together. Any one could lead you to the others.

With this shopping list in mind, there are several approaches you could take to finding a topic. The suggestions below range across a spectrum from fairly passive alertness to active research.

As a *first* approach, be alert to ideas that just happen to cross your path as you go through your day.

- A teacher has commented that the box at the back of the room holds old textbooks that have gone out of date. What has made them go "out of date"? Are your current textbooks giving you the truth, or just a version that is "in date"?
- You notice that your friend's mother has a very different attitude from your own mother about the oil pipeline that has had people in your town going to protests. How is it that they have such different perspectives?
- A friend of yours hesitates to go to a party because of what it said in her horoscope. Why does she believe, and why don't you? Are there some interesting questions about justifications for belief and confirmation bias hidden in this possible topic?

As a *second*, keep all possibilities open and look in the news for real-life situations or debates that catch your interest.

- Find out what people are talking about. In newspapers, check the editorials, opinion columns, and letters to the editor. Online, check blogs that accompany news sites or others that deal with special topics. There are almost always lively discussions on science, nutrition, medicine, and technology.

- Deliberately read the news from sources that comment from different positions on the political spectrum. Sometimes accounts of events are startlingly different, and could provoke some interesting questions of knowledge.

Or, *third*, start with personal interests and go looking for situations or knowledge questions related to them.

- If you love sports, are there any topics currently generating intense discussion, such as ethical issues surrounding performance-enhancing drugs?
- If you're good at photography and digital modification, are there current hot topics about representation of reality on which you might have some insight?
- If you enjoy astronomy, movie-making, dancing, sailing, orienteering, or gymnastics – just to name a few – could they yield questions of knowledge?

*Fourth*, perhaps decide in advance that a particular issue of local or global significant is one you want to investigate, somehow. Any major global issue is alive with questions of knowledge. You might find knowledge questions through thinking about some of the topics we've raised in this book:

- definition and its implications for how we think about topics and investigate them (for instance, "faith", "culture", "poverty").
- classification and its implications
- symbolic representation such as language, photographs, maps, or statistics that can be used factually and/or persuasively
- causal connections that can be drawn differently according to different concepts of cause and different perspectives.

Similarly, *fifth*, start with perspectives you want to learn more about, and then figure out a topic that could focus them. You might want to team up with one or two others from the class from different cultural or religious communities to talk about how you see things – and then go looking for your real-life situation.

- If there is a debate on differences in a multicultural society, could there be a specific incident or legal challenge that raises knowledge questions?

- Is there a particular life experience that you might examine from different perspectives for the different ways you understand it?

Or even, *sixth*, start centred in a particular academic subject or area of research, perhaps one that you're studying. You might team up with others from one of your IB classes.

- If you are history students, could you look for current topics that use your understanding developed in history class? Are there official apologies for the past in the news, or truth and reconciliation commissions, or national replacement of historic monuments with others?
- If you are biology students, is there any current breakthrough that illustrates characteristics of science?

You are likely to go back and forth repeatedly between different real-life situations and possible knowledge questions to explore before you settle on one. When you have a proposal, you should consult with your teacher to make sure that you are on the right path, and to get advice. As your ideas develop, you are permitted to consult a second time with your teacher.

## STEP 4: Identify knowledge questions

If you've chosen your real-life situation as we've suggested here, you have some good raw material for creating a good presentation. But now you have to shape it!

The most important point to remember about your presentation is that it is *about knowledge*. It is not really about your topic: it is *not* a report describing your real-life situation, giving information. It is about the inquiry that animates that situation – the *knowledge questions* that the topic illustrates. Your real-life situation becomes your grounding example for the questions that arise from it.

Now, do this: put into words, in two or three sentences, what your topic has to do with knowledge. Use the word "knowledge" or "know". If you are working with teammates, all of you should do this independently, exchange your sentences, and discuss them. Don't worry about shaping a clear knowledge question yet. Just come to grips with whatever *ideas about knowledge* your real-life situation raises.

It might help to phrase your sentences with familiar vocabulary for central concepts: for example, perspectives, ways of knowing (and specific ones), areas of knowledge (and particular ones), knowledge claims, justification, evidence, certainty/uncertainty, prediction, causation, fallacies, methodology, confirmation bias, cognitive biases, truth, assumptions, values.

Only after you've figured out roughly what you want to talk about should you try to phrase the knowledge question that will focus your presentation. You can probably see several possible directions any presentation could take, depending on what you emphasize. Choose one, the one that you think will best be able to unify your ideas and bring out the really interesting features of your real-life situation. It will be your focus for developing your exploration.

*Example 1*

- *real-life situation:* In October 2012 a court in Italy found a group of scientists guilty of failing to give adequate warning to the people of Aquila of a devastating earthquake in 2009, and sentenced them to six years in prison.
- *rough ideas:* There is a lot of controversy about holding scientists responsible for warning people when the knowledge of earthquakes is uncertain, and does not allow prediction. If scientists don't have the justifications for a time-based prediction, they can't be expected to warn people. Scientists around the world are protesting the verdict, but people who lost families and homes think they should have been given better information about risks, and the court agrees. One consequence is that other disaster experts are quitting their jobs in case they might be next.
- *knowledge question:* To what extent can we predict with confidence in the sciences? or Are scientific experts ethically responsible for warning the public of possible dangers?

*Example 2*[3]

- *real-life situation:* A video by Invisible Children went viral on YouTube, Facebook, and Twitter in March 2012 and raised widespread support for bringing to justice Joseph Kony, wanted for war crimes for his exploitation of child soldiers in Uganda. Called "Kony 2012", it

---

[3]  Eileen Dombrowski, "Kony 2012: viral videos, responsibility, action", 9 March 2012. http://blogs.triplealearning.com/2012/03/diploma/dp_tokglobal/kony-2012-viral-videos-responsibility-action/

stirred up support but also major criticism for its representation of a complex issue.

- *rough ideas:* Perspectives are easy to find here. The video makers seemed genuinely to mean well and can point out that Kony had violated human rights, abducting and brutalizing children, and was still on the loose. But many Ugandans protested that the information was out of date, that the video oversimplified and misrepresented a complex situation, that it did more harm than good in giving notoriety to a war criminal who no longer had power in any case, and that it misdirected resources that could have been used better to help the former child soldiers. Some felt the video as a western do-gooder insult to African competence to deal with their own problems.
- *knowledge question:* What is the impact of new media on knowledge? or How do we judge when we have enough knowledge to act responsibly?

## Example 3

- *real-life situation:* In May 2012 the National Science Advisory Board for Biosecurity in the United States recommended censoring scientific studies on bird flu virus (avian H5H1 influenza virus) because the information could be used by bioterrorists.
- *rough ideas:* There are different perspectives on whether scientific knowledge should be censored – whether conjectured national security or scientific freedom is more important, or even if it's even practical to try to restrict information. Who decides what should be censored, and with what justification? Would censorship conflict with the fundamental methodology of the sciences as shared knowledge? If we want to think ethically about social responsibility, do we judge according to guiding principles or according to evaluation of likely consequences?
- *knowledge question:* Are ethical restrictions on the sharing of scientific knowledge ever justified? If so, on what grounds? If not, why not?

## Example 4

- *real-life situation:* In 2010 the last speaker of the Bo language died at the age of 85, on an island east of India.
- *rough ideas:* This incident got press coverage, with articles saying that the extensive death of

languages is a significant loss. Bo might have been the carrier of knowledge that is now also lost. But on the other hand, knowledge is always changing in any case and maybe it's more useful for communicating knowledge if people speak fewer languages anyhow, and have fewer language barriers. Does it matter if languages die out?

- *knowledge question:* To what extent does the knowledge of a culture depend on its language? or In what ways does the immense variety of languages affect knowledge?

## Example 5[4]

- *real-life situation:* In France in 2012, the findings of a study on rats linked large tumours with their being fed genetically modified food. It seemed to be revealing health problems concealed by GM industries and created enormous public concern.
- *rough ideas:* If sound, the study points towards possible human health dangers previously unrecognized. It seems to confirm public suspicion of GM industries justified on other grounds. However, the study has been seriously criticized for its methodology and has been rejected by the European Union.
- *knowledge question:* To what extent is it important to understand the methodology of science in order to evaluate scientific knowledge claims presented in the media? or How can the line be drawn between sensationalistic reporting and responsible "whistleblowing" journalism?

## Example 6

- *real-life situation:* In December 2011, Médecins Sans Frontières (MSF)/Doctors without Borders announced in its regular newsletter two projects to convey important social issues: the multimedia Urban Survivors and a fundraising music album Positive Generation, songs about living with HIV/AIDS.
- *rough ideas:* MSF regularly uses numerous ways of communicating, using newsletters, personal blogs, statistical information, and such. What's interesting about these projects is the use of the arts to inform us, engage our imaginations, and make us care. MSF talks about "shedding light" on a humanitarian

---

4  Theo Dombrowski, "Guest blog: GM foods and the French rats", 5 October 2012. Triple A Learning blogsite. http://blogs.triplealearning.com/2012/10/diploma/dp_tokglobal/guest-blog-gm-foods-and-the-french-rats/

crisis, with implications for how we should respond and act.

- *knowledge question:* What is the role of the arts in giving us knowledge and understanding of social issues? or What ways of knowing can the arts use to give us understanding beyond just facts? or In what ways can the arts give understanding of ethical responsibility?

Do you recognize what we're doing in these examples? We're taking you from the real-life situation on the ground up, up into the overview of knowledge, where the situation becomes an *example* of an open and general question of knowledge. (See page 49.) We're zooming back and up, from close-up to panorama! What we look for, then, is what makes the selected real-life situation alive with interest and challenges to explore, with knowledge questions also applicable to other examples that we can see around us.

The subject guide for TOK speaks of "extracting" the knowledge question from the real-life situation, using a metaphor for drawing out of the particular event an essential question about *how we know*.

The development thereafter will be an analysis of the knowledge question, with grounded reference to the real-life situation. It will surely bring out further knowledge questions in the process, and differing perspectives.

## STEP 5: Identify perspectives

At this point, you've identified perspectives along with your knowledge question. We need to add very little further advice.

Remember, though, that you shouldn't just describe perspectives: A says this, B says that. This may be your starting point as you investigate the topic, but go further. Be analytical about the ways that those perspectives work to shape conclusions on your real-life situation: stay aware of the assumptions, values, selection of facts, different process of validation, and implications. (See familiar page 28.) What justifications are offered from different points of view, and how do you evaluate the relative merits of the different conclusions?

Take care not to make some silly assumptions about perspectives:

- Don't assume that there are just two and that they are distinct, without overlap.

- Don't assume they necessarily oppose each other rather than both (or all) adding something different to the discussion.
- Don't assume that a particular view can be attributed firmly to any group, since communities have internal variability.

Be analytical about the perspectives. Ask yourself, for example:

- Who holds the perspective? Why does this group care or get involved?
- Does there seem to be self-interest behind the perspectives?
- Do people communicate their views explicitly and give justifications for their conclusions, or do they imply them, or communicate them otherwise? Do some perspectives seem to get a lot more attention than others?
- If communication is public, how are the ideas presented? Is the viewpoint apparent in the selection of information to put forth, the emphasis placed on some information, the apparent colouring given by values and emotions, or the placement in context? (Check the Critical Thinking pages after chapter 8.)
- What are the implications of accepting each perspective?

You will also want to be aware of your own assumptions and values as you take your own perspective.

## STEP 6: Organize your ideas in preparation

Leave nothing to chance or last minute spontaneity. You're taking responsibility for a slice of class time, so have to be well prepared for your own success and for the sake of the rest of your class.

During your planning in steps 2 to 5, you had support and advice from your teacher. At the point of more detailed organization, he or she will provide you with a copy of the IB planning document (form TK/PPD), which will help you to concentrate on the order of your ideas. Several days in advance of the presentation, you are expected to give a completed copy to your teacher and have a final consultation. Listen closely to any advice at this point; you and your teacher both want a presentation that will show your ideas at their best and also benefit the rest of the class.

The planning document requires that you follow a particular sequence, a template that ensures an appropriate presentation. You have to be clear and compact: you are expected not to exceed 500 words or the two sides of the planning form (typed in 12 point font).

Do *not* expect this step to be easy. It's *always* challenging to organize fuzzy and interconnected ideas. It is painful to cut and discard some appealing ideas as you recognize that your time is limited and you have to focus. Below are the five instructions to which you will respond, followed by our advice for each one.[5]

### 1. Describe your real-life situation.

You have to be ready to give essential features of the situation so that the audience will understand, but spend little time in doing so. This is just preamble.

### 2. State your central knowledge question.

Usually, many possible knowledge questions could come out of a real-life situation, but you must extract a single central one as your primary focus. Put it clearly into words and keep it in front of you as you do all the rest of your planning.

### 3. Explain the connection between your real-life situation and your knowledge question.

Putting the connection into words, briefly, can be enormously helpful to your own sense of control. In this step, you are thinking at a high level of generality for your knowledge question, but at the applied and particular level for the real-life situation that acts as the focusing example for your analysis.

### 4. Outline how you intend to develop your presentation, with respect to perspectives, subsidiary knowledge questions and arguments.

Here you give your plan for your analysis of the knowledge question. Use bullet points or a skeleton outline to do the following:

- identify the perspectives you will explore that are relevant to the knowledge question
- outline the main arguments you will make

- indicate any secondary knowledge questions that will come up in the development of your ideas.

On the planning document, don't give details. You don't have space. What you need to provide here for your teacher, and for any examiner who might also read your form, is the skeleton of your ideas.

### 5. Show how your conclusions have significance for your real-life situation and beyond.

Where point 4 above was concerned with the conceptual and analytical level of the presentation, point 5 is concerned with the grounded and particular level. You should not lose sight of the sustained example *at any point* while you actually do the presentation; it is your reference point. For this form, though, you need to state only how the analysis, in its conclusions, applies to your real-life situation. How do the different perspectives, for instance, illuminate it, and what would you conclude about it?

In point 5, the words "and beyond" indicate a last expectation. As a final stage of your planning, you are asked to step back from your chosen real-life situation to think more broadly. In what ways is your central knowledge question and the analysis you have given it relevant to other real-life situations? This is your chance to indicate why the presentation topic you have chosen is important to knowledge, by showing it to apply also to other cases. The application of the knowledge question "beyond" is likely to be the final stage of your presentation as you deliver it.

Completing the planning form imposes considerable discipline on your thinking and compels you to think through your ideas in a particular way. If you give it your full attention and prepare yourself to frame a particular event or situation in the world with analytical thinking, you gain a double benefit: for the immediate practicality, you will be prepared to do a good TOK presentation; for longer term usefulness, perhaps for the rest of your life, you will have practised one form of applying your critical thinking to the world.

## STEP 7: Prepare your delivery

With your ideas clearly organized, you can think now about how to communicate them most effectively – how to bring them to life so that you

---

[5] *Theory of knowledge guide.* P 42.

enjoy doing the presentation and others become interested and involved.

Why did you choose your topic originally? Bring back to mind what drew you to that situation and why you think it is important. Can you formulate to yourself what your *purpose* is in speaking on this topic – why you *care*?

What form of presentation best conveys the ideas? How will you alternate voices for variety, and balance speaking turns within your total time allowed? The TOK guide is very clear on the possibilities for how to do the presentation.

> Presentations may take many forms, such as lectures, skits, simulations, games, dramatized readings, interviews or debates. Students may use multimedia, costumes, or props to support their presentations. However, under **no circumstances** should the presentation be simply an essay read aloud to the class. While pre-recorded inserts **within** a presentation are permissible, the presentation itself must be a live experience and not a recording of the presentation.[6]

Use your imagination, bring the ideas to life for your class, and do so in a way that conveys your ideas most effectively. If you do choose to dramatize your presentation, remember that the role play has to function *to support the ideas.* You will be graded on clarity and effectiveness, not on acting ability and the quality of your costumes and props.

Regardless of the form of the presentation, rehearse your delivery – your verbal delivery of ideas to your audience.

- Keep your head up and make eye contact with your audience.
- Speak loudly, so that everyone can hear. Project your voice outward.
- Speak clearly, sounding every word.
- Speak with expression, modulating your voice.
- Do not rush your words. It is better to be a little on the slow side than too fast.
- Even if you are interacting with another student in a discussion or role play, turn to your audience as you speak. Realism in drama is not as important as audibility and clarity of speech.

When you rehearse, pay attention to the total timing of roughly 10 minutes per presenter and do not run over the total time you are given for your presentation. All student presentations have to be graded on the same basis to be fair. Even for people experienced in oral presentation, the timing is one of the hardest parts to control. The solution? Rehearsal!

That does not mean at all, though, that *within* the presentation each student has to speak for exactly 10 minutes – nor that each has to take the 10 minutes in a single block. Alternating voices more frequently and creating interaction between presenters is one way of making the presentation more dynamic. The number of speaking minutes per person need not be precise, since the count may be affected by roles, but it should be approximately so. It is important that no one dominate the others, and that no one be marginalized. After the presentation, there should ideally be some time left in class for discussion.

Plan to give your audience a brief outline of the major points you are making, particularly in a longer presentation. Such an outline should be kept to very short headings. It can be written in advance on a classroom board or handed out on slips of paper.

It may be possible that you have the facilities at your school to do a computer projection of your key points as you speak. If so, beware of the seductions of technology! Many students are tempted to invest a huge proportion of their preparation time into making flashy slides, forgetting entirely that what matters is the quality of their ideas. Indeed, a computer projection can undermine the very purpose for which it is supposedly used – the clarity of communication and the quality of connection with the audience.

If you plan to use a computer projection to support your presentation, keep the following in mind:

- Just because the software can do it, that doesn't mean *you* should. Avoid dazzling transitions and needless animations that distract from your points.
- Give headings or keywords only, not sentences or blocks of text. The projection is an outline of the major points you are making, not a report.
- For maximum clarity, keep the design simple and consistent. Make sure the font is large enough to read at the back of the room.
- Never turn your back to your audience to read out text.

---

6 *Theory of knowledge guide.* Page 41.

- The earlier advice on verbal delivery still applies. You, and not your slides, should be connecting with your audience.

Computer projections, if well done, can be helpful in some cases, for example when images are an important component of a presentation, or when presenters or members of the audience have trouble with the language or accent of presentation. Still, they are not an expectation and often cause more difficulties than they solve.

You are allowed to incorporate audience reaction into your presentation as you run it, and in a longer presentation you may want to engage the class actively in some kind of reaction to keep their attention (voting on a proposal, standing and saluting, attempting to repeat aloud words in an unfamiliar language, singing along, etc.). But remember that you are not being graded for what others do, and that it is easy to lose control of the timing when unscripted others are spontaneously responding. So be very clear on what role you give your audience in this case, and how you will open and close their participation.

## STEP 8: Do the presentation

The first seven steps have all been planning and rehearsing. Actually performing is a minor part of a successful presentation.

It is entirely possible that you will be nervous. Remember, though, that your ideas are interesting, that you are prepared – and that your audience is on your side. Aim to finish on time, and to conclude firmly. And then…enjoy your moment of triumph. You have just completed a fine TOK presentation! You have surely also learned more about applying your critical skills to understanding knowledge in the world.

## How to write a really good TOK essay

Unlike the topics for your class presentations, the possible topics for your TOK essay – called "prescribed titles" – come from the IB and will be given to you by your teacher. Two thirds of your final TOK mark for the Diploma Programme rests on how well you can demonstrate the breadth and depth of your TOK learning through an essay in response to one of these titles.

Your essay will be evaluated according to criteria that emerge from the single summary question:

> Does the student present an appropriate and cogent analysis of knowledge questions in discussing the title?[7]

The answer, if you plan well, will be "yes" – and the grade will reward you.

Treat your teacher as a valuable – and valued – resource. Although you can choose any title, you should consult with your teacher to make sure that you are clear on what each one actually means. When you have chosen your title and pulled your ideas roughly together, you are permitted to consult your teacher again for help to finalize a plan. Then, when you have a draft of your essay, you are permitted to ask for general written comments and advice – but not corrections or editing. After that one draft, you can ask your teacher only specific questions. The essay is yours and the thought has to be your own.

## TOK essay: myth and fact

**Myth:** Every subject requires a different kind of essay.

**Fact:** Although there are some surface differences in approach, all IB subjects, the extended essay, and theory of knowledge demand some fundamental qualities in a good essay:

- a demonstrated understanding of the topic under discussion
- a demonstrated skill in analytical thinking in the form learned in the particular subject, applied in development of the topic
- a well-organized and clearly written presentation of the ideas, with control of overall argument
- honesty in not plagiarizing, and formalization of this principle by following accepted practices for footnotes and bibliography.

Gaining control of essay writing in any one part of your IB helps in all other parts.

---

[7] *Theory of knowledge guide.* Page 44.

## TOK essay assessment instrument

### Does the student present an appropriate and cogent analysis of knowledge questions in discussing the title?

| Aspect | Level 5 Excellent 9–10 | Level 4 Very good 7–8 | Level 3 Satisfactory 5–6 | Level 2 Basic 3–4 | Level 1 Elementary 1–2 | Irrelevant 0 |
|---|---|---|---|---|---|---|
| | | | **Typical characteristics** | | | |
| Understanding knowledge questions | There is a *sustained focus* on **knowledge questions** *connected* to the prescribed title—**developed** with *investigation* of **different perspectives** and **linked** *effectively* to **areas of knowledge** and/or **ways of knowing**. | There is a *focus* on **knowledge questions** *connected* to the prescribed title—**developed** with *acknowledgement* of **different perspectives** and **linked** to **areas of knowledge** and/or **ways of knowing**. | There is a *focus* on *some knowledge questions connected* to the prescribed title—with *some* **development** and **linking** to **areas of knowledge** and /or **ways of knowing**. | *Some knowledge questions* that are *connected* to the prescribed title are considered, but the essay is largely *descriptive*, with *superficial or limited* **links** to **areas of knowledge** and/or **ways of knowing**. | The essay **is mainly irrelevant** to the prescribed title— relevant points are *descriptive*. | The essay is not a response to one of the prescribed titles on the list for the current session. |
| Quality of analysis of knowledge questions | **Arguments** are *clear*, supported by *effective* **real-life examples** and are *effectively evaluated*; **counterclaims** are *extensively explored*, **implications** are *drawn*. | Arguments are *clear*, supported by **real-life examples** and are *evaluated*; **counterclaims** are explored. | *Some arguments* are *clear* and supported by **examples**; some **counterclaims** are *identified*. | *Arguments* are *unclear* and/or *not supported by effective* **examples**. | **Assertions** are offered but are not *supported*. | |
| | | | **Some possible characteristics** | | | |
| | Cogent Accomplished Discerning Individual Lucid Insightful | Pertinent Relevant Thoughtful Analytical Organized Credible | Typical Acceptable Mainstream Adequate Competent Predictable | Underdeveloped Basic Unbalanced Superficial Derivative Rudimentary | Ineffective Elementary Descriptive Incoherent Formless | |

The TOK essay can be a great pleasure to write. It's your chance to show your own keen mind at work, truly engaged with significant questions of knowledge. It's your chance to demonstrate that you have thought about the huge range of ideas raised in TOK and are ready to speak about them in your own voice, taking your own perspective and being *aware* that you are doing so. These are sophisticated skills, but as you emerge from a TOK course thoughtfully followed, you are ready to demonstrate them. If you can do a fine TOK paper, you will have reason for immense satisfaction as you graduate with your IB diploma.

As we suggested for the presentation, think of the essay as a performance in which you demonstrate particular skills that will be evaluated according to particular criteria – rather like Olympics gymnastics, as you move confidently along a balance beam or control your stunts on the hand rings. Admittedly, you will not have an audience to give you thunderous applause nor a stadium of fans to cheer as you step onto the winner's podium. But if you can be clear about your goals in performance and meet them *as well as you can,* you will have achieved a private triumph. In the upcoming section, we will give you advice on setting these goals – and we encourage you to aim high. Go for gold!

## STEP 1: Know what is expected

Read the instructions and re-read the assessment criteria. You will not be given a top evaluation for gymnastics if what you perform is ice skating – or even gymnastics with required routines left out. You will not be give a top evaluation for your essay either, if what you hand in does not fulfill the appropriate expectations.

**(a)** First read over the criteria according to which your essay will be marked. Pay attention to the top descriptor to set in your mind the standard of excellence towards which you are aiming. You have to know what is required to get the gold.

**(b)** Next, read closely the general instructions found at the top of the prescribed title list. These apply to all TOK essays, regardless of the title. These instructions tell you exactly what you are expected to do in your essay. (e.g. "Always justify your statements…")

**(c)** Read the title you have chosen, paying attention to its particular instructions. What exactly are you being told to do?

## STEP 2: Select a title from the IB list

Do not instantly seize upon a prescribed title that sounds appealing and plunge into it headlong. Often titles that at first glance seem easy are really the most difficult of all, so *really read* all six titles on the list. Remember that you may not change the title to something else that you *wish* you had been asked, but must respond exactly to what the IB has given.

Which two or three titles allow you to demonstrate *best* your understanding of TOK knowledge questions and your own skills of thinking critically? Of those, which ones *most*

### What are the key words of instruction?

Identify any tasks the title asks you to undertake by paying attention to action words. If you are told to "assess" or "evaluate" a claim, then you are supposed to consider the arguments both for and against it, taking into account any ambiguities in interpreting it. Possible responses, for example, are:

- that the claim is justified in *these* ways or up to *this* point, but not justified in *those* ways or beyond *that* point. (Acknowledge the counter-claims, or what can be said *against* a point of view!)
- that whether or not the claim is justified depends on what is meant by one of its key words or concepts, so that if you understand the key word *this* way the claim is justified, but if you understand it *that* way it is not.
- that although some justification (such as the following…) can be offered for this point of view, the claim is really an oversimplification of a question which needs to be understood with awareness of the following complexities…

If you are asked "to what extent" a statement is justified – or whether a given statement is true – then you are still being asked to evaluate a knowledge claim. You will still respond with *the degree* to which you agree, and *the degree* to which (counter-claim!) you do not agree…or to which you see things otherwise.

## Discussion Activity

### Follow an argument

This activity is best done with pairs of students working together to compare understanding. If different pairs work on the same article, or on articles expressing contrary views, they could benefit from small group discussion as they compare work at the end.

### Instructions for a single article

- Find an article that puts forward an argument on an issue that is relevant to your own life or your community. Newspaper editorials, opinion columns, or blogs are likely places to find views expressed.

- Look for the article's central argument – its main point or thesis. It is often in a sentence at the end of the first paragraph.

- Trace the overall sequence of ideas in support of its central point from beginning to end, looking for its main points and supporting points. Main points are often placed in the opening sentence of each paragraph (its topic sentence). What is the *line of reasoning* that holds all the parts together?

- Look for any counter-arguments, points that acknowledge what could be said from a contrasting perspective. These could be raised for serious consideration or seemingly stated only in order that the writer can present and dismiss them.

- Try to identify any implicit assumptions – that is, unstated ideas that contribute to the overall argument.

- Notice any examples that the writer uses to illustrate points.

- Identify the conclusions the writer reaches.

- Last, take an active role yourself. Write a statement of what main point you would make yourself on this topic, with two or three further points that support it.

### Extending to different perspectives

If you are able to find two articles that put forward arguments from different perspectives on the same issue, you will find this activity particularly beneficial. Do contrasting opinion pieces refer to the same pool of evidence and examples, or do they dip into quite different pools? To find articles expressing contrary points of view, go to different media sources, perhaps taking into account their ownership and political leaning.

It is helpful to think of opinion pieces as *putting ideas into play* as part of a larger social conversation that bounces ideas around. Feel free to make analogies to sports! No one writer treats the whole of a topic or considers all relevant arguments, and all writers are likely to pick out for comment the issues that are important from their own perspectives. Following an argument involves tracing the reasoning and supporting justifications *from a particular point of view*. Following an issue more broadly involves noticing ideas as they are picked up and tossed to readers, and volleyed back and forth between commentators with different perspectives.

### Transitions to connect ideas

Notice words and expressions that indicate connections between ideas:

- adding a point to one already made: in addition, furthermore, moreover, also, besides, beyond that, for one thing/for another, first/second/third

- conceding a point to an opposing interpretation: certainly…but, granted that, no doubt, to be sure, admittedly

- comparing: likewise, similarly, in like manner, in the same way

- contrasting or introducing a counter-claim: however, nevertheless, on the contrary, on the other hand, even though, instead, despite

- giving examples: for example, for instance, as a case in point, in particular, such as

- qualifying with some uncertainty: perhaps, maybe, it is possible that, possibly

- emphasizing: above all, most important, surely, indeed

- concluding: consequently, therefore, thus, as a result, clearly, in brief, on the whole, to sum up

**Know what's expected**
You will not be applauded in a gymnastics competition if what you perform is contemporary dance. Nor will you receive an excellent evaluation for a TOK essay unless you demonstrate the appropriate thinking and writing skills. In preparing your essay, familiarize yourself with the marking criteria and aim to show your skills at their best.

## What are the key concepts?

There are some key words you will find in each of the titles, for example, "evidence", "belief", "knowledge", "methodology" and "justification". Are you clear about what they mean? Are there multiple possible meanings or ambiguities in their meaning? Think back on class discussions and check your notes. Refresh your memory on chapters in this book that are particularly relevant.

Put the title into your own words to make sure you understand what is being asked, and check your understanding with your teacher.

Identify explicitly what is/are the central knowledge question(s) of the title. If after having given it some thought you still aren't sure about this, choose a different title, no matter how much time and effort you have expended. Without clarity regarding the knowledge question(s) involved in the title, you will not be able to write a good TOK essay.

catch your personal interest and give you a sense that you have something to say that will show your perspective as a knower?

## STEP 3: Gather your ideas

Brainstorm in several sweeps across the ideas. Have paper in front of you, and a pen ready for quickly jotting down your ideas, or else be ready with a new document on your computer screen.

### First sweep: think openly

You've already understood the knowledge questions in the title and your instructions. Now – what comes to your mind? Write or type it quickly. What assumptions might there be within the title? What areas of knowledge and ways of knowing will you talk about in your essay? What kind of comparisons will you make between them? What examples can you think of already? Don't give *any* attention to sentence structure or beautiful phrasing. Just write quickly until your mind storm, inevitably, passes.

### Second sweep: think more deliberately

Use circles, arrows, links, bold highlighting, colour or whatever other markings work for

you to connect up the main jotted ideas on the page in front of you. Cluster them: group them for similar points. Then focus your mind again on the knowledge questions of the title, and *brainstorm again*, pushing your thoughts more deliberately now. Are there perspectives other than the ones you have noted – perspectives from other cultures, other age groups and interest groups, other areas of knowledge than the ones that came to you first? Within an area of knowledge, do different theories provide different perspectives? Can you notice any assumptions that you are making yourself, or any values that come with your own point of view? What key words do you find yourself using, and are you entirely clear over what they mean? Scribble down your thoughts. If they obviously and instantly belong to your first clusters, add them there, but otherwise *just write*.

### Third sweep: counter-think

Read over everything you have written and mark new clusters forming. Then focus your mind again on the questions of knowledge of the title, and *brainstorm again*, this time giving much more deliberate attention to what you have gathered so far. Think in reverse. What can be said *against* the points you are starting to make? What counter-claims might expose their limitations or add a level of complexity? What are the implications of your main points? If you accept them then what else do you end up also accepting? Could someone else object to the conclusions you reach and, if so, on what grounds? Without discarding anything yet, start to highlight the main points towards an essay that will treat the topic with balance and awareness of counter-claims.

### Fourth sweep: develop ideas

Now enrich your immediate ideas by going back over notes from your TOK class to remind yourself of discussions that are relevant to your title. Go back through this book, using chapter titles and headings – and, of course, memory – to locate relevant ideas and refresh your memory on them. What areas of knowledge and ways of knowing, from among the first ones you noted, would be the *best* ones to use? Gather examples to illustrate your points from notes and texts from your other IB courses, the media, people you know, your own experience, or any other relevant sources. But remember that the TOK essay is not a research paper: you will not find your response to the title in a book or on a website. Books and other sources give you only the raw material from which you, as knower and author, must shape your *own* response.

## STEP 4: Organize your ideas in preparation for writing

Now comes probably the greatest challenge – to move from scribbled notes towards a plan for an essay that lays out a sequence of arguments that clearly respond to the title. If you find this

## Patterns of development: thesis first or thesis last

### 1. Thesis first

In this pattern of development, you place your thesis in your introductory paragraph (usually as its final sentence after an opening to catch attention and a sentence or two to establish your topic) so that your central argument hits the reader right at the beginning. Each subsection of the body of the essay then supports and develops the thesis to create a sustained argument.

The overall argument is created by the sequence of main points: the thesis gives the main argument and the topic sentences of paragraphs give the supporting arguments. The conclusion picks up the thesis again, restating it in somewhat different words as an argument that you have, by that point, firmly established.

Note that the thesis will often have counter-claims built right into it (e.g. "*Although* X has some justification, Y is more convincing."). You will usually treat counter-claims or counter-arguments at the beginning, in order to lay them aside. Move on to give arguments that you think are better justified – with the most persuasive at the end, in order of climax.

### 2. Thesis last

In this pattern of development, you place in your introduction (usually as its final sentence, just as

with the thesis first pattern) a focused question raising for discussion the knowledge question(s) of your title.

Each subsection of the body of the essay then treats aspects of the question or possible answers to it, usually in order of climax with the most convincing answer at the end. The thesis then emerges firmly at the end of the essay as the conclusion of the argument, the answer to the question posed at the beginning.

This pattern simulates the process of thinking and reaching a conclusion. Do not be fooled, though, into thinking that you really can just think and write as you go. This pattern demands just as much advance planning as the other; you will need to know before you start to do the actual writing exactly what your introductory question will be, exactly what your answer will be at the end, and the sequence of questions that will lead your reader through the simulated reasoning process from beginning to end.

Different school systems or writers favour one pattern or the other. If you are in doubt about which to use or unsure of your writing skills, however, the thesis-first pattern is safer in immediately getting your argument on track and giving a reader confidence in your control of ideas.

step difficult, remember that no one is born already knowing how to write an essay. It takes concentration and practice to learn to swim, to tango . . . or to organize ideas for an essay. Allow yourself only a few minutes to wail "But I *can't* . . .!" and then settle down to start planning.

### (a) Identify your thesis.

At this point, you should concentrate on identifying your *thesis* – that is, the central point that you want to make about knowledge questions in response to the title, the *argument* that emerges from your thoughts on your rough material. Distill this argument into a single sentence to write at the top of your plan. Your *thesis* is the single most important sentence in your entire essay. *Make*

sure that it responds to the title and focuses on its central knowledge questions.

### (b) Consider counter-claims.

Will you agree with the title's assertion (if it makes one) or will you disagree? Most of the best essays agree (or disagree) *with reservations*. What will these be? There is almost always something to be said for different perspectives and for different sides of an argument. Consider alternate views and be as critical (or as forgiving) of your own perspective as you are of others.

### (c) Plan your sequence.

To write a golden essay, have a golden plan. The sequence of ideas as you move from subsection to

## The essay: assessment criteria

### The essay: assessment criteria

*Does the student present an appropriate and cogent analysis of knowledge questions in discussing the title?* [8]

The judgment about the TOK essay is to be made on the basis of the following two aspects:

#### 1. Understanding knowledge questions

Knowledge questions addressed in the essay should be shown to have a direct connection to the chosen prescribed title, or to be important in relation to it.

Depth of understanding is often indicated by drawing distinctions within ways of knowing and areas of knowledge, or by connecting several facets of knowledge questions to these.

Breadth of understanding is often indicated by making comparisons between ways of knowing and areas of knowledge. Since not all prescribed titles lend themselves to an extensive treatment of an equal range of areas of knowledge or ways of knowing, this element in the descriptors should be applied with concern for the particularity of the title.

Relevant questions to be considered include the following.

- Does the essay demonstrate understanding of knowledge questions that are relevant to the prescribed title?

- Does the essay demonstrate an awareness of the connections between knowledge questions, areas of knowledge, and ways of knowing?
- Does the student show an awareness of his or her own perspective as a knower in relation to other perspectives, such as those that may arise, for example, from academic and philosophical traditions, culture or position in society (gender, age, and so on)?

#### 2. Quality of analysis of knowledge questions

This aspect is concerned only with knowledge questions that are relevant to the prescribed title.

Relevant questions to be considered include the following.

- What is the quality of the inquiry into knowledge questions?
- Are the main points in the essay justified?
- Are the arguments coherent and compelling?
- Have counter-claims been considered?
- Are the implications and underlying assumptions of the essay's argument identified?
- Are the arguments effectively evaluated?

Analysis of a knowledge question that is not relevant to the prescribed title will not be assessed.

---

[8] *Theory of knowledge guide.* Pp 44–45.

subsection in the body of your essay must develop your thesis, which in turn must respond to the title. Generally it should be possible to follow the argument of your essay simply by reading your thesis in the introduction, the opening topic sentence of each of your paragraphs, and the restated thesis in your conclusion, clinching the argument.

## STEP 5: Write your draft essay and revise it

The actual writing is only a small part of a good essay.

Before you start, be aware of some of the most common pitfalls that assessors of TOK essays can recognize in an instant. Things to avoid:

- Avoid sweeping claims (overgeneralization and oversimplification). If you do not intend to show that you are aware you are making a large generalization or to analyse it in some way, do not make it.
- Avoid caricatures and stereotyping: for example, all historians are unaware of their biases; all adherents to religion possess blind, perfect faith in what their religion tells them to believe; because of their professions, scientists rely on reason, artists on emotion, always. Go back to the section on reason as a way of knowing for a review of the dangers of the hidden "all" and possible fallacies, and go back to the section on classification to remind yourself of its possible dangers.
- Avoid an essay composed principally of questions, paragraph upon paragraph of questions: What is truth? Can we ever be certain? How can we know? If you do not try to answer the questions, they will be considered to be empty rhetoric and you will gain no credit.
- Avoid quoting other people's words unless you will analyse them or otherwise use them directly in argument. An essay that merely pastes quotations together does not achieve the critical analysis and argument that you are expected to do in your own words.
- Avoid full-blown preaching. Absence of counter-claims and acknowledgment of alternative perspectives significantly undermines the quality of an essay.
- Avoid using this book as a substitute for thought. We have written it to stimulate your

own thinking – to encourage you to consider thoughtfully a multitude of knowledge questions with a perspective of your own of which you are increasingly aware. You should not need to quote us. Put ideas entirely into your own words. You do not need to borrow the examples we use to illustrate ideas. Find your own examples. Have confidence in yourself. After a course in TOK, you are entirely ready to fly on your own.

Now write. Use your introduction to:

- catch your reader's attention
- establish the title that you are going to discuss
- give your thesis.

The taste for stylistic flourishes and fine writing in an introduction varies from culture to culture, but be warned that the marking criteria do not reward elegance of style. But they do count the words in a preamble as part of your maximum allowed.

As you write, *develop ideas in proportion* to their importance in your overall plan. Your essay must not be more than 1,600 words in length, so control the degree to which you expand on an idea as you go. Doing so is not easy, but it is easier than trying to readjust the whole essay at the end.

*Clarify concepts as you go,* defining and/or exemplifying terms if they are key terms necessary to your argument.

Things to avoid:

- Do not pad your essay with definitions of terms which are not particularly ambiguous.
- Do not drop into your essay lumps of definition which are not clearly linked to your argument and are ignored thereafter.
- Do not, above all, use a dictionary definition to bypass complexities: no assessor will be impressed if, after a course in which you discuss possible understandings of "truth" or "knowledge", you resolve this question of ambiguity and different perspectives by plunking down a citation from the dictionary as if you have thereby settled the matter.

*Use examples* to develop and illustrate your arguments. Examples do not *prove* a point. Remember all that you learned about the evidence base necessary for sound inductive conclusions. However, well-chosen examples can bring arguments to life, clarify concepts, expand upon points, and demonstrate your understanding. In your brainstorming, you have already gathered possible examples from which you now have to *select*.

*Select examples for breadth.* Take your examples from a variety of sources and areas of knowledge as a major means of demonstrating the breadth of your understanding. Draw from the media, books that you have read, lectures on special topics that you have heard, cultural issues of which you are aware, documentary films that you have seen, and so on. Draw from your other IB courses and course textbooks. Do not just make up your examples or suppose them in a hypothetical way ("If a historian were to write from an American perspective, he might…"). Then, out of the wide range of examples select the ones that seem most effective for illustrating your points. Your goal is not to stuff your essay with as many examples as possible, but to have breadth within the ones selected as best.

*Use the examples effectively.* Think strategically to use those examples to give the best support you can to your ideas. Will you use a single sustained example in a paragraph in order to demonstrate, in some detail, how knowledge works in a particular area? Or will you use two or three smaller examples, giving them brief development to ensure that they do play their part to clarify points and illustrate your argument?

*Reference your work.* Give the source of any quotation or unusual pieces of information, using accepted conventions of footnotes and bibliography. Acknowledge any source that has contributed significantly to your thinking. If you are not sure whether to footnote or not, it is better to footnote too much than too little.

*Check your facts* as you bring in examples and support generalizations. Are your assertions accurate, sufficiently specific and detailed?

*Polish the essay as you finish writing.* Check for mistakes in sentence structure, grammar, word choice and spelling. Errors can interfere with the clarity of your communication.

You are almost finished, but there is still an essential step between the draft and your final version: you have to make sure that you have not drifted from the expectations of a top performance that you had in mind as you began. With the marking criteria in hand, go through the essay to confirm that it is as close as you can make it to the description of the top achievement. Read carefully, check, and pick out features of your essay that you may still strengthen and polish. This done, you are ready, triumphantly, for the final step.

## STEP 6: Hand it in – and celebrate!

A good TOK essay demands that you think deeply about questions about knowledge that thread themselves through all areas of your life. If you have done your best to take a significant question and make it your own, you have achieved a goal central to TOK and your International Baccalaureate diploma – and important in the growth of your own thinking.

Congratulations! Regardless of what the mark on the essay ends up being, you have reason for celebration. You have won the gold.

# Index